To Carl & Maria

D1713330

# NOT UNDER THE LAW

From Mitchell
& Michael

# NOT UNDER THE LAW:

*Paul's Gospel from a Hebrew Mindset*

by:  Brother Mitchell W. Morris

YouTube Channel: www.Hebrewmindset.info

Facebook: Hebrew Mindset

Email: Hebrewmindsetministries@gmail.com

Hebrewmindsetministries.org

Voicemail: (407) 720-8862

ISBN: 9798533995221

*All Scripture, both the Tanak (OT) and the Messianic Writings (NT), regardless of the language in which we receive them, were written by men with a Hebrew mindset and from a Hebrew culture. The Father, in His Infinite Wisdom, established the Foundations of Our Faith in the Hebrew language, culture and mindset.*

*It is our duty to keep this understanding firmly in our minds as we read and interpret the Father's Word to accurately determine His intent. It is imperative that we conform our way of thinking so that it conforms to the mindset of the Hebrew Scripture.*

*Furthermore, the Messianic Writings (NT) are founded upon the writings of the Tanak. As we read and interpret the writings of the Messiah and His disciples we first must do so from a Hebraic mindset and secondly, we must understand that much of what they say is given from the presumption that their readers understand that the Tanak is the foundation of what they're saying.*

*In other words, the Messianic writers assume that everyone in the Belief who reads the Scripture already has some basic knowledge of the Tanak and an understanding of their responsibility to obey the Torah (Law) as it was given by YHWH to Moses at Mount Sinai.*

*To these writers it was a foregone conclusion that obedience to the Torah is the only Way to live righteously and set-apart before a Righteous and Set-Apart Elohim (God).*

(**Emphasis ours throughout** and unless otherwise noted, all scripture quotes are from "The Scriptures" 2009 version – https://isr-messianic.org)

v

# Testimony

I guess you could say that I was born a Baptist, if such a thing is possible. My family, however, didn't actually "practice" their Baptist Faith until I turned 12 years old. This was my first real introduction to the Bible, which I read all the way through many times during my adolescence.

I was taught that the WHOLE Bible was the "Word of God" and that "the LORD" was immutable (unchanging). I was also taught that the WHOLE "Word of God" was Truth and that within it there were no contradictions.

Even as a child I wholeheartedly believed this to be true, just as I do today. However, the more I listened to Pastors teach the Bible the more the Bible seemed to contradict itself. It wasn't until much later in life that I realized my mistake. Unlike most "believers", I was actually reading the WHOLE "Word of God" as "THE WORD OF GOD!"

I, in what many of the Christian Elders assured me was my ignorance, couldn't understand how certain portions of the "Old Testament" applied to us, mostly all the blessings, but that a great portion of it no longer applied to us.

My Pastors assured me that the "Law" no longer applies to "New Testament" believers, even though the Law itself says, in many places, it is never to be added to nor was anything to be taken from it (Deut 4:2; 12:32; Ecc 3:14; Pro 30:6 and Rev 22:18-19) and that it applies to both the native born and the stranger (Gentile) that sojourns with them (Num 15:15-16) because once the Gentile joins Yisra'el in covenant with YHWH, they are no longer to be considered Gentile, but a member of the Household of YHWH, which is the Children of Yisra'el (Lev 19:33-34; Eph 2:11-19).

This was especially confusing for me because the Messiah Himself said He had not come to destroy (diminish) the Law and for as long as the heaven and earth remained, not a single jot or tittle should past from the Law. This perplexed my young mind and as I matured the reasoning's given by my Pastors made less and less sense to me. Eventually, I lost heart in my belief, figuring that I was just too dumb to figure it out. After all, all these adults understood it, or at least claimed to, and all these highly educated "Theologians" couldn't possibly be wrong, could they?

Little did I know at the time that what the enemy had meant for evil, the Father would use for my good. At the lowest point of my life, when my heart was shattered and my spirit contrite, I cried out to

Him for knowledge and prayed for understanding, so that I could walk before Him spotless and blameless.

In His mercy, He heard me and flipped the "Light" switch of my perception, giving me eyes to see and ears to hear, because I had developed a heart that was prepared to obey Him at all costs.

This book is my sincere and well thought out attempt to show you, the reader, what the Father of Light wants us to understand about the "Good News" of His Son, our Master and Savior Yahushua, whom the world calls Jesus Christ.

May His mercy and blessing be upon me, and you as we search the WHOLE Scripture to find His Truth, the true Good News of our salvation.

Brother Mitch.

P. S.    This book is meant to be a companion to the Bible so you can compare scripture with scripture, not trusting in our words but in the Words of He who called us to salvation. Shalom

# BODY

# Table of Contents

# Glossary

Herein are the words, terms and names used in this book, that come directly from the original Hebrew text. These words, terms and names of the original Hebrew are used throughout this book for several reasons:

1. The English words are derived from pagan idolatry.
2. The English word doesn't truly express the meaning of the Hebrew word.
3. The English word is a mistranslation of the Hebrew word or the intent of the context.

יהוה    stgs #**H3068** "YHWH", from H1961 (to exist); (the) self-existent or eternal.

The personal name of the Creator. The only 'name' He gave us by which we are to call upon Him. There is a debate about the actual pronunciation of these Hebrew letters, so we have chosen to allow the reader to choose for themselves how to pronounce the Name. However, the opinion of the author may be found in the section on translation (see Preface, beginning of pg. xvi). This Name has been removed from Modern bibles over 6800 times and replaced with the title 'the LORD' and in eight places the Name has been wrongly transliterated as Jehovah.

יה    stgs #**H3050** "Yah", contracted for H3068 (YHWH), meaning the same, i.e., eternal.

The shortened, intimate form of the personal name of the Creator. This form of the Name has been removed from modern bibles 48 times and replaced with the titles, "the LORD" and "GOD". One time it is wrongly transliterated as Jah.

Note:    Both the Jewish Scribes have intentionally mis-vowel pointed the Name of Both the Father and the Son so the common wouldn't pronounce it properly. Christian Translators have mis-transliterated these names, as well as many other names in Scripture.

**Master:**      stgs #**H136** "יָנֹדֲא - 'ădônâI", an emphatic
form of H113 (to rule); (my) Master.

**Elohim:**      stgs #**H430** " אֵלֹהֽיׅם - 'ĕlôhîym" plural of
H433 (deity [?]); generally, a reference to the
"gods" of the nations. This Hebrew word is
the plural form of 'eloah', meaning 'mighty
one', as a title for one in authority.

The Scripture uses this same word for YHWH and for the
Malakim (angels), and for men (kings, judges, etc.). The word
"elohim" DOES NOT mean deity, as the Strong's Concordance
defines it, it refers specifically to those in authority. It is the primary
title that YHWH uses for Himself

**יהושע**   stgs #**H3091** "yehôshûa'", from H3068 and H3467;
Jehovah-saved; Jehoshua (that is, Joshua), the Jewish
leader: - Jehoshua, Jehoshuah, Joshua.

Yahusha (Yah Saves) or Yahushua (יהושוע - "Yah's
Salvation") is the proper Hebrew Name of the Messiah, which is the
exact same name as the man called Joshua in English.

**Note:**      Both the Jewish Scribes have intentionally mis-vowel
pointed the Name of Both the Father and the Son so
the common wouldn't pronounce it properly. Christian
Translators have mis-transliterated these names, as
well as many other names in Scripture.

**Mashiach:** stgs #**H4899** "חׅישָׁמ", from H4886 (to
rub with oil, to anoint) anointed;
specifically, the Messiah.
The Hebrew word translated as Messiah is used specifically to
one anointed to do the work of YHWH. In the Messianic Writings
(NT) the word Christ (Gk: Christos) is wrongly used as a replacement
of the Hebrew word.

The Greek language already has a word that translates the
Hebrew word Mashiach:

Stgs #**G3323** "Μεσσίας – Messias", of Hebrew origin [H4899
- Mashiach].

xii

This Greek word is used in John 1:41 and 4:25, and it is this word that we get the English word 'Messiah'.

Christos' was a title used specifically for the initiates of the secret pagan sun cults of ancient Greece and was used by these pagans to slander of the assemblies of Messiah in Antioch (Acts 11:26) and was later used by scribes to Hellenize the "New Testament" and confuse the way we view the writings.

All the writings of the Messianic text must be viewed from the mindset of a 1st century Hebrew and not the Greco/Roman mindset of the modern world. In this writing the English word Messiah will be used wherever appropriate.

> **Torah**: stgs #**H8451** "הָרוֹת - tôrâh", from H3384 (to flow out as water); a precept or statute, especially the Decalogue or Pentateuch: - law.

The Hebrew word wrongly translated as 'Law', which comes from the verbal root 'yarah' which means, 'to flow out' and when used in the context of speech, is translated as 'to teach'. Torah is the noun form of yarah and means teaching or instruction.

The best Scriptural statement that describes the meaning of Torah is given in Deut 8:3 and quoted by Messiah in Matt 4:4, "Man shall not live by bread alone but by **every word** that proceeds from the mouth of Elohim".

In Exodus 19:5 the text tells us to "obey my voice", so the word Torah refers to everything YHWH has spoken in His Word. The Greek word that translates the Hebrew word Torah is 'Nomos' and comes from an unused root word, 'nemo', meaning to 'parcel out', and has the same fundamental meaning as Torah, i.e., Instructions.

Though Torah has law in it, the word itself has a much broader meaning than the word law and includes all forms of instructions found in the Scripture, including shadow pictures, metaphors, idioms, patterns and parables.

> **Set- Apart**: stgs #**H6944** "שְׂדֹק – qôdesh", from H6942 (to be clean); a sacred place or thing;

This phrase refers to being 'set aside for a purpose or distinction'. It is the actual meaning of the English words: holy, sanctified, sanctify (to set apart), sanctification (the process of being set apart), saints (those who are set apart). It refers to a state of being separated from the world and submitted to the Will and Word of YHWH.

**Other important words and their meanings:**

Grace: stgs #H2580 "חֵן - chên", from H2603 (chânan, a primitive root; properly to bend or stoop in kindness to an inferior), graciousness, favor.

The Hebrew word 'chen' comes from 'chanan', which refers to a superior kneeling down to help an inferior). It is from this meaning and the context of Scripture that we get the idea of 'unmerited favour'.

The Greek word for grace is 'charis', which means "graciousness (as gratifying)" and does not refer to the extension of 'favour' but the attitude (emotion) of the recipient.

Note: While studying the Greek language of the Messianic Writings can be helpful, we should NEVER give the Greek meanings more relevance in our study then similar Hebrew words.

Faith: stgs #H530 "הֱנוּמֱא - ĕmûnâh," feminine of H529 (established); literally firmness; faithfulness.

The word "emunah" refers to standing steadfast or immovable. It carries the meaning of a life lived consistent with the principles of what they say they believe.

The Greek word for belief is 'pistis', which means 'persuasion' and refers to being persuaded by argument. This is not the same as the Hebrew 'emunah', which refers to a position from which the Believer shall not be moved.

Righteousness: 'in right standing' – there are two forms of righteousness, one is the righteousness of belief (spiritual), which delivers or acquits us **FROM** sin and its penalty, death (also known as **'justification'**, i.e., to be made right). We receive this righteousness freely because of our belief in the Messiah.

The other form of righteousness is the standard of righteous behavior **In Which We Live**, that is outlined in the Torah/Law (also known as 'sanctification', i.e., to live right).

> **Note**: We must always remember the duality of the Two-Part Principle (TPP see chapter called the Two-Part Principle [Sec. 1, Ch. 4]) when we interpret anything in the Scripture because the duality of spiritual things and physical things cannot be separated and is in every doctrinal part of the Good News (gospel) of Scripture.

So, there are two forms of justification, i.e., justification **FROM** death and the justification **OF** life, meaning that Messiah 'made us right" **from** sin and death through belief in Him, and that 'in Him' we are **to live** justified/righteous/set-apart (holy) lives before Him, through obedience to the Torah/Law of the Father, which Messiah did perfectly.

He was our example, and we are told to "imitate" Him (1Cor 11:1) and "walk as He walked" (1Jn 2:3-6). He made us righteous, justified us, set us apart (sanctified us) **through** His blood and we are to walk/live righteously, justified, set-apart (sanctified) **in** Him, as His people, through obedience to the Torah/Law.

> **Repentance**: The Greek word for repentance is "metanoeō" (**G3340**), from two words meaning, accompaniment (**G3326**) and to exercise the mind (**G3539**); to reconsider or think differently.

The Hebrew words for repentance are, (1) 'nacham', (G5132) meaning, to sigh, and can be interpreted differently depending on the context of the passage it is in, i.e.,, to be sorry, or to pity, or to console (oneself) or to rue or avenge, all carrying an emotional element, and (2) 'shub', (G7725) meaning, to turn back, and can also be used in a multitude of ways based on the context; however, this word has no emotional element but is strictly an action.

The words "shub" and "metanoeo" are not exactly the same because "metanoeo" is an intellectual exercise, a changed mind, while "shub" is the physical response to a changed attitude. The Hebrew mind understands the word "repent" from an overall understanding of what the Scripture teaches concerning man's relationship with YHWH and what He requires of those who would call themselves His people.

Yah created mankind for Himself and it was ALWAYS our duty to live according to His instructions (Torah). It was when we stopped obeying Him we lost our position as His people. He sent Messiah to restore ALL mankind back to Himself, as He promised Abraham (Gen 12:1-4). In the foundational context of Scripture, repent can only mean one thing, it means to **RETURN** to YHWH through believing in His Son Yahushua AND living in obedience to His instructions, i.e.,, Torah/Law. Scripturally, repentance is a way of life, a path and not just the act of turning.

| | |
|---|---|
| **Redeem(ed)**: | to pay the price owed (to be bought back for a price) |
| **Propitiation**: | the price paid to "Cover" (atone) a debt |
| **Adoption**: | to bring in from outside and be granted full rights and inheritance |
| **Yisra'el**: | 'to struggle with El and overcome', meaning to struggle with Him but not against Him and sometimes takes on the concept of ruling alongside Him. Generally, this name refers to "the Nation", YHWH's people. |

This is the name given to Jacob (Ya'aqob) when he wrestled with the man at Peni'ĕl (face of El) in Genesis 32:28. Literally this name refers to the descendants of this man.

These descendants, however, are not only those people that have been born in the bloodline of this man Jacob, for it also applies to any person that would 'struggle with El and overcome'. The Children of Yisra'el are the 'overcomers' spoken of in Revelation Chapter 2 and 3!

The Scripture says that the Children of Yisra'el consist of both the native born and the stranger that sojourns with them (Lev 19:33-34). The Messianic Writings use the phrase 'Jew and Gentile' for those who believe and are no longer two separate groups of people but a single group/family through the Messiah, who is, prophetically, the True Man, Yisra'el.

| | |
|---|---|
| **Gentile**: | Gk- ethnos (from which we get the word ethnic) referring to a tribe or clan or group other than Yisra'el. The word means 'nations', as in everyone who is not a part of |

the Nation of Yisra'el. From the Scriptural point of view there are only two types of people in the world, the Yisra'eli and the Gentile, the believer who is a child of YHWH and an unbeliever who is a child of Satan, the devil.

Despite what the 'Church' teaches, there is no such entity in Scripture as a Gentile Church. The Scripture would consider a 'Gentile Assembly' a group pagan idolaters. A Gentile (Heb: Goy) that forsakes his Gentile heritage and joins Yisra'el in covenant with YHWH is considered a Yisra'eli by adoption (Consider: Lev 19:33-34). Ruth is a perfect example of a Gentile that forsakes all to partake of the blessings of Yisra'el.

| | |
|---|---|
| **Rth 1:16** | But Ruth said, "Do not urge me to leave you, or to go back from following after you. For wherever you go, I go; and wherever you stop over, I stop over. Your people is my people, and your Elohim is my Elohim. |
| **Rth 1:17** | "Where you die, I die, and there I shall be buried. יהוה do so to me, and more also – for death itself parts you and me. |

The doctrine of Gentile inclusion into the household of Yisra'el is in both the Tanak (OT) and the Messianic Writings (NT). (Ex 12:37-38, 49; Lev 17:8-15; 19:34; Num 9:14; 15:15-16, 29; Eze 47:21-23; Rom 2:28-29; 4:1-25: 9:1-8; 11:1-36; Gal 3:26-29; Eph 2:8-22.)

The Scripture puts no restriction upon who can and cannot become an Yisra'eli, a chosen of YHWH. Anyone, from any background or ethnic heritage who will trust in Him by belief, in His Son Yahushua Messiah, and will walk-in whole-hearted obedience to His Torah, with an attitude of mercy and love, can be a member of the Household of Yisra'el.

| | |
|---|---|
| **Ha'Satan**: | "The Adversary", which is a title and not a name. The Hebrew 'name' translated as 'Lucifer' in English (Isaiah 14:12) is "Helel": |
| | stgs #**H1966** "לֵילָה - hêylêl", from H1984 (to be clear; shine); the morning star. |

The name "Lucifer" actually means 'light-bringing' in Latin and is similar to, but not exactly the same as the Hebrew "Helel", which means to be clear or to shine. The title "morning star" is what the planet Venus used to be called when it arose in the morning.

The name "Satan" is actually a title, it refers to the 'Devil' as our Adversary who "leads all the world astray" and is the "accuser of the brothers" (Revelation 12:9-10). In this writing, we will use the phrases "Ha'Satan" or "the Devil" to describe this entity.

# INTRODUCTION

The most important concept that we hope to instill in every one of our readers is the necessity of reading and evaluating the Scripture from a Hebraic mindset.

What we mean is, YHWH (יהוה), in His infinite and infallible wisdom chose the Hebrew people and the Hebrew language as the vehicle by which He would reveal Himself to the world. The Hebrew language and mentality are significantly different than almost all others on the planet.

For instance, the Hebrew language is a verb or action-based language, so we must understand that even the nouns have a component of action in them because they are based on verb roots.

As an example, the Greek word for belief is "pistis" and means, 'to be persuaded by argument'. This is a mental exercise that has no intrinsic requirement of action. However, the Hebrew word for belief is "emunah" and means, 'steadfastness'. This word has an intrinsic requirement to act upon what is believed.

A Hebrew mindset is vital if we truly desire to understand the Scripture and our responsibility to it as believers in the Messiah. However, a clear distinction must be made between the "Jewish" mindset and the "Hebrew" mindset. Yes, Jews are Hebrews, but the Jewish mindset is formed and founded in accordance with the Jewish Religion and not the Hebrew Scripture only.

Judaism is founded on the "traditions of the Rabbis" most of which are an addition to or a subtraction from the Torah of YHWH, something we are instructed repeatedly not to do. The Jewish mindset is founded in the Talmud and not the Torah only. They only give lip service to the Torah.

The Hebrew mindset is one in which only the Hebrew Scriptures are used to formulate the basis of understanding and doctrine. Messiah Himself was founded solely and completely on the Torah and went out of His way to intentionally violate the Takanot (Rabbinical edicts) and Ma'asim (Behavioral precedent set by a Rabbi) of the teachers of Judaism.

We too need to be founded solely and completely on the Torah as it was given to Mosheh, without adding anything to it or taking anything from it. It is this practice of Judaism, trusting in manmade traditions, that blinded the Jews of the presence of their own Messiah. True "Sola Scriptura" (Scripture only) is the only way to find the Truth.

# PREFACE

## "A Word about Translation"

The author grew up using the King James Version of the Bible exclusively, however, after having put in a little bit of study of Hebrew and Greek, he found that virtually all the English versions are plagued with translational and transliteration errors.

Some of these errors are major obstacles to understanding the correct English word or phrase needed to convey the original meaning. There are also theological errors, where translators added words to the text to 'help' us ignorant sheep understand the "meaning" of the passage.

The following are two examples of translator additions to the text that do not exist in the Greek text but have influenced the meaning of the passage in a negative manner.

### Example #1

| | |
|---|---|
| **Col 2:16** | Let no man therefore judge you in meat, or in drink, or in respect of an holyday, or of the new moon, or of the sabbath *days:* |
| **Col 2:17** | Which are a shadow of things to come; but the body *is* of Christ. |

Later in this book we will carefully examine the whole context of this passage to come to a fuller understanding of what Paul intends us to understand here, but for now we need to focus on a single word.

If you look closely you will notice that the word 'is' in v. 17 is italicized, meaning it was added by the translators to 'help' us understand the meaning of this passage.

If the publisher of your bible has any integrity at all you should be able to find a section on translation in the front of your bible that will verify the use of italics. If you find a good Greek Interlinear Bible (i.e.,, J. P. Green's is the best I've found) and look up this passage you will find that there is no 'is' in verse 17. J. P. Green used the 'is' in the verse but he placed it within brackets to show that it was added.

Typically, the phrase 'but the body **is** of Messiah' is interpreted by Christian teachers to mean that since the Body of Messiah 'is of' Messiah we are no longer required to keep any of the things mentioned in verse 16, which is the exact opposite of what Paul intends his readers to understand.

If you remove the 'is' from the passage it reads, "but the Body of Messiah', which is completely different. It implies that we are to keep the things mentioned in verse 16 but only the "Body of Messiah" can judge us in how to keep them.

This is further proved in the context of chapter 2 which concerns being led astray by "philosophy and vain deceit, after the tradition of men, after the rudiments of the world, and not after Messiah" (v.8), who by the way, kept all the things mentioned in verse 16.

The believer's responsibility to obey the Word of Elohim has been removed from the text by translator's addition of this single little word. This little 'is' has led millions of well-meaning believers down the path of disobedience and lawlessness.

### Example #2

**Joh 1:17**     For the law was given by Moses, ***but*** grace and truth came by Jesus Christ.

Again, we have a little word in italics, the word 'but'. 'But' is a conjunction like 'and', except where 'and' generally brings two or more things together, 'but' generally separates things or creates a contrast between ideas.

The use of the 'but' in this passage has caused many people to think that a contrast is being made here between the law and grace and this is simply not the case. The 'but' does not belong here, without it and with a little bit of word study, we find something profound.

This passage says that Moses gave us the Torah, though we know it actually came from YHWH through Moses, 'but' that grace AND truth came by the Messiah. However, did you know that the Scripture refers to the Torah (law) as truth?

**Psa 119:142**     Thy righteousness *is* an everlasting righteousness, and **thy law *is* the truth.**

So, what's really being said here? Moses only gave us the Torah, but the Messiah gave us both grace and the Torah. Later in this book we will see that it was Messiah's work on the cross that allowed us to 'establish the law' in our lives (Rom 3:31).

The grace of YHWH, which we receive when we believe in Yahushua, allows us to live in obedience to the Torah with a clear conscience and without fear of future condemnation when we struggle. Messiah is the Truth that we trust in for salvation, but the Torah is the

Truth we walk in as servants of the YHWH Most-High. (Jn 14:6; 17:17)

Further examples of translator error that have caused confusion has to do with the taking of "Poetic License" in the inconsistent translation of a single Hebrew or Greek word with more than one English word.

**Ex:**  (stg# **G458**) - 'Anomia', meaning, illegality: A compound word (a-nom-ia) meaning, no law doing.

1.  The 'a' is a negative participle meaning 'no or not'.

2.  The 'nom' is the conjugated form of 'nomos', translated as law, however, 'nomos' is the Greek word that translates the Hebrew word 'Torah', which is also translated law but actually means, instructions, so then 'nomos' also must carry this same meaning.

3.  The 'ia' is an active participle meaning 'to do or doing'.

So, the actual meaning of the Greek word 'anomia' is "no law (instructions) doing" and, in fact, in 1 John 3:4 the King James translators translated 'anomia' as "transgression of the Law".

**1Jn 3:4**  Whosoever committeth sin transgresseth also the law (*anomia*): for sin is the transgression of the law (*anomia*).

The King James translators knew that this word meant 'no law doing' or 'lawlessness' and yet this verse in 1st John is the only place they translated it correctly. In the other places they translated it as follows:

**Mat 7:23**  And then will I profess unto them, I never knew you: depart from me, ye that work iniquity (*anomia*).
*   *   *

**Mat 13:41**  The Son of man shall send forth his angels, and they shall gather out of his kingdom all things that offend, and them which do iniquity (*anomia*);

**Mat 23:28**   Even so ye also outwardly appear righteous unto men, but within ye are full of hypocrisy and iniquity (*anomia*).

***

**Mat 24:12**   And because iniquity (*anomia*) shall abound, the love of many shall wax cold.

***

**Rom 4:7**   *Saying,* blessed *are* they whose iniquities (*anomia*) are forgiven, and whose sins are covered.

***

**Rom 6:19**   I speak after the manner of men because of the infirmity of your flesh: for as ye have yielded your members servants to uncleanness and to iniquity (*anomia*) unto iniquity (*anomia*); even so now yield your members servants to righteousness unto holiness.

***

**2Co 6:14**   Be ye not unequally yoked together with unbelievers: for what fellowship hath righteousness with unrighteousness (*anomia*)? and what communion hath light with darkness?

***

**2Th 2:7**   For the mystery of iniquity (*anomia*) doth already work: only he who now letteth *will let,* until he be taken out of the way.

***

**Tit 2:14**   Who gave himself for us, that he might redeem us from all iniquity (*anomia*), and purify unto himself a peculiar people, zealous of good works.

***

**Heb 1:9**   Thou hast loved righteousness, and hated iniquity (*anomia*); therefore God, *even* thy God, hath anointed thee with the oil of gladness above thy fellows.

In the following verse 'anomia' is part of a larger compound word 'paranomia' which stems from the word 'paranomeo' meaning, 'to be opposed to the law'.

| **2Pe 2:16** | But was rebuked for his iniquity (*paranomia-opposition to the law*): the dumb ass speaking with man's voice forbad the madness of the prophet. |
|---|---|

As you can see, the single Greek word, 'anomia' has been translated as:

1. Transgression of the Law
2. Iniquity
3. Unrighteousness

Talk about confusing, how is anyone supposed to come to a coherent understanding of the Scripture when the Translators have confused the meanings of important words like 'anomia'?

Next, we need to understand the difference between translation and transliteration.

| **Translate:** | To express the sense (or meaning) of a word in another language. Ex: |
|---|---|

1. Hebrew word: 'aziqqim'
2. Greek word: 'halusis'
3. English word: 'chains'

All of these words have the same basic meaning, which today would best be understood to mean handcuffs or shackles, depending how they are used in the context of the passage, or can actually mean 'chains' if used in the context of binding an animal, etc.

Translation is a 'meaning for meaning', between languages, about objects or actions. You never 'translate' proper names unless it is used alongside the name as a descriptive.

| **Ex:** | **Gen 17:5** | "And no longer is your name called Abram, but your name shall be Abraham because I shall make you a father of many nations. |
|---|---|---|

Here we see that YHWH changed the name of Abram (High Father) to Abraham (Father of many), because of His promise to multiply his seed like the stars of heaven (15:5). YHWH did not call him 'father of many' but gave him a name that meant 'father of many'.

It is in situations like this that proper names are translated but not at any other time. If someone asks you for your name, do you give them your name, or the meaning of your name? Of course, you give them your name, not its meaning, unless they go a step further and ask you its meaning. The meaning of your name is not you; your name is you.

**Transliterate**: A representation of a word or name in the closest possible corresponding sounds of letters or characters from the alphabet of a different language.

1. Hebrew Name: אדם
2. Greek Name: Αδαμ
3. English Name: Adam

All three of these alphabets have letters or characters that represent the syllables "Ah-dahm", though the letters look different, when put together they have the same basic sound.

Proper names are always transliterated, 'sound for sound' so that our name in English sounds the same, or nearly the same, in all other languages.

**Ex**: My proper name is Mitchell, where the 'ch' carries the same sound as in the word '<u>ch</u>urch', however, in Hebrew the letter transliterated as 'ch' does not carry that sound, but instead carries the hard sound as in 'Bach', almost a 'kh' sound and very guttural. In Hebrew, the closest letter to the 'ch' sound in my name is the 'shin' (ש), which is the 'sh' sound you find in '<u>sh</u>irt'.

So, in Hebrew, the closest thing to my name is - מיטשל – pronounced 'meet- shel'. However, once I taught the Hebrew speaker to pronounce my name correctly, they could repeat it with little effort, but they couldn't spell it in Hebrew and come up with the exact sound.

Below is an example of where the English translators erred in the transliteration of a Hebrew name into English.

**Ex**: Eve - pronounced in English - 'ee-veh'
in Greek - 'you-ah'
in Hebrew - 'Khaw-ah'

The proper transliteration of this name from Greek into English should have been 'eua', not 'eve'. However, neither of these forms actually convey the proper sound of the Hebrew name 'Chawwah'. Names and words are about sounds and when it comes to names especially, if you don't make the proper sound you are unlikely to get an answer from the person you call to.

The proper pronunciation of the name 'chawwah' is 'Khaw-ah' or 'Khav-ah', if you adhere to the modern rabbinical pronunciation of the letter 'waw' (ו). The problem the translators had, was there is no Greek or English or even Latin letter that carries the sound of the Hebrew letter 'cheit' (ח), which has a harsh, guttural, 'h' sound similar to the 'ch' in 'Bach' but harsher.

Because they couldn't replicate that letter, they simply dropped it and began the name with the following vowel. As time passed and more languages got thrown into the mix the name evolved. It is likely that we got the 'v' in eve from the conversion of the name from Greek, that uses a 'u', to Latin, where the 'u' looks like a 'v', into English as a 'v'. Who knows for sure?

Other examples of Hebrew names where a letter was dropped are:

1.    Abel, who is actually, 'Hebel', הבל
2.    Enoch, who is actually, 'Chanok', חנוך

Also, there has never been a 'J' in the Hebrew language, in fact, there is no 'J' in the Greek language either. What we think of as a 'J', with the 'gd' sound, didn't exist until about the late 16th century.

The 'J' originally was the capital form of the Greek 'i' or 'iota' (ι), when it was used at the beginning of a sentence or at the beginning of a proper name. Even then, it carried the double 'ee' sound of the 'i or y'.

Examples of improper transliterated names in the Scripture:

| 1. | Moses | – | Mosheh |
| 2. | Isaac | – | Yitschaq |
| 3. | Jacob | – | Ya'aqob |
| 4. | Joshua | – | Yahushua |
| 5. | Isaiah | – | YeshaYahu |
| 6. | Ezekiel | – | Yechezqel, etc. |

Furthermore, we need to discuss intentional deception, caused by man-made religious error in direct violation of the Scripture.

## The Name of the Father?

Unquestionably, the greatest translator error of the Scripture has to do with the proper name of the Creator Himself. You may have heard pastors or teachers give a lesson on the "Names of God", which is nothing more than theological error.

In all the Scripture, the Creator has given us only One name by which He was to be called and set that Name apart above all other names so as to distinguish Himself above all other would be authorities. However, He has many titles:

| | | |
|---|---|---|
| 1. | El, Eloah, Elohim – | "Mighty One(s), at its base it means authority (god, God). |
| 2. | Ab, Abba – | Father |
| 3. | Adonai – | Master (lord). |
| 4. | El Shaddai – | Almighty El. |
| 5. | El Elyon – | El Most High. |

He has other descriptive titles attached to His Name:

| | | |
|---|---|---|
| 1. | YHWH-Nissi | – | YHWH our Banner |
| 2. | YHWH-Yirah | – | YHWH our Provider |
| 3. | YHWH-Rapha – | YHWH our Healer, etc. |

When ask by Mosheh what His Name was, YHWH said (read from right to left),

אהיה אשר אהיה ◄————
Eheyah asher eheyah

This phrase is translated as 'I Am that I Am'. The true meaning of these Hebrew words is 'exist which exist' and can better be understood to mean, eternal.

He is the Eternal One, which is what is said about Him in Revelation 1:4 where He is called, "He that was, He that is and He that is to come". Mosheh was told to tell them that the "Eternal One" had sent him, however, this is not His proper name, but the meaning of His Name.

The Creator told Mosheh, in Exodus 3:16, to:

**Exo 3:16**  Go, and gather the elders of Israel together, and say unto them, The LORD God of your fathers, the God of Abraham, of Isaac, and of Jacob, appeared unto me, saying, I have surely visited you, and *seen* that which is done to you in Egypt:

Here we see that the Elohim, our Mighty One, gives us His proper name, however, the translators hid the Name from us by substituting it with a title, the LORD, just as the Jewish rabbis had done before them.

In this verse, 'the LORD' has been put in place of the Hebrew Name, יהוה (YHWH). If we go back to what He told Mosheh about His Name we will once again see the word, אהיה (eheyah).

The root verb for this word is 'hayah' (היה – stg# H1961) and it means, 'to exist'. If you notice the last two Hebrew letters in this word you will see (יה), which everyone agrees should be pronounced, 'Yah'. If we go back to the Name in Exodus 3:16, we see that the first two letters of the Name are also, 'Yah" (יה). So, the first part of His Name means, 'to exist'.

The last two letters of His Name are (וה) and it's in these two letters that the controversy rests. How do we pronounce these two letters?

Well, if we look carefully at the Hebrew word 'hawah', (הוה – stg# H1933) we will find that this word also means, 'To breathe or be', as in existing or living. The last two letters of this Hebrew word are (וה), just like the last two letters of the Creator's Name, 'wah'.

So, the translators should have transliterated the Creators name as 'Yahwah', or, if they believed it should have three syllables, then Yahuah, but instead they hid it from us and replaced it with a title some 6823 times in the Tanak alone.

There is serious disagreement as to how the Name should be pronounced, and just like the pagans around us we argue and bicker about it, allowing our opinions to separate us, instead of coming together in one heart and one mind to serve Him as we have been instructed. What a shame!

The Name of the Father can be pronounced in a few different ways; Yahwah, Yahweh, Yahvah, Yahveh, , or it can simply be spelled out, Yod-Hey-Wah-Hey, Yod-Hey-Vav-hey, etc. The Name should end with an "ah" sound or an "eh" sound, not a 'ey' or 'ay' sound.

It is our opinion that when the Name is writings, it should be spelled out in the Hebrew (יהוה) or with the English transliteration, i.e., the letters representing the Hebrew characters (YHWH), and let the reader pronounce it as they may.

There is one thing we all agree on... YAH is our Elohim.

As has already been mentioned, the Name has been removed from the Text of Scripture some 6823 times, transliterated wrongly as 'Jehovah' only 8 times. The short form of the Name, 'Yah', has been removed 48 times and transliterated as 'Jah' one time. There are many, many other times the Name is used within the name of a person in the text, i.e., YeshaYahu (Isaiah) and in every case the Name was obscured by transliterating it as 'iah'.

This practice of hiding the Name of the Most-High is actually a practice of unbelieving pagan idol worshippers, who thought that saying the name of their highest deity was forbidden, only for the highest priest among them. Interestingly enough, during the second temple era the only time the Name was spoken was at the Day of Atonement, Yom Kippur, and then, only by the High Priest.

Amazingly, the Christian translators took up this pagan practice, along with many others, and have hidden the only True Name of El Shaddai. Even though we are told many times, in many ways to call upon His Name, to lift up His Name, to swear by His Name, etc. and we are called by His Name, almost no 'believer' today actually knows His Name, and the few that do spend more time bickering over how to pronounce it than they do magnifying it.

In closing, let me say that despite all the confusion and bickering about the Name and how to pronounce it, I think it is as easy as pronouncing each letter and allowing the sound to come through.

י        - Yod (Y) is the same sound as the 'i' in most
           languages and has the double 'ee' sound.

ה        - Hey (H) is a breathy sound, like a sigh,

ו        - Waw (W) is the same sound as a 'u' in most
           languages and has the double 'oo' sound

So, YHWH (יהוה) is: ee – ha – oo – ha   (or)   ee – ah – oo – ah allowing the 'ee' and 'oo' sounds to end in a sigh.

Some suggest that there should be 3 syllables in the Name because of the way it is constructed, and I accept the possibility of this being true. If so, the Name would be pronounced, ' Ya-hu-ah'.

Lastly, the Hebrew language began as a pictograph language, wherein all the letters were represented by pictures.

The Name of the Father was pictured like this (read from right to left):

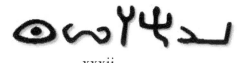 The first letter is a "yod" meaning: hand.

The second letter is a "hey" meaning: behold or reveal.

The third letter is a "waw" meaning: fastener or nail.

The fourth letter is a "hey" meaning: behold reveal.

"Behold the nail and behold the hand."

**REMEMBER**, when the disciple Thomas first heard that the Master had been raised from the dead, he said that he would not believe it until he could put his finger in the nail holes in His hands (John 20:24-29).

Could the Father's Name be connected to Messiah's nail scarred hands? We believe so.

**As for the Name of the Messiah?**

**Psalms 118:14** "**Yah** is my strength and song, And He has become my **deliverance**."

The word here for deliverance is feminine form , 'yeshuah', so Yah has become our yeshuah! The name transliterated as Joshua is, 'Yahushua' and means, "Yah our Deliverance". The Messiah's Name is the same as that of Joshua, who in turn is a shadow picture of the Returning Messiah.

YHWH our Elohim and Yahushua, His Redeemer!

The Messiah's name in pictograph form (read from right to left):

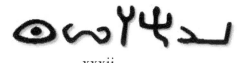

The first letters are the same as that of the Father.

The first letter is a "yod" meaning: hand.

The second letter is a "hey" meaning: behold or reveal.

The third letter is a "waw" meaning: fastener or nail.

The last two letters are:

The fourth letter is a "shin" meaning: sharp, teeth, press (down as in chewing) and some connect to the pressure and/or a consuming fire.

The last letter is a "ayin" meaning eye, as in seeing or watching.

"Behold the nailed hand that sees our troubles", may be a possible meaning to His Name.

**Note:** An interesting side note, is what the word Torah means in pictograph form.

The firsts letter is a "tau" meaning mark or sign.

The second letter is a "waw" meaning: fastener or nail.

The third letter is a "resh" meaning: head or man.

The last letter is a "hey" meaning behold or reveal.

"Behold, the man nailed up is a sign" may be a possible meaning of the word Torah.

Lastly, let's take a moment to talk about the Hebrew style. Though we read the Scripture in English today, it is a fundamental error to view and interpret Scripture from an English grammatical perspective.

The whole Bible, regardless of whether you believe the 'Messianic Writings' to have originally been written in Greek or Aramaic or Hebrew, was written originally in the Hebrew grammatical style and from the mindset of ancient Hebrews. Hence, it must be viewed and interpreted in this same way.

I know, you don't speak Hebrew and that's ok. Obviously, if we all still did, we wouldn't have the interpretational confusion we have today. Our rebellion at Babel is responsible for our modern confusion of the linguistics of Scripture and yet we still haven't learned our lesson.

Rebellion causes confusion; however, a submitted heart can gain the wisdom and understanding needed to live before Abba YHWH (Deut 6:1-5; Ps 119:95-104). Understanding the Hebrew style isn't really that difficult to learn.

There are just a few major things to consider:

1.  Hebrew writers use synonymous words and phrases, covering the same topics from various viewpoints, while adding smaller elements of information to eventually develop a complete picture.
2.  Hebrew writers use "contrasting" as a form of teaching to encourage abstract thought in doctrinal development.
3.  Due to the nature of the Hebrew language, Hebrew writers allow the immediate context of the argument to define a word or a term's meaning.
4.  Hebrew writers establish a base context, which is always consistent to foundational Truth (Torah), and then develop topics and arguments consistent with the immediate context, never allowing the debate to wander beyond the boundaries of the base context. There is a 'contextual flow' within Hebrew writings that must never be deviated from.

**Ex**:    In the book of Galatians, Paul is arguing against a teaching that says that Gentile believers have to be circumcised 'TO BE SAVED' (Acts 15:1), as if being physically circumcised is a pre-salvation requirement.

So, the question in Galatians is, "By what are we Saved?" Therefore, the entire book of Galatians is debating **how we get saved** and has nothing to do, contextually, with **how we live as saved people**. However, once this is understood there is clear evidence in Galatians as to how we should live as saved people.

Ironically, modern teachers misunderstand and therefore misinterpret what Paul is saying. We will see that Paul actually teaches the exact opposite of what they think he is saying.

Because they do not have his knowledge of the Hebrew Scriptures or its style, they turn the meaning of what he is saying upside down. They suggest that he is teaching that the "Law" (Torah) no longer has a place in the lives of believers because they were saved by faith and not by works.

However, Paul is saying we were saved from the condemnation of death by belief and not works, but once we are saved, we must live in obedience to the Word of YHWH, which is the "Law" (Torah). They don't see this truth because they are not founded in the same knowledge and style that Paul was founded in (2 Peter 3:14-17).

It is imperative that we do not confuse the Hebrew Perspective with the "Jewish" perspective when interpreting the Scripture. The "Jewish" perspective is shrouded in the Talmudic teachings of the 'non-believing' rabbis of Orthodox Judaism. The Hebrew Perspective is founded solely and completely on the Torah, the Prophets, and the Writings (Tanak -Old Testament) without additions or subtractions.

# SECTION 1

# Section 1:    Foundations

Ch. 1 -  Torah, its Meaning, Purpose, and Importance

Ch. 2 -  Cultural, Religious and Social Context of the
Messianic Writings

Ch. 3 -  Paul:  A Foundational Perspective

Ch. 4 -  Two Parts

Ch. 5 -  The Jerusalem Council

# Chapter 1: Torah

"Its Meaning, Purpose and Importance!"

The Hebrew word 'torah' has been wrongly translated in our English Bibles as 'Law', however, our English word law doesn't convey the full meaning of the word 'torah'.

Torah comes from the root verb 'yarah', meaning 'to flow out', and when used in the context of speech and information, it carries the meaning, 'to teach or instruct'. Torah is the noun equivalent of 'yarah' and defines *what* is taught, i.e.,, teachings or instructions.

Scripturally and traditionally, the phrase 'Torah of YHWH' refers to the first five books of the Bible that were authored by Moses (Mosheh), These are the instructions that YHWH gave Moses to give to the people (you and me) at Mt. Sinai.

There is an error afoot today that makes a distinction between the phrases 'Law of Moses' and 'Law of God'. These two phrases are synonymous since the entire Torah was spoken by YHWH to Mosheh (Moses).

Other words in the Tanak (OT) that are used as synonyms to Torah are:

Word – Way – Statutes – Ordinances – Judgments, etc.

It is a foundational principle within all Hebrew writings that many synonymous words and phrases, as well as, idioms, metaphors, parables, shadow pictures, patterns etc., are used to teach Scriptural Truth and they all must agree. This is true in both the Tanak (OT) and the Messianic Writings (NT).

| | |
|---|---|
| **Psa 19:7** | The **Torah of יהוה** is perfect, bringing back the being; The **witness of יהוה** is trustworthy, making wise the simple; |
| **Psa 19:8** | The **orders of יהוה** are straight, rejoicing the heart; The **command of יהוה** is clear, enlightening the eyes; |
| **Psa 19:9** | **The fear of יהוה** is clean, standing forever; The **right-rulings of יהוה** are true, they are righteous altogether, |
| **Psa 19:10** | More desirable than gold, Than much fine gold; And sweeter than honey and the honeycomb. |

| | |
|---|---|
| **Psa 19:11** | Also, Your servant is warned by them, In guarding them there is great reward. |

In this passage of Psalms, all the highlighted phrases are synonymous with one another and are used to express slightly different characteristics of the Torah. They express the blessedness of all YHWH has promised to those will obey Him.

They have more value than the purest gold and are sweeter than the sweetest food. They warn us, His servants, on how to please Him and bring us great reward when we do them. This is the most consistent teaching throughout the totality of Scripture.

| | |
|---|---|
| **Deu 30:15** | See, I have set before you today life and good, and death and evil, |
| **Deu 30:16** | in that I am commanding you today to love יהוה your Elohim, to walk in His ways, and to guard His commands, and His laws, and His right-rulings. And you shall live and increase, and יהוה your Elohim shall bless you in the land which you go to possess. |
| **Deu 30:17** | "But **if your heart turns away**, and **you do not obey**, and **shall be drawn away**, and **shall bow down to other mighty ones and serve them,** |
| **Deu 30:18** | "I have declared to you today that **you shall certainly perish**, you shall not prolong your days in the land which you are passing over the Yardĕn to enter and possess. |
| **Deu 30:19** | " I have called the heavens and the earth as witnesses today against you: I have set before you life and death, the blessing and the curse. Therefore you shall **choose** life, so that you live, both you and your seed, |
| **Deu 30:20** | to love יהוה your Elohim, to obey His voice, and to cling to Him – for He is your life and the length of your days – to dwell in the land which יהוה swore to your fathers, to Aḇraham, to Yitsḥaq, and to Yaʿaqoḇ, to give them." |

Here again, we see several synonymous terms used; love, ways, commandments, statutes, judgments, obey and cleave, all of which are given in the context of life and blessing if we obey them and death and cursing if we do not obey them.

4

The Torah or Instructions of YHWH is like a fence running through the course of our lives. If we keep and obey them, we will dwell on the 'life' side of the fence, but if we do not keep and obey them, we will dwell on the 'death' side of the fence.

This is the Truth of the written Word of YHWH, given to Moses at Mt. Sinai for all the children of Yisra'el, both the native born and the stranger (Gentile) that would sojourn with them (Num 15:15-16; Lev 19:33-34), an "ordinance FOREVER, throughout your generations".

Messiah Yahushua defined the meaning of Torah in Matthew 4:4, when He said:

> **Mat 4:4** But He answering, said, "It has been written, **'Man shall not live by bread alone, but by every word that comes from the mouth of יהוה.'** " (Deut 8:3)

The phrase 'comes from the mouth' clearly expresses the same meaning as 'flows out of the mouth', which would be the meaning of 'yarah' in this context. Yarah, remember, is the root word from which we get the word 'torah'. The true 'key' phrase here though is 'every word'. It is every word, law, statute, instruction, etc., that gives life to the man who does, keeps, obeys, and lives in them.

This truth cannot change because YHWH does not change (Mal 3:6), and it cannot be added to nor taken away from (Deut 4:2; 12:32; Ecc 3:14; Rev 22:18-19), which Messiah said that He did not come to do (Mat 5:17-19), nor could He, for if He had He would have been a false prophet (Deut 13:1-5).

The Greek word 'nomos' is the word used in the Messianic Writings that translates the Hebrew word 'torah'. Since the Hebrew is the foundational language upon which all doctrine must be understood and developed, then the Hebrew meaning of Torah must be applied to the Greek word 'Nomos'. However, let's see what 'nomos' actually means in Greek.

> **Law:** stg's #G3551 - "nomos", meaning, law **(instructions);** From a primary word (nemō) meaning, to *parcel* out, (especially *food* or *grazing* to animals); *law* (through the idea of prescriptive *usage*), generally (*regulation*), specifically (of Moses [including the volume];

5

Nomos comes from an unused root word, 'nemo', which means to 'parcel out' or 'give out by portion'. Again, like Torah, when used in the context of speech or information it refers to what is parceled out, i.e.,, instructions. Nomos has nearly the same exact meaning as Torah.

In Greek, the letter 'a' at the beginning of a word is a negative participle, meaning no or not, and when it is a prefix for 'nomos' we get, 'anomos' meaning, 'no law or lawless'. If we add the active participle 'ia' to the end of 'anomos' we get 'anomia' meaning, 'no law doing or lawlessness'.

**1Jn 3:4**        Everyone doing sin also does lawlessness (*anomia*), and sin is Lawlessness (*anomia*).

The King James Version translated 'anomia' here in 1 John 3:4 as 'transgression of the law', which I've already mentioned before, and will do again several times in this study, because it is vital to understand that sin is by definition, a violation of the Torah.

The purpose of the Torah has been misunderstood for millennia. Nowhere in the Scripture is the Torah referred to as our salvation or that obeying Torah gives us salvation. The Torah of YHWH was given to His people for several reasons, among them was to teach us how to live right (righteousness) before YHWH (Deuteronomy 6:24-25).

The reward for living right (obeying Torah) was, as stated above, to give us life, good and blessing. Torah teaches us how to love YHWH, and to fear Him, and to walk in His ways. The Torah was **NEVER** given to "make us right" before YHWH...BUT...to show us **HOW** to "live right" as His children.

The Torah, however, also teaches us what evil is, and what brings cursing and death upon us. It gives us the knowledge of sin (Romans 3:20), both of what sin is (Romans 7:7 and the 1 John 3:4) and what the consequence of committing sin is (Romans 6:16, 23; 8:13).

The Torah itself is the standard of what is "holy, just and good" (Romans 7:12), as well as defining the meaning of "spiritual" (Romans 7:14).

Paul says that the Torah is a "Schoolmaster" that leads us to Messiah Yahushua (Galatians 3:19-24), and that it is the authority from which sin gets the power to kill us (1 Corinthians 15:56), for when the Torah says "thou shalt not...for thou shall surely die", and we go ahead and disobey, then the Torah requires death as the penalty for our sin, for sin is not obeying the Torah (1 John 3:4).

The Torah will condemn us if we do not obey it or it will prove us, if we do obey it. But once the Torah has condemned us, it can no longer prove us righteous, because there is a penalty of death over us that must be paid. This is how the Torah teaches us our need of the Messiah.

The importance of Torah should be obvious; however, some would teach that once we've received the forgiveness of our sins and gain the redemption, through belief in the death, burial, and resurrection of Yahushua Messiah, we no longer have to live according to the righteous standard of the Torah, as if we are now exempt from righteous living.

The Torah is holy, just, and good, so the man who would live a holy, just (righteous) and good life before YHWH, would live in obedience to Torah. Torah is spiritual (Romans 7:14), so the man who would live a spiritual life, one led by The Spirit, would live a life in obedience to the Torah.

Torah teaches us to love, fear and walk in the ways of YHWH. So, the man who would love YHWH and fear Him by walking in His ways would live in obedience to the Torah. These principles are true after salvation, for the unsaved man has no desire or ability to serve YHWH. The Torah is the "Family Rules" for those who would be YHWH's children.

Since the Torah of YHWH is synonymous with the Word of YHWH, and the Word became flesh in Messiah Yahushua, then Yahushua is the Torah of YHWH by which we are to live.

Yahushua lived His entire life in perfect obedience to the Torah and we, His disciples, should do as we see our teacher doing (Matthew 10:25; Luke 6:40; John 13:14) we should imitate Him (1 Corinthians 11:1) and we should walk out our lives the same way He walked out His (1 John 2:6).

The mind of our Master Yahushua should also be in us (Philippians 2:5), so that we too should offer up our own fleshly bodies as a living sacrifice (Romans 12:1-2) unto YHWH, as He offered His for us, to live holy and acceptable, as a sacrifice, just as He did (i.e., obeying the Torah).

Listen to what Moses had to say about the Torah when he spoke to the children of Yisra'el just prior to entering the Promised Land:

> **Deu 8:1**      "**Guard to do every command** which I command you today, that you might **live**, and

|         | shall **increase**, and **go in**, and shall **possess** the land of which יהוה swore to your fathers. |
| Deu 8:2 | "And you shall remember that יהוה your Elohim led you all the way these forty years in the wilderness, to **humble** you, **prove** you, to **know what is in your heart, whether you guard His commands or not.** |
| Deu 8:3 | "And He humbled you, and let you suffer hunger, and fed you with manna which you did not know nor did your fathers know, to make you know that man **does not live by bread alone, but by every *Word* that comes from the mouth of יהוה.** |

Now listen to what Messiah Yahushua said to the enemy towards the end of His 40 days in the wilderness:

| Mat 4:4 | But He, answering, said, "It has been written, **'Man shall not live by bread alone, but by every word that comes from the mouth of יהוה.' "** |

This is a powerful statement, because Messiah is identifying with the wilderness wandering of Yisra'el and the trials that came along with it. In quoting this verse He was reinforcing the fact that our primary responsibility in serving Him, as being His children and trusting Him as our Elohim, was to obey EVERY WORD He had spoken. It's important to note that, when Moses gave this word to the people, it was after they had been saved from Egypt and crossed the Red Sea.

It was after their fathers had died in the wilderness for not obeying the Torah. The meaning, purpose and importance of the Torah is clear, and they are all summed up in one word:

| Mat 22:37 | And יהושע said to him, "'**You shall love יהוה your Elohim with all your heart, and with all your being, and with all your mind.'** |
| Mat 22:38 | "This is the first and great command. |
| Mat 22:39 | "And the second is like it, '**You shall love your neighbour as yourself.'** |

(Deuteronomy 6:5-6; Leviticus 19:18; Matthew 22:36-40; 1 John 2:3-6; 5:2-3)

8

# Chapter 2: Context

"The Cultural, Religious and Social Context
of the
Messianic Writings"

The 1st century was a very chaotic time in the Land YHWH promised Abraham, Isaac (Yitschaq) and Jacob (Ya'aqob). In the three centuries prior to the Messiah's birth the social environment of the Land went through radical upheaval. After the house of Judah (Yahudah) began its return from captivity in Babylon it was still under the authority of the Medo-Persian Empire.

Alexander the Great (356-323 BCE) conquered Medo-Persia and spread his religious culture (i.e., Hellenism) all throughout the known world, including the Land of Judea. After Alexander's death his empire was divided into four smaller kingdoms, two of which would fight over the Land (i.e., Egyptian and Seleucid kingdoms).

In approximately 168 BCE, the king of the Seleucid kingdom, Antiochus IV Epiphanies, attempted to completely Hellenize the land and the Jews. He conspired with certain Jews who had already succumbed to Hellenism and defiled the altar and the holy place, burned Torah scrolls, outlawed the keeping of the Sabbath, the feast days, and the dietary laws, even executing mothers who had circumcised their children. Antiochus and his forces were finally defeated by Jonathan Maccabaeus, under whom the Hasmonaean Dynasty was founded.

In the mid-first century BCE, Rome took control of the lands of Judea and Samaria and would ultimately destroy the Temple and the city of Yerushalayim in 70 CE. Rome would later outlaw the observance of the Jewish Religion (later called Judaism) throughout the entire Roman Empire (c. 135 CE.).

Because of the continual and severe control over the Jews by their Gentile enemies, the Jews were continually contentious against them and ethnically distant. The Jews were waiting for the imminent appearance of the Messiah, who they believed would deliver them from the Roman oppressors.

Back when the House of Judah was still in Babylonian captivity, the Jews began to rely heavily on the teachings of their scribes and rabbis. Throughout the years leading up to Messiah's ministry, these "Jewish sages" began creating oral traditions in an effort to "protect" the Torah from the people and the people from the Torah.

These traditions added thousands of man-made regulations and rituals, along with behavioral precedents from the practice of the rabbis themselves, to the Torah given by YHWH to Mosheh at Mount Sinai.

These "Oral Laws" (known today as the Talmud) began to take on more authority than the scriptural law (the Torah) among practicing Jews. The entire culture of the land of Judea in the time of Messiah was based on these "Rabbinic Traditions", which by now had become a man-made religion associated to the Scripture by name only. In the 1st century there were several "Houses" of rabbinical thought, as well as other divisions; Sadducees, Essences, Zealots, etc.

The two main houses of 1st century Pharisaic thought were that of Shammai and Hillel. Hillel, who was president of the Sanhedrin died, circa 10 CE and was replaced by Shammai, who went on to add 18 edicts based on his own opinions that did not conform to those of Hillel. These edicts of Shammai were mostly concerning ritual purity and the exclusion of Gentiles as part of the Jewish religion.

> **Note**: The grandson of Hillel was Gamliel, Paul's teacher, succeeded Shammai as president of the Sanhedrin in 30 CE, likely just after the death of Messiah. The teachings of Shammai continued to dominate Jewish religious practice and culture until the destruction of the Temple in 70 CE. However, we are told that a "voice from heaven" spoke and nullified the rulings of Shammai, which is why modern Judaism follows the teachings of Hillel and not Shammai.

Judaism is willing to include Gentiles into their belief if said Gentile will undergo certain "pre-requisite" qualifications. Among these are circumcision, baptism (mikvah), Torah obedience BEFORE they were allowed into the religion of the Jews (Galatians 1:13), however, a Gentile convert is never considered a Jew.

There are also the teachings concerning a 'righteous Gentile', which is one who adheres to the Noachian Laws, instituted in Babylonian Talmud (Sanhedrin 59a, see also Tosafot ad. loc.) and , interestingly, signed into law in the USA in 1991 by both Houses of Congress and President George H. W. Bush.

It was these man-made religious traditions, that the Messiah and His Apostles would deal with in the Messianic Writings.

> **Note**: Judaism, as a religion, had not been formalized into such at the time of the Messiah. Jews considered

11

themselves the chosen of YHWH and their adherence to the Torah as it was given through Mosheh was still their primary association, however, by the first century the "traditions of the rabbis" had transformed the true belief into one drowning in man-made thoughts and opinions (i.e., religion).

It wasn't until much later that the religion of Judaism was formalized in the Talmud. The appellation, Judaism, is a creation of Christian dogma which focuses on the differences between their man-made dogma and that of the Jews, instead of the things they have in common. They cannot do this, of course, because Christianity has rejected the Tanak (OT) as the foundation of their Belief.

Due to the social, religious, and cultural differences going on at the time, there were many questions as to what actually "saves" us and how we serve YHWH among the non-believing cultures that we live in. Both the Pharisees of the Jewish religious cast and the pagan religious cultures of the Gentiles were vying for the attention of the Messianic Believers, both Jew and Gentile.

Pagan religions, of course, taught idol worship, which YHWH hates, but to which many of the former Gentile believers had been a part. The Greek culture of Hellenism was heavily influenced by man-made intellectual thought, known as philosophy, which is a form of understanding generated by human reasoning alone.

Pharisaic teachers were going around attempting to convince believers that they couldn't be saved until AFTER they adhered to the Torah (i.e., legalism), Torah observance "to be saved" and specifically that of circumcision.

To a Pharisee of the first century, if you were not a Jew by birth and had been physically circumcised to show that you were a descendent of Abraham, you couldn't be saved. Beyond this they also confused the issues with other man-made traditions.

It was into this environment the Messiah was born and lived, and it was against those religious and cultural enemies (i.e., man-made religion and ideology) that Messiah and the Messianic writers had to deal.

Most all the Messianic letters of Paul (Sha'ul), James (Jacob) and Peter (Kepha) are attempting to answer questions that were asked of them, questions that were not preserved in Scripture, so we must

12

carefully examine those letters to find out what the overriding issues were that the 1st century Assemblies struggled with.

**Remember**, the Scripture is written to the Bride, so it can only be understood by those who have submitted themselves as the Bride. It is written to the "diligent seekers" who will search the entire Word, comparing Scripture with Scripture, not adding to, nor taking from the Scripture as a whole.

All doctrine must be consistent throughout the Scripture and there is nothing new under the sun or in the "New Testament" (not even doctrine).

| | |
|---|---|
| **Ecc 3:14** | I know that, whatsoever God doeth, it shall be forever: **nothing can be put to it, nor any thing taken from it**: and God doeth *it,* that *men* should fear before him. |
| **Ecc 3:15** | That which hath been is now; and that which is to be hath already been; and God requireth that which is past. (KJV) |

This was quoted from the King James Version so that comparison can be made between what that version says and what is actually said in the Hebrew.

But first consider, it says "whatever Elohim does", which would include the redemption plan, the Torah and everything else He has done… "is FOREVER!!!" Nothing can be added to it, meaning no one can change what it says, which includes taking anything from it. He does this so that man would fear Him.

Now, this doesn't mean He gave them to us so we would be afraid of Him, but He gave His Instructions, His Teachings (Torah) to man, so that man would know how to reverence Him throughout all generations.

> **Note**: Only those who reject Him need truly be afraid of Him.

YHWH's standards and requirements are FOREVER, and they NEVER change! The next verse begins with the Scriptural principle, there is "nothing new under the sun", then finishes with "God requires that which is past".

What's interesting about this last part of the verse, is that, in the Hebrew it actually says He "seeks what is pursued". This means, that from the very beginning, even before the foundation of the world,

13

YHWH set forth the redemption plan, and part of this redemption plan was a righteous standard of living, which is called the Torah.

It also means that this redemption plan, including the righteous way of living, is set in stone forever, it will never change, and it's always going to be the same. However, YHWH is seeking what's in the heart of man, in what he is pursuing, i.e., the intent of his heart.

The question now is, what are we pursuing? Are we pursuing Him according to our own thoughts and feelings? Have we created a "God" in our own image or are we totally and completely submitted to the instructions that He set forth before the foundation of the world that His people should live by?

# Chapter 3: Paul

"A Foundational Perspective"

The Messianic writer whose works have generated and is generating, the greatest doctrinal problems within believing assemblies today, is those of Paul of Tarsus.

This man was a native born Yisraeli, from the tribe of Benjamin, who on the day of his circumcision, was named Sha'ul (meaning, asked) as is the custom among the Hebrews (see Luke 1:57-63).

However, he also had the Roman name of Paulus (meaning, little), because he was born a Roman citizen in the city of Tarsus, which was in the area that used to be called Asia minor, but is now called Turkey.

Paul spent most of his life under the tutelage of one of the most highly honored rabbis of his day, Gamliel. Gamliel was the grandson of Hillel the First from whom a large portion of modern Judaism gets its teachings. Paul, as a Pharisee, would have had a very strict religious upbringing.

The word Pharisee comes from the Hebrew word "parash" and refers to a person who has been separated for some purpose, in this case, as a student of the religious sect of Pharisees (Acts 26:1-5). An ancient Pharisee is what we would call a Rabbi today.

Paul would have had to have almost encyclopedic knowledge of the Tanak (OT) by the time he was an adult. On top of this he would have had proficient knowledge of the oral traditions (Oral Law) of the Jewish religion, i.e., Judaism.

It is important to know that there is a distinction between the written Word or Torah (Law) given by YHWH through Mosheh and the Oral Law of the Pharisees.

What's vitally important to know about Paul, is that his entire life and point of view was that of a Hebrew, Torah obedient, scholar. All his writings are written from the perspective of a Torah observant Hebrew teacher and they were all written to people already in the assembly of believers, most of these assemblies having been started by Torah observant Jews, or Gentiles who had already been going to Jewish synagogues (Acts 13:14-49).

To truly understand what Paul is teaching in his writings, you have to look at them from a Hebrew/Torah perspective or you will misinterpret his meaning. To attempt to explain or teach Paul's intent without the Hebrew/Torah perspective is like trying to understand the meaning of a conversation of which you've only heard one side.

16

1.     To the assembly at Corinth, he wrote answers to questions the assembly had already sent to him.
2.     To the assemblies in Galatia, he sent a letter rebuking the assemblies there and clarifying the doctrine for which they were in error.
3.     To Rome he wrote a letter of introduction that covered the entire Good News (gospel), as well as how to live as believers. He also covered other topics, such as, who we are in Yahushua, how to behave towards unbelieving societies we are part of, and other questions that had come up throughout the Body of Messiah generally.
4.     Ephesians through 2nd Thessalonians were sent to answer a lot of the same questions already mentioned and warned the assemblies concerning the waywardness and influence of both the Jewish religion and Gentile idol worship (religious and philosophical ideologies).
5.     Both books of Timothy and the book of Titus were to these specific brothers about the organization of assemblies and the appointing of elders and servants, as well as personal encouragement to them.
6.     Philemon is a personal letter to a fellow believer concerning how the brother should behave towards his ex-servant, now brother.

Though open to some debate, the order of Paul's writings are as follows.

1.     Galatians
    2.     1st Thessalonians
    3.     2nd Thessalonians
    4.     1st Corinthians
    5.     2nd Corinthians
    6.     Romans
    7.     Philemon
    8.     Colossians
    9.     Ephesians
    10.     Philippians
    11.     1st Timothy
    12.     Titus
    13     2nd Timothy

There is reason to believe that the book of Hebrews was written by Paul also, however, there are a few elements that could be evidence of another writer. Personally, the author believes Hebrews is one of Paul's writings, however, it has been somewhat tainted by scribal or translational error.

Key principles to remember when attempting to understand Paul's writings are:

1. That he was a Sabbath keeping, Torah observant, Hebrew speaking, believer of Messiah (Acts 17:2; 21:20-24, 22:1-3; Philippians 3:3-6).
2. That he lived this way until his death (Acts 24:10-16; 25:7-8) and he claimed to be an imitator of the Messiah, who Himself lived in obedience to the Torah His entire life (1 Corinthians 11:1; 2 Corinthians 5:20-21; 1 Peter 2:21-22).
3. That though he surely spoke other languages, he wrote his books in a distinctively Hebrew style.
4. That he proved the doctrines he taught from quoting the Torah and prophets (Old Testament) exclusively (Acts 28:23)
5. That the Word or Scripture he refers to in his writings is a reference to the Tanak (Old Testament), because the Messianic Writings (New Testament) had not yet been written.
6. That the stories in the Tanak are parables or pictures to help us learn the doctrines of salvation written in the Messianic Writings. They are examples for us to learn from. (1Corinthians 10:1-12; Hebrews 4:1-11; 2 Peter 2:4-6; Jude 7)
7. That all his readers were already fellow believers, saved by Messiah, and so, all his warnings and teachings must be understood in light of this fact.
8. That the Assemblies already had prior teachings upon which they were founded, to which he elaborates upon in his writings.
9. That the majority of the first Gentile believers had already been participating in the Jewish synagogue system (Acts 13).
10. That the Bereans, after they heard Paul's message, went to the Scriptures (i.e., the Tanak) to check to be sure that what he said could be believed (Acts 17:10-11).

These 10 principles must be firmly established before we begin  trying to understand Paul's writings.

**Foundational principles of Scriptural thought and doctrine.**

| 2Ti 3:16 | **All Scripture** *is* given by inspiration of God, and *is* profitable for doctrine, for reproof, for correction, for **instruction in righteousness**: |
|---|---|
| 2Ti 3:17 | That the man of God may be perfect, thoroughly furnished unto all good works. (KJV) |

"All Scripture", from Paul's perspective, is a reference to the Tanak (OT).

| Deu 30:15 | "See, I have set before you today **life and good**, and **death and evil,** |
|---|---|
| Deu 30:16 | in that I am commanding you today to **love** יהוה your Elohim, to **walk in His ways**, and to **guard His commands**, and **His laws,** and **His right-rulings**. And you shall live and increase, and יהוה your Elohim shall bless you in the land which you go to possess. |
| Deu 30:17 | "But **if your heart turns away, and you do not obey**, and shall be drawn away, and **shall bow down to other mighty ones and serve them,** |
| Deu 30:18 | "I have declared to you today that **you shall certainly perish**, you shall not prolong your days in the land which you are passing over the Yardĕn to enter and possess. |
| Deu 30:19 | "I have called the heavens and the earth as witnesses today against you: I have set before you life and death, the blessing and the curse. Therefore you shall **choose life**, so that you live, both you and your seed, |
| Deu 30:20 | **to love** יהוה your Elohim, **to obey** His voice, and **to cling** to Him – for He is your life and the length of your days – to dwell in the land which יהוה swore to your fathers, to Aḇraham, to Yitsḥaq, and to Yaʻaqoḇ, to give them." |

To obey the Torah brings life, good and blessing, while disobeying the Torah brings death, evil and curses.

| Deu 6:24 | And יהוה commanded us to do **all** these laws, **to fear** יהוה our Elohim, **for our good always, to keep us alive**, as it is today. |
| Deu 6:25 | And **it is righteousness for us when we guard to do all** this command before יהוה our Elohim, as He has commanded us. |

The Torah is for our good always and by obeying it we show that we both fear YHWH and that we are living righteously before Him.

| Num 15:15 | **One law** is for **you of the assembly and for the stranger who sojourns with you** – a law that have **forever** throughout your generations. As you are, so is the stranger before יהוה. |
| Num 15:16 | **One Torah and one right-ruling is for you and for the stranger who sojourns with you.** |

***

| Lev 19:33 | 'And when a stranger sojourns with you in your land, do not oppress him. |
| Lev 19:34 | 'Let the **stranger who dwells among you be to you as the native among you**, and you shall love him as yourself. For you were strangers in the land of Mitsrayim. I am יהוה your Elohim. |

That both, the native born Yisra'eli and the stranger (Gentile: ger) that joins them, are equal before YHWH, like adopted sons, and one Torah is for both (There is neither Jew nor Gentile in Messiah for we are all ONE in Him-Galatians 3:28).

| Deu 28:13 | "And יהוה shall make you the head and not the tail. And you shall be only on top, and not be beneath, **if you obey** the commands of יהוה your Elohim, which I command you today, to guard and do. |
| Deu 28:14 | "**And do not turn aside from any of the Words** which I am commanding you today, right or left, to go after other mighty ones to serve them. |

To turn to the right or to the left of **anything** YHWH has
spoken through Mosheh is the same as serving another deity.

**Deu 13:1**    "When there arises among you a prophet or a
dreamer of dreams, and he shall give you a
sign or a wonder,

**Deu 13:2**    and the sign or the wonder **shall come true**,
of which he has spoken to you, saying, 'Let us
go after other mighty ones *(turning to the left
or the right of **anything** YHWH has spoken)* –
which you have not known – and serve
them,'

**Deu 13:3**    **do not listen** to the words of that prophet or
that dreamer of dreams, for יהוה your **Elohim**
**is trying you to know whether** you love יהוה
your Elohim with all your heart and with all
your being.

**Deu 13:4**    "**Walk** after יהוה your Elohim and **fear** Him,
and **guard** His commands and **obey** His
voice, and **serve** Him and **cling** to Him.

**Deu 13:5**    "And that prophet or that dreamer of dreams
is put to death, because **he has spoken
apostasy against יהוה** your Elohim – who
brought you out of the land of Mitsrayim and
ransomed you from the house of bondage – **to
make you stray** from the way in which יהוה
your Elohim commanded you to walk. Thus,
you shall purge the evil from your midst.

YHWH will send false prophets and workers of wonder to do
mighty signs among us, **to test us**, to see whether we love Him (by
obeying Him) or whether we will follow the lies and deceptive powers
of the false prophet.

**2Th 2:7**    For the secret of **lawlessness** is already at
work – only until he who now restrains comes
out of the midst.

**2Th 2:8**    And then the **lawless one** shall be revealed,
whom the Master shall consume with the
Spirit of His mouth and bring to naught with
the manifestation of His coming.

| 2Th 2:9 | The coming of the *lawless one* **is according to the working of Satan**, with all power and signs and wonders of falsehood, |
|---------|---------|
| 2Th 2:10 | and with **all deceit of unrighteousness in those perishing**, because they **did not receive the love of the truth,** in order for them to be saved. |
| 2Th 2:11 | And for this reason **Elohim sends them** a working of delusion, for them to believe the falsehood, |
| 2Th 2:12 | in order that all should be judged **who did not believe the truth but have delighted in the unrighteousness.** |

A False leader will come doing "signs and wonders" and YHWH will allow a lie to be believed because people refuse to believe the Truth. What is the Truth, in Scripture?

1.  Yahushua is the Truth!  John 14:6
2.  The Word is Truth!  John 17:17
3.  YHWH is Truth!  Romans 3:4
4.  The Torah is Truth!  Psalms 119:142

What is righteousness?

1.  Belief is the spiritual part. Hab 2:4/Gal 3:11
2.  Obeying Torah is the physical part.
    Deut 6:24-25/Rom 2:13

Note: Living righteously and being a just person means the same thing in Hebrew (STG# H6662): Tsaddiq, and in Greek (STG# G1342 and 1343): dikaios/dikaiosune.

***Strong's, under "just", reads 6622, but it is an error***

YHWH/Yahushua is Truth, and the Word/Torah is Truth!

| Joh 1:14 | And the Word became flesh and pitched His tent among us, and we saw His esteem, esteem as of an only brought forth of a father, complete in favour and truth. |
|---------|---------|

Yahushua and the Torah are one and cannot be separated!

**Isa 8:20**      To the Torah and to the witness! If they do not speak according to this Word, it is because they have no daybreak (light).
                                    ***

**Rev 14:12**      Here is the endurance of the set-apart ones, here are those guarding the commands of Elohim and the belief of יהושע.

See also:

1.      Revelation 1:2, 9; 6:9, 12:17 / Word/Commands and testimony
2.      Revelation 3:8; 19:13 / Word and the Name
3.      Revelation 12:11 / Blood and Word
4.      Revelation 15:3 / Songs of Moses and the Lamb
5.      Revelation 20:4 / Witness and Word

**Rev 22:12**      "And see, I am coming speedily, and My reward is with Me, to give to each according to his work.

**Rev 22:13**      "I am the 'Aleph' and the 'Taw', the Beginning and the End, the First and the Last.

**Rev 22:14**      "Blessed are those **doing His commands**, so that the authority shall be theirs unto the tree of life, and to enter through the gates into the city.

Both the witness of Messiah Yahushua **AND** the obedience to the Torah are **REQUIRED** to be complete and endure to the end.

**Psa 119:105**      Your word is a lamp to my feet and a light to my path.
                                    ***

**Pro 6:23**      For the command is a lamp, and the Torah a light, and reproofs of discipline a way of life,

The Word/Torah is the light that shows us the path we should walk; it's the way we are to live. But it cannot save us from our sins or the penalty for sin, which is death. What is sin?

23

| 1Jn 3:4 | Whosoever committeth sin transgresseth also the law: for sin is the transgression of the law. (KJV) |

One act of disobedience, one transgression of the Torah makes us guilty of sin (James 2:10) one act of sin brings the penalty of death upon us (Romans 6:23; 1 Corinthians 15:56). The only way to be forgiven for sin and saved from the death penalty, is for someone innocent to die in our place, for only death can free us from the death penalty (Romans 6:7) and only blood can pay for our sin (Hebrews 9:22).

Therefore, once we have disobeyed the Torah, which everyone has (Romans 3:23), the Torah can no longer "make us right", with YHWH (Romans 3:20), only a blood sacrifice can do that.

However, once we receive the blood sacrifice and gain forgiveness for our past sin, can we go on disobeying the Torah? "God forbid!" (Romans 6:15)

If we continue to live in disobedience to the Torah we will once again bring death upon our heads (Romans 6:15; 8:13; Gal 2:20-25; Hebrews 6:4-8; 10:26-31).

| Psa 119:89 | Forever, O יהוה, Your word stands firm in the heavens. |

\*\*\*

| Deu 4:1 | "And now, O Yisra'ĕl, listen to the laws and the right-rulings which I am teaching you to do, **so that you live**, and shall **go in** and **possess** the land which יהוה Elohim of your fathers is giving you. |
| Deu 4:2 | **"Do not add to the Word which I command you, and do not take away from it, so as to guard** the commands of יהוה your Elohim which I am commanding you. (See also Deu 12:32; Pro 30:6; Rev 22:18-19) |

\*\*\*

| Deu 4:5 | "See, I have taught you laws and right-rulings, as יהוה my Elohim commanded me, **to do** thus in the land which you go to possess. |
| Deu 4:6 | "And you shall **guard and do** them, for **this is your wisdom and your understanding** before the eyes of the peoples who hear all these laws, and they shall say, 'Only a wise |

24

and understanding people is this great nation!'

We are not to add to the Torah or to take anything away from it. We are to obey it **ALL** without adding to it or taking from it and it is by doing this we gain wisdom and understanding (Psalms 119:95-104).

> **Mat 5:17**  "Do not think that I came to destroy the Torah or the Prophets. I did not come to destroy but to complete.
>
> **Mat 5:18**  "For truly, I say to you, till the heaven and the earth pass away, one yod or one tittle shall by no means pass from the Torah till all be done. (Luke 16:17)

In the above quoted verses, the word "destroy" is the Greek word "καταλύω" (*kataluō*), which is a compound word meaning, "to loosen down", and refers to a doing away with or reducing or diminishing in some capacity. Scripturally speaking, and in the context of these verses, it refers to causing the Torah to "pass away".

Modern teachers would have us believe that because of the death, burial and resurrection of Yahushua the Torah no longer applies to us, it has been "done away with" by the blood of Messiah, no longer having relevance in a believer's life.

The very concept of this is foreign both to the entire Scripture and to what the Messiah Himself, is saying in this very passage.

The word "complete" in verse 17 is the Greek word "πληρόω" (plēroō), which means "to make replete, that is to cram (full)". This Greek word has the meaning of making something full as in the process of filling something up, like taking a half a glass of water and filling it to the brim.

As we have said before, the Torah cannot be added to nor taken away from, by ANYONE, so the Messiah cannot, in any way, intend for us to interpret this passage, to mean that the law no longer applies to us.

What the Messiah is saying, is that the Torah, in its totality, shall not be diminished from, in any way.

The Torah is as relevant today as it was when it was given two and a half millennia ago, and it remains today the only standard of righteous living for which believers can live righteously before YHWH. Consider Ephesians 2:10,

25

**Eph 2:10**     For we are his workmanship, created in Christ Jesus **unto good works**, which God hath **before ordained that we should walk in them.** (KJV)

I hear this verse quoted a lot; however, no one takes the time to critically think about what is being said here. In fact, your average everyday believer today is not encouraged to think critically about anything the pastor tells them.

Looking at Ephesians 2:10, we see that believers in Yahushua are supposed to walk in the good works that YHWH ordained before the Messiah came to die.

The only standard of "good works" set forth in the Scripture is that which YHWH gave through Moses to the children of Yisra'el on Mount Sinai. The Torah IS the "good works" that YHWH before ordained that we should walk in them.

The word "fulfilled" or "completed" in verse 18 is the Greek word "γίνομαι" (ginomai), which has a wide variety of meanings based on the context in which you choose, however in this context it takes on the meaning of "completely full" or finished.

What's significant about verse 18 is that nothing shall pass from the Torah until **ALL** is completed.

Now, as far as I can tell, there is not a single Christian or Jewish teacher in the world that suggests everything that's been written in the Scripture has been finished, we are all still waiting for something to be finished, i.e., the return of Messiah.

So, according to this passage, the Torah is still relevant and in force today. Any teaching that says that the Torah is no longer necessary to live by today, is a false teaching according to YHWH, through Moses (Deuteronomy 4:2; 12:32; 13:1-5) and Messiah Himself (Matthew 5:17-18).

Any teaching that says you don't have to obey the Torah is teaching you to serve another deity (Deuteronomy 28:14) and no matter how many miracles accompany the teaching, it's still a false teaching (Deuteronomy 13:1-5; Matthew 7:22-23). Any teaching that says Torah "is for Jews" and that Gentiles don't have to obey it, is a false teaching (Exodus 12:49; Numbers 15:15-16).

**Ecc 3:14**     I know that whatever Elohim does is **forever**. There is no adding to it, and there is no taking from it. Elohim does it, that men should fear before Him.

\*\*\*

| | |
|---|---|
| **Mal 3:6** | "For I am יהוה, **I shall not change**, and you, O sons of Yaʿaqob̲, shall not come to an end. (See also: James 1:17) |

***

| | |
|---|---|
| **Ecc 1:9** | What has been is what shall be, what has been done is what shall be done, and there is **no new *matter* under the sun**. |

The foundational perspective of how to understand Messianic doctrine, is founded on the principles laid out below.

1. YHWH does not change His commands once they are given. (Isaiah 55:11)
2. The Torah (law) that YHWH gave to Mosheh is as authoritative and binding today as it was when He gave them to Yisra'el on Mount Sinai. (Matthew 5:17-18).
3. Not a single commandment has been done away with, they are all binding today. (Deuteronomy 4:2; 12:32; Ecclesiastes 3:14; Proverbs 30:6; Revelation 22:18-19)
4. Messiah did not change the Torah or our obligation to keep it today. (Matthew 5:17-18; Galatians 2:17
5. Nothing can be taken from the Torah or added to it by anyone. (Deuteronomy 4:2; 12:32; Ecclesiastes 3:14; Proverbs 30:6; Revelation 22:18-19 and Deuteronomy 13:1-5
6. Obeying the Torah is "by definition"; life, good and blessing. (Deuteronomy 30)
7. Not obeying the Torah is "by definition"; death, evil and a curse. (Deuteronomy 30)
8. Not obeying the Torah is "by definition"; (sin). (1 John 3:4)
9. Obeying the Torah is how we live righteously. (Deuteronomy 6:24-25)
10. Obeying the Torah makes us wise and understanding. (Deuteronomy 4:5-6)
11. Though the Torah cannot save us from past sin, it can keep us from sinning in the future if we obey it. (Romans 6:15-16)

Since all these principles are scripturally true, how then can we understand the writings of Paul, considering our teachers tell us that Paul says, we are no longer required to obey the Torah, or keep the Sabbath, or obey the dietary laws, etc.?

Yah willing, this book will help you find answers to your "New Testament" questions in an "Old Testament" understanding and will explain why the Jews throughout the history of "Christianity" have vehemently rejected the good news of Messiah Yahushua.

# Chapter 4: The Two-Part Principle

In this next section, we are going to discuss one of the most important and overlooked doctrines in the Scripture. Most modern teachers give lip service to the distinction between spiritual and physical but do not actually understand this principle, nor do they apply it to themselves or teach others to apply it properly.

> **Ecc 3:1**     "know that **whatever** Elohim does is **forever**. There is **no adding to it, and there is no taking from it**. Elohim does it that men should **fear** before Him."

The most overlooked principle in modern teachings of the Scripture, as well as the least understood, is the *Two-Part Principle*. And the reason it is so misunderstood is because modern teachers do not practice the Way of understanding, neither do they teach it.

> **Deu 4:5**     "See, I have taught you laws and right rulings, as יהוה my Elohim commanded me, to do thus in the land which you go to **possess**.
>
> **Deu 4:6**     "And you shall **guard** and **do** them, for **this is your wisdom and your understanding** before the eyes of the peoples who hear all these laws, and they shall say, 'Only a wise and understanding people is this great nation!

To know what the Scripture says is a far cry from understanding what it means. There is a process that must take place if we hope to gain true understanding. King David once said that he had more understanding then all his teachers and elders because he "studied" and "observed" the orders, instructions, and Laws of YHWH. [Ps 119: 95-104]

We must never forget that His ways and understanding are far, far greater than ours. We must NEVER rely on our own thoughts, opinions, or feelings, or those of other men, but must submit ourselves to the understanding of YHWH as He has given in His Word.

> **Isa 55:8**     "For My thoughts are not your thoughts, neither are your ways My ways," declares יהוה.

| | |
|---|---|
| **Isa 55:9** | "For as the heavens are higher than the earth, so are My ways higher than your ways, and My thoughts than your thoughts. |
| **Isa 55:10** | "For as the rain comes down, and the snow from the heavens, and do not return there, but water the earth, and make it bring forth and bud, and give seed to the sower and bread to the eater, |
| **Isa 55:11** | so is My Word that goes forth from My mouth – it does not return to Me empty, but shall do what I please, and shall certainly accomplish what I sent it for. |

***

| | |
|---|---|
| **Pro 3:1** | My son, do not forget my Torah, and **let your heart** watch over my commands; |
| **Pro 3:2** | For length of days and long life and peace they add to you. |
| **Pro 3:3** | Let not kindness and truth forsake you Bind them around your neck, Write them on the tablet of your heart, |
| **Pro 3:4** | Thus finding favour and good insight in the eyes of Elohim and man. |
| **Pro 3:5** | **Trust in יהוה with all your heart**, and **lean not on your own understanding**; |
| **Pro 3:6** | **Know Him in all your ways**, And He makes all your paths straight. |
| **Pro 3:7** | Do not be wise in your own eyes; **Fear יהוה** and turn away from evil. |

YHWH wants us to know Him. However, there is a far better position we should be seeking to attain. That is a position where He will claim to know us (compare Mat 7:21-23). There is a huge distinction between these two statements and a clear and simple evaluation of the Scripture bears this out.

Some might scoff at this and say that YHWH is both Creator and Elohim of all things, so of course He knows us and all men.

This statement expresses a clear ignorance of the nature of YHWH and His Word. Of course, He knows "of" all men, even their deepest, darkest thoughts, however, He only knows those that have trusted in Him and who strive daily to seek Him out.

| Jer 29:11 | 'For I know the plans I am planning for you,' declares יהוה, 'plans of peace and not of evil, to give you a future and an expectancy. |
| Jer 29:12 | 'Then you shall call on Me, and shall come and pray to Me, and I shall listen to you. |
| Jer 29:13 | 'And you shall seek Me, and shall find Me, when you search for Me with all your heart. |

***

| Heb 11:6 | "But without belief it is impossible to please Him, for he who comes to Elohim has to **believe that He is**, and that He is a **rewarder of those who earnestly seek Him.** |

As an example of these two distinctions (us knowing Him and Him knowing us), let's go back in time to our father Abraham.

| Gen 12:1 | And יהוה said to Abram, "Go yourself out of your land, from your relatives and from your father's house, to a land which I show you. |
| Gen 12:2 | "And I shall make you a great nation, and bless you and make your name great, and you shall be a blessing! |
| Gen 12:3 | "And I shall bless those who bless you and curse him who curses you. And in you all the clans of the earth shall be blessed." |
| Gen 12:4 | So Abram left, as יהוה had commanded him, and Lot went with him. And Abram was seventy-five years old when he set out from Haran. |

Abram was called out of Haran into the land of Kena'an and was promised that land as an inheritance for himself and his seed. He questioned YHWH about him having an heir in Chapter 15.

| Gen 15:1 | After these events the word of יהוה came to Abram in a vision, saying, "Do not be afraid, Abram. I am your shield; your reward is exceedingly great." |
| Gen 15:2 | And Abram said, "Master יהוה, what would you give me, seeing I go childless, and the heir of my house is Eliʿezer of Damascus?" |

31

| Gen 15:3 | And Abram said, "See, You have given me no seed, and see, one born in my house is my heir!" |
| Gen 15:4 | And see, the word of יהוה came to him, saying, "This one is not your heir, but he who comes from your own body is your heir." |
| Gen 15:5 | And He brought him outside and said, "Look now toward the heavens, and count the stars if you are able to count them." And He said to him, "So are your seed." |
| Gen 15:6 | And he believed in יהוה, and He reckoned it to him for righteousness. |

At that time YHWH declared Abram righteous because he had heard the word of promise that YHWH had spoken and believed it. This is vitally important to see because it is a witness to part one of our "Two Part" principle.

The second part is expressed in the offering up of Yitschaq (Isaac).

**The Binding**

| Gen 22:1 | And it came to be after these events that Elohim tried Abraham, and said to him, "Abraham!" And he said, "Here I am." |
| Gen 22:2 | And He said, "Take your son, now, your only son Yitshaq, whom you love, and go to the land of Moriyah, and offer him there as a burnt offering on one of the mountains which I command you." |
| Gen 22:3 | And Abraham rose early in the morning and saddled his donkey, and took two of his young men with him, and Yitshaq his son. And he split the wood for the burnt offering, and arose and went to the place which Elohim had commanded him. |
| Gen 22:4 | And on the third day Abraham lifted his eyes and saw the place from a distance. |
| Gen 22:5 | So Abraham said to his young men, "Stay here with the donkey while the boy and I go over there and worship, and come back to you." |

| Gen 22:6 | And Abraham took the wood of the burnt offering and laid it on Yitshaq his son. And he took the fire in his hand, and a knife, and the two of them went together. |
|----------|------------------------------------------------------------------------------------------------------------------------------------------------------------------------|
| Gen 22:7 | And Yitshaq spoke to Abraham his father and said, "My father!" And he said, "Here I am, my son." And he said, "See, the fire and the wood! But where is the lamb for a burnt offering? |
| Gen 22:8 | And Abraham said, "My son, Elohim does provide for Himself the lamb for a burnt offering." And the two of them went together. |
| Gen 22:9 | And they came to the place which Elohim had commanded him, and Abraham built an altar there and placed the wood in order. And he bound Yitshaq his son and laid him on the altar, upon the wood. |
| Gen 22:10 | And Abraham stretched out his hand and took the knife to slay his son, |
| Gen 22:11 | but the Messenger of יהוה called to him from the heavens and said, "Abraham, Abraham!" And he said, "Here I am." |
| Gen 22:12 | And He said, "Do not lay your hand on the boy, nor touch him. For now I know that you fear Elohim, seeing you have not withheld your son, your only son, from Me." |
| Gen 22:13 | And Abraham lifted his eyes and looked and saw behind him a ram caught in a bush by its horns, and Abraham went and took the ram and offered it up for a burnt offering instead of his son. |
| Gen 22:14 | And Abraham called the name of the place, 'יהוה Yireh,' as it is said to this day, "On the mountain יהוה provides." |

Here we see that YHWH instructed Abram, (now Abraham) to offer up his son as an ascending offering. Notice in verse 12 that Elohim prevented him from taking the fatal blow and then, said something interesting.

"… for **now I know** that you fear Elohim, seeing you have not withheld your son, your only son, from Me." 12b

YHWH had already declared Abraham righteous in Genesis 15:6, however, He did not state that He knew Abraham feared Him, until after he had fully committed to killing his own son.

Yes, the Scriptures declares that Elohim knows the hearts of men, even better than we know our own, yet it wasn't until Abraham acted upon the command to offer Yitschaq that he proved, to both YHWH and to himself, that He loved and trusted YHWH more than all else.

These are the Two Parts {Trust and Action} that make true "Belief" perfect (complete). Let's now start at the beginning, literally, to see that this *Two-Part Principle* was at work even then.

## CREATION

**Gen 1:1**      In the beginning Elohim created **the heavens and the earth**.

The act of creation, mentioned in Scripture, included two parts: Heavenly things and Earthly things. It is important to recognize that everything in creation resides within these two parts. Heavenly and Earthly, working together, side by side, embody the whole (complete) creation and everything else derives from within them.

## MAN

**Gen 2:7**      And יהוה Elohim **formed the man out of dust from the ground**, and **breathed into his nostrils breath of life**. And **the man became a living being**.

It says that Elohim "formed" man. The Hebrew word for formed is (Strong's # [stg#] H3335), "yatsar": to mould into a form; from a word meaning to press or squeeze.

This expresses that Elohim took the dust into His own hands and molded man into shape just as a potter molds the clay. Here we see, from the ground (earthly) man received his physical body.

The Hebrew phrase: "nishmat chayim", means, breath of lives (which suggests a breath from which life comes). The word "nishmat" is associated to "neshamah" [stg# 5397], also translated as breath but means a "puff" of air or wind.

This word is translated as spirit in Job 26:4, where it says of man "whose spirit comes from you", and Pro 20:27, which says, "The spirit of man is the candle of YHWH searching all his inward parts".

34

See how the word for both breath and spirit are related? This is also true for the primary word for spirit in the Hebrew, i.e., "ruach" [stg# 7307], meaning wind and associated to breath from stg# 7306.

Notice how the physical body came from the earth while the breath or spirit came directly from YHWH, who is Spirit (Jn 4:24). Here again we see that the heavenly (spirit) and the earthly (body) are together, side by side, to accomplish some purpose. What purpose did they accomplish here?

"And the man became a living soul". 7c (KJV)

The word "became" is from the Hebrew, "hayah" [stg# 1961], meaning, to exist. There is a debate among, so called, scholars as to the actual meaning of this word and it has caused huge theological schisms within modern doctrine.

Like all Hebrew words, this one has a root meaning, which gives us a starting place in trying to translate it. Also, the word must be translated within the immediate context of the passage where it's used.

In this context we see it used in relation to something "coming into existence" that did not exist before, i.e., the man became alive. So, then, we see that it took the spirit and the body working together to produce life.

This is confirmed by Brother James (2:26), where he says, "the body without the spirit is dead".

## ISAIAH

There are many examples of this principle at work in virtually every story and teaching in Scripture, however here we are going to just look at a few clear examples from the whole of Scripture.

| | |
|---|---|
| **Isa 8:13** | "יהוה of hosts, Him you shall set apart. Let Him be your fear and let Him be your dread. |
| **Isa 8:14** | "And He shall be for a set-apart place, but a stone of stumbling and a rock that makes for falling to both the houses of Yisra'ĕl, as a trap and a snare to the inhabitants of Yerushalayim. |
| **Isa 8:15** | "And many among them shall stumble and fall and be broken and snared and taken." |
| **Isa 8:16** | Bind up the witness, seal the Torah among my taught ones. |

35

| | |
|---|---|
| **Isa 8:17** | And I shall wait on יהוה, who hides His face from the house of Yaʿaqoḇ. And I shall look for Him. |
| **Isa 8:18** | Look, I and the children whom. יהוה has given me – for signs and wonders in Yisra'ĕl from יהוה of hosts, who dwells in Mount Tsiyon. |
| **Isa 8:19** | And when they say to you, "Seek those who are mediums and wizards, who whisper and mutter," should not a people seek their Elohim? Should they seek the dead on behalf of the living? |
| **Isa 8:20** | **To the Torah and to the witness**! If they do not speak according to this Word, it is because they have no daybreak. |

At the time of this writing, Isaiah was dealing with false prophets and priests who were teaching the people to go in a way that was different then they had been taught by Moses. This was, and still is, a direct violation of the Torah (Instruction, i.e., Law).

| | |
|---|---|
| **Deu 13:1** | "When there arises among you a prophet or a dreamer of dreams, and he shall give you a sign or a wonder, |
| **Deu 13:2** | and the sign or the wonder shall come true, of which he has spoken to you, saying, 'Let us go after other mighty ones – which you have not known – and serve them,' |
| **Deu 13:3** | do not listen to the words of that prophet or that dreamer of dreams, for יהוה your Elohim is trying you to know whether you love יהוה your Elohim with all your heart and with all your being. |
| **Deu 13:4** | "Walk after יהוה your Elohim and fear Him, and guard His commands and obey His voice, and serve Him and cling to Him. |
| **Deu 13:5** | "And that prophet or that dreamer of dreams is put to death, because he has spoken apostasy against יהוה your Elohim – who brought you out of the land of Mitsrayim and redeemed you from the house of bondage – to make you stray from the way in which יהוה your Elohim commanded you to walk. Thus you shall purge the evil from your midst. |

In Isaiah 8, YHWH is warning that the true "Word" that is true "Light" is one that has both the Torah and the Testimony/Witness (The Two Parts).

You don't get a clearer statement of fact than that, yet the "church" can't seem to grasp it. Our complete salvation, complete redemption, is based on a teaching that incorporates both belief and works, Yahushua and the Torah.

This is obviously an "Old Testament" passage, and some would claim that it no longer applies to the "New Testament Church". To those men I would offer the end time prophet John.

> **Rev 14:12**     Here is the endurance of the set-apart ones,
> here are those **guarding the commands of
> Elohim and the belief of יהושע.**

In some versions they use the word "patience" in verse 12, but the Greek word is, "hupomone" [stg#5281], meaning, cheerful (or hopeful) endurance. It comes from stg# 5278, "hopomeno", which means, to stay under (or behind).

"Hopomeno" is used in Matthew 24:14, another end time passage, where Messiah Himself said, "He that shall endure to the end shall be saved." This is meant to express the idea of staying faithful and obedient under, or beneath, the hardship of this life and, specifically, of that time.

So today, and in a time to come, there are things that must be endured to receive the promise of complete redemption. Those who will endure it, according to Rev 14:12, are those who "keep the commandments of Elohim AND have belief in Yahushua Messiah". Here we see clearly that the *Two-Part Principle* is at work even in the last days.

Once understood, this *Two-Part Principle* can be seen in every doctrine, passage, and statement of belief in the Scripture. Yes, even in the so-called "New Testament" (Messianic Writings).

You need to understand that all salvation is a "New or Renewed Covenant" promise from YHWH, through Yahushua, to all peoples, both Jew and Gentile. One People, One Yisra'el!

## The Brit Chadashah (Renewed Covenant) or Messianic Writings

Now, before we go to the Messianic Writings to see this principle at work there and how it applies today, let's look at the "New or Renewed Covenant" promise.

| | |
|---|---|
| **Jer 31:31** | "See, the days are coming," declares יהוה, "when I shall make a new covenant with the house of Yisra'ĕl and with the house of Yehuḏah, |
| **Jer 31:32** | not like the covenant I made with their fathers in the day when I took them by the hand to bring them out of the land of Mitsrayim, My covenant which they broke, though I was a husband to them," declares יהוה. |
| **Jer 31:33** | "For this is the covenant I shall make with the house of Yisra'ĕl after those days, declares יהוה: I shall put My Torah in their inward parts, and write it on their hearts. And I shall be their Elohim, and they shall be My people. |

***

| | |
|---|---|
| **Eze 36:22** | "Therefore say to the house of Yisra'ĕl, 'Thus said the Master יהוה, "I do not do this for your sake, O house of Yisra'ĕl, but for My set-apart Name's sake, which you have profaned among the Gentiles wherever you went. |
| **Eze 36:23** | "And I shall set apart My great Name, which has been profaned among the Gentiles, which you have profaned in their midst. And the Gentiles shall know that I am יהוה," declares the Master יהוה, "when I am set-apart in you before their eyes. |
| **Eze 36:24** | For I will take you from among the heathen, and gather you out of all countries, and will bring you into your own land. |
| **Eze 36:25** | Then will I sprinkle clean water upon you, and ye shall be clean: from all your filthiness, and from all your idols, will I cleanse you. |
| **Eze 36:26** | A new heart also will I give you, and a new spirit will I put within you: and I will take away the stony heart out of your flesh, and I will give you an heart of flesh. |
| **Eze 36:27** | and put My Spirit within you. And I shall cause you to walk in My laws and guard My right-rulings and shall do them. |
| **Eze 36:28** | "And you shall dwell in the land that I gave to your fathers. And you shall be My people, and I shall be your Elohim. |

First, notice that in Jeremiah YHWH is addressing the Houses of Yisra'el and the House of Judah, while Ezekiel is addressing the House of Yisra'el. I emphasize this because it is a huge factor in understanding to whom the Master is making promises or giving warnings.

It's important that the promises are to the children of Yisra'el, NOT to the nations (Gentiles). It must be clearly stated, however, that the nations can enter into the Promises through belief in Yahushua Messiah (Eph 2:11-19). The Torah calls these people… "the strangers that sojourn among you."

It is clear in both the Tanak (OT) and the Messianic Writings (NT) that when the people of the nations (Gentiles) believe in Yahushua as Saviour, they join alongside the children of Yisra'el in covenant with YHWH.

> **Lev 19:33** 'And **when a stranger sojourns with you** in your land, do not oppress him.
>
> **Lev 19:34** 'Let the stranger who dwells among you **be to you as the native among you**, and **you shall love him as yourself**. For you were strangers in the land of Mitsrayim. I am יהוה your Elohim.

We see here that, to YHWH, once a non-Yisra'eli joins with Yisra'el in the covenant they are no longer to be considered strangers but are to be granted the same dignity and position as any native born Yisra'eli.

This, by the legal definition, is called adoption. Any Gentile who forsakes his old life and joins with Yisra'el, through belief in Yahushua, has been adopted into the household of Yisra'el, YHWH's Chosen People. A perfect picture of this can be seen in the story of Ruth.

Ruth was a Moabite and she married a Yisra'eli man who had left the Promise Land with his father's house because of a drought in the Land. While still in Moab, Ruth's husband died.

When her Mother-in-law, Naomi, decided to return to The Promised Land after the drought, she tried to convince Ruth to return to her father's house, for Naomi had nothing to offer her since both Naomi's husband and sons were dead. Consider Ruth's response.

> **Ruth 1:16** But Ruth said, "Do not urge me to leave you, or to go back from following after you. For

| | wherever you go, I go; and wherever you stop over, I stop over. Your people is my people, and your Elohim is my. |
|---|---|
| Ruth 1:17 | "Where you die, I die, and there I shall be buried. יהוה do so to me, and more also – for death itself parts you and me." |

(Also, consider Messiah's words in Mat 19:29)

See how Ruth was willing to leave everything she had ever known, to go to the Promised Land with Naomi? The shadow picture here is undeniable. Naomi represents the House of Yisra'el who had left the Land in a time of drought. The drought that Naomi fled from was one of water, but the drought that Yisra'el experienced was a spiritual drought.

In the scripture, water often symbolizes the spirit or spiritual things. In the time before the northern house, the House of Yisra'el, went into exile among the nations (722 BCE), it was suffering the worst kind of drought possible, that is, they were in a spiritual drought of misunderstanding because of disobedience, which led them to destruction.

Like Naomi, Yisra'el's Husband, YHWH, became dead to her because of her rebellion. When she turned to make her way back (repented) to the Land of Promise, which she (Yisra'el) will do in the last days, she will bring with her, her Gentile daughter-in-law.

That daughter-in-law, Ruth, represents all those Gentiles that heard the message of their salvation in Yahushua Messiah and believed. Those who have forsaken their old pagan ways, their "old man" , and joined their mother-in-law, Yisra'el, in covenant with YHWH through the redemption that only comes through belief in Yahushua Ha'Mashiach.

Brother Paul explained this in both Romans and Ephesians, where he showed us that Gentiles who believe in Yahushua are "no longer strangers and foreigners, but fellow citizens with the set-apart ones and members of the house-hold of Elohim," (Eph 2:19) and that those "wild olive branches" (Gentiles) who have trusted in Yahushua have been grafted into the "natural olive tree" (Yisra'el-Rom 11:5-24) and should be treated just as native born Yisra'elis, as commanded in Leviticus 19:33-34.

So, we have established that the "New or Renewed Covenant" promises were for the Children of Yisra'el and for the Gentiles who would join with them in covenant with YHWH through belief in Yahushua Messiah.

Now, let's move on to the *Two-Part Principle*, as taught in the Brit Chadashah (NT) and since it is Paul whose writings have been so erroneously interpreted by modern teachers, let's begin with his letters. First, however, let's remember what Brother Peter said concerning these types of men and Paul's writings.

| | |
|---|---|
| **2Pe 3:14** | So then, beloved ones, looking forward to this, do your utmost to be found by Him in peace, spotless and blameless, |
| **2Pe 3:15** | and reckon the patience of our Master as deliverance, as also our beloved brother Paul wrote to you, according to the wisdom given to him, |
| **2Pe 3:16** | as also in all his letters, speaking in them concerning these matters, in which some are hard to understand, which those who are **untaught and unstable** twist to their own destruction, as they do also the other Scriptures. |
| **2Pe 3:17** | You, then, beloved ones, being forewarned, watch, lest you also fall from your own steadfastness, being led away with the delusion of the lawless, |

There are several significant things being said here that need to be understood.

| | |
|---|---|
| **(1) -** | Peter expected us (the brethren) to live our lives "spotlessly and blamelessly" before YHWH. This phrase is referring to our righteous lifestyle as believers. See what Paul said concerning this manner of living. |

| | |
|---|---|
| **Php 2:5** | For, let this mind be in you which was also in Messiah יהושע, |
| **Php 2:6** | who, being in the form of Elohim, did not regard equality with Elohim a matter to be grasped, |
| **Php 2:7** | but emptied Himself, taking the form of a servant, and came to be in the likeness of men. |

41

| | |
|---|---|
| **Php 2:8** | And having been found in fashion as a man, He humbled Himself and became obedient unto death, death even of a stake. |
| **Php 2:9** | Elohim, therefore, has highly exalted Him and given Him the Name which is above every name, |
| **Php 2:10** | that at the Name of יהושע every knee should bow, of those in heaven, and of those on earth, and of those under the earth, |
| **Php 2:11** | and every tongue should confess that יהושע Messiah is Master, to the esteem of Elohim the Father. |
| **Php 2:12** | So that, my beloved, as you always obeyed – not only in my presence, but now much rather in my absence – work out your own deliverance with fear and trembling, |
| **Php 2:13** | for it is Elohim who is working in you both to desire and to work for His good pleasure. |
| **Php 2:14** | Do all things without murmurings and disputings: |
| **Php 2:15** | in order that you be blameless and faultless, children of Elohim without blemish in the midst of a crooked and perverse generation, among whom you shine as lights in the world, |
| **Php 2:16** | holding on to the Word of life, for a boast to me in the day of Messiah, that I have not run in vain or laboured in vain. |

Our question then, what is the standard of righteousness that we are to live by?

It is obvious that it should be the same standard of righteousness that Yahushua Himself lived by, wouldn't you think?

| | |
|---|---|
| **1 Cor 11:1** | "Be imitators of me, as I also am of Messiah." |
| | *** |
| **1Jn 2:6** | "The one who says he stays in Him ought himself also to walk, even as He walked. |

The standard of righteous living that He lived by is the same standard that we are to live by. It's the standard of the Torah, as it was given by YHWH, through Mosheh, to His people Yisra'el, without additions or subtractions.

| Deu 6:24 | 'And יהוה commanded us to do all these laws, to fear יהוה our Elohim, for our good always, to keep us alive, as it is today. |
| Deu 6:25 | 'And it is righteousness for us when we guard to do all this command before יהוה our Elohim, as He has commanded us. |

Sounds simple, right? It really is that simple, unfortunately we have allowed men to interfere with the simplicity of the scripture, which is Peter's next admonishment.

**(2) -** Peter knew some of the things Paul had written were hard to understand and that certain men would sneak into the Assembly and misuse Paul's writings to subvert the Truth. His statement that these men would be untaught and unstable is an important one.

**Untaught:** stg's #**G261** "amathēs" from (G1 - as a negative particle) no, not and (G3129) to learn; ignorant: - unlearned. This word suggests that these men did not have the same knowledge of the Scripture that Paul had and therefore could not correctly interpret his intent.

**Unstable:** stg's #**G739** "astēriktos" from (G1 - as a negative particle) no, not and (a presumed derivation of G4741) to set fast; unfixed, that is, (figuratively) vacillating: - unstable.— This word suggests that these men have no fixed foundation from which to correctly understand Paul's writings.

Let us remember what the Messiah Himself said about foundations.

| Mat 7:24 | "Therefore everyone who hears these words of Mine, and does them, shall be like a wise man who built his house on the rock, |
| Mat 7:25 | and the rain came down, and the floods came, and the winds blew and beat on that house, |

43

| | and it did not fall, for it was founded on the rock. |
|---|---|
| Mat 7:26 | "And everyone who hears these words of Mine, and does not do them, shall be like a foolish man who built his house on the sand, |
| Mat 7:27 | and the rain came down, and the floods came, and the winds blew, and they beat on that house, and it fell, and great was its fall." |

These men who neither have Paul's learning, nor his foundation of hearing and doing the Word, will have a great fall.

This great fall is Peter's next point, but before we go there, I want to stress a point that I have already alluded to.

Wisdom and Understanding of the Word of YHWH isn't something we get from KNOWING what the Word says, they come from DOING what the Word says. Consider the following, again.

| Deu 4:2 | "Do not add to the Word which I command you, and do not take away from it, so as to guard the commands of יהוה your Elohim which I am commanding you. |
|---|---|
| | *** |
| Deu 4:5 | "See, I have taught you laws and right rulings, as יהוה my Elohim commanded me, to do thus in the land which you go to possess. |
| Deu 4:6 | "And you shall guard and do them, for this is your wisdom and your understanding before the eyes of the peoples who hear all these laws, and they shall say, 'Only a wise and understanding people is this great nation!' |
| | *** |
| Psl 119:89 | Forever, O יהוה, Your word stands firm in the heavens. |
| Psl 119:90 | Your trustworthiness is to all generations; You established the earth, and it stands. |
| Psl 119:91 | According to Your right-rulings They have stood to this day, For all are Your servants. |
| Psl 119:92 | If Your Torah had not been my delight, I would have perished in my affliction. |
| Psl 119:93 | Let me never forget Your orders, For by them You have given me life. |
| Psl 119:94 | I am Yours, save me; For I have sought Your orders. |

| Psl 119:95 | The wrong have waited for me to destroy me; I understand Your witnesses. |
| Psl 119:96 | I have seen an end of all perfection; Your command is exceedingly broad. |
| Psl 119:97 | O how I love Your Torah! It is my study all day long. |
| Psl 119:98 | Your commands make me wiser than my enemies; For it is ever before me. |
| Psl 119:99 | I have more understanding than all my teachers, For Your witnesses are my study. |
| Psl 119:100 | I understand more than the aged, for I have observed Your orders. |
| Psl 119:101 | I have restrained my feet from every evil way, That I might guard Your word. |
| Psl 119:102 | I have not turned aside from Your right-rulings, For You Yourself have taught me. |
| Psl 119:103 | How sweet to my taste has Your word been, More than honey to my mouth! |
| Psl 119:104 | From Your orders I get understanding; Therefore, I have hated every false way. |
| Psl 119:105 | Your word is a lamp to my feet and a light to my path. |

It is the combination of KNOWING what the Word says and the DOING of what it commands that gives us the wisdom and understanding to walk the True Way and teach it.

Thus, if the teachers today know what the Word, the Torah (law), of YHWH commands but do not obey all that it says, then they are the untaught and unstable men that Peter is referring to in his letter.

> **(3) -** Peter tells us that these men twist Paul's writings as well as the other Scripture to their own destruction (remember the warning that Messiah gave about the foundation that was built on sand in Matthew 7—they had a great fall).

It is this great fall that Peter is warning the brethren about in this passage and he goes further to warn us not to be led away by this delusion of the lawless. This phrase in modern translations is "error of the wicked," which is pretty vague.

**Delusion**: stg's #G4106 "planē" (the feminine of G4108 - as abstraction) roving; objectively

|            | fraudulence; subjectively a straying from orthodoxy or piety: - deceit, to deceive, delusion, error. —This word suggests a straying away from a specific path or way of living, a deceitful or false teaching. |
|------------|---|
| **Lawless**: | stg's #**G113** "athesmos" from (G1 - as a negative particle) no, not and (a derivative of G5087 -in the sense of enacting) to place; lawless, that is, (by implication) criminal: - wicked. —This word is clear, it refers to a specific standard of law or instruction that has been put in place or enacted, which is not being adhered to. |

Peter is trying to warn us that there are men who will take Paul writings and will twist them, either knowingly or innocently, because they do not have Paul's foundation and knowledge.

These men will be destroyed because of their corruption of the teaching and if we follow them, we too will be led away into their destruction. These men will not be men of obedience but will teach a lie of disobedience.

You know the lie I am referring to. The lie that says, "because we have been saved by the blood of the Messiah, we no longer have to keep the 'Old Testament Law.'" That is the lie of the Anti-messiah, the Lawless One.

Now, back to Paul's "Two Part" teaching and let's start with a "Paulian" conundrum. How can Paul say:

| **Rom 3:20** | "Therefore by works of Torah no flesh shall be declared right before Him, for by the Torah is the knowledge of sin". |
|------------|---|

…when he has already told us:

| **Rom 2:13** | "For not the hearers of the Torah are righteous in the sight of Elohim, **but the doers of the Torah shall be declared right**." |
|------------|---|

Is Paul contradicting himself? Is he confused? NO, of course not, it is those who call themselves teachers of the Word that are confused by what Paul means, blind to the distinction between the two types of justifications referred to in these passages.

46

| **Declared Right**: | stg's #**G1344** "dikaioō", from (G1342) to render; (that is, show or regard as) just or innocent: - free, justify (-ier), be righteous. Refers to being regarded as innocent. |

There are two types of justification, one is Spiritual and can only be received through belief in the atoning work of Yahushua Messiah. The spiritual justification is the justification from the condemnation of Death.

The other justification is physical and is received through obedience to the Torah, **AFTER** we have received the Justification from Death through belief in Messiah. This is the Justification of Life.

You have heard what Brother James (Ya'aqob) said?

| **Jam 2:14** | My brothers, what use is it for anyone to say he has belief but does not have works? This belief is unable to save him. |
| **Jam 2:15** | And if a brother or sister is naked and in need of daily food, |
| **Jam 2:16** | but one of you says to them, "Go in peace, be warmed and be filled," but you do not give them the bodily needs, what use is it? |
| **Jam 2:17** | So also belief, if it does not have works, is in itself dead. |
| **Jam 2:18** | But someone might say, "You have belief, and I have works." Show me your belief without your works, and I shall show you my belief by my works. |
| **Jam 2:19** | You believe that Elohim is one. You do well. The demons also believe – and shudder! |
| **Jam 2:20** | But do you wish to know, O foolish man, that the belief without the works is dead? |
| **Jam 2:21** | Was not Aḇraham our father declared right by works when he offered Yitsḥaq his son on the altar? |
| **Jam 2:22** | Do you see that the belief was working with his works, and by the works the belief was perfected? |
| **Jam 2:23** | And the Scripture was filled which says, "Aḇraham believed Elohim, and it was |

| | reckoned to him for righteousness." And he was called, "Elohim's friend." |
|---|---|
| **Jam 2:24** | You see, then, that a man is declared right by works, and not by belief alone. |
| **Jam 2:25** | In the same way, was not Raḥaḇ the whore also declared right by works when she received the messengers and sent them out another way? |
| **Jam 2:26** | For as the body without the spirit is dead, so also the belief is dead without the works. |

Brother James and the Assembly at large were obviously dealing with the same type of errors back then as we face today. There were false teachers rising up, teaching a lawless doctrine that 'saved' us but didn't require anything from us in return. This is contrary to everything the Scripture, in its totality, teaches about YHWH.

Throughout the Scripture, from Genesis to Revelation, YHWH consistently says, "If you do this, then I will do that." He has always given us a choice and consequences for those choices.

Obedience brings blessings, while disobedience brings curses. Those who live lives worthy of blessings also inherit eternal life, but those who live lives worthy of curses inherit destruction and death.

Two Parts, one spiritual and one physical, one His work and one our work, both vital to the fullness of the Truth, both required for the Kingdom and eternal life.

Lastly, consider Brother Paul's statement to the brethren of the Assembly in Roman.

| **Rom 6:15** | What then? Shall we sin because we are not under Torah but under favour? Let it not be! |
|---|---|
| **Rom 6:16** | Do you not know that to whom you present yourselves servants for obedience, you are servants of the one whom you obey, whether of sin to death, or of obedience to righteousness? |

The definition of 'sin' in 1 John 3:4 is 'transgression of the Law" (lawlessness), so the first thing Paul is asking is whether we who have believed in Yahushua should transgress (violate or disobey) the Law/Torah).

His answer is "Let it not be!" (KJV) "God forbid!") which is a resounding NO!!! We are not to continue disobeying the Torah (Law). Modern teachers call it the 'Old Testament Law' and tell you that it no longer applies to the "Gentile Church", which is found nowhere in Scripture.

The Torah, which was given through Moses to the Children of Yisra'el, both the native born and the stranger sojourning with them, is the same Torah/Law/Instructions that Messiah lived by and Paul lived by, as well as Peter, John, James, etc, etc, etc.

It is the height of arrogance and deception to think that we no longer must live by the standard of righteousness that all these great men of belief lived by and died for.

| | |
|---|---|
| **Mat 5:17** | "Do not think that I came to destroy the Torah or the Prophets. I did not come to destroy but to complete. |
| **Mat 5:18** | "For truly, I say to you, till the heaven and the earth pass away, one jot or one tittle shall by no means pass from the Torah till all be done. |
| **Mat 5:19** | "Whoever, then, breaks one of the least of these commands, and teaches men so, shall be called least in the reign of the heavens; but whoever does and teaches them, he shall be called great in the reign of the heavens. |

The True Belief is founded in the blood of Yahushua and lived out in obedience to all the Torah/Law commands, with all our heart and mind and strength, every day.

The last element, the one that binds all things together is an attitude of Love. Without love we have nothing.

| | |
|---|---|
| **1Co 13:1** | If I speak with the tongues of men and of messengers, but do not have love, I have become as sounding brass or a clanging cymbal. |
| **1Co 13:2** | And if I have prophecy, and know all secrets and all knowledge, and if I have all belief, so as to remove mountains, but do not have love, I am none at all. |
| **1Co 13:3** | And if I give out all my possessions to feed the poor, and if I give my body to be burned, but do not have love, I am not profited at all. |
| **1Co 13:4** | Love is patient, is kind, love does not envy, love does not boast, is not puffed up, |
| **1Co 13:5** | does not behave indecently, does not seek its own, is not provoked, reckons not the evil, |

| | |
|---|---|
| **1Co 13:6** | does not rejoice over the unrighteousness, but rejoices in the truth, |
| **1Co 13:7** | it covers all, believes all, expects all, endures all. |
| **1Co 13:8** | Love never fails. And whether there be prophecies, they shall be inactive; or tongues, they shall cease; or knowledge, it shall be inactive. |
| **1Co 13:9** | For we know in part and we prophesy in part. |
| **1Co 13:10** | But when that which is perfect has come, then that which is in part shall be inactive. |
| **1Co 13:11** | When I was a child, I spoke as a child, I thought as a child, I reasoned as a child. But when I became a man, I did away with childish matters. |
| **1Co 13:12** | For now we see in a mirror, dimly, but then face to face. Now I know in part, but then I shall know, as I also have been known. |
| **1Co 13:13** | And now belief, expectation, and love remain - these three. But the greatest of these is love. |

We are told here that love DOES NOT rejoice over unrighteousness and yet the church teaches that believers no longer need to obey the only standard of righteous living ever given.

Deuteronomy 6:24-25 states that it is righteousness for us when we guard and do all that the Torah says.

By teaching that believers no longer need to obey the Torah, modern teachers are telling them to love unrighteousness, which is contrary to love as YHWH defines it.

Paul goes on to say that love rejoices in the truth, yet the church only teaches believers to have half of the truth, which is a whole lie.

Messiah Himself said that He was the truth (John 14:6) but He also said that the Word was truth (John 17:17), which is a direct reference to the Torah, the words spoken by YHWH to His people.

The Torah is called the truth in Psalms 119:142, so modern teachers are teaching believers to love unrighteousness and NOT rejoice in all the truth, just some of it.

Who gave the church the authority to change the definitions of love and truth? If it was not YHWH or Yahushua, then who was it?

There is only one other "father" out there to whom service can be given and it is he that teaches the lie.

| Joh 8:39 | They answered and said to Him, "Abraham is our father יהושע said to them, "If you were Abraham's children, you would do the works of Abraham. |
|----------|-------------------------------------------------------------------|
| Joh 8:40 | "But now you seek to kill Me, a Man who has spoken to you the truth which I heard from Elohim. Abraham did not do this. |
| Joh 8:41 | "You do the works of your father." Then they said to Him, "We were not born of whoring, we have one Father: Elohim." |
| Joh 8:42 | יהושע said to them, "If Elohim were your Father, you would love Me, for I came forth from Elohim, and am here. For I have not come of Myself, but He sent Me. |
| Joh 8:43 | "Why do you not know what I say? Because you are unable to hear My Word. |
| Joh 8:44 | "You are of your father the devil, and the desires of your father you wish to do. He was a murderer from the beginning, and has not stood in the truth, because there is no truth in him. When he speaks the lie, he speaks of his own, for he is a liar and the father of it. |
| Joh 8:45 | "And because I speak the truth, you do not believe Me. |
| Joh 8:46 | "Who of you proves Me wrong concerning sin? And if I speak the truth, why do you not believe Me? |
| Joh 8:47 | "He who is of Elohim hears the Words of Elohim, therefore you do not hear because you are not of Elohim." |

As has been shown, the Truth is Messiah Yahushua and the Word/Torah, the Two Parts of redemption, belief worked out through obedience to the Torah of YHWH.

Lastly, Paul said that three things remained, belief, expectation (hope) and love, but the greatest of these is love.

Belief is the first part of the *Two-Part Principle*, the spiritual part, wherein the inner man is born again through belief in Yahushua and justified from the condemnation of death for past sin.

Expectation (hope) is the second part of the *Two-Part Principle*, the physical part, wherein the "new" inner man brings the "old" outer man into subjection to the righteousness of YHWH, which is His Torah.

51

Paul said as much in Philippians.

| | |
|---|---|
| **Php 3:1** | For the rest, my brothers, rejoice in יהוה. To write the same matters to you is truly no trouble to me, and for you it is safe. |
| **Php 3:2** | Look out for dogs, look out for the evil workers, look out for the mutilation! |
| **Php 3:3** | For we are the circumcision, who are serving Elohim in the Spirit, and boasting in Messiah יהושע, and do not trust in the flesh, |
| **Php 3:4** | though I too might have trust in the flesh. If anyone else thinks to trust in the flesh, I more — |
| **Php 3:5** | circumcised the eighth day, of the race of Yisra'ěl, of the tribe of Binyamin, a Hebrew of Hebrews, according to Torah a Pharisee, |
| **Php 3:6** | according to ardour, persecuting the assembly; according to righteousness that is in the law, having become blameless. |

These were all the things he had been trusting in BEFORE he came to understand his need in Yahushua for justification.

| | |
|---|---|
| **Php 3:7** | But what might have been a gain to me, I have counted as loss, because of Messiah. |
| **Php 3:8** | What is more, I even count all to be loss because of the excellence of the knowledge of Messiah יהושע my Master, for whom I have suffered the loss of all, and count them as refuse, in order to gain Messiah, |
| **Php 3:9** | and be found in Him, not having my own righteousness, which is of the law, but that which is through belief in Messiah, the righteousness which is from Elohim on the basis of belief, |

This section shows Paul understood that all those things he had been trusting, including the righteous acts of Torah, were of no redemptive value to him and that he needed to place his trust in Yahushua.

Once we understand that ONLY the blood of Messiah can justify us from the condemnation of death for sin, we place our trust in

Him ONLY, considering all other things as inconsequential as a means of justification.

This passage shows the first part of the *Two-Part Principle* at work in Paul's life.

This is not the end of Paul's lesson, however. Being justified from death is not the end of the story of redemption, there is still the second part of the *Two-Part Principle*, which concerns how we live AS justified believers in Him.

| | |
|---|---|
| **Php 3:10** | to know Him, and the power of His resurrection, and the fellowship of His sufferings, being conformed to His death, |
| **Php 3:11** | if somehow I might attain to the resurrection from the dead. |

Paul wants to come to all the knowledge of Him and the things associated to having believed in Him and is committed to conforming his life to the righteousness of Messiah's life by conforming to His death, i.e., dying to self (Romans 6:3-4) by offering his body as a living sacrifice (Romans 12:1-2).

Paul is committed to doing this in the "hope" of attaining something, i.e., the Resurrection.

| | |
|---|---|
| **Php 3:12** | Not that I have already received, or already been perfected, but I press on, to lay hold of that for which Messiah יהושע has also laid hold of me. |
| **Php 3:13** | Brothers, I do not count myself to have laid hold of it yet, but only this: forgetting what is behind and reaching out for what lies ahead, |
| **Php 3:14** | I press on toward the goal for the prize of the high calling of Elohim in Messiah יהושע. |

We see here that Paul does not consider himself to have securely attained the promise of the resurrection simply because of his belief in Messiah.

He knows that the resurrection is something to be worked out and he is pressing forward to attain it. He has forgotten all the things he once trusted in, placing his trust in Yahushua alone, yet he knows that there is only one way to LIVE righteously before YHWH to confirm his place at the resurrection.

The only standard of righteous living that ends in inheriting the promises of YHWH is the Torah as it was given by YHWH,

53

through Mosheh, to the people of YHWH, both native born and stranger, at Mt. Sinai, without additions or subtractions, in an attitude of compassion for others.

Belief in Yahushua Messiah and striving to reach the Hope of the resurrection, through obedience to the Torah, with a heart of Love towards our fellow man, especially the household of YHWH, is the formula for complete redemption.

**Remember**, love overcomes a multitude of sins and mercy overcomes judgment.

# Chapter 5: The Jerusalem Council

"Acts 15:1-21 - Circumcised to be saved?"

One of the biggest bones of contention in the 1st century among believers, was what constituted "salvation" for Gentiles who wanted to join the Body of Messiah. The confusion arose because you had two kinds of people coming into one body of belief.

The first were the Jews (Yahudim), who came from a culture that included the Torah of YHWH as it had been given through Moses at Mount Sinai.

The other group, made up of Gentiles, was coming, primarily, from a background of Greek paganism and philosophy which had never included the Torah of YHWH.

It must be noted; the first Gentile believers were people who had already been a part of the synagogue system or had prior knowledge of the Torah.

The conversion of those in Samaria by Philip in Acts 8, are from the latter group who had prior knowledge of the Torah having been descended from those put into the land by the Assyrians after the northern house of Yisra'el was sent into exile in 722 BCE (see: 2 Kings 17).

Acts 13 and 14 represent those who had been a part of the synagogue services prior to hearing the good news of Messiah Yahushua.

Paul (Sha'ul), as was his habit, first preached in the synagogues on the Sabbath day and when some of the Yahudim rejected his message, he turned to those Gentiles who were already experienced in the Torah culture.

Peter (Kepha)'s experience with the Gentile man named Cornelius is an example of a Gentile with prior knowledge of the Torah.

Acts 10:2 says that Cornelius was "a devout man, and one that feared Elohim with all of his house". This statement is clear evidence that Cornelius had pre-conversion knowledge and adherence to the Torah.

As mentioned, there were two groups of people who were coming to Messiah in the 1st century, the Torah experienced and those with no Torah knowledge.

The Jews, already having the Torah, came to understand that they needed to add belief in Messiah to their lives.

However, many struggled in understanding that the Gentiles could come into the belief even though they had never obeyed the Torah.

A controversy ensued because some Jews were teaching that the Gentiles had to be circumcised according to the Torah **BEFORE** they could be saved. This debate led to the Jerusalem Council in Acts 15.

| | |
|---|---|
| **Act 15:1** | And certain men came down from Yehuḏah and were teaching the brothers, "Unless you are circumcised, according to the practice of Moses, you are unable to be saved." |

Some debate that these were believing Jews who were simply in error, while others claim them to be unbelievers. Sha'ul clarifies the issue by calling them "false brothers" (see: Galatians 2:4).

| | |
|---|---|
| **Act 15:2** | So when Sha'ul and Barnaḇa had no small dissension and dispute with them, they arranged for Sha'ul and Barnaḇa and certain others of them to go up to Yerushalayim, to the emissaries and elders, about this question. |

The words "dissension" and "disputation" come from Greek words meaning," to stand" and "to debate". So, Paul and Barnaba stood against these "false brothers" in what appears to be a heated discussion. The conclusion of this debate was that a group of brothers be sent to Jerusalem to inquire with the leadership there.

| | |
|---|---|
| **Act 15:3** | So, being sent on their way by the assembly, they passed through Phoenicia and Shomeron, relating the conversion of the nations. And they were causing great joy to all the brothers. |
| **Act 15:4** | And having arrived in Yerushalayim, they were received by the assembly and the emissaries and the elders. And they reported all that Elohim had done with them. |
| **Act 15:5** | And some of the **believers** who belonged to the sect of the Pharisees, rose up, saying, "It is necessary to circumcise them, and to command them to keep the Torah of Moses." |

Clearly the Pharisees here are believers and yet the discussion returns to circumcision and keeping the Torah. The question, then, is in what way is the Torah associated to our salvation, or is it at all?

| | |
|---|---|
| **Act 15:6** | And the emissaries and elders came together to look into this matter. |
| **Act 15:7** | And when there had been much dispute, Kĕpha rose up and said to them, "Men, brothers, you know that a good while ago Elohim chose among us, that by my mouth the nations should hear the word of the Good News and believe. |
| **Act 15:8** | "And Elohim, who knows the heart, bore witness to them, by giving them the Set-apart Spirit, as also to us, |
| **Act 15:9** | and made no distinction between us and them, cleansing their hearts by belief. |

To understand Peter's statement here, you need to understand his involvement in the conversion of the Gentile named Cornelius. I encourage you to stop now and read that passage (Acts 10).

To summarize Acts 10, Kepha was given a dream which he interpreted to mean, YHWH would accept any "man" who believed in Yahushua, and that these "men" were no longer to be considered common or unclean, as non-believing Gentiles were (See: Acts 10:28).

The sign that confirmed YHWH's acceptance of Cornelius was the Set-Apart (Holy) Spirit that came upon him and his household.

It was this experience that confirmed to Peter that YHWH had accepted Gentiles into the assembly when they believed, no longer considering the Gentile a foreigner but a son, just like the native-born son (Compare Leviticus 19:33-34).

It is important to see here that Cornelius' belief had already been proven by his previous obedience; however, he was still considered an outsider by the religious Jews.

YHWH's point in this passage is to express that Cornelius' belief had made him right and that having been cleansed through belief he could no longer be considered an outsider.

| | |
|---|---|
| **Act 15:10** | "Now then, why do you try Elohim by putting a yoke on the neck of the taught ones which neither our fathers nor we were able to bear? |

This verse is misunderstood by most teachers today because they believe the "yoke" that was on the fathers and their descendants was the Torah, but that is not the case at all.

The yoke that they couldn't bear, was the additional religious dogma (Oral Law, later to be codified in the Talmud) that required works (Torah observance) **as a means of acceptance** before YHWH. Their pseudo-obedience to the Torah, through their man-made religious dogma, lacked the element of belief.

> **Heb 4:2**     For indeed the Good News was brought to us **as well as to them**, but the word which they heard did not profit them, **not having been mixed with belief** in those who heard it.

They had made the Torah a religious rite of acceptance when it was never meant to be such. The Torah was given to those who were already following YHWH, so that they would know how to please Him by how they lived.

Did not YHWH deliver Yisra'el from Egypt by the blood of the Passover lamb **BEFORE** He gave them the Torah to live by?

Yes, He did! He saved them from the death Angel through the blood, delivered them out of Pharaoh's power by the death of the firstborn, baptized them in the Red Sea and gave them the "Living Waters" at the rock of Horeb, all **BEFORE** He gave them the Torah.

This same pattern happens in our salvation today. We are saved by the blood of Yahushua, the Passover Lamb, delivered from the power sin and Satan through the death of YHWH's "only begotten Son", we are then baptized in the waters for the remission of sin and receive the "Living Waters" of His set apart Spirit, all **BEFORE** we are required to obey the Torah.

What is the promise of the "New Covenant?"

> **Jer 31:31**    "See, the days are coming," declares יהוה, "when I shall make a renewed covenant with the house of Yisra'ĕl and with the house of Yehudah,
>
> **Jer 31:32**    not like the covenant I made with their fathers in the day when I strengthened their hand to bring them out of the land of Mitsrayim, My covenant which they broke, though I was a husband to them," declares יהוה.
>
> **Jer 31:33**    "For this is the covenant I shall make with the house of Yisra'ĕl after those days, declares

| | |
|---|---|
| **Jer 31:34** | יהוה: I shall put My **Torah** in their inward parts, and write it on their hearts. And I shall be their Elohim, and they shall be My people. "And no longer shall they teach, each one his neighbour, and each one his brother, saying, 'Know יהוה,' for they shall all know Me, from the least of them to the greatest of them," declares יהוה. "For I shall forgive their crookedness and remember their sin no more." |

The "New Covenant" is, firstly, to the house of Yisra'el and the house of Yahudah, no Gentiles mentioned here. Secondly, it is the Torah in our inward part (spiritual man) that shall be written on our fleshly (pliable and compliant) heart.

| | |
|---|---|
| **Eze 36:22** | "Therefore say to the house of Yisra'ĕl, 'Thus said the Master יהוה, "I do not do this for your sake, O house of Yisra'ĕl, but for My set-apart Name's sake, which you have profaned among the nations wherever you went. |
| **Eze 36:23** | "And I shall set apart My great Name, which has been profaned among the nations, which you have profaned in their midst. And the nations shall know that I am יהוה," declares the Master יהוה, "when I am set-apart in you before their eyes. |
| **Eze 36:24** | "And I shall take you from among the nations, and I shall gather you out of all lands, and I shall bring you into your own land. |
| **Eze 36:25** | "And I shall sprinkle clean water on you, and you shall be clean – from all your filthiness and from all your idols I cleanse you. |
| **Eze 36:26** | "And I shall give you a new heart and put a new spirit within you. And I shall take the heart of stone out of your flesh, and I shall give you a heart of flesh, |
| **Eze 36:27** | and put **MY SPIRIT WITHIN YOU. AND I SHALL CAUSE YOU TO WALK IN MY LAWS AND GUARD MY RIGHT RULINGS AND SHALL DO THEM.** |

Do you see that the "New Covenant" in Messiah's blood was to give us a new heart, and that this new heart was not going to be stony (stubborn and rebellious) but a heart of flesh (humble and submissive)? Upon this heart of flesh, He was going to write His Torah so that we would **desire** to obey Him.

He was going to give us a new spirit, into which He was going to put His Torah, so we would know Him. Then He was going to put His Spirit in us to cause (lead) us **into obeying His Torah**.

However, the new covenant needed to be established in the blood of His Son Yahushua, because all of us had already been convicted as sinners by the Word (Romans 3:23) and condemned to death for our disobedience.

So, we needed to take on the Messiah's blood by belief, to be justified (made right-acquitted) from that condemnation BEFORE any of this work could be accomplished in us. Belief first, Torah second!

The yoke Peter is referring to in acts 15:10 is the yoke of legalism (Torah observance **TO BE SAVED**), which is a religious doctrine of men and not spiritual truth!

**Now back to Acts 15**,

Act 15:11          "But through the favour of the Master יהושע Messiah we trust to be saved, in the same way as they."

Here Peter brings the decision full circle. First, he had stated that the Gentiles are accepted because they believe, as Cornelius had, and that despite having the Torah, they, the Jews, also had to believe in Yahushua to be saved. **THE TORAH SAVES NO ONE!**

The Torah was not given to save anyone! The Torah did not save Yisra'el from Egypt, it was given to them AFTER they were saved from Egypt! Here, the Council will determine the same conclusion for the Gentiles.

Act 15:12          And all the crowd was silent and were listening to Barnaḇa and Sha'ul declaring how many miracles and wonders Elohim did among the nations, through them.
Act 15:13          And after they were silent, Ya'aqoḇ answered, saying, "Men, brothers, listen to me:
Act 15:14          "Shim'on has declared how Elohim first visited the nations to take out of them a people for His Name.

61

| | |
|---|---|
| **Act 15:15** | "And the words of the prophets agree with this, as it has been written: |
| **Act 15:16** | 'After this I shall return and rebuild the Booth of Dawiḏ which has fallen down. And I shall rebuild its ruins, and I shall set it up, |
| **Act 15:17** | so that the remnant of mankind shall seek יהוה, even all the nations on whom My Name has been called, says יהוה who is doing all this,' |
| **Act 15:18** | who has made this known from of old. |

James (Ya'aqob) is quoting from Amos 9:11-12 to show the Gentile inclusion was always in YHWH's plan.

| | |
|---|---|
| **Act 15:19** | "Therefore I judge that we should not trouble those from among the nations who are turning to Elohim, |

The context here is Torah obedience, specifically circumcision "**TO BE SAVED**". Works as a pre-salvation requirement, which is something James is saying they should **not** demand of the Gentiles.

No work, whether circumcision or other Torah commandment, is a prerequisite for acceptance into the body of Messiah Yahushua. We are saved by belief and not by works, yet that does not eliminate the requirement of works **AFTER** we are saved.

| | |
|---|---|
| **Act 15:20** | but that we write to them to abstain from [a] the defilements of idols, [b] and from whoring, [c] and from what is strangled, [d] and from blood. |

| **Note**: | a. | Exo 22:20; Lev 17:7; Deu 32:17; Deu 32:21; 1Co 10:14; 1Co10:20-21. |
|---|---|---|
| | b. | Num 25:1-3; Lev 17:7. |
| | c. | Gen 9:4; Eze 33:25 (Strangled - One way of eating meat with blood); Pro 21:25. |
| | d. | Lev 17:10-14. |

Today, many teachers say these four commands are the only commandments the Gentiles must obey. They take up a Rabbinical Jewish Tradition that says the Gentiles are only subject to the "Noahide Laws" (laws given to Noah).

However, this doctrine is not founded in the Scripture but is, as I've said, part of the Rabbinical Tradition. The Scripture says that there is only one Torah for both the native born Yisra'eli and the stranger (Gentile) who sojourns with them.

> **Num 15:15**      **One law** is for you of the assembly and for the stranger who sojourns with you – **a law forever throughout your generations**. As you are, so is the stranger before יהוה.
>
> **Num 15:16**      **One Torah** and one right-ruling is for you and for the stranger who sojourns with you.' "

In verse 15 an interesting statement is made, that says, "as you are so is the stranger before YHWH". What do you think this means? The answer is in Leviticus 19.

> **Lev 19:33**      'And when a stranger sojourns with you in your land, do not oppress him.
>
> **Lev 19:34**      'Let the stranger who dwells among you **be to you as the native among you**, and you shall love him as yourself. For you were strangers in the land of Mitsrayim (Egypt). I am יהוה your Elohim.

The phrase "stranger that sojourns with you" is referring to a Gentile who has joined with Yisra'el in covenant with YHWH. These Gentiles are to be considered the same as a native born Yisra'eli, a co-heir with Yisra'el of the promises and covenants.

Paul refers to the Gentiles as those who have been "grafted in" to Yisra'el through belief in Yahushua (Romans 11) and that we are both (native born and stranger) one in Messiah (Ephesians 2:11-19; Galatians 3: 28).

This "both, one" doctrine is NOT a "New Testament" doctrine but is in fact, a Torah commandment! It has always been YHWH's intention to have one people for Himself from every nation and tribe and tongue, and that they would all keep one law, one Torah!

These four rules mentioned in acts 15:20 are not for the "Gentile Church" as some teach, for there is no such thing.

These four commands are in fact, all associated to pagan idol worship. The pagan priest would strangle the sacrifice to get the blood into all the animal's muscles and then they would cut its throat and drain its blood into a chalice from which adherents would drink. Then, they would eat the meat that was full of blood and top their celebration off with an orgy.

63

**Note:** All four of these rules are Torah commands: Genesis 9:4; Exodus 22:20; Leviticus: 3:17; 17:7, 10-12, 26; Numbers 25:1-3; Deuteronomy 12:23-24; 32:17, 21; Ezekiel 33:25; Acts 21:25; 1 Corinthians 10:14, 20-21.

Verse 20 of acts 15 is not given to the Gentiles as "pre-salvation" rules, nor are they given as the only rules for a so-called "Gentile Church".

These four rules were given so the new Gentile believers would no longer participate in pagan idolatry, which would allow them to participate in this Shabbat services in the local synagogues where they could then learn from the Torah.

**Act 15:21** "For from ancient generations Moses has, in every city, those proclaiming him – being read in the congregations every Sabbath."

The entire context of the debate is about pre-salvation requirements, which all the apostles, including Paul, agreed were not valid. There are no works of Torah that could give salvation because it was the Torah that condemned us to death for sin when we disobeyed.

This passage is NOT, however, teaching that the works of the Torah are done away with or that they don't apply to the Gentiles.

This passage is a contextual argument about what we are saved by. According to the totality of Scripture, especially in the Messianic Writings, salvation comes by belief in the Good News of Yahushua the Messiah and not by any works of any kind, whatsoever. There is no such thing as pre-requisite works to receive the justification of belief.

Torah works are a **post salvation** requirement to prove or perfect our belief (James 2:17-26; Deuteronomy 8:1-3). Torah obedience is a heart matter to prove our sonship and has nothing to do with our justification (salvation) from the death penalty for past sin.

The death, burial and resurrection of Yahushua, the Son of YHWH, as the Lamb of Elohim, saves us from the death penalty for sin, through His blood, and delivers us from the power of Satan and the bondage to sin.

Just as the Passover Lamb's blood saved Yisra'el from the death Angel and the death of the firstborn delivered them from the power of Pharaoh and their bondage to slavery in Egypt.

64

The Torah came **after** their salvation and deliverance from Egypt, just as Torah observance comes **after** our salvation and deliverance.

"There is nothing new under the sun", according to the wisest man that may have ever lived, King Solomon, and all the stories, yea every jot and tittle, in the Tanak are relevant to our salvation today, in words and pictures, patterns and Truth.

# SECTION 2

**Section 2**:  Paul's Good News to the Romans


Ch. 1 ------------- Romans 1-3

Ch. 2 ------------- Romans 4

Ch. 3 ------------- Romans 5

Ch. 4 ------------- Romans 6

Ch. 5 ------------- Romans 7

Ch. 6 ------------- Romans 8

Ch. 7 ------------- Romans 9

Ch. 8 ------------- Romans 10

Ch. 9 ------------- Romans 11

Ch. 10 ----------- Romans 12-16

# Chapter 1: Romans 1 - 3

As noted, Paul was not anti-Torah, but was, in fact, pro-Torah his entire life. The question in the Messianic Writings was not whether we should obey the Torah of YHWH, but whether the keeping of the Torah was a pre-salvation requirement. Paul's answer was "Let It Not Be!

In his letter to the Assembly in Rome, whom he had yet to visit, Paul covers a multitude of topics, if we went verse by verse, it would be a whole book unto itself. In this writing our specific intent is to see what he taught about "how to be saved" and how the Torah of YHWH applies, if it does, to the believers in Yahushua Messiah today.

Our primary text in this section will be Romans 5 thru 9 and 11, however, we will do a basic overview of each chapter as we go through the letter, covering more closely the portions that relate to our primary text, drawing together all aspects of his teachings.

We will also draw from Paul's other writings, comparing them with still other writings from both the Tanak and the Messianic Writings to come to a full understanding of what truly constitutes the Good News of Yahushua.

### Chapter 1

| | |
|---|---|
| **Rom 1:1** | Sha'ul, a servant of יהושע Messiah, a called emissary, separated to the Good News of Elohim, |
| **Rom 1:2** | which He promised before through His prophets in the Set-apart Scriptures, |

Notice that the "Good News" he was "set apart" to preach, was promised in the "Holy Scriptures". The Scriptures he is referring to are the Torah, Prophets and Writings of the Tanak (O.T.)-(See also: 1 Corinthians 15:1-4).

It is important to note, that at the time the "Messianic Writings" were being written, the Tanak or the Hebrew Writings were the only "Scripture" in existence from which to teach the "Good News" of the Messiah Yahushua.

This is absolutely and fundamentally key to getting a true understanding of everything Paul taught, about both our salvation and how we live as the people of YHWH in Yahushua Messiah.

Here's why!

| Amo 3:7 | For the Master יהוה does no matter unless He reveals His secret to His servants the prophets. |
|---|---|

***

| Isa 46:9 | "Remember the former *events* of old, for I am Ěl, and there is no one else – Elohim, and there is no one like Me, |
|---|---|
| Isa 46:10 | declaring the end from the beginning, and from of old that which has not yet been done, saying, 'My counsel does stand, and all My delight I do,' |

***

| Ecc 3:14 | I know that whatever Elohim does is forever. There is no adding to it, and there is no taking from it. Elohim does it, that men should fear before Him. |
|---|---|
| Ecc 3:15 | Whatever is has already been, and what shall be has been before. But Elohim seeks out what has been pursued.* |

[* i.e.,, "the intent of a man's heart". It must be noted here that in the King James Version the last part of this verse has been incorrectly translated as "requires that which is past".]

| Deu 29:29 | The secret *things belong* unto the LORD our God: but those *things which are* revealed *belong* unto us and to our children for ever, that *we* may do all the words of this law. |
|---|---|

These passages are clear, YHWH knows everything that will happen before it does, and He doesn't do anything unless He reveals it through His prophets **beforehand,** so we will know it is from Him.

Also, what He has revealed to us, is for us to do, "all of it", that we might fear before Him, to test our hearts. The "all" mentioned here has to do with everything YHWH has spoken, both the things of belief and the things of works, none of which can be added to nor taken away from by the teachings of men.

(Read also: Isaiah 29:18-24, about false teachers and compare Isaiah 8 [esp. vs 20], which speaks prophetically of both the Torah [foundation] and Messiah [the Cornerstone] that shall be a stumbling stone for the people who disobey.)

| Rom 1:7 | To all who are in Rome, beloved of Elohim, called, set-apart ones: Favour to you and peace from Elohim our Father and the Master יהושע Messiah. |
|---|---|

Paul here, identifies who this teaching is intended for, those "called to be set apart ones".

| Mat 20:16 | "So the last shall be first, and the first last: for many be called but few chosen". |
|---|---|

The Greek word here for "chosen" is "eklektos" (stgs# G1588) meaning, "select" and comes from the root word, "eklegomai" meaning, "to select". So, one may argue, the word chosen here could easily be understood to mean "choose", i.e., "for many are called but few choose".

As we go through the teachings of Paul, we will come to see that many are called to be the people of YHWH through belief in Yahushua the Messiah, but all will not be "chosen" as sons because they do not submit to the Torah of YHWH.

Notice, however, that there will be some who answer the call, who have the heart to obey Him but, due to false doctrine, lack the understanding to obey Him completely or correctly.

These may well find mercy under the grace of YHWH through their devoted hearts. "For love overcomes a multitude of sin" and "His mercies are renewed every morning".

| Rom 1:9 | For Elohim is my witness, whom I serve with my spirit in the Good News of His Son, how unceasingly I make mention of you, |
|---|---|

This statement, at first glance, may seem of little import; however, Paul's reference to serving YHWH in his spirit, Paul's spirit, will be immensely important as we progress through Romans, as it relates to living out our belief.

| Rom 1:16 | For I am not ashamed of the Good News of Messiah, for it is the power of Elohim for deliverance to everyone who believes, to the Yehuḏi first and also to the Greek. |
|---|---|
| Rom 1:17 | For in it the righteousness of Elohim is revealed from belief to belief, as it has been |

71

written, **"But the righteous shall live by belief."**

(See: Habakkuk 2:4 and compare: Hosea 14)

Here we clearly see Paul's teaching on what saves us, it is through the Good News of Yahushua's death, burial and resurrection alone (1 Corinthians 15:1-4) that we have the power to be saved and we gain access to that salvation through our belief in what Yahushua has done.

**Note**: It is YHWH's righteousness that is revealed here - not ours - later in chapter 3 Paul is going to explain how YHWH could overlook our sin and free us from the death penalty we owed, and still be righteous Himself.

**Ex:** During the Passover chronicled in Exodus 12, YHWH gave Moses instructions concerning the killing of a Lamb and the placing of the blood over the doorpost and lintel of every house. This instruction is significant in two ways.

First, it shows us how YHWH was going to fulfill his promise to Abraham concerning the deliverance of his seed, in a way that allowed YHWH to remain righteous even though they had been living un-righteously in the pagan world. The blood of the Lamb was going to cover them when death came upon Egypt.

Secondly, it's going to show us something about belief and how it works. When Moses returned to the Yisra'elis and instructed them concerning the Passover Lamb, they were given a choice.

Do they believe what YHWH has said and act accordingly by painting the blood of the doorpost, or do they disbelieve what YHWH has said and not paint the blood on the doorpost and lintel?

The answer is, of course, to receive the deliverance from death they had to paint the doorpost with the blood, or their firstborn would die, just as the firstborn of Egypt did.

So, there belief was the catalyst that brought deliverance from death when they acted upon belief. And the same holds true today.

This is what Paul means when he says the righteousness of YHWH is revealed "from belief to belief". See, it was their belief in what He said that delivered them from death at the beginning of their deliverance in Egypt and it was the belief of Yahushua (Joshua), Caleb and the second generation that brought them into the Promised Land, completing their deliverance.

It is Paul's intention for us to understand that our deliverance, whether it be from the penalty of sin and death or from the wilderness of this life into the Messianic Kingdom, is all about belief from "beginning to end".

It's important to see here that the price of our deliverance was blood and not just the blood of an animal, but the blood of Yahushua Himself. It is this sacrifice, and this sacrifice alone that allowed us to be delivered from the penalty of death for our past sins, and yet allow YHWH to remain righteous.

However, just like Yisra'el's deliverance began with their choice to act on what they believed concerning the Passover Lamb and their children's choice to act in obedience to the Torah which allowed them into the promised land, so to do we have a choice to make.

First, we must choose to believe what YHWH has said about His Son so that we might be covered by the blood of Yahushua and delivered from the penalty of death.

However, unlike what the modern church would have us believe; this is not the end of our choosing. We are still required to make a choice to obey the Word/Torah of YHWH so that we might inherit the Kingdom of Messiah. "There is nothing new under the sun."

| | |
|---|---|
| **Rom 1:18** | For the wrath of Elohim is revealed from heaven against **all** wickedness and unrighteousness of men, who suppress the truth in unrighteousness, |

*** 

| | |
|---|---|
| **Rom 1:28** | And even as they did **not think it worthwhile** to possess the knowledge of Elohim, Elohim gave them over to a worthless mind, **to do what is improper,** |

*** 

| | |
|---|---|
| **Rom 1:32** | who, though they **know** the righteousness of Elohim, that those that who **practice such deserve death**, not only **do the same but also approve** of those who **practice** them. |

Please, go back and carefully read the entire context of chapter 1, where you'll see that man had no excuse for denying YHWH's existence, because all creation testifies of Him, yet instead of honoring Him, man created false forms of worship that allowed them to live as they pleased, and not only that, but they taught that their own man-made doctrines were the will of YHWH.

And this is nothing new, if you go back to the Exodus story when Moses was up on the mountain and the people began to grow restless, they went to Aaron demanding he build them an Elohim to go before them. Consider:

| | |
|---|---|
| **Exo 32:3** | "And all the people took off the golden earrings which were in their ears, and brought them to Aharon. |
| **Exo 32:4** | And he took *this* from their hand, and he formed it with an engraving tool, and made a moulded calf. And they said, **"This is your mighty one, O Yisra'ĕl, that brought you out of the land of Mitsrayim!"** |
| **Exo 32:5** | And Aharon saw and built a slaughter-place before it. And Aharon called out and said, **"Tomorrow is a festival to יהוה."** |

Moses had not been gone a hot month and a half, and not only did the people rebel, but their soon to be High Priest, Aaron, not only violated the Torah they had been given by creating a graven image but violated it again by teaching them to worship it, calling the image "YHWH". And what was YHWH's response to this? Judgment and death, to the tune of 3000 beings.

As time went by YHWH allowed Yisra'el to live in the folly of their own man-made teachings because they refused to acknowledge Him in their behavior even though they knew the truth of what He requires of man and what the price of disobeying Him would be.

Despite this knowledge, they chose to follow their own fleshly desires, created doctrine to support it, and taking pleasure in associating with others who did the same, even teaching them to do so.

Compare carefully what the Messiah said to the Pharisees:

| | |
|---|---|
| **Mat 23:15** | "Woe to you, scribes and Pharisees, hypocrites! Because you go about the land and the sea to **win one convert**, and when he is won, **you make him a son of GĕHinnom twofold more than yourselves.** |

74

GĕHinnom is a valley in Jerusalem where refuse is burned and is used in the Messianic Writings as a shadow picture of the Lake of Fire.

As we move through Romans you will see this truth of "Rabbinic/Jewish Hypocrisy" to which Yahushua is referring. We will also see how this error has been brought into the "new belief" and created what might be called "The Christian Apostasy". Before we go there though let's carefully dissect what is said in Roman 1:18, 28 and 32.

**Vs. 18**

| | |
|---|---|
| **Ungodliness**: | **G763** "asebeia", meaning not reverent or having no reverence for YHWH - no fear, as a way of life. |
| **Unrighteousness**: | **G93** "adikia", a legal term meaning, not just or doing what is not right as a way of life |

Notice, no fear and no obedience, tied together. So, the concept of fearing YHWH or having reverence for Him is directly tied to our obedience to His Word/Torah.

It is this type of disobedient and irreverent behavior, this rebellious attitude that brings the wrath of YHWH upon mankind. **Consider:**

| | |
|---|---|
| **Eph5:5** | For this you know, that **no one** who whores, nor unclean one, nor one greedy of gain, who is an idolater, **has any inheritance in the reign of Messiah and Elohim**. |
| **Eph 5:6** | Let no one deceive you with **empty words**, for because of these the wrath of Elohim comes upon the **sons of disobedience**. |
| **Eph 5:7** | Therefore do not become partakers with them. |
| **Disobedience**: | stg's #*G543* "apeitheia", from *G545* (*unpersuadable*, that is, *contumacious: -* disobedient.); *disbelief (obstinate and rebellious): - disobedience, unbelief. This word can be used interchangeably, depending on the context, from disbelief to disobedience.* |

75

> *It is key to remember that this is referring to a so-called belief lived in disobedience to the Torah.*

Notice, Paul is referring to believers (Ephesians 1:1-6), instructing US in how to follow YHWH (Ephesians 5:14) then reminding us that certain behaviors exclude us from inheriting the Kingdom (Ephesians 5:5), telling us that the wrath of YHWH will come upon these "children of disobedience" (Ephesians 5:6) and telling us not to take part in it with them (Ephesians 5:7).

Wrath will come upon the "Children of Disobedience" at the return Yahushua Messiah (2 Thessalonians 1:7-10) and we don't want any part of that (compare Colossians 3:1-6). If it is not possible for us to lose our inheritance, why this warning?

And this is not the only one, for there are many such warnings in the Messianic Writings. We will answer this in more detail as we go through Romans.

**Vs. 28**

> **Truth**: *G225 "alḗtheia", from G227 (not hidden); truth: - true, X truly, truth, verity.*

\*\*Do a complete word study on the word "truth" from the entire Scripture! \*\*

**Consider**:

| | |
|---|---|
| **John 14:6** | יהושע said to him, "I am the Way, and the Truth, and the Life. No one comes to the Father except through Me. |
| **John 17:17** | "Set them apart in Your truth – Your Word is truth. |

(See also: Psalms 119:142, 151 and 160)

Messiah is the Truth, the Word/Torah is Truth and Messiah is the Word/Torah made flesh.

| | |
|---|---|
| **John 1:14** | And the Word became flesh and pitched His tent among us, and we saw His esteem, esteem as of an only brought-forth of a father, complete in favour and truth. |

76

Now, Messiah is complete in favour AND truth.

**Compare**:

| | |
|---|---|
| **Psl 119:1** | Blessed are the perfect in **the way**, Who walk in the Torah of יהוה! |
| **Psl 119:30** | I have chosen the way of truth; Your right-rulings I have held level. |
| **Psl 119:42** | The righteousness of Your witnesses is **forever**; Make me understand, that I might live. |

***

| | |
|---|---|
| **Pro 3:1** | My son, do not forget my Torah, and let your heart watch over my commands; |
| **Pro 3:2** | For length of days and long life and peace they add to you. |
| **Pro 3:3** | Let not loving-commitment and truth forsake you – Bind them around your neck, Write them on the tablet of your heart, |
| **Pro 3:4** | Thus finding favour and good insight in the eyes of Elohim and man. |

The Torah of YHWH is the foundation of the Way we live our life in the Truth of YHWH and Messiah Yahushua, who Himself is the Torah made into human flesh through whom we receive the favor (grace) of YHWH by belief in Him.

Once we believe in Yahushua we are called to live in obedience to the Torah, in our spirit man, with all of our heart, our being, and our strength (Deuteronomy 6:4-5).

When Paul states in Acts that he is a follower of the Way, he means he is a Torah observant believer in Yahushua Messiah. (Messiah and Torah: Isaiah 8:20; Revelation 14:12)

Going back now to verse 28 of Romans 1, we see it is because man did not choose to "retain Elohim in their knowledge", He gave them over to a "reprobate mind" to do those things which are inconvenient, meaning, that they chose not to accept the knowledge of Him as He had revealed Himself to them in the Scripture (read again vs. 19-23 and compare Proverbs 3:5-8), so He gave them over to worthless thinking, to believe a lie and be damned.

| Reprobate: | stg's #**G96** - "adokimos", meaning, unapproved; from two words meaning: not and acceptable. Refers to a mind that is focused on doing what is not acceptable - a rebellious mind. |
|---|---|
| Note: | This word is associated to the word unrighteousness (G93: adikia: unjust) in v 18. |
| Convenient: | stg's #**G2520** - "katheko", meaning, to reach; it comes from two words that mean, to arrive and down, and refers to not arriving or not measuring up. A more accurate translation would be "to do those things which are improper". (Compare Romans 1:24-27) |

Versus 29-31 give several examples of behavior that is "improper", that, if we do them, we "shall not inherit the kingdom of Elohim" (Galatians 5:19-21; 1 Corinthians 6:9-10). All of these examples can be boiled down to a single saying, "those who 'sin willfully'" (Hebrews 10:26-31).

Before we go any further, we want to clearly define the meaning of the word "sin".

| Sin: | stg's #**G266** - "hamartia", meaning, sin; from a word meaning, to miss the mark (compare to Hebrew: "chata" - to miss [sin]). This presumes that there is a mark or standard of righteous living that has not been lived up to -a sinner lives "improperly" (Romans 1:28). |
|---|---|

However, the actual mark or standard of righteous living is the Torah (law) according to Deuteronomy 6:24-25. The Torah of YHWH is how men live righteously but if we do not live according to the Torah of YHWH then we are guilty of improper behavior, i.e., Sin.

| 1Jn 3:4 | Everyone doing sin also does **lawlessness**, and sin is **lawlessness**. |
|---|---|

The word lawlessness here in 1 John 3:4 is the Greek word "anomia" (G458) meaning, illegality or doing what is illegal. Technically, this word anomia has three parts which breakdown to literally mean "no law doing".

It is the Law/Torah of YHWH that defines what is legal and what is illegal in the matters that concern His people.

**Willfully**: stg's #**G1596** -"hekousios", meaning, voluntarily; refers to an act done intentionally with full knowledge of the truth.

So, to sin willfully is to intentionally disobey the Torah when you know it's required of you to obey it (See again, Rom 1:32).

**Rom 1:32** who, though they know the righteousness of Elohim, that those who practice such deserve death, not only do the same but also approve of those who practice them.

See here, these people "know" what YHWH has determined as the right way of living and yet in their knowledge they intentionally chose to violate, this standard of right living (Torah) and teach others to do so as well.

**Note**: The totality of Scripture revolves around one key concept…knowledge. Adam ate willfully (voluntarily) from the tree of the knowledge of good and evil. Was it the knowledge that was sinful? Was it having that knowledge that condemned him to death? To both questions the answer is, NO! It was in HOW HE OBTAINED the knowledge of good and evil - through disobedience - that condemned him.

**Pro 1:7** The fear of יהוה is the beginning of knowledge; Fools despise wisdom and discipline.

Knowledge is a KEY component to understanding Paul's writings, especially this letter to the Romans.

Paul's conclusion of chapter 1 is that mankind has no excuse for not knowing YHWH and not living correctly before Him. Also, there are people out there who know the right way but refuse to live by it and teach others not to live by it. It is to these people, those believers who know and refuse to obey, that the wrath of YHWH shall come.

It's upon this conclusion that Paul begins chapter 2. Keep in mind that this letter is written to brothers and that the warnings of chapter 1 are to us, and so, it is to us that the teaching of chapter 2 is intended.

**Chapter 2**

This chapter begins with the word "therefore" so Paul is telling us that because of what he just explained in chapter 1 we should behave a certain way.

That way begins in verses 1-4 concerning judging other people. The words "judgest" and "judgment" in these verses refer to making a decision, specifically, a decision against other people.

The context of this form of decision or judgment is one of condemnation. Not one of us has the right or authority to condemn another person, because all mankind is guilty of sin (disobeying the Torah) before YHWH (Romans 3:23; Galatians 3:22).

Paul warns us, if we do condemn others, we too shall be condemned in the judgment of YHWH (compare Matthew 6:14-15) and we need to understand that it is by His goodness and mercy that people - even us - come to repentance.

> **Rom 2:5**     But according to your **hardness and your unrepentant heart** you are treasuring up for yourself wrath in the day of wrath and revelation of the righteous judgment of Elohim,

Notice, a "heart condition" is mentioned concerning some "among the brethren", which causes them to "treasure up" or "store up" wrath upon themselves. Again, this concerns those who are unforgiving and unmerciful within the brotherhood of belief.

**Consider**:

> **1Jn 2:7**     Beloved, I write no fresh command to you, but an old command which you have had from the beginning. The old command is the Word which you heard from the beginning.
>
> **1Jn 2:8**     Again I write you a fresh command, which is true in Him and in you, because the darkness is passing away, and the true light now shines.
>
> **1Jn 2:9**     The one who says he is in the light, and hates his brother, is in the darkness until now.

| | |
|---|---|
| **1Jn 2:10** | The one who loves his brother stays in the light, and there is no stumbling-block in him. |
| **1Jn 2:11** | But the one who hates his brother is in the darkness and walks in the darkness, and does not know where he is going, because the darkness has blinded his eyes. |

Here again we see a heart condition, a condition that blinds our eyes to the way we should be going. This heart condition keeps us out of the true light that we have received in Him. This is exactly what Paul is teaching in Romans 2:1-5.

| | |
|---|---|
| **Hardness**: | stg's #**G4643** - "sklerotes", meaning, callousness; from a word meaning, dry or parched. Refers to a heart without mercy, unforgiving, and unloving. |
| **Impenitent**: | stg's #**G279** - "ametanoetos", meaning, unrepentant; refers to a heart or attitude that has not turned away from the old ways to walk in the ways of YHWH. |

Paul's accusation here in Romans 2:5 is that some brothers have not turned away from their fleshly, condemning, and loveless behavior.

I contend that, since all the Torah hangs on or is founded on these two; love YHWH and your neighbor, that these brothers have not applied the Torah of YHWH to their lives in an attitude of humility but have instead used their knowledge of the Torah to belittle and condemn their brethren, so as to elevate themselves, something Paul sternly warns against in Galatians 6:1-7.

| | |
|---|---|
| **Rom 2:6** | who **"shall render to each one according to his works"**: |
| **Rom 2:7** | everlasting life to those who by persistence in good work seek for esteem, and respect, and incorruptibility; |
| **Rom 2:8** | but wrath and displeasure to those who are self-seeking and do not obey the truth, but obey unrighteousness; |
| **Rom 2:9** | affliction and distress on every human being working what is evil, of the Yehuḏi first, and also of the Greek; |

81

| **Rom 2:10** | but esteem, respect, and peace to everyone working what is good, to the Yehudi first and also to the Greek. |
| **Rom 2:11** | For there is no partiality with Elohim. |

**REMEMBER**, this letter is to the brethren in Rome, to believers! Paul uses the phrase "by patient continuance" which in the Greek is only one word.

**Patient Continuance**: stg's #**G5281** - "hupomone", meaning cheerful (or hopeful) endurance; from a word meaning, to stay under. It refers to a heart condition that joyfully endures the trials of this life in the hope of the reward that awaits them.

The believer that seeks "glory, honor, and immortality (eternal life)" with a cheerful endurance - a true believing heart - shall receive them. "BUT" (2:8) is a word of contrast that reveals another possibility.

The word Paul uses in contrast here is "contentious" which is two words in Greek.

**Contentious**: stg's #**G1537**- "ek", meaning, place of origin (i.e., from or out of);

stg's #**G2052** - "eritheia", meaning, intrigue; from a word meaning, a quarrel or wrangling.

These two words used together refer to a heart condition that is argumentative and disobedient, rebellious. A heart attitude like this has NO place among the brethren. This heart condition, according to Paul in verse 8, does not obey the truth.

There are two parts of truth identified by Messiah that together make up the Truth. There is only one Truth, but this truth has two components.

Yahushua is the Truth (John 14:6) that gains us access to the Father, and the Word/Torah Is the Truth that sanctifies or sets us apart unto Him in our daily life (John 17:17; Psalms 119:142).

The *Two-Part Principle* of the Truth (one-part belief and one-part obedience) is self-evident.

82

| | |
|---|---|
| **Isa 8:20** | To the Torah and to the witness! If they do not speak according to this Word, it is because they have no daybreak (light). |

***

| | |
|---|---|
| **Rev 14:12** | Here is the endurance of the set-apart ones, here are those guarding the commands of Elohim and the belief of יהושע. |

Our belief must be expressed in how we live.

| | |
|---|---|
| **Jam 2:14** | My brothers, what use is it for anyone to say he has belief but does not have works? This belief is unable to save him. |
| **Jam 2:15** | And if a brother or sister is naked and in need of daily food, |
| **Jam 2:16** | but one of you says to them, "Go in peace, be warmed and be filled," but you do not give them the bodily needs, what use is it? |
| **Jam 2:17** | So also belief, if it does not have works, is in itself dead. |
| **Jam 2:18** | But someone might say, "You have belief, and I have works." Show me your belief without your works, and I shall show you my belief by my works. |
| **Jam 2:19** | You believe that **Elohim is one.** You do well. The demons also believe – and shudder! |
| **Jam 2:20** | But do you wish to know, O foolish man, that the belief without the works is dead? |
| **Jam 2:21** | Was not Aḇraham our father declared right by works when he offered Yitsḥaq his son on the slaughter-place? |
| **Jam 2:22** | Do you see that the belief was working with his works, and by the works the belief was perfected? |
| **Jam 2:23** | And the Scripture was filled which says, **"Aḇraham believed Elohim, and it was reckoned to him for righteousness."** And He called him, **"he who loves Elohim."** |
| **Jam 2:24** | You see, then, that a man is declared right by works, and not by belief alone. |
| **Jam 2:25** | In the same way, was not Raḥaḇ the whore also declared right by works when she |

|  | received the messengers and sent them out another way? |
|---|---|
| **Jam 2:26** | For as the body without the spirit is dead, so also the belief is dead without the works. |

Since this letter is to believers in Rome, they have already accepted the Truth of Messiah, however, they refuse to live in the Truth of Messiah by obeying the Torah of YHWH - they are rebellious.

**REMEMBER**, the true word that is true light by which we, the saints, endure contains both the Law/Torah and the Witness/Testimony of Yahushua Messiah (Isaiah 8:20; Revelation 14:12).

These two heart conditions reside within the body of Messiah today; the right heart condition that wants to obey and the un-right (not right) heart that refuses to obey.

What is Paul's conclusion concerning them? The right heart shall inherit eternal life, while the un-right heart inherits wrath. Whether Jew or Gentile, the same rule applies, YHWH does not see bloodlines, only heart condition (consider Hebrews 4:12).

> **Note**: A comparative study of 2 Peter 2:18-22 with Hebrews 6:4-8 and 10:26-31 Clearly shows that even amongst the brethren (fellow believers) there can be an attitude of rebellion that will lead that believer back into condemnation, which is the second death. (See appendix: 3 The Second Death on Pg. 554).

In verse is 12 and 13, Paul is going to teach us certain universal truths. Then, in 14-16, he is going to teach us a knowledge principle as it pertains to Gentiles, who have never heard what the Torah says, though they have believed in Messiah, and as it pertains to the Yahudim who have grown up knowing the Torah.

This principle is hugely important in understanding the teaching on HOW we receive salvation. This principle will help us clearly understand the decision of the Jerusalem Council in Acts 15, as well as Messiah's own statement in Matthew 5:19 concerning who shall be greatest or least in the kingdom.

It is a distinction between Jewish salvation and Gentile salvation, both dependent on Yahushua, but each originating from different backgrounds, beliefs and knowledge.

84

| | |
|---|---|
| **Rom 2:12** | For as many as **sinned without Torah shall also perish without Torah**, and as many **as sinned in the Torah shall be judged by the Torah**. |
| **Rom 2:13** | For not the hearers of the Torah are righteous in the sight of Elohim, but **the doers of the Torah shall be declared right**. |

The word "sinned" means to have transgressed/disobeyed the Torah of YHWH (1 John 3:4).

> **Perish**: stg's #**G622** - "apollumi", meaning, to destroy fully; from two words meaning: away and destruction. Refers to death but goes further to express being taken away into destruction.

First, verse 12 shows that both the Jew and Gentile who refused to obey the Torah will be condemned by the Torah, because the wages of sin is death (Romans 6:23).

This principle applies universally to both believers and nonbelievers (compare Romans 6:16; 8:13; Hebrews 6:4-8; 10:26-31; John: 1-7).

Verse 13 also applies universally and teaches us that to be righteous before YHWH, we must obey the Torah. So, there is a form of justification that comes from Torah obedience.

Before we go any farther let's define a couple of words

> **Just**: stg's #**G1342** - "dikaios", meaning, equitable (as in character or act from a word meaning, right (as in a place of). Refers to a person who is righteous or in right standing before YHWH, he is innocent.

> **Justified**: stg's #**G1344** - "dikaioo", meaning, to render or regard as righteous or innocent. Refers to being "made or declared right", either from a previous state of unrighteousness or as being in a state of righteousness.

> **Ex**: If a person has violated the Torah of YHWH and been condemned to death for that violation, which we **ALL** have, then that person must be justified or declared right **from** past sin **before** YHWH will accept them. However, if a person has obeyed the Torah all their

life, as Messiah Yahushua did, then that person is justified or declared right based on the righteous standard of the Torah. Yahushua qualified to be the Messiah because the Torah declared Him worthy due to His sinlessness.

**Note**: We were all first condemned to death because of the sin of our human father, Adam, and then we all became guilty of sin due to our own disobedience to the Torah.

Yahushua did not have a human father, so he did not inherit the penalty of Adam's sin, furthermore, He never violated any requirement of the Torah. Thus, He was completely without sin.

According to Paul, someone who obeys the Torah is righteous before YHWH, He regards them as innocent.

**Deu 6:24** And יהוה commanded us to do all these laws, to fear יהוה our Elohim, for our good always, to keep us alive, as it is today.

**Deu 6:25** And it is righteousness for us when we guard to do all this command before יהוה our Elohim, as He has commanded us.

This is a universal principle! So, how can Paul later say:

**Rom 3:20** Therefore by works of Torah **no flesh shall be declared right before Him,** for by the Torah is the knowledge of sin.

Is Paul contradicting himself? NO! If man would obey, he would be regarded as innocent before YHWH. The question then is, has he?

Paul will answer this question for us, helping us to understand the contrast between Rom 2:13 and 3:20, and how it all works in our lives today, as we continue through this letter.

**Rom 2:14** For when nations, who do not have the Torah, by nature do what is in the Torah, although not having the Torah, they are a torah to themselves,

**Rom 2:15** who show the work of the Torah written in their hearts, their conscience also bearing

86

| | witness, and between themselves their thoughts accusing or even excusing, |
|---|---|
| **Rom 2:16** | in the day when Elohim shall judge the secrets of men through יהושע Messiah, according to my Good News. |

This passage is profoundly important to understand. Teachers today have used it to excuse "Gentile" rebellion, teaching them that they no longer need to obey the Torah, which is not Paul's intent here. Paul is challenging the Jewish brethren, who have condemned the Gentile brethren for their lack of Torah observance or knowledge (2:1-5).

The Jewish brethren didn't have compassion towards the Gentile brethren's ignorance of the Torah. Instead of admonishing them in love they condemned them for their ignorance while they themselves were guilty of not obeying, as we shall see, however, let's consider what Paul is saying here.

**REMEMBER**, this teaching is to believers and is contrasting between two kinds of believers. The first group, the Jews, who have knowledge of the Torah and know how to live righteous before YHWH, while the other group, the Gentiles, are mostly new to the Torah and don't know the first thing about how to live righteously.

Paul warned that sinners, Jew and Gentile, will be accountable for their sin (v12), and that it is the obedient that are justified (v13). Here in verse 14-16, Paul is going to explain Gentile acceptance and judgment, as it relates to their ignorance.

The Gentile believer who has little or no knowledge of the Torah, but upholds the principles of Torah (love, justice, belief, mercy, etc.), prove that the "new covenant" promise of the Torah placed on the heart and mind (Jeremiah 31:31-33), is working in them, thus "they are a law unto themselves", and then it is their conscience (their inner voice) that will determine what the true intent of the heart was.

| **Conscience**: | stg's #**G4893** -"suneidesis", meaning, co-perception; from two words meaning, union and to see, as in perceive or know. Refers to the part of us that allows us to understand contrasting concepts: specifically, the difference between right and wrong, good and evil, etc. |
|---|---|

The Gentile believer's conscience will either accuse them if their intent was evil, or it will excuse them if their intent was righteous, on that day Messiah returns to judge His people (1 Cor 3:11-15; Rev 11:18).

It is imperative to remember that though a man is accountable for what he knows, he is also expected to learn and grow (bear fruit- John 15:1-10) and when he hears the truth he is to turn and live by it (Acts 17:30).

> **Note**: This is what James meant in Acts 15:21, after he had admonished the Jewish believers to not place upon the new Gentile believers any pre-acceptance requirements, but that they should abstain from idolatry, which is what the four things mentioned in Acts 15:20 represent (i.e., abstain from the defilements of idols, and from whoring, and from what is strangled, and from blood).

James had admonished them to refrain from these four things because anyone participating in idolatry would not be allowed to enter the synagogue where the Torah was taught every Sabbath (v21).

James intention was for the Jewish believers to accept the Gentiles, purely based on their confession of belief, and admonished the new believers to not participate in any form of idolatry, because they needed to be able to enter the synagogue on the Sabbath to learn what the Torah actually said.

Once they heard what the Torah said, then they were required to obey it. However, to learn it on their own, directly from the Word itself, they had to qualify to hear it read in the synagogues on Sabbath, which they couldn't do if they still practiced with the pagans.

Next, Paul is going to admonish the Jews (vs 17-29), being very critical to those who consider themselves knowledgeable but are guilty themselves, reinforcing his accusations toward the Jewish believers in vs. 1-5. We are going to look at a specific portion of this passage that will be needed later in the book.

**Rom 2:17**     See, you are called a Yehudi, and rest on the Torah, and make your boast in Elohim,
**Rom 2:18**     and know the desire *of Elohim*, and approve what is superior, being instructed out of the Torah,

First, the Jews were being arrogant about their better understanding of the things of YHWH and in the verses that follow, Paul is going to tell them that trusting in their knowledge, or their ethnic ancestry (bloodline) means nothing if they themselves are not actively obeying the Torah.

The main point we need to realize as truth here, is not the Jew's error, but what Paul says concerning the will of YHWH.

He says that the Jews "know His will" and can approve of "more excellent things" because they have been "INSTRUCTED BY THE TORAH"!

| Instructed | stg's #G2727 - "katecheo", meaning, to sound down, as in to speak into the ear; from two words meaning, down and to make noise. Refers to being taught or indoctrinated by the Torah, i.e., trained by it. |

It is the Torah itself that trains us to know the will of YHWH for our lives and how to make right decisions or judgments and other matters.

| Deu 4:5 | "See, I have taught you laws and right-rulings, as יהוה my Elohim commanded me, to do thus in the land which you go to possess. |
| Deu 4:6 | "And **you shall guard and do them, for this is your wisdom and your understanding before the eyes of the peoples** who hear all these laws, and they shall say, 'Only a wise and understanding people is this great nation!' |

Here Moses states that it is from the practical application of the Torah in our day-to-day lives (our complete obedience to it) that we get the wisdom and understanding YHWH desires us to have, and that in our obedience to the Torah we will be a light of wisdom and understanding to the world and the unbelievers around us.

Consider the following:

| Pro 3:1 | My son, do not forget my Torah, And let your heart watch over my commands; |
| Pro 3:2 | For length of days and long life And peace they add to you. |
| Pro 3:3 | Let not loving-commitment and truth forsake you – Bind them around your neck, Write them on the tablet of your heart, |

| Pro 3:4 | Thus finding favour and good insight In the eyes of Elohim and man. |
|---------|----------------------------------------------------------------------|
| Pro 3:5 | Trust in יהוה with all your heart, And lean not on your own understanding; |
| Pro 3:6 | Know Him in all your ways, And He makes all your paths straight. |
| Pro 3:7 | Do not be wise in your own eyes; Fear יהוה and turn away from evil. |

(Isa 5:21; Job 28:28.)

Notice, the context is established in the first verse where it talks about not forgetting the Torah, which is another way of saying to obey it, and setting your heart on watching over or obeying the commandments.

Everything after this is associated to that context of remembering the Torah and having a heart set on obedience. If you have this heart and mind, then long life and peace will be added to you (Romans 8:6).

Verse 3 goes on to say that we are not to let loving commitment (mercy) and truth forsake us, for we are to bind them around our neck and write them upon our heart.

This is simply trying to tell us that we should let truth (belief [John 14:6] and works [John 17:1]) and mercy (compassion) be the intent of our heart and the yoke that guides us. It is basically teaching us the binding element.

Remember the *Two-Part Principle*, belief in Yahushua Messiah and obedience to the Torah, must be lived out in an attitude of compassion, which is the foundation of everything the Scripture is trying to tell us. Love, mercy, compassion is the heart attitude of a True Believer.

The reward for this obedient and compassionate heart is that we will have favour (grace) and good insight (understanding/wisdom) in the eyes of both YHWH and men. **Remember** Deuteronomy 4:5-6 where it's our obedience to all the commandments that gives us understanding and wisdom?

The last three verses have been quoted, *ad nauseam,* out of context but once looked at in the proper context it's easy to see what the Scripture is trying to tell us.

We are to not live our lives according to the thoughts and desires of our flesh (Rom 8:1-7, 12-13) but to trust and reverence YHWH by conforming our lives to the commands of Torah (Rom 12:1-2), thus allowing Him to make straight our way.

90

In this last section of Romans 2, Paul is going to show us that the only "condition" that matters is our heart condition.

| | |
|---|---|
| **Rom 2:25** | For circumcision indeed profits if you practise the Torah, but if you are a transgressor of the Torah, your circumcision has become uncircumcision. |
| **Rom 2:26** | So, if an uncircumcised one watches over the righteousnesses of the Torah, shall not his uncircumcision be reckoned as circumcision? |
| **Rom 2:27** | And the uncircumcised by nature, who perfects the Torah, shall judge you who notwithstanding letter and circumcision are a transgressor of the Torah! |
| **Rom 2:28** | For he is not a Yehudi who is *so* outwardly, neither is circumcision that which is outward in the flesh. |
| **Rom 2:29** | But a Yehudi is he who is *so* inwardly, and **circumcision is that of the heart**, in Spirit, not literally, whose praise is not from men but from Elohim. |

It is imperative to understand, that in the time Paul was writing this, the title of "Jew" had several meanings. One, it meant that you were a descendent of the Tribe of Yehudah (Judah).

Two, it meant that you dwelt in the land of Judea, and three, you were an adherent to the Jewish religion.

Paul's statements in vs 28 & 29 were very radical in his time, and even today causes great confusion among those coming into the whole Truth of Scripture. Remember that the context of this passage has to do with the acceptance of Gentiles within the Body of Messiah.

This was a foreign concept to the Jewish brethren, because of the influence of what we now call religious Judaism, which had abandoned the principle of Gentile inclusion taught by Moses.

Keeping this in mind, we see Paul telling the Jews that their physical circumcision and knowledge of Torah will not help them if they are not actually obeying the Torah.

On the other hand, the Gentiles lack of knowledge of the Torah and the uncircumcision of their flesh ,will not count against them when their fulfilling the principles of the Torah in their day-to-day life (vs. 14-16).

Paul goes on to tell the Jews that if they do not obey the Torah, the Gentiles who do obey the Torah will be judges over them in

91

that Day, even though they have none of the advantages of being the natural seed.

Being a "Jew" is not about bloodlines, Torah knowledge or physical circumcision, but has everything to do with having a heart completely submitted (circumcised) to YHWH.

The reference to "in the spirit, and not the letter" will come up again in chapter 7 and is expressing the distinction between a heart that is trusting in the Master Yahushua's work and not the works of the Torah alone, both refer to obeying the Torah but only one can make us right before YHWH.

It's interesting that most Christians believe the circumcision of the heart is the "New Testament" idea when in fact it comes from the Torah.

However, there's an interesting duality to circumcision of the flesh in the Torah, by this I mean there's a promise that YHWH will circumcise the heart and yet there is a command for each of us individually to circumcise our own heart.

| | |
|---|---|
| **Deu 30:6** | "And יהוה your **Elohim shall circumcise your heart** and the heart of your seed, to love יהוה your Elohim with all your heart and with all your being, so that you might live, |
| **Deu 30:7** | and יהוה your Elohim shall put all these curses on your enemies and on those who hate you, who persecuted you. |
| **Deu 30:8** | "And you shall turn back and obey the voice of יהוה and do all His commands which I command you today. |

As you can see here, the purpose of YHWH circumcising our heart is to **CAUSE** us to repent (turn back to YHWH) and to obey all the commands of Torah.

| | |
|---|---|
| **Deu 10:12** | "And now, Yisra'ĕl, what is יהוה your Elohim asking of you, but to fear יהוה your Elohim, to walk in all His ways and to love Him, and to serve יהוה your Elohim with all your heart and with all your being, |
| **Deu 10:13** | to guard the commands of יהוה and His laws which I command you today for your good? |
| **Deu 10:14** | "See, the heavens and the heaven of heavens belong to יהוה your Elohim, also the earth with all that is in it. |

| **Deu 10:15** | "יהוה delighted only in your fathers, to love them. And He chose their seed after them, you above all peoples, as it is today. |
| **Deu 10:16** | **"And you shall circumcise the foreskin of your heart**, and harden your neck no more. |

We see here now that we are commanded to circumcise our own heart and not to be stiff-necked (stubborn).

Notice the context here concerns guarding the commands of YHWH and His laws, His Torah, which is how we (1) fear Him, (2) walk in His ways, (3) love Him and (4) serve Him. We are to dedicate our whole heart (desires) and our whole being (conscious mind) to obedience to the entire Torah, for this is what it means to have a circumcised heart.

One thing we do have to be careful about though, when it comes to the teaching of the circumcision in the Messianic Writings, is the Christian misunderstanding that believers should no longer have to be circumcised. Paul says some things in the "New Testament" concerning circumcision that have confused the issue.

| **1Co 7:19** | The circumcision is naught, and the uncircumcision is naught, but the guarding of the commands of Elohim *does matter*! |

In this passage, as in certain others, Christian teachers have taught that believers no longer should be circumcised or circumcise their children because neither circumcision or uncircumcision matter.

However, Paul can never say that we should not circumcise our children, but that circumcision in and of itself has no redemptive properties, it is not a prerequisite for salvation as the Jews were teaching.

Circumcision, just like all the other commands of Torah, only applies to the new believer after he has accepted Messiah and become part of the nation of Yisra'el.

Circumcision is not a requirement TO BE SAVED, however it is a command of the Torah, which according to 1 Corinthians 7:19, does matter.

Having said this let me clarify the circumcision commandment, Abraham himself was commanded to be circumcised and his entire household, both the native born and the stranger (Gentile) in Genesis 17.

Then he was told that every generation of his descendents should be circumcised as well, as a sign of the covenant Abraham had with YHWH. Circumcision is a sign that we are in covenant with YHWH, but before we can get this sign we need to enter into the covenant, not before.

During the first century, the teaching of the Jewish rabbis concerning the prerequisite of circumcision (to be saved) had become such a bone of contention that Paul suggested that if we come to salvation as an uncircumcised Gentile that it would be better for us not to be circumcised at all than to be confused by the doctrine that circumcision was a requirement "to be saved", after all it's the circumcision of the heart to obey all the Torah that's most important.

A grown man who comes into the belief should not be circumcised unless and until he fully understands what circumcision means and its place in his salvation.

However, if after the man becomes a believer and has a son, he should circumcise that son on the eighth day, according to commandment, as a sign that his household is committed to the covenant.

The overall conclusion of chapter 2, which we need to understand, is that in the early years after the Messiah's ascension there were issues between the Jew and Gentile believer that caused Paul to define what a true "Jew" is, and that the more knowledge we have of the standard of righteous living (Torah), the more accountable we are to both live it ourselves and extend mercy to those of us who lack knowledge.

We cannot use our knowledge as a hammer by which we condemn less knowledgeable brothers. Again, our life in the Messiah Yahushua comes down to a heart condition. Our hearts must be circumcised or fully submitted to obeying the Torah of YHWH, however, we are to place our trust in the Messiah only and not in the works themselves.

Those of us who do so prove that we are seeking "glory and honor and immortality" and shall receive the peace of our assurance of everlasting life, whether we're a Jew or a Gentile.

However, if our hearts are hard and rebellious, refusing to obey the truth of obedience to Torah in our belief, and live unrighteously, with bitterness and wrath towards our brothers, then we will suffer "tribulation and anguish" for our evil.

The other side of this, which is not plainly stated, says if we obey the Torah, trusting in the works themselves and not in the blood of Messiah which has redeemed us, we will also suffer "tribulation and anguish" for our legalism (Trusting in works).

Furthermore, as we shall see, we can cause ourselves to be re-condemned to death and eternal judgment because of our hardhearted and hardheaded rebellion.

## Chapter 3

In chapter 3, Paul is going to speak of the Jews as a whole in their calling as the people of YHWH and explain the advantages of being a Jew. Paul's reference to "Jew" here must be understood in the proper context.

He's going to mention how they were given the Oracles or Word of YHWH, however, we know that the Scripture says the Word was given to the entire nation of Yisra'el, and not the "Jews" only.

**Note:** The promise of rule and scribe was given to the Jews, i.e., the children of Yahudah.

**Gen 49:10** "The sceptre (rule) shall not turn aside from Yehuḏah, nor an Inscriber (scribe) from between his feet, until Shiloh comes, and to Him is the obedience of peoples.

Messiah is prophesied here as the future King of the Jews, i.e., "Shiloh", and He is the Inscriber (scribe/lawgiver). The House of Yahudah (Jews) encompasses the tribes of Yahudah, Benjamin and Levi, and have safe-guarded the Hebrew Scripture and the Temple since the division of Yisra'el after the death of Solomon.

Paul's reasoning for saying that these advantages belong to the Jews instead of all Yisra'el has to do with the division of the two houses, Yisra'el and Judah (Yahudah). Paul goes on to ask them a question.

**Rom 3:3** For what if some did not believe? Shall their unbelief nullify the trustworthiness of Elohim?

**Rom 3:4** Let it not be! But **let Elohim be true, and every man a liar,** as it has been written, **"That You should be declared right in Your words, and prevail in Your judging."**

This passage is interesting because it is associated with two passages from the Tanak.

| | |
|---|---|
| **Hab 2:4** | "See, he whose being is not upright in him is puffed up. But the righteous one lives by his steadfastness. |
| **Being**: | stg's #**H5315** - "nephesh", meaning, a breathing creature; referring to the living person (conscious being) that we became when we were created (see: Genesis 2:7) or conceived. |
| **Puffed up**: | stg's #**H6075** -"aphal", meaning, to swell; referring to pride, arrogance or stubbornness within a man's heart or mind. |

A man resting (trusting) in himself, i.e., his own righteousness, is proud and arrogant, however, the righteous stand (place their trust) on their belief. It's about what our trust is based on and not on our capacity for obedience.

Though obedience is both required and relevant, it is the heart that is willing to obey perfectly that matters and not the perfection of our obedience.

| | |
|---|---|
| **Upright**: | stg's #**H3474** - "yashar", meaning, to be straight or even; refers to a state of righteousness or trustworthiness. |
| **Righteous**: | stg's #**H6662** - "tsaddiq", meaning, just or lawful; from a word meaning, to be right. Refers to someone who is in a "right position" (righteous) before YHWH. |
| **Steadfastness**: | stg's #**H530** - "emunah", meaning, to be firm; from a word meaning, to build up or support. Refers to a position of stability or steadfastness, a position in which the object shall not be moved (faithful). |

This passage is quoted by Paul in Galatians 3:11 and refers to a person who has taken a position upon which he shall live and from which he shall not be moved, and because of his stance, he is declared by YHWH to be a righteous (holy, set apart, etc.) person. (Genesis 15:1-7).

Here in Romans 3:3, Paul is stating that there are some natural Jews who did not stay fixed on the position (covenant) to which they and their fathers had been founded (read Exodus 19:1-8 and 24:1-8). He is associating their "self-righteousness" (their heart condition) with their inability to believe in Yahushua.

Then he asked whether their "unbelief", means that having belief in Yahushua is of "no effect."

No Effect: stg #**G2673** - "katargeo", meaning, to be entirely idle; from two words meaning, down and to be idle. Refers to a position of uselessness.

Paul wants to know if it's useless to believe in YHWH's promises, just because some Jews chose not to live true to their part of the bargain. To this he exclaims, "God forbid!"

God forbid: stg's #**G3361** - "me", meaning, a negation; -and-

stg's #**G1096** - "ginomai", meaning, to cause to be; or, let it be.

These two words combine to state in emphatic denial, "let it not be" or in modern language, **"Absolutely Not!"**

Paul goes on in verse 4 to confirm that YHWH is true and that it's mankind who errs. The trustworthiness of YHWH cannot be measured by the untrustworthiness of men.

Think of it in this way; what YHWH says…He does, without partiality and without failure, however, man wants what YHWH has promised…but does not want to comply with what he has agreed to, i.e., "All YHWH says we shall do" (Exodus 19:8 and 24:7).

YHWH is faithful and true to those who have showed themselves, in their heart, to be faithful and true. Paul goes on to refer to Psalms 51.

Psa 51:4 Against You, You alone, have I sinned, And done evil in Your eyes; That You might be proven right in Your words; Be clear when You judge.

Here, King David is making confession to YHWH concerning his murder of Uriah and adultery with his wife Bathsheba. He acknowledges that ultimately these crimes (sins) were not just against Uriah and Bathsheba but more specifically against YHWH Himself.

As a person upon whom YHWH's Name has been called, David understood that to defile the Torah of YHWH was to defile His Name as well, and thus, as believers, our disobedience is always against YHWH regardless of who it might affect otherwise.

Furthermore, David states that his sins gave YHWH the right to judge him for them, because YHWH is righteous, and David acted un-righteously.

If you look at the difference in the Hebrew of Psalms 51:4, which makes YHWH the object, you see the verse saying, "and be clear when You judge," compared to the Greek of Romans 3:4, which says, "and might overcome when you are judged," you see a different meaning, since YHWH judges, but is never judged.

The Greek version seems to change the object away from YHWH, the judge, to man, he that is judged. The Greek text reads:

*"kai nikeses en to krinesthai se"*
*-and prevail in the (things) you're judging-*

The verse in Romans 3 is meant to be an exact quote of Psalms 51:4. But Paul is going to reverse the logic of David's statement to question the fairness of YHWH's judgment on us.

**Rom 3:5**  But if our unrighteousness establishes the righteousness of Elohim, what shall we say? Is Elohim unrighteous who is inflicting wrath? I speak as a man.

**Rom 3:6**  Let it not be! Otherwise how shall Elohim judge the world?

Basically, Paul is asking how we can be punished for doing wrong, if the wrong we do actually prove how righteous YHWH is. Paul is using man-made reasoning in his question, which men have used to justify wrong behavior, as an accusation towards the Jews of chapter 2.

His conclusion is, if this reasoning was accurate, then YHWH could not judge the unbelieving world. YHWH has the right to judge us even though our unrighteous behavior proves that He is righteous, because He is, in fact, righteous and we are not.

Paul is going to revisit this question from a different angle because he has been accused of saying this very thing (that he taught that believers no longer needed to obey the Torah).

***

| | |
|---|---|
| **Rom 3:7** | For if the truth of Elohim has increased through my lie, to His esteem, why am I also still judged as a sinner? |
| **Rom 3:8** | And *why* not *say*, "Let us do evil so that the good might come"? – as we are wrongly accused and as some claim that we say. Their judgment is in the right. |

Paul is asking why he is being judged as a sinner (someone who disobeys the Torah-1 John 3:4) if he teaches a lie about the truth of YHWH, when the lie proves that what YHWH has said is true. The way Paul phrases his questions is always interesting because it requires us to take a moment to step back and say, "What?!"

This argument has risen up because Paul has taught that man cannot be justified (made right from sin and death) through obeying the Torah, which caused certain Jews to accuse Paul of teaching that believers don't have to obey the Torah at all, which is a prominent Christian doctrine. (See our study: Acts 21:17-26)

Paul himself here, clearly and unreservedly, declares that these Jews have wrongfully accused him of teaching this. To be wrongly accused of something is to be lied about and slandered.

According to Paul, the idea that believers no longer have to obey the Torah of YHWH is a LIE!!! This lie has been taken up by modern Christian teachers and taught as truth. (See also the false accusation made by the Jewish leadership against Brother Stephen in Acts 6:8-14).

Paul's question was meant to challenge those Jews who criticize the new Gentile believers, while they themselves were disobeying the Torah, yet calling themselves the "children of Elohim".

Paul says, those who say such things (about him) deserve damnation, however, Paul clarifies that he is no better than them.

| | |
|---|---|
| **Rom 3:9** | What then? Are we better *than they*? Not at all, for we have previously accused both Yehuḏim and Greeks that they are all under sin. |

Paul goes on in verses 10-18 to quote extensively from the Tanak (Psalms 14:1-; 53:1-4; 140:3; 10:7; Proverbs 1:16; Isaiah 59:7;

99

Psalms 36:1) to prove that all men are sinners (transgressors of the Torah), however, his statement that "we" have proved both Jew and Gentile are "under sin" is a reference to his own teachings.

He already stated in chapter 2:13 that both the Jew and the Gentile who disobey the Torah shall answer for it. His "proof" though comes also from his previous writings to other assemblies, which we will covered in a future study.

What we really want to show from this verse is the meaning of "under sin" because this is going to come up over and over in various forms as we cover Paul's writings.

We have already shown that the definition of sin is "the transgression of the law (Torah-1 John 3:4) and it's very imperative that we don't lose sight of this, as we move through Romans.

> **Under**: stg's #G5259 - "hoopoe", meaning, under; referring to a place or position. In the context of sin, it refers to sin's authority over us.

> **1Cor 15:56**    And the sting of death is sin, and the power of the sin is the Torah.

> **Sting**: stg's #G2759 - "kentron", meaning, a point; refers to the point of or reason for (death).

> **Power**: stg's #G1411 - "dunamis", meaning, force; from G1410, "dunamai", meaning, to be able.

So, you see, the reason we die is because we do not obey the Torah (sin-1 John 3:4) and so sin has the authority to kill us because of the Torah, which says, "the being that sins shall die" (Ezekiel 18:4). It is the Torah that gives sin the authority to kill us, so we become "under" the authority of sin (death) because of disobedience.

To be "under sin" means to be condemned to death, but to be "under the Torah" also means to be under the condemnation of death, because it is the Torah that gave sin the authority to kill us. In fact, Paul uses these two phrases, "under sin" and "under the Torah" synonymously throughout his writings.

**Ex:**    **Gal 3:22**    But the Scripture has shut up all *mankind* **under sin**, that the promise by belief in יהושע Messiah might be given to those who believe.

| | |
|---|---|
| **Gal 3:23** | But before belief came, we were being guarded **under Torah**, having been shut up for the belief being about to be revealed. |
| **Gal 3:24** | Therefore **the Torah became our trainer unto Messiah**, in order to be declared right by belief. |
| **Gal 3:25** | And after belief has come, we are **no longer under a trainer**. |

Notice here, Paul states that all men are under (the condemnation of death because of) sin and that before we had belief in Messiah we had been under (the condemnation of death required by the) Torah, because of sin.

So, the Torah became our teacher or trainer to teach us that we are guilty of sin and in need of the Messiah.

However, once we've come to understand our need for Messiah and been declared right by Him through belief, we are no longer under (the condemnation of) the trainer.

> **Note**: As mentioned above, the standard of righteous living that all believers are to live by is the Torah (Deuteronomy 6:24-25) and so, to sin or do something unrighteous, would be to violate the Torah.

Also, the Greek word used for law in the Messianic Writings is "nomos", which comes from the unused root "nemo", meaning to parcel out. Nemo is the Greek word used to translate the Hebrew word Torah.

Both the root word for Torah (yarah) and Nemo carry the sense of giving out or passing along, and when used in the context of Scripture means instructions, or what is spoken.

Messiah said in Matthew 4:4 that man does not live by bread alone but by "every word that proceeds out of the mouth of Elohim". He was given the perfect definition of what the word Torah (Nomos) means.

| | |
|---|---|
| **Deu 30:15** | "See, I have set before you today life and good, and death and evil, |
| **Deu 30:16** | in that I am commanding you today to love יהוה your Elohim, to walk in His ways, and to guard His commands, and His laws, and His right-rulings. And you shall live and increase, |

| | |
|---|---|
| | and יהוה your Elohim shall bless you in the land which you go to possess. |
| **Deu 30:17** | "But if your heart turns away, and you do not obey, and shall be drawn away, and shall bow down to other mighty ones and serve them, |
| **Deu 30:18** | "I have declared to you today that you shall certainly perish, you shall not prolong your days in the land which you are passing over the Yardĕn to enter and possess. |
| **Deu 30:19** | "I have called the heavens and the earth as witnesses today against you: I have set before you life and death, the blessing and the curse. Therefore, you shall choose life, so that you live, both you and your seed, |
| **Deu 30:20** | to love יהוה your Elohim, to obey His voice, and to cling to Him – for He is your life and the length of your days – to dwell in the land which יהוה swore to your fathers, to Aḇraham, to Yitsḥaq, and to Ya'aqoḇ, to give them." |

Here's a thought, if YHWH is our Father because of our belief in Yahushua (Galatians 3:29), then the promise of the land belongs to us who believe also, the land of promise in the Tanak is a shadow picture, a hidden mystery, of the Kingdom of Messiah in the last day, the millennial (1000 year) reign of Messiah.

Notice, here in Deuteronomy 30, Moses equates life and death with obedience or disobedience to the Torah (commandments, statutes, judgments, ordinances, orders, etc.).

Also, that obeying (living by the Torah) is equated to:

1.  Loving YHWH,
2.  Walking in His Way,
3.  Good and Blessing,
4.  Cleaving To YHWH.

Obedience to the Torah is life because YHWH, who gave us the Torah to live by (Leviticus 18:5), is our life and the length of our days (Proverbs 3:1-2; Romans 8:6).

However, not obeying the Torah is equated to:

1.  Worshiping and serving other gods (Deut 28:14; demons – 1Corinthians 10:19-20)
2.  Evil and Cursing,

3.      Perishing (death).

Once again, it is the Torah of YHWH that teaches us how to live, but it also teaches us why we die, and that reason is disobedience (sin). It is the Torah that says, "You shall not murder and the man that murders he shall die".

Thus, the Torah is the authority through which sin has the power to kill us (condemn us to death). To be "under sin" or "under the Torah" is to be condemned to death because of sin.

\*\*\*

**Rom 3:19**       And we know that whatever the Torah says, it says to those who are in the Torah, so that every mouth might be stopped, and all the world come under judgment before Elohim.

The phrase "in the Torah" here, says "under the Law" in most of the new English translations including the (KJV), however, the Greek word translated a in/under in this verse is "en" and not the word "hupo" that is used in verse 9.

**en:**       stg's #**G1722** - "en", meaning, position (in place, time or state); though used in many different applications this word (translated as "under" in most English versions) does not carry the same meaning of authority as "hupo" in verse 9. This word does not imply authority as much as a position in or of something.

From the first chapter of Romans, we have had the theme of "knowledge" weaving its way through the context and it should be applied here. Remember what chapter 2:12 said, "...as many as have sinned in the law shall be judged by the law".

The word for "in", in 2:12, translates the Greek word, "en", just as in 3:19.

Paul is telling us, in 3:19, that the Torah speaks to those people who HAVE or KNOW the Torah, so they too will have no defense when YHWH judges them. This is connected directly to 2:12, and to verify this conclusion, we need to continue to the next verse.

**Rom 3:20**       Therefore by works of Torah **no flesh shall be declared right before Him, for by the Torah is the knowledge of sin.**

103

The phrase "in the Torah" in verse 19, carries the meaning of "knowledge of the Torah", as stated here in verse 20. By translating both the Greek words "en" and "hupo" as under, the English translators have obscured the meaning of this passage and raised all sorts of confusion.

Here in verse 20, Paul states that the deeds of the law (obeying it) will not be able to declare right (justify) a man because from the Torah comes the knowledge of sin.

> **Declare right**:  stg's #G1344 - "dikaioo", meaning, to render just; from a word meaning, right. Refers to the act of making a person right from sin. Sin makes a man un-right and justifying him makes him right again.

Why can't the Torah, which "if a man obeys it he shall live (Leviticus 18:5)", make a man right from sin?

Because the entire world is **already guilty** before YHWH (v. 19) as sinners (v. 9), and since it was the Torah that declared us guilty for disobeying it, it cannot declare us right again until the penalty it condemned us to (i.e., death), is paid for.

The Torah teaches us what sin is and that we are guilty of disobeying it, therefore it teaches us that we are deserving of death and cannot escape it by our own works.

| | |
|---|---|
| **Rom 3:21** | But now, apart from the Torah, a righteousness of Elohim has been revealed, being witnessed by the Torah and the Prophets, |
| **Rom 3:22** | and the righteousness of Elohim is through belief in יהושע Messiah to all and on all who believe. For there is no difference, |
| **Rom 3:23** | for all have sinned and fall short of the esteem of Elohim, |

Paul just told us in verse 20 that doing the works of the Torah cannot make us right before YHWH, but now he is showing us that we can be made right again if we believe in the Good News of Messiah's death, burial and resurrection. Why?

As we shall see, Messiah became the sacrifice of atonement through which we can be made right with YHWH again.

He clearly states that this "righteousness", that makes us right again or justifies us, is witnessed in the law and the prophets, it is NOT A NEW DOCTRINE!

The "Gospel" is not a "New Testament" doctrine! It is, in fact, an "Old Testament" doctrine revealed to the 1st century Brethren in the person of Messiah Yahushua.

Paul references a righteousness that comes by belief in Messiah. He is talking about the righteousness referred to in Habakkuk 2:4 - "the just shall live by belief."

There is an important doctrinal point being made here that is obscured by modern Christian dogma and misunderstood by the church to its ultimate destruction. The doctrinal point I'm referring to is called the *Two-Part Principle* and refers to the scriptural fact of both a spiritual element and a physical element to the redemption process.

When man was created, he was created from the dust of the earth (his physical body) which was totally inert, having no life in it. Then, YHWH breathed into the man's nostrils the breath of life. The Hebrew words "neshamah" and "rauch" are both translated as spirit in our English Bibles, yet both words are related to air or breath.

We need to understand that when the breath entered the body the person became alive. For man to have life, required a physical body that was part of the physical creation and a spark (breath) that came directly from YHWH the Creator. It took the physical and a spiritual together to make life.

This same principle is true for eternal life as well. For a sinner who is under the penalty of death for disobeying the Torah, to be made right again and to inherit the Kingdom of YHWH and eternal life, requires them to be redeemed in the spirit-man, which only happens through belief in the blood of Yahushua Messiah.

Then, they need to be redeemed in the physical man, which takes place at the resurrection of the dead, when we receive our new (redeemed) bodies.

The problem is, like Yisra'el before us, we are living in the wilderness of this life that began with the Passover Lamb (Yahushua) and ends when we enter into the Promised Land (the Kingdom).

And, just like Yisra'el in the wilderness we are required to submit to the authority of YHWH according to His Torah in belief, trusting that He will see us through the wilderness and defeat our enemies before us.

The question then is, did everyone that escaped Egypt enter into the Promised Land? The answer is a big fat emphatic **NO!!!**

Just as some of those who escaped Egypt did not enter into the Promised Land because they would not obey, so too some of us who have escaped the penalty of death and the power of this world by confession of Yahushua as our Messiah, if we refuse to obey His Torah, shall die in the wilderness of this life and never inherit the Kingdom.

Back in verse 22, Paul said that this righteousness is "unto all and upon all who believe", which is a reference to the two types of believers (i.e., Jewish, who had the Torah and the Gentile, who did not have it). YHWH is not a respecter of persons; He receives all who will believe.

This phrase "unto all" is a reference to the Jew who had the Torah but needed to believe, while the phrase "upon all" is a reference to the Gentile who did not have the Torah.

The distinction lies in the fact that since the Jew already had the Torah, they needed to add belief to their way of life, but the Gentile who had never heard of the Torah needed to believe first and then learn the Torah way of life afterwards. We'll see this again shortly.

The question one might ask is, "how can a righteous Elohim forgive the sin of unrighteous men and still be righteous Himself?" Because YHWH is completely righteous and completely just, it would seem impossible for Him to forgive the sins of unrighteous men, because once He has said that death was required for sin, He cannot change it, He is immutable (unchanging).

The answer lies in the blood of Yahushua.

| | |
|---|---|
| **Rom 3:24** | being declared right, without paying, by His favour through the redemption which is in Messiah יהושע, |
| **Rom 3:25** | whom Elohim set forth as an atonement, through belief in His blood, to demonstrate His righteousness, because in His tolerance Elohim had passed over the **sins that had taken place before,** |
| **Rom 3:26** | to **demonstrate at the present time His righteousness, that He is righteous and declares righteous the one who has belief in** יהושע. |

Remember, being justified refers to our being made right again from our past wrongness (sin), and this was done freely (it cost us nothing), it was a gift (Ephesians 2:8-9). How did this happen?

YHWH made Messiah a propitiation (atonement) for us so that we could be redeemed from our past sin debt, i.e., death.

106

| | |
|---|---|
| **Redemption**: | stg's **#G629** - "apolutrosis", meaning a ransom; from two words meaning, off and loosen. Refers to being released from a debt because the ransom price (the debt) has been paid. |
| **Atonement**: | stg's **#G2435** - "hilasterion", meaning, expiatory; refers to one who paid a price for a debt. Yahushua Messiah became the ransom price that was paid for us so that we could be made right again in the eyes of YHWH. |

Yahushua's life was the price that was paid so that we could be redeemed (set free) from the death penalty we owed. Just like Yisra'el was saved from the death Angel by the blood of the Passover Lamb applied to the doorpost and lintel of the house.

He gave up His life in exchange for ours, the righteous for the unrighteous, it was by this act (giving His Son to die) that YHWH was able to accept us, the sinner, and still remain righteous Himself.

Consider that YHWH gave the Torah, which says that a person who sins shall die (Ezekiel 18:4) so, if He forgives our sins without making us die for them, He Himself has broken the Torah, making Himself unrighteous.

However, He provided a perfect sacrifice (a death) as a substitute for our own death, which allowed Him to forgive our sins and still be righteous.

Messiah's death allowed YHWH to forgive our sins without breaking His own Torah, so now, YHWH is free to give forgiveness and redemption to anyone He chooses. However, He will only extend that forgiveness to those who will believe in what Messiah Yahushua did for us.

Our belief in Him, Yahushua, gives us access to the redemption that He paid for, in His own blood. This is one thing; Christians will wholeheartedly agree with.

However, the fact that they believe they no longer have to obey the Torah, is a violation of everything Yahushua said and did. It is, in fact, the apostasy He foretold, and the Great Deception/Powerful Delusion spoken of by Paul in 2 Thessalonians 2:11-17. (See Appendix: 5 – The Great Deception on Pg. 570).

| | |
|---|---|
| **Rom 3:27** | Where, then, is the boasting? It is shut out. By what torah? Of works? No, but by the torah of belief. |

107

| | |
|---|---|
| **Rom 3:28** | For we reckon that a man is declared right by belief without works of Torah. |

Paul concludes that, YHWH provided a sacrifice for us, while we were still in our sin, that Messiah paid the price for our sin debt while we were still guilty of sin, and that through this work of Messiah we regained our freedom from death, when we believe in Him. So then, do we have anything to boast of in ourselves?

We should never boast in anything but Him, especially anything that WE might have done, because WE didn't do ANYTHING of redemptive value!

Yahushua did it all and since He did it all for us, then our justification comes only from Him and not from anything we have done. So, the only way to be made right from our past sins, from the death penalty we owed, is by belief in Yahushua only.

| | |
|---|---|
| **Rom 3:29** | Or *is He* the Elohim of the Yehuḏim only, and not also of the nations? Yes, of the nations also, |
| **Rom 3:30** | since it is one Elohim who shall **declare right the circumcised by belief and the uncircumcised through belief.** |
| **Rom 3:31** | Do we then nullify the Torah through the belief? Let it not be! **On the contrary, we establish the Torah.** |

YHWH is the Master of all men, He created us all, Jew and Gentile, so His Work is to all men who would believe. That's Paul's conclusion, however, he is not finished. He once again makes a distinction between the Jew (circumcised) and the Gentile (uncircumcised) as to how they receive this gift.

The Jew receives it by belief, which is a reference to the fact that they already had the Torah and just needed to add belief in Yahushua, to be complete in the Truth of YHWH.

| | |
|---|---|
| **Joh 14:6** | יהושע said to him, "I am the Way, and the Truth, and the Life. No one comes to the Father except through Me. |
| | *** |
| **Joh 17:17** | "Set them apart in Your truth – Your Word is truth. |

(Ps 119:142; 119:151; 119:160)

108

Messiah is the Truth! The Word (Torah-Psalms 119:142) is Truth! The Messiah and the Torah!

This is what YHWH spoke to Isaiah concerning those false priests and prophets who would lead His people to disobey the Torah.

**Isa 8:20**          To the Torah and to the witness! If they do not speak according to this Word, it is because they have no daybreak (light).

When the messenger was speaking to John concerning those set-apart ones (saints) that would endure to the end, in Revelation, he described them thusly.

**Rev 14:12**         Here is the endurance of the set-apart ones, here are those guarding the commands of Elohim and the belief of יהושע.

**Endurance**:        stg's #**G5281** - "hupomone", Meaning, cheerful or hopeful endurance; from two words meaning, to stay and under. Refers to remaining in position, planted like a tree, no matter the circumstances.

The way we stay in position during the trials and tribulations of the last day is to be among those who both, believe in the Messiah Yahushua **AND** obey the Torah of YHWH. Paul is going to confirm this a bit later

As we've said, the Jewish believer is saved by belief in Yahushua, because he already has the Torah and by adding belief, he completes the Truth.

However, the Gentile does not HAVE or KNOW the Torah and so must come to the Messiah through belief first and then complete the Truth by learning to walk in the Torah.

Both must have belief to be justified and both can only be saved from the death penalty by believing in the Messiah. The Torah cannot help us at all, but to be complete (perfect) in the Truth the Jews have a head start because they know the righteous standard of living, the Torah.

The Gentiles must learn about the Torah and their need to obey it **AFTER** they are saved (justified) by favor through belief. This takes us right back to chapter 2 when Paul was accusing the Jewish brethren for condemning the Gentiles, he told them that the Gentile

109

believer doing the principles of Torah in his heart is a law to himself, it's all connected.

Paul was not telling the Gentiles in chapter 2 to follow their heart, as some would suggest, however he was saying that if they are living in a manner of behavior and attitude that is consistent with the Torah, then their lack of knowledge will not condemn them.

This does not mean, as some Christian teachers would have you believe, that new believers are not required to learn the Torah and do it.

Paul is clear in all his writings that we are supposed to be obeying the Torah; it's just that modern teachers do not understand what he is saying, because they don't obey the Torah, as he did all his life. It is through obedience to the Torah, that we get wisdom and understanding (Deuteronomy 4:5-6) and Paul knew this.

Paul's statement in verse 31 is significant enough to repeat. Even though we are not justified by the law... "Do we then make void the law through belief? Let it not be: yea, we establish the law."

Is the Torah void (katargeo - made useless) in our lives? NO!

| Establish: | stg's #G2476 - "histemi", meaning, to stand; compares to a word (tithemi), meaning, to place. Refers to upholding or making something stand in its rightful place. |
|---|---|

| Note: | As we have shown, the Hebrew word for belief is "Emunah" and means "steadfastness" or standing firm. We see here, Paul saying that our belief in Messiah "establishes" the Torah and the Greek word for establish also carries the meaning of standing firmly. |
|---|---|

The Torah is **how** we stand in our belief, but our belief in Yahushua is **where** we take our stand. In other words, our belief is firmly founded in the Good News of Messiah's death, burial and resurrection and we live out that belief through obedience to the Torah of YHWH.

The Torah is not useless in the life of a believer. In fact, in our belief, it has taken its rightful place in our lives, secondary to belief. Belief saves us, while Torah is how we live!

| 1Ti 1:8 | And we know that the Torah is good if one uses it legitimately, |
|---|---|

There is a legitimate use of the Torah for believers in Messiah and that is in how we live righteously as believers. To boast in the Torah or depend on the Torah for your justification is an illegitimate use of the Torah and leads to death because your trust is in it and not in Messiah.

Consider what Paul said to Timothy by way of allegory.

| | |
|---|---|
| **2Ti 2:4** | No one serving as a soldier gets involved in the affairs of this life, in order to please *only* him who enlisted him as a soldier. |
| **2Ti 2:5** | And if anyone competes in a game, he is not crowned unless he competes according to the rules. |
| **2Ti 2:6** | The hard-working farmer ought to be first to receive his share of the crops. |

Verse 4 is teaching Timothy a principle of belief; a soldier forsakes his entire life that he might please the one who enlisted him (Yahushua).

Verse 5 is teaching Timothy a principle of work, in that those who compete in the game (race) only receive their reward if they compete according to the <u>rules</u> (G3545 - "nomimōs" - lawfully).

Notice in the word "nomimos" that the first three letters are "nom", which is the conjugated form of the word Nomos (law/Torah) and refers to doing things according to the rules/law/Torah.

So, our race to get to the Kingdom must be ran or lived, according to the rules of Torah.

Verse 6 is teaching Timothy a principle of reward, in that the hard-working farmer receives the best share of the reward. Thus, the hard workers of the belief, those who are diligently committed to obeying the Torah with their whole heart and mind and strength, shall have the greatest reward.

| | | |
|---|---|---|
| **Note**: | **Mat 4:4** | But He answering, said, "It has been written, **'Man shall not live by bread alone, but by every word that comes from the mouth of יהוה.'** |

This verse takes place just after Ha'Satan tried to get the Messiah to make bread out of stones. What is interesting in this verse is, Messiah mentions two things by which men have life. This is important because it supports other things already mentioned in the Scripture (Isaiah 8:20; Revelation 14:12).

111

Here Messiah says that man does not live by bread alone but by EVERY WORD that comes out of the mouth of YHWH. This is a quote from Deuteronomy 8:1-3, where it teaches that we are to obey EVERY WORD YHWH has spoken so we might live and inherit.

He gave us His Word (Torah) to humble us and to prove (test) us to determine whether we will obey His Torah, even during this time of wondering as we await the return of Messiah (See Eccl. 3:14)

Also, when Messiah said that man does not live by bread alone, He was saying something much deeper than is understood by modern teachers.

You see, Messiah refers to Himself as the Bread of Life in John 6:48. This is significant because He's identifying the fact that man does not live (have eternal life) by belief in Him alone, but that he must live by EVERY WORD that proceeded out of the mouth of YHWH (His Torah, without additions or subtractions - Deuteronomy 4:2; 12:32; Ecclesiastes 3:14; Proverbs 30:6 and Revelation 22:18-19; compare also Jam 2:14-25).

**REMEMBER**, from Paul's perspective, our obedience to the Torah as a believer is assumed. The debate in Paul's letters is not whether we should obey the Torah but whether or not Torah obedience alone can justify us (make us right) from past sin. The question was, "is Torah obedience required TO BE SAVED" as many Jews insisted (Acts 15:1)?

Paul's emphatic answer is NO!!! ONLY belief in Yahushua can save us from the death penalty we owed because of past sin, He paid the price for us and set us free (justified us) from that debt.

This Truth BY NO MEANS absolves us from the responsibility to live righteously in obedience to His Torah, and Paul is going to say so as we move forward.

# Chapter 2: Romans 4

Paul (Sha'ul) is going to do something in this chapter that we believers would do well to emulate. He is going to use the story of our father Abraham to prove a doctrinal point, something he admonishes us to do several times when he tells us to use what happened in the Tanak as examples to learn from.

| | |
|---|---|
| **Rom 15:4** | For whatever was written before was **written for our instruction,** that through endurance and encouragement of the Scriptures we might have the expectation. |

***

| | |
|---|---|
| **1Co 10:1** | For I do not wish you to be ignorant, brothers, that all our fathers were under the cloud, and all passed through the sea, |
| **1Co 10:2** | and all were immersed into Mosheh in the cloud and in the sea, |
| **1Co 10:3** | and all ate the same spiritual food, |
| **1Co 10:4** | and all drank the same spiritual drink. For they drank of that spiritual Rock that followed, and the Rock was Messiah. |
| **1Co 10:5** | However, with most of them Elohim was not well pleased, for they were laid low in the wilderness. |
| **1Co 10:6** | And **these became examples for us,** so that we should not lust after evil, as those indeed lusted. |
| **1Co 10:7** | And do not become idolaters as some of them, as it has been written, **"The people sat down to eat and to drink, and stood up to play."** |
| **1Co 10:8** | Neither should we commit whoring, as some of them did, and in one day twenty-three thousand fell, |
| **1Co 10:9** | neither let us try Messiah, as some of them also tried, and were destroyed by serpents, |
| **1Co 10:10** | neither grumble, as some of them also grumbled, and were destroyed by the destroyer. |
| **1Co 10:11** | And **all these came upon them as examples, and they were written as a warning to us, on whom the ends of the ages have come,** |

| 1Co 10:12 | so that <u>he who thinks he stands, let him take heed lest he fall.</u> |
|---|---|

***

| Heb 4:6 | Since then it remains for some to enter into it, and those who formerly received the Good News did **not enter in because of disobedience**, |
|---|---|
| Heb 4:7 | He again defines a certain day, **"Today,"** saying through Dawiḏ so much later, as it has been said, **"Today, if you hear His voice, do not harden your hearts."** |
| Heb 4:8 | For if Yehoshua had given them rest, He would not have spoken of another day after that. |
| Heb 4:9 | So there remains a Sabbath-keeping for the people of Elohim. |
| Heb 4:10 | For the one, having entered into His rest, has himself also rested from his works, as Elohim *rested* from His own. |
| Heb 4:11 | Let us therefore **do our utmost to enter into that rest, lest anyone fall after the same example of disobedience.** |
| Heb 4:12 | For the Word of Elohim is living, and working, and sharper than any two-edged sword, cutting through even to the dividing of being and spirit, and of joints and marrow, and able to **judge the thoughts and intentions of the heart.** |
| Heb 4:13 | And there is no creature hidden from His sight, but all are naked and laid bare before the eyes of Him with whom is our account. |
| Note: | The word "disobedience" in vs. 6 and 11 is translated in the King James Version as "unbelief", which in a strictly scriptural sense is correct but causes the Christian reader to misunderstand what the writer is actually saying and what actually happened in the wilderness that kept Yisra'el from entering into the rest. |

The Greek word used here as disobedience is, "apeitheia" (#G543), meaning, *disbelief* (**obstinate and rebellious**): - disobedience, unbelief; from "apeithes" (#G545), meaning, *unpersuadable*, that is, ***contumacious***: - disobedient.

From a purely scriptural viewpoint, there is no distinction between unbelief and disobedience; they mean the same thing to YHWH. The Greek word here is used interchangeably as both unbelief and disobedience depending on the context, or unfortunately, the translator's point of view.

If we adhere strictly to the shadow picture of Yisra'el to define what is meant here, we see that the first generation of Yisra'eli men did not enter into the Promised Land because they refused to enter the land when YHWH told them to.

Ten of the twelve spies that were sent into the Land to do reconnaissance came back with a fearful report and frightened the camp, persuading them that there was no way they could take the Land.

The other two spies, Caleb, and Joshua (Yahushua) had complete belief that YHWH would go before them and defeat their enemies, just as He promised He would.

Unfortunately, the camp sided with the 10 and that lack of belief in YHWH motivated them to disobey. Their disobedience equaled unbelief and the result was YHWH's judgment that none of the men of that generation would enter into the rest of the Promised Land. All of them died in the wilderness and did not inherit the Land, except for Caleb and Joshua.

Going back to Brother Paul, we see that he is going to use Abraham as a picture of how righteousness is imputed to us by belief. Before we get into chapter 4 though, let's go back to the Tanak and review what happened with Abraham.

| | |
|---|---|
| **Gen 15:1** | After these events **the word of יהוה came to Abram in a vision,** saying, "Do not be afraid, Abram. I am your shield, your reward is exceedingly great." |
| **Gen 15:2** | And Abram said, "Master יהוה, what would You give me, seeing I go childless, and the heir of my house is Eliʿezer of Dammeseq?" |
| **Gen 15:3** | And Abram said, "See, You have given me no seed, and see, one born in my house is my heir!" |
| **Gen 15:4** | And see, the word of יהוה came to him, saying, "This one is not your heir, but he who comes from your own body is your heir." |
| **Gen 15:5** | And He brought him outside and said, "Look now toward the heavens, and count the stars if |

116

you are able to count them." And He said to him, "So are your seed."

**Gen 15:6**     **And he believed in יהוה, and He reckoned it to him for righteousness.**

The first and most interesting thing we see in this passage is that it was "The Word" of YHWH that "came unto Abraham in a vision" and spoke to him. How does a word appear to someone and speak?

This is most likely a pre-incarnate (before He became a man) appearance of Yahushua Messiah (the physical manifestation of YHWH) who is the Word of YHWH made flesh (Jn 1:1-3,14).

Second, we see that Abram was curious as to how YHWH was going to fulfill His promise that through him YHWH was going to bless all the families of the earth (12:1-3), seeing that he had not had any children yet.

YHWH tells Abram that he will have a son from his own body and through that son he will have descendants more numerous than the stars of the heavens. Verse 6 says that Abram "believed in YHWH" and this terminology is important. The Hebrew actually says:


"vᵉha'emin bay YHWH"
***
"and the support in YHWH"


This phrase should be understood to mean that Abram had placed all his trust in **WHO** YHWH is and not just what He had said. This kind of belief is a heart condition that causes us to act upon our belief by doing whatever YHWH requires us to do. Brother James (Ya'aqob) has this to say about this passage.

**Jam 2:14**     My brothers, what use is it for anyone to say he has belief but does not have works? **This belief is unable to save him.**

**Jam 2:15**     And if a brother or sister is naked and in need of daily food,

**Jam 2:16**     but one of you says to them, "Go in peace, be warmed and be filled," but you do not give them the bodily needs, what use is it?

**Jam 2:17**     So also belief, if it does not have works, is in itself dead.

| Jam 2:18 | But someone might say, "You have belief, and I have works." Show me your belief without your works, and **I shall show you my belief by my works**. |
| --- | --- |
| Jam 2:19 | You believe that **Elohim is one**. You do well. The demons also believe – and shudder! |
| Jam 2:20 | But do you wish to know, O foolish man, that the **belief without the works is dead?** |
| Jam 2:21 | Was not Aḇraham our father **declared right by works when he offered Yitsḥaq** his son on the slaughter-place? |
| Jam 2:22 | Do you see that the belief was working with his works, and by the works the belief was perfected? |
| Jam 2:23 | And the Scripture was filled which says, **"Aḇraham believed Elohim, and it was reckoned to him for righteousness."** And He called him, **"he who loves Elohim."** |
| Jam 2:24 | You see, then, **that a man is declared right by works, and not by belief alone**. |
| Jam 2:25 | In the same way, was not Raḥaḇ the whore also declared right by works when she received the messengers and sent them out another way? |
| Jam 2:26 | For as the body without the spirit is dead, so also the **belief is dead without the works.** |

It is obvious that Abraham's whole-hearted trust in **Who** YHWH is, is what was counted towards him as righteousness.

**Counted:**   stg's #**H2803** - "chashab", meaning, to plate (to braid or weave); referring to an act of intertwining something within something else.

**Righteousness:** stg's #**H6666** - "tsedaqah", meaning, rightness; referring to a state of being right.

Because Abram had fully trusted YHWH, the state of righteousness was placed **within** him. He was declared to be right because of what he believed, or better, because of Whom he believed in.

118

| Rom 4:1 | What, then, shall we say Abraham our father, to have found, according to the flesh? |
| Rom 4:2 | For if Abraham was declared right by works, he has *ground for* boasting, but not before Elohim. |
| Rom 4:3 | For what does the Scripture say? **"Abraham believed Elohim, and it was reckoned to him for righteousness."** |
| Rom 4:4 | And to him who is working, the reward is not reckoned as a favour but as a debt. |
| Rom 4:5 | And to him who is not working but believes on Him who is declaring right the wicked, **his belief is reckoned for righteousness,** |

Paul here is simply showing that we come to the same state of righteousness that Abraham received by the same way he received it. If we claim, as some in Paul's time were, that works of the Torah are required to make us right before YHWH, then YHWH would owe us righteousness.

However, since we are already guilty of being unrighteous (3:23) the only thing that can save us is YHWH's favor (grace), which only comes through believing in the work of His Son, Yahushua (3:23-26). Because of this we cannot claim glory in ourselves but can only glorify Him.

We, like Abraham, are not declared righteous because we believe in what YHWH has said about His Son, we are declared right because we believe in **Who** YHWH is, which leads us to act upon what He said in regard to His Son, Yahushua.

Though we call on Yahushua for salvation, our belief/trust is founded in **Who** YHWH is and so we believe in Yahushua. This belief then, allows our trust in the Father to transfer to the Son because of the nature of the relationship between them. To have the Messiah in us through belief, is to have the Father in us as well (John 14:8-24).

It is important to make a distinction concerning the type of righteousness (justification) being referred to here. No amount of works can justify anyone from the penalty of death, which we are all **under** before we confess Messiah.

The Torah is the standard of righteous living (justification/sanctification) that we live by after we've been justified from sin and death through belief in Yahushua.

In verses 6-8, Paul confirms what he's teaching by quoting David, from Psalms 32:1-2. In this passage the word, "impute" is used in place of the word counted.

119

**Impute:**       stg's #**H2803** - "chashab", (see above).

stg's #**G3049** - "logizomai", meaning, to take an inventory; from a word meaning, something said (or thought) as in laying out.

The Hebrew word, as stated, refers to having righteousness "weaved" within us. The Greek word here refers to having it "placed on our account" as a deposit is placed in a ledger.

Obviously, since Paul is using the story of Abraham as our foundation it is the Hebrew meaning that takes precedent.

In Romans 4:8, we are told that YHWH did not "impute" (logizomai) sin against us. So, when we believe in Messiah it removes the condemnation for our disobedience and its penalty, death, and replaces it with the righteousness of Yahushua, thus putting us in right standing before YHWH.

We go from the state of condemned sinner to the state of righteous man, because His grace only, through our belief. Our pre-belief works having no merit at all.

> **Rom 4:9**       Is this blessing then upon the circumcised *only*, or also upon the uncircumcised? For we affirm: **Belief was reckoned unto Abraham for righteousness.**
>
> **Rom 4:10**      How then was it reckoned? Being in circumcision, or in uncircumcision? Not in circumcision, but **in uncircumcis**ion.

Paul's question here is simple; was Abraham declared righteous before he was circumcised or after? Abraham was counted as righteous in Genesis 15:6 but did not receive circumcision until Genesis 17. Abraham's belief came before his circumcision.

This is an important pattern established in the Tanak. Belief must always precede works, for any works that took place before we believe, have no merit.

> **Note:**       Many teach that the righteousness that comes through belief is a "New Testament" doctrine for the "New Covenant Gentile Church". However, Paul here and in many other places teaches that righteousness through belief is an "Old Testament" doctrine. This is why he calls those of us who have accepted Messiah,

120

"Abraham's seed and heirs according to the promise" (Galatians 3:29).

| | |
|---|---|
| **Hab 2:4** | "See, he whose being is not upright in him is puffed up. **But the righteous one lives by his steadfastness.** |

The word "steadfastness" used here is translating the Hebrew word "emunah", which is the word for belief in Hebrew.

| | |
|---|---|
| **Ecc 1:9** | What has been is what shall be, what has been done is what shall be done, and there is no new *matter* under the sun. |

***

| | |
|---|---|
| **Rom 4:11** | And he received the **sign of circumcision**, a **seal** of the righteousness of the belief *while* in uncircumcision, for him to be a father of all those believing through uncircumcision, for righteousness to be reckoned to them also, |
| **Rom 4:12** | and the father of circumcision to those who not only are of the circumcision, but who also **walk in the steps of the belief** which our father Abraham had in uncircumcision. |

Here again, Paul mentions that the righteousness of belief must **proceed** that of obedience. Does our righteous belief nullify the need for obedience? **NO!** (3:31). It places us in the proper position to be obedient, walking in the steps of belief, and inherit the reward.

Paul is saying that circumcision was a sign, (Genesis 17:11 - says token).

**Token**: stg's #**H226** - "oth", meaning, a signal; from a word meaning, to come; refers to a visible sign of a future event.

**Sign**: stg's #**G4592** - "semeion", meaning, an indication; from a word meaning, a mark; refers to a visible indication of something.

Again, the Hebrew meaning clarifies the intent of the Greek. The physical circumcision was a sign that YHWH was going to do what He promised Abraham and this sign was to be placed on **all** the members of his household, **both those of his own flesh and those foreigners born or brought into his house** (Genesis 17:11-12).

    This physical circumcision was an outward sign of Abraham's inner heart condition.

> **Seal:**    stg's #**G4973** - "sphragis", meaning, a signet; a more strengthened form of a word meaning, a fence. Referring to the fencing in of something in order to protect it, a sense of genuineness.

    Paul is saying, circumcision was a sign of the **authenticity**, or **proof**, of the righteousness of Abraham's belief. Abraham's circumcision was **confirmation** that he would be a father of many nations and the fact that he received it **after** he had been counted righteous, was the evidence he would be a father of the Gentiles who believed, even though they were not circumcised.

    Abraham is our father by belief, not by physical bloodlines or Torah obedience (circumcision).

    Abraham's story is also a blueprint of how men gain access to the kind of righteousness YHWH accepts. We all gain it, both those of the circumcision (the physical bloodline) and those of the uncircumcision (Gentiles), by belief.

> **Rom 4:13**    For the promise that he should be the heir of the world, was not to Abraham or to his seed through the Torah, but through a righteousness of belief.

> **World:**    stg's #**G2889** - "kosmos", meaning, orderly arrangement; from a word meaning, to tend or care for. Today we use the word "cosmos" to refer to the ordered universe, however, it really refers to what has been put in order.

    The promise to Abraham was not the world as a whole, but to the land of the Canaanites which is a shadow picture of the coming Messianic Kingdom.

> **Gen 12:1**    And יהוה said to Abram, "Go yourself out of your land, from your relatives and from your father's house, to a land which I show you.

| | |
|---|---|
| **Gen 12:2** | "And I shall make you a great nation, and bless you and make your name great, and you shall be a blessing! |
| **Gen 12:3** | "And I shall bless those who bless you, and curse him who curses you. **And in you all the clans of the earth shall be blessed."** |
| | *** |
| **Gen 12:6** | And Aḇram passed through the land to the place of Sheḵem, as far as the terebinth tree of Moreh. At that time the Kenaʿanites were in the land. |
| **Gen 12:7** | And יהוה appeared to Aḇram and said, **"To your seed I give this land**." And he built there a slaughter-place to יהוה, who had appeared to him. |

So, it was to Abraham and **to his seed**, the land of Canaan was given. But…

| | |
|---|---|
| **Gal 3:16** | But the promises were spoken to Aḇraham, and to his Seed. He does not say, "And to seeds," as of many, **but as of one**, **"And to your Seed" who is Messiah.** |

Paul tells us here that the promises given to Abraham were not given to him and to his seeds, as in plural, which are the thousands and millions of his physical seeds that have arisen since the promise was given, but to One seed, to just One of his physical descendants, and that One was Yahushua Messiah.

The unconditional promise of Inheritance of the Promised Land was to Abraham himself and to his promised seed, the Seed of a woman promised to Adam in the Garden, and that Seed is Messiah. And that promise was not extended to Yitschaq (Isaac), Yaʾaqob, Yoseph, Mosheh, Dawid, or Eliyahu because of their physical bloodline, it was extended to them because of their belief and trust in the Elohim of Abraham.

The land of Kanaʾan (the Land of Promise) is Yahushua's inheritance as King of Yisraʾel, i.e., the Millennial Kingdom of Messiah, from where He will rule the whole world, and for which He is coming again to take possession (Revelation 11:15-17).

Messiah is the Seed of Abraham to which the inheritance of this Land/Kingdom was given and NOT to any other seed, however, THROUGH Him we too can become heirs of the promise (Galatians

3:27-29) and co-heirs with Messiah (Romans 8:14-17). Is this promise extended to us because we obey the Torah/Law? **NO!**

Romans 4:14 is telling us that if it was possible to become heirs through obedience to the Torah, there is then, no need for belief, because we could EARN the inheritance through our obedience to the Torah, thereby nullifying the Promise of YHWH. If that is true, the Messiah died in vain (Galatians 2:21).

However, though our obedience to the Torah cannot earn us the inheritance, the Torah is the "good works, which Elohim prepared beforehand that we should walk in" (Ephesians 2:10), whereby we **prove** or **perfect** (complete) our belief (James 2:14-26), without which our belief has no life, and ends in death, i.e., the Second Death.

Verse 15 has thrown the truth of the Torah into a tailspin in the lives of believers today. This verse must be understood in the context of knowledge as in 3:20 - "for by the Torah is the knowledge of sin".

> **Rom 4:15**      for the Torah works out wrath, for where there is no Torah there is no transgression.

How does the Torah work wrath in us? It defines what is good and what is evil, what gives life and what brings death, what leads to blessing and what causes curses (Deuteronomy 30:11-26), it defines sin and commands judgment on the sinner.

If no Torah (instructions) existed there would be no way to disobey it and where there is no transgression, there is no guilt and no punishment.

However, where Torah exists there is a standard of right and wrong and if we do not live by the standard of what is right, we are guilty of doing wrong. Doing wrong has a consequence, a penalty, which is death.

The wrath of YHWH comes upon **the sons of disobedience** (Ephesians 2:2-3; 5:6; Colossians 3:6).

> **Wrath**: stg's #G3709 - "orge", meaning, desire; referring to a burning passion, which in the context of judgment means a violent passion or punishment.

Before we go on, we need to remember what was determined in chapter 3. There are two types of believers in the assembly of Rome, one that knows the Torah (mostly Jews) and one who is just being introduced to the Torah (Gentiles).

This distinction is clear throughout this book and it is one of the things Paul is contending against. One group thinks itself superior because of their knowledge, circumcision and bloodline. Paul is telling us that there is no difference in how both groups get saved, everybody must come through Messiah.

There IS a difference, however, in the position of these two groups prior to their knowledge of Messiah, which affects how they are to live as believers before YHWH.

The Jews have always had the Torah, while the Gentiles are just being taught it for the first time. Paul uses Abraham's experience to show that both the circumcised and the uncircumcised must be declared righteous (from death) by belief.

Once they had been declared right by belief, then Abraham becomes the father of both (Jew and Gentile) because belief always comes first, overcoming the condemnation demanded for our disobedience and restoring us to righteousness before Him.

Belief, however, does not do away with or in any way nullify the Torah or our responsibility to obey it (3:31).

> **Note:** Once in the belief, both groups have to forsake something, the Gentiles need to forsake the practices of their old pagan beliefs, while the Jews need to forsake all the rabbinical teachings that have added to and taken away from the Torah of YHWH.

Paul is now going to express the kind of belief that Abraham had, which resulted in him being counted righteous.

| | |
|---|---|
| **Rom 4:17** | as it has been written, **"I have made you a father of many nations"** in the presence of Him whom he believed, even Elohim, who gives life to the dead and calls that which does not exist as existing, |
| **Rom 4:18** | who against *all* expectation did believe, in expectation, so that he should become father of many nations, according to what was said, **"So shall your seed be."** |
| **Rom 4:19** | And not having grown weak in belief, he did not consider his own body, already dead, being about a hundred years old, and the deadness of Sarah's womb, |

Compare this passage to the following:

125

**v. 17**

| | |
|---|---|
| **Gen 12:1** | And יהוה said to Aḇram, "Go yourself out of your land, from your relatives and from your father's house, to a land which I show you. |
| **Gen 12:2** | "And I shall make you a great nation, and bless you and make your name great, and you shall be a blessing! |
| **Gen 12:3** | "And I shall bless those who bless you, and curse him who curses you. And in you all the clans of the earth shall be blessed." |
| | *** |
| **Heb 11:17** | By belief, Aḇraham, when he was tried, offered up Yitsḥaq, and he who had received the promises offered up his only brought-forth son, |
| **Heb 11:18** | of whom it was said, **"In Yitsḥaq your seed shall be called,"** |
| **Heb 11:19** | reckoning that Elohim was able to raise, even from the dead, from which he received him back, as a type. |

**v. 18**

| | |
|---|---|
| **Gen 15:1** | After these events the word of יהוה came to Aḇram in a vision, saying, "Do not be afraid, Aḇram. I am your shield, your reward is exceedingly great." |
| **Gen 15:2** | And Aḇram said, "Master יהוה, what would You give me, seeing I go childless, and the heir of my house is Eliʽezer of Dammeseq?" |
| **Gen 15:3** | And Aḇram said, "See, You have given me no seed, and see, one born in my house is my heir!" |
| **Gen 15:4** | And see, the word of יהוה came to him, saying, "This one is not your heir, but he who comes from your own body is your heir." |
| **Gen 15:5** | And He brought him outside and said, "Look now toward the heavens, and count the stars if you are able to count them." And He said to him, "So are your seed." |

126

| | |
|---|---|
| **Gen 15:6** | And he believed in יהוה, and He reckoned it to him for righteousness. |

***

**v. 19**

| | |
|---|---|
| **Gen 18:1** | And יהוה appeared to him by the terebinth trees of Mamrĕ, while he was sitting in the tent door in the heat of the day. |
| **Gen 18:2** | So he lifted his eyes and looked, and saw three men standing opposite him. And when he saw them, he ran from the tent door to meet them, and bowed himself to the ground, |
| **Gen 18:3** | and said, "יהוה, if I have now found favour in Your eyes, please do not pass Your servant by. |
| **Gen 18:4** | "Please let a little water be brought, and wash your feet, and rest yourselves under the tree. |
| **Gen 18:5** | "And let me bring a piece of bread and refresh your hearts, and then go on, for this is why you have come to your servant." And they said, "Do as you have said." |
| **Gen 18:6** | So Abraham ran into the tent to Sarah and said, "Hurry, make ready three measures of fine flour, knead it and make cakes." |
| **Gen 18:7** | And Abraham ran to the herd, took a tender and good calf, gave it to a young man, and he hurried to prepare it. |
| **Gen 18:8** | And he took curds and milk and the calf which he had prepared, and set it before them, and he stood by them under the tree as they ate. |
| **Gen 18:9** | And they said to him, "Where is Sarah your wife?" And he said, "See, in the tent." |
| **Gen 18:10** | And He said, "I shall certainly return to you according to the time of life, and see, Sarah your wife is to have a son!" And Sarah was listening in the tent door which was behind him. |
| **Gen 18:11** | Now Abraham and Sarah were old, well advanced in age, and Sarah was past the way of women. |

| Gen 18:12 | And Sarah laughed within herself, saying, "After I have grown old, shall I have pleasure, my master being old too?" |
| Gen 18:13 | And יהוה said to Aḇraham, "Why did Sarah laugh, saying, 'Shall I truly have a child, since I am old?' |
| Gen 18:14 | "Is any matter too hard for יהוה? At the appointed time I am going to return to you, according to the time of life, and Sarah is to have a son." |
| Gen 18:15 | But Sarah denied it, saying, "I did not laugh," for she was afraid. And He said, "No, but you did laugh!" |

***

| Heb 11:8 | By belief, Aḇraham obeyed when he was called to go out to the place which he was about to receive as an inheritance. And he went out, not knowing where he was going. |
| Heb 11:9 | By belief, he sojourned in the land of promise as a stranger, dwelling in tents with Yitsḥaq and Ya'aqoḇ, the heirs with him of the same promise, |
| Heb 11:10 | for he was looking for the city having foundations, whose builder and maker is Elohim. |
| Heb 11:11 | By belief also, Sarah herself was enabled to conceive seed, and she bore a child when she was past the normal age, because she deemed Him trustworthy who had promised. |
| Heb 11:12 | And so from one, and him as good as dead, were born **as numerous as the stars of the heaven, as countless as the sand which is by the seashore.** |

***

| Rom 4:20 | he did not hesitate about the promise of Elohim through unbelief, but was strengthened in belief, giving esteem to Elohim, |
| Rom 4:21 | and being completely persuaded that what He had promised He was also able to do. |
| Rom 4:22 | Therefore also **"it was reckoned to him for righteousness."** |

Abraham's belief was so strong that when the unbelievable, the impossible, was promised to him he didn't doubt, but believed fully in Him, YHWH, who had promised it. Knowing that He was able to perform everything He had promised because He speaks things into existence that never existed before (v. 17).

| | |
|---|---|
| **Rom 4:23** | And not because of him alone was it written that **it was reckoned to him,** |
| **Rom 4:24** | but **also because of us, to whom it shall be reckoned, to us who believe in Him who raised up יהושע our Master from the dead,** |
| **Rom 4:25** | who was delivered up because of our trespasses, and was raised for us to be declared right. |

Paul follows up his explanation of Abraham's type of belief by qualifying what type of belief we need, to have righteousness imputed on to us. We need to, not only believe that Yahushua died for our sins, but that He also rose again from the dead. Why?

Because it was His death that atoned for our sins (delivered us from the death penalty) but it was His resurrection that verifies our justification, for by it He proved He had the power to fulfill the promise of everlasting life and by His new life He is able to intercede for us (1 John 2:1-2).

Paul's conclusion in chapter 4 is that all men, Jew and Gentile, find redemption from sin and death, and justification into new life only through Yahushua Messiah, who died for our sins and was raised again.

No amount of righteous behavior can accomplish this. Righteous behavior is for those who have already received redemption and justification into the new life (a new obedient and righteous lifestyle).

# Chapter 3: Romans 5

Beginning in this chapter, Paul is going to get into the meat and potatoes of the Good News of Yahushua Messiah. The why's and wherefores of Messiah Yahushua and how we are to live our lives **AFTER** our salvation.

**REMEMBER**, Paul is a Hebrew Torah scholar and writes like one, so you must think like one to understand his writings. Here is what Brother Peter (Kepha) has to say about Paul's writings and how certain men have mishandled them.

| | |
|---|---|
| 2Pe 3:15 | and reckon the patience of our Master as deliverance, as also our beloved brother Paul wrote to you, according to the wisdom given to him, |
| 2Pe 3:16 | as also in all *his* letters, speaking in them concerning these *matters*, in which **some are hard to understand**, which those who are **untaught and unstable twist to their own destruction**, as they do also the other Scriptures. |
| 2Pe 3:17 | You, then, beloved ones, being forewarned, watch, **lest you also fall** from your own steadfastness, being led away with the **delusion of the lawless**, |
| Unlearned: | stg's #G261 - "amathes", meaning, ignorant; from two words meaning, no and to learn. Refers to not having the knowledge or understanding of a topic. |
| Unstable: | stg's #G793 - "asteriktos", meaning, unfixed (wavering or shaky); from two words meaning, no and to set fast (to stand firm). Refers to being in a position of instability, like building a house on shifting sand… |
| Mat 7:24 " | Therefore everyone who hears these words of Mine, and does them, shall be like a wise man who built his house **on the rock**, |
| Mat 7:25 | and the rain came down, and the floods came, and the winds blew and beat on that house, |

and **it did not fall**, for it was founded on the rock.

1.  YHWH is our Rock / Deuteronomy 32:3-4
2.  YHWH is our Fortress / Psalms 18:2
3.  YHWH is our Salvation / Psalms 62:2
4.  YHWH of Host/Rock of Offense Isaiah 8:11-14
5.  Yahushua Messiah is that Rock 1 Kepha 2:1-8

| | |
|---|---|
| **Mat 7:26** | "And everyone who hears these words of Mine, and does not do them, shall be like a foolish man who built his house **on the sand**, |
| **Mat 7:27** | and the rain came down, and the floods came, and the winds blew, and they beat on that house, **and it fell**, and great was its fall." |

Peter is saying that certain men among the brethren, didn't have Paul's knowledge and neither was their understanding built upon the same foundation Paul's understanding was built on.

Paul was a Torah expert, and he understood the deeper mysteries of the Torah and the prophets because Messiah Himself had revealed them to him (Galatians 1:11-12).

In Romans, Paul is explaining salvation as it applies to both the Jew and the Gentile, even though his primary calling was to teach Gentile inclusion into the body of believers (i.e., Yisra'el) through Messiah.

Peter went on to say in chapter 3:15-17, that these ignorant men, who were not founded on the rock, had twisted Paul's words to teach, what the (KJV) calls an "error of the wicked."

| | |
|---|---|
| **Twist**: | stg's #**G4761** - "strebloo", to *wrench* or to *torture (fig: to **pervert**);* from **G4762**. |
| | stg's #**G4762** - "strephō", meaning, to *twist (turn* around or ***reverse**).* |
| **Note**: | It is Peter's intent for us to understand that men who did not have the same learning and foundational background in the Scripture that Paul had, were taking the things he had written and turning them upside |

down, making them mean the opposite of what Paul intended them to mean. As we shall see this is exactly what has happened and is still happening today.

**Error**:  stg's #**G4106** - "plane", meaning, **fraudulence** (a deception); from a word meaning, roving (like a tramp). Refers to a teaching or a doctrine that is false, that causes the hearer to stray from the true path.

**Wicked**:  stg's #**G113** - "athesmos", meaning, **lawless**; from two words meaning, no and to place. Refers to someone who is not living or teaching according to the correct path, i.e., lawless person.

Scripturally, living and teaching that we are to obey the Torah is good, but to live and teach that we are not to obey the Torah is evil (Deuteronomy 30:15-20; comp. Matthew 5:17-19).

So, an evil or wicked person is one who does not teach us to obey the Torah, which Peter says is a deception, a false teaching.

**REMEMBER**, Deuteronomy 13:1-5 warns us that anyone who is teaching us to go in a way other than the Way YHWH told us to go from Mount Sinai, even if that person does signs and miracles and prophecies, that person has taught us to stray from YHWH and we are to purge them from our midst, they are a false prophet.

Peter goes on to say, these people who teach such will receive destruction and he emphatically warns us to "**BEWARE**" least we also fall into the same destruction.

For those who would tell us that the Torah of YHWH, given to us through Moses, no longer applies to us today, we admonish them to repent! For they have twisted Paul's writings to teach a lie.

Furthermore, to those who say, once you have accepted Messiah as Savior, you can never step out of your position and wind up being destroyed with the wicked, we admonish them to repent! For they do not know the importance of proving your belief by your works (James 2:14-26) as a son who loves his father.

***

| | |
|---|---|
| **Rom 5:1** | Therefore, having been declared right by belief, we have peace with Elohim through our Master יהושע Messiah, |
| **Rom 5:2** | through whom also we have access by belief into this favour in which we stand, and we |

132

exult in the expectation of the esteem of Elohim.

Pretty simple right? We were, before Messiah, enemies of YHWH (v. 10; Colossians 1:21), but once we trusted in His work on the tree we have come into peace with YHWH, having received His grace (favor) as a gift (Ephesians 2:8-9) because we believed. It is in this position of grace that we "stand".

> **Stand**: stg's #**G2476** - "histemi", meaning, to stand; compares to a word (tithemi), meaning, to place; refers to upholding or making something stand in its rightful place. (Similar to #**G3306** - "meno", to abide (to stay or continue); John 15:1-7.

Both words have the basic meaning of remaining in place, "meno" is used by Messiah in John 15 where He instructed us to remain in Him and His Word in us, for it is the only way we can bear fruit of righteousness. The word "histemi" is used here by Paul in relation to our hope, stating that we stand in our belief while we await the promise to come.

> **Hope**: stg's #G1680 - "**elpis**", meaning, expectation or confidence; from a primary word meaning to anticipate, usually with pleasure. Refers to a hope of something in the future that is founded in something that gives us confidence we shall receive it.

> **Heb 11:1**    Now faith is the substance of things hoped for, the evidence of things not seen. (KJV)

The word used here in Hebrews is "elpizo" (#G1679 -to hope or confide; trust) and again holds the meaning of a confident expectation.

> **Note**:    It is imperative that we understand what "elpizo" really means before we move on. Though there is a subtly difference in the English words 'hope' and 'expectation' according to Webster, we think that the way humans generally understand these two words can cause confusion when reading this text.

The word 'hope' is generally understood to refer to something we are looking forward to without true confidence that it we will receive it, while 'expectation', on the other hand, is generally understood to refer to looking forward to something that we have confidence will take place, likely because of some experience that proves to us or within us that our expectation is valid.

We've heard this verse interpreted many different ways by many different people, however the meaning is fairly simple.

Our belief is what makes our hope real to us and true belief is, evidence within us that what we hope for will come true. Belief is the substance and the evidence, that what we hope for will be ours even though we cannot see it.

Speaking of belief/faith there are two verses we need to consider.

**Rom 10:17**  So then faith *comes* by hearing, and hearing by the word of God. (KJV)

When you see the word "hear" in the Scripture we must remember that in the Hebrew language all words have a deeper active meaning. So, when the Scripture says that our belief comes by hearing and our hearing by the word of Elohim, it's referring to hearing it with the intent to obey it.

In truth, hearing from a Hebrew perspective is something you're doing with your heart and not just your ears. To hear the word of Elohim means to hear it with the intent, the heart attitude, to obey it. To truly hear something is to submit to what is heard.

**Heb 11:6**  But without faith it *is* **impossible** to please *Him:* for he that comes to God must believe that He is, **and** *that* He rewards those that diligently seek Him. (KJV)

Just like the word "hear" has the assumed intent of obedience, so too does "belief" (faith). The belief referred to throughout Scripture is a belief that acts out in response to what is believed.

So, when we see that it is impossible to please Elohim without belief, we know it is referring to a belief that has to be acted out in accordance with of His Word, which is proven out in the next two phrases.

The writer of Hebrews goes on to say, "we must **believe** that He is (belief part/spiritual part) and that He rewards those who **diligently seek** Him (works part/physical part)".

134

It is our belief in Him that motivates us to seek Him diligently through obedience, that we might receive the reward, i.e., eternal life.

Back in Romans 5:2, where it says, "we rejoice in the hope of the glory of Elohim", Paul is referring to the whole hope, that of the resurrection and everlasting life in the kingdom.

This resurrection, called the first resurrection (Revelation 20), is for the just, those who have believed in Yahushua Messiah and lived in obedience to the Torah of YHWH (Revelation 14:12).

This resurrection is our hope, the hope of our high calling in Yahushua Messiah that Paul refers to in Philippians 3. Many times, this resurrection is downplayed by "the church" as if it's secondary to what it calls the Rapture.

In truth, the "Catching away" (rapture) of the living at the time of Messiah's return is a secondary event to the resurrection.

This Catching Away only needs to take place because some believers will still be alive at His return (1 Thessalonians 4:13-18; 1 Corinthians 15:51-52; Matthew 24:29-31).

| | |
|---|---|
| **Rom 5:3** | And not only this, but we also exult in pressures, knowing that pressure works endurance; |
| **Rom 5:4** | and endurance, approvedness; and approvedness, expectation. |
| **Rom 5:5** | And expectation does not disappoint, because the love of Elohim has been poured out in our hearts by the Set-apart Spirit which was given to us. |

| | |
|---|---|
| **Note:** | In the King James Version the word "Ghost" is used here instead of Spirit, which is an absolute travesty. The Greek word translated as ghost is "pneuma". |

| | |
|---|---|
| **Ghost:** | stg's #G4151 - "pneuma", meaning, **breath**; from a word that means, a current of air. This word is generally translated as **spirit** but is also translated as ghost and soul. It is best understood to be a translation of the Hebrew words "neshamah" (the breath/spirit given to us) and "ruach" (the breath/spirit within us). |

There is another word in Greek translated as spirit and soul, and that word is "psuche" (#G5590), from where we get the word psyche. This word means breath and is typically used by scholars to

135

refer to the sentient life forms of animals, rather than humans, while "pneuma" is used to refer to the rational or immortal soul of humans.

In the Hebrew there is no distinction between the "soul" of humans and that of animals, because both are referred to as "nephesh". The word nephesh simply means living breathing creature and would be best translated by the Greek word "psuche", where the word "pneuma" should be translated as spirit. The soul (living breathing "conscious" person) is not immortal until the resurrection.

Paul, in Romans 5:3-5, is showing us the purpose for trials and tribulation in the life of the believer. When we receive the redemption that is in Yahushua Messiah we are not fully redeemed from all pain, suffering or temptation.

The fullness of that redemption comes at the return of Messiah when we receive the new resurrected body (1 Corinthians 15:35-39). Between then and now, we who have believed, have received the redemption of the "inner man" or spirit-man, which continues to reside within this physical body.

Before Paul leads us into this teaching, he needs to set the stage so we can fully understand how we overcome in Messiah, until the fullness of that blessed hope (new body) comes.

When we endure trials and tribulation but remain faithful, we learn to wait patiently and YHWH who has promised us deliverance, not just from the penalty of sin (death) but also from the entire wretched man-made (Satan inspired) worldly system.

As we wait on Him, we experience the goodness of His mercy as we learn how much He loves us. It is in the experiencing of His love, despite our troubles and throughout them, that confirms in our hearts the hope of the future glory He has promised to those who "stand fast" and "endure to the end" (Matthew 24:14; Galatians 5:1; Ephesians 6:10-13; 1 Thessalonians 3:8).

Here's the part most people don't understand, when the Scripture tells us to stand fast or endure…it is referring to something very specific about our belief.

It not only means that we need to keep believing in what Messiah has done for us and what YHWH has promised because of that, it also refers to our responsibility to remain obedient to the Torah, despite what the world might say or do.

We are to stand fast in our belief, in obedience to the Torah, all the way to the end (Revelation 14:12), at which time we will receive everlasting life. Paul is going to make this much clearer in chapter 6 of Romans.

| Rom 5:6 | For when we were still weak, Messiah in due time died for the wicked. |

"Weak" is a reference to our inability to be justified (made right from death) by works of Torah, because we are already guilty of sin (3:23) having lived "ungodly" (irreverent-not giving Him the respect/obedience He deserves).

Yet even though we were not giving Him the honor He deserves, He still sent Yahushua to die for us. He expressed His love and mercy towards us in the most profound way, in the death of His Own Son!

Paul, in typical Hebrew style, is going to make the same statement three (3) times within the next four verses. Anytime a Hebrew writer repeats himself, he is emphasizing something important.

| Rom 5:7 | For one shall hardly die for a righteous one, though possibly for a good one someone would even have the courage to die. |
| Rom 5:8 | But Elohim proves His own love for us, in that while we were still sinners, Messiah died for us. |

First, Paul spoke of our own inability to help ourselves, here he highlights that YHWH proved His love toward us, despite our disobedience to Him (His Torah). He is expressing the kind of love YHWH has for us in contrast to how we define love (emotional).

Very few men would willingly die for the greatest of men, some might risk their lives for a good man, but YHWH gave His Own Son to die for the most wretched of sinner. That's true love when you give your best in exchange for the worst.

| Rom 5:9 | Much more then, having now been **declared right by His blood**, we **shall be saved from wrath through Him**. |
| Rom 5:10 | For if, being enemies, we were restored to favour with Elohim through the death of His Son, much more, having been restored to favour, we shall be saved by His life. |
| Rom 5:11 | And not only this, but we also exult in Elohim through our Master יהושע Messiah, through whom we have now received **the restoration to favour**. |

There is a lot going on here, and all of it is important. The "justification by His blood" is a reference to the Torah's requirement of death for disobedience. If someone rebels against the Torah the penalty is death and the only way that penalty can be taken away is if someone dies.

A person's sin cannot be forgiven unless blood is shed to cover them (Hebrews 9:22). This was the purpose of the sacrificial system, not that it did away with sin, but that it pointed to the future sacrifice that YHWH would give, which could take away the guilt of sin and remove the penalty of death we owed, that sacrifice was Yahushua Messiah.

His blood is the atonement spoken of in verse 11 which we received through belief. The Hebrew word for atonement is "kaphar" (#H3722) and means, a covering. However, the Greek word is "katallage" (#G2643) meaning, exchange. These two words have different meanings but they both express the truth of what Messiah did by dying for us.

"Kaphar" denote His blood sprinkled on the mercy seat in heaven that paid the price of our debt, while "katallage" denote the exchange that took place when He died on that tree instead of us. It also refers to the exchange that takes place between our unrighteousness before the Father with His righteousness before the Father.

Paul tells us that since we have received this atonement, we no longer need be subject to the wrath of YHWH, on the Day of YHWH, when Yahushua shall return with flaming fire, taking vengeance upon those who do not know YHWH and have not obeyed the Good News of Yahushua (2 Thessalonians 1:7-10).There is, however, a much more interesting statement in verse 10 that must be understood.

Paul says we have been reconciled to YHWH (past tense) but that we shall be saved (future tense). Paul is showing us that though we have been reconciled to YHWH, our salvation is incomplete.

This is imperative for us to grasp! Our salvation is a two-part process that begins with our belief in Yahushua Messiah, which justifies us before YHWH, but it will not be complete until we receive what we hope for, i.e., the new body (resurrection). Paul is revealing to us, the *Two-Part Principle* (see: *Two-Part Principle* on Pg. 25).

In short, our spiritual rebirth of the inner-spirit-man, which is given to us freely by belief in Yahushua, is still awaiting the physical rebirth of the outer-physical-man, which takes place at the resurrection.

Between our confession of belief and our resurrection we are in the wilderness of this life, just as Yisra'el was in the wilderness between the crossing the Red Sea and the crossing of the River Jordan into the Promised Land.

Just like Yisra'el in the wilderness, we have a choice to make, do we trust in YHWH enough to obey His Torah and thereby enter into the Promised Land (Kingdom) like Caleb and Joshua (Yahushua).

Or, do we "do our own thing" instead of obeying His Torah and die in the wilderness of this life without inheriting the Kingdom. It's our choice, this is the burden of free will, and we cannot have free will without a requirement to act responsibly with it

He provided everything needed in Messiah, for us to be both justified from sin and death and to be resurrected into the new body at Messiah's Return, to enter eternal life in the Kingdom.

However, because of free will we too have a part to play, and that part is willful and deliberate obedience. We must have a heart to obey Him no matter what He says or what the consequences are.

Don't let those "lawless men" currently spouting off Christian dogma, which says, in Yahushua Messiah (Jesus Christ) we no longer have to obey the Torah (law). We are **NOT** saying that we are to **TRUST** in the Torah, because our trust is **FULLY AND COMPLETELY** resting in the work of Yahushua Messiah.

However, it is a believer's responsibility **to live** righteous and set apart (holy) before YHWH **in his belief**. The only way scripturally to do that is through obedience to the Torah, which YHWH laid down for all His people, both the native born and the Gentile who sojourns with them, to live by before the advent of Messiah (Ephesians 2:10).

The *Two-Part Principle* recognizes that there's a spiritual part that only YHWH can do and a physical part that we are responsible for, and these two parts need to work together to accomplish our ultimate deliverance.

He did the work we could not do for ourselves through the sacrifice of His beloved Son, Yahushua Messiah, and it is our responsibility to do the work (Torah) He set forth for us to do, so as to humble us and prove us, to know whether we will obey Him or not (Deuteronomy 8:1-3). It's a heart thing; He wants us to prove to Him where our heart is.

> Note: There are three things that men do, in their so-called belief, that turns the truth of the Scripture into a man-made religion.
>
> 1. They add to or take away from what YHWH

gave to Moses. (Deuteronomy 4:2; 12:32; Ecclesiastes 3:14; Proverbs 30:6 and Revelation 22:18-19)

2.    They attempt to please YHWH according to their own desires and understanding and not according to the word that He set forth. (Proverbs 3:1-7)

3.    They listen to voices other than His, (Genesis 3:17; Isaiah 29:13 [see also: Matthew 15 and Mark 7]) which can only be tested and proven through what He gave to Moses and the prophets. (See Appendix 4: Religion on Pg. 563)

***

Rom 5:12    For this reason, even as through one man sin did enter into the world, and death through sin, and thus death spread to all men, because all sinned –

Rom 5:13    for until the Torah, sin was in the world, but sin is not reckoned when there is no Torah.

Rom 5:14    But death reigned from Adam until Mosheh, even over those who had not sinned according to the likeness of the transgression of Adam, who is a type of Him who was to come.

**REMEMBER,** the word "law" (Hb - Torah / Gk - Nomos), when referring to the five books of Moses, means YHWH's instructions, i.e., every word that has proceeded out of His mouth (Deuteronomy 8:3; Matthew 4:4), which includes Genesis 2:16-17.

When Adam disobeyed, the penalty of death came upon him, this death penalty passed on to his sons and his daughters because they were born in his image and likeness (Genesis 5:3).

Exo 20:5    you do not bow down to them nor serve them. For I, יהוה your Elohim am a jealous Ěl, **visiting the crookedness of the fathers on the children to the third and fourth *generations*** of those who hate Me,

In this verse we see how the curse (death) was placed upon Adam for his sin, and that curse has passed from the fathers (not mothers) to their children.

The entire Scripture is patriarchal and so the sins of the fathers are passed down to the children, both male and female. This is how

140

Yahushua could have been born of a human woman and yet not born under the curse of sin and death. He had no human father, for the spirit of YHWH came upon Miriam and He was conceived.

Part of the curse given for disobedience, was that man would have to labor hard daily to eat and that thorns and thistles would grow, making growing food difficult (Genesis 3:17-19).

This is also true in the spiritual sense because within each man and woman are the thorns and thistles of our fleshly passions that make it difficult to produce the fruit of righteousness that YHWH desires of His children.

The flesh, or as the Jews say, our "evil inclinations", brings us into captivity to sin. The flesh acts according to the desires of our physical and mental senses. Therefore, even though we haven't committed the exact same transgression (sin) that Adam did, we are still guilty of sin and are subject to the death penalty that we inherited from him.

Romans 5:13 has been misunderstood by most of the teachers I've heard, because of the word "imputed". As we've seen earlier in chapter 4, righteousness was imputed to Abraham because of his belief.

In that instance the word "imputed" is the Greek word "logizomai", which is translated in the King James as "imputeth",

**Imputed:**      stg's **#G3049** - "logizomai", meaning, to *take an inventory;* a middle voice from G3056.

stg's **#G3056** - "logos", meaning, something *said* (including the *thought*); From G3004 (to lay down).

In certain circles Yahushua is referred to as the "Logos" because He is the Word made flesh. The word "logos", whose root word "lego", means to lay down or out. It is the Greek word that represents something said or thought.

It's similar to the Hebrew word "torah", whose root word "yarah" means to flow out, and the Greek word "nomos", whose root word "nemo" means to parcel out.

As can be easily recognized, "logos" is part of the word "logizomai" and in this case should be understood to mean something that was laid down on Abraham's account.

If you think of it in banking terms, righteousness was deposited into Abraham's account because of his belief. This is the sense of this Greek word and is how it should be understood.

However, in Romans 5:13, the King James also translates a different but similar word as "imputed". The word imputed in chapter 5 is the Greek word "ellogeō".

**Imputed:**   stg's **#G1677** - "ellogeō", meaning, to *reckon in;* From G1722 and G3056 .

stg's **#G1722 -** "en", A primary preposition denoting (fixed) *position* (in place, time, or state)

stg's **#G3056 -** "logos", meaning, something *said* (including the *thought*); from G3004 (to lay down).

If you look in the Strong's concordance under this word "ellogeo" and read the entire description they will give you basically the same exact definition (to place on account) as the word in chapter 4, "logizomai". However, these words are very different and despite what Mr. Strong says, "ellogeo" does not, in this context, mean to place on account.

You see, the "en" in front of "logeo" (logos) represents a time, place, or state and we have to remember that the entire context of this passage concerns our knowledge of sin.

Romans 3:20 says that "for by the Torah is the **knowledge** of sin" and we are going to see in Romans 7:7 Paul saying, "...I did not **know** sin, except through the Torah. For also the covetousness I **knew** not if the Torah had not said. "You shall not covet."

So, this word usage in 5:13 must be understood in this vein. What Paul is saying here is that before the Torah came there was no **knowledge of sin**, or what sin was. The word "ellogeo" is referring to a "state of word or thought", that's what en + logos means when put together.

Paul is simply telling us that before the Torah was given, men were sinning (disobeying the Torah) and dying because of it, even though they didn't **know** that what they were doing was sin.

It's important to understand this distinction between these two Greek words and how they are applied in chapters 4 and 5, because some teachers today think and teach that these two words mean the same thing and by doing so, they apply an erroneous meaning to 5:13.

This erroneous doctrine suggests that all the people who died before the Torah was given at Mt. Sinai, did not have their sins "counted against them" or "imputed against them".

142

From this idea has sprouted several other doctrines, which are either ambiguous in nature or complete heresy.

Once again, at the risk of belaboring the point, both "logizomai" and "ellogeo" come from the word "logos", which is translated as "word" in the Messianic Writings. The word "Legos" itself comes from the word "Lego" which means "to lay forth", i.e., instructions.

The word "Legos" means something spoken or thought, a topic or reasoning, motive, or computation. The word "en", which is connected to logos in this word "ellogeo", means, a position (in time, place, or state); in, at, on, by, etc.

In Romans 5:13, this word "ellogeo" is meant to refer to a state of reasoning or a position of knowledge (see Scripture references above).

One last Scripture reference on this topic of "knowledge of sin" comes from Galatians.

> **Gal 3:24**     Wherefore the law was our schoolmaster *to bring us* unto Christ, that we might be justified by faith. (KJV)

Here Paul clearly teaches that it is the Torah that acts as our **schoolmaster** to lead us (teach us our need for) Messiah. The Torah teaches us the meaning of sin, that we are sinners and that because of sin, we are in a position of or **under** the condemnation of death. This knowledge is what motivates us to seek out and receive the redemption offered by Yahushua Messiah.

Some people might think it's harsh that YHWH would condemn men for disobedience to commands they did not know existed. However, in Leviticus chapter 4, we see that sins committed by mistake, when the guilt is hidden from us, we are still guilty even in our lack of knowledge.

However, when we find out that we are guilty of violating the Torah, we can offer an offering (a sin offering) that will cover that sin and make us right before YHWH again. This was the whole point of the sacrificial system.

YHWH be praised! He sent His Son Yahushua, who is the Messiah (Anointed One) to be a sin offering for us so when we realize, through the Torah, we are sinners, all we have to do is call out to Him (1 John 1:19).

This is one of the reasons the Torah is still important in the lives of believers today, it reveals where we are lacking and whether our heart is devoted to Him more than to our own pursuits.

143

Paul also mentions in 5:16, that Adam is a figure of Him that was to come. This statement is important because it confirms a very important principle that we have already mentioned; that the people and stories of the Tanak are figures or shadow pictures of things going on in our lives today and that we need to know and understand these pictures if we are going to really understand our salvation and how to live in it today.

Let's have a brief discussion about the two Adams, one earthly and one heavenly.

**1Co 15:45** And so it has been written, "The first man Adam **became a living being,**" the last Adam a life-giving Spirit.

In everything there are two parts, the physical part and the spiritual part, but these two can NEVER be divided or separated.

The first Adam, of Genesis, was created in the image and likeness of YHWH, pure and undefiled, until sin was found in him. Adam failed to walk in the righteousness of YHWH and so this "earthly" (fleshly) Adam has condemned all his descendants to death.

The second Adam, Yahushua, was born in the image and likeness of Elohim, in that He was not subject to the curse of death, which all other men inherited, because He did not have a human father, as we mentioned above.

Both these Adams began life sinless, pure, and undefiled, however only the second Adam, Yahushua, lived His entire life in perfect obedience to the Torah of YHWH.

He was without sin (1 John 3:5) and so, the penalty of death was never against Him. He was what the Scripture refers to as perfect (complete both spiritually and physically).

In His completeness He alone was worthy to be the atonement sacrifice for His brethren, so that, through our belief and trust in Him we too might receive a righteous standing before YHWH. By belief in Yahushua's sacrifice, we escape the penalty of death that we all owe.

Since Paul says that the things in the Torah are for our instruction (Romans 15:4 and 2 Timothy 3:16-17)) and are examples to us (1 Corinthians 10:11), then let's consider the Exodus story as it relates to the teaching of the Good News of Messiah.

**Yisra'el in Egypt (Exodus 12)**

Yisra'el was in bondage to Egypt, under the authority of Pharaoh when YHWH sent Moses to deliver (save) them. Let's consider the events that led up to their leaving Egypt.

First YHWH disseminated Egypt, having proven His power and authority over the elohim (gods) of Egypt through plagues, leaving only one to deal with, i.e., Pharaoh himself.

To deal with Egypt's last elohim, YHWH was going to send Death upon Egypt to kill all the firstborn, from the firstborn of Pharaoh to the firstborn of their animals.

The Children of Yisra'el were instructed to paint the blood of the Pesach (Passover Lamb) on the door posts and lintel of their houses so they could escape the death of their own firstborn.

When the people heard this message they immediately went out and got a Passover Lamb and, on the day instructed, they kill the Passover Lamb and painted the door posts and lintel with its blood.

When the death Angel came into Egypt, Yisra'el's firstborn, who were under the blood of the Lamb, were spared. This also would have, and likely did, apply to any Egyptian that had heard the message and painted the blood on their door as well.

Note:  It is important to note that the blood of the Lamb **only** spared them from the death Angel and **did not** deliver them from Egypt. The sacrifice and blood of the Pesach was only the first step in a **process** that would deliver (save) them from Egypt (bondage) and lead them into the Promised Land (inheritance).

When Pharaoh discovered that his son was dead, he sent for Moses and Aaron, telling them to take all Yisra'el out of the land of Egypt as YHWH had commanded. It was the death of Pharaoh's son that prompted him to set Yisra'el free from their bondage.

Note:  Consider the Pictures

1.  Bondage in Egypt is a picture of our bondage to sin and death.
2.  Egypt is a picture of this world and its elohim (god) Pharaoh who is a picture of Satan.
3.  The Passover Lamb is Yahushua Messiah.
4.  Pharaoh, who was the ultimate authority in Egypt and the self-proclaimed elohim. His son also represents Yahushua, who is the Son of the true Elohim, YHWH.

145

How are the Passover Lamb and the son of Pharaoh both shadow pictures of Yahushua?

The blood of the Lamb (Yahushua) was placed upon the doorpost and lintel of each man's house (heart) and the blood protected (saved) them from the penalty of death that had come upon all men, because all had sinned (Romans 3:23-25; 5:12-21).

The death of the firstborn (Yahushua; the only begotten of the Father-John 1:14) delivered us from the bondage to sin and this world, as well as the authority of all other so-called elohim (both spiritual [demons] and physical [men]-Colossians 2:13-15).

Salvation in Yahushua removes the death penalty we owed for our past sins (Romans 3:25), delivers us from sin's authority to kill us and from the authority of this world system and its elohim, Satan (Ephesians 2:1-2; 2 Corinthians 4:3-4).

However, was Yisra'el's deliverance from Egypt the end of the story? Did everyone who was "saved" from the death Angel and delivered out of Egypt enter into the Promised Land (Kingdom)?

_NO,_ on both counts!!! (Read: numbers 13:1-14:39 and compare to Hebrews 3:1-4:11; 6:4-8; 10:26-31. Also, John 15:1-7 and 2 Kepha 3:1-22)

***

| | |
|---|---|
| **Rom 5:15** | But the favourable gift is not like the trespass. For if by the one man's trespass many died, much more the favour of Elohim, and the gift in favour of the one Man, יהושע Messiah, overflowed to many. |
| **Rom 5:16** | And the favourable gift is not as by one having sinned. For indeed the judgment was of one to condemnation, but the favourable gift is of many trespasses unto righteousness. |
| **Rom 5:17** | For if by the trespass of the one, death did reign through the one, much more those who receive the overflowing favour and the gift of righteousness shall reign in life through the One, יהושע Messiah. |
| **Rom 5:18** | So then, as through one trespass there resulted condemnation to all men, so also through one righteous act there resulted righteous-declaring of life to all men. |
| **Rom 5:19** | For as through the disobedience of one man many were made sinners, so also through the |

obedience of the One many shall be made righteous.

This is another one of Paul's more scholarly explanations, written in the true Hebrew style.

First, Paul compares Adam's sin, which caused him and all his descendants to inherit the curse of death, to Yahushua's righteousness, which causes us, through belief, to receive the grace (favor) of YHWH and escape the curse of death.

Second, Paul says that it was the sin of Adam (singular) that brought the condemnation of death upon all men, but the free gift of grace covers many different kinds of sins to bring us all into right standing (justification) before YHWH.

Third, Paul reaffirms that Adam's sin brought the condemnation of death upon all men. The phrase "death reigned" is meant to express that death has authority over all men, but YHWH's gift of grace has been poured out more abundantly on those who would believe in Yahushua, making them right again from the sin debt and bringing them under the authority of life.

Lastly, Paul concludes that Adam's sin condemned all men to death because through his disobedience all men became sinners (through having been born in the image and likeness of his sinful flesh - Genesis 5:3).

However, the free gift of YHWH (grace/favor) is offered to all men to make them right before Him so they can inherit life, when they believe in Yahushua Messiah, who proved His righteousness before YHWH through His obedience, making Himself the "spotless Lamb" through whom all men can be restored to the Father, YHWH.

So, Paul has clarified the situation, all men face the condemnation of death for their sin. He has also shown that the only way we can be delivered (saved) from this condemnation, is belief in Yahushua Messiah. He alone has lived a life worthy of eternal life and it's only through trusting in Him that man can come into right standing with YHWH and inherit that eternal life. Now then, the big question is, why the Law (Torah)?

Before we go there though, we want to go back to the Tanak and see some more pictures.

There is a mixed multitude of people who were delivered (saved) out of Egypt with Yisra'el by the death of Pharaoh's son (Exodus 12:37-38), who are called the strangers (Gentiles) who sojourn with Yisra'el (Exodus 12:49; Numbers 15:15-16), who were to be treated as native born Yisra'elis (Leviticus 19:33-34).

147

All the firstborn that were under the blood of the Passover Lamb, whether of Native Born or Gentile, were saved from death by the blood of the Lamb. All were delivered from the authority of Pharaoh and their bondage in Egypt, by the death of the firstborn of Pharaoh.

All of them (Native Born and Gentile), went through the Red Sea to escape Pharaoh and his army. The Red Sea is a type/picture of baptism wherein the enemies of Yisra'el (Pharaoh's Army/Sin and Death) were washed away by the water, never to come against them again.

Lastly, all of them stood at the base of Mt. Sinai to hear the Torah and all agreed to keep the covenant and obey YHWH's voice.

(Exodus 12-19)

1. The Lamb is Yahushua the firstborn of YHWH (John 1:29)
2. The Red Sea is water baptism (1 Corinthians 10:1-12)
3. The Rock of Horeb represents the Messiah, when struck down, gave us the life-giving waters of the Holy Spirit (John 4:1-26)
4. Mt. Sinai is the Word/Torah through which we are sanctified

(John 17:17: Psalms 119:142) when we obey it.

Notice the progression, i.e., pattern, the Blood of the Lamb, then Baptism, then the Set-Apart Spirit, then the Torah.

YHWH told Moses to build the tabernacle according to the pattern he had seen while on the mountain. This establishes the fact that YHWH has a set pattern of how things are supposed to work.

The pictures mentioned above establish a pattern, which describes a process where the Torah comes AFTER deliverance by the blood. The covenant is confirmed in blood and then the covenant makers adhere to the rules of the covenant, according to that pattern.

**Note**: Consider the pattern of the Tabernacle.

1. The Gate
2. The Altar
3. The Basin
4. The Holy Place

148

a.     The Lampstand (Menorah – Spirit)
b.     The Table of Shewbread – Word)
c.     The Golden Altar of Incense – Prayer)
5.     The Most Holy Place
a.     The Ark/Mercy Seat/Presence of YHWH

This is the same pattern shown in Exodus, where the Blood (altar) is before the Baptism (basin) where we get access to the Spirit and the Word/Torah and the Intercessor (golden altar), which is prayer in the Name of Messiah, through whom we gain access the Father.

***

| | |
|---|---|
| **Rom 5:20** | And the Torah came in beside, so that the trespass would increase. But where sin increased, favour increased still more, |
| **Rom 5:21** | so that as sin did reign in death, even so favour might reign through righteousness to everlasting life through יהושע Messiah our Master. |

The Torah was given at Mt. Sinai to reveal to us the depth of our sinfulness and the depravity of our nature. It was given to show us what the righteousness of YHWH is and how we are to walk/live in it (Deuteronomy 6:24-25).

It was given to us so that we would know and understand our position before Him, so that we could live in His wisdom and according to His good pleasure (Deuteronomy 4:1-6).

It was also given to teach us that we were sinners deserving of death so we would reach out to Yahushua for deliverance (Romans 7:7-11; Galatians 3:22-24).

Lastly, it was given to humble us and prove us, to see if we would obey Him (Deuteronomy 8:1-3). The Torah is a "heart test" to prove our sonship.

The phrase "might grace reign through righteousness" is important here. We know that the Torah says it is our righteousness before YHWH. It is how we live righteous before Him (Deuteronomy 6:24-25) because we know that it results in long life and peace to those who obey it (Proverbs 3:1-2).

However, the righteousness that leads to eternal life comes ONLY from Yahushua Messiah, as Paul has clearly shown. So then, the question is, "Is the Torah of any use to believers in Messiah Yahushua today?"

Chapter 6 is going to tell us that it **IS**. To see it though, we need to let the Word define itself and **REMEMBER**, Paul has just taught us the first part of the process of salvation (spiritual part), which is deliverance **FROM** the condemnation of death and sin's authority to kill us.

Now, in Chapter 6, he is going to begin teaching us the second part of the process of salvation (physical part), which is how we **LIVE** righteously before YHWH, **THROUGH** belief in Yahushua, and the struggles we will go through while still in the fleshly body as we await the resurrection.

Before we go there, however, I want to show you that the process Paul teaches Chapter 6 is present here in Chapter 5 as well.

As we mentioned earlier, verse 13 says that "until the Torah, sin was in the world, but sin is not reckoned when there is no Torah" and we showed how the word "reckoned" (imputed) was 'ellogeo', meaning a place or state of word or thought, i.e., a state of knowledge or understanding.

Basically, Paul is saying that before the Torah came there was sin in the world, but sin was not known or understood to be sin until the Torah explained what sin is and the consequences of committing it.

Paul will state this very thing in Chapter 7:7 where he says, "I did not know sin except through the Torah. For also the covetousness I knew not if the Torah had not said, "You shall not covet."

Verses 14-19 teach the Good News of Messiah as the Second Adam who would come and fulfill the duty of obedience that the First Adam failed to do, and that through Him, all who believe can access that same right-standing that had been imputed to Abraham (4:13-25).

Verse 20 refers to the same thing as verse 13 and 7:7, i.e., knowledge of Torah teaches us what sin is and our position 'under' the condemnation of the Torah for having violated it (Galatians 2:21-29).

Paul is saying that all mankind was condemned to death for sin, first Adam's sin and then their own, even though they didn't know it. The Torah was given to show mankind that they were all guilty of sin even though they had not sinned in the same way Adam had.

So, the knowledge of Torah caused our understanding of what sin is to increase but the favour (grace) of Elohim, which we receive through belief in Yahushua (Ephesians 2:8-9), increased that much more because His blood would atone for all sin (1 John 2:2).

This was the first part, the spiritual part of the Salvation Process, and in verse 21 he is going to mention the second part, the physical part, of the process as a prelude to Chapter 6, where he is going to lay the whole process out.

> **Rom 5:21**      so that as sin did reign in death, even so favour might reign[1] **through** righteousness[2] **to** everlasting life[3] **through** יהושע Messiah our Master.[4]

1. The Good News of Justification from sin and death through belief in Messiah (Ephesians 2:8-9).
2. Our responsibility to live righteously in the Grace of Elohim, which can only be done by obeying the Torah just as Messiah, our example, did (Ephesians 2:10; 1 John 2:3-6).
3. The Grace of YHWH gives us access to the righteousness of Messiah, through which we are justified from sin and death (spiritual part), working together with our wholehearted commitment to live in the righteousness of the Torah (physical part), ends in everlasting life (Romans 6:22).
4. This is the most important part!!! Our expectation (hope) **DOES NOT** rest in our obedience to Torah or how well we are able to keep it. Our expectation rest**, SOLELY AND COMPLETELY**, on the shed blood of Yahushua Ha-Mashiach, and it is through this **sincerity of heart** that the Grace of YHWH continues to cover our mistakes as we "workout our salvation with fear and trembling" (Philippians 2:12).

This pattern or process of salvation is taught throughout the whole of Scripture and confirmed by Paul in numerous places, if you have "eyes to see and ears to hear", which is a phrase that refers to a heart condition. The words "see" and "hear" come from verbal roots in Hebrew and as such, they refer to an active seeing and hearing, meaning that a person sees or hears with the intent to obey.

# Chapter 4: Romans 6

**Rom 6:1**        What, then, shall we say? Shall we continue in sin, to let favour increase?

**Rom 6:2**        Let it not be! How shall we who died to sin still live in it?

**REMEMBER,** Paul has just told us that sin/death did increase to all Adam's descendants due to both his own sin and theirs, but now, through belief in Messiah, grace/favor has increased to forgive all sins because Messiah lived righteously. **DON'T LOSE SIGHT OF THIS TRUTH!**

Paul's question here is about whether we should continue to sin (violate the Torah/Law – 1 John 3:4) now that we've been delivered from the penalty of sin and death, so that YHWH's grace/favor can increase even more? His answer is a resounding, **Absolutely Not!!!**

**1Jn 3:4**        Everyone doing sin also does lawlessness, and sin is lawlessness.

Though there are many errors in the church today there is none greater than how it defines sin!

**Sin:**      stg's #G266 - "hamartia", meaning, sin; from two words meaning, not and at a distance. Refers to an archer who is aiming at a distant target and has missed it. Contextually, it refers to a mark or standard of right behavior that we have not lived up to, due to our disobedience.

**Transgression of the Law:**      stg's #G458 - "anomia", meaning, illegality; from two words meaning, no and law (instructions). Refers to the standard of right living (Deuteronomy 6:24-25) that we are suppose live by (Eph 2:10) but haven't. We have sinned (missed the mark of righteousness) because we did not obey the Torah of YHWH.

**Note:**    Nomos is the Greek word used to translate the Hebrew word Torah, which means the **instructions** of YHWH (everything that has proceeded out of His mouth - Matthew 4:4).

Anomia actually means:

1.   "a"      = no
2.   "nom"    = Law/Torah
3.   "ia"     = doing.

Now, understanding the definition of sin, hear what Paul is actually asking us.

> **Rom 6:1**   Shall we continue to sin (disobey the Torah), that grace may abound?

His answer: God forbid! **<u>ABSOLUTELY NOT!!!</u>** Why?

> **Rom 6:2**   How shall we, that are dead to sin (disobedience), continue living in it (disobedience to the Torah).

Disobeying the Torah (instructions) of YHWH is what made us guilty and condemned us to death in the first place, just like it condemned Adam before us.

> **Rom 6:3**   Or do you not know that as many of us as were immersed into Messiah יהושע **were immersed into His death**?
>
> **Rom 6:4**   We were therefore buried with Him through immersion into death, that as Messiah was raised from the dead by the esteem of the Father, so also we **should walk in newness of life**.

Paul is showing how Messiah's death has been applied to us through the act of baptism, which is what the shadow picture of the Red Sea crossing teaches us. Our baptism washes away our old enemy (sin) just like the Red Sea washed away Pharaoh and the armies of Egypt.

Baptism is a picture of our burial with Yahushua, and so, having died to our past disobedient lifestyle, we are now to live our lives in the newness of an obedient lifestyle. How does a child of YHWH live?

| Lev 18:4 | 'Do My right-rulings and guard My laws, to walk in them. I am יהוה your Elohim. |
| Lev 18:5 | 'And you shall guard My laws and My right-rulings, which a man does and lives by them. I am יהוה. |

However, the Torah is not about belief.

| Gal 3:11 | And that no one is **declared right by** Torah before Elohim is clear, for **"The righteous shall live by belief."** |
| Gal 3:12 | And the Torah is **not of belief**, but **"The man who does them shall live by them."** |

No one ever gets this right. **REMEMBER,** Yisra'el was saved from death by the blood of the Passover Lamb, **LONG BEFORE** the Torah was given to them at Mt. Sinai. So then, the Torah comes into the life of the believer **AFTER** he has believed and **NOT BEFORE!!!**

We live **BY BELIEF**, but we live **IN THE TORAH!!!** Belief proved by works (James 2:14-25), the Torah and Messiah, the whole gospel of complete salvation (Isaiah 8-20 and Revelation 14:12).

The church misses this simple principle and constantly quotes Ephesians 2:8-9 out of the full context, to teach a lawless salvation (i.e., "error of the wicked"-2 Peter 3:14-17).

| Eph 2:8 | For by favour you have been saved, through belief, and that not of yourselves, it is the gift of Elohim, |
| Eph 2:9 | it is not by works, so that no one should boast. |

Hallelujah, what a gift, however, this is not the end of the quote.

| Eph 2:10 | For we are His workmanship, created in Messiah יהושע **unto good works, which Elohim prepared beforehand that we should walk in them**. |

What standard of "good works" did YHWH ordain that we, His people, should live by, **BEFORE MESSIAH CAME?** (Leviticus 18:4-5; Deuteronomy 28:1-65; 30:11-20)

154

| | |
|---|---|
| **2Ti 3:16** | **All Scripture** is breathed out by Elohim and **profitable for teaching**, **for reproof**, **for setting straight**, <u>**for instruction in righteousness**</u>, |
| **2Ti 3:17** | that the man of Elohim might be fitted, **equipped for every good work**. |

What "Scripture" is Paul referring to here? <u>**"ALL SCRIPTURE"!!**</u> Paul was referring to the Torah, the Prophets, and the Writings (the Tanak). The so-called "New Testament" did not exist in that time; it was in the process of being written.

Romans 6:3-4; Ephesians 2:8-10 and many others we will look into, are telling us that we get saved from the condemnation (death penalty) for our past disobedience to the Torah, ONLY through belief in Yahushua Messiah.

However, **AFTER** we have been saved from condemnation, the Torah is **how we live** unto YHWH, as it was given to Yisra'el in the wilderness, **without additions or subtractions** (Deuteronomy 4:2; 12:32).

"There is nothing new under the sun" (Ecclesiastes 1:9) and Paul confirms to Timothy that it's through the Torah and the Prophets, or the "Old Testament" (Tanak), that we develop doctrine and reprove false doctrine. It is how we protect ourselves from error and from it we learn the way of righteousness, so that we will be fully prepared to do <u>**"EVERY GOOD WORK"**</u>.

The church does not understand this because it refuses to obey the Torah, for it is through obeying the Torah that we get wisdom and understanding (Deuteronomy 4:5-6). They are under the misguided conclusion that they are not part of Yisra'el but are instead some "New Testament Gentile Church". This concept is completely and utterly foreign to **ALL SCRIPTURE.**

Continuing in Ephesians chapter 2, you will see that Paul teaches the Gentile believer, he is NO LONGER A GENTILE but a fellow citizen of Yisra'el, and a partaker of all the covenants, promises and hopes prophesied for Yisra'el in the Tanak (See: Sec 2, Ch 9 - Romans 11 on pg. 268).

***

| | |
|---|---|
| **Rom 6:5** | For if we have come to be grown together in the likeness of His death, we shall be also of the resurrection, |

When we believe in Messiah, our first act of obedience is baptism, which is a shadow picture of the Two-Part process of redemption.

The first part, the immersion (baptism), is a picture of taking part in His substitutionary death. This is the Spiritual New Birth.

The second part, when we emerge from the water, is a picture of our FUTURE resurrection, at His return (1 Corinthians 15:35-55). This is the Physical New Birth when we shall be like Him (1 John 3:2).

> **Rom 6:6**    knowing this, that our old man was impaled with Him, so that the body of sin might be rendered powerless, to serve sin no longer.

We died in Messiah and our physical body, which still contains the sinful flesh, no longer has power to continue to force us to disobey the Torah.

The phrase "serve sin" means exactly what it says. By definition, to sin is to disobey the Torah (1 John 3:4) so to "serve sin" is to live in disobedience to the Torah (law). Paul clearly tells us in verse 6 that "henceforth we should not serve sin", which means that from now on we should be obeying the Torah.

> **Rendered Powerless**:    stg's #G2673 - "katargeo", meaning, to be entirely idle; from two words meaning, down and to be idle. Refers to being useless or powerless.

When Paul mentions in verse 6 the "body of sin", he is referring to our physical body that is no different than an animal. It is subject to our five senses and reacts by emotion and instinct. Later, Paul is going to call this "body of sin" our flesh.

Paul is saying, because we have died with Messiah through baptism, the work He has done in us, makes our flesh powerless to continue living in disobedience. But is that true?

After you have believed in Yahushua and received the Spiritual New Birth, does your body still desire to sin?

If Paul is saying that being born again in Yahushua prevents our physical body from dragging us back into disobedience, then what does he mean in Chapter 7, where he says, "Though I wish to do good, evil is present in me...bringing me into captivity to the torah of sin which is in my members"? (Rom 7:21 and 23)

Paul is NOT telling us that our belief in Messiah prevents our physical body from having power over us, to cause us to sin. He is telling us that now, in our belief, we have the power to resist our physical body, because our spirit man is alive again. This will be explained more in Chapter 7.

Some have used this verse to teach they can do whatever they want, and that is true. However, though we are free to do all things, not everything we can do is beneficial to us (1 Corinthians 6:12), because things like "willful sin" (Hebrews 10:26-31), lead us back into condemnation (death).

> **Rom 6:7**     For he who has died has been made right from sin.

Hear this? We **were** all sinners and condemned to death because we disobeyed YHWH's Torah, however, once a man dies, he has paid the physical debt he owed for his sin.

Due to Adam's disobedience the curse of death came upon all men, as Paul told us in Chapter 5. This curse of death that came upon man, cursed his whole being, both physical and spiritual.

Unfortunately, without the redeeming blood of Yahushua Messiah, it is impossible for the spirit man to be born again and so the death of the physical man is the righteous judgment for his sin.

Once a man dies, the inheritance (eternal life) is no longer available to him because though he has paid the physical price for sin, the spirit man was never born again. Without spiritual rebirth there is no resurrection to life, only the second death.

To help us, YHWH sent Yahushua to die in our place, so that, if we trust in Him, His death pays the penalty for our sin (death-Romans 3:23-26), making us free from the penalty of death.

However, this begs the question, how do we, as free men, live in Him?

> **Rom 6:8**     And if we died with Messiah, we believe that we **shall also live with Him**,
> **Rom 6:9**     knowing that Messiah, having been raised from the dead, dies no more – death no longer rules over Him.
> **Rom 6:10**    For in that He died, He died to sin once for all; but in that He lives, **He lives to Elohim.**

Verse 8 reveals the promise of the resurrection to all those who have trusted in Yahushua Messiah and that all those who have believed in Him shall be raised to meet Him at His return.

Messiah is now immortal, having received in Himself everlasting life through what He has suffered, having paid the penalty for sin once for everyone for all time. He now lives to do the work of YHWH, which is to bring many brethren to the same everlasting life (Romans 8:29).

**Rom 6:11**    So you also, **reckon yourselves to be dead indeed to sin, but alive to Elohim in Messiah יהושע our Master.**

As Messiah has died to put away our sin debt and now lives to do the will of the Father, so we also should consider ourselves dead to the "old man" of rebellion and disobedience and live unto YHWH as "new creatures" (2 Corinthians 5:17) of obedience to the Word/Torah of YHWH, doing so through belief in Yahushua.

Torah obedience is a post-salvation requirement, **NOT** a pre-salvation requirement. We obey the Torah, NOT TO BE SAVED, but because WE ARE SAVED and members of the household of YHWH, i.e., Yisra'el (See: Eph. 2:10-19). The Torah is a **heart test**, to prove who we serve (Deuteronomy 8:1-3), Him, others, or ourselves.

**REMEMBER,** Torah observance alone cannot make us righteous before YHWH because it only teaches us how to live righteously. We must never put our trust in the Torah to make us right from our sin, for our flesh is too weak to keep it perfectly (Romans 8:3) neither does it wish to (Rom 8:7).

To fail in even one point in the Torah is to be guilty of all of the Torah (James 2:10-11), so to place our trust in the Torah, means that we have to keep it perfectly (Galatians 3:10), which we have shown above is impossible because of our fleshly desires.

However, once we have been made right through belief in Yahushua Messiah, we need to live righteously before Him with all of our heart, mind and strength (Deuteronomy 6:4-5; Mark 12:19) by steadfast continuance in doing the good works of YHWH/Torah (Romans 2:6-7, 10, 13).

Now that we have come to this understanding clarify how the blood of Messiah continues to cleanse the Believer once they have been justified from sin and death by belief.

In the process of salvation taught in the totality of Scripture, the first step is belief in the blood, i.e., Messiah, the second step is Baptism, the third is Obedience to the Torah. As mentioned above, if we have placed our TRUST in the Torah, we have to keep every jot and tittle of it to avoid being re-condemned when we stumble, however, it also tells us that if we have believed in Messiah but refuse to obey the Torah/Law of YHWH, we re-condemn ourselves, proving that we are transgressors (Galatians 2:15-18; Hebrews 10:26-31).

We **MUST** understand that obeying the Torah of YHWH is a **REQUIREMENT** for **ALL** believers, the Household of YHWH is not a democracy, it is a theocracy and as such, obedience to the Torah of YHWH is non-negotiable.

However, keeping the Torah perfectly as a believer is possible IF we understand the *Two-Part Principle* and how the blood of Messiah works on behalf of the Believer post-justification.

English words that translate Hebrew words do not always mean the same thing as the English word. In English, as a verb, 'perfect', refers to being "completely free from faults and defects", which is how we understand this word, however, as an adjective in refers to (1) "having all the required or desirable elements, qualities or characteristics, as good as it is possible to be" and (2) "absolute; complete".

In Hebrew there are several words translated as perfect in modern Bibles and each of these words carry similar meanings, to which the context where they are used heavily influences the meaning intended. Generally, though, the Hebrew words refer to 'completeness', but not necessarily in the same way this word is understood in English.

In the Scripture, the word completeness or perfection refers to a state of being more than a state of flawlessness. When the Scripture refers to perfection it is referring to being completely whole, both spiritually and physically. This means that your belief in Messiah MUST be accompanied by the works of Torah.

| | |
|---|---|
| **Psa 119:1** | Blessed are the **perfect** in the way, who **walk** in the Torah of יהוה! |
| **Psa 119:2** | Blessed are those who **observe** His witnesses, **who seek Him with all the heart!** |
| **Psa 119:3** | Yes, **they shall do no unrighteousness**; They **shall walk in His ways**. |
| **Psa 119:4** | You have commanded us to **guard Your orders** diligently. |
| **Psa 119:5** | Oh, that my ways were established to guard Your laws! |
| **Psa 119:6** | Then I would not be ashamed, When I look into all Your commands. |

| | |
|---|---|
| **Psa 119:7** | I thank You **with uprightness of heart**, When I learn the right-rulings of Your righteousness. |
| **Psa 119:8** | **I guard Your laws**; Oh, do not leave me entirely! |

First of all, this passage is clearly written by someone (Dawid) who believed in YHWH.

Secondly, we see that he clearly understood both the advantages (perfection, blessing, not ashamed) for obeying the Torah of YHWH and consequences (leaving me entirely) for not obeying the Torah of YHWH.

Thirdly, we see that he understood that his flesh was a problem because it was not "established to guard Your laws", though it was his desire (Rom 7:7-8:7).

And lastly, the standard of 'physical' acceptance was "seeking Him with all the heart", guarding "Your orders diligently" and being thankful "with uprightness of heart".

Even in the Tanak (OT), pleasing YHWH was not about how perfectly you obeyed the Torah, but it was, is and will always be about our heart condition. When we strive "diligently" with "all of our heart" to obey His desire (Torah) and are thankful for all He has done for us in uprightness (sincerity) of heart, He accepts us.

It is imperative, however, that we see that Dawid's love/belief/trust was present when he wrote this passage. He cried out this psalm from a believers heart and strived to live out the Torah (way, witnesses, orders, laws, commands, righteousness) of YHWH because of that love/belief/trust. He was not trusting in the Torah itself, but in the Giver of the Torah who required him to obey, and he did it in sincerity and diligence (1 John 5:1-4).

| | |
|---|---|
| **Rom 6:12** | Therefore **do not let sin reign** in your mortal body, **to obey it** in its desires, |
| **Rom 6:13** | neither present your members as instruments of unrighteousness **to sin**, but present yourselves to Elohim as being alive from the dead, and your members as instruments **of righteousness to Elohim**. |
| **Rom 6:14** | For sin shall not rule over you, for you **are not under the law but under favour.** |

This is another passage of Scripture completely misunderstood by so-called Bible teachers today. This passage has been taught as

160

PROOF that believers are not "under the law" TO OBEY IT, since they are "under grace". It is most ironic because this passage is telling them the exact opposite and they can't see it.

**REMEMBER,** "sin is a transgression of the law (Torah-1 John 3:4)", so to avoid being called sinners, we must obey the Law/Torah of YHWH. This seems pretty simple to figure out doesn't it?

Prior to verse 12, Paul was using the word "sin" in reference to our behavior. Beginning here in verse 12 he is going to use the word "sin", in reference to our flesh (the mind of the flesh), the part within us that desires to live according to its own way.

Paul says our fleshly mind is the "law of sin and death" (Romans 7:25; 8:2), because it doesn't subject itself to the Torah of YHWH (Romans 8:7). To Paul's way of thinking, every person is of two minds, one spiritual and one physical.

The spiritual mind is the rational part of our mind, the part that can observe facts and make choices based on the facts without being unduly influenced by our five senses or the emotions they evoke.

The physical mind is the instinctual part of our mind, the part that is controlled by our five senses and their emotions. This is the part of us that is similar to the animals because it is reflexive and impulsive.

Paul is trying to let us know that we have a choice as to which mind controls us. Do we give in to the impulses of our physical mind and its fleshly desires or do we allow our spiritual/rational mind to lead us into righteous behavior in accordance with the Torah, despite how it feels, or the consequences of right living in a sinful world.

So, in verse 12, Paul is telling us not to allow our flesh to control our physical body, to obey its desires, and neither are we to allow the members of our physical body (i.e., heart, mind, hands, etc.) to be used as tools by our flesh to cause us to live in disobedience to the Torah.

We are to commit our members as tools to do righteousness, which is obedience to the Torah (Deuteronomy 6:24-25) in service to YHWH. Our fleshly mind only has the power to bring us back into the condemnation of death if we **willfully** give our fleshly mind (sin) rule over our physical body.

If, however, we make our members subject to what is righteous (Torah) with all of our heart, mind and strength, then our servant's heart protects us from sin's ability to condemn us again when we fail, because of our belief in Yahushua Messiah.

The intended purpose of the Torah was to give us life (Leviticus 18:5; Deuteronomy 30:11-16) but if we make a **willful**

161

choice to disobey it, our disobedience brings upon us the penalty of death (Deuteronomy 30:17-18), it is our choice (Deuteronomy 30:19).

If we choose to disobey the Torah, we choose death for ourselves, and the Torah gives sin the authority to kill us (1 Corinthians 15:56).

Here in Romans 6:12-14 we are told again to make better choices as to how we live as believers. If we choose well, obedience, then Torah will no longer condemn us when we fail, but if we choose to disobey, our choice proves that we don't have the heart of the Son.

| | |
|---|---|
| **Gal 2:16** | knowing that a man is **not declared right by works of Torah**, but through belief in יהושע Messiah, even we have believed in Messiah יהושע, in order to be **declared right by belief** in Messiah and not by works of Torah, because **by works of Torah no flesh shall be declared right**. |
| **Gal 2:17** | "And if, **while seeking to be declared right by Messiah**, we ourselves also are **found sinners**, is Messiah then a servant of sin? Let it not be! |
| **Gal 2:18** | "For if **I rebuild what I *once* overthrew, I establish myself a transgressor**. |
| **Gal 2:19** | "For through Torah I died to Torah, in order to live to Elohim. |

What Paul is saying here couldn't be clearer if you understand what Paul teaches. Paul is stating clearly that justification (being made right from sin and death) comes from belief in Yahushua Messiah and not by works of the law.

However, if we are expecting to be justified by our belief in Yahushua, but we continue to disobey the Torah, has Messiah became our servant to allow us to disobey? Paul's answer is an emphatic **NO!!!**

Does not the "New Testament Christian Doctrine" say that once you've been justified by belief in "Jesus Christ" you no longer need obey the "Old Testament" Law/Torah?

IF, by definition, sin is the transgression of the law (1 John 3:4), then for Christian teachers to say that belief in Messiah allows them to no longer obey the law, THEY HAVE MADE the Messiah a servant of sin.

They are teaching us that we are now allowed to sin because Messiah justified us, making Him sin's servant.

Paul concludes his argument with, "if I build again the things I once destroyed, I make myself a transgressor". Consider this a moment.

**Destroyed:** stg's **#G2647** - "kataluō", meaning, overthrow or overcome; from two words meaning, down and to loosen. Refers to the act of tearing down or destroying something that has held someone down or held them back.

In the context of this passage, we have to understand the word "kataluō" to mean what we have overcome through our belief in Yahushua Messiah. Our belief in Yahushua Messiah has justified or made us right from the condemnation of death. So, we have overcome (kataluō) the condemnation of death.

Paul says, if he builds again or rebuilds upon himself the condemnation of death, which he overcame in Yahushua Messiah, then **he** "makes" **himself** a transgressor.

**Make:** stg's **#G4921** - "sunistaō", meaning, to set together or prove; from two words meaning, to gather and to stand. Refers to concluding something based on the evidence.

What Paul is trying to tell us, is that once we have come to the Messiah to be justified from past sin and we continue to be disobedient, we prove that we are transgressors and build for ourselves again the condemnation of death we had overthrown (been justified from) when we believed in Messiah. (See also: Hebrews 6:4-8; 10:26-31; 2 Peter 2:18-22).

Consider for a moment what the wisest man in the world (King Solomon) once said.

**Ecc 3:14** I know that **whatever Elohim does is fore**ver. There is **no adding to it, and there is no taking from it.** Elohim does it, **that men should fear before Him.**

**Ecc 3:15** Whatever is has already been, and what shall be has been before. But Elohim **seeks out what has been pursued.**

Notice the word "whatever", which means absolutely everything YHWH has said or done, including every command in the

163

Torah, stands forever (Psalms 119:89). EVERY WORD, EVERY COMMAND, EVERY PROMISE, EVERY JUDGMENT, EVERYTHING REMAINS FOREVER. Do we still live in forever?

Note also, **NOTHING** can be added to it or taken from it. Not one jot nor one tittle (Matthew 5:17-19) can be added to or taken from the Scripture **forever**. No command, once given, can be removed, rescinded, or reinterpreted. Why?

YHWH laid this proclamation down so that **ALL** men everywhere and from every time would know how to fear (reverence and worship) Him in the Way He expects to be feared.

He did it to test us, to see who would serve Him as He wishes to be served, showing the difference between a son and those who really just want to live according to our own fleshly feelings or opinions or motivations.

There is nothing new under the sun (Ecclesiastes 1:9), which Solomon confirms, when he says, what was in the past was still present in his time and what is to be in the future has already been in the past.

The last portion of this passage is the most interesting because the King James says, "and God requires that which is past", leading some to interpret it to mean that YHWH requires us to do the things He commanded in the past.

Unfortunately, we don't have the authority to just make it mean what we think it should mean, we have to tell you what it says.

This verse actually says, "and Elohim seeks that which is pursued". This seems like a big difference between what it says in the King James, however, this is not the first time the King James translators have woefully misunderstood what is being said.

**Requireth:** stg's **#H1245** - "bâqash", a primitive root meaning, **to search out.**

**Past:** stg's **#H7291** - "râdaph", a primitive root meaning, **to run after**.

So, these two words mean 'to search out what is ran after' or 'seek out what is pursued'.

What this passage actually means, is that YHWH has set before men the **Way** He expects them to reverence and worship Him, which is through trusting in Him, specifically Yahushua, and walking in obedience to His Torah.

However, when He judges those who are trusting in Him, He doesn't judge them based on how perfectly they were able to obey His Torah but rather, on how diligently they pursued it.

In other words, YHWH is going to judge the hearts of men to see if they really had a heart to obey Him. The Messianic Writings support this when in Hebrews 4:12 it says that the Word can "discern the thoughts and intents of the heart".

Like the Scripture says, there is nothing new under the sun and nothing changes. The words and works of YHWH that were spoken at Mount Sinai are equally alive and potent today.

The future was in existence long ago, for YHWH does not change (Malachi 3:6) and neither is there any shadow of turning from anything He has said (James 2:17).

Though the standards of Torah are a requirement today, just as they always have been, YHWH is not seeking the man who walks perfectly in the Torah but the man whose heart is sold out to Him, to obey the Torah with all of his might.

Abraham was not perfect, but YHWH received him. Neither was Isaac nor Jacob perfect, but YHWH received them. King David stole a man's wife and then plotted to murder the man in such a way that would not only kill that man but would put many other men's lives at risk and yet YHWH said he was a man after His own heart and received him.

YHWH's standard of right living has never changed and has always been based on trusting in Him (belief) and obeying His Torah with a true heart. In judgment, it will not be the perfection of our Torah obedience that gains us the Kingdom, but the perfection of our INTENT TO OBEY, it's all about the heart.

Our rewards are based on our Torah obedience, our works (1 Corinthians 3:11-15), at the Bema seat, the seat of Messiah's judgment.

***

| | |
|---|---|
| **Rom 6:15** | What then? **Shall we sin because we are not under Torah** but under favour? Let it not be! |
| **Rom 6:16** | Do you not know that to **whom you present yourselves servants for obedience, you are servants of the one whom you obey**, whether of **sin to death**, or of **obedience to righteousness**? |

**REMEMBER**, "sin is the transgression of the law (Torah)". I know you must be tired of hearing this but with Christian doctrine the way it is today, it cannot be stressed enough.

165

In verses 12-14 Paul associates' sin with our rebellious flesh and now, in 15-16, he is referring to both our fleshly desire and our behavior.

First, he asked, shall we disobey the Torah (sin)? He then goes ahead and answers his own question, **NO!!!**

As in verse 1 and verse 14, Paul contrasts behavior (v.1) and fleshly desire (v.14) to not being under the condemnation of death (the law of sin and death - Romans 8:2).

Paul is asking, even though the Torah no longer condemns us because of the grace of YHWH, through our belief in Yahushua Messiah, should believers continue to disobey the Torah (sin)? **NO!!!**

Why? "You are servants to who you obey!" If believers serve/obey sin (our fleshly nature) they shall die, however, if they obey (the Torah), they will be righteous (Deuteronomy 6:24-25).

Let's look ahead a little to chapter 8 of Romans.

| | |
|---|---|
| **Rom 8:12** | So then, **brothers**, we are not debtors to the flesh, **to live according to the flesh**. |
| **Rom 8:13** | For **if you** live according to the flesh, **you are going to die**; but if by the Spirit you put to death the deeds of the body, you shall live. |

Paul is obviously talking to the "brethren" and states that, if they live according to the flesh (obey sin) they **SHALL DIE.**

Believers must choose between obeying or disobeying, between life and death, between the blessing and the curse (Deuteronomy 30:11-20) just as our forefathers in the wilderness.

| | |
|---|---|
| **Eze 18:26** | "When a righteous one **turns away from his righteousness**, and does unrighteousness, and **he dies in it**, it is because of his unrighteousness which he has done that he dies. |
| **Note:** | This verse in the King James Version uses the word "iniquity" instead of the word "unrighteousness". |
| **Iniquity:** | stg's **#H5766** - "evel", meaning, evil; from a word meaning, to distort. Refers to living in a way contrary to the Torah. |

Notice, if a righteous man turns away from living righteously and dies without repenting for it, he dies in his sin. He has a heart of rebellion.

| | |
|---|---|
| **Eze 18:27** | "And when the wrong **turns away from the wrong** which he has done, and he does right-ruling and righteousness, **he keeps himself alive**. |

| | |
|---|---|
| **Note:** | In the King James Version, the word "wrong" is translated as "wicked" (wickedness). |

| | |
|---|---|
| **Eze 18:28** | "Because he sees and **turns away from all the transgressions** which he has done, he shall certainly live, **he shall not die**. |

| | |
|---|---|
| **Wicked(ness):** | stg's #H7563 (64) - "rasha" (rish'ah), meaning, wrong; refers to a person or behavior that is contrary to YHWH's standard of right (Torah). |

These prophetic passages are referring to eternal life or death (the second death) and refers equally today for believers who refuse to obey the Torah, due to their rebellious heart.

You might say, but my trusted Pastor has assured me the Bible says my Belief alone gives me eternal security.

Your pastor, or priest, etc., has ignored Scripture, and allowed you to believe that Messiah will keep you, if you reject the Torah (2 Peter 3:14-17).

It is true, eternal security is possible, if your heart remains steadfast in belief by striving daily to obey the Word/Torah, to the very end. However, if you know what the word requires of a believer (Torah obedience) and you refuse to obey it, your place in the Kingdom is forfeit.

This is about KNOWING what Scripture says and obeying it, NOT agreeing with what others SAY it means or choosing an alternate interpretation. Scripture **DEMANDS** obedience (Genesis-Revelation), according to YHWH's Torah and not man's interpretation.

| | |
|---|---|
| **Heb 6:4** | For it is impossible for those who were once enlightened, and have tasted the heavenly gift, and have become partakers of the Set-apart Spirit, |

167

| | |
|---|---|
| **Heb 6:5** | and have tasted the good Word of Elohim and the powers of the age to come, |
| **Heb 6:6** | and fall away, to renew them again to repentance – having impaled for themselves the Son of Elohim again, and put Him to open shame. |

And again,

| | |
|---|---|
| **Heb 10:26** | For if we sin purposely after we have received the knowledge of the truth, there no longer remains a slaughter *offering* for sins, |
| **Heb 10:27** | but some fearsome anticipation of judgment, and **a fierce fire which is about to consume the opponents.** |
| **Heb 10:28** | Anyone who has disregarded the Torah of Mosheh dies without compassion on the witness of two or three witnesses. |
| **Heb 10:29** | How much worse punishment do you think shall he deserve who has trampled the Son of Elohim underfoot, counted the blood of the covenant by which he was set apart as common, and insulted the Spirit of favour? |
| **Heb 10:30** | For we know Him who has said, **"Vengeance is Mine, I shall repay, says יהוה."** And again, **"יהוה shall judge His people."** |
| **Heb 10:31** | It is fearsome to fall into the hands of the living Elohim. |

Don't let the man-made doctrine of disobedient men lead you astray from doing the truth of Yahushua Messiah and the Torah (Isaiah 8:20; Revelation 14:12). We must believe in Him first, then walk in obedience to His Law/Torah!

Paul finishes up Romans 6:16 by saying, if we live as servants of obedience unto YHWH (by obeying the Torah) we shall be righteous (compare Romans 2:13; Deuteronomy 6:24-25).

If we, as believers, hear what the Torah requires us to do, and we don't do it we are deceiving ourselves (James 1:22).

**Note:** **REMEMBER**, in the Hebrew language the word for "hear" comes from "shama", which implies active intent. To "hear" in Hebrew means to LISTEN with the INTENT to OBEY.

| Rom 6:17 | But thanks to Elohim that you **were** servants of sin, **yet you obeyed from the heart** that form of teaching to which you were entrusted. |
| Rom 6:18 | And having been **set free from sin**, you became **servants of righteousness.** |

Paul is referring to the current state of behavior among the believers in Rome. They **USED TO BE** disobedient to the Torah and condemned to death for it, **BUT NOW** they have obeyed the Good News of deliverance in Yahushua Messiah.

Once they were "saved" from there past condemnation, they "became" servants of YHWH to live in righteousness, which comes from Torah obedience.

| Rom 6:19 | I speak as a man, because of the weakness of your flesh. For even as you **did** present your members as servants of uncleanness, and of lawlessness resulting in lawlessness, **so now** present your members as servants of righteousness resulting in set-apartness. |

| Note: | Notice that "did" is past tense and "now" is present tense. |

Paul is now going to teach us the "process" of salvation that began with our confession of belief in Yahushua Messiah, which delivered us from the death penalty and the authority of sin, making us born again in the inner-spirit-man.

This process is finished at the resurrection, the redemption of this body (Rom 8:23). The physical new birth delivers us from our state of mortality and the corruption of our flesh and transforms us into a new body that cannot die when we inherit the Kingdom of Messiah.

The Two-Part process of salvation, the spiritual part comes through belief and the physical part comes through obedience, which leads to complete salvation. The spiritual part is given freely by belief in Yahushua and the physical part is accomplished by us through obedience to the Torah, from a sincere heart.

<u>NO,</u> we are not suggesting that the Torah accomplishes our salvation, Messiah alone accomplishes that, however, because YHWH has created us with the privilege of free will, we must surrender our free will as sons, to obey the Torah.

It is **NOT** about how well we obey it, but that we have surrendered (circumcised) our hearts to obey it every day with all of our strength. Only those with the heart of a child will inherit the Kingdom (Matthew 18:1-4).

Paul says, because of the weakness of our flesh, he is going to reveal a principle to us, the principle of yielding.

**Yield**: stg's #G3936 - "paristemi", meaning, to stand beside; from two words meaning, to stand and near. Refers to taking a position that is consistent with or exhibits certain behaviors or beliefs.

Before Messiah, we all took a position that was contrary to the Torah of YHWH, which led to a state of uncleanness and lawlessness, i.e., sin.

**Uncleanness**: stg's #G167 - "akatharsia", meaning, impurity; refers to doing things that make us unclean before YHWH, which are given in the Torah; idolatry, eating unclean animals, etc.

**Iniquity** stg's #G458 - "a-nom-ia", meaning, illegality (doing what is illegal or against the law); from two words meaning, no and law doing. Refers to someone not obeying the Law/Torah of YHWH.

This verse says that uncleanness and lawlessness are both lawlessness, encompassing all the forms of uncleanness and disobedience as lawlessness.

Now that we are in Messiah, we are to take a position that is consistent to the Torah and exhibits the righteous standard of the Torah, through which we will make ourselves set apart (holy) unto YHWH.

**Set-Apartness**: stg's #G38 - "hagiasmos", meaning, to make holy (distinct form others); from a word meaning, sacred. This is the same word used for sanctification (being set apart), as the children of YHWH.

Our submission to living righteously (Torah obedience) leads to set apartness (sanctification) as children of YHWH (John 17:17). Paul is going to add to this in a moment, but first he is going to challenge us about past behavior and current behavior.

| | |
|---|---|
| **Rom 6:20** | For when you **were** servants of sin, you **were** free from righteousness. |
| **Rom 6:21** | What fruit, therefore, **were** you having then, over which you are **now** ashamed? **For the end thereof is death**. |

We need to see that when we submit ourselves to our fleshly desires, we have no righteousness in us, for our flesh is unable to subject itself to the righteousness of Torah (Romans 8:7).

Before we knew Messiah, most of us didn't even know what the standard of righteousness was, even the Jews who had the Torah, were unable to produce the righteousness of YHWH, not having founded their works in belief (Romans 9:31-32).

When the knowledge of righteousness came to us, we were ashamed of our previous way of life because we understood it brought the death penalty upon us (Torah is our schoolmaster that brought us to Messiah - Galatians 3).

| | |
|---|---|
| **Rom 6:22** | But **now**, having been **set free from sin**, and having **become servants of Elohim**, you have your **fruit resulting in set-apartness**, and **the end, everlasting life.** |

**BUT NOW!** Do you see there is a change that should take place, from the old works (sin) that we are ashamed of, because they lead to death, to the new works (of Torah), that lead to righteousness and set apartness?

In Messiah, we have been freed from the condemnation death in order to serve YHWH, by bearing the fruit of righteous living (Torah obedience-Deuteronomy 6:24-25) which leads to set apartness as children.

This set apartness will end in our having eternal life, our belief + our works of obedience to the Torah = Eternal Life (spirit part + physical part = life).

| | |
|---|---|
| **Heb 12:14** | **Pursue peace** with all, **and *pursue* apartness** without which **no one shall see the Master.** |

171

**Heb 12:15** See to it that no **one falls short of the favour of Elohim,** that no root of bitterness springing up causes trouble, by which **many become defiled,**

(Also: 1 Corinthians 4:9-10; Galatians 5:9-21; Ephesians 5:1-9)

If we refuse to live a life of righteousness through obedience to the Torah, in belief that Yahushua is the Messiah, we shall not see the Master nor inherit His kingdom. Romans 6:23 confirms this for believers.

**Rom 6:23** For the wages of sin is death, but the favourable gift of Elohim is everlasting life in Messiah יהושע our Master.

Paul will carry on this teaching of our need of obedience to the Torah, **AFTER** believing in Messiah, in chapter 7 and 8.

# Chapter 5: Romans 7

Let's remember, in the original text there are no chapter and verse numbers, so this book is one big continuous teaching. The elements of Chapter 5 flow into 6 and then into 7 and onward throughout the whole book. This is called 'contextual flow' and we must always keep in mind the overall context.

The book of Romans is Paul's "Good News" to the **BELIEVERS** in Rome. The first verse of chapter 7 is a word play on what Paul has already taught in 3:20, 24; 4:15; 5:20 and 6:19-20. It is also the lead-in to a metaphor that explains 3:24-25; 4:16, 23-25; 5:8-19, 21; 6:3-4, 6-11, 17-18.

All Hebrew Scripture is written in this manner; however, no other Messianic writer was as intellectual as Paul, so his writings are sometimes hard to understand. Even well-meaning, highly educated, teachers of Scripture err in understanding Paul. To get it right, you must view his writings with his eyes and interpret it from his Hebraic, Torah oriented, mindset.

> **Rom 7:1**    Or do you not know, brothers – for I speak to those **knowing the Torah** – that the Torah **rules over a man** as long as he lives?

Paul is setting up his listeners, specifically the Jewish believers, by asking them a question that he has already given them the answer to in 3:20-23. There he stated that "no man can be justified by the Torah, because by the Torah comes the knowledge of sin", specifically what sin is (a violation of the Torah) and that all men are guilty of it (compare 5:20).

Knowledge is the overall idea of all Scripture. Adam failed by attempting to acquire knowledge through disobedience, i.e., sin. Throughout the prophets YHWH warns the people to stop trying to figure Him out or worship Him according to their own man-made understanding (see Proverbs 3:1-7 and Isaiah 54:8-11).

Romans 7:1 and 6:7 are contrasting thoughts on the same idea. In 6:7, Paul says that a man who is dead is free from sin. Why?

The penalty of sin (disobeying the Torah-1 John 3-4) is death, once a man dies, he is no longer guilty of his sin, he has paid the penalty.

However, once we are dead, we are beyond the hope of redemption because salvation requires a conscious willful acceptance of the "Good News" and a confession (Rom 10:10). If we haven't done that before we die, it's too late.

In a deeper aspect, Romans 6:7 is letting us in on a little tidbit of information that Paul will cover later, concerning the separation of the redeemed "inner-spirit-man" and the unredeemed "outer-physical-man", the fleshly body.

This fleshly body does not overcome the sentence of death until it dies. Even though the spirit is renewed, our flesh remains condemned. We will not receive the new body until Messiah's return.

Verse 1 of chapter 7 is a play on 6:7 from the opposite direction. Remember, the Torah condemns sin and the wages of sin is death (Romans 6:23), sin being the "transgression of the Law" (Torah – 1 John 3:4). Paul will further explain in chapter 7 that it is not the Torah that condemns us, it's our own fleshly desires that have caused us to sin, and the Torah condemns sin.

| | |
|---|---|
| **Jam 1:13** | Let no one say when he is enticed, "I am enticed by Elohim," for Elohim is not enticed by evil *matters*, and He entices no one. |
| **Jam 1:14** | **But each one is enticed when he is drawn away by his own desires and trapped.** |
| **Jam 1:15** | **Then, when desire has conceived, it gives birth to sin. And sin, when it has been accomplished, brings forth death.** |

However, the power to kill us for disobeying comes from the Torah (1 Cor 15:56). So, according to 7:1, the Torah "has dominion", over man until he dies.

| | |
|---|---|
| **Dominion**: | stg's #G2961 - "kurieuo", meaning, to rule. From a word meaning, supreme authority or control. |

How does the Torah "have dominion" over a man? The Torah has no authority over a man until he violates the Torah, which brings upon him condemnation for his disobedience, which is death.

When a man violates the Torah the sentence of death hangs over him until he dies, then he is free from that sin and the death penalty associated to it, according to 6:7.

Once we have received Yahushua's death as a substitute for our own, through belief in Him (6:3-4), we are **no longer under** the dominion of sin and thus it no longer has the power to kill us, as the Torah has decreed.

Also, we are not to let our flesh have dominion over us (6:8-13) because if we do, "serve sin" (disobey the Torah), we will reap the corruption of death again (6:16; 8:12-13; Hebrews 6:4-8; 10:26-31; 2 Peter 2:20-22, etc.).

We need to understand Paul's use of the words sin and Torah, they are connected and refer to the "law of sin and death" (8:2), which is simply the condemnation of death for sin. You are never condemned to death for obeying the Torah, only for disobeying the Torah.

Paul knew this would turn heads when he said it, which is why he quickly ask another question in verse 7, "Is the law sin? Let it not be!"

We will cover that passage as we get to it, but it is imperative to understand Paul's use of the phrase, "law has dominion", which is not about our need to obey it pre- or post-salvation, it's about the condemnation of death the Torah requires for disobeying it.

Once we accept Messiah we are "free" from that condemnation. However, our belief in Him does **NOT** "free" us from the requirement to obey the Torah. Continuing to disobey the Torah (i.e., sin) reaps the wages of sin, which is death (compare 1 John 3-4 with Romans 6:23; 8:12-13; Galatians 2:15-18; Hebrews 10:26-31).

So, Paul has asked those who know the Torah, if they understand that the Torah has condemned man to death for his sin, and he remains under the condemnation demanded by Torah until he dies to pay that debt.

Now, Paul is going to use a woman's position, under the authority of her husband, as a metaphor for us who were under the authority of the Torah's condemnation.

| | |
|---|---|
| **Rom 7:2** | For the married woman has been bound by Torah to the living husband, **but if the husband dies, she is released** from the Torah *concerning* her husband. |
| **Rom 7:3** | So then, while her husband lives, she shall be called an adulteress if she becomes another man's. But if her husband dies, **she is free** from that *part of the* Torah, so that she is not an adulteress, having become another man's. |

Any Jew that heard this would comprehend a couple different levels of doctrine, the first one we want to cover has to do with the specific condemnation that applies to each of us as individuals.

Notice, although this passage is correct scripturally, it is not really about marriage per se. However, when it says that the woman is "free" it is referring to the part of the Torah concerning her husband, not the entire Torah.

175

To clarify this just a little bit; the Torah says a woman is bound to her husband until her husband dies but when he dies, she is free to marry another man.

However, her freedom does not allow her to violate any other command(s) of the Torah. If she does, she will then be under the authority (condemnation) of the Torah for that sin.

The husband in this metaphor is the Torah of sin and death, which refers to the condemnation of death for sin decreed by the Torah.

The woman who is bound (under the condemnation of death, decreed by Torah), represents mankind who is guilty of sin.

Mankind is bound to the condemnation of death until the Torah of sin and death loses its authority. Once the authority of sin and death is removed, because of our belief in Yahushua Messiah, we are free from condemnation.

Another level of doctrine concerns mankind's union (marriage) to YHWH, but man chose to disobey the Torah of YHWH and came under the condemnation of death (Genesis 3:16-19).

From YHWH's point of view, when Adam listened to his wife (who had been tricked by the adversary) instead of obeying the command of YHWH, the man committed **spiritual adultery**.

Adam's obedience to another voice other than that of YHWH, is the same as a married woman's submission to another man's sexual advances. Man commits spiritual adultery every time he disobeys the Torah of YHWH or listens to any teaching of men or angels, which is inconsistent with YHWH's Torah.

The only way for mankind to be reconciled back to YHWH was for a death to take place.

**Rom 7:4**    So my brothers, you also were put to death to the Torah through the body of Messiah, for you to become another's, the One who was raised from the dead, that we should bear fruit to Elohim.

By accepting the "Good News" of Yahushua Messiah, His death became our propitiation (atonement price) so that we could be free from what we were bound to (i.e., sin and death) and be re-married to YHWH through Yahushua.

YHWH (our husband) gave of Himself, in Yahushua, to be the ransom so we could become His Bride, and as the Bride we are to bear fruit unto YHWH. What kind of fruit? The fruit of righteousness unto holiness (6:17-21), which leads us into everlasting life (6:22).

176

What is the standard of righteousness the people of YHWH are to live by to make them set apart (holy) unto Him? The Torah! (Deuteronomy 6:24-25; Romans 2:13; James 1:21-25; 1 John 2:3-5; 5:2-3; Revelation 14-12)

Now to the final level, every Jew in Rome was aware of Deuteronomy 24:1-4.

| | |
|---|---|
| **Deu 24:1** | "When a man takes a wife and shall marry her, then it shall be, if she finds no favour in his eyes because he has found a matter of **uncoveredness** in her, and he shall write her a certificate of divorce, and put it in her hand, and send her out of his house, |
| **Deu 24:2** | and if she left his house and went and **became another man's wife,** |
| **Deu 24:3** | and the latter husband shall hate her and write her a certificate of divorce, and put it in her hand, and send her out of his house, or when the latter husband dies who took her to be his wife, |
| **Deu 24:4** | then her former husband who sent her away is **not allowed to take her back to be his wife after she has been defiled,** for that would be an abomination before יהוה. And do not bring sin on the land which יהוה your Elohim is giving you as an inheritance. |

Did you get that? Once a man puts away his wife, he is not to marry her again after she has been with another man. It's an abomination! It is a sin that defiles the land.

When the Two Kingdoms (Yisra'el and Judah) were divided in the time of King Rehoboam, the son of Solomon, the northern kingdom of Yisra'el followed Jeroboam into idolatry and never repented. Because of this they were eventually conquered by Syria and exiled into the nations and have not as yet been allowed to return (1 Kings 12:1-2 Kings 17:23).

Yisra'el's problem was that idolatry was spiritual adultery to YHWH, and so He divorced them and sent them into exile.

| | |
|---|---|
| **Jer 3:1** | *Elohim* said, "**If a man puts away his wife, and she goes from him and becomes another man's, does he return to her again?** Would not that land be made greatly |

177

| | |
|---|---|
| | unclean? But you have committed whoring with many lovers. And would you return to Me?" declares יהוה. |
| **Jer 3:2** | "Lift up your eyes to the bare heights and see: where have you not lain with men? Besides the ways you have sat for them like an Araḇian in the wilderness. And you made the land unclean with your whorings and your evil. |
| **Jer 3:3** | "Therefore the showers have been withheld, and there has been no latter rain. You have had a whore's forehead, you refuse to be ashamed. |
| **Jer 3:4** | "Shall you not from now on cry to Me, 'My father, You are the guide of my youth? |
| **Jer 3:5** | Does one bear a grudge forever? Does one keep it to the end?' See, you have spoken and done the evils that you could." |
| **Jer 3:6** | And יהוה said to me in the days of Yoshiyahu the sovereign, "Have you seen what backsliding Yisra'ĕl has done? She has gone up on every high mountain and under every green tree, and there committed whoring. |
| **Jer 3:7** | "And after she had done all these, I said 'Return to Me.' But she did not return. And her treacherous sister Yehuḏah saw it. |
| **Jer 3:8** | "And I saw that for all the causes for which backsliding Yisra'ĕl had committed adultery, I had put her away and given her a **certificate of divorce**; yet her treacherous sister Yehuḏah did not fear, but went and committed whoring too. |
| **Jer 3:9** | "And it came to be, through her frivolous whoring, that she defiled the land and committed adultery with stones and wood. |

Now, according to the Torah in Deuteronomy 24:1-4, YHWH **CANNOT** restore Yisra'el as His bride without violating His own Torah. He cannot sin nor change what's already been spoken!

Their spiritual adultery (idolatry) forced YHWH to make a sacrifice of Himself, so restoration could be possible.

Yahushua said clearly that He had come to save the "lost house of Yisra'el" (Matthew 15:24) and it was to them only that He sent His twelve disciples (Matthew 10:1-6). He was not referring to the house of Judah, they were not lost, they were in the land with Him. He was a Jew!

Messiah was speaking to the "sheepfold" of the house of Judah but mentioned that he had "another sheepfold", that being the house of Yisra'el (John 10:26; compare Ezekiel 37).

There is a "Two House" doctrine in the Scripture, however, this doctrine has been twisted by men in these last days, so one must be very careful to allow the Scripture itself to define this doctrine.

As mentioned above, the Kingdom of Yisra'el was divided after the death of King Solomon into the Northern House of Yisra'el and the Southern House of Judah.

When Messiah came the first time, He came to bring salvation to the House of Judah, and then He sent His disciples out among the nations to show the path of salvation to the lost House of Yisra'el, so at His return He can restore the two houses back into one (Ezekiel 37:15-28).

In Romans 7:2-4, Paul explains how YHWH can bring Yisra'el back to His Household despite their adultery, i.e., the death of Messiah. The Torah in Deuteronomy 24:1-4 that "bound" Yisra'el into condemnation because of her adultery was "put to death" in Messiah, so that Yisra'el could be remarried (renewed in covenant) with YHWH, who was alive evermore in the resurrected Yahushua! Praise Yah!

| | |
|---|---|
| **Rom 7:5** | For when we **were in the flesh**, the passions of sins, through the Torah, were working in our members to bear fruit to death. |
| **Rom 7:6** | But now we have been released from the Torah, having died to what we were held by, so that we should serve in newness of Spirit and not in oldness of letter. |

The phrase "were in the flesh" here refers to the time before we believed in Messiah.

| | |
|---|---|
| **Passions:** | stg's **#G3804** - "pathema", meaning, something undergone, as in the hardship of pain (also emotion or influence); from a word meaning, to experience a sensation (feeling, passion) or impression (hurt or suffering). Refers here in context to the influence or desire of our flesh. |

179

The next phrase, "which were by the law" in Greek actually reads:

$$\tau\alpha \ \delta\iota\alpha \ \tau\text{ou}$$

Both "τα" and "του" (**G5120**) are related to other Greek forms that refer to the definitive article "the", which is sometimes translated into the English and sometimes it is omitted. The "του" does however; suggest a masculine possessive, i.e., "his".

> **By:** stg's #**G1223** - "dia", meaning the channel of an act; refers to where or how something took or takes place, i.e., through.

So, verse 5 could be understood in two ways:

1. The sufferings of sin, which were through the law.
2. The passions of sins, through the law.

Paul is telling us that before we were saved by Messiah (in the flesh) the sinful passions of our flesh led us into behavior that brought us under the condemnation of death, because of what the Torah says.

Basically, Paul is saying that our fleshly nature desires to do the opposite of what the Torah requires of us, and he's going to say it again in 8:7.

**Remember**, Paul has already warned us not to let our rebellious flesh have rule over us to obey it (6:12-13) and neither are we to allow our members (heart, mind, and body parts) to be tools of our rebellious flesh to cause us to live in disobedience (sinfully).

Contextually, Paul is saying, when we were not desiring to serve YHWH, our sinful desires caused a schism in our relationship with Him, because of our disobedience, and it was the Torah that gave sin the authority to condemn us to death.

**"BUT NOW...",** This little phrase is one of my favorites in the Scripture because it denotes that a change has taken place. Before we lived "in the flesh" not desiring to please YHWH, **BUT NOW,** "having obeyed from the heart that form of doctrine" (6:17) by which we were saved, through belief in Yahushua Messiah, He has delivered us from the condemnation of the Torah, thereby making us dead to the penalty that held us captive and the fleshly desires that captured us.

180

In Yahushua, we are to serve (obey) "the Torah of Elohim" (7:25) in our spirit man and have no trust in the letter of the law alone! The phrases "in the flesh" and "in the spirit" are going to be introduced here by Paul, because he is about to explain our part in overcoming our rebellious flesh. He is going to discuss how the "Two Parts" of man are at work in believers (i.e., the spirit man who has been redeemed and the physical man who is awaiting the "redemption of the body" [Romans 8:23]).

To fully understand the way Paul uses this language we must understand his use of synonymous phrases.

**Ex**: In the flesh:

1. Servant of sin (6:16)
2. Servant of uncleanness and lawlessness (6:19)

(Both of which lead to death[6:16, 23 and 8:13])

In the spirit:

1. Servant of obedience (6:16)
2. Servant of righteousness (6:18)
3. Servant of Elohim (6:22)

(All of which lead to righteousness [v. 16], holiness [v. 19] and in the end to everlasting life [v. 22] in Yahushua Messiah)

Before we continue, I want to give you a sign to look for to know whether you are in the flesh or in the spirit.

1. In the flesh:   does not subject itself to the law. (Torah - Romans 8:7)
2. In the spirit:   is working in you both to will and to do YHWH's good pleasure (Philippians 2:13), also **walks** in the spirit (Galatians 5:25) by obeying the Torah, which itself is holy, just, good, and spiritual (Romans 7:12, 14)

You can know whether you're in the spirit by examining your heart, do you desire to do the things YHWH has commanded us to do (obey the Torah)? If you truly desire to live in a way that pleases Him, more than doing your own sinful pleasures, then that's a good sign you are living "in the spirit", even amidst your struggles.

I want to make sure we clearly understand that the discussion between being "in the flesh" and "in the spirit" is a discussion based on two contrasting points of view. To be "in the flesh" is to behave in a manner that is controlled by the lust of our desires/flesh and our five senses, despite what the Scripture says.

To be "in the spirit" is to behave in a manner that is controlled by our desire to obey and serve YHWH according to His Word/Torah, despite how we feel or what we think to be true.

It is important to know, in the latter part of Romans 7 and most of chapter 8, the word spirit should not be capitalized, as if referring to the Spirit of YHWH, but is a reference to our personal inner-spirit-man.

***

**Rom 7:7**        What, then, shall we say? Is the Torah sin? Let it not be! However, I did not know sin except through the Torah. For also the covetousness I knew not if the Torah had not said, **"You shall not covet."**

Paul is asking whether the "letter of the Torah" is itself sinful. His answer, of course, is **ABSOLUTELY NOT!** The opposite is true in fact (1 John 3:4). Paul is adamant that it was and is the Torah that defines what sin is and what the penalty is for sinning.

Paul is telling us that he did not know what "sin" was until after he knew what the Torah said. He didn't know that lust was sin until the Torah told him he was not to covet.

None of us knew the price of disobeying the Torah was death until the Scripture said, "that the man that sins shall die".

Paul here is restating concepts that he had already discussed in Romans 3:20; 5:13 and 20, which are, it is through the Torah we came to understand the definition of sin and the consequences of committing it, Torah became our schoolmaster teaching us our need for Messiah (Gal 3:22-25).

**Rom 7:8**        But sin, having taken the occasion through the command, did work in me all *sorts of* covetousness. For apart from Torah sin is dead.

**Sorts of covetousness**: stg's **#G1939** - "epithumia", meaning, a longing; from two words meaning,

182

superimposition and passion refers to our fleshly desires causing us to "set our hearts" towards sin. (The word concupiscence is used here in the (KJV)

**Dead**: stg's #G3498 - "nekros", meaning, dead (in both literal and figurative sense). Refers here to sins lack of life in us before we knew the law.

First off, Paul is letting us know that our rebellious flesh is a treacherous enemy and when it heard what the Torah said, it caused us to desire the things the Torah condemned.

It's kind of like a child, he might not ever want something until you tell him he cannot have it, then it is all he can think about.

The last part of this passage has confused people to no end, it simply refers to our lack of knowledge of both what sin is and what the consequences of sin are. **Remember**, Paul's teachings, as well as that of all Scripture, is about knowledge.

Before we knew Yahushua, we were in a sense "in the flesh" in both our spiritual man and our physical man, and so our whole heart and mind was only evil continually (Genesis 6:5; Jeremiah 17:9; Ecclesiastes 9:3).

However, part of the Renewed Covenant promise was that YHWH would put within us "a new heart and a new spirit", and then put "His spirit in us to cause us to obey His law" (Ezekiel 36:26-27) because He was going to write His Torah on our hearts and place it in our inner parts (inner-spirit-man - Romans 7:22; and read Jeremiah 31:31-33).

Here in Romans 7:8, Paul is personifying our fleshly desire, giving it willful intelligence, by saying that it made use of the Torah to cause us to desire sinfulness. He will go on later to show that within the believer there are two minds, one of the flesh, which is in our members (physical body), and one of the spirit (8:5-6).

We will cover this thoroughly when we get there, but it's important to see that within us is a dangerous enemy and for that reason the Torah was given, to help us understand it.

**Rom 7:9**     And I was alive apart from the Torah once, but when the command came, the sin revived, and I died.

183

Some teachers will tell you that before the Torah was given at Mt. Sinai, men were not subject to the death penalty, however, that is a direct contradiction of Paul's own words in chapter 5:14.

We must remember, the Torah is about knowledge, and so, when Paul said he was alive once without the law, he is saying, in his knowledge he was alive (not condemned to die) but when he heard the Torah, the knowledge of his sinful state became known to him, and he understood that he was **under** the sentence of death.

| | |
|---|---|
| **Rom 7:10** | And the command which was to result in life, this I found to result in death. |
| **Rom 7:11** | For sin, having taken the occasion through the command, deceived me, and through it killed *me*. |

The Scripture says, if we obey the Torah we shall live (Leviticus 18:5), however, once we knew what it said our sinful flesh caused us to desire to disobey it and through our disobedience our flesh condemned us to death.

It is key here to see that if we think or believe that we don't have to obey the Torah it's our flesh convincing us we don't have to, because it doesn't want to (Romans 8:7) and men have "constructed" doctrines to fit our desires and not the truth (2 Timothy 3:1-7; 4:1-4).

| | |
|---|---|
| **Rom 7:12** | So that the Torah truly is set-apart, and the command **set-apart, and righteous, and good.** |
| **Rom 7:13** | Therefore, has that which is good become death to me? Let it not be! But the sin, **that sin might be manifest**, was working death in me through what is good, **so that sin through the command might become an exceedingly great sinner**. |

If the Torah is holy and the commandment holy, just, and good, as Paul says it is, would not a person commanded to live a holy, righteous (just) and good life be expected to obey the Torah?

Of course, the answer is **YES**, however, as Peter said (2 Peter 3:14-17), lawless men have twisted Paul's writings upside down to make them mean something Paul did not intend them to mean.

Paul asked again, whether there is something wrong with the Torah, and his answer is the same, **ABSOLUTELY NOT!** It was to show us we have a vile, rebellious flesh which is attempting to destroy us by making us desire the very things that YHWH despises.

We need to get it through our heads that somewhere inside of us is the worst kind of sinner and that sinner wants nothing more than to destroy us.

The word "sinful" is used here in verse 7 of many modern Bible versions, however, the Greek word here is "hamartolus", and it refers to a personage, i.e., a sinful person.

In Messiah, we, our inner being, is no longer a sinner, however, within us, in our bodies, is an exceedingly great sinner, our flesh. The determining factor of our eventual reward rests in who we allow to control us; flesh unto death or spirit unto righteousness and eternal life (Romans 6:16-22).

| | |
|---|---|
| **Rom 7:14** | For we know that **the Torah is Spiritual**, but I am fleshly, sold under sin. |
| **Rom 7:15** | For what I work, I know not. For what I wish, that I do not practise, but what I hate, that I do. |
| **Rom 7:16** | But if I do what I do not wish, I agree with the Torah that it is good. |

If the Torah is spiritual, would not the spiritual man live by it? Once again, of course, our answer to that is a resounding **YES,** however, and unfortunately, many modern teachers would say no, or they, as men, would pick and choose which of the commandments apply today, as if they had that authority. Something not even Messiah did (Matthew 5:17-19).

Paul recognizes that our fleshly bodies are sold out to our rebellious fleshly desires (v. 25) and so it is contrary to the Torah. Therefore, no matter how hard he (Paul) attempts to do what the Torah requires, his fleshly desires continually pressure him to do what is improper.

This battle within us proves to us that the Torah is good, but we (our bodies) are corrupt.

| | |
|---|---|
| **Rom 7:17** | And now, it is no longer I that work it, but the sin dwelling in me. |
| **Rom 7:18** | For I know that in me, that is in my flesh, dwells no good. **For to wish is present with me, but to work the good I do not find.** |
| **Rom 7:19** | For the good that I wish to do, I do not do; but the evil I do not wish to do, this I practise. |

185

| Rom 7:20 | And if I do that which I do not wish, it is no longer I who work it, but the sin dwelling in me. |
| Rom 7:21 | I find therefore this law, **that when I wish to do the good, that the evil is present with me.** |

Notice, Paul is always referring to himself (i.e., I, my, me, etc.) saying that in **him** is a law that when **he** is intent on doing what is right, within **him** lies an evil flesh that strives against **his** good desires.

Any "Religious Person", and there are many, who tells you they have not experienced this in their own life is almost certainly lying to you or have never actually been born again. This is the natural experience of a newborn believer, and Paul is attempting to assure new believers of this because he suffers it himself, and to explain why they shouldn't allow this to discourage them.

He is going to show us how we remain "in Messiah" though we have struggles against this rebellious flesh. Before we move on though, you need to read the article on the "Two parts", if you haven't (See: Sec 1, Ch. 4 - The *Two-Part Principle* on Pg. 25).

To summarize, all men are of two parts, one part is spiritual given to us by YHWH when He breathed into the nostrils of Adam, and the other part is physical and comes from the dust of the ground from which YHWH molded Adam. It took these two, the spiritual breath plus the physical form, for the man to become a living creature.

Adam's sin contaminated both the spiritual and the physical sides of man and brought the curse of death upon him. Through belief in Yahushua Messiah, the spiritual side, the inner man, has been born again, however, the physical side, the outer man (our flesh), is still condemned to die until the redemption of this body (Romans 8:25) at the resurrection.

Starting here in verse twenty-two, Paul is going to teach this *Two-Part Principle* and how we are to live in Messiah.

| Rom 7:22 | For **I delight in the Torah of Elohim according to the inward man,** |
| Rom 7:23 | but I see another **torah in my members,** battling against the torah of my mind, and bringing me into captivity to the torah of sin which is in my members. |

As a believer, Paul delights in the Torah of YHWH, why? Modern teachers would have us believe that our belief in Yahushua

Messiah exempts us from having to obey the Torah and if you tell them otherwise, they have no delight in it.

According to the Renewed Covenant, the Torah of YHWH has been written on the hearts of every believer and placed within them, even Christians (Jeremiah 31:31-32).

The promise of the Spirit of YHWH, to reside within the "new covenant" believer, says His Spirit would **"CAUSE"** us to walk in His laws and statutes.

But, within Paul's physical body is a great sinner, known as his flesh, and it battles against Paul's attempt to obey the Torah and causes him to desire and do disobedience.

It is important to see the contrast here and how Paul uses synonymous phrases. Here he contrasts his inner man, that delights to do the Torah, with his members (physical body), that wants to bring him into captivity to sin.

He also uses the phrase "torah of my mind" as a synonym for his inner man stating that it, his spiritual mind, is in battle against his physical body (Galatians 5:16-18).

> **Rom 7:24** Wretched man that I am! Who shall deliver me from this body of death?

Paul, the believer, is pressured by his body (physical man) to behave in disobedience, and asks how he can be delivered from this body, which is trying to kill him?

How many of us truly desire to live lives pleasing to YHWH, yet are continually burdened by those strong desires to do the contrary? Sure, in time we can and will get stronger, but initially it's a tremendous battle. How do we survive it?

> **Rom 7:25** Thanks to Elohim, through יהושע Messiah our Master! So then, **with the mind I myself truly serve the Torah of Elohim**, but with the flesh the torah of sin.

His answer is simple, but it reflects the first stage of a process that eventually leads either to the Kingdom of Messiah or to the Lake of Fire. We overcome this treacherous body by belief in Yahushua Messiah, however, there's more.

There are two things going on in believers every day; one of the spirits and one of the flesh. The spirit-man **sets his heart, mind and strength** towards obeying the Torah, even while his old rebellious flesh continues to try to turn his heart away from YHWH to follow its own passions.

**LISTEN!!!...** Satan is our enemy, and he is a powerful enemy, but he cannot make you do anything against your own will. He can only tempt your flesh to do things and your flesh is more than willing to obey him.

Your greatest enemy, **BAR NONE**, is your own sinful desires, your own flesh. Your flesh can, all by itself, influence you to turn away from the truth of YHWH if you are not diligently seeking Him out and striving to serve Him day in and day out.

Even as believers in Yahushua Messiah this is true, so, through our belief in Yahushua Messiah we strive diligently to know and to obey (serve) the Torah of YHWH, just as He says to, without adding to it or taking anything away from it. We serve Him as He commands us, not how men have taught us (read very carefully-Isaiah 9:13-21).

It is a requirement for us, our calling, to walk in obedience to the Torah even though our body/flesh is striving to serve sin.

**REMEMBER,** there are no chapter and verse headings in either the Hebrew or the Greek text, these were added by men. Paul's discussion in chapter 7 flows directly into Chapter 8.

# Chapter 6: Romans 8

Most English Bibles capitalize the word "spirit" here when it shouldn't be. The Spirit of YHWH doesn't enter this discourse until verse 9.

The previous discussion in chapter 7:22-25 concerned our inner-spirit-man that was renewed by belief in Yahushua Messiah (Ephesians 3:14-16; 4:20-24; Philippians 3:3; 2 Timothy 4:22; Philemon 25). In our belief, Paul says he serves the Torah of YHWH (Romans 1:9), but the outer-fleshly-man (the body) continues to serve its own rebellious passions.

The spirit man lives in obedience (6:16) through the righteousness of Torah (Deuteronomy 6:24-25; Romans 7:22, 25), while the fleshly man lives in disobedience (Romans 6:16; 7:23-25), which leads to death. These two principles never...ever change.

Obedient men live righteous lives that set them apart from all other men, which culminates in everlasting life, because of their belief in Yahushua Messiah (Romans 6).

Disobedient men, however, live unrighteous, sinful lives that lead to death. We all reap what we sow (Galatians 6:7-8).

Knowing this, we see in Romans 8:1-2 that Paul is expressing the same rule, those who walk according to the spirit man, which seeks to obey the Torah of YHWH (7:25), shall reap eternal life from the Spirit of YHWH (8: 2, 13), but if we walk according to the fleshly man we shall die (6:16; 8:2, 13).

Don't be fooled by sweet words of man-made doctrine that guarantee you eternal salvation by belief alone, without a heart committed to obeying the Torah of YHWH. Consider:

| | |
|---|---|
| **Joh 15:1** | "I am the true vine, and My Father is the gardener. |
| **Joh 15:2** | "Every branch in Me that **bears no fruit He takes away**. And every branch that bears fruit He prunes, so that it bears more fruit. |
| **Joh 15:3** | "You are already clean because of the Word which I have spoken to you. |
| **Joh 15:4** | "Stay in Me, and I *stay* in you. As the branch is unable to bear fruit of itself, unless it stays in the vine, so neither you, unless you stay in Me. |
| **Joh 15:5** | "I am the vine, you are the branches. He who stays in Me, and I in him, he bears much fruit. |

| | Because without Me you are able to do naught! |
|---|---|
| Joh 15:6 | **"If anyone does not stay in Me, he is thrown away as a branch and dries up. And they gather them and throw them into the fire, and they are burned.** |
| Joh 15:7 | "If you stay in Me, and My Words stay in you, you shall ask whatever you wish, and it shall be done for you. |

Do you hear what Yahushua our Master (The Word) is saying? The phrase "in me" refers to us being a branch of the Vine (a believer).

Any branch (believer) that **does not bear fruit is "TAKEN AWAY"** from the Vine by the Father. However, every branch (believer) that **does bear fruit** is pruned by the Father so that it can bear more fruit.

| Prunes: | stg's #G2508 - "kathairo", meaning, to cleanse; from a word meaning, clean. Refers to the act of cleansing the branch so that it can produce more (the word "clean" in verse 3 is a root word of kathairo, i.e., G2513 - "katharos"). |
|---|---|

Before we go further, let's determine what the Master means by bearing fruit. Fruit of what?

Many people want to say that we are to bear the "fruit of the Spirit" mentioned in Galatians 5:22-23 (i.e., love, joy, peace, long-suffering, gentleness, goodness, faith, meekness, temperance), however, these are the fruits of the Spirit that YHWH bears in us when we "walk in the spirit" (Gal 5:25) or do the work of the spirit in our daily lives, through the leading of the Spirit of YHWH.

Messiah, in John 15, is referring to the fruit that we believers bear unto Him **AFTER** we have believed in Him, let's let the context of John 14 and 15 give us the answer to the question, fruit of what?

| Joh 14:6 | יהושע said to him, "I am the Way, and the Truth, and the Life. No one comes to the Father except through Me. |
|---|---|

Yahushua Messiah Is the "Word" by which we were originally "cleansed" or made right from our sins (John 15:3; Romans 6:17). Our belief in the "Good News" of His death, burial, and resurrection (1 Corinthians 15:1-4) cleanses us from all sin (1 John 1:7) both at our first confession (Romans 10:9-10) and throughout our life after salvation (1 John 1:9).

Yahushua was talking to His disciples in John 14 and 15, so when He made the following statement in 14:6 He was referring to them and He then followed it up with this.

| | |
|---|---|
| **Joh 14:10** | "Do you not believe that I am in the Father, and the Father is in Me? The words that I speak to you I do not speak from Myself. But the Father who stays in Me does His works. |
| **Joh 14:11** | "Believe Me that I am in the Father and the Father in Me, otherwise believe Me because of the works themselves. |

| | |
|---|---|
| **Note**: | The "works" Messiah is referring to here are all His works, not just those miracles that He accomplished. It includes the works of righteous living and love that made Him the "spotless Lamb" who would take away the sins of the world (Hebrews 9:14; John 1:29). |

| | |
|---|---|
| **Joh 14:12** | "Truly, truly, I say to you, he who believes in Me, the works that I do he shall do also. And greater *works* than these he shall do, because I go to My Father. |
| **Joh 14:13** | "And whatever you ask in My Name, that I shall do, in order that the Father might be esteemed in the Son. |

We are to do all the works of Messiah and even greater works.

| | |
|---|---|
| **Joh 14:15** | "If you love Me, you shall guard My commands. |
| **Joh 14:16** | "And I shall ask the Father, and He shall give you another Helper, to stay with you forever – |
| **Joh 14:17** | the Spirit of the Truth, whom the world is unable to receive, because it does not see Him or know Him. But you know Him, for He stays with you and shall be in you. |

191

We are to do the works Yahushua did and obey His commandments, He then will give us the "Spirit of Truth" that will "teach us all things" (v. 26), who will testify of Messiah (15:26) and who will "guide us into all truth" (16:7-14).

Compare John 14:6, 17:17 and Psalms 119:142. Also, review the promise of the Spirit in Ezekiel 36: 27-28, which declares that the Spirit of YHWH would "**cause us to obey** His laws and right rulings".

| | |
|---|---|
| **Joh 14:21** | "He who **possesses My commands and guards them**, it is he who loves Me. And he who loves Me shall be loved by My Father, and I shall love him and manifest Myself to him." |

***

| | |
|---|---|
| **Joh 14:23** | יהושע answered him, "If anyone loves Me, he shall **guard My Word**. And My Father shall love him, and We shall come to him and make Our stay with him. |
| **Joh 14:24** | "He who does not love Me **does not guard My Words**. And the Word which you hear is not Mine but of the Father Who sent Me. |

We must do His works and obey His commandments, if so He and the Father will make their abode within us.

| | |
|---|---|
| **Stay**: | stg's **#G3438** - "mone", meaning, a staying; from #G3306 - "meno", meaning, to stay. Refers to the Father and Son staying or abiding (G3306) with us, in us (v. 17). This word is the active tense of the word abide in chapter 15. The word stay here is translated as abode in the (KJV). |

Again, **obeying and doing** is the prerequisite for having the Father and the Messiah dwelling in us. And the thing Messiah is telling us to obey and do, are the words of the Father spoken beforehand (Ephesians 2:10), not something new. Verse 24 is the fulfillment of Deuteronomy 18:15-19.

John 15:1-10 is saying the exact same thing that John 14 is saying, only in a slightly different way, which is a typical Hebrew teaching style.

The fruit we are to bear in 15:1-7 is the fruit of obedience unto righteousness (Deuteronomy 6:24-25; Romans 6:16, 22 and carefully compare John 14:6, 15 to Romans 6: 16-17, 22).

In John 15 Yahushua is saying that any believer who does not bear the fruit of obedience is "**TAKEN AWAY**" by the Father (v. 2) and withers up to be cast into the Lake of Fire, eternal judgment (compare v. 6 to Hebrews 6:4-8 and 10:26-31).

He also states, however, that **if** we abide in Him, by obeying the commandments (14:15 and 15:10) **then** He and the Father will abide in us (14:23), which is the only way for us to really bear the fruit of obedience unto righteousness. Why?

Because our flesh does not wish to obey (Romans 7:14-25 and 8:7) but, if we remain in Messiah, by belief, and produce the fruit of obedience (to Torah) then the Father will "prune" (cleanse) us from all sinful mistakes that we do in our salvation, when we confess them (1 John 1:9).

Obedience to the Torah is REQUIRED, post-salvation, **through** belief, as proof of our belief (James 2:14-26), for the Torah is the tester of the thoughts and intents of our heart (Hebrews 4:12).

A heart committed to obedience sets us apart (makes us holy) unto YHWH because of our belief in Yahushua and allows us to receive whatever we ask of Him (John 14:13-14; 15:7; 1 John 3:20-24) and ends with our receiving eternal life (Romans 6:22).

If our lack of obedience proves that we do not have the heart condition of a son, who bears fruit unto righteousness and holiness, then we will be cast into the fire (John 15:6; Hebrews 6:4-8; 10:26-31).

This is Yahushua Himself warning us to "stay" in Him by "obeying" the Word/Torah which His Father gave Him, which He in turn has given us. The question then is, does what we've seen in John 15 concur with what Paul is saying in Romans 8?

Again, Paul says that with his inner-man (spirit mind) he serves the Torah of YHWH (Romans 1:9; 7:22, 25), now, Romans 8:1-8.

| | |
|---|---|
| **Rom 8:1** | There is, then, now no condemnation to those who are in Messiah יהושע, **who do not walk according to the flesh**, but according to the Spirit. |
| **Rom 8:2** | For the torah of the Spirit of the life in Messiah יהושע has set me free from the torah of sin and of death. |
| **Rom 8:3** | For the Torah being powerless, **in that it was weak through the flesh**, Elohim, having sent His own Son in the likeness of flesh of sin, |

| | |
|---|---|
| | and concerning sin, **condemned sin in the flesh,** |
| Rom 8:4 | so that the **righteousness of the Torah should be completed in us who** do not walk according to the flesh but **according to the Spirit.** |
| Rom 8:5 | For those who live according to the flesh set their minds on the *matters* of the flesh, but those *who live* according to the Spirit, the *matters* of the Spirit. |
| Rom 8:6 | **For the mind of the flesh is death,** but the mind of the Spirit is life and peace. |
| Rom 8:7 | **Because the mind of the flesh is enmity towards Elohim, for it does not subject itself to the Torah of Elohim,** neither indeed is it able, |
| Rom 8:8 | **and those who are in the flesh are unable to please Elohim.** |

There is so much stuff in this passage that an entire book could be written on it alone. First, we need to examine the context to determine again what Paul means by, in the flesh and in the spirit.

> **Note:** The Torah of YHWH is holy, just and good (7:12), it is also spiritual (7:14) and Paul delights in it with all his "inner-man" (7:22) as he serves YHWH with his spirit (1:9) by serving (obeying) the Torah of YHWH with his mind (7:25).

Now this might seem overly simple, but the true "Good News" is really that simple. The holy (set apart), righteous (just), good and spiritual man who would serve YHWH in his spirit, does so by delighting in and giving service (obedience) to the Torah of YHWH, which is itself holy, righteous, good and spiritual.

Any doctrine that says a man in Messiah can be spiritual, who does not obey the Torah, is a false doctrine, with no light (Isaiah 8:20).

Furthermore, those doing and teaching such, will not endure to the end (Revelation 14:12) and will, if they make it, be least in the Kingdom of YHWH (Matthew 5:17-19).

There is some debate about the meaning of this phrase in Matthew 5:19 which says, "shall be least in the kingdom". Some believe that even though these teachers do not keep the Torah themselves and neither do they teach other people to keep it, that in their ignorance they might still get into the kingdom but will be "the least" of those who inherit.

The problem with this idea is that there are numerous examples in both the Tanak and the Messianic Writings that seem to clearly teach that without obedience to the Torah there is no inheritance, and that ignorance is not an excuse.

Others look to passages that say things like the smoke of their torture (Lake of Fire) will be rising forever and ever (Revelation 14:11), suggesting that this smoke will be visible in the kingdom because of what Daniel 7:10-11 says concerning the "stream of fire" going forth from the Presence, and the beast being cast into it.

What's interesting here, is that the very next verse in Revelation 14 (12), right after it talks about the smoke of this torture rising forever, it talks about those who have endurance, as the ones that believe in Yahushua Messiah and keep the commandments (Torah)].

Let us now see a list of things that Paul says here in Romans about "the flesh" and compare it to a list of what he says concerning "the spirit".

**IN THE FLESH**       (serving sin/disobedience - 6:16)

| | |
|---|---|
| uses the commandment to kill us | 7:8-11 |
| Is an exceedingly great sinner | 7:13 |
| nothing good dwells in it | 7:18 |
| is evil | 7:21 |
| wars against us | 7:23 – |
| | (Galatians 5:17) |
| brings us into captivity to sin | 7:23 |
| serves the law of sin | 7:25 |
| focuses its mind on fleshly things | 8:5 |
| brings us into death | 8:6 - (Rom 6:16, 23; 8:13) |
| is an enemy of YHWH | 8:7 |
| does not submit to the Torah | 8:7 |
| cannot submit to the Torah | 8:7 |
| does not please YHWH | 8:8 |

**IN THE SPIRIT**     (serves obedience - 6:16)

| | |
|---|---|
| wills to do good | 7:15-21 |
| agrees that the Torah is good | 7:16 - (12, 14) |

| | |
|---|---|
| delights in the Torah | 7:22 |
| wars against the flesh | 7:23 |
| serves the Torah of YHWH | 7:25 |
| keeps us from condemnation | 8:1 |
| gives us life in Yahushua | 8:2 |
| fulfills the righteousness of Torah | 8:4 |
| focuses its mind on spiritual things | 8:5 - (7:14) |
| is life and peace* | 8:6 - (comp. Pro 3:1-2) |
| is an ally of YHWH | 8:7 |
| submits to the Torah | 8:7 |
| Pleases YHWH | 8:8 |
| puts to death the deeds of the flesh | 8:13 |

[*contrasted against the flesh which brings cursing and death*]

Seeing this comparison and remembering what has been said in Romans 8:1; John 15:6; Hebrews 6:4-8; 10:26-31, etc., we see that after we believe in Yahushua Messiah and have been made right again from the condemnation of death (Romans 6:3-7) that held us (7:6) because of past sins (Romans 3:24-25) we are to stop living to satisfy our rebellious flesh or it will kill us (6:16; 8:13) again (Galatians 2:17-19) bringing us back into condemnation (8:1).

But some might ask, "Once I'm saved, I can't lose my salvation, can I?" If by "lose it", you mean accidentally dropping it somewhere without knowing it? Then no! However, if by "lose it", you mean having a hard heart of rebellion against the Torah? Then yes!

| | |
|---|---|
| **Heb 3:12** | Look out, brothers, lest there be in any of you a **wicked heart of unbelief in falling away from the living Elohim,** |
| **Heb 3:13** | but encourage one another daily, while it is called "Today," lest any of you be **hardened by the deceivableness of sin.** |
| **Heb 3:14** | For we have become partakers of Messiah **if we hold fast** the beginning of our trust firm to the end, |
| **Heb 3:15** | while it is said, **"Today, if you hear His voice, do not harden your hearts as in the rebellion."** |

| Heb 3:16 | For who, having heard, rebelled? Was it not all who came out of Mitsrayim, led by Mosheh? |
| Heb 3:17 | And with whom was He grieved forty years? Was it not with those who sinned, whose corpses fell in the wilderness? |
| Heb 3:18 | And to whom did He swear that they would not enter into His rest, **but to those who did not obey?** |
| Heb 3:19 | So we see that **they were unable to enter in because of unbelief**. |

**Unbelief** (vs. 12, 19): stg's **#G570** - "apistea", meaning, faithlessness or disbelief; from two words meaning, not and convinced. Refers to a state of doubtfulness or lack of trust.

**Deceivableness:** stg's **#G539**- "apate", meaning, delusion; from a word meaning, to cheat. Refers to the trickery of our flesh in desiring what is forbidden (Romans 7:7-21) and convincing us that it is okay. The word "deceivableness" here is translated as deceitfulness in the (KJV).

**Trust:** stg's **#G5287** - "hupostasis", meaning, a setting under; from two words meaning, under and to stand. Refers to what supports us, i.e., our trust in Yahushua. The word trust here is translated as "confidence" in the (KJV).

[v. 14 - **if we hold on firmly** to the beginning of our trust (Yahushua) to the end.]

**Rebellion:** stg's **#G3894** - "parapikraino" (parapikrasmos), meaning, to come bitter alongside; from two words meaning, near and to be bitter. This word is translated as "provocation" in the (KJV)

Verse 15 is a quote from Psalms 95:7-8, where the word in Hebrew is "meriybah" (#H4808), meaning, quarrel; from a word meaning, to toss or grapple.

The Hebrew word "meriybah" refers to the waters of strife in Exodus 17, when Yisra'el murmured and complained against Moses, because of the bitter waters.

The author of Hebrews is using this passage on complaining to show our heart condition, which acts contrary to the will of YHWH by NOT trusting in Him enough to do as He says without complaint. This heart condition (attitude) provokes YHWH to act against those who have it.

| | |
|---|---|
| **Was it not** (v 16): | stg's **#G235** - "alla", meaning, other things or counter wise (and, but [even], indeed, nevertheless, etc.); From a word meaning, else or different. This phrase is translated as "howbeit" in the (KJV). |

[vs. 16b - **but** not everyone who came out of Egypt with Moses...]

| | |
|---|---|
| **Did not obey** (v 18): | stg's **#G544** - "apeitheo", meaning, to disbelieve (willfully and perversely); from two words meaning, no and to convince or not be convinced. This phrase is translated as "believe not" in the (KJV). |

Though the Greek word "apeitheo" is usually translated as "unbelief" in this and other passages by modern Christian translators, the Greek words "apeitheia" (G543), "apeitheo" (G544) and "apeithes" (G545) are all translated as disobedient or disobedience in:

1.   G543 -  Ephesians 2:2; 5:6; Colossians 3:6
2.   G544 -  Romans 10:21; 1 Peter 2:7-8; 3:20
3.   G545 -  Luke 1:17; acts 26:19; Romans 1:30; 2 Timothy 3:2 and Titus 1:16; 3:3

They are words that can mean either not believing or not obedient depending on the context. So, what is the author of Hebrews trying to tell us?

He gives us a warning in verse 12, specifically calling to the "brethren", so we know it's for believers. He warns us about having an "evil heart of unbelief", but are we not all believers?

The author is trying to warn us that it is still possible, after we've been saved, to later develop an evil (hard) heart of unbelief that will cause us to depart from the living Elohim. He is not casting us away; rather we choose to depart from Him (Hebrews 6:4-8).

He warns us not to allow our flesh to delude or trick us into hardening our hearts against the things of YHWH, specifically His Torah (Romans 7:7-11). He says that we are partakers (sharers) of Messiah, as coheirs (Romans 8:16-17), **"IF"**; ← this "IF" denote that there is a condition set in place to determine whether we become coheirs with Him or not.

There was no condition set for being saved (justified from death) by Him (John 3:16) it was a free gift (Ephesians 2:8-9), however, there is a condition associated to our coheirship in Him in the "rest" (Romans 8:11), or the Kingdom.

This is seen clearly in the Tanak, where the promise to Abram (later, Abraham) and his Seed, meaning Messiah (Genesis 12:1-4, 7; Galatians 3:16) was unconditional, being based solely on Abram's belief (Genesis 15:6). So, the unconditional promise of inheritance of the Land/Kingdom, which Joshua did not bring Yisra'el into (Heb 4), was promised ONLY to Abram and Messiah, no one else.

Then we see Abraham's descendants, specifically the Children of Abraham, Isaac (Yitschaq) and Jacob (Ya'aqob), i.e., Yisra'el, delivered from death by the Passover Lamb (Messiah), delivered from bondage in Egypt and the authority of Pharaoh by the death of Pharaoh's firstborn son (Messiah), baptized in the Red Sea, given the 'Living Waters' (token of the Spirit) at Mt. Horeb and standing at the foot of Mt. Sinai awaiting YHWH's voice.

| | |
|---|---|
| **Exo 19:3** | And Mosheh went up to Elohim, and יהוה called to him from the mountain, saying, "This is what you are to say to the house of Yaʻaqob̠, and declare to the children of Yisra'ĕl: |
| **Exo 19:4** | 'You have seen what I did to the Mitsrites, and how I bore you on eagles' wings and brought you to Myself. |
| **Exo 19:5** | 'And now, **IF you DILIGENTLY obey My voice, AND shall guard My covenant, THEN** you shall be My treasured possession |

|              | above all the peoples – for all the earth is Mine – |
|--------------|----------------------------------------------------|
| **Exo 19:6** | 'and you shall be to Me a reign of priests and a set-apart nation.' Those are the words which you are to speak to the children of Yisra'ĕl." |
| **Exo 19:7** | And Mosheh came and called for the elders of the people, and set before them all these words which יהוה commanded him. |
| **Exo 19:8** | And all the people answered together and said, **"All that יהוה has spoken we shall do."** So Mosheh brought back the words of the people to יהוי. |

Now, Mosheh is a forerunner or shadow picture of Messiah, who came from the Father with a message to His people concerning the "Kingdom of Heaven", the Messianic Kingdom.

To gain access to this kingdom, His people, Yisra'el, first had to "repent", meaning that they had to turn away from their old life, and 'return' to YHWH, the Elohim of their fathers (Belief), secondly, they had to serve Him through obedience to His Torah (Works), Two-Parts, spiritual (Belief) and physical (Works).

Notice that this covenant is conditional, "IF you DILIGENTLY obey my voice (works) AND guard my covenant (belief), THEN…". Also, in another place (Deuteronomy 9:4-5), YHWH tells Yisra'el that He did not deliver them from Egypt because they were bigger or more righteous than any other nation, but He delivered them because of the evil of the nations and to "establish the word" He had sworn to the fathers, and because He loved their fathers (Deuteronomy 4:37).

When YHWH spoke to them, saying that He had brought them out to give them the land, He also commanded them "to **do** all these laws, to **fear** יהוי our Elohim, for **our good always**, to **keep us alive**, as it is today" and that it was our righteousness when "we **guard to do ALL** this command" before YHWH our Elohim (Deuteronomy 6:23-25).

It is important to understand that the unconditional part of the covenant is deliverance from sin and death through belief in Messiah. By believing in Him we get access to His inheritance IF we walk in the righteousness that YHWH requires for all His people. Justification from death is FREE, i.e., a gift (Ephesians 2:8-9), but our final inheritance is conditional upon our submission to His Torah.

200

The Torah does not and cannot 'save' us, but it is the Path of Salvation that all Believers are to 'live by' because it teaches us the "Way" of Inheritance.

So then, what must we do to be partakers of this rest (inheritance)? We must hold on firmly to the beginning of our belief (trusting only in the Good News of Yahushua Messiah) with a pure heart (of obedience) without turning or wavering to the end (Revelation 14:12).

> **Mat 24:13**  "But he who shall have endured to the end **shall be** saved.

Future tense! There is a salvation still to come.

> **Rom 13:11**  And *do* this, knowing the time, that it is already the hour for us to wake up from sleep, for now our deliverance **is nearer than when we did believe.**

Wasn't our salvation complete when we believed? **NO**, it began a process! Just being delivered from bondage in Egypt did not guarantee that generation of Yisra'elis inheritance in the Promised Land, neither does being delivered from the bondage from sin and death, through belief in Messiah, guarantee us inheritance in the Kingdom to come.

The author of Hebrews warns us again, not to harden our heart as those in the wilderness hardened theirs. Why is their example important to modern believers?

Paul says that their experience coming out of Egypt is **an example for us**, so that we "take heed lest we fall" (Corinthians 10:1-12).

We see in Hebrews 3:16, that some of the people that came out of Egypt with Mosheh had heard the "Good News" (Hebrews 4:2) just like we have, but these people grieved YHWH and died in the wilderness never having received the "rest" of the Promised Land (Kingdom).

Why? They sinned (disobeyed; 17-18), which proved that they did not truly believe (19).

The picture here is a powerful one because we know that every firstborn that survived the death Angel in Egypt, did so because of the blood of the Passover Lamb. They were saved from death by the blood, just as Messiah's death saves us from the death penalty that we owed.

Yisra'eli was allowed to flee Egypt because YHWH killed the firstborn of all Egypt. It was the death of Pharaoh's firstborn child that crushed the will and authority of Pharaoh (Satan) and allowed YHWH's people to escape Egypt (bondage to sin and death and this world).

**ALL** of these people were saved (delivered) from death and bondage because of the blood of the Lamb (Yahushua) and the death of the firstborn of Egypt.

However, not everyone that was delivered by the blood, entered the Promised Land, which is a picture of the Messianic Kingdom. Because they refused to obey (rebelled against) the Word of YHWH when He told them to take the Land. The people feared the giants and their strongholds more than they trusted YHWH and so, they would not obey Him.

Their rebellion, which was already raising its ugly head when they grumbled to Mosheh at Massah and Mᵉriyeah, led to the condemnation of death which came upon the entire first generation of Yisra'el, save only Caleb and Joshua (Yahushua), who trusted YHWH with their whole heart.

This picture is important because it shows that though we have been saved from the penalty of death for our sin by the blood of Yahushua Messiah, the Lamb of Yah (John 1:29) and have been delivered from the authority of sin, Satan and the world, it is still possible for us to "harden our hearts", like in the rebellion of Yisra'el in the wilderness.

By refusing to trust YHWH enough to do what He has commanded of us, we can bring upon ourselves again the condemnation of death that we had once overcame by belief in Yahushua (Galatians 2:18).

| **Heb 4:1** | Therefore, since a promise remains of entering into His rest, let us fear lest any of **you** seem **to have come short of it.** |
| | *** |
| **Heb 4:11** | Let us therefore do our utmost to enter into that rest, lest **anyone fall after the same example of disobedience.** |

We need to see a principle back in Romans 8 that is often missed or is at least misunderstood.

We have been told that the **doer** of the Torah is made right before YHWH (Romans 2:13) but that it cannot justify us (Romans 3:20) because we are all sinners (Romans 3:23) having disobeyed the

202

Torah (1 John 3:4) and so we must now depend on a form of righteousness that comes only by belief in Yahushua Messiah (Romans 5:21-22).

However, once we are **in Messiah,** we are to bear fruits of obedience (John 15:4-5; Romans 6:16) unto righteousness and holiness (Romans 6: 16, 19) which will end in everlasting life (Romans 6:22).

Paul says Messiah's death might allow favor (grace) to reign through righteousness unto eternal life in Yahushua (Romans 3:21) through whom we can fulfill the righteousness of the Torah in ourselves, if we walk in accordance to the spirit (Romans 8:4).

If we still struggle and commit sin after we have been saved, because of the influence of our rebellious flesh, how can we fulfill the righteousness of the Torah?

Doesn't James say that to violate the least commandment of the Torah means that I violated the whole Torah (James 2:10)?

Yes, it's true that violating one command of the Torah is to violate the entire Torah, however, it is also true that we can fulfill the righteousness of the Torah, though we stumble in our ability to obey it. How?

Since we are not trusting in the Torah, but in the blood of Messiah, His blood can continually cleanse us from future unrighteousness **IF** we don't harden our hearts in rebellion.

| | |
|---|---|
| **1Jn 2:1** | My little children, I write this to you, so that you **do not sin**. **And if** anyone sins, we have an Intercessor with the Father, יהושע Messiah, a righteous One. |
| **1Jn 2:2** | And He Himself is an atoning offering for our sins, and not for ours only but also for **all the world**. |

John says we are **NOT** to disobey the Torah (sin – 1 John 3:4), but that if we commit a transgression of the Torah, Messiah has paid the price for not only our sins but the sins of the whole world and can act as our Intercessor.

> **Note:** the word "and" in verse 1 is the Greek word "kai" which can be translated as "and", however, when used with other small words like "if" this Greek word can also be translated as "but" to show a counter position.

This is all about the intent of our heart and we who are in the Messiah never intentionally disobey even the least of the commands in the Torah (sin). However, because of the rebellious nature of our flesh we are in a continual struggle with and against our fleshly desires, and sometimes they cause us to stumble into an act of disobedience.

Since the intent of our hearts are steadfast and true towards obeying the Torah, our stumbling is not counted against us. Messiah will cleanse us when we confess (John 1:9).

| | |
|---|---|
| **1Jn 2:3** | And by this we know that we know Him, **if we guard His commands**. |
| **1Jn 2:4** | The one who says, "I know Him," and **does not guard His commands, is a liar, and the truth is not in him.** |
| **1Jn 2:5** | But whoever **guards His Word**, truly the love of Elohim has been perfected in him. By this we know that we are in Him. |
| **1Jn 2:6** | The one who says he stays in Him **ought himself also to walk, even as He walked**. |

How do we know for sure that we know YHWH? By obeying His Torah!

What if some would say, they know Him but will not obey the Torah? John calls that person a "liar" saying that the truth of Yahushua is not in them (1 John 2:3-4).

How do I perfect the love of YHWH within myself? Obey His Torah! (1 John 2:5).

How do we know for sure that we abide in the Master Yahushua? If we "walk as he walked" by living our life the same way He lived His (i.e., obeying the entire Torah, without additions and subtractions, every day, with all our heart, mind and strength, and loving others as He loved us [See the authors study: "The Epistles of John"]).

| | |
|---|---|
| **1Jn 5:3** | For this is the love for Elohim, that **we guard His commands, and His commands are not heavy,** |

**Heavy**: stg's #G926 - "barus", meaning, weighty; from a word meaning, a burden. Refers to a heart condition that feels burdened by the commands of the Torah.The word heavy here is translated as "grievous" in the (KJV).

204

The phrase "are not heavy" refers to a heart condition that "delights" in the Torah (Rom 7:22) to obey it (Rom 7:25).

**Note**:  A person that looks into the truth of the Torah and resists it or has a heart of rebellion towards what it commands, is not a heart that has the love of YHWH within it.

**Ex**:  If I learned that the Torah says, I cannot eat pork and I say, "okay" and never willingly or knowingly eat pork again, my heart is right in line with the love of YHWH.

However, if once I've seen the command to not eat pork and, instead of submitting gladly to the command, I rummaged through the Scripture trying to find a loophole that will allow me to eat what YHWH has declared unclean, even though the command is clear and unmistakable, I have proven that my heart is not in the love of YHWH, but in my own stomach.

While trusting in the Messiah, we are to strive diligently to obey the whole Torah every day. If we do this, our stumbles will be covered by Messiah's blood and through Him we will perfect (complete) or establish (Romans 3:31) the righteousness of Torah in our inner-spirit-man. Then what of this fleshly body?

According to Romans 8:3, one of the things Messiah did was to condemn sin in this body. Even though the sins of our past are no longer counted against us in the spirit man, they still have authority to kill this body. Therefore, we still must endure physical death after salvation.

This condemnation, however, does not prevent us from inheriting the Kingdom and the new body at the resurrection, **"IF"**: we walk in the spirit (Rom 8:1) by obeying the Torah of YHWH (Rom 7:25) with our whole heart.

This physical body must be transformed into a spiritual body through the process of resurrection before we can inherit the Kingdom of YHWH (1 Corinthians 15).

The only exception to this is for those believers who have walked in obedience to the Torah of YHWH and are still alive at the return of Messiah. These believers will be "caught up together" with the resurrected believers at that time (1 Thes 4:13-18; 1 Cor 15:51-52).

| Rom 8:12 | So then, **brothers**, we are not debtors to the flesh, to live according to the flesh. |
| --- | --- |
| Rom 8:13 | **For if you live according to the flesh, you are going to die; but if by the** Spirit you put to death the deeds of the body, you shall live |

According to Romans 8:12-13, the believer that "walks in the flesh" (does not submit to the Torah - vs. 7) is going to die, but the believer that "puts to death the deeds of the flesh" shall live.

The phrase "puts to death the deeds of the flesh" means the same thing as overcoming evil with good. We know that the Torah of YHWH is "holy, just, and good" (Rom 7:12) and is spiritual (Rom 7:14). We also know that the flesh is hostile towards the things of YHWH and refuses to submit to the Torah of YHWH (Rom 8:7).

So, to "put to death the deeds of the flesh" in our lives we must make alive the deeds of the spirit or walk in the spirit by doing the exact opposite of the things the flesh desires and does, replacing its evil behavior with the spirit's good behavior.

If the flesh does not "subject itself to the Law/Torah of YHWH", by contrast the spirit does subject itself to the Law/Torah of YHWH.

In plain English, this passage is telling us that we are to stop living in disobedience to the Torah and start walking in obedience to the Torah, which is consistent with everything the Scripture says, Genesis to Revelation.

Our belief in Yahushua is **walked out** or lived out **in obedience to the Torah of YHWH**, as it was spoken by Him to Mosheh at Mount Sinai, without additions or subtractions (Deut 4:2; 12:32; Pro 30:6; Ecc 3:14 and Rev 22:18-19).

The concept that "Messiah obeyed the Law/Torah, so we don't have to" is in absolute opposition to everything the Scripture teaches from Genesis to Revelation. Messiah Himself said:

| Mat 5:17 | "Do not think that I came to destroy the Torah or the Prophets. I did not come to destroy but to complete. |
| --- | --- |
| Mat 5:18 | "For truly, I say to you, till the heaven and the earth pass away, one yod or one tittle shall by no means pass from the Torah till all be done. |

Now, no one would argue that the heaven and the earth are not still in the sky, nor would they claim that everything the Torah and the Prophets spoke about has been accomplished.

There are still things that must happen before the whole of what Scripture has said comes to an end, yet modern teachers will twist this very passage to say that Messiah's death did away with the Torah in the lives of believers, which is the exact opposite of what is being said.

|  |  |
|---|---|
| **Destroy:** | stg's #**G2647** "kataluō", from two words meaning (G2596) down and (G3089) loosen; to loosen down (disintegrate), that is, (by implication) to demolish (literally or figuratively); specifically (compare G2646) to halt for the night: - destroy, dissolve, be guest, lodge, come to nought, overthrow, throw down. |

To "loosen down" conjures the image of someone loosening the anchor ropes that hold a boat securely to the dock. To do so puts the craft in danger of destruction, which is how this word is translated here.

However, in the context this word is used, it must be compared to other things the Scripture says concerning the Torah, such as, no adding to or taking away from (Deut 4:2; 12:32; Ecc 3:14; Pro 30:6; Rev 22:18-19) and not turning to the left or right of anything it says (Deut 28:14) or that anyone teaching us to go in a way other than the Way YHWH told us to go is a false Prophet (Deut 13:1-5).

Considering all this, we understand Messiah was saying that He did not come to take away (diminish) from anything the Torah or the Prophets had spoken. He, in fact, came to fulfill (increase) our knowledge and understanding of it until the time when all of it would be fulfilled (completely full).

Yahushua had to live in complete obedience to the Torah of YHWH for two reasons. The first is so He would qualify to be the spotless Passover Lamb of YHWH who would take away the sin of the world, and the second was to be an example of how we, His people, should live in this world, walking out our belief, "even as He walked" out His (1 John 2:6). Consider what Paul says in Galatians 5.

| | |
|---|---|
| **Gal 5:16** | And I say: **Walk in the Spirit, and you shall not accomplish the lust of the flesh**. |

207

| Gal 5:17 | For the flesh lusts against the Spirit, and the Spirit against the flesh. And these **are opposed to each other**, so that you do not do what you desire to do. |
| Gal 5:18 | **But if you are led by the Spirit, you are not under Torah.** |
| Gal 5:19 | And the works of the flesh are well-known, which are *these*: adultery, whoring, uncleanness, indecency, |
| Gal 5:20 | idolatry, drug sorcery, hatred, quarrels, jealousies, fits of rage, selfish ambitions, dissensions, factions, |
| Gal 5:21 | envy, murders, drunkenness, wild parties, and the like – of which I forewarn you, even as I also said before, that those who practise such as these shall not inherit the reign of Elohim. |
| Gal 5:22 | But the fruit of the Spirit is love, joy, peace, patience, kindness, goodness, trustworthiness, |
| Gal 5:23 | gentleness, self-control. Against such there is no Torah. |
| Gal 5:24 | And those who are of Messiah have impaled the flesh with its passions and the desires. |
| Gal 5:25 | **If we live in the Spirit, let us also walk in the Spirit.** |

This passage is continuously quoted by modern teachers, yet they teach it incorrectly. The very first statement made in this passage is that **IF** we "walk in the spirit we shall not fulfill the lust of the flesh". So, to put to "death the deeds of the flesh" (Rom 8:13) we need to "walk in the spirit".

He goes on to tell us that the flesh and the spirit are in complete opposition to one another, in constant battle within us (Rom 7:7-21). The spirit mentioned here, by the way, is the spirit within us and not the Spirit of YHWH.

Verse 18 is the most interesting, because Paul clearly states that "IF" we walk in the spirit we are not under the Law/Torah. This is really confusing for people because they do not understand what it means to be "under the Law/Torah".

Now, as we mentioned before, to be "under the Law/Torah" is to be under the condemnation of Torah for disobeying it. By definition, sin is the transgression (disobedience) of the Law/Torah (1

John 3:4) and the consequence or "wage" of sin is death (condemnation-Rom 6:23).

We've also already shown that the mind of the flesh "does not subject itself to the Law/Torah" (Rom 8:7). Here Paul clearly states that the spirit and the flesh are contrary to one another, "polar opposites".

Walking in the flesh means to walk in disobedience to the Torah i.e., sin, which leads to death, while walking in the spirit means to walk in obedience to the Torah i.e., righteousness.

Consider again Romans 6:15-16 (words in parentheses added for clarification)

| | |
|---|---|
| **Rom 6:15** | What then? Shall we sin (disobey the Torah) because we are not under (the condemnation of) Torah but under favour (through belief in Yahushua Messiah)? **LET IT NOT BE!** |
| **Rom 6:16** | Do you not know that to whom you **present yourselves servants for obedience, you are servants of the one whom you obey,** whether of sin (disobedience to the Torah, which leads) unto death, or of obedience (to the Torah, which leads) unto righteousness? |

Once again, according to Deuteronomy 6:24-25, it is by obedience to **ALL** that YHWH gave to Yisra'el, through Mosheh, that we live righteously in the Physical Realm.

| | |
|---|---|
| **Deu 6:24** | And יהוה commanded us **to do ALL these laws, to fear יהוה our Elohim,** for our good always, **to keep us alive,** as it is today. |
| **Deu 6:25** | And **it is righteousness for us when we guard to do ALL this command** before יהוה our Elohim, as He has commanded us.' |

Going on in Galatians 5:19-21, Paul lists the "works of the flesh", all of which, of course, are in violation of the Torah, and he ends this passage by saying that those who **practice** these shall not inherit the kingdom of Elohim.

| | |
|---|---|
| **Practice:** | stgs# **G4238** "prassō", A primary verb meaning to "practise"; that is, to *perform repeatedly* or *habitually*. |

209

This Greek word is important because it shows the distinction between the "practice" of disobedience (rebellion) and an act of disobedience done without willful intent.

Sometimes mistakes are made that we truly regret, mistakes that were not our intent but that circumstances and the overt rebelliousness of our flesh combined to bring us into captivity to a particular sin (Rom 7:23).

Modern Christians would say that they do not "practice" any of these things, however, we beg to differ. For instance, the Christian church is guilty of uncleanness, because it has rejected the Torah through which we understand what makes us clean and unclean, i.e., unclean meats, blood guilt (consumption of blood and blood of menstruation), etc.

Furthermore, the church is guilty of idolatry through all the pagan practices of Christmas and Easter and Valentine's Day etc. etc. etc. Also, it is guilty of dissensions and factions which are now called denominations. I could go on and on and on, but you get the point.

Christianity has, through the teachings and doctrines of men, relegated the Torah to the dung heap of history to fulfill its own fleshly desires and to bring their fellow men into the bondage of man-made religion, which is nothing more than man-made rebellion.

Scripture says obedience to the Torah is life and peace and good and blessings, while disobeying the Torah is death and evil and cursing, but we, like the ancient Yisra'elis before us, are a hardheaded stiff-necked people who have changed the Truth into a lie and who deserve the judgment and condemnation afforded those who do such things (Rom 1:32).

Starting in verse 22 of Galatians 5, Paul is going to talk about the "fruit of the spirit". Again, the spirit mentioned here is your spirit not the Spirit of YHWH. The "fruit of the spirit" here is used in opposition to "works of the flesh" in verse 19.

It is important to understand the difference between fruit and work. Work produces fruit. Paul stated earlier that the "fruit" of practicing the works of the flesh was **NOT** inheriting the Kingdom.

In this passage he starts out with fruit of the spirit, not mentioning any works of the spirit, why? Because he has already told us in vs. 16-18 that walking in, or doing the works of the spirit, helps us to overcome the lust of the flesh, which is contrary to the spirit, and prevents us from inheriting the Kingdom.

Walking in the spirit or doing the works of the spirit ensures our inheritance of the kingdom by contrast and prevents us, according to verse 18, from falling back under the condemnation of death required by Torah.

Since he has already mentioned walking in the spirit in verse 16, he doesn't feel the need to repeat himself here, instead he moved right onto the fruit that is produced in us when we walk in obedience to spiritual things, which is the Torah (Rom 7:14).

Now he lists the fruits that will be born in us in our obedience, and these are: love, joy, peace, patience, kindness, goodness, trustworthiness, gentleness, and self-control, all of which are things promised or revealed to us in the Torah for those who would obey it.

Paul goes on to say that there is no Law/Torah against or contrary to these things. In other words, a person that walks in obedience to the Torah produces all these things within themselves because it is how the Torah trains us to be, and those who have produced these character traits in themselves and walk in them will not be condemned by the Torah.

Christians might say "I live like this; I live in love towards my fellow man, and I have joy in my heart, and I try to live in peace with all men" etc. etc. etc., however, the one that they always struggle with the most, is self-control.

Self-control is connected to "offering your body as a living sacrifice, holy and acceptable unto Elohim", which is what the Law/Torah, in its entirety, requires of us, and which Paul summarizes for us in Romans 12:1-2.

Self-control requires us to forfeit the things that are not pleasing to YHWH and submit to the things that are, i.e., all the words of His Law/Torah without additions and subtractions.

Paul alludes to this in the very next verse where he says that those who are of Messiah "have impaled the flesh with its passions and the desires".

So, anybody that says they have the fruits of the spirit, yet does not obey the Torah is in fact, living a lie, and no matter how "spiritual" they claim to be or seem to be, they are in the flesh, having twisted the truth to their own desires.

The last verse in this passage, says that "if we live in the spirit, let us also walk in the spirit." Once again this is referring to our spirit. To be "in the spirit" means the exact same thing as being "of Messiah" in the previous verse. This phrase is a reference to those who have "trusted" in Messiah as their Savior and have been "born again" in the inner-spirit-man.

To "walk in the spirit" means the exact same thing as "impaling the flesh with its passions and desires" mentioned in the previous verse. If we have trusted in the Messiah for our salvation of the inner man then the spiritual man should put to death the physical

211

man daily to bring him into subjection to the Law/Torah of YHWH, which will produce in the spiritual man the fruit of the spirit.

What this all breaks down to is quite simple, those who claim to be believers in Yahushua Messiah should walk in obedience to the Torah with compassion towards our fellow man, which is the foundational understanding of the *Two-Part Principle*.

> **Note:** It is important to understand that the "fruit of the spirit" is contrasted here by the "works of the flesh", so it is our spirit that bears this fruit as we submit to the Torah, however, it is the Spirit of YHWH that bears this fruit in us as we follow His lead.

Don't forget the *Two-Part Principle* is at work at every level of doctrine and this is no different. The *Two-Part Principle* teaches that in all things there is what YHWH does for us and what we do in response to it.

In this case, He gave Messiah as a sacrifice for our sins so that we could be made righteous through Him, and it is our responsibility to live righteously in Him through obedience to the Torah.

As we walk in the spirit, we produce the fruit of righteousness through obeying the Torah, which produces in us the fruit of the Spirit, who is leading us into all truth. This connection between our spirit and His Spirit is what it means to be in Him and Him in us.

Having said all this, let us go back to Romans 8:1 and go through this passage verse by verse to show what's really being said. Keep in mind though the things we've already discussed. Also, let's recap for a moment the last two verses of chapter 7.

If you remember in chapter 7 Paul is discussing the conflict between his inner-spirit-man, which delights in the Law/Torah YHWH, and the outer-fleshly-man, which only wants to follow its own desires and passions.

> **Rom 7:24** Wretched man that I am! Who shall deliver me from this body of death?

In verse 24, Paul states that he is wretched, which is true of all of us, and he asked the question, "Who shall deliver me from this body of death?"

He is telling us that this body that we live in seeks only its own desires, even desires that would destroy it because it does not subject itself to the Law/Torah, it sins. (Rom 8:7)

**Rom 7:25**     Thanks to Elohim, through יהושע Messiah our
Master! So then, with the mind I myself truly
serve the Torah of Elohim, but with the flesh
the torah of sin.

In verse 25, Paul answers the question of how we are going to
get delivered from this "body of death", i.e., through belief in
Yahushua Messiah.

Then, he explains how the believer is to live an overcomer's
life, despite the battle that is raging between his inner man and his
outer man.

We get deliverance (salvation) through belief in the Messiah
Yahushua and Him alone, however, being **in Him** requires that we
also **walk in Him,** which means to live righteously, set apart (holy)
unto the Father YHWH just as Messiah Himself did.

> **Note**:    Christians today, wear bracelets that say "WWJD?"
> (What Would Jesus Do?) and attempt to live their
> lives in the same love and compassion that He did.
> However, Yahushua learned to live His life in love
> and compassion through obedience to the Law/Torah.
>
> No one that has ever lived held the Law/Torah in
> greater esteem than Messiah Himself and proved it
> day in and day out through His absolute obedience to
> it.
>
> If you want to know "What Would Jesus Do?", He
> would obey the Law/Torah in EVERY situation in
> life. So, to "Walk in Him" is to live a life in absolute
> obedience to the Law/Torah with all our heart, mind
> and strength, as He did.

What Paul is trying to tell us in vs 24 & 25 is that there is a
distinction between our spirit man and our fleshly man. He talks as if
his fleshly man, which is his physical body, is a separate entity from
his spiritual man which resides inside him, i.e., the inner man.

He states that his fleshly man continues to strive to live,
according to its own selfish passions and sinful desires, but his spirit
man sets all its heart, mind and strength to honoring the Father through
obedience to His Law/Torah, diligently seeking Him every day.

It is to this contrast that Paul is referring in Romans 8 and
Galatians 5:16-25. He says that there is a battle going on between

213

these two parts of himself, the physical part, and the spiritual part, and he is going to tell us that the only way to avoid future condemnation is to live out our lives through the guidance of the inner/spirit man, which delights in and serves the Law/Torah.

> **Note:** Our fleshly man is the instinctual part of us, it is the part of us that is like the animals. To be fleshly minded is to live in obedience to our "animal mind", that is to make our choices based on our feelings and emotions. It is the "fight or flight" mind.
>
> Our spirit man is the rational part of us, it is the part of us that is made in the image and likeness of YHWH. To be spiritually minded is to live in obedience to the Word/Torah of YHWH, that is to make our choices based on a rational consideration of the circumstances and the application of the Torah in each particular circumstance. It is the "rational" mind that distinguishes us from the animals.

This is one of the most important passages in all Paul's writings because it defines what it means to be "in Messiah" and confirms the promises to those who walk in Him.

> **Rom 8:1** There is, then, now no condemnation to those who are in Messiah ,יהושע **who do not walk according to the flesh**, but according to the Spirit.

Despite the new chapter heading, which were added by translators and is not in the original text, Chapter 8 is a continuation of the argument Paul is making in chapter 7.

The "there is, then, now" that starts this chapter is Paul's way of expressing the consequences of our choices as it relates to what he said in verse 25 of the last chapter.

There Paul made a distinction between his desire to serve the Torah of YHWH and his body's desire to NOT obey the Torah of YHWH but serve sin instead.

Keeping in mind what he has already said in Romans 6:15; that we are "servants to whom we obey, whether sin unto death or obedience unto righteousness". Paul is saying the exact same thing here in verse 1 of chapter 8.

In fact, all of chapter 7 and chapter 8 reflects what was taught in chapter 6 but from a slightly different angle and in more depth.

For instance, Paul began chapter 7 (1-4) by teaching us how we, as the bride, have escaped the authority of the Law/Torah that had condemned us, through the death, burial and resurrection of Yahushua Messiah, to whom we are now remarried.

Then, Paul explains how we learn what sin is and the consequences of sin, and exposes this evil flesh, which desires to do what is contrary to what we should do, i.e., obey the Torah (vs. 5-23).

Paul goes on to tell us, both how to overcome in this battle, i.e., belief in Yahushua, and how we are to live in Him, i.e., through obedience to the Law/Torah (vs. 24-25).

In chapter 6, Paul asked the question, "Shall we continue to sin, that grace may abound" and he answered himself with a resounding **"Let it not be!"**

Remember, the definition of sin is, "the transgression of the Law/Torah" (1 John 3:4), so we can clearly see that Paul is instructing the new believer to walk in obedience to the Torah, just like he does in chapter 7:25.

He goes on in 6:15, to ask, "Shall we sin, since we are not under the law but under grace" and again, he answers himself with a resounding "Let it not be!"

He follows this up with, "Do you not know that to whom you present yourselves servants for obedience, **you are servants of the one whom you obey**, whether of sin to death, or of obedience to righteousness?"

Can you see it? Paul's question, "Shall we sin", followed by his resounding "Let it not be", is an indirect command to believers to walk in obedience to the Law/Torah.

Also, his statement in 7:25 that "with the mind I myself (a believer) truly serve the Torah of Elohim" is a more direct confirmation of a believers need to obey the Torah once he has trusted in Messiah.

Now, Paul's statement about, "being a servant to whom you obey" in 6:25 and his statement in 8:1 is to be understood to mean the same thing.

> **6:25 -** "whether of sin to death, or of obedience to righteousness?"
>
> ***
>
> **8:1 -** There is, then, now no condemnation to those who are in Messiah, יהושע **who do not walk according to the flesh, but according to the Spirit.**

I know this might not be obvious to the new believer, but from a Hebrew mindset it's very clear. In this verse of chapter 8, Paul is making a distinction between "walking in the flesh" and "walking in the spirit" and he is associating these two in the context of condemnation (death).

As we have stated before and we shall show again in the rest of chapter 8, the principle of "walking in the spirit" is associated to the inner man's delight and service to the Torah of YHWH (7:22, 25), while the principle of "walking in the flesh" is associated with the outer man's desire to serve sin (7:23, 25).

So then (Rom 6:16 = Rom 8:1):

1.  "whether of sin unto death" = "walking in the flesh"
2.  "obedience unto righteousness" = "walking in the spirit"

As you can see, Paul is simply reconfirming in chapters 7 and 8 what he has already said in Chapter 6, which is, if we serve obedience (6:16) by walking in the spirit (8:1), we will be declared righteous (6:16), avoid condemnation (8:1) and have our place in eternal life (6:22).

However, if we choose to serve sin (disobey the Torah, walk in the flesh) we will earn the condemnation of death (Rom 8:13; Gal 2:17-18).

Though not expressly stated in 8:1, there is a huge "**IF**" implied there, which gives believers the choice to walk in the spirit and be free of condemnation **OR** walk in the flesh and fall back into the condemnation of death. This principle is reconfirmed in the next verse.

**Rom 8:2**     For the torah of the Spirit of the life in Messiah יהושע has set me free from the torah of sin and of death.

What does "For the torah of the spirit of the life in Messiah Yahushua..." mean?

Those believers who walk in the spirit, by obeying the Torah, are free from future condemnation, **NOT** because they walk in perfect obedience to the Torah, but because the favor (grace) of YHWH is

216

extended to those who have believed in His Son Yahushua, whose hearts are perfectly committed to obey.

**Mat 5:48**     "Therefore, be perfect, as your Father in the heavens is perfect.

It's not about perfect obedience but about perfect commitment. The word "perfect" in Hebrew does not mean the same thing as perfect in English. The word for perfect in Hebrew is "tamiym" and is better translated as entire or complete.

The concept of completeness in the Scripture has nothing to do with absolute perfection as we think of it in the English. Completeness has to do with a heart condition that is committed to trusting and obeying in an attitude of compassion. This is what it means to be complete or perfect from a Hebrew point of view.

In vs. 2, the phrase "torah of the spirit of the life in Messiah" is a roundabout way of saying those who are in Messiah live a life in submission to the instructions of the spirit man, i.e., walk in the spirit.

When we walk in the spirit, we have been made free from the torah of sin and death. What does "The torah of sin and death..." mean? The Scripture defines sin as the transgression of the Law/Torah and if you remember, at the beginning of this book we defined Law/Torah as instruction, there are many types of instruction.

There is the instruction or Torah of YHWH, which leads to life for those who obey it and death to those who do not obey it. The Torah of YHWH has condemned all men to death because no one obeyed it.

YHWH had another set of instructions which we call the "Torah of Belief" or as Paul said, "the torah of the spirit of the life in Messiah".

This is what we also call the "Torah of Two Parts", a set of instructions that includes belief in Yahushua Messiah followed by obedience to the Torah of YHWH, without additions or subtractions, in a heart of compassion for your fellow man.

"The torah of sin and death" is everything that is contrary to, a contradiction of, or has added to and taken away from the Torah of YHWH. So, the phrase, "Torah of sin and death" means the same thing as serving sin (disobeying the Torah of YHWH) which leads to death (6:16).

To sum this up, Paul is trying to tell us that after we have placed our belief in Yahushua Messiah, we are required to obey the Torah of YHWH with all our heart, all our mind and all our strength, as the Torah commands, with an attitude of love towards one another

217

(1 John 2:10-11), i.e., "The Torah of Belief". If we do this, then we are set free from any future condemnation when we stumble and commit some violation of the Torah.

What we have called "The Torah of Belief" acts as a safety net for those who are of the belief which protects them from condemnation if they are overcome by some sin.

The favor (grace) of YHWH is extended to those believers who are fully committed to obeying everything the Torah says from a pure heart of compassion.

In contrast to this, the grace of YHWH which is extended to all who have believed in Yahushua Messiah; **DOES NOT** sustain those that walk in willful disobedience to the Torah of YHWH (John 15:1-6; Hebrews 6:4-8; 10:26-31; 2 Peter 2:20-22). WILLFUL DISOBEDIENCE IS REBELLION, for which favor (grace) is not extended.

| Rom 8:3 | For the Torah being powerless, **in that it was weak through the flesh**, Elohim, having sent His own Son in the likeness of flesh of sin, and concerning sin, **condemned sin in the flesh**, |
| Rom 8:4 | so that the **righteousness of the Torah should be completed in us who** do not walk according to the flesh but **according to the Spirit.** |

Now, everything we have just said about what Paul has written in chapters 6:1 through 8:2 and the conclusions we have made based on them, are verified by Paul here in verses 3 and 4.

Paul states that the Torah of YHWH had no power to make us righteous in and of itself, because of our rebellious flesh, but YHWH made a way for us by sending His Son Yahushua. Yahushua was born human with all our frailties and temptations and was tempted in every way that we are (Hebrews 4:15) and yet He overcame by:

1. Being born with no earthly father and so did not inherit the condemnation of death passed down from father to his children since the fall of Adam.

2. Trusting in His Father, YHWH, so completely that He obeyed everything His Father's Torah required of Him with a heart of compassion towards His fellow man, even though they executed Him for it.

218

Having overcome, He was able to act as our Passover Lamb, sacrificing His own life so that through His death His blood could atone for our sins (Romans 3:24-25). This is what Paul means when he said, Messiah came "in the likeness of flesh of sin and concerning sin".

As the word of YHWH, He took on flesh (John 1:14) and by dying for us, He took away sins authority to condemn us to death.

Paul goes on to say that He "condemned sin in the flesh". By this, Paul is telling us that the penalty of sin that was once upon us, the whole man, now rests only in our body, which is why we must still die.

When we confessed Yahushua Messiah for salvation, we were only "born again" in the inner-spirit-man, **NOT** in the whole man. The outer-physical-man is not "born again" until the resurrection of this body (1 Corinthians 15:35-49).

Paul concludes in verse 4 that everything that Messiah did for us, allows us to accomplish the righteousness demanded by the Torah of YHWH when we walk according to the spirit.

Walking according to the flesh does not allow us to accomplish the righteousness of Torah because, as we are about to see, the flesh is contrary to everything YHWH expects of us.

Once again, we see the "Torah of Belief". A belief in Yahushua Messiah (8:3) that is lived out or walked out according to the desires of the spirit-man. This enables a believer to accomplish the righteous requirements of the Torah of YHWH because he is trusting in the "good news" of Yahushua Messiah and striving to diligently obey the Torah of YHWH every day with a heart of compassion towards his fellow man.

This is the whole truth of what it means to be a servant of YHWH through belief in His Son, Yahushua.

Now, Paul is going to explain the difference between two mindsets, one that leads to death and the other which leads to life. This entire teaching is attempting to express to us, that in every man there are two minds:

1. **The fleshly mind**: makes choices based on its passions and desires, according to the will of its five senses and instincts.

2. **The spiritual mind**: that makes choices based on his commitment to the principles of belief for which he stands, according to a well thought out

219

| Rom 8:5 | For those who live according to the flesh set their minds on the *matters* of the flesh, but those *who live* **according to the Spirit, the matters of the Spirit**. |
| Rom 8:6 | For the mind of the flesh is death, **but the mind of the Spirit is life and peace**. |
| Rom 8:7 | Because the mind of the flesh is enmity towards Elohim, for **it does not subject itself to the Torah of Elohim**, neither indeed is it able, |
| Rom 8:8 | and those who are in the flesh are unable to please Elohim. |

There are couple interesting points that need to be identified here. First, the fleshly mind sets its intent on fleshly things, i.e., things that please the flesh, even if they are contrary to the Torah of YHWH.

Second, the mind of the spirit sets its intent on spiritual things, i.e., things that please YHWH in accordance with His Torah.

Third, the mind of the flesh leads to death because it is contrary to the things of YHWH, the Life Giver, while, in contrast, the mind of the spirit leads to life and peace, because it submits itself to the things of YHWH, the Life Giver. Consider and compare:

| Pro 3:1 | My son, **do not forget my Torah**, And let your heart **watch over my commands**; |
| Pro 3:2 | For **length of days and long life And peace they add to you**. |

Contrary to popular belief, Paul is simply teaching you a Torah principle directly from the mouth of King Solomon. It cannot be stressed enough what Paul says here in verse 7, where he states that the mind of the flesh is "enmity" towards YHWH.

| Enmity: | stg's #**G2189** "echthra", (Fem of **G2190**; to hate) *hostility*; a position of hostility or hatred towards a given thing or principle. |

The mind of the flesh **HATES** the things of YHWH and, as we've stated, is contrary to them. Paul confirms our stance here and explains why the flesh is so hateful or hostile to the things of YHWH.

220

The mind of the flesh "does not subject itself to the Torah" of YHWH, and "neither indeed is it able".

Why? The mind of the flesh is unable to subject itself to the Torah of YHWH because of its passions and desires. The flesh is selfish and self-centered; it only cares about the things that please itself. The flesh does not care who it upsets or who it hurts or what it destroys to accomplish its own purposes.

YHWH requires a totally different "mindset". YHWH defines love as sacrifice.

> **Joh 3:16**     "For Elohim **so loved the world that He gave** His only brought-forth Son, so that everyone who believes in Him should not perish but possess everlasting life.

The mind of the spirit **DOES** subject itself to the Torah of YHWH because it trusts in Him. The spirit is compassionate, generous, patient, kind, it does not condemn, does not consider itself, it serves, and it sacrifices. The mind of the spirit is peace and love everlasting for it is the reflection of the Spirit of YHWH, Who is love.

Paul continues by saying "that those who were in the flesh are not able to please" YHWH. Wow!!!

There is an entire "Church" out there claiming to be "The Way". They are more than two billion strong, in its many denominations, all of whom claim to be the children of YHWH. They all claim to be "in the Spirit", however and unfortunately, they are actually in the flesh and unable to please the very One they claim to serve.

I know, I know, that seems harsh and judgmental, but is it? Does not Paul, the Apostle they supposedly give so much credence to, state very, very, very clearly in this passage that the mind of the flesh **"does not subject itself to the Law/Torah"** of YHWH.

The **entire** "Church" has founded itself upon the principle that those who believe in 'Jesus' are **no longer required to subject themselves to the Law/Torah** of YHWH, the Old Testament Law.

Now, we did not say that Paul did, and he goes on to say that those people, including those in the "Church", who are not subjecting themselves to the Torah of YHWH are not only in the flesh but are not pleasing the Father, and to the "Church", we say, "repent for the Kingdom of Elohim is near", much nearer than before.

The word repent does not mean "to turn", as you've been taught by the "Church". The Hebrew word for repentance is "teshuvah" and it carries a direct meaning of **"return".**

221

YHWH is calling out to mankind, to all who have went astray from His Torah (instructions), to return to Him in obedience to His Torah, through belief in His Son Yahushua.

It is imperative we understand that both the Tanak and the Messianic Writings confirm our responsibility to have both belief in Him and obedience to His Torah.

Scripture says that Abraham, our father in the belief (Galatians 2:7, 29), was declared righteous by YHWH because of his **belief** (Genesis 15:6) and that he had **obeyed all the Torah** of YHWH (Genesis 26:5), so that if we claim to be of the belief of Abraham, then our belief should include obedience to all the Torah as his did.

At Mount Sinai, YHWH instructed Mosheh to tell the people that **IF** they would **"diligently obey His voice and guard His covenant"** (Exodus 19:5) **THEN He** would make them His treasured possession.

In this promise there was a condition that applied to both the native born Yisra'eli and the stranger that sojourns with them (Numbers 15:15-16; Leviticus 19:33-34), which was that they had to both obey Him and protect His covenant.

The *Two-Part Principle* can be seen here, the spiritual part being the covenant and the physical part being obedience to His Voice. Covenant refers to blood, i.e., the blood of Yahushua Messiah, and obedience to His Voice refers to His Law/Torah, i.e., everything He has spoken, without additions or subtractions.

Isaiah (YeshaYahu), when talking about the priest and prophets, stated that they must speak a word that includes both the **Torah and the Witness** or they have no light in them (Isa. 8:20), so then, if we claim to be in the light, we must have both the Torah and the Witness of Messiah.

Messiah Himself, when confronted by Satan (Matthew 4:4), quoted from Deuteronomy 8:3, saying that "man does not live by bread alone, but by **every word** that proceeds out of the mouth of Elohim".

Messiah refers to Himself as the bread of life (John 6:33, 35, 48 and 51) but has stated that man does not live by bread alone, but by **EVERY WORD** that proceeds out of the mouth of Elohim.

The bread represents the covenant in Messiah's blood and **EVERY WORD** represents the voice of YHWH that spoke from the mountain.

"The Torah and the Witness", applied to Abraham, is required by Isaiah and was reinforced by Messiah; why would we think it doesn't apply to us?

Messiah told His disciples (which includes believers today) that He is "the Way, the Truth and the Life, and that no man came to the Father but through Him" (John 14:6) yet He also asked the Father to sanctify (set apart) us "in Your Truth, Your Word is Truth" (John 17:17). Here we see the Witness of Messiah and the Word/Torah of YHWH.

Yahushua, in His Revelation given to John (Yochanan), refers many times to "the Word of Elohim and the Witness of Yahushua Messiah".

1.  The angel bore witness of them (1:2),
2.  John was in prison on the island of Patmos because of them (1:9),
3.  The martyrs of the Fifth Seal are those who are slain for them (6:9),
4.  When Satan accuses the brethren, they overcome him by them (12:10-11) and when Satan could not destroy the woman, Yisra'el, he went after the remnant of her seed, those who had them (12:17),
5.  The Saints that will endure are those that have them (14:12),
6.  At the end of the thousand years, thrones are set up for those who had been beheaded for them (20:4).

Here are a few more obscure references to this *Two-Part Principle* of Witness and Torah working together. Some of these may need a bit of critical thinking to understand.

This first one is pretty simple, it was given to the assembly of Philadelphia to whom Messiah had nothing negative to say but commended them for this one thing, that they "guarded **My Word** and have not denied **My Name**" (Revelation 3:8).

This next one is a reference to the Whore of Babylon (false church) that rides on the back of the Beast.

"And I saw the woman, **drunk with the blood of the set-apart ones, and with the blood of the witnesses of יהושע** (Rev 17:6)

To understand this, you must remember that Messiah said in John 17:17 that it is the Word that sanctifies (sets apart) us. The only reason to state that "she was drunk on the blood of both the set apart

223

ones and those of the blood of the witness" is to reaffirm this *Two-Part Principle* of Witness and Torah.

This third reference is mentioned in the context of the Bride of Messiah, so Part-One of the *Two-Part Principle* (Witness) is assumed, but this verse acknowledges the second part (Torah).

"And to her it was given to be dressed in fine linen, clean and bright, for the fine linen is **the righteousness of the set-apart ones**". (19:8)

**Remember**, again, it's through obedience to the Torah that we live righteously (Deut 6:24-25) and it is through this Word that we are set apart (John 17:17). The fine linen mentioned in this verse represents the works part of belief, it is how we have lived righteous and set apart through obedience to the Torah.

This final reference is even more obscure, mostly because it must be understood from the opposite point of view, meaning that while the other references are referring to the saints, those with the Witness of Messiah who obey the Torah, these two references are referring to those who shall endure the wrath of YHWH, and specifically, why they do.

"they **blasphemed the Name** of Elohim who possesses authority over these plagues. And **they did not repent**, to give Him esteem". (6:9)

-and-

"they **blasphemed the Elohim** of the heaven for their pains and their sores and, **did not repent** of their works". (v. 11),

They rejected the only Name by which they could avoid these plagues and they refused to turn away from their "fleshly" ways and **return** to Him through obedience to the Torah.

\*\*\*

Returning to Romans 8, we see that Paul makes an obvious and yet terrifying proclamation.

**Rom 8:9**  But you are not in the flesh but in the Spirit, <u>if</u> indeed **the Spirit of Elohim dwells in you**. And if anyone does not have the Spirit of Messiah, **this one is not His**.

The first "spirit" mentioned here refers to our inner-spirit-man and should not be capitalized.

Here Paul makes a condition concerning whether we are in the spirit or in the flesh, and that condition concerns the Spirit of YHWH dwelling inside of us.

How do you know "if indeed the Spirit of Elohim dwells in you"? It's important to remember that being "in the spirit" is a principle of belief and that Paul has told us in Galatians 5:25 that if we are "in the spirit" we should be "walking in the spirit".

He has already told us that to be "in the flesh" is to have a mind that refuses to subject itself to the Torah of YHWH and is therefore the enemy of YHWH, hating the things of YHWH (Romans 8:7-8).

We know that according to John those who love YHWH are those who "guard His commands" and do not consider obeying His commands, "heavy" or a burden (1 John 5:3).

According to the Tanak, when YHWH places His Spirit within us, His Spirit "**shall** cause you to **walk** in My **laws** and **guard** My **right-rulings** and **shall do them**."

> **Eze 36:27**     and put My Spirit within you. And I shall **cause you to walk in My laws and guard My right-rulings and shall do them**. (See also: Eze 11:19-20)

Messiah Himself said that when His Spirit came to us, to dwell in us, He would witness of Messiah Yahushua and lead us into all truth, and as we have already shown, Messiah determined that He was truth (John 14:6) and the Word was truth (John 17:17).

Now for some reason, Christians arbitrarily accept the "Word" as a reference to the Scripture in its totality but seem to conveniently forget that the "Word" that is **Truth**, is both Messiah (John 14:6) and the Torah (Psalms 119:142).

As it says in Isaiah 8:20, The Word that must be spoken includes both the Torah and the Witness or it has no light. Messiah is the Word made flesh (John 1:14) and the Torah is the written Word given at Mt. Sinai, i.e., The Witness and the Torah.

The Truth is Messiah and the Torah! Together they are the Scripture, they are the Word! They cannot be separated, or they are no longer Truth.

The Scripture teaches us what righteousness is and how we get cleansing if we fail to live righteously. Messiah is the cleansing, but once cleansed we must still live righteously, and the Torah is the only standard of righteousness ever laid down for man to live by.

Christianity also seems to ignore the fact that Paul himself told Timothy that "all Scripture" is inspired by Elohim and good for teaching.

| | |
|---|---|
| **2Ti 3:16** | All Scripture is breathed out by Elohim and profitable for **teaching**, for **reproof**, for **setting straight**, for <u>**instruction in righteousness**</u>, |
| **2Ti 3:17** | that the man of Elohim might be fitted, equipped for every good work. |

In the Messianic Writings, when the writers used the words "Scripture" or "Word" or "Law" they were always referring to what was written in the Tanak because the so-called "New Testament" did not exist and was only then in the process of being written.

So, Paul's reference to "all Scripture" in 2 Timothy is a clear and undeniable reference to the Tanak or "Old Testament", which unquestionably includes the Torah. Clearly, Paul's statement here about "instruction in righteousness" is a reference to Deuteronomy 6:24-25, where we are told that it is "righteousness for us when we guard to do **all** this command".

Now, having said all this, what does Paul mean when he tells the Romans in 8:9 that "we are not in the flesh but in the spirit if the Spirit of Elohim dwells in us"?

Having the Spirit of Elohim dwelling in us is clearly a reference to obedience, as Messiah said in John 14:21-24.

| | |
|---|---|
| **Joh 14:21** | "He who **possesses My commands and guards them**, it is he who loves Me. And he who loves Me **shall be loved by My Father**, and I shall love him **and manifest Myself to him.**" |
| | *** |
| **Joh 14:23** | יהושע answered him, "If anyone loves Me, **he shall guard My Word. And My Father shall love him**, and **We shall come to him and make Our stay with him.** |
| **Joh 14:24** | "He **who does not love Me does not guard My Words.** And the Word which you hear is not Mine but of the Father Who sent Me. |

To be able to claim that Messiah lives in us, that the Spirit of YHWH is in us, we must be walking in obedience to the

226

Command/Word/Torah. If we do not "guard to do" the commands/Word/ Torah then we have proven that we do not love Messiah and neither He nor His Father nor the Spirit of His Father shall dwell in us.

In the context of chapter 8 of Romans and in the context of the entire Scripture, we are not truly "in the spirit" if we are not "walking in the spirit" by obedience to His Torah, and if this is the case then the Spirit of Messiah is not in us, and we are not His.

Ouch, there is a whole lot of so-called believers claiming to have the Spirit of YHWH in them and yet the very fact that they choose, through man-made doctrines, to reject the Torah of YHWH as the standard of righteous living for them, proves, by their attitude towards the Torah, that they are not in the Messiah nor the Messiah in them, which then begs the question, what spirit is in them?

| | |
|---|---|
| **1Jn 3:4** | Everyone doing sin also does lawlessness, and **sin is lawlessness** (Gk - anomia: no law doing). |
| **1Jn 3:5** | And you know that He was manifested to take away our sins, and **in Him there is no sin** (we walk as He walked-2:6-in obedience). |
| **1Jn 3:6** | Everyone staying in Him **does not sin**. Everyone sinning has neither seen Him nor known Him. (Staying in Him obeying-John 15:10) |
| **1Jn 3:7** | Little children, let no one lead you astray. **The one doing righteousness is righteous, even as He is righteous**. (It is righteousness for us when we **guard to do** all His command-Deut 6:25) |
| **1Jn 3:8** | **The one doing sin** (not obeying the Torah) **is of the devil,** because the devil has sinned from the beginning. For this purpose the Son of Elohim was manifested: to destroy the works of the devil. |
| **1Jn 3:9** | Everyone having been born of Elohim **does not sin** (disobey the Torah), because His seed stays in him, and he is powerless to sin, because he has been born of Elohim. |
| **1Jn 3:10** | In this the children of Elohim and the children of the devil are manifest: **Everyone not doing righteousness is not of Elohim,** neither the one not loving his brother. |

**1Jn 4:1**   Beloved ones, **do not believe every spirit,**
**but prove the spirits, whether they are of**
**Elohim,** because many false prophets have
gone out into the world.

**Note:**   For a more in-depth study of 1 John see the author's
booklet, "The Epistles of John".

We have a choice, because there are only two possible fathers
and two possible spirits, you are either of the Spirit of YHWH,
through belief in His Son and obedience to His Torah (Witness and
Torah), or you are of the spirit of error, Satan, who has disobeyed the
Torah from the beginning.

**Rom 8:10**   And if Messiah is in you, **the body is truly**
**dead on account of sin, but the Spirit is life**
**on account of righteousness.**
**Rom 8:11**   And if the Spirit of Him who raised יהושע
from the dead dwells in you, He who raised
Messiah from the dead **shall also give life to**
**your mortal bodies** through His Spirit
dwelling in you.

There are some important distinctions made here and in the
verses prior to them that is important for us to understand, some refer
'spiritual' things and some to "physical" things. Consider the
similarity between verse 10 and verse 3. In verse 3 we are told that:

**Rom 8:3**   For the Torah being powerless, in that it was
**weak** through the flesh, Elohim, having sent
His own Son in the likeness of flesh of sin,
and concerning sin, **condemned sin in the**
**flesh,**

Paul's argument here is that man cannot put their trust in the
Torah alone because, before he believed in Messiah, it is powerless to
make him righteous. It was powerless because his inner-spirit-man
was dead, so YHWH sent Yahushua so that everyone who believes in
Him could be 'born again' in the spirit-man (Ephesians 2:1-6; Romans
7:24-25).

However, it is ONLY the spirit-man that has been born again
NOT the outer-physical-man, i.e., the body (flesh). The physical body

is still condemned to death, which is what "condemned sin in the flesh" means here in verse 3.

It is the same thing that verse 10 is saying, "the body is truly dead on account of sin". However, our belief in Messiah has made our inner-spirit-man alive again and so 'walking in the spirit' (our spirit, not His) is life on account of righteousness.

"Life on account of righteousness" refers to both forms of righteousness, i.e., the righteousness of Messiah that delivered us from sin and death and the righteousness of an obedient life (Torah obedience). This goes back to what Paul said in Romans 7:22-8:13, where Paul states that **HE** "delights in the Torah (Law) of Elohim according to the **INWARD MAN**".

Once again, it is important to note that Paul is and has been talking about his own personal experience. He says that there is a struggle going on within him, between his "inward man" i.e., inner-spirit-man, which has been born again in Messiah, and his "members", i.e., outer-physical-man, who is still dead (dying) because of trespasses and sin.

He states that in Yahushua Messiah he as that "with the mind I truly serve the Torah of Elohim, but with the flesh the torah of sin. This does NOT mean that he gives his physical body free reign, but recognizes that it, his flesh, desires to serve sin.

The "mind" is a reference to the inner-spirit-man that is SERVING or OBEYING the Torah. Beginning in verse 1 of Chapter 8, he goes on to give an 'if and then' statement that begins with "There is, then, now no condemnation to those who are in Messiah יהושע, **WHO DO NOT** walk according to the flesh, but according to the Spirit.

If there is no longer any condemnation for those who DO NOT walk according to the flesh, then there IS condemnation to those who DO walk in the flesh, and he says so in two places, one in verse 6a, "For the mind of the flesh is death", which refers to a mind that is focused on living according to the desires of the flesh, and verse 13a, "For if **you LIVE ACCORDING TO THE FLESH, you are going to die**".

How does Paul then define, "live according to the flesh"? He explains it in verse 7, "Because the mind of the flesh is enmity towards Elohim, for **IT DOES NOT SUBJECT ITSELF TO THE TORAH OF ELOHIM**", and because of this, the flesh is "unable to please Elohim" (v.8).

If "walking according to the flesh" leads to death because it "does not subject itself to the Torah", then "walking according to the spirit, which leads to "life and peace" (6b, 13b), does subject itself to the Torah.

Why? Because the Torah of YHWH is "holy, just and good" (7:12- KJV) and it is "spiritual" (7:14), so the follower of Messiah that wishes to be set-apart (holy), just (righteous), good and spiritual, would subject themselves (obey) the Torah of Elohim.

Believers in Messiah are alive in their inner-spirit-man because they have walked according to the spirit unto righteousness, having proven their "mind" (heart condition) by their diligent obedience to the Torah of YHWH, and because of this, the Spirit of YHWH that raised Yahushua from the dead and dwells in us, shall also resurrect us on that Day.

| Rom 8:12 | So then, **brothers**, we are not debtors to the flesh, to live according to the flesh. |
| Rom 8:13 | **For if you live according to the flesh, you are going to die**; but if by the Spirit you put to death the deeds of the body, you shall live. |

Here is Paul's clearest and last admonition on this matter, in this chapter. He clearly and unequivocally states that we believers are not to live according to the flesh.

According to Paul, just a few verses ago, the flesh does not submit to the Torah, so it is clearly Paul's intent that we are to obey the Torah, which is the same thing he said in 6:1 and 6:15 and 6:19 and 7:22 and 25 and 8:1.

He confirms unequivocally that if we continue to live according to the flesh (disobeying the Torah) **we are going to die**, which is what he said in 6:15 and 6:23 and 8:1.

He says that we need to put to death the deeds of the flesh so that we might live, which we do "by walking in the spirit". As we've stated before this is a reference to overcoming evil with good, i.e., obeying the Torah.

If the flesh and the spirit are contrary to one another, as Paul states clearly in Galatians 5:17, then the only way to do away with the deeds of the flesh is to walk in the deeds of the spirit, AND if the flesh DOES NOT subject itself to the Torah of YHWH, then the spirit DOES subject itself to the Torah of YHWH!

This teaching was meant for any 12-year-old Hebrew child to understand, so if we just accept it for what it says and obey what it says. Instead, we have allowed "untaught and unstable" men to twist and turn the meanings of these passages, ignoring the first two thirds of the book as a means of understanding, until we've created a doctrine of lawlessness that leads to destruction.

Which is exactly what Peter warned us about.

| | |
|---|---|
| **2Pe 3:14** | So then, beloved ones, looking forward to this, do your utmost to be found by Him in peace, **spotless and blameless** (obedient) |
| **2Pe 3:15** | and reckon the patience of our Master as deliverance, as also our beloved brother Paul wrote to you, according to the wisdom given to him, |
| **2Pe 3:16** | as also in all *his* letters, speaking in them concerning these *matters*, **in which some are hard to understand**, which those who are **untaught and unstable twist to their own destruction**, as they do also the other Scriptures. |
| **2Pe 3:17** | You, then, beloved ones, being forewarned, watch, **lest you also fall from your own steadfastness, being led away with the delusion of the lawless,** |

The whole so-called "Church" believes that it no longer needs to obey the Old Testament Law and has adopted a doctrine of lawlessness, which Peter says is a delusion that will lead us astray and cause us to fall.

This is the exact same thing Yisra'el was guilty of when they came out of Egypt, they offered the Passover Lamb, saw all the miracles of YHWH, but when it came time to obey the Torah, they didn't want to do it and so they all died in the wilderness, none of them inheriting the Land.

Wait a minute, two of them did inherit the land, Caleb, and Joshua (Yahushua), the two that believed that YHWH was bigger than all their obstacles and He could be trusted to keep His promises and so they were willing to act on what He told them regardless of the things they saw ahead of them.

As the Messianic Writings tell us, we are those who "walk by belief and not by sight" (2 Corinthians 5:7), just like Caleb and Joshua (Yahushua).

| | |
|---|---|
| **Rom 8:14** | For as many as are led by the Spirit of Elohim, these are sons of Elohim. |

231

You know whether you're being led by the Spirit of Elohim based on what that spirit leads you to do. If that spirit leads you to obey the Torah of YHWH (Eze 11:19-20; 36:27) through belief in Yahushua, who came in the flesh and was raised from the dead, then it is the Spirit of YHWH (1 John 4:2).

However, if that spirit leads you to believe that the Torah of YHWH no longer applies to you or that Yahushua did not come in the flesh (1 John 4:3) and that He was not born of a virgin, and was not raised from the dead, then that spirit is not the Spirit of YHWH.

> **Rom 8:15** For you did not receive the spirit of bondage again to fear, but you received the Spirit of adoption by whom we cry out, "Abba, Father."

The fear Paul is referring to here, is that of condemnation. Paul has already expressed to us that if we "walk in the spirit" there is no more condemnation awaiting us (8:1) and so he is reaffirming that to us here. We no longer need to be afraid of stumbling and falling back under the bondage to the fear of death that we escaped, because of our belief in Yahushua.

The key to understanding this, which the "Church" has missed, is our requirement to "walk in the spirit" in obedience to the Torah of YHWH through belief.

**REMEMBER**, the Word/Torah is a two-edged sword (Hebrews 4:12) that judges the thoughts and intents of the heart. The Torah will give life to those who obey it and it will destroy those who do not obey it.

This applies to both believers and non-believers; therefore, we are told that it judges the **"thoughts and intents of the heart"**. Non-believers do not know YHWH and neither do they want to, so they do not believe in His Son nor obey His Torah, and they shall be judged for it.

Believers, come in three types; the first type have confessed the Messiah as their Savior but have been led astray by false prophets who teach lying doctrines, which tell them they no longer must obey the Torah, to whom Peter has something to say.

> **2Pe 2:1** But there also came to be false prophets among the people, as also **among you there shall be false teachers**, who shall secretly **bring in destructive heresies**, and deny the

|        |                                                                 |
|--------|-----------------------------------------------------------------|
|        | Master who bought them, bringing swift destruction on themselves. |
| 2Pe 2:2 | And **many shall follow their destructive ways, because of whom the way of truth shall be evil spoken of,** |
| 2Pe 2:3 | and in greed, **with fabricated words,** they shall use you for gain. From of old their judgment does not linger, and their destruction does not slumber. |

Note: The "Way of Truth" does and has always included both obedience to the Torah of YHWH and belief in the Witness of Messiah (Isaiah 8:20).

Modern teachers have taught that the Torah of YHWH no longer applies to those who have the Witness of Messiah, in direct violation of Isaiah 8, going so far as to say that if a believer obeys the Torah of YHWH they have somehow "fallen from grace", which is a phrase from Galatians chapter 3 that has been interpreted out of context, twisted as Peter says in 2 Peter 3:14-17, to support their lawless dogma.

|          |                                                                 |
|----------|-----------------------------------------------------------------|
| 2Pe 2:18 | For speaking **arrogant nonsense,** they entice **– through the lusts of the flesh, through indecencies –** the ones who **have indeed escaped** from those living in delusion (unbelievers), |
| 2Pe 2:19 | promising them freedom, though themselves being slaves of corruption – **for one is a slave to whatever overcomes him.** (Compare this to Romans 6:15) |
| 2Pe 2:20 | For if, **after they have escaped the defilements of the world through the knowledge of the Master and Saviour יהושע Messiah,** they are **again entangled in them and overcome,** the latter end is worse for them than the first. |
| 2Pe 2:21 | For it **would have been better for them not to have known the way of righteousness** (Torah and Witness), **than having known it, to turn from the set-apart command delivered unto them** |

| | |
|---|---|
| **2Pe 2:22** | For them the proverb has proved true, **"A dog returns to his own vomit,"** and, "A washed sow *returns* to her rolling in the mud." |

The second type of believer is the one that has confessed Yahushua Messiah as their Savior but have intentionally chosen to disobey and/or dishonor the Torah of YHWH, to whom the book of Hebrews has a couple things to say.

| | |
|---|---|
| **Heb 6:4** | For it is **impossible** for those who were **once enlightened**, and have **tasted the heavenly gift**, and have become **partakers of the Set-apart Spirit**, |
| **Heb 6:5** | and have **tasted the good Word** of Elohim and the **powers of the age to come**, |
| **Heb 6:6** | <u>**and fall away**</u>, to renew them again to repentance – having <u>**impaled for themselves the Son of Elohim again**</u>, and put Him to open shame. |
| **Heb 6:7** | For ground that is drinking the rain often falling on it, and is bearing plants fit for those by whom it is tilled, receives blessing from Elohim, |
| **Heb 6:8** | but if it **brings forth thorns and thistles** it is rejected and near to being cursed, and ends up by being burned. |

**Enlightened**: Need for Messiah (Passover Lamb)

**Heavenly Gift**: Grace through Belief (Red Sea Crossing)

**Partakers of the Spirit**: Received the Comforter (Rock of Horeb)

**Good Word**: Training in the Torah (Mount Sinai)

**Power**: Gifts of the Spirit (the Presence with Us)

While it is true that most Christians have not experienced all these things in the wake of so much false doctrine, it is vitally important that they hear this message and repent, for once you received all these things and turned away from them to walk according

234

to your own way, according to the flesh and in rebellion against the Torah of YHWH, it is **IMPOSSIBLE** to be restored again to repentance.

| | |
|---|---|
| **Heb 10:26** | For if **we sin purposely** after we have received the knowledge of the truth, there no longer remains a slaughter *offering* for sins, |
| **Heb 10:27** | but some fearsome anticipation of judgment, and **a fierce fire which is about to consume the opponents.** |
| **Heb 10:28** | Anyone who has disregarded the Torah of Mosheh dies without compassion on the witness of two or three witnesses. |
| **Heb 10:29** | How much **worse punishment** do you think shall he deserve who has **trampled the Son of Elohim underfoot**, counted the blood of the covenant by **which he was set apart** as common, and insulted the Spirit of favour? |
| **Heb 10:30** | For we know Him who has said, **"Vengeance is Mine, I shall repay, says .יהוה"** And again, **"יהוה shall judge His people."** |
| **Heb 10:31** | It is fearsome to fall into the hands of the living Elohim. |

This passage has been distorted ad nauseam but the understanding of it is quite simple if we pay attention. If you were to look up this passage in your Bible and go back to verse 19 you would see that it begins with "so, brothers…".

He begins verse 26 with "for if we", clearly identifying this passage is relevant to the body of believers, including himself. He follows that with "sin purposely after we come to the knowledge of the truth", which should not be hard to understand anymore after all we've said.

"… sin is the transgression of the law" 1 John 3:4

| | |
|---|---|
| **Purposely:** | stg's #**G1596** "hekousiōs", an adverb from a root stem meaning to volunteer: - wilfully, willingly. A word to express intent, i.e., knowing the truth and willfully and intentionally disobeying. |

235

As we have already stated, knowing the truth concerns both belief in Messiah (John 14:6) and obedience to the Word/Torah of YHWH (John 17:17; Psalms 119:142).

Paul follows this up with "there no longer remains a slaughter *offering* for sins, but some fearsome anticipation of judgment, and **a fierce fire which is about to consume the opponents**".

The word "opponents" in this verse translates the Greek word "hupenantios", which comes from two other Greek words, meaning, "under" and "opposite". This word expresses the idea of someone who is against or is an adversary of a certain position.

Since the context is "sin" and sin is contrary to or against the Torah, then it is clear that these people called "opponents" here, refers to those who are contrary to the Torah, i.e., disobedient. Paul has something to say about these kinds of people.

| | |
|---|---|
| **Eph 2:1** | And you **were** dead in trespasses and sins, |
| **Eph 2:2** | in which you **once walked** according to the course of this world, according to the ruler of the authority of the air, of **the spirit that is now working in the sons of disobedience**, |
| **Eph 2:3** | among whom also **we all once lived in the lusts of our flesh**, doing the desires of the flesh and of the mind, and were **by nature children of wrath**, as also the rest. |

Here Paul is referring to our position before we confessed Messiah for salvation, being "dead in trespasses and sins" which refers to the fact that, at that time, we were under the condemnation of death because of our disobedience to the Torah of YHWH.

He goes on to say that this behavior (disobedience) was the way of the world, according to the world's ruler (Satan) who is the spirit working in the hearts and minds of those who are **disobedient**. He states clearly that we were all once living this way, according to the lust of our flesh, which we know Paul says "does not subject itself to the Torah" of YHWH (Romans 8:7).

This last verse states that when we **were** sons of disobedience, we "**were** by nature children of wrath". This should not be hard for us to understand because it's what the Scripture says Genesis to Revelation, that those who refuse to obey shall suffer the judgment, the wrath of YHWH.

Those who **are** "in Messiah" **are** not appointed to wrath (1 The 5:9) at His coming, but as we have already shown it is possible to be in Him by belief at confession and yet walk out from under the protection of His favor if we "fall away" (Heb 6:6), by not obeying the Law/Torah, i.e., "sin purposely"(Heb 10:26).

We are clearly told in John 14 that Him being in us and us being in Him is connected to obedience and that abiding or staying in Him has to do with the obedience (John 15:10).

It is only those of us who have called on the Name of Yahushua for salvation and remain in Him through obedience to the Torah of YHWH that are not appointed to wrath at His return.

Those who at some point were part of us but have intentionally or even unwittingly walked in rebellion against the Torah of YHWH are still "children of wrath" because they have proven they are "sons of disobedience", just as with the Children of Yisra'el, all of them were saved by the blood of the Lamb but not all of them inherited the Promise Land because of disobedience/disbelief (Hebrews 4:1-11).

| | |
|---|---|
| **Eph 5:5** | For this you know, that no one who whores, nor unclean one, nor one greedy of gain, who is an idolater, **has any inheritance in the reign of Messiah** and Elohim. |
| **Eph 5:6** | Let no one deceive you with **empty words**, for because of these (sins) the wrath **of Elohim comes upon the** sons of disobedience. |
| **Eph 5:7** | Therefore **do not become partakers with them**. |
| **Eph 5:8** | For you were once darkness, but **now *you are* light** in the Master. **Walk as children of light** |

The people who willingly practice acts of disobedience have no inheritance in the Messianic Kingdom. Any teaching or doctrine which states that a believer in Yahushua Messiah is no longer required to obey the Torah of YHWH, is nothing more than empty words intended to deceive you.

Any person, even a believer, who accepts these empty words as truth and walks in disobedience to the Torah of YHWH will not inherit the kingdom of YHWH but will, in fact, endure the wrath of YHWH as sons of disobedience.

They will be one of those to whom Messiah Himself was referring in Matthew 7:21-23.

| | |
|---|---|
| **Mat 7:21** | "Not everyone who says to Me, 'Master, Master,' shall enter into the reign of the |

|            | heavens, **but he who is <u>doing</u> the desire of My Father in the heavens.** |
| ---------- | ------------------------------------------------------------------------------ |
| Mat 7:22   | "Many shall say to Me in that day, 'Master, Master, have we not prophesied in Your Name, and cast out demons in Your Name, and done many mighty works in Your Name?' |
| Mat 7:23   | "And then I shall declare to them, 'I never knew you, **depart from Me, you who work lawlessness!'** |

"First off, we see that those who are "doing the desire of My Father" shall inherit the Kingdom and not necessarily those who called on His Name or did works in His Name or invoked power through His Name.

Those who inherit are those who are "**DOING**" His will. As we've shown in Romans 2:17-18, those who know the "will of Elohim" are those who have been "instructed out of the Torah".

Notice that even though they did all these great miracles, according to His Name, He rejected them, saying that He never knew them, because they performed the works of lawlessness, meaning that they did not obey the Law/Torah of YHWH.

The word "lawlessness" here translates the Greek word "anomia". This is the same Greek word in 1 John 3:4 that is translated as "transgression of the law" in the (KJV). The word "anomia", as we have stated many times, means "no law doing" and is a specific reference to the Law/Torah of YHWH or what the Christians call the Old Testament or Mosaic Law.

There is another passage in Paul's writings that covers this same topic, and it is in Colossians 3:4-11. Keeping in mind what's been said, go read it yourself and consider critically what is being said.

Going back to Romans now, remembering what has already been spoken in verses 12-13 about believers living in the flesh being cursed to condemnation and the admonition to put those deeds to death by walking in the spirit by obedience to the Torah of YHWH.

For we are those who are led by the Spirit of Elohim, which causes us to obey the laws and right rulings of YHWH (Ezekiel 36:27) by leading us into all the truth (John 16:13) of Messiah (John 14:6) and obedience to the Word/Torah of YHWH (John 17:17). We are of the adoption because we are loyal and obedient sons.

Note:    The "adoption" mentioned in this verse is a reference to the inner-spirit-man, spiritual adoption, which is

238

different than the physical adoption of the outer-physical-man mentioned in verse 28.

| Rom 8:16 | The Spirit Himself bears witness with our spirit that we are children of Elohim, |
| Rom 8:17 | and if children, also heirs – truly heirs of Elohim, and co-heirs with Messiah, **if** indeed we suffer with Him, in order that we also be exalted together. |

How does His Spirit bear witness with our spirit that we are His children?

1. Giving us the desire to obey His Torah,
2. By revealing understanding of the Scripture to us in a way that is consistent Genesis to Revelation,
3. Gifting's of the Spirit,
4. The increase of belief as we walk in the Word/spirit,
5. Our personal growth.

These are just a few of the ways His Spirit bears witness in us that we are His sons, for the Spirit can only bear witness to us in ways that are consistent with what the Scripture says He will do for He can't go beyond what is written.

Being His children, we have become coheirs with Messiah of the everlasting covenant and promises which include the resurrected body and the eternal kingdom. We could go on for days explaining what all that meant but let's just say it's a reference to Messiah being the true Yisra'el, of whom Jacob (Ya'aqob) was only a shadow picture.

YHWH told Abram that He would give the land to his "seed" (Genesis 12:7) and we know that Paul says that "seed" was not referring to the seed as in many seeds but as one seed, that Seed being Yahushua (Galatians 3:16).

YHWH told Pharaoh that "**Yisra'ĕl is My son, My first-born**" (Exodus 4:22) and we know that Yahushua is the "only begotten of the Father" (John 1:14).

YHWH told Hosea that "**When Yisra'ĕl was a child, I loved him, and out of Mitsrayim (Egypt) I called My son**" (Hos 11:1) and Matthew, when Joseph brought Yahushua and his mother back from Egypt to Nazareth (Mat 2:15), claimed this act to be the fulfillment of that prophecy.

Taking these and other relevant Scriptures into account, it seems clear that the man Jacob, whose name was changed to Yisra'el, was just a shadow picture of a future man who would be the fulfillment of that shadow picture.

The man Yisra'el then, is Yahushua Messiah and its through Him and by Him that we become members of the household of Yisra'el and inheritors (coheirs with Him) of the promises.

> **Note:** This truth of who we are in Messiah will be explained more clearly when we talk about Romans 11.

Paul goes on to say that we are "coheirs with Messiah" **if** we "indeed suffer with Him, in order that we might be exalted together".

Now, while it's true that at some point in our life, especially if these truly are the last days, we who are servants of the Most High, shall be tortured and killed as the Messiah was, however, that is likely not the type of suffering referred to here by Paul.

Contextually, it seems clear that the suffering Paul is referring to is the battle between our fleshly nature and our spirit man. For we know, Scripture says that Messiah was tempted and yet overcame that He might help us who are tempted as our High Priest (Hebrews 2:17-18).

And even though He was tempted in every way, the same way we are, He was able to endure it and overcome it without committing sin (Hebrews 4:15) so that we could know that it was possible for us to emulate Him.

Temptation comes more from within than from without, for it is our own fleshly desires that (James 1:14) tempt and entice us to sin.

Ha'Satan (the adversary), whispers in our ear and accuses us before the Father, but it is our own flesh that draws us into sin. That is why Paul admonishes us repeatedly to **NOT** walk according to the flesh, but to walk according to the spirit.

> **Rom 8:18** For I reckon that the sufferings of this present time are not worth comparing with the esteem that is to be revealed in us.

This is a reference to the resurrected body in the kingdom to come.

> **Rom 8:19** For the intense longing of the creation **eagerly waits for the revealing of the sons of Elohim.**

| Rom 8:20 | For the creation was subjected to futility, not from choice, but because of Him who subjected it, in anticipation, |
| Rom 8:21 | that the creation itself also **shall be delivered from the bondage to corruption into the esteemed freedom of the children of Elohim.** |
| Rom 8:22 | For we know that all the creation groans together and suffers the pains of childbirth together until now. |
| Rom 8:23 | And not only so, but even we ourselves who have **the first-fruits of the Spirit**, we ourselves also groan within ourselves, eagerly waiting for the adoption, the redemption of our body. |

The creation was subject to futility (entropy), not because of anything it had done but because of what Adam did when he ate of the tree of the Knowledge of Good and Evil. Adam had been given dominion of the earth and his disobedience required death, so the curse of death that was placed on him was also placed upon his entire domain.

So, both the creation and the children of Adam are subject to gradual death (entropy). We groan within ourselves awaiting their deliverance that is to come at the resurrection (the adoption, the redemption of the body) and it is at that time that the whole of creation will be delivered or restored to its rightful condition.

It's important for us to remember that the phrase "the first-fruits of the Spirit" refers to the down payment of the Spirit given to believers and does not represent the fullness of the Spirit that we receive at the resurrection. There is a huge error floating around that suggests that believers have the fullness of the Spirit dwelling in them and so their full redemption is sealed.

This couldn't be farther from the truth. As believers we are given a token or down payment of the Spirit to assist us in overcoming this body of death **IF** we submit to His leading. This first-fruits of the Spirit seals, or better marks, us for redemption, however, the fullness of our redemption rests upon a heart of submission.

The book of Hebrews states that Messiah is the "Author and Finisher" of our belief, and this is true, however it ignores the totality of what Scripture teaches to suggest that we have no part or responsibility in our salvation. We do have a very significant part to play, and that part has to do with humility and submission.

I am in no way suggesting that **how well we obey the Torah** determines whether we received the fullness of our redemption, because our capacity to obey is hindered in the struggle between the spirit man who wants to obey and the fleshly man who does not.

It is this struggle that Paul refers to repeatedly in his writings and it is our trust in Yahushua's sacrifice that gives us the hope of the resurrection, which is our complete redemption. Messiah's sacrifice, however, does not excuse willful disobedience.

| | |
|---|---|
| **Rom 8:24** | For in this expectation we were saved, but expectation that is seen is not expectation, for when anyone sees, does he expect it? |
| **Rom 8:25** | And if we expect what we do not see, we eagerly wait for it with endurance. |

In our salvation, we have this expectation or hope of the resurrection even though we do not yet see it. Because we do not see it, we eagerly await it through all the suffering and tribulation that comes our way.

It is this, a belief walked out in obedience to His Torah, that sets us apart (sanctifies us) from the world and makes us its enemy, because we live in the righteousness of YHWH and that righteousness sheds light on the unrighteousness (darkness) of the world, condemning it.

It is this righteousness, a belief walked out in obedience to His Torah, that gives us the hope of redemption at the resurrection and reveals to the world the futility of their philosophies and religions that only lead to the second death.

| | |
|---|---|
| **Rom 8:26** | And in the same way the Spirit does help in our weaknesses. For we do not know what we should pray, but the Spirit Himself pleads our case for us with groanings unutterable. |
| **Rom 8:27** | And He who searches the hearts knows what the mind of the Spirit is, because He makes intercession for the set-apart ones according to Elohim. |

The Ruach Ha'Qodesh (Holy Spirit) is given to us to "lead us into all truth" (John 16:13) and to cause us to walk in obedience to His laws and right rulings (Ezekiel 36:27). Our spirit is a lamp through which YHWH searches the innermost parts of men (Proverbs 20:27) and this is what Paul is referring to here.

In Romans 8:16 we are told that the Spirit of Elohim bears witness to our spirit that we are sons of Elohim and as part of that He searches the innermost parts of our hearts and minds through the conduit of our spirit which is born again in Him.

The things that we cannot articulate, i.e., the things that we desire so much to seek the Father for but cannot seem to put into words, His Spirit articulates for us as an intercessor between us and the Father.

**Note**:    Many in the church teach that this passage is specifically referring to speaking in tongues, but there is no evidence of that. We are not saying that speaking in tongues is not possible or that it isn't a way that the Spirit relates our unutterable needs to the Father, we are just saying that this passage doesn't say that, nor is speaking in tongues the only way the Spirit can communicate with the Father on our behalf.

>**Rom 8:28**      And we know that all *matters* work together for good to those who love Elohim, to those who are called according to *His* purpose.

This passage does not suggest that nothing bad will happen to the believer, for as the Scripture teaches "time and chance meets with all" men (Ecc 9:11), so sometimes stuff just happens either by chance or because of our own actions.

>What this passage in Romans 8 does promise is that no matter what happens, YHWH has promised to work it out for our eventual good. However, there is a qualifier in this verse that is generally either overlooked or misunderstood.

>This passage says that the promise is unto all those who "love Elohim" and to those "who are called according to His purpose". So, there is a very select group of people to which this promise is given.

>First, we must ask ourselves what does it mean to "love Elohim"?

**1Jn 5:3**      **For this is the love for Elohim**, that we **guard His commands**, and His commands are **not heavy**.

>So, those who love Him obey His Torah! Our next question then should be, what does it mean to be "called according to His purpose"?

243

| | |
|---|---|
| **Purpose:** | stg's #G4286 "πρόθεσις" (prothesis), from G4388 (to place before); a *setting forth*, that is, (figuratively) *proposal* (*intention*). |

We must ask ourselves then, what did the Father "set forth" for His called ones to accomplish?

| | |
|---|---|
| **Eph 2:10** | For we are **His workmanship**, created in Messiah יהושע unto good works, **which Elohim prepared beforehand that we should walk in them.** |

What standard of "good works" did YHWH set forth before Messiah came that His people should live by? The answer is, of course, His Torah.

The "purpose" of YHWH is that all His children do His will. The Greek word translated as "His will" in Romans 2:18 is: "θέλημα" (thelēma - stg's #**G2307)** from the prolonged form of G2309; a *determination* (properly the thing), that is, (actively) *choice* (specifically ***purpose***, *decree*; abstractly *volition*) or (passively) *inclination:* - desire, pleasure, will.

What we are trying to get you to see here, is that His will and His purpose refers to the same thing, that we obey Him.

So, to love Him and be called according to His purpose is associated to trusting in Him and obeying His Torah.

Now, this brings what Paul is saying here in Romans 8:28 into absolute and complete agreement with everything else this picture says about those who will "guard and do" His Torah (Deuteronomy 28:1-13).

| | |
|---|---|
| **Rom 8:29** | Because those whom He knew beforehand, He also ordained beforehand to be conformed to the likeness of His Son, for Him to be the first-born among many brothers. |
| **Rom 8:30** | And whom He ordained beforehand, these He also called, and whom He called, these He also declared right. And whom He declared right, these He also esteemed. |

244

| **Rom 8:31** | What then shall we say to this? If Elohim is for us, who is against us? |
|---|---|

This passage concerns what is called predestination, which has been sorely mis-used and abused over the millennia. Huge dissension and division within the body has taken place because of the argument between pre-ordained destiny (predestination) and free will.

The argument holds that YHWH is absolutely sovereign and, in His sovereignty, He has preordained some to be His children and some not be His children, even though Scripture says that He wants none to perish but that all come to repentance (2 Peter 3:9).

Admittedly, there are passages in the Scripture that suggest or at least seem to suggest that we have no free will, and everything happens because it's ordained. However, there are equally as many passages in Scripture that teach a clear and unarguable position of choice and free will within man.

There is a passage where it says that YHWH has created the wicked for the day of evil (Proverbs 16:4) and yet He has also told us that He has put before us both good and evil of which we are to choose for ourselves (Deuteronomy 30:14-20).

> **Note**: Before we move on I want to explain the difference between pre-destination and fate. Fate is a belief that no matter what choices we make in our life, our destiny is set by forces outside our control.

Pre-destination, on the other hand, at least as it is taught in the Scripture, refers to YHWH's knowledge of our destiny based on His foresight, meaning that we do absolutely have free will to make our own destiny, however, He already knows where those choice will lead, even though we don't and need to experience them ourselves.

Any thorough and unprejudiced view of Scripture will produce the truth of both absolute sovereignty and free will. This seems problematic, however, if, in His absolute sovereignty, YHWH declared man to have free will then both are true. YHWH has sovereignty, and, in that sovereignty, He granted man free will.

If this is true, how then can anyone be pre-ordained or predestined by YHWH? Well, Paul himself gives us the answer in this very passage, and it has to do with YHWH's "knowing beforehand" or foreknowledge of what would take place.

There are plenty of examples of His foreknowledge in the Scripture, for example, we are told in the Scripture that He tells us the "end from the beginning".

| | |
|---|---|
| **Isa 46:9** | "Remember the former *events* of old, for I am Ĕl, and there is no one else – Elohim, and there is no one like Me, |
| **Isa 46:10** | **declaring the end from the beginning,** and **from of old that which has not yet been done,** saying, 'My counsel does stand, and all My delight I do,' |

Through foreknowledge, YHWH predestines those who will, in the future, trust in Him through His Son Yahushua and walk in obedience to His Torah. Because He knows beforehand the thoughts of a man's mind and the choices of a man's heart, YHWH calls him, justifies him and shall esteem him both in this life and in the world to come.

Because this is true, those who have proven their love for Him, by confessing the name of His Son and walking in obedience to His Torah, have nothing to fear, for if YHWH is on our side nothing can stand against us.

| | |
|---|---|
| **Rom 8:32** | Truly, He who did not spare His own Son, but delivered Him up on behalf of us all – how shall He not, along with Him, freely give us all else? |

If YHWH loved us so very much that He offered Yahushua up to die on our behalf, then how could we not expect Him to give us all that He has promised in Yahushua, having become coheirs with Him.

| | |
|---|---|
| **Rom 8:33** | Who shall bring any charge against Elohim's chosen ones? It is Elohim who is declaring right. |
| **Rom 8:34** | Who is he who is condemning? It is Messiah who died, and furthermore is also raised up, who is also at the right hand of Elohim, who also makes intercession for us. |

No one and nothing, in heaven or in the earth or under the earth, can bring any charge against those of us who have named the name of Messiah and have committed our hearts and our minds and our strength to obeying the Torah.

Messiah Himself has died for us and the Father has raised Him up again from the dead and has sit Him at His right hand, with all power and authority, so the Messiah can and will intercede on our behalf when we call upon Him.

Anyone, no matter who they claim to be, can ever justly bring up your past to use it against you once you have believed. Anyone who does so is an 'accuser of the brethren' and a child of the Devil (Revelation 12:10).

| | |
|---|---|
| Rom 8:35 | Who shall separate us from the love of the Messiah? Shall pressure, or distress, or persecution, or scarcity of food, or nakedness, or danger, or sword? |
| Rom 8:36 | As it has been written, **"For Your sake we are killed all day long, we are reckoned as sheep of slaughter."** |
| Rom 8:37 | But in all this we are more than overcomers through Him who loved us. |
| Rom 8:38 | For I am persuaded that neither death nor life, nor messengers nor principalities nor powers, neither the present nor the future, |
| Rom 8:39 | nor height nor depth, nor any other creature, shall be able to separate us from the love of Elohim which is in Messiah יהושע our Master. |

This is a very comforting passage; unfortunately, it has been used to suggest something that is not true.

The "once saved, always saved" proponents have twisted this passage to suggest that once you've called on the name of "Jesus", you are part of the predestinated ones, that nothing more is required of you and that no one can ever take you out of his hand, thus granting you eternal security.

There are two very interesting things in this passage. First, as we mentioned when discussing verse 28, there were two qualifiers, which are "loving Elohim" and being "called according to His purpose". We went on to show how these qualifiers are a reference to our obedience to His Torah through belief.

Well, that same qualifier is found here in verse 39. Nothing and no one can "separate us from the love of Elohim" which we have through belief in Yahushua Messiah. However, to have this protection, to have His love as a guard against being separated from Him, we must be in His love. The key phrase here is that the love of Elohim is with those who are **"IN"** Messiah Yahushua. What does it mean to be "in Messiah"?

247

Being "in Messiah" and being "in the spirit" mean the exact same thing. We have trusted in the promises of YHWH through belief in His Son Yahushua, which has caused us to be born again in the inner-spirit-man.

This "new man" is required to "walk in the spirit", which is our righteousness (Deut 6:24-25; Rom 6:16, 18-19, 22) and which leads us into set apartness (holiness), which ends in eternal life, so that he does not "accomplish the works of the flesh", which is rebellion and ends in the second death.

The spirit man is in continual daily battle against the fleshly man for control over our behavior (Gal 5:17) and Paul gives us many instructions as to how to overcome the fleshly man, and all of them have to do with obedience to the Torah. Paul tells us in Romans 12:1-2 to make a sacrifice.

> **Rom 12:1**     I call upon you, therefore, brothers, through the compassion of Elohim, **to present your bodies a living offering** – set-apart, well-pleasing to Elohim – your reasonable worship.
>
> **Rom 12:2**     And do not be conformed to this world, but **be transformed by the renewing of your mind**, so that you prove what is that good and well-pleasing and perfect **desire of Elohim**.

We are to present our body's as a living sacrifice "holy and acceptable" unto Elohim. We are to transform the way we think by renewing our mind to a new standard of thinking and acting that will prove the perfect will of YHWH.

We have already shown that those who know the desire or will of Elohim are those who have been trained by the Torah (Romans 2:17-18). We know the Messiah "sets apart and cleanses" His bride through the "washing of water by the Word" (Ephesians 5:6).

What is interesting about that statement in Ephesians 5:6 is that water is used many times in Scripture as a metaphor for the Spirit of YHWH. Paul of course knows this and is explaining here in Ephesians that the Spirit of YHWH cleanses and sets us apart (makes us holy) through the washing of the Word, i.e., He causes us to walk in obedience to the laws and right rulings of YHWH (Ezekiel 36:27).

We are transformed by the renewing our mind in the same manner. The Spirit of YHWH is sent to us to lead us into **ALL TRUTH,** which includes both the spiritual truth of our need to believe in Yahushua Messiah for justification from death **AND** the physical truth of our need to walk in the justification of life through obedience to the Torah.

So, we must "renew our mind" by washing it through the Word of YHWH. What we mean by this is that we are to set aside our old thoughts and opinions and understanding of the way things are, or the way we think things should be, and we must transform our thinking so that it is consistent and in total agreement with the Word/Torah of YHWH.

We do this by reading and meditating on the Word/Torah of YHWH day and night.

|  |  |
|---|---|
| **Psa 1:1** | Blessed is the man who shall not walk in the counsel of the wrong, and shall not stand in the path of sinners, and shall not sit in the seat of scoffers, |
| **Psa 1:2** | But **his delight is in the Torah of** יהוה, and he meditates in His Torah day and night. |
| **Psa 1:3** | For he shall be as a tree Planted by the rivers of water, that yields its fruit in its season, and whose leaf does not wither, and whatever he does prospers. |

Do you remember what Paul said of himself as the new believer in Romans 7:22? He said that he "delights in the Torah of YHWH in the inner man". Paul was just quoting David as a man who has been blessed by the favor of YHWH through belief in His Son Yahushua.

What else does David say about the Torah?

|  |  |
|---|---|
| **Psa 119:89** | **Forever**, O יהוה, Your Word stands firm in the heavens. |
| **Psa 119:90** | Your trustworthiness is to **all generations**; You established the earth, and it stands. |
| **Psa 119:91** | According to Your right-rulings they have stood to this day, for all are Your servants. |
| **Psa 119:92** | If Your Torah had not been **my delight**, I would have perished in my affliction. |
| **Psa 119:93** | Let me never forget Your orders, **for by them You have given me life.** |
| **Psa 119:94** | I am Yours, save me; **For I have sought Your orders**. |
| **Psa 119:95** | The wrong have waited for me to destroy me; I understand Your witnesses. |

| | |
|---|---|
| **Psa 119:96** | I have seen an end of all perfection; Your command is exceedingly broad. |
| **Psa 119:97** | **O how I love Your Torah! It is my study all day long.** |

(See also Psa 119:113, 119, 127, 163, 165, 167)

| | |
|---|---|
| **Psa 119:98** | **Your commands make me wiser than my enemies; For it is ever before me.** |
| **Psa 119:99** | **I have more understanding than all my teachers, For Your witnesses are my study.** |
| **Psa 119:100** | **I understand more than the aged, for I have observed Your orders.** |
| **Psa 119:101** | I have restrained my feet from every evil way, that I might guard Your word. |
| **Psa 119:102** | I have not turned aside from Your right-rulings, For You Yourself have taught me. |
| **Psa 119:103** | How sweet to my taste has Your Word been, more than honey to my mouth! |
| **Psa 119:104** | **From Your orders I get understanding**; Therefore I have hated every false way. |
| **Psa 119:105** | **Your word is a lamp to my feet And a light to my path.** |

YHWH has called David a "man after Mine own heart" (1 Samuel 13:14; Acts 13:22) and it's because of David's attitude towards the Torah, fully and completely expressed in Psalms 119, that He has said this. David understood that to declare YHWH your Elohim was to take upon yourself all that YHWH had spoken and to make it your own, for in it is our hope.

Now, I know what you're thinking, there's no hope in the "law" for all our hope is in Yahushua Messiah.

Well, as with some things taught by Christians this last statement is true, but only half true. It is the Scripture that teaches us both how to live righteously before YHWH and how to receive cleansing when we fail. It is the Scripture, specifically the Torah, which teaches us our need for the Messiah.

Without the Torah there is no knowledge of sin and without the knowledge of sin there is no understanding our need for a Redeemer. It is the Torah that teaches us we are sinners deserving of death and it is the Torah that teaches us our need for a Redeemer, as well as how that atonement can be achieved.

250

Paul teaches us clearly in Galatians 3:24 that "the Torah became our trainer unto Messiah, in order to be declared right by belief." That's why David delighted so much in the Torah because it trained him to both trust in the promises of YHWH that would be fulfilled in Yahushua Messiah and how to walk out that trust in righteous obedience.

Remember what Paul says in Romans 8:7-8 concerning the mind of the flesh, that it "does not subject itself to the Torah of Elohim, neither can it, and that those who are in the flesh cannot please Elohim".

A man with David's heart and David's understanding has no problem discerning the truth from the error because he "observes" the orders, commands, witnesses (Torah), etc., of YHWH, for it is through the **DOING** of His Torah, **ALL HIS TORAH**, that we receive the wisdom and understanding He has set before us (Deuteronomy 4:5-6) and it is righteousness for us when we both guard and do it (Deuteronomy 6:24-25).

Let's also consider a couple things that King Solomon said…

| | |
|---|---|
| Pro 3:1 | My son, **do not forget my Torah, And let your heart watch over my commands;** |
| Pro 3:2 | For length of days and long life and peace they add to you. |
| Pro 3:3 | Let not loving-commitment and truth forsake you – Bind them around your neck, **Write them on the tablet of your heart,** |
| Pro 3:4 | Thus **finding favour and good insight** In the eyes of Elohim and man. |
| Pro 3:5 | **Trust in יהוה with all your heart, and lean not on your own understanding;** |
| Pro 3:6 | **Know Him in all your ways**, And He makes all your paths straight. |
| Pro 3:7 | Do not be wise in your own eyes; **Fear יהוה and turn away from evil.** |
| Pro 3:8 | It is healing to your navel, and moistening to your bones. |

Once again, we see that the Torah of YHWH is at the center of our "length of days and long life and peace" as well as our ability to find "favor (grace) and good insight (understanding)" in the eyes of both YHWH and men.

To "trust in YHWH with all of our heart and not lean upon our own understanding" means that our trust in Him is reflected in

251

everything we say and do in accordance with what He has said and done.

We don't trust in our own feelings or our own opinions, we trust only in what He has said and walk in obedience to what He has said. It is in doing this that we find the hope through which we receive the inheritance He has promised.

Proverbs 28:26 says that "the man who follows his own heart is a fool but he who **walks wisely** is delivered (saved)". How do we walk wisely?

| | |
|---|---|
| **Deu 4:5** | "See, I have taught you laws and right-rulings, as יהוה my Elohim commanded me, **to do** thus in the land which you go to possess. |
| **Deu 4:6** | "And **you shall guard and do them, for this is your wisdom and your understanding** before the eyes of the peoples who hear all these laws, and they shall say, 'Only a wise and understanding people is this great nation!' |

There is a doctrine floating around out there among Messianic Congregations, that suggests the Torah only applies to us when we live in the land and since we do not live in the land it does not apply to us today.

This could not be farther from the truth, for the Scripture says that when we are living among the nations in the last day and we turn our hearts back to YHWH to obey all His Torah then He will deliver us and restore us.

| | |
|---|---|
| **Deu 30:1** | "And it shall be, when all these words come upon you, the blessing and the curse which I have set before you, and you shall bring them back to your heart **among all the nations where יהוה your Elohim drives you,** |
| **Deu 30:2** | **and shall turn back to יהוה your Elohim and obey His voice, according to <u>all</u> that I command you today, with all your heart and with all your being, you and your children,** |
| **Deu 30:3** | **then יהוה your Elohim shall turn back your captivity,** and shall have compassion on you, and He shall turn back and gather you from all |

252

|  | the peoples where יהוה your Elohim has scattered you. |
|---|---|
| Deu 30:4 | "If any of you are driven out to the farthest parts under the heavens, from there יהוה your Elohim does gather you, and from there He does take you. |
| Deu 30:5 | **"And יהוה your Elohim shall bring you to the land which your fathers possessed, and you shall possess it. And He shall do good to you, and increase you more than your fathers.** |
| Deu 30:6 | "And יהוה your Elohim shall circumcise your heart and the heart of your seed, to love יהוה your Elohim with all your heart and with all your being, so that you might live, |
| Deu 30:7 | and יהוה your Elohim shall put all these curses on your enemies and on those who hate you, who persecuted you. |
| Deu 30:8 | "And **you shall turn back and obey the voice of יהוה and do all His commands which I command you today.** |
| Deu 30:9 | "And יהוה your Elohim shall make you have excess in all the work of your hand, in the fruit of your body, and in the fruit of your livestock, and in the fruit of your ground for good. For יהוה turns back to rejoice over you for good as He rejoiced over your fathers, |
| Deu 30:10 | **if you obey the voice of יהוה your Elohim, to guard His commands and His laws which are written in this Book of the Torah, if you turn back to יהוה your Elohim with all your heart and with all your being.** |

The other interesting thing mentioned in Roman 8:38-39, is that nowhere in this section does it say that we cannot, of our own free will, choose to walk away from the security that is in Yahushua Messiah.

Some might say that we come under the heading of no "other creature", suggesting that we cannot make a free will choice to walk away, however, there are several other Scriptures that not only suggest that we can, but emphatically teach so.

We've quoted these passages ad nauseam, so we are only going to list them here, but we implore you to take the time to go back and read them again remembering what we've spoken to you concerning these things.

(Hebrews 6:4-8 [comp. John 15:1-7]; 10:26-31; 2 Peter 2:18-22)

Consider one of the things Solomon said in Ecclesiastes.

**Ecc 12:13**    Let us hear the conclusion of the entire matter: Fear Elohim and guard His command, for this applies *to* all mankind!

Before we go on to chapter 9, let us review a few Scriptures.

**Hos 14:9**    Who is wise and understands these *words*, discerning and knows them? For the ways of יהוה are straight, and **the righteous walk in them**, but the <u>transgressors</u> stumble in them.
***

**Hos 6:6**    "For I delight in loving-commitment and not slaughtering, and in **the knowledge of Elohim** more than ascending offerings.
***

**1Sa 15:22**    Then Shemu'ĕl said, "Does יהוה delight in ascending offerings and slaughterings, as in obeying the voice of יהוה? Look, **to obey is better than a slaughtering, to heed is *better* than the fat of rams.**

**1Sa 15:23**    "For **rebellion** is as the sin of divination, and **stubbornness** is as wickedness and idolatry. Because you have rejected the word of יהוה, He also does reject you as sovereign."

If man would have walked in obedience there would have been no need for a sacrifice.

Divination, wickedness and idolatry are things the Scripture calls abomination, which in Hebrew is called "tô'ĕbah" (stg's #**H8441**, meaning disgusting), the foulest word in the Hebrew language.

It is very important we understand that YHWH is associating rebellion (willful and intentional disobedience) with stubbornness and says that they are the same to Him as witchcraft and idolatry. Do you hear that?

He also associates turning to the left or to the right of **ANYTHING** He has commanded to be equal to serving a different deity (Deut 28:14).

The Gate is narrow, and the Way is hard, and few will find it. (Mat 7:13-14).

# Chapter 7: Romans 9

Here, Paul (Sha'ul) goes on to teach concerning the concept of predestination, but we must never lose sight of what he said in verse 29, where it says, "those whom He knew beforehand, He also ordained beforehand".

Everything YHWH says about Him choosing to have mercy on whom He would have mercy, and how He chose Jacob over Esau while they were still in the womb, must be understood from His position of pre-knowledge or foreknowledge.

| | |
|---|---|
| Rom 9:1 | I speak the truth in Messiah, I do not lie, my conscience also bearing me witness in the Set-apart Spirit, |
| Rom 9:2 | that I have great sadness and continual grief in my heart. |
| Rom 9:3 | For I myself could have wished to be banished from Messiah for the sake of my brothers, my relatives according to the flesh, |
| Rom 9:4 | **who are *the children* of Yisra'ĕl, to whom is the adoption, and the esteem, and the covenants, and the giving of the Torah, and the worship, and the promises,** |
| Rom 9:5 | **whose are the fathers, and from whom is the Messiah according to the flesh,** who is over all, Elohim-blessed forever. Amĕn. |
| Rom 9:6 | However, it is not as though the word of Elohim has failed. **For they are not all Yisra'ĕl who are of Yisra'ĕl** |
| Rom 9:7 | **neither are they all children because they are the seed of Aḇraham, but, "In Yitsḥaq your seed shall be called."** |

Paul is making a distinction between what seems like two different Yisra'el's. The "church" has divided these up into spiritual Yisra'el and physical Yisra'el, and even though we are a huge proponent of the *Two-Part Principle* of physical and spiritual, we take exception to the concept that there is a physical Yisra'el and a spiritual Yisra'el, mostly because of the way these terms have been interpreted doctrinally.

(See: Sec. 2, Ch. 9 on Pg. 268 for a thorough explanation of who we become in Yahushua Messiah.)

257

Scripturally, the idea of a "spiritual Yisra'el" has merit because the true Yisra'eli are not solely those born into the physical bloodline of Abraham, Isaac, and Jacob (Yisra'el), but, in truth, constitutes all who have claimed the name of Yahushua the Mashiach and walk in the Torah of YHWH, both native born and Stranger (Gentile – Leviticus 19:33-34; Numbers 15:15-16).

As we have stated before, the man Jacob who was later called Yisra'el was a shadow picture of the true man Yisra'el, that is Yahushua. Does this mean that the physical seed of Jacob have no Kingdom inheritance?

Of course not! What YHWH has promised in the physical is not undone by the fulfillment of the spiritual, once He has spoken something it cannot be revoked, however what He accomplishes in the spiritual overshadows the physical shadow pictures.

What we mean is, the promise to Abraham, Isaac and Jacob is still valid, and He has promised that a **remnant** of their seed shall be saved, but they are saved just like everyone else, through belief in Yahushua Messiah.

Paul touches on that in this very passage when he says, "For they are not all Yisra'ĕl who are of Yisra'ĕl". Paul is reaffirming that there is a Yisra'el, in Yahushua Messiah, but that Yisra'ĕl does not incorporate all those who were born in the bloodline of Abraham, Isaac and Jacob.

It is only those who have come to belief in Yahushua Messiah, the true man Yisra'ĕl, that will inherit the Kingdom, both native born and stranger (Gentile), **IF** they walk in obedience to the Torah.

The reason we take exception to the Christian concept of a "spiritual Yisra'ĕl" is because they use it in conjunction with the idea of dispensational and replacement theologies, wherein they say that Yisra'ĕl and the "church" are separate entities that YHWH relates to in separate ways, requiring a different set of rules.

This is a doctrine of demons, intended to separate the body of Messiah into Jew and Gentile even though Paul clearly states in Galatians 3:28 that there is no distinction between Jew or Gentile for those who are in the body of Messiah (see also, Num 15:15-16 and Lev 19:33-34).

Technically, the adoption of a Gentile into the congregation of Yisra'ĕl is a legal matter commanded in the Torah and is meant as an instruction to the native born so they do not treat the Gentile convert differently than they would each other.

Both the "native born and the stranger that sojourns with them" are one people with the same standard of righteous living in the same covenants of promise.

| | |
|---|---|
| **Lev 19:33** | 'And when a stranger sojourns with you in your land, do not oppress him. |
| **Lev 19:34** | 'Let the stranger who dwells among you **be to you as the native among you**, and you shall love him as yourself. For you were strangers in the land of Mitsrayim. I am יהוה your Elohim. |

***

| | |
|---|---|
| **Num 15:15** | **One law** is for you of the assembly and for the stranger who sojourns with you – **a law forever throughout your generations. <u>As you are, so is the stranger before יהוה</u>.** |
| **Num 15:16** | **One Torah and one right-ruling** is for you and for the stranger who sojourns with you.'" |

Do you see, Gentile inclusion into the belief is a matter of legal precedent, commanded by YHWH to the children of Yisra'ěl. This has always been the truth and it is the truth still today. What Christians fail to consider is that the very redemption that we receive in Yahushua Messiah is a matter of legal precedent as well.

The Torah provides a legal remedy for violation of its instructions, namely the sacrificial system which is a shadow picture of the sacrifice Yahushua would make on our behalf. It is how YHWH was able to redeem the sinner without violating His own righteousness.

A righteous and just Elohim cannot arbitrarily forgive sin, His perfect righteousness and set apartness (holiness) rules out any possibility of compassionate judgment. This is why He instituted the concept of "substitutionary redemption".

By substituting the life of an innocent for the life of a sinner He has made a way to redeem the sinner from the condemnation of death he deserves. This is what Paul is saying in Romans 3:23-26.

| | |
|---|---|
| **Rom 3:23** | for all have sinned and fall short of the esteem of Elohim, |
| **Rom 3:24** | being declared right, without paying, by His favour **through the redemption which is in Messiah יהושע,** |

| Rom 3:25 | whom Elohim set forth as an atonement, through belief in His blood, **to demonstrate His righteousness**, because in His tolerance Elohim had passed over the sins that had taken place before, |
| Rom 3:26 | **to demonstrate at the present time His righteousness, that He is righteous and declares righteous the one who has belief in** יהושע. |

By offering up His Son, Yahushua, YHWH has made a way to remain absolutely righteous and still justify the unrighteous who would believe in Yahushua Messiah, His death as a substitute for ours, His blood the price of atonement for our sin.

So, both our redemption and our adoption are legal matters, not spiritual matters, even though they are only available to us through a belief (spiritual matter) that is lived out in obedience to the Torah of YHWH (physical matter), so that we might be complete (perfect) in Him, having done all that is required of us to stand.

In verse 9, Paul said "neither are they all children because they are the seed of Abraham, but **'In Yitshaq your seed shall be called'**".

This is very interesting and yet could be quite confusing because the spiritual meaning here seems contrary to the literal context of the promise to the seed through Isaac (Yitschaq). We know that Isaac was a direct seed of Abraham, so what does this mean.

Paul is telling us that just because someone is of the natural seed, a native born descendent of Abraham, Isaac, and Jacob, does not mean that they are children of the promise that shall inherit the Kingdom. We have already stated that the heirs of the Kingdom are those who have trusted in Yahushua Messiah and walk in obedience to the Torah of YHWH.

And not just here, but all of Scripture says the very same thing. Paul's statement that "In Yitshaq your seed shall be called" has to do with promise and not genealogy. All through his writings Paul makes it clear that there is no distinction, in the eyes of YHWH, between native born seed and the foreign seed that joins in covenant with Him through belief in Yahushua.

And not only Paul, but as we have seen, even Moses shared this doctrine. Paul rebuked the Jews in Romans 2:23-29 for trusting in fleshly issues like genealogy and he made it clear in his letter to the Philippians (3:1-14) that he was not relying upon his physical genealogy nor in his own ability to obey the Torah. His whole trust and hope were in Good News of Yahushua Messiah.

The inheritance of the Kingdom does and always has relied solely upon the promises of YHWH to those who would trust in Him and walk according to His command. What did He say to Yisra'el at Mount Sinai?

| | |
|---|---|
| **Exo 19:3** | And Mosheh went up to Elohim, and יהוה called to him from the mountain, saying, "This is what you are to say **to the house of Ya'aqob, and declare to the children of Yisra'ĕl**: |
| **Exo 19:4** | 'You have seen what I did to the Mitsrites, and how I bore you on eagles' wings and brought you to Myself. |
| **Exo 19:5** | 'And now, <u>if</u> **you diligently obey My voice, and shall guard My covenant,** <u>then</u> you shall be My treasured **possession above all the peoples** – for all the earth is Mine – |

There's a deeper theological meaning in this first verse than most people understand. Any time the Scripture repeats something, especially repeating it one right after another, it is trying to tell us something of significance and the second mention of it is generally referring to something deeper than its first mention.

That is the case here, for when YHWH mentions "the house of Jacob" He is referring to the natural seed of the man Jacob, however His second mention of "the children of Yisra'el" means something much more. The "children of Yisra'el" includes the strangers (Gentiles) that sojourned from Egypt with them.

We know from Exodus 12:37-38 that there was a "mixed multitude" that came out of Egypt with the people of Yisra'el. As we've already shown in Leviticus 19:34, the stranger that sojourns with Yisra'el, in covenant with YHWH, are to be treated as native born Yisra'elis.

So, the conditional promise given to Yisra'el in Exodus 19:5 applied both to the natural seed and to those strangers that were with them. What is that conditional promise?

It says that **"IF"** we do these two things: 1) diligently obey His voice and 2) keep His covenant **"THEN"** He will make us a treasured possession (segulah) above all peoples.

The word "segulah" in Hebrew refers to a treasure that is so special to its owner that he never relies on anyone else to take care of it, but he holds it in his hands and never let's go.

| | |
|---|---|
| **Joh 10:27** | "My sheep **hear My voice**, and I know them, and **they follow Me.** |
| **Joh 10:28** | "And I give them everlasting life, and they shall by no means ever perish, and **no one shall snatch them out of My hand**. |
| **Joh 10:29** | "My Father, who has given them to Me, is greater than all. And **no one is able to snatch them out of My Father's hand.** |

This is the promise for those of us who have trusted in Yahushua and walk in obedience to the Torah of YHWH with a heart of compassion for each other. I know some might look at this passage and ask, "Where does it say here that we have to obey the Torah?"

The fact that some people can look at this passage and not see our requirement to obey the Torah in it, just shows that we as a people do not look at the Scripture from the right mindset.

First, we must understand that the Hebrew Scripture is the underlying foundation upon which all things said in the Messianic Writings must be compared and interpreted. The phrase "hear My voice" refers to a heart condition and not just the act of hearing some words.

The Hebrew word generally translated as **hear** is "Shama" and means more than just the act of hearing something. Like all Hebrew words, this word is active, meaning that there is intent behind it. When the Scripture says to **hear** something, it is referring to a heart condition which acts upon what it is hearing and should best be understood to mean "hear with the intent to obey".

This would be better translated as **"Listen!"** because when a father says this word to his child, he expects the child to obey what is being said. It is the same for the Father, because when He tells us to "hear" something He means to obey what He says.

So, when Messiah here says that His sheep "hear My voice", He is automatically referring to sheep that will obey it when they hear it. And if that isn't enough, He follows that up with saying that they "follow Me". To follow someone is to walk the same path that they walk, just as John says in 1 John 2:3-6.

| | |
|---|---|
| **1 Jn 2:3** | And by this we know that we know Him, **if** we guard His commands. |

| 1Jn 2:4 | The one who says, "I know Him," and **does not guard His commands, is a liar, and the truth is not in him.** |
|---|---|
| 1Jn 2:5 | But whoever guards His Word, truly the love of Elohim has been perfected in him. By this we know that we are in Him, |
| 1Jn 2:6 | The one who says he stays in Him ought himself also to **walk, even as He walked.** |

How exactly did Messiah "walk" out His life? The word **walk** refers to how we live our life, and the Messiah lived His life in absolute obedience to the Torah of YHWH. So, we see that Messiah is not only saying that we should **hear** His voice with a submitted heart but that we are to follow His example of complete obedience to the Torah of YHWH.

Just like YHWH spoke at Mount Sinai, that we are to "diligently obey *His* voice" and "keep (guard) *His* covenant", so the Messiah says that those who are in covenant with Him, "hear *His* voice" and "follow *Him*".

That phrase simply means, we willingly obey His instructions to us when we hear them and because of that, we are in His hands, for we are the **segulah** that the Father promised we'd be at Mount Sinai.

> Note: Before we move forward, we want to say one last thing about the phrase **"For they are not all Yisra'ěl who are of Yisra'ěl"**. The name "Yisra-el" is said in the Scripture to mean, **"because you have striven with Elohim and with men, and have overcome"** (Genesis 32:28).

As we have mentioned, Yahushua is the second man, Yisra'ěl, through whom we all receive the covenant promises, for He is the man who truly "struggled with El and overcame" of whom Jacob was a shadow picture.

So, this statement by Paul in Romans 9 is a play on words, where the native seed of Yisra'el are not necessarily the "overcomers" or the true Yisra'el of YHWH.

> **Rom 9:8** That is, those who are the children of the flesh, **these are not the children of Elohim,** but the children of the promise are reckoned as the seed.

263

| | |
|---|---|
| Rom 9:9 | For this is the word of promise, **"At this time I shall come and Sarah shall have a son."** |
| Rom 9:10 | And not only so, but Riḇqah having conceived by one, our father Yitsḥaq. |
| Rom 9:11 | Yet, before they were born or had done any good or evil – in order that the purpose of Elohim, according to choice, might stand, not of works but of Him who calls – |
| Rom 9:12 | it was said to her, **"The greater shall serve the lesser,"** |
| Rom 9:13 | as it has been written, **"Yaʿaqoḇ I have loved, but Ěsaw I have hated."** |
| Rom 9:14 | What, then, shall we say? Is there unrighteousness with Elohim? Let it not be! |
| Rom 9:15 | For He says to Mosheh, **"I shall favour whomever I favour, and I shall have compassion on whomever I have compassion."** |
| Rom 9:16 | So, then, it is not of him who is wishing, nor of him who is running, but of Elohim who shows favour. |

Again, Paul is referring to the predestination of believers, which is based on the mercy and compassion of YHWH and not based on wishing for it or the striving of men. However, both Paul (8:29) and Peter (1 Peter 1:1-2) suggests that our predestination is based on His foreknowledge.

It is our opinion, and what we believe the totality of Scripture suggests, that our predestination is based on His foreknowledge of the thoughts and intents of our hearts at the **end** of our journey. Knowing this, He has chosen us and set us apart to be saved while we were still in our mother's womb and has throughout our lives sent His messengers to guard us (Hebrews 1:14).

The mention, first of Sarah and then Ribqah (Rebecca), in this passage is a specific reference to the lineage of the promise. What we mean, is that the promises given to Abraham by YHWH were based on what YHWH Himself would do through Abraham and his seed, and not on what Abraham or his seed would accomplish themselves.

When Abraham listened to his wife Sarah and bore Yishma'el through her servant Hagar, he was attempting to accomplish the promise of a seed through his own fleshly mechanisms. Instead of waiting on YHWH, who intended to accomplish this promise by supernatural means, i.e., giving him a son through his barren wife Sarah.

Isaac (Yitschaq) and his birth from a barren womb is a shadow picture of the Messiah Yahushua's supernatural birth from a virgin womb. The promise of the Messiah (the Seed of Abraham) was through a work done by YHWH and not by men.

So, the mention of Isaac here in Romans 9:10, is a reinforcement of what was said in verse 7 concerning the line of promise (spiritual) versus the natural bloodline (physical), which was based on Abraham's belief. In all of Paul's writings you will see this same train of thought woven throughout of his arguments.

Before we move on, lets clarify the "heart issues" that distinguished Jacob (Jacob) over Esau.

As the firstborn son of Isaac and Rebecca, Esau was to inherit both the birthright of authority and the double portion blessing. His status as the first to exit the womb was in itself all that was necessary for him to inherit these things and so he is the picture of the natural (physical) line.

Now Jacob, having been the second son to exit the womb, had no portion in either the birthright or the blessing but what he did have was respect for the covenant and the inheritance, which his brother Esau did not have. This is seen clearly in Genesis 25:29-34.

| | |
|---|---|
| **Gen 25:29** | And Ya'aqob cooked a stew, and Ěsaw came in from the field, and he was weary. |
| **Gen 25:30** | And Ěsaw said to Ya'aqob, "Please feed me with that same red stew, for I am weary." That is why his name was called Edom. |
| **Gen 25:31** | But Ya'aqob said, "Sell me your birthright today." |
| **Gen 25:32** | And Ěsaw said, "Look, I am going to die, so why should I have birthright?" |
| **Gen 25:33** | Then Ya'aqob said, "Swear to me today." And he swore to him, and sold his birthright to Ya'aqob. |
| **Gen 25:34** | Ya'aqob then gave Ěsaw bread and stew of lentils. And he ate and drank, and rose up and left. **Thus Ěsaw despised his birthright.** |

As you can see, Esau "despised" the birthright and because of his **heart attitude** towards it and the things of YHWH (the covenant) he not only lost his birthright but would later also lose the blessing of the double portion (Genesis 27).

265

Thus, the firstborn right, the promise, past from the firstborn Esau (the natural heir) to the second son Jacob (the heir of promise) because of an attitude, more specifically a heart issue as it relates to the things of YHWH.

Because it is YHWH who knows the hearts of men, even more so than we know our own hearts, He, in His foreknowledge, extended love, mercy and the promise to Jacob and rejected Esau before either one of them had even exited the womb or made any choices of their own.

All that remained then, was for the truth of the matters to be proven out through the lives of these men, to show both the wisdom and foresight of YHWH.

It was not something He needed to do for Himself, for He knows all things from the beginning, but it was something that needed to be done both in them and for us, so we would know and understand both the futility of our own nature and His absolute sovereignty, which can be seen in the very next passage.

| | |
|---|---|
| **Rom 9:17** | For the Scripture says to Pharaoh, **"For this same purpose I have raised you up, to show My power in you, and that My Name be declared in all the earth."** |
| **Rom 9:18** | So, then, He favours whom He wishes, and He hardens whom He wishes. |

**Note:** It is imperative we understand that even though YHWH predestined Jacob over Esau, He did not force or in ANY way influence Esau to make the choices he made.

Esau was free to make his own choices and did so. YHWH foresaw the choices Esau would make of his own free will and rejected him. Then foreseeing Jacob's love for Him and His promises, YHWH predestined Jacob instead of Esau.

His purpose for doing things the way He does is to show who He is and that He is worthy of all praise and esteem, which is what this passage is expressing.

The Torah was given as a proof text, which determines whether we are children of YHWH or children of the adversary, Ha-Satan.

| | |
|---|---|
| **1Jn 3:7** | Little children, **let no one lead you astray**. **The one doing righteousness is righteous**, even as He is righteous. |
| | *** |
| **Deu 6:24** | And יהוה commanded us to **do all these laws**, to fear יהוה our Elohim, for our good always, to keep us alive, as it is today. |
| **Deu 6:25** | And **it is righteousness for us** when we **guard to do all this command** before יהוה our Elohim, as He has commanded us.' |
| | *** |
| **1Jn 3:8** | **The one doing sin is of the devil**, because the devil has sinned from the beginning. **For this purpose the Son of Elohim was manifested: to destroy the works of the devil.** |
| | *** |
| **1Jn 3:4** | Whosoever committeth sin transgresseth also the law: for **sin is the transgression of the law**. (KJV) |
| | *** |
| **1Jn 3:9** | Everyone having been born of Elohim **does not sin** *(disobey the Torah)*, because His seed stays in him, and he is powerless to sin, because he has been born of Elohim. *(Added for clarification)* |
| **1Jn 3:10** | **In this the children of Elohim and the children of the devil are manifest**: **Everyone not doing righteousness is not of Elohim**, neither the one not loving his brother. |

We see that **ALL** the Law/Word/Torah is given to us to prove whose son we are. Everyone who refuses to walk in the righteousness of the Torah is a son of the devil, however, all those who set their hearts, minds and strength on obedience to the Torah ,without additions and subtractions, shall be the sons of Elohim.

Yahushua Messiah did not come to give a "New Covenant" in the sense of something that never existed before, but He did come to make the "old" covenant new again, or renew it, through His blood and death.

He did not add to, take away from nor change anything established at Mount Sinai between YHWH and Yisra'el, not a single jot nor a tittle thereof (Matthew 5:17-19)!

| Rom 9:19 | Then you shall say to me, "Why does He still find fault? For who has resisted His counsel?" |
|----------|---|
| Rom 9:20 | But who are you, O man, to talk back to Elohim? **Shall that which is formed say to him who formed it, "Why have you made me like this?"** |
| Rom 9:21 | Does not the potter have authority over the clay, from the same lump to make one vessel for value and another not for value? |

This is one of man's arguments against the "fairness" of YHWH and predestination. It also stems from the idea that the biblical concept of predestination means that YHWH chose arbitrarily to give some people mercy and others not. If you believe in predestination based on an arbitrary choice of the Creator, it denies the very existence of our free will.

Since the Scripture clearly and unambiguously teaches that man has the choice to obey or disobey then our predestination cannot, by definition, be based on an arbitrary choice of the Creator. His predestination of us must be influenced, in some way, by the choices we are making or His knowledge of the choices we will make.

Since both Paul and Peter confirm the fact that our having been chosen is a byproduct of His foreknowledge, then the obvious explanation is that our predestination is a determination made by Him which is based on His foreknowledge of our future heart condition, towards Him and His covenant.

This being true then, we cannot make the argument that is stated above, namely, that it's His fault we are the way we are, not our fault. After all, "He made me this way", which many men throughout history have resorted to as an excuse for their own debauchery.

In truth, what the Scripture is actually saying in passages like this, is not that He created us evil but that He created us with the potential of evil, if we so choose. Furthermore, knowing beforehand that some of us would choose to be evil, He created us anyway. The only question is, why?

| Rom 9:22 | And if Elohim, **desiring to show wrath, and to make His power known,** with much patience tolerated the vessels of wrath prepared for destruction, |
|----------|---|

268

| | |
|---|---|
| Rom 9:23 | and **that He might make known the riches of His esteem on vessels of compassion, which He had prepared beforehand for esteem,** |
| Rom 9:24 | even whom He called, not only us of the Yehuḏim, but also of the nations? |
| Rom 9:25 | As He says in Hoshĕa too, **"I shall call them My people, who were not My people, and her beloved, who was not beloved."** |
| Rom 9:26 | **"And it shall be in the place where it was said to them, 'You are not My people,' there they shall be called sons of the living Elohim."** |
| Rom 9:27 | And Yeshayahu cries out on behalf of Yisra'ĕl, **"Though the number of the children of Yisra'ĕl be as the sand of the sea, the remnant shall be saved.** |
| Rom 9:28 | **For He is bringing a matter to an end, and is cutting it short in righteousness, because יהוה shall cut short a matter on the earth."** |
| Rom 9:29 | And as Yeshayahu said before, **"If יהוה of hosts had not left us a seed, we would have become like Seḏom, and we would have been made like Amorah."** |

He created mankind with the choice to either trust Him and to prove that trust daily through obedience or to deny Him by living our life according to our own fleshly desires, which according to Deuteronomy 28:14 is the same as serving a different Elohim, i.e., Ha-Satan (the adversary).

Though He knew the choices we would make, He allowed us to be born, to live and thrive anyway, tolerating the unrighteous until the day of wrath, and to show His power to them, as He extends His mercy to those of us who have trusted and obeyed Him.

YHWH truly does not want anyone to perish but all to come to repentance (2 Peter 3:9).

It was based upon His foreknowledge that He chose some to be destroyed and some to be redeemed, that's the only reasonable conclusion that man can come to through a sincere and thorough study of the totality of Scripture.

Paul's quotes of Hosea (2:23; 1:10) and Isaiah (YeshaYahu 10:22-23; 1:9) are specifically relevant to the natural seed of Jacob,

269

specifically the northern tribes of the House of Yisra'el that were scattered among the nations (Gentiles) in approximately 722 BCE.

Today, the northern House of Yisra'el is still lost among the nations and, in fact, cannot distinguish themselves from the nations. It is through this scattering of Yisra'el throughout the nations that allows those of the nations (Gentiles) to join with Yisra'el in covenant with YHWH through His Son Yahushua.

When Messiah was speaking with His disciples, a "Gentile" woman from Canaan approached Him asking that He heal her daughter from demon possession.

| | |
|---|---|
| **Mat 15:21** | And יהושע went out from there and withdrew to the parts of Tsor and Tsidon. |
| **Mat 15:22** | And see, a woman of Kena'an came from those borders and cried out to Him, saying, "Have compassion on me, O Master, Son of Dawiḏ! My daughter is badly demon-possessed." |
| **Mat 15:23** | But He did not answer her a word. And His taught ones came and asked Him, saying, "Send her away, because she cries after us." |
| **Mat 15:24** | And He answering, said, "**I was not sent except to the lost sheep of the house of Yisra'ěl.**" |
| **Mat 15:25** | But she came and was bowing to Him, saying, "Master, help me!" |
| **Mat 15:26** | And He answering, said, "It is not good to take the children's bread and throw it to the **little dogs**." |
| **Mat 15:27** | But she said, "Yes Master, for even the little dogs eat the crumbs which fall from their masters' table." |
| **Mat 15:28** | And יהושע answering, said to her, "O woman, **your belief is great!** Let it be to you as you desire." And her daughter was healed from that hour. |

Now Messiah clearly states here that He was sent to bring the "lost sheep of the House of Yisra'el" back into the fold, because it had been scattered among the nations since 722 BCE. And He goes on to say that it was not good to take the children's (Yisra'el) bread and give it to the little dogs (Gentiles).

270

In that day, it was common for Jews to refer to Gentiles as dogs, a dog being an unclean domesticated animal. It was basically a slur; however, the Messiah uses it here to express a very interesting point, which is, even a Gentile (unclean dog) who places his trust in Yahushua can find healing.

> Note: This principle is exactly what Peter's "sheet dream" in Acts 10 was about. He understood that the Spirit was not referring to YHWH making "unclean animals" clean so we could eat them, but that He was making "all men" clean through Yahushua Messiah (see Acts 10:28).

It's important to see the pictures here. Messiah came to restore all of Yisra'el, the northern House of Yisra'el and the southern House of Yahudah, back into a single house, which is exactly what the prophet Ezekiel said would happen.

| | |
|---|---|
| Eze 37:15 | And the word of יהוה came to me, saying, |
| Eze 37:16 | "And you, son of man, take a stick for yourself and write on it, 'For **Yehuḏah and for the children of Yisra'ĕl, his companions**.' Then take another stick and write on it, **'For Yosĕph, the stick of Ephrayim, and for all the house of Yisra'ĕl, his companions**.' |
| Eze 37:17 | **"Then bring them together for yourself into one stick, and they shall become one in your hand.** |
| Eze 37:18 | "And when the children of your people speak to you, saying, 'Won't you show us what you mean by these?' |
| Eze 37:19 | say to them, 'Thus said the Master יהוה, "See, I am taking the stick of Yosĕph, which is in the hand of Ephrayim, and the tribes of Yisra'ĕl, his companions. And I shall give them unto him, with the stick of Yehuḏah, and **make them one stick, and they shall be one in My hand.**" ' |
| Eze 37:20 | "And the sticks on which you write shall be in your hand before their eyes. |
| Eze 37:21 | "And speak to them, 'Thus said the Master יהוה, "See, **I am taking the children of** |

271

| | |
|---|---|
| | Yisra'ĕl from among the nations, wherever they have gone, and shall gather them from all around, and I shall bring them into their land. |
| Eze 37:22 | "And I shall make them one nation in the land, on the mountains of Yisra'ĕl. And one sovereign shall be sovereign over them all, and let them no longer be two nations, and let them no longer be divided into two reigns. |
| Eze 37:23 | "And they shall no longer defile themselves with their idols, nor with their disgusting *matters*, nor with any of their transgressions. And I shall save them from all their dwelling places in which they have sinned, and I shall cleanse them. **And they shall be My people**, and I be their Elohim, |
| Eze 37:24 | while Dawiḏ My servant is sovereign over them. **And they shall all have one shepherd and walk in My right-rulings and guard My laws, and shall do them.** |
| Eze 37:25 | "And they shall dwell in the land that I have given to Ya'aqoḇ My servant, where your fathers dwelt. And they shall dwell in it, they and their children and their children's children, forever, and My servant Dawiḏ be their prince forever. |
| Eze 37:26 | **"And I shall make a covenant of peace with them – an everlasting covenant it is with them.** And I shall place them and increase them, and shall place My set-apart place in their midst, forever. |
| Eze 37:27 | "And My Dwelling Place shall be over them. And **I shall be their Elohim, and they shall be My people.** |
| Eze 37:28 | **"And the nations shall know that I, יהוה, am setting Yisra'ĕl apart, when My set-apart place is in their midst -   forever." ' "** |

Now this is pretty clear, sometime in the future YHWH is going to send His Son Yahushua back to gather all the tribes of the northern house out of the nations and into the Promised Land or what we understand will be the Kingdom of Messiah.

This is what Messiah meant when He said He had come for the "lost House of Yisra'el". The purpose for His death, burial and resurrection was specifically to restore the two Houses of Yisra'el back into a single house, and reign as King over them.

In His mercy, though, YHWH had made a promise to Abraham that through His Seed, He would bless all the clans of the earth (Genesis 12:1-4) and according to Paul this "Seed" was Yahushua Himself (Galatians 3:16).

So, because of this, the death, burial and resurrection of Yahushua not only made a way for the two Houses of Yisra'el to be restored but also made a way for the believing Gentile to come into that covenant with them.

This is the "mystery" that Paul was called to teach among the Gentiles, "Messiah in you, the hope of glory" (Colossians 1:27).

So, the Gentiles were never the intended heirs of this promise but are a byproduct of the immense power and mercy of YHWH, through the redemptive work of Yahushua Ha-Mashiach.

We, the Gentiles, have received this mercy, like the little dogs eating the breadcrumbs from the Master's table, as a result of His restoration of the children of Yisra'el.

And so, as Messiah said, when He was lifted up, He became a light to the Gentiles through which He would fulfill the promise to Abraham of blessing all the clans of the earth through his seed.

**Isa 49:1**     Listen to Me, O coastlands, and hear, you peoples from afar! יהוה has called Me from the womb, from My mother's belly He has caused My Name to be remembered.

This is the prophetic verse referring to the "Servant" of YHWH, Yahushua.

**Isa 49:2**     And He made My mouth like a sharp sword, in the shadow of His hand He hid Me, and made Me a polished shaft. In His quiver He hid Me."

**Isa 49:3**     And He said to Me, 'You are My servant, O Yisra'ĕl, in whom I am adorned.'

It's interesting here that YHWH names His servant "Yisra'el" in reference to Yahushua the Messiah, because it is this Man Yisra'el, through which our inheritance comes.

273

Read carefully and you'll see that the Yisra'el mentioned here in verse 3, is going to deliver the people of Yisra'el in the following verses.

| | |
|---|---|
| **Isa 49:4** | And I said, 'I have laboured in vain, I have spent my strength for emptiness, and in vain. **But my right-ruling is with יהוה, and my work with my Elohim.'** " |
| **Isa 49:5** | And now said יהוה – who formed Me from the womb to be His Servant, **to bring Ya'aqoḇ back to Him**, though Yisra'ěl is not gathered to Him, yet I am esteemed in the eyes of יהוה, and My Elohim has been My strength – |
| **Isa 49:6** | and He says, "Shall it be a small *matter* for You to be My Servant **to raise up the tribes of Ya'aqoḇ, and to bring back the preserved ones of Yisra'ěl? And I shall give You as a light to the nations, to be My deliverance to the ends of the earth!"** |
| **Isa 49:7** | Thus said יהוה, the Redeemer of Yisra'ěl, their Set-apart One, to the despised, to the loathed One of the nation, to the Servant of rulers, "Sovereigns shall see and arise, rulers also shall bow themselves, because of יהוה who is steadfast, the Set-apart One of Yisra'ěl. And He has chosen You!" |

Notice, this "Servant", that YHWH is sending to redeem Yisra'el, will also be a light to the nations (Gentiles) and furthermore, YHWH calls this same Servant, "the despised and loathed one of the nation and a servant of rulers", saying that all the rulers of the nations shall rise up and bow down to him.

This is a hint as to who this "Servant" would be, for He would be considered loathsome and be despised by "the nation". Later on, Isaiah tells us about a "servant" who would come to suffer on behalf of the nation (Isaiah 52:12-53:12).

Needless to say, this "Servant" is a reference to Yahushua the Messiah, who came and died for the sins of the world, having been despised by His own people and killed to redeem all mankind back to YHWH.

In Luke 2:22-35, Shim'on was waiting in the temple for the coming of Messiah when he spotted Yoseph and Miriam with the child Yahushua and when he saw them he blessed them, saying over

274

Yahushua, that He was the salvation of YHWH and that He would be a light for the unveiling of the Gentiles, and the glory of His people Yisra'el.

In Acts 26:23, Paul says the resurrection of Yahushua would be a light to both the peoples (Yisra'el) and to the Gentiles. He also told the Jews in Acts 13:47, that since they had refused the message of Yahushua, that the Master has called him and Barnaba to be a light to the Gentiles (quoting from Isaiah 49:6), emphasizing his ministry into the Gentiles.

| | |
|---|---|
| **Rom 9:30** | What shall we say then? That nations not following after righteousness, have obtained righteousness, even the righteousness of belief, |
| **Rom 9:31** | but Yisra'ĕl following after the Torah of righteousness, has not arrived at the Torah of righteousness. |
| **Rom 9:32** | Why? Because *it was* not of belief, but as by works of Torah. For they stumbled at the **Stone of stumbling.** |
| **Rom 9:33** | As it has been written, **"See, I lay in Tsiyon a Stone of stumbling and a Rock that makes for falling, and everyone who is believing on Him shall not be put to shame."** |

This passage is very important to understand, because if you do, you'll understand a great many things in Paul's writings that the church completely misunderstands and because of it they have created a lot of false doctrine.

The problem is, the "devil is in the details" as they say. Coming to understand the meaning of this passage and many other passages in Paul's writings, rests on the understanding of a very small word, namely the word "of".

This passage is making a distinction between the righteousness that comes from obedience to the Torah and the righteousness that comes by belief in Yahushua Messiah.

This distinction is important because it determines where our "trust" lies, whether we are trusting in Yahushua by belief, which brings life or trusting in our works of the Torah, which leads to death.

It's a focus of trust and whether that trust is placed in our belief or in our works. Paul is continually criticizing the Jews because they have placed their trust in their obedience to the Torah and their physical genealogy and not in YHWH Himself, through His Son Yahushua.

Verses 30-31 states two interesting positions:

The Gentiles who **WERE NOT** attempting to live their lives in the righteousness that comes from obedience to the Torah, were actually declared to be righteous because of their belief,

-and-

The Jews (natural Yisra'el) who **WERE** attempting to live their lives in obedience to the righteousness of Torah, never actually achieved the Torah of righteousness because they lacked belief.

Now many modern Christian teachers believe they understand what this passage is saying, but most of them really don't because they think this passage, like several others, is telling them they do not have to live in the righteousness of Torah, which is just not the case.

This passage has absolutely nothing to do with how we "**live**" righteously **after** we have become declared righteous by belief. This passage is wholly and completely about **how** we are made righteous (justified) before YHWH.

Can a man be justified (made righteous) by the works of the Law/Torah? Absolutely not!

**Rom 3:20**     Therefore by works of Torah **no flesh shall be declared right before Him,** for by the Torah is the knowledge of sin. (Psalms 143:2)
\*\*\*
**Gal 3:11**     And that no one is declared right by Torah before Elohim is clear, for **"The righteous shall live by belief." (Hab 3:4)**

So, both the Tanak and the Messianic Writings say that you cannot be made righteous by the works of Torah but by belief only. This being the true facts of the matter, verse 32 asks, why?

Because the Gentiles, who did not know the Torah, neither were they trying to obey the Torah, were made right to the Torah by belief in Yahushua. Yes, before they believed, the Torah had condemned them to death because of their disobedience, even though they did not know the Torah existed or what it required of them.

It was their belief in Yahushua Messiah that delivered them from that penalty of death and made them right in the sight of YHWH,

as it is written in Habakkuk 3:4, a man has always been declared right by YHWH because of his belief and not his works. The works of Torah are, however, how a man lives righteously before YHWH.

The Yisra'elis, however, had the Torah and attempted to live in the righteousness of it, but they were not able to accomplish Torah righteousness because they did not believe. Yes, they walked in the righteousness of Torah, but their lack of belief prevented them from being declared right in the sight of YHWH.

It is in this teaching that both Christianity and Judaism fail to fully understand the two-part nature of all things. All things must have both the spiritual part and the physical part to be fulfilled or complete.

The Christians understand that the works of the Law/Torah cannot make them right before YHWH; however, they take this truth and stretch it out of proportion until it is no longer the truth.

For example, they teach everyone their need to believe in Yahushua Messiah to be made right or justified **from past sins**, which is correct, but they don't stop here, instead they push the idea of justification "by grace through faith" beyond its intended meaning, to include present and future sins in a doctrine that promotes lawless behavior (sin).

They teach that once you have been justified from sin through belief in Yahushua Messiah, they are no longer required to live in obedience to the Torah. This is a clear sign that they understand the spiritual principle of belief but not the physical principle of obedience.

Judaism on the other hand understands the scriptural requirement to walk in the righteousness of the Torah of YHWH, so they do not sin before Him. However, they totally and completely misunderstand the principle of justification by favor (grace) through belief and as a result they have lost sight of their need for Yahushua Messiah.

They believe in YHWH, that He is the Creator of all things and that He is the only Redeemer, which is right, but unfortunately, they put so much of their trust in the works of Torah, and the teachings of their rabbis, that their belief is no longer belief, as it is taught in Scripture.

They believe that obedience to the Torah makes them right in the sight of YHWH, which by itself is an error, they understand the physical principle of obedience but have missed the spiritual principle of belief.

As we've said before, our belief in Yahushua Messiah must be lived out in obedience to the Torah, but it is not our obedience to Torah that makes us right, it is our belief in Yahushua Messiah that

277

makes us right, so that we place our trust in Yahushua Messiah and not the works of the Torah.

As the *Two-Part principle* teaches, the spiritual righteousness that comes by belief must be joined with the physical righteousness that comes through obedience to the Torah, and these must be done with a heart attitude of compassion, for us to be complete before YHWH.

Romans 9:32 says that Yisra'el "stumbled at the stumbling stone". The stumbling stone Paul is referring to here is, of course, Yahushua Messiah. It is important to remember that the Torah is the foundation upon which all the Scripture is based, however, Yahushua is the chief cornerstone of that foundation.

The cornerstone is the very first stone laid in a foundation and all the other stones of the foundation are laid down in a way that makes them completely square or in complete agreement with the cornerstone. So, this metaphor of a cornerstone is letting us know that Yahushua is the cornerstone upon which all the Torah foundation is laid down.

He is the Torah and the Torah is Him, they cannot be separated, they cannot be added to and they cannot be taken away from. You cannot claim to have Yahushua and ignore the Torah (Christianity) and neither can you claim to have the Torah and ignore Yahushua (Judaism), it does not work that way. Yahushua Messiah is the Torah/Word made flesh (John 1:14).

This idea of a stumbling stone comes from the prophet Isaiah (YeshaYahu) in 8:13-15 and 28:14-20. In both cases YHWH is referring to a disobedient nation who has been led astray by disobedient teachers.

| Isa 8:13 | "יהוה of hosts, **Him you shall set apart. Let Him be your fear, and let Him be your dread**. |
| Isa 8:14 | "And He shall be for a set-apart place, but a **stone of stumbling and a rock that makes for falling to both the houses of Yisra'ĕl, as a trap and a snare to the inhabitants of Yerushalayim.** |
| Isa 8:15 | "And many among them shall stumble and fall, and be broken and snared and taken." |

The phrase, "יהוה of hosts" is a messianic title, so every time you see it you know it's referring to Yahushua. It is through our belief in Him that we become a Set Apart Place of YHWH.

| Eph 2:18 | Because **through Him** *(Yahushua)* we both have access to the Father by one Spirit. |
| Eph 2:19 | So then you *(Gentiles)* are no longer strangers and foreigners, but fellow citizens of the set-apart ones and members of the household of Elohim, |
| Eph 2:20 | having been **built upon the foundation of the emissaries and prophets, יהושע Messiah Himself being chief corner-stone**, |
| Eph 2:21 | in whom all the building, being joined together, grows into a set-apart Dwelling Place in יהוה, |
| Eph 2:22 | **in whom you also are being built together into a dwelling of Elohim in the Spirit.** |

In Isaiah 8, both houses of Yisra'el are falling into a trap and a snare because they were listening to disobedient teachers and being disobedient themselves. They were supposed to make YHWH of hosts their fear and their dread. They were supposed to set Him apart in their lives, but they did not. Both of these things they were supposed to do are a reference to obeying His Torah.

This all stems back to what YHWH said to Yisra'el at Mount Sinai, that "IF" they would "diligently obey My voice and keep My covenant, then I shall make you a treasured possession above all peoples".

Obeying His voice is the physical part and keeping His covenant is the spiritual part. The Torah is the physical part and Yahushua Messiah is the spiritual part. YeshaYahu goes on to say this very thing in verse 20.

| Isa 8:20 | **To the Torah and to the witness**! If they do not speak according to this Word, it is because they have no daybreak *(light)*. |

The true word that is true light, is the Word that speaks of both the Torah (the physical part) and the witness (covenant/Yahushua-the spiritual part).

| Isa 28:14 | Therefore hear the **Word of יהוה, you men of scorn, who rule this people who are in Yerushalayim,** |

279

| Isa 28:15 | because you have said, **"We have made a covenant with death, and with She'ol we have effected a vision. When the overflowing scourge passes through, it does not come to us, for we have made lying our refuge, and under falsehood we have hidden ourselves."** |
| Isa 28:16 | Therefore thus said the Master יהוה, "See, **I am laying in Tsiyon a stone for a foundation, a tried stone, a precious corner-stone, a settled foundation. He who trusts shall not hasten away.** |
| Isa 28:17 | **And I shall make right-ruling the measuring line, and righteousness the plummet.** And the hail shall sweep away the refuge of lying, and the waters overflow the hiding place. |
| Isa 28:18 | And your **covenant with death** shall be annulled, and your vision with She'ol not stand. When an overflowing scourge passes through, then you shall be trampled down by it. |
| Isa 28:19 | As often as it passes through it shall take you, for it shall pass through every morning, and by day and by night. And it shall be only trembling to understand the message." |
| Isa 28:20 | For the bed shall be too short for a man to stretch out on, and the covering shall be too narrow to wrap himself in it. |

| Note: | For a much more in-depth study and understanding of what this passage is saying, see the author's study entitled "Isaiah 28" at Hebrewmindsetministries.org. |

The context of this whole chapter has to do with the Word; about how it was written, and to what type of person He would give understanding to, and how the Word would affect us, based on how we respond to it.

Earlier in verse 12 the prophet is told that the Word is the rest and the refreshing for the people of Yisra'el but that they would not "hear" it.

As we have said before, the Hebrew word "shama" is the root word translated as "to hear" in the Tanak. As an active root it carries intent and implies doing something in response to what you hear and should best be understood to mean, listen with the intent to obey.

Bearing this in mind we see that the Word/Torah was intended to be our rest and refreshing if we would hear and obey it but Yisra'el did not hear it with the intent to obey.

As the Torah says multiple times, obedience to the Torah brings life and blessing, while disobedience to the Torah brings death and cursing (Deuteronomy 28 and 30).

Deuteronomy 4:5-6 tells us that YHWH gives wisdom and understanding to those who will "guard and do" all the things mentioned in the Torah. Because Yisra'el did not hear the Word with the intent to obey it, they did not understand it, instead of becoming their rest and refreshing it became, to them, a stumbling block, which caused them to stumble backward, and be broken and snared and taken captive (Isaiah 28:13).

Verse 14 begins with "Therefore", which tells us that because of what was just spoken before something new is about to be said. And ironically it tells them to **hear** the Word of YHWH, which of course is a reference to obeying it. Also, the phrase "Word of YHWH" is a messianic title referring to Yahushua.

Isaiah goes on to talk about these false teachers or men of scorn who ruled over Yisra'el and who say they have made a "Covenant of Death" that will protect them when the overflowing scourge (wrath) passes through, because they have made **"lying our refuge and under falsehood we have hidden ourselves"**.

Now anyone with half a thought process should be able to understand that any covenant that is connected to death, lying and falsehood can in no way protect someone from the wrath of YHWH when it comes. But what is meant by the phrase "Covenant of Death"?

There are two possible covenants associated to the Torah (Deuteronomy 30). There is a covenant of life associated to obeying the Torah and there is a covenant of death associated to not obeying the Torah. This is why YHWH says over and over again that obedience brings life and disobedience brings death.

> **Note**: There is a "covenant of death" mentioned in Isaiah 28, where it says:

> **Isa 28:14** Therefore **hear** the Word of יהוה, you men of scorn, who rule this people who are in Yerushalayim,

> 1. "hear" in Hebrew means to hear with the

intent to obey.

**Isa 28:15**    because you have said, "We have made a **covenant with death**, and with She'ol we have effected a vision. When the **overflowing scourge** passes through, it does not come to us, for we have made **lying** our refuge, and under **falsehood** we have hidden ourselves."

2.    "Covenant of Death" refers to a covenant that allows the people to sin.

3.    "Overflowing scourge" refers to the Wrath of YHWH in the last day.

4.    "Lying our refuge" (rest) and "under falsehood we have hidden" (cover) means that the covenant of death is based on false doctrine.

**Isa 28:16**    Therefore thus said the Master יהוה, "See, I am laying in Tsiyon a stone for a foundation, a tried stone, a precious **corner-stone**, a settled foundation. He who trusts shall not hasten away.

5.    "Corner-stone" refers to Messiah, specifically a covenant of life through Him.

**Isa 28:17**    And I shall make **right-ruling** the measuring line, and **righteousness** the plummet. And the hail shall sweep away the refuge of lying, and the waters overflow the hiding place.

6.    "Right-ruling (judgment)… and righteousness" refers to the standard by which all the people of Messiah will be measured, i.e., the Torah/Law (Deuteronomy 6:24-25; Romans 6:15).

**Isa 28:18**    And your covenant with death shall be **annulled**, and your vision with She'ol not stand. When an overflowing scourge passes through, then **you shall be trampled down by it.**

7.    "Annulled" refers to being cut off or out.

282

8.	"You shall be trampled down by it" refers to the people that are placing their trust in this covenant of death, that is based in false doctrine, i.e., a belief (Messiah) without works (Torah – See: James 2:14-26), who will be "cut off" when the Wrath of YHWH is poured out in the last day.

**Isa 28:19**	As often as it passes through it shall take you, for it shall pass through every morning, and by day and by night. And it shall be only **trembling to understand the message."**

9.	"Trembling to understand the Message" refers to the confusion of those who have trusted in the covenant of death and believed that it would prevent the Wrath from coming upon them, while their suffering through it.

**Isa 28:20**	For **the bed shall be too short** for a man to stretch out on, and **the covering shall be too narrow** to wrap himself in it.

10.	"The bed shall be too short" refers to the thing they were resting in, which will not be enough for them to "stretch out on" (find rest on). This refers to their works, the physical part.

11.	"The covering shall be to narrow" refers to what they are trusting in, which will not be enough for them to "wrap" themselves in. Thes is about their belief, the spiritual part.

Basically, this is an end-time prophesy concerning the end-time 'church' (Yisra'el) who are trusting in a covenant (blood sacrifice) that doesn't require them to obey (works) the Law/Torah of YHWH, as it was given to His people at Mt. Sinai, through Mosheh.

The conclusion of the matter is that these people believe that this 'lawless' covenant will deliver them from the wrath of Elohim, however, the covenant that YHWH as set forth is based in the Corner-stone, Yahushua Messiah, and lived in the righteousness of the Torah of YHWH.

Because of this, the covenant they are hoping in will not deliver them from the wrath and as they suffer through it they will tremble trying to understand why.

Both Judaism and Christianity are in danger of being in this position at the return of the Master. Judaism is trusting in a covenant that is not based in belief and Christianity is trusting in a covenant with no works, at least not the works of Torah, which is what is required.

Another example of this 'covenant of death' can be found in Hebrews 10:26-31.

| | |
|---|---|
| **Heb 10:26** | For **if we sin purposely after we have received the knowledge of the truth**, there no longer remains a slaughter *offering* for sins, |
| **Heb 10:27** | **but some fearsome anticipation of judgment, and a fierce fire which is about to consume the opponents.** |
| **Heb 10:28** | Anyone who has disregarded the Torah of Mosheh dies without compassion on the witness of two or three witnesses. |
| **Heb 10:29** | How much **worse punishment** do you think shall he deserve who has trampled the Son of Elohim underfoot, counted the blood of the covenant by which he **was** set apart as common, and insulted the Spirit of favour? |
| **Heb 10:30** | For we know Him who has said, **"Vengeance is Mine, I shall repay, says** יהוה**."** And again, **"**יהוה **shall judge His people."** |
| **Heb 10:31** | **It is fearsome to fall into the hands of the living Elohim.** |

Now, you notice in verse 26, that the writer starts out with the pronoun "we". To find out who this "we" is we need to back up verse 19, which starts out "So, brothers".

Now it seems pretty obvious that this author was writing to believers, he surely would not be writing to unbelievers and call them brothers, but the lack of critical thinking within the Christian mindset today is frightening, so we felt it necessary to clarify who the "we" is referring to.

So, the author is addressing fellow believers and tells them that "if **we** sin purposely after **we** have received the knowledge of truth" that we have nothing to look forward to but fiery judgment. This sounds pretty serious and is almost completely contrary to everything Christianity teaches, yet here it is.

To "sin purposely" is more about a heart condition of rebellion than it is doing something you know is not right. This is a reference to people who know they're supposed to obey the Torah but refuse to for whatever reason. Most people today do not obey the Torah for the same reason the Yisra'elis of old did not, because of false teachers.

This is **NOT** referring to people who are striving every day with all their heart and mind and strength to obey the entire Torah, but struggle and stumble along the way. This is referring to those people who **do not care** what the Torah says and have **no intention** of obeying anything it says no matter what you tell them.

These people will receive a "worse punishment" than those who never believed at all, because they have trampled the Messiah underfoot, counted the blood of the covenant that **had** justified them as nothing and insulted the Spirit of favor, through which they **were** saved.

This is a covenant of death, a covenant that allows them to disobey the Torah. Sure, they "believe" that YHWH exists, but they don't give Him the honor He deserves by obeying His Torah, just like the demons (Jam 2:19). Because they are trusting in these lies and falsehoods, the wrath they think is going to pass by them, is actually going to roll right over them.

Believing in Messiah Yahushua and walking in obedience to the Torah, without additions and subtractions, in a heart of compassion for your fellow man is the narrow road that ends in the Kingdom and everlasting life.

Because the peoples mentioned here and in Isaiah 28 have put their trust in a covenant of disobedience, they will have to endure the wrath of YHWH when it comes.

When it does, the trust the Jews have placed in their Torah obedience, will give them no rest and the covering the Christians have put their trust in, will not cover them.

285

# Chapter 8: Romans 10

There are eleven quotes from the Tanak in this chapter which is evidence that Paul wanted us to know that our belief is founded in the Tanak (OT).

| | |
|---|---|
| **Rom 10:1** | Truly brothers, my heart's desire and prayer to Elohim for Yisra'ĕl is for deliverance. |
| **Rom 10:2** | For I bear them witness that they have an ardour for Elohim, **but not according to knowledge.** |
| **Rom 10:3** | **For not knowing the righteousness of Elohim, and seeking to establish their own righteousness, they did not subject themselves to the righteousness of Elohim**. |
| **Rom 10:4** | For Messiah is the **goal** of the 'Torah unto righteousness' to everyone who believes. |

Paul seriously desired that his fellow Yisra'elis, the native born, would find salvation, for they truly have a zeal for YHWH, however the zeal they have for Him is not based in true knowledge.

As we have already shown, our belief must have two parts; one based in belief, which is spiritual, and one based in obedience, which is physical.

As Habakkuk 2:4 states, "… But the righteous one lives by his steadfastness."

> **Steadfastness:** stg's **#H530** "emunah", Feminine of H529 (established); literally *firmness*; (fig.) s*ecurity*; (mor.) *fidelity:* - faith (-ful, -ly, -ness).

The word "emunah" is the Hebrew word for belief. Paul quoted this passage in Galatians 3:11 where he said, "that no one is declared right by Torah before Elohim is clear, for **'The righteous shall live by belief.'"**

In fact, the King James Version uses the word "faith" instead of steadfastness here in Habakkuk 2:4. So we see that righteousness has always been about our belief not about our works, however, righteous men live righteously and the only way to do that is to live in obedience to the Torah of YHWH.

| Deu 6:24 | And יהוה commanded us to do **all these laws**, to fear יהוה our Elohim, for our good always, to keep us alive, as it is today. |
| Deu 6:25 | And **it is righteousness for us when we guard to do <u>all</u> this command before יהוה our Elohim**, as He has commanded us.' |

Yisra'el had attempted to be declared righteous because of their works and not because of their belief. They had not put their trust steadfastly in YHWH but in themselves. Because of this the Scripture states that they had a "form of knowledge", but that knowledge was not based in truth.

In Romans 2:20, while admonishing the Jews, Paul stated that they had "…the form of knowledge and of the truth in the Torah". Having a **form** of knowledge means that they did not have the fullness of knowledge, their knowledge was incomplete. The same goes for truth, if you have a form of truth then your truth is incomplete and thus, not truth at all.

In his discussion with Timothy concerning the type of men that would exist in the last days, Paul states that they are "always learning and never able to come to the knowledge of the truth" (2Ti 3:7).

This is true today in both Judaism and Christianity because, as we have already stated, they are both guilty of subverting the truth of YHWH through the traditions and doctrines of men.

The Jews claim to have the righteousness of Torah, yet without the righteousness of belief and Christians claim to have the righteousness of belief but don't walk in the righteousness of Torah, so neither one of them have the truth, which is the righteousness of belief in Yahushua Messiah lived out in the righteousness of Torah.

This is what Paul is referring to in Romans 10:3 when he says that Yisra'el didn't know the righteousness of Elohim (belief lived in works) so they were boasting (trusting) in their own righteousness, which for them was their natural lineage and observance of the Torah.

Paul admonished them for putting their trust in the Torah from two points of view; the first being, not having a circumcised heart in Romans 2:23-29

| Rom 2:23 | You who **make your boast in the Torah**, through the transgression of the Torah do you disrespect Elohim? |

| | |
|---|---|
| Rom 2:24 | For **"The Name of Elohim is blasphemed among the nations because of you,"** as it has been written. |
| Rom 2:25 | For circumcision indeed profits **if you practise the Torah**, but if you are a transgressor of the Torah, your circumcision has become uncircumcision. |
| Rom 2:26 | So, if an uncircumcised one watches over the righteousnesses of the Torah, shall not his uncircumcision be reckoned as circumcision? |
| Rom 2:27 | And the uncircumcised by nature, **who perfects the Torah**, shall judge you who notwithstanding letter and circumcision are **a transgressor of the Torah**! |
| Rom 2:28 | For he is not a Yehuḏi who is *so* outwardly, neither is circumcision that which is outward in the flesh. |
| Rom 2:29 | But a Yehuḏi is he **who is *so* inwardly, and circumcision is that of the heart**, in Spirit, not literally, whose praise is not from men but from Elohim. |

Here Paul is saying that knowing the Torah and having the Torah does you no good if you're not obeying the Torah. He further states that a non-native or Gentile who perfects the Torah will judge those who have the Torah and are circumcised but does not obey the Torah.

Here we see heart issues again, what YHWH is looking for is the thoughts and intents of our heart (Hebrews 4:12) and not our genealogy or even our perfect obedience to the Torah.

When this passage refers to those who "perfect" the Torah it is not a reference to those who walk in it perfectly, as our Western minds define perfect, but refers to the Hebrew idea of completeness, which is a heart issue.

Perfection, scripturally, is a reference to fullness or completeness and is about the heart as it relates to the "two part" principle, meaning that it is about a heart condition within us that trusts in YHWH so completely that we live in sincere obedience to all He has said, even though we may stumble occasionally.

| | |
|---|---|
| Psa 119:1 | Blessed are **the perfect in the way, Who walk in the Torah of** יהוה! |

| | |
|---|---|
| **Psa 119:2** | Blessed are those who observe His witnesses, **Who seek Him with all the heart!** |
| **Psa 119:3** | Yes, they shall do no unrighteousness; They shall walk in His ways. |
| **Psa 119:4** | You have commanded us To guard Your orders diligently. |
| **Psa 119:5** | **Oh, that my ways were established To guard Your laws!** |
| **Psa 119:6** | Then I would not be ashamed, When I look into all Your commands. |
| **Psa 119:7** | I thank You with **uprightness of heart**, When I learn the right-rulings of Your righteousness. |
| **Psa 119:8** | I guard Your laws; Oh, do not leave me entirely! |

As we see here in Psalms 119, David, who was a man after YHWH's heart, defines perfection as a heart issue of seeking and obeying. Seeking YHWH diligently with all your heart is a two-part phrase because it associates believing in YHWH to the degree that you act upon that belief.

| | |
|---|---|
| **Heb 11:6** | But without belief it is impossible to please Him, for he who comes to Elohim has to **believe that He is**, and that **He is a rewarder of those who earnestly seek Him.** |

So, first we must believe that He exists and secondly, we must believe that He rewards those who "earnestly seek Him". To earnestly seek Him means the exact same thing as diligently seeking Him and is a reference to what David said in Psalms 119.

Diligently seeking YHWH is about getting to know what He has spoken to us, what He has done for us and what He requires of us, and then acting on these things on a day-to-day basis.

In the context of our salvation, we believe that YHWH does exist and that He has set forth a way of salvation for us through His Son, Yahushua Ha-Mashiach. Furthermore, in our belief we are to set our heart, or circumcise our heart, to love Him through obeying the things He has required of us, i.e., the Torah.

This is what Paul refers to as the "knowledge of Elohim" that Yisra'el did not understand. Yes, they had the Torah, but they did not have belief, because they believed themselves righteous because of their calling and their circumcision.

The fact that they were trusting or boasting in their calling, as the native born, and the fact of their physical circumcision, yet were not obeying the other principles of Torah, like mercy and justice and belief (Mat 23:23), was evidence that they did not have a heart for YHWH.

To say that you believe in Him is to live out your life in obedience to what He has said, because we trust in Him and all that He has promised.

All the promises that YHWH has given us are founded in Yahushua Messiah. The Torah and all that it teaches is intended to lead us to the knowledge of Yahushua that we might believe in Him unto salvation.

The Torah is our "schoolmaster" (Gal 3:24) to lead us to Messiah, which is what Paul means here in Romans 10 when he says that Messiah is the goal of the Torah unto righteousness for everyone that believes.

We, both Jew and Gentile, were all guilty of sin (Romans 3:23) and deserving of death (Romans 6:23) so that we could not be made right again or justified by the works of the Torah (Romans 3:20) because it is the Torah that gave sin the power to kill us (1 Corinthians 5:56).

So, YHWH sent His Son, Yahushua Messiah, so that whoever believes in Him should not perish but receive everlasting life (John 3:16).

Now, His blood paid the atonement price for our sin when we put our belief in Him (Romans 3:24-25); and so, the righteousness that comes from belief was imputed to us (Romans 4) as it was to our father Abraham some 430 years before the Torah was given at Mount Sinai (Gal 3:16-17).

The promises of YHWH are, and always have been, based on a heart of belief that is lived out through obedience to the Torah.

Therefore, the shadow pictures of Abraham come before the giving of the Torah, so that we see how YHWH imputes righteousness upon those who believe first and then those who believe, walk in the righteousness of Torah, thus the two parts are completed. Belief + works = life, however, belief - works = death (James 2:20).

It's true that, in the King James Version, Romans 10:4 says that Messiah is the "end" of the Torah for righteousness and because of this, modern teaching suggests that our belief in Messiah has put an end to the Torah in the life of believers, meaning that believers are no longer required to obey the Torah unto righteousness. This idea is complete and utter heresy!

| Goal (end): | stg's #**G5056** "telos", from a primary word tellō (to *set out* for a definite point or *goal*); properly the point aimed at as a *limit*. |

As has been stated, the Torah was given to lead us to belief in Yahushua Messiah so that Messiah was the "goal" of the Torah, which is to lead us to the righteousness that comes by belief.

However, this by no means puts an end to the Torah in the life of the believer because the righteousness that comes from belief must be lived out righteously, and the only way to do that is to obey the Torah as mentioned above (Deut 6:24-25).

Paul is going to compare the righteousness which comes from obedience to the Torah to the righteousness that comes from belief.

| **Rom 10:5** | For Moses writes about the righteousness which is of the Torah, **"The man who does these shall live by them."** |

This is a quote from Leviticus 18:5, which sits between the teaching of unlawful blood consumption and unlawful nakedness.

| **Lev 18:1** | And יהוה spoke to Mosheh, saying, |
| **Lev 18:2** | "Speak to the children of Yisra'ĕl, and say to them, 'I am יהוה your Elohim. |
| **Lev 18:3** | '**Do not do as they do in the land of Mitsrayim**, where you dwelt. **And do not do as they do in the land of Kena'an**, where I am bringing you, and do not walk in their laws. |
| **Lev 18:4** | 'Do My right-rulings and guard My laws, **to walk in them**. I am יהוה your Elohim. |
| **Lev 18:5** | 'And you shall guard My laws and My right-rulings, **which a man does and lives by them**. I am יהוה. |

It is important to understand what's being said here, because it describes what it means to be a child of YHWH. We don't live according to the way we used to live before we believed, and we do not live according to the ways of the people or the society in which we now reside, but we live according to what YHWH has spoken and Him only do we serve.

Paul is restating in Romans 10:5, what YHWH said through Moses in Leviticus 18, that the righteousness of Torah has to do with

292

how we live, but there is another form of righteousness that is required.

| Rom 10:6 | But the righteousness of belief speaks in this way, **"Do not say in your heart, 'Who shall ascend into the heavens?'** – that is, to bring Messiah down; or, |
| Rom 10:7 | " 'Who shall descend into the abyss?' " – that is, to bring Messiah up from the dead. |
| Rom 10:8 | But what does it say? **"The word is near you, in your mouth and in your heart"**– that is, the word of belief which we are proclaiming: |

This passage is a quote from Deuteronomy 30:11-13, which sits between the end time promise of restoration, that YHWH has planned for those who turn back to Him with all their heart and all their being, to do all that He has commanded, **and** the teaching of blessings (for obedience) and cursing (for disobedience), in which He tells us to "choose life"(v. 19).

| Deu 30:11 | "For this command which I am commanding you today, it is not too hard for you, nor is it far off. |
| Deu 30:12 | "It is not in the heavens, to say, 'Who shall ascend into the heavens for us, and bring it to us, and cause us to hear it, so that we do it?' |
| Deu 30:13 | "Nor is it beyond the sea, to say, 'Who shall go over the sea for us, and bring it to us, and cause us to hear it, so that we do it?' |
| Deu 30:14 | "For the Word is very near you, in your mouth and in your heart – **to do it.** |

As shown, this passage sits between a promise to those who repent and a teaching on the consequences associated with both obedience and disobedience. Don't lose sight of the fact that the context is about repentance and obedience.

Between these two teachings sits this passage, which in its original form is basically telling the people that the command they were given was not too hard for them to accomplish and was not hidden from them, but was in fact, right there before them. Thus, the promises associated to the command, was right there before them, if they would obey.

Paul's use of this passage in Romans 10 is a revelation of Yahushua in the original text, though not specifically referenced, which is very typical of how Paul uses quotes from the Tanak. Let us remember that just before this passage in Deuteronomy is the end time promise of restoration for those who repent.

This context is a revelation of what Paul has already said many times, that all have sinned and fallen short of the glory of Elohim, that none are righteous no not one, and that all need repentance.

As Paul has taught before, the Torah is of no use to us who are declared unrighteous because of sin, however, our belief in Yahushua Messiah can make us righteous again before YHWH.

There is a process going on, which Paul is trying to explain to us, that is hidden within the text of Deuteronomy 30.

The process begins in verses 1-10 concerning a heart of repentance, next is the passage quoted by Paul concerning belief righteousness and concludes with the instruction to choose life, which comes from obedience to the commandments of YHWH. Do you see it?

1.  Repentant Heart
2.  Belief Righteousness
3.  Works Righteousness
4.  The Promise of Eternal Life

This is the same exact process taught by Paul in Romans Chapters 3, 5-6.

1.  There is none righteous no not one, we are all guilty before Him - Romans 3
2.  We have all inherited death through Adam because of sin, but are justified through belief in Yahushua - Romans 5
3.  We do not continue to sin (disobey the Torah -1 John 3:4) because we are under righteously unto set apartness (sanctification/holiness), which ends in eternal life - Romans 6

Paul has taken the admonishment of Deuteronomy 30:11-15, which concerns the Written Torah (that leads us to Messiah) and reveals the Living Torah (that is Messiah) in it, by asking us about the Word, which is in our mouth and in our heart. His answer is, the Word of Belief, i.e., Yahushua Messiah.

| Rom 10:9 | That **if you confess** with your mouth the Master יהושע **and believe in your heart** that Elohim has raised Him from the dead, you shall be saved. |
| Rom 10:10 | **For with the heart one believes unto righteousness, and one confesses with the mouth, and so is saved.** |

Here again we see the process, belief followed by action equals salvation. Belief brings righteousness and confession completes salvation. This is an example of the *Two-Part Principle* as it relates contextually to spiritual justification.

What do we mean by this? Well, Paul is using this passage specifically for the purpose of teaching justification from past sin through belief in Yahushua Messiah, which is our spiritual justification. This is the first part of complete justification (sanctification, redemption, salvation, etc.).

In this first part however, Paul reveals a *Two-Part Principle* concerning what's going on with our hearts and how it affects our actions.

Let's go back and consider what happened on the original night of Passover in Egypt. YHWH told Moses to go back and tell the people that He was sending death through Egypt and that all the firstborn would die.

He went on to tell Moses that the people were to find a spotless Lamb and to kill it on the fourteenth day of the first month and to paint its blood on the doorpost and lintel of each house. YHWH assured them that those who had the blood painted on their door post and lintel would be spared death.

The people of Yisra'el believed what YHWH had spoken through Moses, so much so, that they acted upon it by killing the Lamb and painting its blood on their door post and lintel, thus sparing their firstborn children.

The point we're making is, even belief, which brings justification from death, has this two-part element associated to it, a belief (spiritual) that causes an action (physical). This is exactly what Paul is saying in Romans 10.

As verse 10 says, "For with the heart one believes unto righteousness (spiritual), and one confesses with the mouth, and so is saved (physical)." So, the Christian idea that there is absolutely no work or physical action associated to our justification is incorrect.

Paul's assertion that no man is justified from death by works has to do with works of the Torah, i.e., circumcision, and not action generally. True belief in something forces action, in this case confession, then a requirement of further action is expected to verify the confession.

This is where the Torah of YHWH comes in. The belief and confession mentioned in Romans 10:10 justifies us from death and the Torah of YHWH teaches us how to live justified before YHWH as righteous men and women.

It is those believers who have been justified from death by belief and live justified lives through obedience to the Torah, as Yahushua did, that shall reign as coheirs with Yahushua at His return.

| | |
|---|---|
| Rom 10:11 | Because the Scripture says, **"Whoever puts his trust in Him shall not be put to shame."** |
| Rom 10:12 | Because there is **no distinction** between Yehuḏi and Greek, for the same Master of all is rich to all those calling upon Him. |
| Rom 10:13 | For **"everyone who calls on the Name of יהוה shall be saved."** |

These last three verses are quotes from the Tanak. Verse 11 is a quote from Isaiah (YeshaYahu) 28:16-17 concerning the chief cornerstone (Yahushua) Who "shall make right-ruling the measuring line, and righteousness the plummet" and shall "sweep away the refuge of lying" (false doctrine) that so many people are trusting in, at His return.

Verse 12 is a reference to Leviticus 19:34, where the native born Yisra'elis were told to "Let the stranger who dwells among you **be to you as the native among you,** and you shall love him as yourself. For you were strangers in the land of Mitsrayim. I am יהוה your Elohim", which itself is connected to Numbers 15:15-16.

| | |
|---|---|
| Num 15:15 | **One law** is for you of the assembly **and** for the stranger who sojourns with you – **a law forever throughout your generations.** As you are, so is the stranger before יהוה. |
| Num 15:16 | **One Torah** and one right-ruling is for you **and** for the stranger who sojourns with you.'" |

And lastly, verse 13 is a quote from Joel 2:32 (also quoted in Acts 2:21) concerning the events at the end of days when redemption and restoration come upon the children of Yisra'el (both Jew and

Gentile) and the wrath of YHWH is poured out on the unbeliever and the disobedient (2 Thessalonians 1).

There seems to be a subliminal message going on here in these verses Paul has chosen to quote and the order in which he quotes them.

The context of Isaiah 28 is about the Word/Torah of YHWH and how it was intended to be the "rest" for His people but they would not "hear" it and so it became a stumbling stone for them that they might be destroyed by it.

The word "hear" in this passage is the word *shama* and refers to the type of hearing that acts. It would be better translated as "Listen" because it carries intent within it. It should be understood to mean, we "hear" with the intent to obey.

So, because Yisra'el did not hear the Word with the intent to obey it, the Word condemned them, as it does all of us who do not obey it. However, Yisra'el continued to trust that YHWH would deliver them because of the covenant He made with their fathers, whether they obeyed or not, which in Isaiah 28 is called the Covenant of Death.

They assumed that their position as the "chosen people" guaranteed their inheritance, which has never been the case, because YHWH has always required obedience and has always destroyed the disobedient. Paul makes this argument clearly in his writings, which we have seen already and will see again before we are done.

Interestingly, Paul follows that quote with the one from Leviticus 19, where he clearly states that there is no distinction between the native born (Jew) and the stranger (Greek). Now in this context, Paul is using this quote to show that YHWH will receive all people regardless of their bloodline, which is the same context as was used in Leviticus.

It must be understood also, this "no distinction" policy of YHWH applies to both the positive and negative sides of the scale. By this we mean that all who believe in the Messiah will find redemption but also, those who do not believe in Messiah will find judgment, both Jew and Gentile.

There is also a "two-edged sword" principle that must be applied to every Scripture passage for us to understand the totality of what's being said. For instance, if sin, which is disobeying the Torah, brings death, then obeying the Torah must give life. Life, good and blessing is always attached to obedience, while death, evil and cursing is always associated to disobedience (Deuteronomy 30).

Lastly, the end times context of Joel 2, quoted in verse 13, speaks of restoration, yet we know that restoration only comes to those believers that live righteously, those who "hear" the word with the intent to obey it, whether native born or stranger.

> **Rom 10:14** How then shall they call on Him in whom they have not believed? And how shall they believe in Him of whom they have not heard? And how shall they hear without one proclaiming?
>
> **Rom 10:15** And how shall they proclaim if they are not sent? As it has been written, **"How pleasant are the feet of those who bring the Good News of peace, who bring the Good News of the good!"**
>
> **Rom 10:16** However, not all obeyed the Good News. For Yeshayahu says, **"יהוה, who has believed our report?"**
>
> **Rom 10:17** So then belief comes by hearing, and hearing by the word of Elohim.
>
> **Rom 10:18** But I ask, Did they not hear? Yes indeed, **"Their voice went out to all the earth, and their words to the ends of the world."**

Again, Paul quotes several verses from the Tanak, the first two being Isaiah 52:7 and 53:1, which lie in the midst of a Messianic revelation.

Isaiah 50 compares the sin of Yisra'el, which caused YHWH to divorce her, and the Servant that would come to deliver her. Isaiah 51 starts out with, "Listen to Me, you who pursue righteousness, seeking יהוה ...", and goes on to encourage them concerning YHWH's ability to deliver them.

Chapter 52 continues this theme of redemption and deliverance until we reach verse 7 quoted by Paul. This chapter goes on, beginning in verse 13 and into chapter 53, to prophesy concerning the "Suffering Servant", which is Yahushua Messiah.

Paul's use of these quotes shows that the truth of Yahushua Messiah was recorded long ago, thereby leaving Yisra'el without excuse.

The other quote in this passage comes from Psalms 19:4 and the reference to "their voice" is to the creation itself. By using it here Paul is going back to chapter 1 of Romans where he said that the creation itself reveals the Creator, so that all men are without excuse.

| | |
|---|---|
| Rom 10:19 | But I ask, Did Yisra'ĕl not know? First Moses says, **"I shall provoke you to jealousy by those who are not a nation, I shall enrage you by an unwise nation."** |
| Rom 10:20 | And Yeshayahu boldly says, **"I was found by those not seeking Me, I was made manifest to those not asking for Me."** |
| Rom 10:21 | And to Yisra'ĕl He says, **"All day long I have stretched out My hands to a disobedient and back-talking people."** |

Again, and again, we see Paul quoting from the Tanak and this is one of the more profound examples of why Yisra'el is without excuse before YHWH.

The first quote comes from Deuteronomy 32:21 and is part of Moses's final speech to the nation wherein he recaps some of their journey, warns them concerning disobedience and prophesies concerning their future.

In this passage, YHWH says, because Yisra'el had provoked Him to jealousy by submitting to the authority of elohim that were not Elohim, i.e., idols (demons), He would provoke them to jealousy by a people that were not a people, and Paul declares that these "people" were the Gentile believers who would put their trust in Yahushua.

The next two quotes come from Isaiah 65:1-2, where YHWH is continuing this theme of provoking Yisra'el through a people who were not even looking for Him, as Yisra'el claimed to be doing, in their words but not in their deeds.

Unfortunately, Paul did not fully quote Isaiah 65:2 and so the full essence of what was being said is not brought forth. To Paul, it was not necessary to quote the entire passage because his message in Romans was primarily to the Jews that lived there, who knew what the Torah said.

The full quote of the passage is interesting and reflects the current status of those who call themselves the people of YHWH.

| | |
|---|---|
| Isa 65:1 | "I have let Myself be inquired of, not by those who asked; I was found, not by those who sought Me. I said, 'Here I am, here I am,' to a nation not calling on My Name. |
| Isa 65:2 | "I have held out My hands all day long to a stubborn people, **who walk in a way that is not good, after their own thoughts;** |

| | |
|---|---|
| **Isa 65:3** | the people who **provoke Me continually** to My face, who slaughter in gardens, and burn incense on slaughter-places of brick; |
| **Isa 65:4** | who sit among the burial-sites, and spend the night in secret places, **who eat flesh of pigs, and the broth of unclean** *meat* **is in their pots,** |
| **Isa 65:5** | **who say, 'Keep to yourself, do not come near me, for I am set-apart to you!'** These are smoke in My nostrils, a fire that burns all day. |
| **Isa 65:6** | "See, it is written before Me: I am not silent, but shall repay, and I shall repay into their bosom, |
| **Isa 65:7** | your crookednesses and the crookednesses of your fathers together," said יהוה, "who burned incense on the mountains and reproached Me on the hills. And I shall measure their former work into their bosom." |

You see, these people walk "after their own way". We are warned multitudes of times in the Scripture not to go our own way but to serve YHWH according to the Way in which He instructed us, without additions or subtractions, but we just find this too difficult to do because of our hard hearts and stiff necks .Consider Proverbs 3:

| | |
|---|---|
| **Pro 3:1** | My son, **do not forget my Torah,** and let your **heart watch over my commands**; |
| **Pro 3:2** | For length of days and long life and peace they add to you. |
| **Pro 3:3** | Let not loving-commitment and truth forsake you – Bind them around your neck, Write them on the tablet of your **heart,** |
| **Pro 3:4** | Thus finding favour and good insight in the eyes of Elohim and man. |
| **Pro 3:5** | Trust in יהוה with **all your heart,** and lean **not on your own understanding**; |
| **Pro 3:6** | **Know Him in all your ways,** And He makes all your paths straight. |
| **Pro 3:7** | **Do not be wise in your own eyes; Fear יהוה and turn away from evil.** |
| **Pro 3:8** | It is healing to your navel, and moistening to your bones. |

The first thing that needs to be seen here is that YHWH is asking for a certain heart condition and that condition is one that concerns His commands. He admonishes us to "**NOT** lean (or trust) in our own understanding" or "to be wise in our own eyes" but to know Him in all the things we do and to fear Him, turning from evil.

If we are not to lean on our own understanding, what understanding are we to lean on?

| | |
|---|---|
| **Deu 4:5** | "See, I have taught you laws and right-rulings, as יהוה my Elohim commanded me, to do thus in the land which you go to possess. |
| **Deu 4:6** | "**And you shall guard and do them, for this is your wisdom and your understanding** before the eyes of the peoples who hear all these laws, and they shall say, 'Only a wise and understanding people is this great nation!' |
| **Deu 4:7** | "For what great nation is there which has Elohim so near to it, as יהוה our Elohim is to us, whenever we call on Him? |

See, the understanding that we are to live in, is not that of our own thoughts and feelings, but is that of the commandments of YHWH and the laws that He set up for us to live by.

| | |
|---|---|
| **Pro 28:26** | He who trusts in his own heart is a fool, But he who **walks wisely is delivered** (saved). |

To "know Him in all your ways" refers to an intimate relationship with Him that causes you to consider Him and His thoughts and feelings concerning everything that you do. The question on your mind in the moment that you make your choices should always be, "what would the Father have me do?", and then do that.

We are to never allow our emotions or even our instincts to control our choices, but we must bring them into conformity with the instructions of the Torah. We must learn to love the things that YHWH loves and hate the things that He hates, despite the way we FEEL about them or what we have been taught by other men.

What does it mean to "fear YHWH" and what is evil?

| | |
|---|---|
| **Deu 10:12** | "And now, Yisra'ĕl, what is יהוה your Elohim asking of you, but to **fear יהוה your Elohim,** |

301

| Deu 10:13 | to walk in all His ways and to love Him, and to serve יהוה your Elohim with all your heart and with all your being, to guard the commands of יהוה and His laws which I command you today for your good? |

We are not sure that it is possible to get any clearer than that! To fear Him means the same thing as walking in His ways (Torah) and loving Him and serving Him and guarding His Law/Torah!!!

| Deu 30:15 | "See, I have set before you today **life and good, and death and evil,** |
| Deu 30:16 | in that I am commanding you today to love יהוה your Elohim, to walk in His ways, and to guard His commands, and His laws, and His right-rulings. And you **shall live** and increase, and יהוה your Elohim shall bless you in the land which you go to possess. |
| Deu 30:17 | "But if your **heart** turns away, and you do not obey, and shall be drawn away, and shall bow down to other mighty ones and serve them, |
| Deu 30:18 | "I have declared to you today that **you shall certainly perish**, you shall not prolong your days in the land which you are passing over the Yardĕn to enter and possess. |
| Deu 30:19 | "I have called the heavens and the earth as witnesses today against you: **I have set before you life and death, the blessing and the curse. Therefore you shall choose life, so that you live, both you and your seed,** |

Notice here how life is associated to what is good and death is associated to what is evil. Life comes to those who obey the commandments (Torah) of YHWH and death comes to those who do not obey the commandments (Torah) of YHWH.

Thus, it is **evil** to disobey the Torah just as **sin is** disobeying the Torah (1 John 3:4). YHWH is the Creator of all things and so He, and He only, can define the difference between what is good and what is evil, and He has done so in His Torah!

To say that you believe in Him, which is good, but to not obey His commandments, His Torah, is to be doing evil, for which the penalty is death. One cannot say that they believe in Him and not obey His Torah; it is heresy to do so!

It needs to be clearly established once again that YHWH is seeking the heart condition of those who claim to be His, which is more important than their absolute perfect obedience because of this fleshly vessel that we inhabit.

Remember, it is with the **heart** one believes unto righteousness (justification) and that heart condition causes a response in us wherein we confess unto salvation (Romans 10:9-10).

Furthermore, it is this **true heart** of belief that works in us the desire to live righteously before Him in obedience to His Torah.

| | |
|---|---|
| **Php 2:12** | So that, my beloved, as you always obeyed – not only in my presence, but now much rather in my absence – **work out your own deliverance with fear and trembling,** |
| **Php 2:13** | for it is Elohim who is working in you **both to desire and to work for *His* good pleasure.** |

It is through the gifting of the Ruach Ha'Qodesh (the Set-Apart Spirit) of YHWH, which He has given to all those who believe, that prompts us to both desire and to do the will of YHWH through obedience to His Word/Torah.

| | |
|---|---|
| **Eze 36:25** | "And I shall sprinkle clean water on you, and you shall be clean – from all your filthiness and from all your idols I cleanse you. |
| **Eze 36:26** | "And I shall give you a new heart and put a new spirit within you. And I shall take the heart of stone out of your flesh, and I shall give you a heart of flesh, |
| **Eze 36:27** | and put My Spirit within you. And I **shall cause you to walk in My laws and guard My right-rulings and shall do them.** |

If **ANYONE** claims to have the Spirit of YHWH in them but teaches that the Spirit has led them to an understanding of Scripture, which allows them to live in disobedience to the Law/Torah that YHWH handed down to Moses, then they are a false teacher listening to a false spirit.

If they claim you can "live righteously" through belief in Yahushua, but you don't have to live in obedience to the Law/Torah of

YHWH, the spirit they are listening to is not the Spirit of YHWH, but a demon in disguise.

Lastly, we want to go back to Romans 10:17 and break down what is being said there.

**Rom 10:17**   So then belief comes by hearing, and hearing by the word of Elohim.

**REMEMBER**, the foundation of our understanding must be rooted in the Hebrew mind and thus the Hebrew language of the Tanak. The English word "hearing" comes from the Hebrew word "shama", which is better understood to mean "listen".

As mentioned earlier, even in English there is a distinction between the word **hear** and the word **listen**, the latter carrying with it intent, meaning that when you tell your children to listen, you are expecting them to follow up what they hear with the actual act of doing what you've told them.

It is the same with the Hebrew, the word "shama" carries within it the intent to act and would be better understood to mean, "Hear with the intent to obey!"

So, when verse 17 says that "belief comes by hearing" it is referring to the type of hearing that has a heart condition of obedience connected to it. So, we must ask ourselves, what are we supposed to be obeying?

"And hearing by the Word (Torah) of Elohim", for it is through obedience to the Word/Torah of YHWH that we gain understanding (Deut 4:5-6) and our belief increases through a greater understanding of both who YHWH is and what He has promised.

This idea of obedience being connected to belief is borne out in verse 21, which expresses why Yisra'el had not been accepted by YHWH. Remember, one of the main arguments here in Romans concerns "Jewish unbelief" because even though they had the Torah, they had not circumcised their own hearts to obey it (Romans 2:25-29).

In verse 21, Paul says that they are a "disobedient and back talking people", quoting from Isaiah 65, where YHWH Himself called them "a stubborn people, who walk in a way that is not good, after their own thoughts".

Once again, we see that people were "walking" in a way that was of their own making and not according to the Way YHWH had commanded them to walk (Torah), and so they lacked the type of belief necessary to be accepted by YHWH.

Never forget, there is no such thing as belief without works to support it and no amount of works that will be accepted without belief to establish them, for one without the other is death.

# Chapter 9: Romans 11

Paul is going to continue with this theme of the Gentile provocation in chapter 11. He begins with a question concerning the rejection of Yisra'el.

This is an important question today especially because there is a very prominent Christian doctrine out there which declares that YHWH no longer deals with Yisra'el, because He has rejected them in favor of itself, the "New or Spiritual Israel".

**Rom 11:1**    I say then, has Elohim rejected His people? Let it not be! For I also am of Yisra'ĕl, of the seed of Aḇraham, of the tribe of Binyamin.

Paul emphatically states that YHWH has not rejected His people Yisra'el, for Paul himself is a Yisra'eli, of the tribe of Benjamin.

**Note:**    It is important to see here that Paul is from the tribe of Benjamin and not from the tribe of Judah, so he is not a Jew by blood. There is a lot of confusion concerning this because at some point Paul does call himself a Jew, however, as was stated at the beginning of this work there is more than one kind of Jew.

Paul referred to himself as a Jew because of one or both of the following reasons:

1)    He lived in the region of Judaea,

and/or

2)    He had been raised among and had been part of the Jewish religious culture of his time, which was founded in what is now called Judaism.

We know it is impossible for YHWH to have rejected Yisra'el completely because He Himself said He would not.

**Mal 3:6**    "For I am יהוה, I shall not change, and you, O sons of Ya'aqoḇ, **shall not come to an end**.

Since YHWH called Yisra'el to be His people, because of His promises to Abraham, Yitschaq and Ya'aqob, He cannot revoke that promise to them as a people. This does not mean, however, that every Yisra'eli that has ever lived will inherit the Kingdom, because inheritance is based on belief followed by obedience regardless of your bloodline.

YHWH has promised that in the last day He would preserve a remnant of Yisra'el (Isaiah 10:22).

| | |
|---|---|
| **Rom 11:2** | **Elohim has not rejected His people** whom He knew beforehand. Or do you not know what the Scripture says of Ĕliyahu, how he pleads with Elohim against Yisra'ĕl, saying, |
| **Rom 11:3** | **"יהוה, they have killed Your prophets and overthrown Your slaughter-places, and I alone am left, and they seek my life"?** |
| **Rom 11:4** | But what does the answer *of Elohim* say to him? **"I have left for Myself seven thousand men who have not bowed the knee to Ba'al."** |

This passage refers to events that took place in 1 Kings 18-19, where Elijah (EliYahu) defeated the priest of Ba'al and fled in fear from Jezebel. YHWH asked Elijah what he was doing, and he answered, that he was alone in his zeal for YHWH and that Yisra'el as a people had forsaken the covenant, they had made with Him.

YHWH told him that there remained some 7000 men who were faithful to Him and had not bowed the knee to the idol.

| | |
|---|---|
| **Rom 11:5** | **So therefore also**, at this present time a remnant **according to the choice of favour** has come to be. |
| **Rom 11:6** | And if by favour, it is no longer of works, otherwise favour is no longer favour. And if it is of works, it is no longer favour, otherwise work is no longer work. |

Paul is using this shadow picture to emphasize the fact that, though Yisra'el as a people had forsaken the covenant with YHWH and refused to accept Yahushua as Mashiach, there were still a select few, like him, that did believe.

The phrase "according to the choice of favour" is a reference to belief, for it is by favour through belief (grace through faith) that we receive salvation. There is some confusion concerning the way the word "choice" is used here, because it begs the question, "Whose choice?"

Once again, we run into that old argument between the sovereignty of YHWH and our own free will as it relates to predestination. As we explained in chapter 8, predestination, or YHWH's selection of us as His people before our actual birth, is founded in His foreknowledge or His ability to see into the future.

Because He can see into the future and know what choices we will make, and the condition of our heart when we make them, He is able to choose us as His people long before He even created people.

So then, His choice of us, is a reflection of our own choices which we have not as yet made, and it is in this context that the phrase "choice of favour" must be understood.

Since YHWH knows the hearts of all men before they do, He can preserve a remnant of people that **will** believe, long before they make the choice to believe.

In verse 6, Paul makes an interesting statement, let's see it again.

**Rom 11:6** And if by favour, it is no longer of works, otherwise favour is no longer favour. And if it is of works, it is no longer favour, otherwise work is no longer work.

If choice (salvation) is a matter of YHWH extending His favour towards us because of our belief in Yahushua, then our salvation is not based on any work that we do.

If our salvation was based on the work we do, then it is no longer the gift of favour.

If our work can earn salvation, then YHWH must grant us salvation as a debt He owes us and not as a free gift, which is the argument being made here.

**Remember**, many Jews, even today, believe they have an inherent right to the promises of YHWH because of who they are as "His people". For them, it has to do with genealogies and covenants made by their fathers that secure their inheritance of the Kingdom, when in fact nothing could be farther from the truth.

A great many of those Yisra'elis that had been delivered from Egypt by Moses died in the wilderness, never having inherited the Promised Land that was promised to their fathers. Why?

| Heb 3:7 | Therefore, as the Set-apart Spirit says, **"Today, if you hear His voice,** |
| Heb 3:8 | **do not harden your hearts as in the rebellion, in the day of trial in the wilderness,** |
| Heb 3:9 | **where your fathers tried Me, proved Me, and saw My works forty years.** |
| Heb 3:10 | **"Therefore I was grieved with that generation, and said, 'They always go astray in their heart, and they have not known My ways.'** |
| Heb 3:11 | **"As I swore in My wrath, 'If they shall enter into My rest...'"** |
| Heb 3:12 | Look out, brothers, lest there be in any of you **a wicked heart of unbelief in falling away** from the living Elohim, |
| Heb 3:13 | but encourage one another daily, while it is called "Today," lest any of you be **hardened by the deceivableness of sin**. |
| Heb 3:14 | For we have become partakers of Messiah if we hold fast the beginning of our trust firm to the end, |
| Heb 3:15 | while it is said, **"Today, if you hear His voice, do not harden your hearts as in the rebellion."** |
| Heb 3:16 | For who, having heard, rebelled? Was it not all who came out of Mitsrayim, led by Moses? |
| Heb 3:17 | And with whom was He grieved forty years? Was it not with those who sinned, whose corpses fell in the wilderness? |
| Heb 3:18 | **And to whom did He swear that they would not enter into His rest, but to those who did not obey?** |
| Heb 3:19 | **So we see that they were unable to enter in because of unbelief.** |

Notice, it states that Yisra'el was rejected and denied entrance into His rest (Promised Land) because of **rebellion,** which he goes on to call **unbelief**. Now, I think it's clear to everyone that rebellion means a refusal to obey and Paul very clearly associates the refusal to obey with unbelief.

So, most of those Yisra'elis, though they had been saved from death and Egypt, died in the wilderness having never received the promise because of rebellion, having refused to obey the Word/Torah of YHWH, which He considers a lack of belief.

Remember, BELIEF WITHOUT WORKS IS DEAD, it does not exist and as a result, **there is no life in it!!!** (James 2:14-26)

> **Note:** Carefully look at what is being said in verses 10-13. YHWH says that He was "grieved" with that generation because they were always going **astray in their heart** and that they did not **know His ways**.

Now, it is obvious that they did know what He expected of them for He told them explicitly. Their rebellious heart was evidence that they truly did not know or understand what He desired from them.

In verse 12 the author of Hebrews is clearly warning us not to allow the same heart attitude, this **wicked heart of unbelief in falling away** to be in us, so that we do not let our hearts be **hardened by the deceivableness of sin** (13).

> **Deceivableness:** stg's **#G539**, "apate", meaning delusion: from **#G538** (apatao), meaning to cheat or delude.

This word "apate", especially used in this context, must be understood to mean to lie or deceive and the author is suggesting that sin will deceive us into hardening our heart against the things of YHWH.

Remember, by definition, **sin is the transgression of the Torah** (1 John 3:4) so the author's use of the word "sin" here is a reference to our rebellious flesh, which is an allusion to something Paul taught us back in chapter 7.

> **Rom 7:10** And the command which was to result in life, this I found to result in death.
>
> **Rom 7:11** For sin, having taken the occasion through the command, **deceived me**, and through it killed *me*.
>
> ***
>
> **Rom 7:21** I find therefore this law, that when I wish to do the good, that the **evil is present with me**.

Several times in the Scripture, a multitude of different authors continually warn us concerning our heart condition and letting things influence our heart against YHWH. It cannot be emphasized enough, that YHWH is interested, not so much in the absolute perfection of our walk, but in a heart attitude of absolute submission and gratitude.

We will be judged concerning the "thoughts and intents of our heart" (Heb 4:12) and not about the stumbling we may do between now and then. As long as we live in this fleshly body we will struggle with temptation and have to continually battle our fleshly, rebellious attitude that seeks to rise up within us and overtake us.

Verse 14 goes on to tell us that we "have become partakers of Messiah **IF** we hold fast the beginning of our trust **firm to the end**". Remaining faithful to the very end is a theme in the Scripture and is a reference to a commitment, especially a heart commitment, to remain true to YHWH through all trials and tribulations and persecution, no matter what may come, until we take our very last breath.

This heart commitment is one of obedience to the Torah or instruction that YHWH gave His people to live by, so that they might be set apart or "holy" before Him, as a beacon to those in the world who do not know Him, that they might see our light and step out of the darkness to join us.

Messiah Himself, when teaching concerning the end of days, spoke concerning our need to endure to the very end.

| **Mat 24:12** | "And because of the increase in lawlessness, the love of many shall become cold. |
| **Mat 24:13** | "But he who shall have endured to the end shall be saved. |

Love, as YHWH defines it, is associated to living lawfully before Him and our fellow man, i.e., we obey His Law/Torah (1 John 5:1-3), and those who endure to the end, in His Love/Law/Torah, shall be saved (future tense), a salvation that is yet to come.

***

Returning to the last part of Romans 11:6, it says, "And if it is of works, it is no longer favour, otherwise work is no longer work", which on the surface we seem to have already explained, however, what does "work is no longer work" mean?

It seems to be just a play on words, and it very well might be, however, it is clear that Paul is trying to make a distinction between favour and work and yet it appears there is something else going on here.

311

As we've already stated, in every doctrine of Scripture there are two parts, one physical and the other spiritual, and it would be foolhardy of us to just speed through interesting passages like this, without taking into consideration this *Two-Part Principle.*

It seems to us that Paul is making the distinction between favour and works for more than just what most people think. Yes, it is true that favour and works, in the context of justification from death, are polar opposites of one another.

If you are justified by favour then it can have nothing whatsoever to do with your work because if you can be justified by work, then favour is unnecessary for you have **earned** your inheritance.

However, we know unequivocally that work has its place in the belief, and it is to this principle we think Paul is alluding. It is only because of the favour of YHWH, through our belief in Yahushua, that we can be justified from sin and death, however this is not the end of the belief, only the beginning.

It is our belief **worked out** in obedience to the Torah that brings us to the end, i.e., the Kingdom of Yahushua and eternal life. The following verse from Romans 6 has been rewritten by this author to *clarify* Paul's intent.

> **Rom 6:22**    But now, having been set free *from past disobedience to Torah* (Rom 3:22-25) *by grace through belief (Eph 2:8-9)*, and having become servants *to obey the Torah* of Elohim (Rom 6:16; 7:22,25), you bear your *righteousness* fruit (John 15:1-10), *the results of which is* set-apartness (Holiness- Heb 12:14), leading to everlasting life.

Once again, we see this process taking place, which begins with our confession of Yahushua and ends with inheritance of the Kingdom and eternal life, a process that is clear in this passage.

1.    Being set free from past sin through belief in Yahushua Messiah.
2.    Becoming servants of YHWH through obedience.
3.    Our obedience brings forth the fruit of righteousness which makes us set- apart or holy before Him (Deut 6:24-25).
4.    We inherit the Kingdom and everlasting life

312

at the Resurrection.

***

| | |
|---|---|
| **Rom 11:7** | What then? Yisra'ěl has not obtained what it seeks, but the chosen did obtain it, and the rest were hardened. |
| **Rom 11:8** | As it has been written, **"יהוה has given them a spirit of deep sleep, eyes not to see and ears not to hear, unto this day."** |
| **Rom 11:9** | Dawiḏ also says, **"Let their table become for a snare, and for a trap, and for a stumbling-block and a recompense to them,** |
| **Rom 11:10** | **let their eyes be darkened, not to see, and bow down their back always."** |

Again, Paul resorts to quoting the Tanak to establish his teaching. Before we get to that though let's consider what he says in verse 7, where he asked the question, "What then?".

This is a reference to the issue of Yisra'el as a people having not entered His rest, but His rest has been extended to the Gentiles.

Paul's answer is that Yisra'el has not obtained what it was searching for, i.e., acceptance by YHWH and inheritance of the Kingdom, but that a select few, a remnant according to the choice of favour, have received it but the rest have had their heart hardened against the things of YHWH, as was prophesied.

First, let's think about what causes YHWH to harden the heart of someone and a perfect example of this is Pharaoh at the time of the Exodus. Pharaoh had proved that he had no respect for YHWH at the very beginning when he said, "Who is הוהי, that I should obey His voice to let Yisra'el go? I do not know הוהי, nor am I going to let Yisra'el go." (Exodus 5:2)

Pharaoh proved this was the true nature of his heart, because despite the things he had seen he refused to repent and let the people go. Even stating at one point that he would let them go and then changing his mind.

Remember, all men have free will that YHWH never violates; however, the Scripture says YHWH hardened his heart, how could that be?

All other things considered, we must accept the fact that it was the true nature of Pharaoh's heart to reject YHWH and all that He commanded. However, his own fear and the influence of the people,

313

caused him to act, or at least consider acting, in a way that showed contrition.

In the deeper recesses of his heart he was never submitted to the will of YHWH. Because of the deceit and double mindedness of his heart, YHWH is free and capable of nudging Pharaoh to a further hardness of heart.

Now, back in verse 8, Paul quotes Deuteronomy 29:4 and Isaiah 29:10. The context of Deuteronomy 29 is the time just prior to Moses's death as Yisra'el was near the river Jordan preparing to cross into the Promised Land.

Chapter 29 is the beginning of Moses' last words to the people and within it we see a heart attitude mentioned which explains why YHWH has allowed hardness to come upon the children of Yisra'el.

| | |
|---|---|
| **Deu 29:19** | "And it shall be, when he hears the words of this curse, that he should **bless himself in his heart**, saying, 'I have peace **though I walk in the stubbornness of my heart**,' in order to add drunkenness to thirst. |
| **Deu 29:20** | "יהוה would **not forgive him**, but rather, the displeasure of יהוה and His jealousy shall **burn against that man**, and every curse that is written in this book shall **settle on him, and יהוה shall blot out his name from under the heavens**. |
| **Deu 29:21** | "And יהוה shall separate him for evil, out of all the tribes of Yisra'ĕl, according to all the curses of the covenant that are written in this Book of the Torah. |

It is because of the heart issue within the nation of Yisra'el, of both native born and stranger, that brought hardship and blindness into the lives and understanding of the people.

| | |
|---|---|
| **Rom 11:11** | I say then, have they stumbled that they should fall? Let it not be! But by their fall deliverance has come to the nations, to **provoke them to jealousy.** |
| **Rom 11:12** | And if their fall is riches for the world, and their failure riches for the nations, how much more their completeness! |

| | |
|---|---|
| **Rom 11:13** | For I speak to you, the nations, inasmuch as I am an emissary to the nations, I esteem my service, |
| **Rom 11:14** | if somehow I might **provoke to jealousy** *those who are* my flesh and save some of them. |
| **Rom 11:15** | For if their casting away is the restoration to favour of the world, what is their acceptance but life from the dead? |

Here we see Paul explaining to the nations that it was Yisra'el's fall that allowed deliverance to come upon the Gentiles and that he quotes from Deuteronomy 32:21 concerning YHWH using the Gentile nations as a means to provoke Yisra'el to jealousy.

| | |
|---|---|
| **Deu 32:21** | "They made Me jealous by what is not Ěl, They provoked Me with their worthless *matters*. But I make them jealous by those who are no people, I provoke them with a foolish nation. |

Notice here that YHWH gives a - because... then I – statement, saying that since they had made Him jealous by things that were not Elohim, i.e., idols of the nations, then He was going to provoke them to jealousy by those same idol worshipers whose example they had followed.

He confirms though, that the blessing of deliverance that we receive because of their fall is nothing compared to the blessing that will be received when they are restored. Now, Paul is going into a discussion concerning Gentile inclusion into the nation of Yisra'el, which the modern church cannot seem to understand.

Today, Christian dogma teaches that the church has replaced Yisra'el as the people of YHWH or that it is something unique unto itself and separate from Yisra'el, i.e., a Gentile Church.

This could not be any farther from the truth, for both the Tanak and the Messianic Writings teach that the Gentile who would come alongside Yisra'el in covenant with YHWH and walk in obedience to that covenant are to be considered native born Yisra'elis.

| | |
|---|---|
| **Lev 19:33** | 'And when a stranger **sojourns with you** in your land, do not oppress him. |
| **Lev 19:34** | 'Let the stranger who dwells among you **be to you as the native among you**, and you shall |

315

love him as yourself. For you were strangers in the land of Mitsrayim. I am יהוה your Elohim.

*\*\**

| Num 15:15 | One law is for you of the assembly and for the stranger who sojourns with you – **a law forever throughout your generations**. As you are, so is the stranger before יהוה. |
| Num 15:16 | **One Torah and one right-ruling is for you and for the stranger who sojourns with you.' "** |

*\*\**

| Gal 3:26 | For you are **all** sons of Elohim through belief in Messiah יהושע. |
| Gal 3:27 | For as many of you as were immersed into Messiah have put on Messiah. |
| Gal 3:28 | There is **not Yehuḏi nor Greek**, there is not slave nor free, there is not male and female, for **you are all one** in Messiah יהושע. |
| Gal 3:29 | And **if** you are of Messiah, **then** you are seed of Aḇraham, and heirs according to promise. |

The totality of Scripture is clear on this point, there is only one group of people from among all the peoples of the world that YHWH has called to be His People, and they are the children of Abraham, Yitschaq and Ya'aqob, i.e., Yisra'el. And it was through this people that the Savior would come to bring all the other people back to YHWH as His children, Yisra'el.

Yahushua is the man, Yisra'el to whom the Scripture was alluding to in the shadow pictures of Ya'aqob in Genesis 32:22-32 and Yisra'el as "My son, My first-born" in Exodus 4:22-23 (Hosea 11:1).

When we place our trust in Him for salvation, we are "in" Him, so as He is the man, Yisra'el, of which the Scripture foretold, we become His People, i.e., Yisra'el through Him.

It is from this understanding of Gentile inclusion into the congregation of Yisra'el that Paul goes on to make his illustration concerning the olive tree in the following verses.

However, before we go forward in Romans 11, we need to firmly establish Paul's position of Gentile inclusion into the congregation of Yisra'el from his own mouth, taught in Ephesians 2.

Let's begin in verse one and continue through the entire chapter.

| Eph 2:1 | And you **were** dead in trespasses and sins, |
| Eph 2:2 | in which you **once** walked according to the course of this world, according to the ruler of the authority of the air, of the spirit that is now working in the **sons of disobedience**, |
| Eph 2:3 | among whom also we all **once** lived in the lusts of our flesh, doing the desires of the flesh and of the mind, and were by nature **children of wrath**, as also the rest. |

The first thing we want to notice is the tense in which Paul is speaking. He uses the words "**were**" and "**once**" expressing a past tense, he is speaking of something that used to be true but is not true anymore.

Notice, he uses two phrases that are synonymous with one another, one is "sons of disobedience" the other is "children of wrath". It's important to know and to realize and to remember that wrath comes upon the children of **disobedience** (Ephesians 5:6).

This passage is reminding us that in the past, before we believed in Yahushua as Messiah and Savior, we too were spiritually dead and condemned to death (the second death) because of the trespasses and sins that we had committed. The main question we must ask ourselves is, what did we trespass against that made us "sons of disobedience" and "children of wrath"?

As we stated earlier, "sin is the transgression of the Law (Torah)" and if you don't believe us go to 1 John 3:4 from which this phrase is quoted. In the so-called "New Testament", John the apostle states that disobeying the Torah, i.e., the Law, as it was given through Moses at Mount Sinai, is a sin.

So, any person who is not obeying the Torah is committing sin and that applies to people today both unbelievers and believers. A sinner is someone who commits sin, i.e., does not obey the so-called Old Testament Law, and our position in or out of the belief doesn't change that.

Even if you have believed in Yahushua Messiah and been cleansed from the sins of the past and been made new in Him through belief but continue to walk in disobedience to the Torah you are by definition a sinner.

| Gal 2:17 | "And if, **while seeking to be declared right by Messiah, we ourselves also are found sinners,** is Messiah then a servant of sin? Let it not be! |

317

| | |
|---|---|
| **Gal 2:18** | "For if I rebuild what I *once* overthrew, **I establish myself a transgressor.** |

Even Paul, who is the author of both Ephesians and Romans, declares it is possible to be trusting in the Messiah for justification and still be found a sinner, because our continual sin stacks up the penalty of death against us, even though we had once overcome it by belief in Messiah.

And there is a penalty, a very severe penalty, for those believers that continue to disobey. And the penalty for disobedient believers is more severe than the penalty for the unbelievers.

| | |
|---|---|
| **Heb 10:26** | For if **WE** sin purposely after we have received the knowledge of the truth, there no longer remains a slaughter *offering* for sins, |
| **Heb 10:27** | but some **fearsome anticipation of judgment, and a fierce fire which is about to consume the opponents.** |
| **Heb 10:28** | Anyone who has disregarded the Torah of Moses dies without compassion on the witness of two or three witnesses. |
| **Heb 10:29** | How much **worse punishment** do you think shall he deserve who has trampled the Son of Elohim underfoot, counted the blood of the covenant **by which he was** set apart as common, and insulted the Spirit of favour? |
| **Heb 10:30** | For we know Him who has said, **"Vengeance is Mine, I shall repay, says יהוה."** And again, **"יהוה shall judge His people."** |
| **Heb 10:31** | It is fearsome to fall into the hands of the living Elohim. |

Now, we have purposely overemphasized the word "we" in verse 26 because we don't want you to miss the **fact** that this verse is written to fellow believers. If you go to this passage in your Bible and look back to verse 19 you will see that the author of Hebrews starts this teaching with the phrase "now brothers".

The book of Hebrews was written by a teacher of the belief, probably Paul or possibly Apollos, who had a deep understanding of the Temple service and Aaronic priesthood and how those things shadow pictured the priesthood of Yahushua and the redemption plan of YHWH.

318

It was written to Hebrew believers of the time because Messiah had prophesied (just as Daniel had before Him) that the Temple and the city were to be torn down (Matthew 24:1-2; Daniel 9:24-26).

The point here was to prove that it is possible to be declared a transgressor, i.e., sinner, even after we have believed in Yahushua Messiah for justification from the penalty of sin and death.

Our position as believers does not exempt us from the requirement of obedience, because belief without works is not real belief (James 2:14-26) and neither will it protect us from the penalty of judgment, which is death, if we choose to walk in willful disobedience.

| | |
|---|---|
| **Eph 2:4** | **But** Elohim, who is rich in compassion, because of His great love with which He loved us, |
| **Eph 2:5** | even when we **were** dead in trespasses, made us alive together with Messiah – by favour you **have been** saved – |
| **Eph 2:6** | and raised us up together, and made us sit together in the heavenlies in Messiah יהושע, |
| **Eph 2:7** | in order to show in the coming ages the exceeding riches of His favour in kindness toward us in Messiah יהושע. |

Notice the word "but" in verse 4. The word "but" here shows that a transition is taking place from something that was true in the past to something that is true now in the present, and this transition is further expressed in the word "were" and the phrase "have been".

We **were** condemned to death because of our past sin **but** we **have been** saved, justified (made right) from that condemnation by our belief in Yahushua Messiah.

Do you see the transition, from a state of unrighteousness into a state of righteousness because of what Yahushua did for us by offering Himself as the payment for our disobedience (Romans 3:23-26)?

Also, Paul says the reason YHWH has justified us through our belief in Yahushua, was so He could show, in the coming ages, how great His favour (grace) was to us, who have believed.

He did not do it for us because we were righteous or better than anyone else, He did it because He said He would (Genesis 3:15; 12:1-4) and He is always trustworthy to do what He has promised, and He does not want us to forget it.

319

Before we move on, I want us to see that this transition shows our movement from a position of spiritual death into a position of spiritual life, which is part one of the two-part process that leads to complete redemption.

Paul is going to restate this in the next two verses but then follows it up in verse 10 with our responsibility to accomplish the second part of the two-part process, which is obedience.

It is imperative that we remember and take into consideration the two-part process whenever we are reading or studying the Scripture, because without it, it is impossible to find true understanding.

Our complete redemption can only be accomplished if both parts of the redemption process are fulfilled, and it is in this misunderstanding that the Christian church continually condemns itself.

Our complete redemption (inheritance) rests in, (1) what He did for us that we could not do for ourselves, i.e., deliver us from the penalty of our past sin through our belief in Yahushua Messiah who died for us to pay that penalty, and (2) what we do in response to what He did for us, i.e., obey His commands (Torah) with all of our heart, mind, and strength.

| **Eph 2:8** | For by favour you **have been** saved, through belief, and that not of yourselves, it is the gift of Elohim, |
| **Eph 2:9** | it is not by works, so that no one should boast. |
| **Eph 2:10** | For we are His workmanship, created in Messiah יהושע unto good works, which Elohim prepared **beforehand** that **we should walk in them**. |

Now, we are getting into one of, if not the most quoted passages in the Scripture. Notice again the tense of this phrase, i.e., **have been**, which points to our present position because of our belief, in contrast to our past position when we were in unbelief and disobedience.

It is important to remind you that Paul is speaking to this congregation from a presumption on his part that they were walking in obedience, as he had taught them.

Paul, like most Messianic writers, assumes that the believers he's writing to understand their need to obey the Torah as the physical

**path** of righteousness that must follow the spiritual **Way** of righteousness, which is belief in Yahushua Messiah.

Notice that verse 10 says we are His "workmanship", which in English means a decree of skill needed to produce or make a product. In Greek, however, the word is "ποίημα - poiema", which is NOT a reference to the skill needed to make a product but refers to the product itself.

We are the produce, the creation, of YHWH in Yahushua Messiah. This 'creation' is the 'new man' or inner-spirit-man that was born again when we believed. As mentioned, verse 8 says we "have been saved", past tense, "by grace through belief", which is the spiritual part of belief that connects us to the unconditional covenant of Abraham and makes us adopted sons of Yisra'el, both the native born and the stranger (Leviticus 19:33-34; Romans 11:11-24 and Eph 2:11-19).

Verse 10, refers to the physical part, our obedience, and what does it say we are supposed to obey? What Elohim prepared "beforehand", meaning before we were saved, but more specifically, that which He laid down before He sent Messiah, i.e., His Torah!!!

Once again, we see that we are justified, or made right, from our past sin and the condemnation of death through our belief in Yahushua Messiah, and this justification is a free gift granted to us by YHWH, our Father. There is nothing we did; indeed, there is nothing we could do to be justified from past sin.

The Torah of YHWH, as it was given to Moses at Mount Sinai, is His standard of righteousness, morality, and holiness (set apartness) that He requires of His people, and it cannot be added to or taken away from (Deut 4:2; 12:32; Ecc 3:14; Pro 30:6; Rev 22:18-19), and neither are we allowed to turn to the left nor to the right of it, lest we be found to serve a different elohim (Deut 28:14).

So, since both things are true and cannot be opposed to one another, then we must dig a little deeper to find out how both can be true and in agreement with one another. To do that we have to begin in 1 Corinthians 15:56, which states, "The sting of death is sin and the power of sin is the Torah".

As we've already said, the definition of sin is not obeying the Torah (1 John 3:4) and the wages of sin is death (Rom 6:23), so then, we were condemned to death because we did not obey the Torah and then the command in the Torah that disobeyed declared us guilty and condemned us to die, because the Scripture says, "the being that sins shall die" (Eze 18:20).

Since it was the Torah that condemned us to death for disobeying it, the Torah itself had no power to free us from that condemnation. There is however, in the Torah, a process through which atonement for sin can be attained and that is substitutional sacrifice, meaning, though I owed a death, some other being could die for me to pay the penalty that I owed.

In the Torah there are shadow pictures in the sacrificial system, that illustrate the giving of a life other than our own for the penalty of sin we owed. In the Torah that other life belonged to sheep and goats and bulls, but the Scripture is clear that the blood of bulls and goats cannot take away the sin debt of men.

Like in the Garden of Eden, where YHWH killed an animal to cover the nakedness of Adam and Chawwah with its skin, the killing of bulls and goats and sheep could only cover or cleanse our physical guilt (nakedness). The writer of Hebrews puts it this way…

| | |
|---|---|
| **Heb 9:13** | For if the blood of bulls and goats and the ashes of a heifer, sprinkling the defiled, **sets apart for the cleansing of the flesh,** |
| **Heb 9:14** | how much more shall the blood of the Messiah, who through the everlasting Spirit offered Himself unblemished to Elohim, **cleanse your conscience** from dead works to serve the living Elohim? |

You see, the sacrificial system instituted by YHWH in the wilderness and performed by Aaron the High Priest, was only for the cleansing of the outer man, the physical man, but it was a shadow picture of a future system of atonement whereby our body becomes the Tabernacle/Temple of YHWH. There Yahushua is the High Priest, and this system cleanses the inner man, the spiritual man (our conscience).

It is through this other, spiritual, system that we receive justification from past sin and the rebirth of the inner-spirit-man, however, our outer-physical-man is still guilty before YHWH to this very day, because there is no physical system through which we can get cleansing.

Since the Temple was taken from us after the death of Yahushua, due to the hardhearted and rebellious hearts of our Yisra'eli forbearers, physical cleansing is impossible today.

This is what Paul and all the rest of the Messianic Writers, including the writer of Hebrews, are trying to teach us concerning the justification from condemnation and the rebirth of the inner man. This, however, does not absolve us from the requirements of the covenant established at Mount Sinai.

**Note:** We find ourselves in an interesting conundrum because Paul, in Galatians 3, makes this very same point from the opposite side of the argument. In the 1st century believers were struggling against the "Jewish religious" traditions and customs that required Torah obedience as a **prerequisite** of acceptance into the congregation, meaning that you had to do acts of the Torah "to be saved" (Acts 15:1).

Of course, all the Messianic Writers, especially Paul, were opposed to this idea because they understood, only the promise of YHWH's favour through belief in Yahushua could deliver us from the condemnation of death and bring us into the household of YHWH, i.e., the congregation of Yisra'el (Eph 2:19).

In his argument against this Jewish idea of works salvation (legalism) Paul used YHWH's covenant with Abraham (Gen 15) as a counterpoint to His covenant with Yisra'el (Ex 19-20), so let's take a look at what he said there.

| | |
|---|---|
| **Gal 3:15** | Brothers, as a man I say it: a covenant, even though it is man's, yet if it is confirmed, **no one sets it aside, or adds to it**. |
| **Gal 3:16** | But the promises were spoken to Abraham, and to his Seed. He does not say, "And to seeds," as of many, but as of one, "And to your Seed," who is Messiah. |
| **Gal 3:17** | Now this I say, Torah, that came four hundred and thirty years later, **does not annul a covenant previously confirmed by Elohim** in Messiah, so as to do away with the promise. |
| **Gal 3:18** | For if the inheritance is by Torah, it is no longer by promise, but Elohim gave it to Abraham through a promise. |
| **Gal 3:19** | Why, then, the Torah? It was added because of transgressions, **until the Seed should come to whom the promise was made**. And it was ordained through messengers in the hand of a mediator. |

Now we will go through this much more in depth in the chapter on Galatians, however we want to point out a couple of things here.

1. Once a covenant is established it cannot be added to or taken away from.
2. A covenant that has been confirmed by Elohim cannot be annulled by any other covenant confirmed by Elohim (All covenants confirmed by Elohim are connected and cannot be added to or taken away from by any man-made doctrine).

The first thing a Christian, when confronted with this passage, will say when told that they are still accountable to obey the Torah is that "the Seed...to whom the promise was made" is Yahushua and He has come, so the Torah no longer has any value in the lives of believers today.

The question you must ask yourself is; "Did Yahushua inherit anything when He came?" or "Did Yahushua give His life so that those who would believe in Him could be co-heirs with Him when He returned?" **Remember** Romans 8?

| | |
|---|---|
| Rom 8:12 | So then, **brothers**, we are not debtors to the flesh, to live according to the flesh. |
| Rom 8:13 | For **if you live according to the flesh, you are going to die**; but if by the Spirit you put to death the deeds of the body, you shall live. |
| Rom 8:14 | For **as many as are led by the Spirit of Elohim, these are sons of Elohim.** |
| Rom 8:15 | For you did not receive the spirit of bondage again to fear, but you received the **Spirit of adoption** by whom we cry out, "Abba, Father." |
| Rom 8:16 | The Spirit Himself bears witness with our spirit that we are children of Elohim, |
| Rom 8:17 | and if children, also heirs – truly heirs of Elohim, and **co-heirs** with Messiah, **if** indeed we suffer with Him, in order that we also be **exalted together**. |

You see, the inheritance that we will share with Yahushua is something we will receive at the same time He receives it; we shall be exalted together.

Not only this, but if you continue reading in Romans 8 you will see that all the creation is waiting for the day when the "sons of Elohim" shall be revealed, which is a reference to the "adoption", i.e., the resurrection, the "redemption of our body" (8:23).

So, since Yahushua has not yet come to inherit the promise, then the statement in Galatians 3:18 that says, "until the Seed comes" is referring to a time in the future when He shall return to gather us together unto Him, to be exalted together with Him.

Having said all that, let us remember the main point, that no covenant confirmed by Elohim can be nullified by any other covenant, even one confirmed by YHWH Himself.

**Remember**, we are the product of YHWH (Ephesians 2:10) which was bought with a price (1 Corinthians 6:20; 7:23), i.e., the blood of His Son Yahushua. He purchased us to do "good works", the same good works that He prepared before Messiah came, that all His people should walk in (live by) and that "all" of Scripture was preparing us for (2 Timothy 3:16-17).

You see, it was never YHWH's intention to do away with our requirement to obey the Torah, when we believed in Yahushua as Messiah, and it is clear that Paul understood this and taught it to all who would listen.

It was never Paul's intention that his readers think that just because we are not saved or justified by the works of the Law/Torah that we are no longer required to obey the Torah in our belief. The very thought of this is heresy of the vilest kind and an insult to all Paul believed and taught. Paul would vomit if he saw what the 'Church' has done with his writings and Messiah will "spit" out all who refuse to repent in these last days.

Not only that, but those who say they are believers in Messiah and yet no longer have to obey the Torah, are guilty of trampling the sacrifice of the Son of Elohim under their feet. They have counted the blood of the covenant by which He set them apart as a common thing and have insulted the Spirit of favour that they claim lives within them (Heb 10:26-31).

They hang Yahushua Messiah back on the cross every day! And, whether their rebellion is ignorant or arrogant, they are denying the Master and all He has done for them, putting Him to open shame through their continued disobedience (Hebrews 6:4-8)..

They do not realize that YHWH will take vengeance on them for this behavior and all their prayers and praising and religious worship will not help them because He does not accept the worship of those who live un-righteously (Isaiah 1:13).

So, we see that Paul was aware of the *Two-Part Principle* and taught it over and over again in his teachings. He understood that belief in Yahushua was the only way to be cleansed from past sin and delivered from the penalty of death that we deserved for it.

Furthermore, he also understood that once we have entered this covenant with YHWH through belief in Yahushua Messiah we are **REQUIRED** to walk righteously in obedience to the Torah, for it is only through fulfilling these two principles, i.e., belief followed by Torah obedience, that we can be declared "perfect".

Now, we get into the meat of Ephesians 2 as it relates to our study in Romans 11.

**Eph 2:11**    Therefore remember that you, **once** nations in the flesh, who are called 'the uncircumcision' by what is called 'the circumcision' made in the flesh by hands,

**Eph 2:12**    that **at that time** you **were** without Messiah, excluded from the citizenship of Yisra'ĕl and strangers from the covenants of promise, having no expectation and without Elohim in the world.

Once again, we need to pay attention to the tense of what is being said here. "**Once**" refers to a time in the past when something was true but is no longer true because something took place that caused a change.

What then, does this passage say was formerly true about these Gentiles, that is no longer true of them as believers?

1.    They **were** Gentiles in the flesh (meaning that they were not born as part of the covenant people, Yisra'el, but were foreigners by nature).
2.    They **did not have** the Messiah (having not

326

been born into the congregation of Yisra'el, the Promise of Messiah was not inherently theirs).

3.  They **were not citizens** of the nation of Yisra'el (not having been born into it).
4.  They **had no place** in the covenant that YHWH made with Yisra'el (because they were not born into it).
5.  They **had no hope** of eternal life (because they were not part of the covenant).
6.  They **were without Elohim** (because He had revealed Himself to Abraham and through his descendants, no one that was outside of Abraham's household had any part with Elohim).

Eph 2:13      **But now** in Messiah יהושע you who **once** were far off **have been** brought near by the blood of the Messiah.

BUT NOW, is a clear and inarguable statement of change and transition, and Paul tells us what that transition is. Before, when we were still Gentiles, we did not have all these things mentioned above, we were not part of Yisra'el and neither did we have a share in any of the promises and covenants associated to Yisra'el, through their father Abraham, we were far off.

BUT NOW, we have been brought near, meaning that although we originally had no part in any of the things mentioned above, our belief in Yahushua Messiah has brought us into all these things:

1.  We have Messiah.
2.  We are no longer Gentiles but citizens of Yisra'el.
3.  We are now part of **ALL** the covenants, including Torah.
4.  We have the hope of eternal life.
5.  We have YHWH as our Elohim.

Because the Christian church has rejected the Torah as a means of righteous living, they are blind to the totality of truth revealed in and through Yahushua Messiah.

Messiah's death, burial and resurrection was never intended to deliver us from having to obey the Torah, He was given to deliver us **from** the death penalty for having disobeyed it and to **RESTORE** us

327

**to** Him so we could obey the Torah of YHWH without fear of future condemnation when and if we stumble.

| Rom 3:31 | Do we then nullify the Torah through the belief? Let it not be! On the contrary, we establish the Torah. |
|---|---|

Once we had been cleansed from the penalty of death, through Yahushua Messiah, we, both Jew and Gentile, are supposed to be established in and to the Torah...

| Deu 27:26 | Cursed is he **who does not establish the Words of this Torah.**' And all the people shall say, 'Amĕn!' |
|---|---|

... for the Torah is holy, just (righteous), good and the spiritual man lives in it by belief.

| Rom 7:12 | So that the Torah truly is set-apart, and the command set-apart, and righteous, and good. |
|---|---|

*** 

| Rom 7:14 | For we know that the Torah is Spiritual, but I am fleshly, sold under sin. |
|---|---|

Nothing has changed since the beginning; nothing has been added to nor taken away from the fullness of the truth that was given to us at Mount Sinai. Messiah did not come to make a "new covenant" in the sense that the "old" one has passed away and is no longer valid.

Messiah came to make **US new** through His blood so that we could be cleansed of the guilt of having disobeyed the so-called "old" covenant. Then, He **RENEWED** the terms of the covenant with us in His resurrection through our belief. This is what Paul meant in Romans 7:1-4.

| Rom 7:1 | Or do you not know, brothers – for I speak to those knowing the Torah – that the Torah rules over a man as long as he lives? |
|---|---|
| Rom 7:2 | For the married woman has been bound by Torah to the living husband, but if the husband dies, she is released from the Torah *concerning* her husband. |
| Rom 7:3 | So then, while her husband lives, she shall be called an adulteress if she becomes another |

|            |                                                       |
|------------|-------------------------------------------------------|
|            | man's. But if her husband dies, she is free from that *part of the* Torah, so that she is not an adulteress, having become another man's. |
| **Rom 7:4** | So my brothers, you also were put to death to the Torah through the body of Messiah, for you to become another's, the One who was raised from the dead, that we should bear fruit to Elohim. |

The Torah has authority to destroy the man because of his sin as long as he lives, but once he dies his sin debt is paid.

| **Rom 6:7** | For he who has died has been made right from sin. |
|------------|-------------------------------------------------------|

Just as a woman is bound to her husband as long as he lives, according to the Torah, so too are we bound under the authority of the Torah unto condemnation until that condemnation is removed through death. Versus 2-3 is just restating metaphorically what Paul already said in verse 1.

In this metaphor the woman represents us (Yisra'el - both native born and Gentile) "who **were** dead in trespasses and sins" (Ephesians 2:1) and the husband represents the Torah, which condemned us to death for our trespasses and sins.

The phrase "bound to her husband" in verse 2 means the exact same thing as the phrase "Torah rules over a man" in verse 1. In both cases a death is required to free us from what we were bound to, i.e., condemnation - **NOT TORAH!!!**

| **Note:** | It is very, very important to understand what these words and phrases mean and how Paul uses them to get his point across. We know that Paul is going to go on to say in chapter 7 that the Torah is "holy, just and good" and also, "what was intended to give life was found to result in death". Paul is NOT saying that the Torah is the problem, but that our rebellious flesh is the problem. |
|------------|-------------------------------------------------------|

In the same way, in Romans 7:1-4, even though Paul says that it is the Torah that rules over a man until he dies, he is not saying that it is the Torah itself that condemned us, it was our disobedience, our sin that condemned us, the Torah only passed sentence on us because it says, "the being (man) that sins shall die".

Paul says that we were "put to death to the Torah" through our belief in Yahushua, he is not saying that our belief in Yahushua Messiah frees us from having to obey the Torah.

What he is saying is that our belief in Yahushua Messiah has freed us from the condemnation of death that the Torah requires for disobedience. We are not free from obeying the Torah, but we are free from the condemnation of death.

Just as the wife (us) is no longer bound to her husband (condemnation) when he dies, so we are no longer under the authority of the condemnation of death, which the Torah requires for sin, when we believe that Yahushua died for us, in our place.

Now, having been set free from the condemnation of death for violating the covenant (Torah) through belief in Yahushua, who died for us, we are free to be restored to the covenant in Messiah, becoming His bride through His resurrection.

So, it is through belief in Yahushua Messiah that the native born Yisra'elis restore themselves to the covenants YHWH made with them and their fathers, and it is through this same belief in Yahushua Messiah that we who were born Gentiles enter the covenants that YHWH made with Yisra'el and the fathers.

**WE JOIN THEM** as fellow citizens, as Yisra'elis (Leviticus 19:33-34; Deuteronomy 15:15-16).

*****THERE IS NO SUCH THING AS A GENTILE CHURCH!!!*****

The very idea of a "Gentile Church" is heresy. Oh, Gentile churches exist but we call them Islam or Buddhism or Mormonism or Evolutionism or even Satanism, or any other "religious" concept(s) that are not strictly founded in what the Scripture teaches, without additions or subtractions.

And yes, this list would include both Judaism and Christianity, both of which are nothing more than man-made pagan ideologies.

> **Note**: It must be said here, that though we teach against the doctrines of both the Christian Church and Judaism, we do not teach against Christians and Jews. We love them and are attempting to draw them away from the errors of their 'religious' folly.

> **Eph 2:14**    For He is our peace, who **has made both one**, and having broken down the **partition of the barrier**,

| | |
|---|---|
| **Eph 2:15** | having abolished in His flesh the enmity – **the torah of the commands in dogma** – so as to create in Himself one renewed man from **the two**, thus making peace, |
| **Eph 2:16** | and to **completely restore to favour both** of them unto Elohim in one body through the stake, having destroyed the enmity by it. |
| **Eph 2:17** | And having come, He brought as Good News peace to **you who were far off, and peace to those near.** |
| **Eph 2:18** | Because through Him we **both** have access to the Father by one Spirit. |

Notice how Paul uses the word **both** here, for he is establishing the fact that both the native born Yisra'eli (i.e., the circumcision – v.11) and the Gentiles (i.e., the uncircumcision) have been brought together as one body of people in Yahushua Messiah, as one Yisra'el.

There are two very important phrases that must be discussed here because they have truly confused the post-justification doctrine of the Messianic Writings.

The phrases **"partition of the barrier"** and **"the Torah of the commands in dogma"** have been used to distort truth; since the church generally understands these two phrases to refer to the "Old Testament Law" (Torah) which separates Yisra'el from the "New Testament, Gentile Church".

This could not be further from the truth, for we have already established that the Torah teaches that the native born and the stranger (Gentile), who come together in covenant with YHWH, are to be treated as equals, i.e., one people.

If this is true then, what does Paul mean by "the Torah of the commands in dogma" and what is the "partition of the barrier" that separated the native born from the Gentile, before Messiah came?

**REMEMBER**, there is more than one kind of law (torah) because both the Hebrew and Greek words that are generally translated as "law", torah and nomos, mean instruction.

| | |
|---|---|
| **Dogma**: | stg #**G1378 -** From the base of G1380 (to think); a *law* (civil, ceremonial or ecclesiastical): - decree, ordinance. |

Doctrine, decree, ordinance' of public decrees, of the Roman Senate, of rulers. The rules and requirements of the law of Moses;

carrying a suggestion of severity and of threatened judgment, of certain decrees of the apostles relative to right living.

(https://www.biblestudytools.com/lexicons/greek/KJV/dogma.html)

By this definition alone it's hard to discern how Paul intended us to interpret this word in this passage; since we've already shown that the word dogma here cannot refer to the Torah (Old Testament or Mosaic Law) because it's the Torah that said the native born and the stranger (Gentile) that sojourns with them are to be one people unto YHWH, with one Torah forever, throughout our generations (Leviticus 19:33-34; Numbers 15:15-16).

The word "dogma" is used in the following contexts in the Messianic Writings.

**A decree was set forth by a pagan ruler:**

**Luk 2:1**      And it came to be in those days that a **decree** went out from Caesar Augustus for all the world to be registered.

**Regulations decided by men:**

**Act 16:4**      And as they went through the cities, they delivered to them the **regulations** to keep, which were decided by the emissaries and elders at Yerushalayim.

**Commands of a pagan ruler:**

**Act 17:7**      whom Jamon has received. And all of them are acting contrary to the **dogmas** of Caesar, saying there is another sovereign, יהושע."

**Man-made philosophy and ideology:**

**Col 2:14**      having blotted out that which was written by hand against us – by the **dogma** – which stood against us. And He has taken it out of the way, having nailed it to the stake.

The meaning of this last one is quite controversial because the same people that wrongly use the word **dogma** in Ephesians 2, as a reference to the Torah of YHWH, make the exact same mistake in this passage, however, if you read all of Colossians 2, the context stated in v.8 and confirmed in v. 22 clarifies the meaning of the use of the word dogma here.

| | |
|---|---|
| **Col 2:8** | See to it that no one makes a prey of you through philosophy and empty deceit, **according to the tradition of men**, according to the elementary matters of the world, and not according to Messiah. |

***

| | |
|---|---|
| **Col 2:20** | If, then, you died with Messiah from the elementary matters of the world, why, as though living in the world, do you subject yourselves to **dogmas**: |

***

| | |
|---|---|
| **Col 2:22** | which are all to perish with use – **according to the commands and teachings of men?** |

**Note**: In Colossians 2:20, the word is **dogmatizo,** which comes from the word **dogma** and has the same basic meaning.

The point here is that in the Scripture, the word **dogma** is always a reference to commands, regulation or teaching that come from the dictates of men and not of YHWH. Typically, when we use the word **dogma** it is a reference to the traditions and policies associated to a group or system.

Technically, dogma could be used in reference to scriptural principles and teachings, however, scripturally it is never used to refer to the teachings of YHWH or any other portion of the Torah, it is always a reference to man-made teachings whether philosophical or theological or ideological, etc.

So, the "partition of the barrier" Paul is referring to in Ephesians 2:14 is not the Torah of YHWH or the Old Testament Law or the Mosaic Law or whatever else you want to call the Covenant YHWH made with His people at Mount Sinai, both native born and stranger (Gentile) that had joined them.

That partition was, in fact, something put into place by the teachings and traditions of men and not something required by YHWH. Accepting this then, we must figure out what partition Paul is referring to.

**Note:**  "In building the temple Herod the Great had enclosed a large area to form the various courts. The temple itself consisted of the two divisions, the Holy Place, entered by the priests every day, and the Holy of Holies into which the high priest entered alone once every year.

"Immediately outside the temple there was the Court of the Priests, and in it was placed the great altar of burnt offering. Outside of this again was the Court of the Sons of Israel, and beyond this the Court of the Women. The site of the temple itself and the space occupied by the various courts already mentioned formed a raised plateau or platform.

"From it you descended at various points down 5 steps and through gates in a lofty wall, to find yourself overlooking another large court--the outer court to which Gentiles, who desired to see something of the glories of the temple and to offer gifts and sacrifices to the God of the Jews, were freely admitted. Farther in than this court they were forbidden, on pain of death, to go.

The actual boundary line was not the high wall with its gates, but a low stone barrier about 5 ft. in height, which ran round (sic) at the bottom of 14 more steps".

(J. Armitage Robinson, D.D., Paul's Epistle to the Ephesians, 59; see also Edersheim, The Temple, Its Ministry and Services as They Were at the Time of Jesus Christ, 46).

"The middle wall of partition was called Coregh and was built of marble beautifully ornamented."

(https://www.biblestudytools.com/dictionary/partition-the-middle-wall-of/ under "Encyclopedias - International Standard Bible Encyclopedia - Partition, The Middle Wall Of")

### The Wilderness Tabernacle

The World (Gentiles)

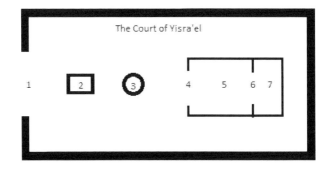

The Court of Yisra'el

1.     The Outer Gate
2.     The Bronze Altar of Burnt Offering
3.     The Bronze Laver
4.     The Outer Veil
5.     The Holy Place
6.     The Inner Veil (Separation)
7.     The Most Holy Place

*****

- The outside of the Tabernacle represents the Gentile (Unbelieving) world.
- Inside the first door is the Court of Yisra'el, which represents the Native Born Yisra'el believers and the Believing Strangers (Gentiles) that sojourn with them.
- The structure within the Courtyard is the Dwelling Place (Tent of Appointment), which includes two rooms:
  - The first is called the Holy Place: where the Priesthood ministers.
  - The Most Holy Place: where YHWH dwells.

Above is a depiction of the original Tabernacle that Moses was instructed to build in the wilderness, which is an earthly replica of the heavenly Tabernacle in which YHWH dwells.

The Tabernacle itself depicts the process of redemption for all men and each element means something specific, however we will only be highlighting a few points as they relate to the discussion at hand.

The Tabernacle represents the people of YHWH, Yisra'el (both the native born and the stranger that sojourns with them), as they are separate or set apart from the world at large around them.

335

The Dwelling Place represents the heart of the people where in YHWH is meant to dwell.

The first veil or door of the Tabernacle represents Yahushua, through whom all who would be in covenant with YHWH must come (both the native born and the stranger). It is through our trust in Yahushua that we **all**, both the native born and the stranger, become members of the household of Elohim, the Yisra'el of YHWH.

The Bronze Altar of Sacrifice represents the sacrifice Yahushua made for us, our Passover Lamb, wherein His blood cleansed us from our sin and delivered us from the condemnation of death that was upon us, as it is upon the entire world.

Those who would come into the door that is Yahushua must take part in the sacrifice, for it alone has the power to cleanse us.

The Bronze Laver represents our baptism, our Red Sea crossing, wherein His death freed us from the authority of Ha-Satan and our bondage to sin and death.

Now that we have been made new through the blood of Yahushua, we have become priests of Yahushua, in the order of Malki-tsedek, and have access to the Holy Place.

Within the Holy Place are three pieces of furniture, each of which represents Messiah, as well as the three elements that every believer requires in this life to live set apart (holy) before YHWH and achieve the eventual reward, i.e., The Kingdom.

It was never the intent of YHWH to bar Gentiles from participating in the Tabernacle services but to do so they had to be identified as part of Yisra'el. The Tabernacle depicts what must take place for all men, both native born and stranger, to become part of the household of YHWH, and so there was never intended to be any barrier that separated the native born (Jew) from the stranger (Gentile) of those who would join together in covenant with YHWH.

As has been shown, the Second Temple, or Herod's Temple, had a barrier that prevented all Gentiles from coming too near the Dwelling Place. Paul uses this actual barrier as a picture of a different barrier that had been erected by the rabbis of what would later be called Judaism.

Paul's reference to the "partition of the barrier" in association with "the torah of commands in dogma" shows us the connection he is making between a real actual man-made wall of separation and man-made traditions of religious doctrine that have become a wall of separation between the native born and the stranger.

As we've shown, it was never the intent of YHWH to have the separation exist and it was man-made doctrine and commands that erected this separation/wall, and through His death, burial and resurrection, Yahushua Messiah tore down this wall of separation, taught in man-made religious dogma, making the two, native born and stranger, into one body, and one Yisra'el, as YHWH had always intended.

Once again, clear and careful understanding of Colossians 2, shows this very principle; how Yahushua "nailed to the tree" all man-made religious dogmas, secular philosophies and elemental matters of idolatry; and in doing so He took authority over all the principalities and powers of creation, both human and nonhuman.

| | |
|---|---|
| **Eph 2:19** | So then you are no longer strangers and foreigners, but fellow citizens of the set-apart ones and members of the household of Elohim, |
| **Eph 2:20** | having been built upon the foundation of the emissaries and prophets, יהושע Messiah Himself being chief corner-stone, |
| **Eph 2:21** | in whom all the building, being joined together, grows into a set-apart Dwelling Place in יהוה, |
| **Eph 2:22** | in whom you also are being built together into a dwelling of Elohim in the Spirit. |

Paul begins verse 19 with "so then", which gives the conclusion of his argument that the Gentiles are no longer strangers and foreigners to the covenant (chosen) people but are fellow citizens with them through our belief in Yahushua Messiah.

All of us, both native born and stranger/Jew and Gentile, are one people, one Yisra'el, which is being built up together as a dwelling place, a Tabernacle, Yahushua Messiah being chief cornerstone thereof and we must remember what the Messiah Himself said concerning His and the Father's residence within us.

| | |
|---|---|
| **Joh 14:23** | יהושע answered him, "If anyone loves Me, **he shall guard My Word**. And My Father shall love him, and We shall come to him and **make Our stay with him**. |
| **Joh 14:24** | "He who does not love Me does not guard My Words. And the Word which you hear is not Mine but of the Father Who sent Me. |

It is those believers who walk in obedience to the Torah of YHWH that are the dwelling place of both the Father and the Son, those workmen who live according to the standard of "good works" that YHWH prepared for His people to live by, before He sent Messiah (Eph 2:10).

Notice, in Ephesians 2:22, that we are called a dwelling place of Elohim "in the spirit". Now, in most of our Bibles this word "spirit" is capitalized, referring to His Spirit, but we must ask ourselves if that is what Paul is referring to.

This phrase by Paul is a reference to us being a dwelling place of Elohim, in our spirit man, that has been redeemed and not the physical man that is awaiting redemption.

Each of us, who have declared Yahushua our Messiah, are a "living stone" of a spiritual Temple.

| | |
|---|---|
| 1Pe 2:4 | Drawing near to Him, a living Stone – rejected indeed by men, but chosen by Elohim and precious – |
| 1Pe 2:5 | you also, **as living stones, are being built up, a spiritual house, a set-apart priesthood**, to offer up spiritual slaughter *offerings* acceptable to Elohim through יהושע Messiah. |
| 1Pe 2:6 | Because it is contained in the Scripture, "See, I lay in Tsiyon a chief corner-stone, chosen, precious, and he who believes on Him shall by no means be put to shame." |
| 1Pe 2:7 | This preciousness, then, is for you who **believe**; but to those who are **disobedient**, "The stone which the builders rejected has become the chief corner-stone," |
| 1Pe 2:8 | and "A stone of stumbling and a rock that makes for falling," who stumble because they are **disobedient** to the Word, to which they also were appointed. |
| 1Pe 2:9 | But you are a **chosen race**, a **royal priesthood**, a **set-apart nation**, a **people for a possession,** that you should proclaim the praises of Him who called you out of darkness into His marvellous light, |
| 1Pe 2:10 | who **once** were not a people, **but now** the people of Elohim; who **had** not obtained compassion, **but now** obtained compassion. |
| 1Pe 2:11 | Beloved ones, I appeal to you as sojourners and pilgrims, to abstain from fleshly lusts which battle against the being, |

338

**1Pe 2:12** **having your behaviour among the nations good** so that when they speak against you as evil-doers, let them, by **observing your good works**, esteem Elohim in a day of visitation.

Peter (Kepha) gives us the same argument that Paul gives concerning our membership in the household (Temple) of YHWH, distinguishing the believers from the disobedient, therefore declaring that being a believer means to walk in obedience.

He goes on to speak of how we were "once" (past tense) not His people, "but now" we have become the people of Elohim through our belief, and he admonishes us to have our behavior (our physical response to our spiritual rebirth) be an example of the good works of YHWH before all the nations.

Now that we have seen Paul's position of Gentile inclusion, which he taught the Ephesians, let us go back to Romans 11.

**Rom 11:16** Now if the first-fruit is set-apart, the lump is also. And if the root is set-apart, so are the branches.

Paul is showing us a principle that it would behoove us to understand. Namely, that a bad tree does not produce good fruit and a good tree does not produce bad fruit.

He does this to let us know that if we declare Yahushua to be our Master, the Vine of which we are the branches (John 15), then as He was set apart so too must we be.

Paul is going to use an olive tree as a metaphor for the children of Yisra'el, as a people, and the branches as individuals within the body of Yisra'el. The natural branches are a reference to the actual physical descendants of Abraham, Yitschaq and Ya'aqob, while the wild olive tree represents the Gentile nations of which a wild branch would be an individual Gentile (nonbeliever).

The Root of the natural olive tree is Yahushua, He is the true man Yisra'el of whom Ya'aqob was a shadow picture.

**Rom 11:17** And if some of the branches were broken off, and you, being a wild olive tree, have been grafted in among them, and came to share the root and fatness of the olive tree,

**Rom 11:18** do not boast against the branches. And if you boast, *remember*: you do not bear the root, but the root *bears* you!

339

Paul gives us a scenario in which some of the natural descendants of Abraham were rejected out of the olive tree that is Yisra'el and some of the wild (Gentile) branches became part of the natural olive tree to share in the root (Messiah) and fatness (blessings) of the natural tree.

He warns these converted wild branches not to speak out or boast against the natural branches that were rejected because if we are to boast we need to boast in the root (Messiah) because we do not bear Him up, or even ourselves, but it is He that bears us up.

| | |
|---|---|
| **Rom 11:19** | You shall say then, "The branches were broken off that I might be grafted in." |
| **Rom 11:20** | Good! By unbelief they were broken off, and you stand by belief. Do not be arrogant, but fear. |
| **Rom 11:21** | For if Elohim did not spare the natural branches, He might not spare you either. |

Now comes the interesting part, wherein Paul says it was the natural branch's (Yisra'el's) unbelief that caused them to be rejected and it was the wild branch's (Gentile's) belief that brought them into acceptance, however, he instructs us not to be arrogant but to fear lest YHWH chooses not to spare us either.

What does it mean to fear YHWH and how does that fear keep us from being rejected as the natural seed was? Consider Ecclesiastes 3:14.

| | |
|---|---|
| **Ecc 3:14** | I know that whatever Elohim does is forever. There is no adding to it, and there is no taking from it. Elohim does it, that men should fear before Him. |

It says that whatever YHWH does, which includes everything He has said or will say, everything He has done or will do, and every choice He makes or will make, is forever, meaning it never changes or goes away or ends. Furthermore, it says that nothing can be added to it and nothing can be taken from it, just as Messiah Himself said, not one jot or tittle shall pass from the Law/Torah (Mat 5:17-19).

It says that YHWH does it this way so that man should fear before Him. This means that YHWH set in order the ONLY path through which men could live righteously before Him and be restored

340

to Him if they stumbled, and nothing and no one can add too or take away from what He has set out as the ONLY Way.

A man can prove that he "fears" YHWH by forsaking his own thoughts and feelings and walking in obedience to the ONLY path of restoration YHWH provided for him.

If we fear YHWH then we will walk in obedience to His Torah without additions or subtractions, for that is the ONLY way to fear Him, the ONLY Way to live righteously before Him.

> **Rom 11:22** See then the kindness and sharpness of Elohim: on those who fell sharpness, but toward you kindness, **if you continue** in *His* kindness, **otherwise you also shall be cut off.**

Paul mentions YHWH's "kindness and sharpness" as relates to both the natural branches that were rejected and the wild branches that were accepted. The natural branches were rejected because they refused to believe, and the wild branches were accepted because they did believe.

So, YHWH is kind to the believer (obedient one) and is sharp or hard on the unbeliever (disobedient one), remembering how both Peter and Paul use the words believer and disobedient in opposition to one another.

What's most interesting about this passage is the warning to the wild branches that if they do not remain in YHWH's kindness (belief/obedience) they could be cut out of the tree once again.

> **Rom 11:23** And they also, if they do not continue in unbelief, shall be grafted in, for Elohim is able to graft them in again.
>
> **Rom 11:24** For if you were cut out of the olive tree which is wild by nature, and were grafted contrary to nature into a good olive tree, how much more shall these who are the natural *branches*, be grafted into their own olive tree?

Paul is reaffirming the fact that the natural branches can come to themselves and repent and return back to the natural tree and be received. This would require them to believe in Yahushua Messiah with a heart of obedience towards the Torah.

| Rom 11:25 | For I do not wish you to be ignorant of this secret, brothers, lest you should be wise in your own estimation, that hardening in part has come over Yisra'ĕl, until the completeness of the nations has come in. |
|---|---|

YHWH told Abraham that it was His intention to bring all nations back to Himself (Genesis 12:1-4) and it was His plan to have the descendants of Abraham, i.e., Yisra'el, to be His prophets and priests (Exodus 19:6) to lead the nations back to Himself.

Unfortunately, Yisra'el chose to walk in rebellion and as a result they were given eyes that could not see and ears that could not hear (understand). So, they were blinded to the truth and their hearts were hardened towards the truth as a body of people, though individuals throughout time have seen the truth and walked it.

Now, this hardening of Yisra'el was to last until the fullness of the Gentiles had come and there are a lot of different ideas being passed around concerning what this means. However, there are actually two similar phrases, this being one and the other being "times of the Gentiles" in Luke 21:24.

Just as there are two parts to righteousness and salvation, these two phrases represent two different things. The phrase "times of the Gentiles" refers to the statue of Nebuchadnezzar in Daniel 2, which is a prophetic illustration of the rise and fall of Gentile nations that lead up to the coming of the Messiah and His Kingdom, which is the context of Luke 21:24.

The phrase "fulness of the Gentiles" refers to Yoseph's second born son, Ephrayim, whose name means 'double fruit'. This is important because, even though he was the second born, Ya'aqob gave him the first born blessing of the double portion.

| Gen 48:19 | But his father refused and said, "I know, my son, I know. He also becomes a people, and he also is great. And yet, his younger brother is greater than he, and **his seed is to become the completeness of the nations**." |
|---|---|

The last phrase, "completeness of the nations", is actually "מְלֹא־הַגּוֹיִם", i.e., "male'-hagoyim", meaning 'fulness the Gentiles'. Ephrayim's seed was prophesied to "become" the "fulness of the Gentiles". Ephrayim, prophetically, is the 'House of Yisra'el' which was sent out of the Land in ca. 722 BCE and is prophesied to be gathered from the 'nations' (Gentiles) when the Messiah returns to gather His Bride.

These two phrases represent the same time frame in the future, one referring to the end of Gentile control of the Land of Yisra'el, when Messiah shall reign as King, and the other referring to Him gathering the people out of the nations and back to the Land.

Paul's statement in verse 25 refers to the time between Messiah's death as the Lamb and His return as King, when Yisra'el shall be blind to the Truth to allow the fulness of the Gentile believers comes to pass and then He shall come to restore the Land and the People to fulfill the promise YHWH made to the fathers, i.e., the remnant.

This promise of a remnant is also likely a two part doctrine, referring to those who believe in this time before Messiah returns, the spiritual seed, who will be resurrected and inherit the Kingdom in the new body, and those who come to believe during the Wrath, the physical seed, who will go into the kingdom in this natural body (to include the 144,000 native born – Revelation 7:1-8; 12:1-17; 14:1-5).

| Rom 11:26 | And so all Yisra'ĕl shall be saved, as it has been written, "The Deliverer shall come out of Tsiyon, and He shall turn away wickedness from Yaʿaqoḇ, |
| Rom 11:27 | and this is My covenant with them, when I take away their sins." |

The "all Yisra'el" that shall be saved here is most likely a reference to all people, both native born and stranger, who have placed their trust and hope in YHWH through belief in Yahushua Messiah.

However, it is possible that it refers also to those who are of the physical descendants of Abraham, Yitschaq and Ya'aqob who do not believe in Yahushua Messiah until His return.

| Rom 11:28 | Truly, as regards the Good News *they are* enemies for your sake, but concerning the choice *they are* beloved for the sake of the fathers. |
| Rom 11:29 | For the gifts and the calling of Elohim are not to be repented of. |

Paul's statement here concerning Yisra'el being an enemy to the good news of Messiah, for the sake of Gentile acceptance, is interesting, because all the original believers were of the natural branches, thousands of them, long before a single Gentile had converted. So, it is not the people as individuals, to which Paul is referring, but to a nation of people.

Despite their unbelief, they are still loved by YHWH because of His promises to their fathers, Abraham, Yitschaq and Ya'aqob. As stated in Ecclesiastes 3:14, once YHWH has made a choice, He does not change His mind, so even despite their unbelief and disobedience the calling of the descendants of Abraham remains valid.

| | |
|---|---|
| **Rom 11:30** | For as you also at one time disobeyed Elohim, but now have obtained compassion through their disobedience, |
| **Rom 11:31** | so also these have now disobeyed, that through the compassion shown you they also might obtain compassion. |
| **Rom 11:32** | For Elohim has shut them all up to disobedience, in order to have compassion on all. |

Think about what would've happened if Yisra'el would have marched right into the Promised Land and conquered Canaan after they came out of Egypt. Think about what would've happened if Yisra'el had never walked in disobedience before YHWH. Think about what would've happened if the whole body of Yisra'el would have received the Messiah at His first coming.

Remember, YHWH knows all things before they happen, He sees the end from the beginning. He knew before anything was created that man would sin, that Yisra'el would walk in disobedience and that the world would become what it is today.

He has not been surprised, in the slightest by anything that has happened, yet He had a plan to redeem, not just all Yisra'el but all mankind back to Himself.

However, since He granted us all free will, He had to allow for things that were not in His perfect will, and one of these things was a heart attitude of rebellion in the people of Yisra'el. Because of this, His plan required that His Son be rejected and killed so that through Him all mankind could be redeemed back to Him.

| | |
|---|---|
| **Rom 11:33** | Oh, the depth of riches, and wisdom and knowledge of Elohim! How unsearchable His judgments and untraceable His ways! |

| | |
|---|---|
| Rom 11:34 | "For **who has known the mind of יהוה? Or who has become His counsellor?"** |
| Rom 11:35 | **"Or who first gave to Him, and it shall be given back to him?"** |
| Rom 11:36 | Because of Him, and through Him, and to Him, are all, to whom be esteem forever. Amĕn. |

# Chapter 10: Romans 12-16

Throughout the book of Romans, Paul has switched between teaching us concerning the redemption of the spirit man and the responsibility of the physical man to walk spiritually, until the day of redemption.

This *Two-Part Principle*, spiritual things and physical things, working together to accomplish eternal life in us, through belief in Yahushua Messiah, is hard for some people to see in the writings of Paul. Paul has made certain presumptions of his readers, namely that they understand the need to walk in obedience to the Torah as believers.

Unfortunately, because of 2000 years of man-made additions and subtractions, there has been a serious distortion of the very basic facts of the true belief, which were fundamental to, and common knowledge among the early believers. In the mind of every early believer was the understanding that the command to repent (teshuvah) was an instruction to **re-turn to YHWH and His Torah.**

This return was a return to Torah, to obedience to everything YHWH had spoken through Moses to the children of Yisra'el. To Paul it was a fundamental principle of the belief that the believer in Yahushua Messiah was to walk in the same obedience to the Torah that Yahushua Himself walked in.

Unfortunately, because of the man-made additions and subtractions that the Jews were already guilty of at the time, the Messiah and His apostles spent a good portion of their time correcting Jewish error. Paul is doing a significant amount of this in Romans because the assembly there was a combination of both Jew and Gentile believers. So, the book of Romans includes Paul's answer to different elements of this man-made Jewish dogma, i.e., Gentile inclusion.

The *Two-Part Principle* is something that Paul was continually trying to express in his writings, which is why he makes a distinction between what is spiritual and what is physical in all his writings.

However, because the church, like the Jews before them, have instituted so much man-made dogma, the basic principles of Scripture have been lost and so the church is unable to clearly understand the distinctions between spiritual and physical, and how these things apply in a believer today.

Yes, if you talk to a Christian teacher or maybe even the Christian layman about whether there is a distinction between spiritual and physical, they will say yes, however, their inability to scripturally support the position and show how both apply in the totality of

Scripture for the believer today, is evidence that they do not really understand.

They have a form of knowledge, but do not walk in the understanding of it, and so they are like the Jews, that have a form of knowledge which is not complete, because of their rejection of the Torah.

The Torah itself tells us, it is through the guarding and doing of the commands of YHWH that we walk in the wisdom and understanding of Him (Deut 4:5-6). Both Judaism and Christianity are full of those people Paul described to Timothy, who are "always learning and never able to come to the knowledge of the truth" (2Ti 3:7).

Fortunately for us, Paul is going to make a clear and definitive statement concerning how we believers are to bring our physical body into subjection to the spirit man and what that means.

Yes, he already clearly did this in chapter 7 and 8, however these first two verses of chapter 12 are difficult to argue against when understood in the right context.

### Romans 12

**Rom 12:1**   I call upon you, therefore, brothers, through the compassion of Elohim, to **present your bodies** a living offering – **set-apart**, well-pleasing to Elohim – your reasonable worship.

**Rom 12:2**   And do not be conformed to this world, but be transformed by **the renewing of your mind**, so that you prove what is that **good and well-pleasing and perfect desire of Elohim**.

We are to present our body, a living sacrifice! He couldn't be much clearer than that. Paul specifically uses this terminology so that we will understand there is a distinction between the born-again spiritual man and the physical man (body) that is still waiting for the adoption (the redemption of the body-Romans 8:23).

Here we see Paul is admonishing us to bring our physical man into obedience, so that it can be "set apart and pleasing to Elohim" which Paul says is the least we should be doing, considering all He's done for us by offering up His Son, Yahushua Messiah, to pay the debt of our sin.

We have stated before, what being "set apart" or holy means, but let's look at it one more time.

348

The word holy or set apart means to be distinctly different than everyone else around you and the admonition for us to be set apart unto YHWH means that we are absolutely committed to Him and to obeying His instructions, despite what the rest of the world is doing. This behavior makes us unique or "set-apart from" all men.

To declare YHWH as our Elohim, is to declare that everything He has spoken or required of us, is the only path upon which we live. His Word is also the basis upon which we form our mindset and worldview, so that we can judge everything we see and hear in this world from His point of view and not that of the world itself and especially our fleshly desires.

This is what Paul means when he instructs us to "not be conformed to this world, but to be transformed by the renewing of our mind". He's telling us to no longer think like the world thinks but to transform the way we think to be consistent and in complete agreement with what YHWH has spoken in His Word.

By conforming our mindset to the Word of YHWH and living out our lives in obedience to that mindset, we prove within ourselves and to the world around us what is the good and well pleasing and perfect will or desire of YHWH. How?

The Word/Torah of YHWH is the good and perfect will of YHWH for His people, it is how His people live in His will, because it protects us from the penalty for disobedience (sin) which is death.

The Torah gives life and blessing to those who obey it and death and cursing to those who do not obey it (Deuteronomy 30). YHWH wants His children to have life and have it more abundantly.

It is the Torah of YHWH that teaches us His will and allows us to approve of what is best.

| | |
|---|---|
| **Rom 2:17** | See, you are called a Yehudi, and rest on the Torah, and make your boast in Elohim, |
| **Rom 2:18** | and **know the desire** *of Elohim*, and approve what is superior, **being instructed out of the Torah,** |

As we can see here, Paul says that the Jews knew the will of YHWH and could approve of what is superior because they had been instructed out of the Torah, however, he goes on to say that they walked in disobedience to the will of YHWH. The knowledge they had did not help them because they refused to apply it in their life.

There are two important principles here, first, the Torah is the foundation upon which we know the will of YHWH and of how we approve of superior things. Second, knowledge of the Torah has no value for you if you're not applying the principles of Torah to how you live.

The one who claims the Name of YHWH upon himself and yet does not live in obedience to the Torah, blasphemes the Name of YHWH.

| | |
|---|---|
| **Rom 2:23** | You who make your boast in the Torah, through the transgression of the Torah do you disrespect Elohim? |

You cannot claim that YHWH is your Elohim and that you have declared Yahushua, His Son, as your Master and Savior and be walking in disobedience to His Torah, it's blasphemy!

| | |
|---|---|
| **Rom 12:3** | For I say, through the favour which has been given to me, to everyone who is among you, not to think *of himself* more highly than he should think, but to think soberly, as Elohim has given to each a measure of belief. |
| **Rom 12:4** | For as we have many members in one body, but all members do not have the same function, |
| **Rom 12:5** | so we, the many, are one body in Messiah, and members each one of one another. |
| **Rom 12:6** | Now having different gifts, according to the favour which was given to us, *let us use them accordingly*: if prophecy, according to the proportion of belief; |
| **Rom 12:7** | if serving, in the serving; or he who is teaching, in the teaching; |
| **Rom 12:8** | or he who encourages, in the encouragement; or he who is sharing, in sincerity; he who is leading, in diligence; he who shows compassion, joyously. |

This passage is an admonition to believers to remember that we are all one body in Yahushua Messiah, whether we are Greek or Jew, male or female, red, white, black or green, it doesn't really matter to YHWH. In Him we are one people, one race, one culture which adheres to His Word.

As a family we always work towards the betterment of the whole, and not just our own personal agendas, and to this purpose YHWH has granted each of us a gift. Some gifts we may have been

350

exercising long before we became believers. We are to use these gifts for the lifting up and growth of the body, in humility and sincerity, lifting others above ourselves.

Too many times in the so-called body of Messiah, we see people utilizing their gifts with arrogance and pride, lording it over the brethren. This mentality is what Yahushua calls in the book of Revelation, the doctrine of the Nikolaites (Nicolaitans) which He hates.

> **Nikolaites:** stg's #**G3531 "Nikolaitēs",** a Nicolaite, that is, adherent of Nicolaus: - Nicolaitane; from stg's #**G3532 "Nikolaos",** **victorious over the people**; Nicolaus, a heretic.

Servants in the body of Messiah are supposed to be just that, servants, not masters, not leaders, not priests or Cardinals or Bishops or Popes or Pastors or any other kind of appellation that stipulates authority.

Yes, of course, there are gifting's that allow people to teach or to Shepherd or to organize, or any other such talents, but these are positions of service to the larger body, for Messiah and only Messiah is the Master and Teacher and Leader of the body, He is the husband, the head of His bride.

| | |
|---|---|
| **Rom 12:9** | Let love be without hypocrisy. Shrink from what is wicked, cling to what is good. |
| **Rom 12:10** | In brotherly love, tenderly loving towards one another, in appreciation, giving preference to each other; |
| **Rom 12:11** | not idle in duty, ardent in spirit, **serving the Master**; |
| **Rom 12:12** | rejoicing in the expectancy, enduring under pressure, continuing steadfastly in prayer; |
| **Rom 12:13** | imparting to the needs of the set-apart ones, pursuing kindness towards strangers. |
| **Rom 12:14** | Bless those who persecute you – bless and do not curse. |
| **Rom 12:15** | Rejoice with those who rejoice, and weep with those who weep. |
| **Rom 12:16** | Be of the same mind toward one another. **Do not be proud in mind**, but go along with the lowly. **Do not be wise in your own estimation**. |

| Rom 12:17 | Repay no one evil for evil. Respect what is right in the sight of all men. |
| Rom 12:18 | If possible, on your part, **be at peace with all men**. |

This should be the mind and heart of all believers toward one another and their fellow men and it is the mindset of the Torah observant believer, for it is the Torah that teaches us to behave this way. It is the Torah that teaches us that a man does no harm to his neighbor.

These are not new commands from a so-called "New Testament", but they are a summary of the attitude of a Torah observant person. Paul is simply summarizing the proper attitude of a believer, instead of quoting the Torah line by line and word by word, but in the end it's all the same thing.

| Rom 12:19 | Beloved, do not revenge yourselves, but give place to the wrath, for it has been written, **"Vengeance is Mine, I shall repay," says יהוה.** |
| Rom 12:20 | **"Instead, if your enemy hungers, feed him; if he thirsts, give him a drink, for in so doing you shall heap coals of fire on his head."** |

It is not the place of the believer to take vengeance on anyone, but it is his duty to put all things at the foot of the Master and trust the Master Himself will fulfill His promise to judge the world on our behalf.

It is a believer's duty to walk humbly before the Master and all men, as a witness of the love and mercy of the Master, walking out our lives in the honesty, humility and compassion in which He lived out His life, while He was on earth.

| Rom 12:21 | Do not be overcome by evil, but overcome evil with good. |

**Romans 13**

| Rom 13:1 | Let every being be in subjection to the governing authorities. For there is no authority except from Elohim, and the |

352

| | |
|---|---|
| | authorities that exist are appointed by Elohim. |
| Rom 13:2 | So he who opposes the authority withstands the institution of Elohim, and those who withstand shall bring judgment on themselves. |
| Rom 13:3 | For those ruling are an object of fear, not to good works, but to evil. Do you wish to be not afraid of the authority? Do the good, and you shall have praise from it, |
| Rom 13:4 | for it is a servant of Elohim to you for good. But if you do evil, be afraid, for it does not bear the sword in vain. For it is a servant of Elohim, a revenger to execute wrath on him who practises evil. |
| Rom 13:5 | Therefore, it is necessary to be subject, not only because of wrath but also because of the conscience. |
| Rom 13:6 | For because of this you also pay taxes, for they are servants of Elohim attending continually to these duties. |
| Rom 13:7 | Render therefore to all what is due to them: tax to whom tax *is due*, toll to whom toll, fear to whom fear, respect to whom respect. |

This has to do with how believers are to live among the Gentile nations and our responsibility to respect the authorities of that given nation. Our responsibility to submit to the authority of these nations, is part of the judgment which we have inherited from our ancestors, until the day the Master returns and restores all things.

It is important to note however, that even though it is not mentioned here, there are certain boundaries within the belief that no authority in the heavens or on the earth can demand of us, nor force us, to violate. No authority in heaven or on earth can command a believer to violate the Torah in any way, shape or form.

Consider the four Jewish young men that had been taken into Babylonian exile around 605 BCE. These men were Dani'ĕl (Bĕlteshatstsar), Ḥananyah (Shaḏraḵ), Misha'ĕl (Mĕyshaḵ), and Azaryah (Aḇĕḏ-Neḡo).

When these young men first got to Babylon, as it is recorded in Daniel 1, they were informed that they would be eating certain succulent meats from the King's table, which to the Babylonians was considered a privilege, but likely included meats that the Scripture had declared unclean.

These young men petitioned the King to be allowed to eat a strictly vegetarian type of diet, in order to avoid violating the commands of the Scripture and found mercy in the eyes of the King.

Later, in chapter 3, three of these young men, Shadrak, Misha'el and Abed-Nego, were put to the test when King Nebuchadnezzar of Babylon built a giant image and required all people in the kingdom to bow down and give reverence to the image. These young men declined to bow down before the image and were brought before the king to be judged.

The King offered them a second chance, they had the choice to bow down to the image or be put to death in a flaming fire, yet these three young men kept true to the belief and in accordance with the command of Torah, refused to bow down.

| | |
|---|---|
| **Dan 3:16** | Shadrak, Měyshak, and Abĕd-Nego answered and said to the sovereign, "O Nebukadnetstsar, we have no need to answer you in this matter. |
| **Dan 3:17** | "For if so, our Elah whom we serve is able to deliver us from the burning furnace of fire and from your hand, O sovereign – He does deliver! |
| **Dan 3:18** | "But if not, let it be known to you, O sovereign, that we do not serve your elahin, nor do we do obeisance to the gold image which you have set up." |

| | |
|---|---|
| **Note:** | This passage was written in Aramaic so the words "Elah" and "elahin" are the Aramaic forms of the Hebrew words "Eloah" and "Elohim" respectively. These of course are words meaning authority or mighty one in our reference to YHWH. |

Though these men had lived in Babylon for a while and had adhered to the laws and requirements of Babylonian society, they refused to compromise the principles of the belief, set forth in the commands of Torah, even at the threat of death.

The prophet Daniel suffered in a similar manner in chapter 6, when his enemies convinced the King to create a decree that forbade anyone praying to any deity other than the King himself, upon point of death.

Daniel, even knowing the consequences for his actions, continued to openly pray to YHWH and was arrested and thrown into the lion's den because of it. In both cases these young faithful men were delivered from the wrath of the King, however, as was quoted in 3:18, whether YHWH delivered them or not, they would not bow down to foreign deities.

This principle applies today as well, as believers we are to be mindful and respectful of the laws and authority of the secular government in which we live, however, we are never to adhere to a law that requires us to violate the Torah in any way, even at the point of death.

| | |
|---|---|
| **Rom 13:8** | Owe no one any *matter* except to love one another, for he who loves another has filled the Torah. |
| **Rom 13:9** | For this, **"You shall not commit adultery," "You shall not murder," "You shall not steal," "You shall not bear false witness," "You shall not covet,"** and if there is any other command, it is summed up in this word, **"You shall love your neighbour as yourself."** |
| **Rom 13:10** | Love does no evil to a neighbour. Therefore, love is completion of the Torah. |

Now, because Paul said this and it sounds like something the Messiah Himself said, men have wrongfully interpret this in several ways.

First, some men say that if we just love my neighbor with all my heart, we have fulfilled the law, therefore we don't need to obey the commands of the law, such as Sabbath and feast days and dietary laws, etc.

Other men say that since these are the only commands specified in the so-called "New Testament", these are the only commandments a new testament believer need obey and so they can disregard the other commands of Sabbath and feast days and dietary laws, etc.

This cannot be any farther from the truth and the fact that men have said so, shows that they have a rebellious heart that serves itself and not a pure heart of service to YHWH, Who never changes and Who's work is settled forever, and cannot be added to or taken away from.

Part of the issue may be the way the Greek word "pleroo" and its companion word "pleroma" are translated in this passage.

**Filled:** stg's #G4137 "pleroo", to make replete, that is, (literally) to cram (a net), level up (a hollow)

**Completion:** stg's #G4138 "pleroma", repletion or completion, that is, (subjectively) what fills (as contents, supplement, copiousness, multitude), or (objectively) what is filled

Paul is saying that love is the fulfillment of Torah, he says this because the Torah teaches us how to love both YHWH and one another according to YHWH's definition of love.

Since we, as humans, generally do not understand how, which day we celebrate on or what type of foods we eat, have anything to do with love, we misunderstand what Paul is saying here.

To YHWH, keeping His Sabbath is an act of love towards Him, to celebrate His feast days, and reject the feast days that are pagan in origin, is an act of love towards Him, and to restrict our meat consumption to only those creatures that He has declared to be food for us is an act of love towards Him.

More than that, committing ourselves to complete obedience to His Torah is not only an act of love towards Him but it is a sign of our loyalty and trust.

The point that Paul is trying to make, is just the simple fact that the Torah, by definition, **is love** just as YHWH Himself is love. Only YHWH can set the standard of what love means and He declared it to us in His Torah.

**Rom 13:11** And *do* this, knowing the time, that it is already the hour for us to wake up from sleep, for now **our deliverance is nearer than when we did believe**.

Paul is saying, there is still a future deliverance (salvation) and he is warning us to wake up and be sober. This is a warning to us, because as we have shown in other places, he's telling us we have to be **doing right** if we expect to be delivered, for if we don't we will be judged.

This is another example of Paul showing us an aspect of the *Two-Part Principle*. Sometimes he refers to our salvation as something that has been completed in the present time and then he says something like this where our salvation is yet in the future.

Not understanding the difference between our present salvation and our future salvation is why we have so many different interpretations of the Good News among denominations. What these groups do not want to accept is that there is more than one deliverance, just like there is more than one righteousness.

There is the righteousness of Yahushua, which covers our unrighteousness and justifies us from the penalty of sin, which is death. This is the spiritual justification or spiritual righteousness, which can only be received through belief in Yahushua Messiah and saves our inner man. This is the righteousness that we receive through belief and not through works.

There is also the righteousness of Torah, which trains us to walk in righteousness and, when we walk in it, sets us apart or makes us holy before Him and the world. This is physical justification or physical righteousness, which is achieved through obedience to the Torah from a pure heart and leads to the salvation of the outer man at the return of Yahushua at the resurrection.

This is the righteousness that we live in, the works which YHWH prepared before He sent Messiah that all His people should live by (Eph 2:10).

| | |
|---|---|
| Rom 13:12 | The night is far advanced, the day has come near. So let us **put off the works of darkness**, and **let us put on the armour of light.** |
| Rom 13:13 | Let us **walk** becomingly, as in the day, not in wild parties and drunkenness, not in living together and indecencies, not in fighting and envy, |
| Rom 13:14 | but put on the Master יהושע Messiah, and **make no provision for the lusts of the flesh**. |

Paul is telling us how to **live** as believers. The reference to the armor of light has to do with something he has told the Ephesians.

| | |
|---|---|
| Eph 6:13 | Because of this, take up the **complete armour of Elohim**, so that you have power to withstand in the wicked day, and having done all, to stand. |
| Eph 6:14 | Stand, then, **having girded your waist with truth,** and having **put on the breastplate of righteousness,** |

357

| Eph 6:15 | and having fitted your **feet with the preparation of the Good News of peace;** |
| Eph 6:16 | above all, having taken up the **shield of belief** with which you shall have power to quench all the burning arrows of the wicked one. |
| Eph 6:17 | Take also the **helmet of deliverance,** and the **sword of the Spirit**, which is the Word of Elohim, |

The complete armor of Elohim, which is also the armor of light, consists of very particular components.

### Girdle (belt) of Truth

Messiah is the truth (John 14:6); the Word is truth (John 17:17; Psalms 119:160); the Torah is truth (Psalms 119:142).

### Breastplate of righteousness:

Messiah is the righteousness that comes by belief (Romans 3:22); the Torah is the works of righteousness that all His people live by (Deuteronomy 6:24-25).

### Sandals of the Good News of peace:

The work of Messiah is the Good News that delivered us from the penalty of sin which is death (Romans 3:24-25); the Torah is the good news of YHWH to His people, which, if we obey it, we shall live by it (Leviticus 18:5).

### Shield of belief:

Belief in Yahushua Messiah is the substance upon which we open and it is the evidence that what we hope for is true even though we have not yet seen it, which gives us the power and strength to fight off the wicked one (Hebrews 11:1); belief without works is dead (James 2:17-18, 22) and Torah is the standard of good works which YHWH prepared for His people to live by (Ephesians 2:10).

### Helmet of deliverance:

Belief in Yahushua Messiah, and the works of Torah which perfect it (James 2:22), protects our minds from the wiles of theenemy, if we live in it.

### Sword of the Spirit (Word of YHWH):

Messiah is the Word made flesh. through whom we overcome the penalty of sin, which is death, and are "born again" in the inner-spirit man; the Torah, which is spiritual (Romans 7:14), is the standard of righteousness in which the new "spirit man" brings the ld "physical man" (flesh) into subjection, so that it too might be "born again" at the
>resurrection on the last day, which is the adoption, the redemption of the body (Romans 8:23).

As you can see, and as we have said repeatedly, every doctrine in the Scripture consists of two parts, one physical and one spiritual. The spiritual side of the Scripture are the things that YHWH does on our behalf and the physical side of the Scripture is how we are to respond to the things He has done for us.

Just as He created us partly of the earth (physical) and partly of His breath (spiritual) so do all things that have to do with life consist of the physical things (the things we do) and the spiritual things (the things He does).

This duality is important because in it we understand the responsibility and accountability of free will. It was His choice to give us free will and in doing so He created a system by which everything He did for us must be reciprocated by us to prove the legitimacy of the thoughts and intents of our heart.

## Romans 14

Chapter 14 has confused and confounded Christianity since it became a religion in the second century CE. We are not going to go in depth here concerning this chapter because it will be covered at length in Section 4: "Food" pg. 485.

What we will do, is give you, the reader, a principle of Scripture interpretation which, if you accept it and then apply it to what you're reading, will make the context of this passage and many others become much clearer.

The primary context of the so-called "New Testament" passages concerning food and eating has to do with eating things that have been or might have been sacrificed to idols and **NOT** about what kind of meat a believer is allowed to eat, because that was already established in the Torah.

This principle of scriptural interpretation that we are going to discuss is, foundational continuity. Foundational continuity is a principle that requires every Scripture passage to be interpreted consistently with all the Scripture that has come before it.

For example, in the beginning (Genesis 2:2-4) YHWH chose the seventh day as the day of rest and set it apart (sanctified it).

| | |
|---|---|
| **Exo 31:12** | And יהוה spoke to Mosheh, saying, |
| **Exo 31:13** | "And you, speak to the children of Yisra'ĕl, saying, 'My Sabbaths you are to guard, by all means, for it is a **sign** between Me and you throughout your generations, to know that I, יהוה, am setting you apart. |
| **Exo 31:14** | 'And you shall guard the Sabbath, for it is set-apart to you. Everyone who profanes it shall certainly be put to death, for anyone who does work on it, that being shall be cut off from among his people. |
| **Exo 31:15** | 'Six days work is done, and on the seventh is a Sabbath of rest, set-apart to יהוה. Everyone doing work on the Sabbath day shall certainly be put to death. |
| **Exo 31:16** | 'And the children of Yisra'ĕl shall guard the Sabbath, to perform the Sabbath throughout their generations as an everlasting covenant. |
| **Exo 31:17** | 'Between Me and the children of Yisra'ĕl it is **a sign forever**. For in six days יהוה made the heavens and the earth, and on the seventh day He rested and was refreshed.'" |

The principle of foundational continuity requires that the seventh day of the week is to be the Sabbath day forever and ever, as a sign of the people of YHWH. Now this statement can never change and it can never be added to or taken away from, because the Scripture says everything that YHWH does is forever, it cannot be added to or taken away from (Ecclesiastes 3:14).

Furthermore, to those who would say this sign is for the people of Yisra'el only, YHWH says there is one law, one Torah for both the native born and the stranger that sojourns with them (Numbers 15:15-16) and that the stranger who sojourns with them is to be treated as a native born among them, an Yisra'eli (Leviticus 19:33-34).

Considering this, the Scriptures states there is only one day set apart for the people of YHWH and that day is the seventh or Sabbath day.

This same principle applies to food. In Leviticus 11 and Deuteronomy 14 YHWH established what living animals are acceptable as food for His people. All the living creatures in these two passages that YHWH says can be eaten are considered food for the people of YHWH.

Likewise, all living creatures listed in these passages that YHWH says cannot be eaten are **NOT** considered food for the people of YHWH.

According to YHWH, a pig is not food and because nothing can be added to or taken away from what YHWH has said, a pig is not now and never will be considered food for the people of YHWH.

Now, because of foundational continuity, any time the so-called "New Testament" is talking about food or the eating of food it is **NEVER** going to be a reference to pig or any other unclean animal.

> **Note**: A lot of people like to argue that Genesis 9 proves that YHWH does change His Torah periodically throughout time. One of the greatest errors in Christian Theology is called Dispensationalism. This teaches that YHWH has treated mankind differently in different 'dispensations' of time. Some say there are three dispensations of time, some say seven, etc., etc., etc.
>
> Unfortunately, for those holding such views, there are a plethora of passages in the Scripture that state that He does not change and that His word is settled in Heaven forever, etc. We will get into this discussion more thoroughly later in the section titled "Food?"
>
> However, since His word is eternal, just as He is, then it cannot change, be added to or taken away from, during any time in history. Thus, the same "Law" that was given to Yisra'el through Moses, is the same "law" that was true for Adam or Noach, etc.

Genesis 9 MUST be understood in light of what YHWH said in Leviticus 11, Deuteronomy 14, Acts 10 and anywhere else in the

Scripture. However, there is His perfect will, i.e., the way He intended things to go in the Garden, and the way things had to go after man choose of his own freewill to violate the instructions (Torah) of his Creator.

**Rom 14:2**      One indeed believes to eat all *food*, but he who is weak eats only vegetables.

**Rom 14:3**      He that eats, let him not despise him who does not eat, and he that does not eat, let him not judge him who eats, for Elohim received him.

As mentioned before, this and most all other passages in the Messianic Writings concerning what is eaten, has to do with eating things offered to idols. Even in times when the context is not referring to eating things offered to idols, it is never a reference to being able to eat what YHWH has already declared unclean, not food for us.

This passage in Romans 14 is a reference to eating things sacrificed to idols, however, it is not referring to what kinds of meat can be eaten but to whether meat should be eaten or only vegetables. It's an argument between eating meat or being a vegetarian and the argument exists because some of the brethren thought it would be better to not eat meat at all than to risk eating a piece of meat that had been offered to an idol by mistake.

We will consider this passage more thoroughly later in this writing, but for now just remember, the only things allowed by YHWH in Leviticus 11 and Deuteronomy 14 are to be considered food for the people of YHWH, and this will never change.

The Messianic writers understood this well and when they mention food or eating it is never a reference to what is unclean, because what is unclean is not food.

The other significant teaching in this chapter is about mature believers watching out for the well-being of the less mature brethren near them. The mature believers understood that eating clean meat was okay, even if you were not sure where it came from (i.e., had been sacrificed to idols).

This right confused some of the immature believers, whose lack of biblical understanding caused them to think that they could eat meat that had been sacrifice to idols.

Paul's admonition to the mature believer was to not do anything which would cause the immature believer to stumble. He also admonished the immature believer, not to judge the mature believer, for things they did not yet understand.

| Rom 15:1 | But we who are strong ought to bear with the failings of the weak, and not to please ourselves. |
| Rom 15:2 | Let each one of us please his neighbour for his good, to build him up. |
| Rom 15:3 | For even the Messiah did not please Himself, but, as it has been written, "The reproaches of those who reproached You fell upon Me." |
| Rom 15:4 | **For whatever was written before was written for our instruction, that through endurance and encouragement of the Scriptures we might have the expectation.** |
| Rom 15:5 | And the Elohim of endurance and encouragement give you to be of the same mind toward one another, according to Messiah יהושע, |
| Rom 15:6 | that with one mind and one mouth, you might praise the Elohim and Father of our Master יהושע Messiah. |
| Rom 15:7 | So accept one another, as Messiah also did accept us, to the esteem of Elohim. |

This chapter begins were chapter 14 left off concerning judging each other, specifically the mature believer's responsibility to bear with the ignorance and immaturity of a new believer, using Messiah Himself is an example.

The most significant verse in this passage is vs. 4, which has a much broader application than just this specific context. It states that whatever was written before (i.e., the Tanak) was written for our instruction.

Everything written in the Torah, the Prophets and the Writings was written to instruct us, so that we would learn endurance and be encouraged through our sojourning, awaiting the return of Yahushua and the beginning of the Kingdom.

This is similar to what Paul told Timothy.

| 2Ti 3:14 | But you, stay in what you have learned and trusted, having known from whom you have learned, |
| 2Ti 3:15 | and that from a babe you have **known the Set-apart Scriptures, which are able to** |

|         | make you wise for deliverance through belief in Messiah יהושע. |
|---------|---------------------------------------------------------------|
| 2Ti 3:16 | **All Scripture** is breathed out by Elohim and **profitable for teaching, for reproof, for setting straight, for instruction in righteousness,** |
| 2Ti 3:17 | that the man of Elohim might be fitted, equipped for every good work. |

Paul encouraged Timothy to remember things he had learned and trusted in, having been taught from his childhood what the Scriptures had told him. The only Scripture available to Timothy in his childhood was the Tanak, which Christians incorrectly call the Old Testament.

Paul tells him, these same Scriptures can make him wise through belief in Yahushua Messiah. Long before Messiah came the Tanak was able to make a man wise unto salvation through belief in Yahushua Messiah. This is the same thing he is saying in Romans 15 concerning what had been written before for our endurance and encouragement of hope we have in Yahushua Messiah.

If you pay close attention to what's being said in 2nd Timothy, you see the *Two-Part Principle* clearly expressed. Verses 14 and 15 refer to the spiritual part of our salvation, which comes through belief in Yahushua Messiah as taught in the Tanak.

Verses 16 and 17 refer to the physical part of our salvation, which comes from a pure heart of obedience towards the Torah of YHWH, without additions or subtractions. The Scripture teaches us, reproves us, sets us on the straight path and instructs us on how to live righteously so that we are prepared to accomplish every good work as men of YHWH.

This is the same thing Paul means when he says, "through endurance and encouragement of the Scriptures we might have the expectation (hope)" we are seeking.

Through obedience to the Scripture (Torah) we are encouraged by the Scripture that we will receive the things we hope for.

Paul says this because the Torah says, if we guard and do all the commands YHWH has set out before us, He will bless us and give us life.

| Deu 28:1 | "And it shall be, **if you diligently obey** the voice of יהוה your Elohim, **to guard to do all** His commands which I command you today, |
|----------|----------------------------------------------------------------|

that יהוה your Elohim shall set you high above all nations of the earth.

**Deu 28:2** "And all these blessings shall come upon you and overtake you, **if you obey** the voice of יהוה your Elohim:

**Deu 28:3** "Blessed are you in the city, and blessed are you in the field.

**Deu 28:4** "Blessed is the fruit of your body, and the fruit of your ground and the fruit of your livestock – the increase of your cattle and the offspring of your flocks.

**Deu 28:5** "Blessed is your basket and your kneading bowl.

**Deu 28:6** "Blessed are you when you come in, and blessed are you when you go out.

**Deu 28:7** "יהוה causes your enemies who rise against you to be smitten before your face – they come out against you one way and flee before you seven ways.

**Deu 28:8** "יהוה commands the blessing on you in your storehouses and in all to which you set your hand, and shall bless you in the land which יהוה your Elohim is giving you.

**Deu 28:9** "יהוה does establish you as a set-apart people to Himself, as He has sworn to you, **if you guard the commands of יהוה your Elohim and walk in His ways.**

**Deu 28:10** "And all peoples of the earth shall see that the Name of יהוה is called upon you, and they shall be afraid of you.

**Deu 28:11** "And יהוה shall make you to have plenty of what is good, in the fruit of your body, in the fruit of your livestock, and in the fruit of your ground, in the land of which יהוה swore to your fathers to give you.

**Deu 28:12** "יהוה opens to you His good treasure, the heavens, to give the rain to your land in its season, and to bless all the work of your hand. And you shall lend to many nations, but you do not borrow.

**Deu 28:13** "And יהוה shall make you the head and not the tail. And you shall be only on top, and not be beneath, **if you obey the commands of**

365

יהוה **your Elohim, which I command you today, to guard and do.**

All the promises given the Scripture are conditional upon our obedience.

| | |
|---|---|
| **Deu 30:11** | "For this command which I am commanding you today, **it is not too hard for you**, nor is it far off. |
| **Deu 30:12** | "It is not in the heavens, to say, 'Who shall ascend into the heavens for us, and bring it to us, and cause us to hear it, so that we do it?' |
| **Deu 30:13** | "Nor is it beyond the sea, to say, 'Who shall go over the sea for us, and bring it to us, and cause us to hear it, so that we do it?' |
| **Deu 30:14** | "For the Word is very near you, **in your mouth and in your heart – to do it.** |
| **Deu 30:15** | "See, I have set before you today life and good, and death and evil, |
| **Deu 30:16** | in that I am commanding you today **to love** יהוה your Elohim, **to walk in His ways**, and **to guard His commands, and His laws, and His right-rulings**. And you shall live and increase, and יהוה your Elohim shall bless you in the land which you go to possess. |
| **Deu 30:17** | "But **if your heart turns away**, and you do not obey, and shall be drawn away, and shall bow down to other mighty ones and serve them, |
| **Deu 30:18** | "I have declared to you today that you shall certainly perish, you shall not prolong your days in the land which you are passing over the Yarděn to enter and possess. |
| **Deu 30:19** | "I have called the heavens and the earth as witnesses today against you: I have set before you life and death, the blessing and the curse. Therefore you shall **choose life**, so that you live, both you and your seed, |
| **Deu 30:20** | to **love** יהוה your Elohim, to **obey** His voice, and to **cling** to Him – for He is your life and the length of your days – to dwell in the land which יהוה swore to your fathers, to Aḇraham, to Yitsḥaq, and to Yaʿaqoḇ, to give them." |

Once again, to inherit life and blessing and good we must obey, which is intrinsically tied to love. Therefore, Messiah Himself associated loving Him to obeying Him (John 14:15).

Notice however, that there's another promise here. This promise has to do with disobedience and the consequences of it, i.e., evil, cursing and death.

Paul is admonishing us to walk with endurance in obedience to the Torah, in order to receive the promises of Torah.

| | |
|---|---|
| **Rom 15:8** | And I say that יהושע Messiah has become a **servant of the circumcised for the truth of Elohim, to confirm the promises made to the fathers,** |
| **Rom 15:9** | and **for the nations to praise Elohim for His compassion,** as it has been written, "Because of this I shall confess to You among the nations, and I shall sing to Your Name." |
| **Rom 15:10** | And again it says, "Rejoice, O nations, with His people!" |
| **Rom 15:11** | And again, "Praise יהוה, all you nations! Praise Him, all you peoples!" |
| **Rom 15:12** | And again, Yeshayahu says, "There shall be a root of Yishai, and He who shall rise to reign over the nations, on Him the nations shall set their expectation." |
| **Rom 15:13** | And the Elohim of expectation fill you with all joy and peace in believing, that you overflow with expectation by the power of the Set-apart Spirit. |

In this passage Paul is showing the Ministry of Messiah, first for the native-born seed to confirm the promises made to their fathers, Abraham, Yitschaq and Ya'aqob, and second, to the strangers (Gentiles) sojourning with them, so they would give praise and esteem to YHWH for His compassion.

In verses 14-21 Paul speaks concerning his calling, which was to preach Messiah among the Gentiles and then, in verses 22-33 he tells the Romans of his plans to travel to them, encouraging them concerning the contribution to the poor believers in Yerushalayim.

**Romans 16**

367

This chapter consists of his greetings to the brethren (1-16), his final instructions to the assembly and his closing remarks concerning the esteem and might of YHWH.

> **Rom 16:17**      Now I call upon you, brothers, watch out for those who cause divisions and stumbling, **contrary to the teaching** which you learned, and turn away from them.
>
> **Rom 16:18**      For such ones do not serve our Master יהושע Messiah, but their own stomach, and by smooth words and flattering speech they **deceive the hearts** of the innocent.
>
> **Rom 16:19**      Your obedience, indeed, is reported to all. Therefore I rejoice concerning you, but I wish you to be wise indeed as to the good, and simple toward the evil.
>
> **Rom 16:20**      And the Elohim of peace shall crush Satan under your feet shortly. The favour of our Master יהושע Messiah be with you. Amĕn.

Let's talk a moment about what's being said here in this closing passage. Paul warns us concerning people among us who cause divisions and stumbling.

It's important to understand what causes divisions within the Body. There are thousands and thousands of divisions among the Christian church and it all revolves around doctrine, as it has been interpreted by individual men throughout time.

To YHWH there is only One Truth, and that truth has two parts, the physical part which is the Torah as He gave it through Mosheh at Mount Sinai and the spiritual part, which is Yahushua Messiah, Whom He gave to be the payment for our sins. The physical Truth and the spiritual Truth working together as One is the only real Truth.

Any teaching that separates the Messiah from the Torah or the Torah from Messiah, and does not include sacrificial love for one another, is a departure from the truth i.e., a division.

Any teaching that does not have Messiah first through belief, followed by obedience the Torah in belief, with the sacrificial heart of love for each other is a lie.

This kind of teaching causes people to stumble in the belief because is not founded in the Truth. Paul clearly shows us here that this division and stumbling has to do with people that have taught contrary to the instructions they have learned.

He tells us to separate ourselves from them because they do not serve YHWH, nor the truth of Yahushua, but they only serve themselves, deceiving the hearts of the innocent for their own personal gain.

The next statement to the Romans concerns their own obedience, which can only refer to the Torah, for the Torah is the only standard of obedience given in the Scripture. It is the standard of obedience Yahushua walked in, as well as His disciples, including Paul.

Please brethren, do not be led astray by the ignorance of men who set themselves above you in the congregation claiming authority over you, while they teach you to walk contrary to the truth in the Scripture.

No one, absolutely positively **NO ONE,** not Paul, not Peter, not the Pope, not the president, not even your Pastor has the right to add to or take away one letter of the Scripture as it was handed down to us in the Hebrew Scriptures.

Yes, there are some translational and scribal issues in the English and the Greek, but these can be easily corrected with a basic understanding of the Hebrew.

What's most important, is that we read the Scriptures from a mindset founded in the Hebrew Scriptures and that continually interpret all Scripture, no matter what language it's translated into, according to the original foundational elements of the Hebrew Scriptures.

Anyone that tells you, that as a believer in "Jesus Christ" you no longer have to obey the "Old Testament Law" is a liar and guilty of Deuteronomy 13:1-5 and Romans 16:17-18.

In closing this section concerning Paul's epistle to the Romans, we pray that your heart will be opened so your eyes can see and your ears can hear the truth of the word which is brought forth to you. We close this section as Paul closed his epistle.

"And to Him who is able to establish you according to my Good News and the preaching of יהושע Messiah, according to the revelation of the secret which was kept silent since times of old, but now has been made manifest, and by the prophetic Scriptures has been made known to all nations, according to the command of the everlasting Elohim, for belief-obedience. To Elohim, wise alone, be the esteem, through יהושע Messiah forever. Amĕn."   Romans 16:25-27

369

# SECTION 3

Section 3: Paul's question to Galatia:

"By what are we saved?"

Ch. 1 --------- Galatians 1

Ch. 2 --------- Galatians 2

Ch. 3 --------- Galatians 3

Ch. 4 --------- Galatians 4

Ch. 5 --------- Galatians 5-6

# Chapter 1: Paul's question to Galatia

By What Then Are We Saved?

The book of Galatians is one of the most misunderstood books in the entire Scripture. It, along with the book of Romans, has been used by modern Christian teachers to completely devalue the very foundations of the belief, which were given to us by the Father when He inspired the prophets to write the Tanak (Old Testament).

That Paul is the author of these books comes as no surprise, considering he was the most knowledgeable of all the apostles concerning the Tanak and like most brilliant intellectuals, his writings are so deep and profound that the language therein confuses most readers.

More than that, Paul wrote from a distinctly Hebrew mindset and from the presumption, that his readers already had a basic foundational understanding of the Tanak and its place in the belief, either because of his own teachings or the teaching of other Hebrew apostles.

There are a lot of presumptions made by modern teachers concerning the things Paul has written, which are not based in the same foundational, Hebraic perspective from which Paul wrote, and because of this they misunderstand what Paul is trying to say.

Furthermore, modern teachers have lost or were never taught how to properly follow the contextual flow of his writings. The Messianic Writings are written in a distinctly Hebrew manner, which is completely different than modern writing styles.

To a Hebrew writer, there is always the foundation of the Tanak flowing within the context of every discussion. Next, is the context of reason, i.e., the reason the discussion is being presented, which is then followed by the immediate context of the passage being cited.

So, there is a flow of contextual elements going on within each passage, all of which must be considered before we can conclude anything concerning what the author intends us to understand.

As a Hebrew, Paul wrote from the presumption that everyone understood, the Tanak, especially the Torah (five books of Moses), was the foundational and unchangeable basis upon which every teaching and doctrine within the Messianic Writings was to be constructed.

Modern theologians do not stand on this principle when they interpret Scripture and because of this they misunderstand much of what the Messianic Writings are saying concerning doctrinal elements.

As we saw in our study in Romans, this distinctly non-Hebrew mindset upon which modern teachers interpret the Messianic Writings, has caused them to twist the writings of Paul into a false religion, thus creating for themselves a false Messiah named Jesus.

In this section we will begin to unravel what is being said in the book of Galatians so that we can see how Paul's argument is consistent with not just what he said in Romans but also everything the Torah teaches.

To begin, we must find out what the actual context of the book is, why was Paul writing this book and what argument was he trying to make, and why?

| | |
|---|---|
| **Act 14:24** | And having passed through Pisidia, they came to Pamphulia. |
| **Act 14:25** | And having spoken the word in Perge, they went down to Attaleia, |
| **Act 14:26** | and from there **they sailed to Antioch**, where they had been committed to the favour of Elohim for the work which they had completed. |
| **Act 14:27** | And having arrived, and having gathered together the assembly, they related all that Elohim had done with them, and that He had opened the door of belief to the nations. |
| **Act 14:28** | And they remained there a long time with the taught ones. |
| **Act 15:1** | And **certain men came down from Yehuḏah** and were teaching the brothers, **"Unless you are circumcised, according to the practice of Mosheh, you are unable to be saved."** |
| **Act 15:2** | So when Paul and Barnaḇa had no small dissension and dispute with |

them, they arranged for Paul and Barnaḇa and certain others of them to go up to Yerushalayim, to the emissaries and elders, about this question.

Acts 15 is the passage most commonly referred to as the Yerushalayim (Jerusalem) Council, where Paul and Barnabas went to Yerushalayim to meet with the apostles concerning the question, "By what then are we saved?"

In Antioch, which was a city in the region of Galatia, several Jews came from Yerushalayim attempting to teach the Gentile believers that they needed to adhere to the commands of the Torah, specifically circumcision, **BEFORE** they would be accepted into the belief.

Their position was that a Gentiles responsibility to obey the Torah is a **pre-requisite** to being saved, basing our acceptance and salvation on the works of Torah and not belief in Yahushua. Paul stood against this idea of a works salvation vehemently, stating clearly that we are saved by belief and not by works.

Unfortunately, modern teachers have taken this argument out of its context and said that since we are not saved by works, but by belief, that we no longer are required to obey the Torah in our belief, which is a gross manipulation of the truth of the Scripture.

Nowhere, not even here in Acts 15, does the Messianic Writings teach that a believer no longer needs to obey the Torah, as it was given through Moses at Mount Sinai.

As we have already seen in our study in Romans, nothing that was spoken at Mount Sinai can be added to or taken away from, for it is how the believer is supposed to live set apart (holy) onto YHWH.

The argument being discussed in Acts 15 is not about whether the believer obeys the Torah **AFTER** he is saved by belief but whether the believer must do the works of Torah **TO BE SAVED**, i.e., as a prerequisite of salvation! This is the question upon which the book of Galatians is predicated, "By what then are we saved?"

> **Note**: Before moving on to the book of Galatians, it is important for the reader to review the

section titled "The Yerushalayim Council" found in Sec. 1, chapter 5,which begins on Pg. 49, so that they understand the decision of this counsel, which is the basis upon which Paul wrote his letter to the assemblies in Galatia.

To paraphrase, certain Jews came to the region of Galatia, specifically to the city of Antioch teaching the Gentiles that they could not be saved unless they were circumcised according to the Torah **TO BE SAVED**.

Paul contested against these Jews saying that all the Gentiles needed to do was believe in Yahushua **to be saved** (justified from sin and death) and join the congregation, while the Jews were saying that they needed to do certain types of works before they would be accepted.

The Jewish Religious Leaders had developed a system by which Gentiles could join **their religion**, called the Proselyte System, despite the fact the totality of Scripture teaches that it's through belief/trust in YHWH that man, both the native born and the Gentile, finds acceptance from YHWH.

### "In Judaism
(from: https://en.wikipedia.org/wiki/Proselyte - emphasis mine)

There are two kinds of proselytes in Rabbinic Judaism: ger tzedek (righteous proselytes, proselytes of righteousness, religious proselyte, devout proselyte) and ger toshav (resident proselyte, proselytes of the gate, limited proselyte, half-proselyte).

A "righteous proselyte" is a gentile who has converted to Judaism, is bound to all the doctrines and precepts of the Jewish religion and is considered a full member of the Jewish people. The proselyte is circumcised as an adult (milah l'shem iur), if male, and immerses in a mikvah to formally effect the conversion.

> A "gate proselyte"[12] is a resident alien who lives in the Land of Israel and follows some of the Jewish customs.[10] They are not required to be circumcised nor to comply with the whole of the Torah. They are bound only to conform to the Seven Laws of Noah[10] (do not worship idols, do not blaspheme God's name, do not murder, do not commit fornication (immoral sexual acts), do not steal, do not tear the limb from a living animal, and do not fail to establish rule of law) to be assured of a place in the World to come."

These two types of converts are based on Jewish Law and not the Torah/Law of YHWH as it was given through Moses. YHWH told Moses that the stranger (Gentile) that sojourned with Yisra'el, meaning one that joined Yisra'el in covenant with YHWH, was to be treated as a native born among them, i.e., the adoption (Num 15:15-16 and Lev 19:33-34).

When a person believes in Yahushua as Messiah, they are 'grafted into' Yisra'el, as part of the adoption (Rom 11; Eph 2:8-19). Once in, they are to live righteously, according to the same standard as the native born, i.e., the Torah.

## Chapter 1

**Remember**, the question upon which this book was written is "By what then are we saved?" Keeping this in mind, let's begin dissecting the words of Paul (Sha'ul) to find out his true meaning.

**Gal 1:1**   Paul, an emissary – not from men, nor by a man, but by יהושע Messiah

| | |
|---|---|
| | and Elohim the Father who **raised Him from the dead** |
| Gal 1:2 | and all the brothers who are with me, to the assemblies of Galatia: |
| Gal 1:3 | Favour to you and peace from Elohim the Father and our Master יהושע Messiah, |
| Gal 1:4 | **who gave Himself for our sins**, to **deliver us** out of this present wicked age, according to the desire of our Elohim and Father, |
| Gal 1:5 | to whom be the praise forever and ever. Amĕn. |

This is how Paul introduced himself to the assemblies of Galatia and notice that he declares clearly that he did not receive this teaching from any man. Paul declares that his understanding of the true "Good News" came from Yahushua Himself.

He also answers the question, "By what then are we saved?" in this very introduction. He states clearly that Yahushua gave Himself for our sins, according to the will of the Father, and then was raised from the dead by the Father, which constitutes the Good News by which we are saved.

| | |
|---|---|
| 1Co 15:1 | But brothers, **I make known to you the Good News**, which I brought as Good News to you, which you also did receive, and **in** which you stand, |
| 1Co 15:2 | **through which also you are being saved**, **if you hold fast that word I brought as Good News to you**. Otherwise, you have believed in vain. |
| 1Co 15:3 | For I delivered to you at the first that which I also received: **that Messiah died for our sins according to the Scriptures, and that He was buried, and that He was raised the third day, according to the Scriptures,** |

This is the Good News that Paul taught the believers, that through the death, burial and resurrection of Yahushua Messiah we receive salvation. Notice, Paul says that this Good News is "according to the Scripture", referring to the Tanak (OT).

Like all good Hebrew teachers, when Paul received a revelation, he went to the Scripture to verify it, because he knows what the Scripture says concerning doctrine.

1. The Scripture cannot be added to nor taken away from (Deut 4:2; 12:32; Pro 30:6; Rev 22:18-19).
2. Guard to do **EVERY WORD** of Elohim so that you may live and increase and go in (Deut 8:1).
3. Man does not live by bread alone but by **EVERY WORD** that proceeds from the mouth YHWH (Deut 8:3).
4. Any prophet or doer of wonders that teaches to go in a way other than that which YHWH has already taught us is a false prophet (Deut 13:1-5).
5. Do not turn to the left or to the right of **ANY** of the commands that YHWH has given us (Deut 28:14).
6. The works of YHWH are FOREVER, they cannot be added to nor taken away from so that man may fear Him (Ecc 3:14), etc. etc. etc.

Once the Father has declared something to be true **nothing** and **no one** can change that, not even Messiah, for if He had He would no longer qualify as the Messiah according to Deuteronomy 13.

We have gotten five verses into the book of Galatians and Paul has already answered the question, it is through Messiah who died for us and was raised from the dead that we receive salvation.

However, just like many of the religious Jews of that time, modern teachers do not have a true understanding of what salvation is, in this context, and neither do they understand the *Two-Part Principle* and how it brings our belief and our works together so that we might receive the full inheritance, thus fulfilling the Good News of Yahushua Messiah.

This principle is evident in this very passage, where Paul says that we are "being saved", referring to the process that begins by belief in Messiah for the justification (salvation) FROM the condemnation of death for sin and extends to our responsibility to life justified (righteous) lives, i.e., belief followed by works (Jam 2:14-26).

In the rest of Galatians, Paul is going to elaborate on this salvation through belief doctrine, which modern teachers **seem** to understand, but he is not going to leave out our responsibility to obey the Torah **AFTER** we've been saved by Yahushua Messiah, something modern teachers completely gloss over and misunderstand.

| | |
|---|---|
| **Gal 1:6** | I marvel that you are so **readily turning away** from Him who called you in the favour of Messiah, to a different 'Good News,' |
| **Gal 1:7** | which is not another, only there are **some who are troubling you and wishing to pervert the Good News of Messiah**. |
| **Gal 1:8** | However, even if we, or a messenger out of heaven, bring a 'Good News' to you beside what we announced to you, let him be accursed. |
| **Gal 1:9** | As we have said before, and now I say again, if anyone brings a 'Good News' to you beside what you have received, let him be accursed. |
| **Gal 1:10** | For do I now persuade men, or Elohim? Or do I seek to please men? For if I still pleased men, I should not be a servant of Messiah. |
| **Gal 1:11** | And I make known to you, brothers, that the Good News announced by me is not according to man. |
| **Gal 1:12** | For **I did not receive it from man, nor was I taught it, but through a revelation of** יהושע **Messiah**. |

First, who are the ones that are "troubling" the believers in Galatia? Remembering the context upon which this book was written, we need to go back to Acts 15:1 where we are told that "certain men from Judah" had come teaching that Gentiles had to do the works of the Torah "**To Be Saved**".

Paul declares this teaching, which these "certain men" had brought them, was an attempt to **pervert the truth of the Good News** of Yahushua Messiah. So, the idea that we must do the works of Torah "**TO BE SAVED**" is a perversion of the truth.

Any teaching then, that requires obedience to the Torah, must be presented in a way that does not detract from the truth that salvation comes through belief in Yahushua.

There must be a definition of salvation that includes both belief in Yahushua Messiah and the requirement to obey the Torah, which is where the *Two-Part Principle* comes in (see Sec.1, Chapter 4 on Pg. 25).

In this passage Paul once again reinforces to the Galatians that the Good News that he received did not come from the teachings of men but as by "revelation of Yahushua Messiah".

| | |
|---|---|
| **Gal 1:13** | For you have heard of my former behaviour in Yehudaism, how intensely I persecuted the assembly of Elohim, and ravaged it. |
| **Gal 1:14** | And I progressed in **Yehudaism** beyond many of my age in my race, being more exceedingly **ardent for the traditions of my fathers**. |
| **Yehudaism**: | stg's #**G2454** "Ioudaismos", from G2450; "judaism" (to become a Judean), that is, the *Jewish faith* and usages: - Jews' religion. |

The word Judaism refers to the religion founded by the Jewish rabbis. However, the Jewish religion is not a part of the true belief that is taught in the Scripture. Yahushua Himself spoke and acted against the principles of Judaism during His ministry.

Judaism, as we know it today, did not exist
in the time of Messiah. The use of this word
as a 'religion' came later, however, the
Messianic Writings use it to refer to the
"traditions of the elders" or "of the fathers"
as Paul uses it here.

Judaism, as a religion, is based on the Talmud
(Rabbinical Writings), which were still only oral traditions in
the first century. These oral traditions were later collected
and written down (ca.600CE). The culmination of these
traditions and the commentaries on them by other Rabbis
became what is today called the Talmud.

There is a plethora of examples of Messiah going
out of His way to violate Jewish religious law while never
actually violating the Torah of YHWH, as it was given
through Moses to the people at Mount Sinai. A good
example of this can be found in Matthew 15 (Mark 7).

**Mat 15:1**      Then there came to יהושע scribes
and Pharisees from Yerushalayim,
saying,

**Mat 15:2**      "Why do Your taught ones
**transgress the tradition of the
elders**? For they do not wash their
hands when they eat bread."

We would challenge the reader to search the Tanak
(Old Testament) and see if you can find a single
commandment where YHWH told His people that they **must**
wash their hands before they eat.

Rest assured, you will find no such command,
because one does not exist. This command that a person
**must** wash his hands before he eats is a creation of the
rabbis, it is called a "takkanah", i.e., a religious man-made
rule that has been added to or that detracts from the
commands of YHWH.

**Note**:      "A **takkanah** is an enactment which (1)
**revises** an ordinance that no longer satisfies
the requirements of the times or
circumstances, or which (2), being deduced
from a Biblical passage, may be regarded as

555

new. ... Takkanot were framed even in the time of the Second Temple in Yerushalayim, those of unknown origin being ascribed to earlier leaders, and they have been promulgated at all subsequent periods of Jewish history." (Emphaize mine, quoted from Wikipedia)

Over the course of history, the Rabbis (like the Cardinals and Popes after them) took it upon themselves to modify or "revise" the Torah of YHWH to fit their own opinions. They went so far as to declare that their collective opinions held greater authority then a voice from heaven.

The religious leaders in Messiah's time (those the Messianic Writings refer to as "the Jews") were following and teaching, religious man-made rules, which they called "the tradition of the elders" or what is known as the "oral law".

Yahushua vehemently opposed these traditions, as is shown here, saying that these man-made additions were a transgression of the Torah of YHWH (i.e., sin).

| **Mat 15:3** | But He answering, said to them, **"Why do you also transgress the command of Elohim because of your tradition?** |

Messiah goes on and gives an example of what He means by this.

| **Mat 15:4** | **"For Elohim has commanded,** saying, 'Respect your father and your mother,' 'He who curses father or mother, let him be put to death.' |
| **Mat 15:5** | **"But you say,** 'Whoever says to his father or mother, "Whatever profit you might have received from me has been dedicated," |
| **Mat 15:6** | is certainly released from respecting his father or mother.' So **you have nullified the command of Elohim by your tradition.** |

556

The Torah teaches clearly that a child should honor and respect their parents and part of that would be caring for them in their old age.

Judaism, however, allows the child to dedicate that portion as an offering, which releases the child from his responsibility to his parents. Yahushua says that this is a nullification or a perversion of the commandment of YHWH, which is, by definition, sin.

Man-made rules that add to or take away from what is written in the Torah of YHWH are **SIN** and should be completely removed from the belief. In other passages Messiah calls these man-made traditions "leaven" and commands us to remove all the leaven from the house (the feast of Matzot/Unleavened Bread is a picture of this).

To leave even a small crumb of leaven (false man-made teaching) in the lump (doctrine) will eventually leaven the entire loaf (belief).

This has happened in the belief today. It is what is destroying both Judaism and Christianity and will be the cause of their ultimate demise at the return of Yahushua Messiah.

To inherit the Kingdom of YHWH, a person must reject the teachings of Judaism and Christianity in the last day and turn to the true Good News that includes belief in Yahushua Messiah, which is followed by obedience to the Torah from a sincere heart of love for YHWH and toward one another.

| Mat 15:7 | "Hypocrites! Yeshayahu rightly prophesied about you, saying, |
| Mat 15:8 | 'This people draw near to Me with their mouth, and respect Me with their lips, but their heart is far from Me. |
| Mat 15:9 | '**But in vain do they worship Me, teaching as teachings the commands of men**.'" |

Here the Messiah quotes Isaiah (YeshaYahu) 29, where the prophet is told, the people give honor to YHWH by the things they say but that their heart is far from Him.

This means that their mouth says they believe in Him, and they trust in Him and they love Him, but they have not surrendered their heart to Him, to obey Him in all that He has commanded them, thus not trusting that His Word is true.

Instead, they worship Him in a way that men have taught them to worship Him, and not according to the way He Himself commanded them.

This is not the first time YHWH had convicted them of such, consider 2Kgs 17:18-19…

**2Ki 17:18**   So יהוה was very enraged with Yisra'ĕl, and removed them from His presence – none was left but the tribe of Yehuḏah alone.

**2Ki 17:19**   Yehuḏah, also, did not guard the commands of יהוה their Elohim, but walked in the laws of Yisra'ĕl **which they made.**

Once again, both the Jews and the Christians are guilty of this because the Jews follow the teachings of the rabbis, who have declared their own commands more authoritative than even a voice from heaven.

The Christians declare a Messiah that delivered them from the requirement to obey the Torah, which is a direct violation of the Torah, and makes their Messiah a false prophet according to Deuteronomy 13.

Furthermore, the Catholic Church, which most Christian churches consider the whore of Babylon (Revelation 17), has declared that it has the authority to change the law, even direct commands of Yahushua Himself. They also declare authority over the Protestant churches because of their continued adherence to Catholic religious traditions, and rightfully so.

It is the Catholic Church, specifically Emperor Constantine (circa 320 CE), that created the so-called "Gentile Church" by declaring that adherence to the so-called "Old Testament" was a violation of the belief, the consequence of which was death.

Over the course of time, it was the Catholic Church that declared the Torah of YHWH of no use to a believer (nullifying it) and instituting its own traditions, i.e., Sunday worship, Christmas, Easter, etc.

The Catholic Church today still declares to have authority over the Protestants because the Protestants still adhere to these well-known man-made "pagan" sun worship practices. Anyone celebrating Christmas is honoring the sun deity, Sol Invictus Mithra. And the same goes for Easter, who is the fertility deity and wife of the sun deity.

There is much more that could be said concerning the paganism in the church today, but my point here is, that once you've added to or taken away from anything commanded in the Torah you are serving a different deity according to Deuteronomy 28:14.

Both the Jews and the Christians may be worshiping a "God", but that entity is not YHWH, the Elohim of Abraham and Yitschaq and Ya'aqob. It is not the Elohim of their fathers but a false authority whose name is known today as Satan. What is not of The Father, YHWH, is of another father, Ha-Satan, the adversary (John 3:6-10).

As Messiah told the Jewish leaders of His time, so too will He tell the Christian leaders of our time at His return.

**John 8:44**     "You are of *your* father the devil, and the desires of your father you wish to do. He was a murderer from the beginning, and has **not stood in the truth**, because there is no truth in him. When he speaks the lie, he speaks of his own, for he is a liar and the father of it.

Consider lastly, Isaiah 8…

**Isa 8:20**     **To the Torah and to the witness**! If they do not speak according to this Word, it is because they have no daybreak.

The true Word that is true Light consists of both the witness of Yahushua Messiah and the Torah of YHWH (Exo 19:1-5; Rev 14:12)

Next, Messiah is going to use an analogy concerning the accusation from the Jewish leaders concerning eating bread without washing the hands. Unfortunately, Christians have used this analogy to twist the meaning of Messiah's teaching.

The context of this passage is clearly eating bread without washing your hands, however Christian teachers have usurped the context of this passage, declaring the passage is about what type of animals can be eaten.

This passage has **ABSOLUTELY NOTHING** to do with the difference between clean and unclean meats and whether the believer can eat them or not. The true context is made very clear in the first two verses in Matthew 15, where it says, "For they do not wash their hands when they eat bread".

| | |
|---|---|
| **Mat 15:10** | And calling the crowd near, He said to them, "Hear and understand: |
| **Mat 15:11** | "Not that which goes into the mouth defiles the man, but that which comes out of the mouth, this defiles the man." |
| **Mat 15:12** | Then His taught ones came and said to Him, "Do You know that the Pharisees stumbled when they heard this word?" |
| **Mat 15:13** | But He answering, said, "Every plant which My heavenly Father has not planted shall be uprooted. |
| **Mat 15:14** | "Leave them alone. They are blind leaders of the blind. And if the blind leads the blind, both shall fall into a ditch." |
| **Mat 15:15** | And Kĕpha answering, said to Him, "Explain this parable to us." |
| **Mat 15:16** | And יהושע said, "Are you also still without understanding? |
| **Mat 15:17** | "Do you not understand that whatever enters into the mouth goes into the stomach, and is cast out in the sewer? |
| **Mat 15:18** | **"But what comes out of the mouth comes from the heart, and these defile the man.** |
| **Mat 15:19** | **"For out of the heart** come forth wicked reasonings, murders, |

560

|  | adulteries, whorings, thefts, false witnessings, slanders. |
| Mat 15:20 | **"These defile the man, but to eat with unwashed hands does not defile the man.** |

Before we go on to explain what this analogy is saying, I want to look at verses 12-14 because they are inserted right in the middle of this discussion, yet they are important.

In verse 12 one of his disciples asked the Messiah whether He knew that the Pharisees had stumbled on what He had said about them, having not understood it. Messiah goes on to tell him that they are blind and that there leading the blind and as such both they and their followers will fall into the ditch (i.e., judgment in the Lake of Fire).

Within this discourse, however, is a statement concerning plants that are of the Father. This brings up two very interesting passages in John 15 and Hebrews 6.

| Joh 15:1 | "I am the true vine, and **My Father is the gardener**. |
| Joh 15:2 | "Every branch in Me **that bears no fruit He takes away**. And every branch that bears fruit He prunes, so that it bears more fruit. |
| Joh 15:3 | **"You are already clean because of the Word which I have spoken to you**. |
| Joh 15:4 | **"Stay in Me**, and I *stay* in you. As the branch is unable to bear fruit of itself, unless it stays in the vine, so neither you, unless you stay in Me. |
| Joh 15:5 | "I am the vine, you are the branches. He who stays in Me, and I in him, he bears much fruit. Because without Me you are able to do naught! |
| Joh 15:6 | "If anyone **does not stay in Me, he is thrown away as a branch and dries up. And they gather them and throw them into the fire, and they are burned.** |

561

| | |
|---|---|
| **Joh 15:7** | "If you stay in Me, **and** My Words stay in you, you shall ask whatever you wish, and it shall be done for you. |
| **Joh 15:8** | "In this My Father is esteemed, that you bear much fruit, and you shall be My taught ones. |
| **Joh 15:9** | "As the Father has loved Me, I have also loved you. Stay in My love. |
| **Joh 15:10** | **"If you guard My commands, you shall stay in My love,** even as I have guarded My Father's commands and stay in His love. |

This, like many other passages, has been thoroughly misunderstood and overlooked by Christian teachers. In this passage Messiah calls Himself the vine and believers the branches.

He says that we are clean because of the Word He has already spoken to us, which is a reference to what He said in John 14:6, i.e., "... I am the Way, and the Truth, and the Life. No one comes to the Father except through Me".

In this passage Messiah refers to our need to "bear fruit", which begs the question "What fruit?" Many teachers today want to refer to Galatians 5:22-25, which says,

| | |
|---|---|
| **Gal 5:22** | But the fruit of the Spirit is love, joy, peace, patience, kindness, goodness, trustworthiness, |
| **Gal 5:23** | gentleness, self-control. Against such there is no Torah. |
| **Gal 5:24** | And those who are of Messiah have impaled the flesh with its passions and the desires. |
| **Gal 5:25** | If we live in the Spirit, let us also walk in the Spirit. |

However, this is not referring to our fruit but the fruit of the spirit that's working in us. This is another *Two-Part Principle* passage that must be understood. This is a contrast between our inner-spirit-man and our outer-fleshly-man.

This passage concerning spiritual fruit begins by saying,

| | |
|---|---|
| **Gal 5:16** | And I say: Walk in the Spirit, and you shall not accomplish the lust of the flesh. |
| **Gal 5:17** | For the flesh lusts against the Spirit, and the Spirit against the flesh. And these are opposed to each other, so that you do not do what you desire to do. |
| **Gal 5:18** | But if you are led by the Spirit, you are not under Torah. |

The word "spirit" in this passage should not be capitalized, because it is referring to our spirit, our inner man that Paul says in Romans 7, "delights in the Torah of Elohim" (v. 22) and "serves the Torah of Elohim" (v. 25).

He says that if we "walk in the spirit" we shall not accomplish the lust of the flesh, meaning that we will not be doing fleshly things and thus overcome its desires. This is the same thing Paul said in Romans 8.

| | |
|---|---|
| **Rom 8:13** | **"For if you live according to the flesh, you are going to die;** but if by the Spirit you put to death the deeds of the body, you shall live." |

He goes further to say that our fleshly-outer man is in battle against our spirit-inner man and sometimes causes us to not do the things we desire to do, i.e., obey the Torah of YHWH (Romans 7:14-21).

So, the context of this passage is about "walking in the spirit". To walk in the spirit means to do the things of the spirit, it's the way we live our lives, in agreement with the spirit. Since, as we have shown, Paul says that the inner or spirit man delights in the Torah of YHWH and serves it, then walking in the spirit means to live in obedience to the Torah of YHWH.

After all, it is Paul who said in Romans 7:14 that the "Torah is spiritual" but that we are fleshly, sold under sin. This phrase simply means that the Torah is how a spiritual man walks but we have proven to be fleshly men, selling ourselves to the authority of sin in our lives, which brought on us the penalty of death.

Here in Galatians 5 he is telling us not to live in a way that sells out to sin but to live in a way that's consistent with the Torah of YHWH and when we do this, we will produce this fruit of the spirit within us, i.e., love, joy, peace, patience, kindness, goodness, trustworthiness, gentleness, self-control, which does nothing contrary to the Torah.

To verify that this interpretation is correct concerning how we receive the "fruit of the spirit" we only need to read on to verses 24-25. Verse 24 clearly talks about us having been impaled with Messiah, i.e., having become a new creature in Him, to live unto YHWH (Romans 6:10-11, 22; 7:25). This is the "spiritual" part of this passage.

Verse 25 then says that if we are "in the spirit", which is a reference to the previous verse about having been made new in Yahushua Messiah, and then says we ought to also "walk in the spirit", which is a reference to our responsibility to obey the Torah, the "physical" part.

Remember, because YHWH created all mankind with free will, our ultimate redemption requires both what He has done for us in Yahushua Messiah (spiritual part) and what we do in response to that, i.e., obey the Torah of YHWH from a heart of compassion (physical part).

So, the fruit that the believer is supposed to bear, in John 15, is not "the fruit of the spirit" but a different kind of fruit. What is the context of the passage prior to John 15?

As mentioned before, within the first 14 verses of John 14 is the proclamation by Yahushua that He is "the way the truth and the life and that no one comes to the Father but through Him" which is the main theme of that section of Chapter 14, Yahushua being in the Father and the Father in Him.

Beginning in verse 15 we see the promise of the giving of the Set Apart Spirit of YHWH to believers. His Spirit is called the Spirit of Truth who shall be with us forever for He shall be "in us".

This is the fulfillment of a promise given to the people of Yisra'el by YHWH in Ezekiel 36.

> **Eze 36:22**    "Therefore say to the **house of Yisra'ĕl**, 'Thus said the Master יהוה, "I do not do this for your sake, O

| | house of Yisra'ĕl, but for **My set-apart Name's sake**, which you have profaned among the nations wherever you went. |
|---|---|
| Eze 36:23 | "And I shall set apart My great Name, which has been profaned among the nations, which you have profaned in their midst. And **the nations shall know that I am יהוה**," declares the Master יהוה, "when I am set-apart in you before their eyes. |
| Eze 36:24 | "And I shall take you from among the nations, and I shall gather you out of all lands, and I shall bring you into your own land. |
| Eze 36:25 | "And I shall sprinkle clean water on you, and you shall be clean – from all your filthiness and from all your idols I cleanse you. |
| Eze 36:26 | "And **I shall give you a new heart and put a new spirit within you**. And I shall take the heart of stone out of your flesh, and I shall give you a heart of flesh, |
| Eze 36:27 | and **put My Spirit within you**. And I shall **cause you to walk in My laws and guard My right-rulings and shall do them.** |

The first thing a Christian teacher might say is, this teaching of the Spirit inside of Yisra'el is not the same thing as the Spirit inside of a Gentile, which is ludicrous because Paul says clearly in Galatians 3:28 that in Messiah there is no Jew or Gentile, for we are all one in Him.

For all those that have been listening, we have shown that the children of Yisra'el has always consisted of both the native born and the stranger (Gentile) that sojourns among them (Leviticus 9:33-34; Numbers 15:15-16).

This promise of the Spirit of YHWH being placed in the believer was to accomplish a single purpose, which was to "**CAUSE** you to walk in My laws and guard My right rulings and shall do them".

The gift of the Spirit of YHWH is to "**CAUSE**" us to live in obedience to the Torah of YHWH, for the Torah is truth (Psalms 119:142) and His Spirit is the Spirit of Truth that would lead us into **ALL** Truth.

The rest of John 14 tells the believer to "guard My Word" and references the fact that those who do guard His Word will be those that He comes into and that He and the Father shall abide in.

The "fruit" that the believer is supposed to bear in chapter 15 is the fruit of obedience, i.e., righteousness, as John said of those that are born of Him.

| | |
|---|---|
| **1Jn 2:29** | If you know that He is righteous, you know that everyone **doing** righteousness has been born of Him. |
| | *** |
| **1Jn 3:7** | Little children, let no one lead you astray. The one **doing** righteousness is righteous, even as He is righteous. |

Let's go back now and review what John 15 says concerning those who are in Yahushua Messiah, the branches.

| | |
|---|---|
| **Joh 15:1** | "I am the true vine, and My Father is the gardener. |
| **Joh 15:2** | "Every branch in Me that **bears no fruit He takes away**. And every branch that **bears fruit He prunes**, so that it bears more fruit. |

First, we will deal with those who "bear no fruit" and what it means for them to be "taken away".

| | |
|---|---|
| **Heb 6:4** | **For it is impossible for those who were** once enlightened, and have tasted the heavenly gift, and have become partakers of the Set-apart Spirit, |
| **Heb 6:5** | and have tasted the good Word of Elohim and the powers of the age to come, |

566

**Heb 6:6**     **and fall away, to renew them again to repentance** – having impaled for themselves the Son of Elohim again, and put Him to open shame.

In the passage above we have highlighted what this passage is trying to explain, for the understanding has been confused a bit, because of all the words used between these two highlighted portions.

These highlighted portions are describing how impossible it is for a certain group of people to come to repentance again AFTER they have fallen away from a certain position. First let's start with the position these particular people are in.

1.  They have been enlightened: this means that this group of people have come to an understanding of something, their eyes have been opened to a certain truth, i.e., belief in Yahushua.

2.  They have tasted the heavenly gift: this refers to the gift of grace that we received through belief in Yahushua Messiah, the justification from the penalty of death.

3.  They are partakers of the Spirit: this refers to the token or down payment of the indwelling of the Set Apart Spirit that all believers receive through their belief in Yahushua Messiah

4.  They have tasted the good Word: this refers to the Torah of YHWH, which those who obey it receive the blessings promised by YHWH (Deuteronomy 28:1- 13).

5.  They experienced the powers to come: this likely refers to the gifting's of the Spirit which are appointed to each believer according to His purpose.

The people referred to in this passage are "believers" who have understood their need for Messiah, and experienced the redemption, and indwelling of the Holy Spirit, and have been introduced to the Word and have been granted the gifts of the Spirit.

567

While it is true that there are many out there who have received a form of understanding and have believed on the Messiah for the justification from death, and have received the Spirit of YHWH, most if not all these so-called Christians have ignorantly rejected the True Word, the Torah of YHWH as the standard by which they conduct their lives.

Because of this it is possible that repentance is not yet out of their reach, even for those who have experienced the gifting's. This author can only guess to the possible truth of this for it is only his opinion.

However, what is very clear, once a believer has come to the full knowledge of redemption that is in Yahushua Messiah and "falls away", **IT IS IMPOSSIBLE FOR THEM TO BE RESTORED TO REPENTANCE** according to this passage.

That said, it is this author's opinion that one of the two following things is true;

1.      That most Christians have not tasted the Good Word of Elohim because of false teachers, who've sown themselves among them and taught them that this Good Word no longer applies to them. It is possible that this ignorance may allow them a chance to repent.

-and-

2.      That the "falling away" is a conscious willful rejection of the truth of Yahushua as their sole means of salvation, that they begin trusting on the works of Torah or the teachings of men for their ultimate redemption (this is something the Galatians are going to be admonished for by Paul).

Its vitally important to remember that even though the Scripture clearly teaches that believers have a requirement to obey the Torah **AFTER** they trusted in Yahushua Messiah for justification from death, nowhere in the Scripture does it say our trust can ever be in the Torah.

It is an emphatic and undeniable FACT that trusting in the works of Torah alone or in the traditions of men leads a man to death. There is absolutely and positively **NO** redemptive value in obeying any form of teaching or law, or even the Torah itself, outside of the belief in Yahushua Messiah.

To teach that a man must obey the works of Torah "TO BE SAVED" is heresy and denies everything Messiah stood for and died for. The problem is, because of the doctrines of the Christian church which have been handed down to us, as well as the dogma of Judaism, people do not understand the process of redemption and how the *Two-Part Principle* (His part and our part) work toward our ultimate redemption and inheritance of the kingdom.

| | |
|---|---|
| **Heb 6:7** | For ground that is drinking the rain often falling on it, and is bearing plants fit for those by whom it is tilled, receives blessing from Elohim, |
| **Heb 6:8** | but if it brings forth thorns and thistles, **it is rejected and near to being cursed, and ends up by being burned.** |

The context of Hebrew 6 is about those who would receive the gifts of redemption and yet fall away from them. Verse 7 and 8 uses a lot of symbology, all of it meaningful. The 'ground' is a reference to our hearts and the rain is about the Word (See: Parable of the Sower in Matt 13:1-9, 18-23).

The plants are the fruits of the works of the believer. The one that bears plants/fruit receives a blessing, however, those who do not bear plants/fruit, but thorns and thistles, is rejected and burned.

| | |
|---|---|
| **Joh 15:3** | "You are already clean because of the Word which I have spoken to you. |
| **Joh 15:4** | "Stay in Me, and I stay in you. As the branch is unable to bear fruit of itself, unless it stays in the vine, so neither you, unless you stay in Me. |
| **Joh 15:5** | **"I am the vine, you are the branches. He who stays in Me, and I in him, he bears much fruit.** |

|          | Because without Me you are able to do naught! |
| Joh 15:6 | **"If anyone does not stay in Me, he is thrown away as a branch and dries up. And they gather them and throw them into the fire, and they are burned.** |

Notice the similarities between what the writer of Hebrews said and what Messiah is saying here.

They're both talking about the bearing of fit plants/fruit, saying that those who bear fruit is staying in Messiah and Messiah in him, but the ones that are not bearing fit plants/fruit are thrown into the fire to be burned.

Admittedly, the context of these two passages is slightly different in that Hebrews 6 is a reference to those who have received all the things of redemption, including the Good Word/Torah of YHWH and did eventually fall away, while John 15 is about those who receive the Messiah through belief and yet have not produced the fruit of righteous obedience.

However, the principle here is the same and soundly agrees with what the totality of Scripture teaches concerning the disobedient.

| Joh 15:7  | "If you stay in Me, and My Words stay in you, you shall ask whatever you wish, and it shall be done for you. |
| Joh 15:8  | "In this My Father is esteemed, that you bear much fruit, and you shall be My taught ones. |
| Joh 15:9  | "As the Father has loved Me, I have also loved you. Stay in My love. |
| Joh 15:10 | **"If you guard My commands**, you shall stay in My love, even as I have guarded My Father's commands and stay in His love. |

Lastly, we have more evidence that the fruit that a believer is supposed to bear has to do with obedience. Messiah says that we stay in Him **IF WE GUARD HIS COMMANDS**.

Going back now to Matthew 15:10-20, we see Messiah saying it is not what goes in a man's mouth that defiles them but what comes out of his mouth. Once again, the Christian church uses this passage to say it doesn't matter what you **eat** because what goes into your mouth doesn't defile you.

As we said before this passage in Matthew 15 has nothing whatsoever to do with the dietary laws or what is clean and unclean meat or whether we can eat them or not. This passage is about eating bread with unwashed hands, meaning dirty hands.

In this context, i.e., dirty hands, Messiah says it's not the dirt on the bread that defiles a man when he eats it but the dirt in a man's heart that defiles him.

| | |
|---|---|
| **Mat 15:18** | **"But what comes out of the mouth comes from the heart, and these defile the man.** |
| **Mat 15:19** | **"For out of the heart** come forth wicked reasonings, murders, adulteries, whorings, thefts, false witnessings, slanders. |
| **Mat 15:20** | "These defile the man, but to eat with **unwashed hands** does not defile the man. |
| **Note**: | The Rabbis taught that because a man's hands were always touching things, even a clean person's hands were potentially unclean by the things they touched, thereby allowing demons into the man, so the hand washing was more about a ritual cleansing of the hands than hygiene. |

Now, there are many other examples of Messiah confronting the "Jews" or religious leaders of His time concerning matters of "Jewish law" that is not part of the Torah. Other examples would be; not healing on the Sabbath, divorcing a wife for any reason, and picking heads of grain to eat them on the Sabbath.

These are all examples of traditions made up by the Jewish rabbis but that are not found in the Torah of YHWH.

\*\*\*

| Gal 1:15 | But when it pleased Elohim, who separated me from my mother's womb and called me by His favour, |
| Gal 1:16 | to reveal His Son in me, that I might bring Him, the Good News, to the nations, I did not immediately consult with flesh and blood, |

This phrase, "separated me from my mother's womb, and called me" is a reference to the fore-knowledge of YHWH, which Paul referred to in Romans 8. It's a reference to the fact that YHWH knows the end of our lives before we begin to live and seeing the condition of our heart in the future, He calls us to a work while still in the womb.

The phrase, "to reveal His Son in me" is generally a reference to Paul's witness before other men, a witness that he had not yet accomplished at his conversion, which is the context of what he is saying here. He goes on to tell us that at his conversion, he did not go to other men to learn the truth.

| Gal 1:17 | neither did I go up to Yerushalayim, to those who were emissaries before me. But I went to Arabia, and returned again to Dammeseq. |
| Gal 1:18 | Then after three years I went up to Yerushalayim to learn from Kĕpha, and remained with him for fifteen days. |
| Gal 1:19 | And I saw no other of the emissaries except Ya'aqob, the brother of the Master. |

| Note: | Paul continues describing his travels immediately after his conversion, but one of the things I want to look at here is how many years he spent in Arabia. |

This may seem silly, but many teachers have said that Paul spent three years in Arabia learning from Messiah and they proved this teaching from this text but is that what this text says.

*Read this text carefully and determine where Paul spent three years?*

It says that Paul went to Arabia and **returned to Damascus, then** after three years he went to Yerushalayim. Now, does it say he was in Arabia three years?

**No**, in fact, if anything it suggests he was in Damascus for three years. I bring this up because it's an example of how men misread Scripture and interpret it their own way to create a false teaching.

| | |
|---|---|
| **Gal 1:20** | And what I write to you, see, before Elohim, I do not lie. |
| **Gal 1:21** | Then I went into the districts of Suria and of Kilikia. |
| **Gal 1:22** | And I was *still* not known by sight to the assemblies of Yehuḏah which were in Messiah, |
| **Gal 1:23** | but they were hearing only that, "The one who once persecuted us now brings as Good News the belief which he once ravaged." |
| **Gal 1:24** | So they were esteeming Elohim in me. |

We see Paul's witness before the world, which the brothers in Yerushalayim heard. Here Paul verifies the fact that he had once persecuted the believers, going as far as to say that he ravaged them.

Those are harsh words, but it is not the only time he says it, he mentions it again Philippians 3:6. Paul went from a persecutor of the message to a preacher of the message and notice, it says "they were esteeming Elohim in me", meaning that they were magnifying YHWH because of the work He had done in Paul. All the esteem and glory and whatever else you want to call it belonged to the Father alone.

# Chapter 2: Galatians 2

Now we are going to see Paul mention his travels to
Yerushalayim with Barnaba (a Jew) and Titus (a Greek) at
what is now called the Yerushalayim Council of Acts 15.

| | |
|---|---|
| **Gal 2:1** | Then after fourteen years I again went up to Yerushalayim, with Barnaba, taking Titos along too. |
| **Gal 2:2** | And I went up by revelation, and laid before them that Good News which I proclaim among the nations, but separately to those who were esteemed, lest somehow I run, or had run, in vain. |

Now 14 years have passed since he started preaching
and then there had been 3 years before that, when he was
either in Damascus or somewhere not mentioned, so this is at
least 17 years after his conversion.

It says that he went up "by revelation", which is a
curious thing considering Acts 15 states he went to
Yerushalayim by agreement, sent on his way by the
assembly, to clarify the issue about Torah obedience as a
prerequisite for salvation.

He had a private meeting with the leaders of the
congregation in Yerushalayim, telling them about his
message to the Gentiles.

Evidently, Paul wanted this private meeting so that
he could present his case for approval, as it were, without
having it influence the rest of the congregation, if in fact
there was contention.

| | |
|---|---|
| **Gal 2:3** | But not even Titos who was with me, though a Greek, was compelled to be circumcised. |

Verse 3 is evidence that Paul had won his argument,
if you remember in Acts 15:1 the debate began when people
from Yerushalayim came claiming that Gentiles had to be
circumcised according to the Law of Moses "TO BE
SAVED".

Paul clearly states that Titus, a Greek, was not forced to be circumcised by order of the Council. Go back and read the discussion about the Yerushalayim Council in Section 1, Chapter 5, pg. 49.

| | |
|---|---|
| **Gal 2:4** | But as for the **false brothers**, sneakingly brought in, who sneaked in to **spy out our freedom** which we have in Messiah יהושע in order **to enslave us,** |
| **Gal 2:5** | to these we did not yield in subjection, not even for an hour, so that the truth of the Good News remains with you. |

Paul calls these "certain Jews" in Acts 15:1 "false brethren" who had come to "spy out our freedom", which we have in Messiah.

Now, modern teachers would have you believe that this liberty Paul is referring to has to do with no longer needing to obey the Torah, but that is not the case.

Ya'aqob (James) calls the Torah the "law of liberty" (1:25; 2:12) because when we are **living out** the Torah, with all our heart, mind and strength, trusting **ONLY** in Messiah and not the work itself, we are free from **both** the restrictions of **man-made religious dogma AND the penalty for sin**, which is death.

The doctrinal position that Torah obedience is required as a PREREQUISITE for salvation is a man-made religious doctrine, created by the Jews, and not substantiated in the Scripture itself. Paul's argument about liberty has to do with man-made religious dogma and not our responsibility to obey the Torah AFTER we are saved.

It's important we understand that our salvation is based in what we trust in, or better Who we trust in, and not obedience to the Torah. However, obedience to Torah is a requirement of the belief because it is how you walk righteously before YHWH in Yahushua Messiah.

Our trust or our boasting must ALWAYS be in the work of Yahushua Messiah and never in the Torah itself. Trusting in the Torah brings death but, living in obedience to the Torah brings life to those who have already been justified from death, through belief in Yahushua Messiah.

575

Modern teachers, as well as the religious Jews in Paul's time, do not understand this *Two-Part Principle* of trust followed by obedience. James understood it perfectly and he discussed it in his book when he said, "belief without works is dead".

He understood that if you say you believe and have placed your trust in YHWH through belief in Yahushua Messiah, but do not obey the works of Torah, you are once again condemned to death because belief alone has no power to preserve you to the end.

When Paul says that these "false brethren" had come to bring us back into bondage again, he was referring to the bondage of man-mad religion and not to the Law/Torah, because the Law/Torah is called the law of liberty, as we stated before, however, going back to the teachings of men that have added to or taken away from the Word/Torah is in itself sin and the penalty of such is death.

Paul vehemently opposes this false dogma of Torah obedience as a prerequisite for salvation and did not give this argument even a moment of his time, so that the true Good News could go forth unmolested by man-made religious dogma.

| | |
|---|---|
| **Gal 2:6** | But from those who were esteemed to be whatever – what they were, it makes no difference to me, Elohim shows no partiality – for those who were esteemed contributed naught to me. |
| **Gal 2:7** | But on the contrary, when they saw that the Good News to the uncircumcised had been entrusted to me, even as Kĕpha to the circumcised – |
| **Gal 2:8** | for He who worked in Kĕpha to make him an emissary to the circumcised also worked in me for the nations. |

Paul shows here that he, like YHWH, is no respecter of persons and those who seem to be important members of the congregation added nothing to him.

Many believe this is Paul speaking in arrogance, but this is not the case, he is saying, these so-called pillars didn't tell him or teach him anything he did not already know. In fact, he proved to them that YHWH had called him to be an apostle to the Gentiles in the same measure that Peter (Kepha) had been called to the Jews.

| | |
|---|---|
| **Gal 2:9** | So when Yaʿaqob, Kĕpha, and Yoḥanan, who seemed to be supports, came to know the favour that had been given to me, they gave me and Barnaba the right hand of fellowship, in order that we *go* to the nations and they to the circumcised, |
| **Gal 2:10** | only that we might remember the poor, which I myself was eager to do. |

In conclusion of the matter, the chief apostles in the group, James, Peter and John (Yochanan) extended the "right-hand of fellowship" to Paul, agreeing that he should go on to teach the Gentiles, but encouraged him to remember the poor which, of course, he was already doing because the Torah teaches it.

The reference to the "right-hand" has to do with authority, Yahushua is at the right hand of the Father and it is to Him all power and authority has been given. Even today we shake hands when we "seal the deal" signifying that we have the authority to make this agreement.

It is extremely important to understand that Paul's primary ministry was the conversion of the Gentiles. If you don't keep this in mind some things he says will confuse you.

| | |
|---|---|
| **Gal 2:11** | And when Kĕpha had come to Antioch, I withstood him to his face, because he was at fault. |
| **Gal 2:12** | For before some came from Yaʿaqob, he was eating with the nations, but when they came, he began to withdraw and separate |

| | himself, in fear of those of the circumcision. |
|---|---|
| **Gal 2:13** | And the rest of the Yehuḏim joined him in hypocrisy, so that even Barnaḇa was led away by their hypocrisy. |
| **Gal 2:14** | But when I saw that they are not walking straight according to the truth of the Good News, I said to Kěpha before them all, "If you, being a Yehuḏi, live as the nations and not as the Yehuḏim, why do you compel nations to live as Yehuḏim? |

Paul is giving an example of how respecting false dogma can lead even the staunchest believer into error and how that influential person's error can lead many others astray.

When Peter visited Antioch, the Jews there invited him to dinner, which he was willing to attend. However, it seems that these Jewish believers were still under the false assumption that they were not to associate with Gentiles.

Peter accepted the invitation knowing that to be accepted by the Jews would require him to separate himself from the Gentiles. His desire to be accepted by these Jews led him to commit an error, which he had already been confronted about by the Spirit of YHWH in Acts 10.

Now, Acts 10 has to do with what is called Peter's "sheet dream", which the Christian church has twisted the meaning of, teaching that in Yahushua we can eat unclean meats.

This, of course, is ridiculous and inconsistent with the totality of Scripture, as well as the context of what's being said in that very passage.

We are not going to discuss that here, but this passage of Scripture will be discussed in the section called "Food" (Sec. 4, pg. 485). For now though, we are only going to take from that passage in Acts 10, the conclusion of the matter in verse 28.

| | |
|---|---|
| **Act 10:28** | And he said to them, "You know that a Yehuḏi man is not allowed to associate with, or go to one of |

578

another race. But Elohim has shown me that I should not call any **man** common or unclean.

As you see here, Peter had already been instructed concerning this man-made religious dogma of separating the Jew from the Gentile. Yet, in Antioch he stumbled right back into the same error and drew many of the Jewish brethren along with him, even Barnaba.

Paul called Peter's behavior hypocrisy, and rightfully so, because he had been shown the truth by the Spirit and yet did something else when he arrived in Antioch, and all because of his respect for these Jewish men and their thoughts.

In another of his epistles Paul instructed us how to deal with an elder who had committed some form of sin or error, which is to speak to them privately. However, in this case Paul chose to rebuke Peter publicly because Peter had committed this serious breach of doctrine publicly.

Peter's error is alive and well, even within Messianic congregations today. Nearly all Messianic believers today came out of either Christianity or Judaism, unfortunately, people who are coming out of these religious errors only dwell in the truth for a short time and then end up back in the same or some other man-made error.

By this we mean, Christians are encouraged to find their "Jewish roots" which lead them into the error of religious Judaism, which is no better than the error of Christianity and religious Jews who have come to the knowledge of their need of Messiah get lost in the confusion of Christianity.

Let me make this clear again, both Judaism and Christianity are false religions as far as Scripture is concerned, because of the doctrine they espouse. Judaism teaches the Torah without Messiah and includes thousands of man-made laws that they must keep, while Christianity teaches the Messiah without the Torah and over-spiritualize nearly every element of the belief.

Both of these man-made religions are drowning in error. Even among Messianic teachers, who are striving to teach the purity of the belief, there is a problem of thinking that little things, little traditional things, have no real significance in the belief, and so they practice these things before their congregations.

The problem is, these "little things" are generally commands of Jewish rabbis, i.e., the wearing of the Tallit (prayer shawl) and the Kippa (yarmulke) etc. or some theology taught by Christian teachers, which place unscriptural requirements on their adherents.

To submit to these teachings and traditions, even those we think are harmless, gives validity to the rabbis or theologians that commanded them and just like Peter, the leader of a congregation that commits a doctrinal error will lead less knowledgeable brethren astray into that same error, even brethren as knowledgeable as Barnaba.

And just telling the people, "well this is a tradition and you don't have to do it" is not sufficient because people learn more by our example than by our words.

Now, verse 14 creates a bit of a problem for most teachers because they don't really understand what Paul is saying, let's see it again.

> **Gal 2:14**  But when I saw that they are not walking straight according to the truth of the Good News, I said to Kĕpha before them all, "If you, being a Yehuḏi, **live as the nations and not as the Yehuḏim**, why do you compel nations to live as Yehuḏim?

This passage is not really hard to understand, but to a Greco-Roman mindset this verse seems to suggest that Peter was "living like a Gentile" and so they assume he was eating unclean meats and doing all the things an unbelieving Gentile might do.

However, Peter had not been associating with UNBELIEVING GENTILES, he was associating with BELIEVERS. As believers that had been taught by Paul, all these Gentile believers would have been obeying the Torah, including the dietary laws.

What Paul is suggesting here has to do with religious dogma and not Torah observance. His position is simple, if Peter had been living among the Gentile believers without any concern for the Jewish dogma, why then should these

Jews expect the Gentile believers to honor these man-made Jewish traditions.

This is the hypocrisy that Paul is referring to. It's as if Peter has two faces, one he shows among the Gentiles and another he shows when the Jews are around, which makes Peter a liar in this circumstance and makes Paul's rebuke of him justified.

Now we are about to get into the meat of Paul's argument and if you are one of those people that believe a "Gentile convert" no longer has to keep the "Old Testament Law "you better hold onto your britches.

| | |
|---|---|
| **Gal 2:15** | "We, Yehuḏim by nature, and not of the nations, sinners, |
| **Gal 2:16** | **knowing that a man is not declared right by works of Torah, but through belief in** יהושע **Messiah**, even we have believed in Messiah יהושע, in order to be declared right by belief in Messiah and not by works of Torah, **because by works of Torah no flesh shall be declared right**. |
| **Gal 2:17** | **"And if, while seeking to be declared right by Messiah, we ourselves also are found sinners, is Messiah then a servant of sin? Let it not be!** |
| **Gal 2:18** | **"For if I rebuild what I** *once* **overthrew, I establish myself a transgressor**. |
| **Gal 2:19** | "For through Torah I died to Torah, in order to live to Elohim. |
| **Gal 2:20** | "I have been impaled with Messiah, and I no longer live, but Messiah lives in me. And that which I now live in the flesh I live by belief in the Son of Elohim, who loved me and gave Himself for me. |
| **Gal 2:21** | "I do not set aside the favour of Elohim, for if righteousness is through Torah, then Messiah died for naught." |

Verse 15 is emphasizing the point that even as Jews they are still sinners, knowing a man is not justified or declared right, through the righteousness of Torah but through the righteousness of belief in Yahushua Messiah.

**REMEMBER**, the context is "by what then are we saved" and the salvation which comes through Yahushua Messiah is a justification from the guilt of sin and its consequence, death.

It is in this context this argument is being made, so the righteousness/justification referred to concerns deliverance from sin and death. Paul is emphasizing that, as Jews they know this, or should, and this principle applies to them as well as to the Gentiles. The most interesting thing is in the next verse, where it talks about sinning (disobeying the law) after being justified by belief in Yahushua Messiah.

The question is, if we are attempting to be justified by belief in Yahushua Messiah and yet are still found to be guilty of violating the Law/Torah (sin), did Messiah sacrifice Himself so that we could continue to disobey the Law? Paul's answer is an emphatic **NO!**

Paul follows this up with, "for if I rebuild again what I once overcame", which is a reference to justification from sin and death. We were condemned to death because of our disobedience but our belief in Yahushua Messiah delivered us, or saved us, from our guilt and its penalty, death.

So, what did we overcome in our belief? The answer is our guilt of sin and the penalty of death attached to it. This passage, then, is suggesting that once we have been delivered from the penalty of sin and death it is possible to return to a position in which we are guilty of sin and condemned to death. Remember, it was the condemnation of death we overcame by belief in Yahushua.

Paul is telling us that, if we continue to sin (disobey the Law) after we have come to the knowledge of Messiah and been cleansed, then we rebuild again our guilt of sin and return to a position of condemnation before Him, because our continual disobedience proves that we are not a son but a transgressor (enemy of the truth).

This is not the only time in the Scripture this principle has been suggested, in fact it is stated again in Hebrews 6:4-8 and 10:26-31, as well as referenced by Peter in 2 Pet 2:18-22.

| 2Pe 2:18 | For speaking arrogant nonsense, they entice – through the lusts of the flesh, through indecencies – **the ones who have indeed escaped from those living in delusion**, |
| 2Pe 2:19 | promising them freedom, though themselves being slaves of corruption – for one is a slave to whatever overcomes him. |
| 2Pe 2:20 | For if, **after they have escaped the defilements of the world through the knowledge of the Master and Saviour יהושע Messiah, they are again entangled in them and overcome, the latter end is worse for them than the first.** |
| 2Pe 2:21 | **For it would have been better for them not to have known the way of righteousness, than having known it, to turn from the set-apart command delivered unto them.** |
| 2Pe 2:22 | For them the proverb has proved true, **"A dog returns to his own vomit,"** and, **"A washed sow *returns* to her rolling in the mud."** |

Contextually, Peter is referring to false teachers in the body who are leading astray those who have "escaped the defilements of the world" through their belief in Yahushua Messiah. He says it would be better if they had never known the truth than to know it and turn from it. He compares these disobedient believers to dogs returning to the vomit and sows to the mud.

The writer of Hebrews is even more clear on the subject.

| Heb 10:26 | For **if we sin purposely after we have received the knowledge of the truth**, there no longer remains a slaughter *offering* for sins, |

| | |
|---|---|
| **Heb 10:27** | but some fearsome anticipation of judgment, and **a fierce fire which is about to consume the opponents.** |
| **Heb 10:28** | Anyone who has disregarded the Torah of Mosheh dies without compassion on the witness of two or three witnesses. |
| **Heb 10:29** | How much worse punishment do you think shall he deserve who has trampled the Son of Elohim underfoot, counted the blood of the covenant by which he was set apart as common, and insulted the Spirit of favour? |
| **Heb 10:30** | For we know Him who has said, **"Vengeance is Mine, I shall repay, says יהוה."** And again, **"יהוה shall judge His people."** |
| **Heb 10:31** | It is fearsome to fall into the hands of the living Elohim. |

The very first word that should catch our eye in this passage is the word "we", because it clearly identifies who this message is to, i.e., we the believers.

Secondly, it begins with the phrase "for if", telling us that something is possible. "If" is a conditional term which suggests there is at least two, generally opposing, points of discussion or consequence.

If we look back in verse 19, we see it starts this passage with the phrase "so, brethren", again identifying who this passage is to. Then in verse 26 it says that if "we" sin purposely AFTER "we" have come to the knowledge of the truth.

As we have shown earlier, the Scripture says that Yahushua is the truth (John 14:6) and that the Word/Torah is truth (John 17:17/Psalms 119:142). So the two together become absolute truth, consisting of spiritual truth (Yahushua) and the physical truth (Word/Torah). The one we trust in (Yahushua) and the one we live by (Word/Torah).

Furthermore, to "sin purposely" after having come to the knowledge of Yahushua and the Torah, refers to a willful and intentional rejection of the requirement to obey the Torah. As we have shown, the definition of sin is

584

lawlessness (anomia-"no law doing"/1 John 3:4) and to willfully disobey is rebellion.

Consider the story of the prophet Samuel when he confronted King Saul for having spared King Aḡaḡ, the Amalekite, instead of killing him as YHWH had commanded.

| | |
|---|---|
| **1Sa 15:22** | Then Shemu'ĕl said, "Does יהוה delight in ascending offerings and slaughterings, as in **obeying the voice of יהוה? Look, to obey is better than a slaughtering, to heed is better than the fat of rams.** |
| **1Sa 15:23** | **"For rebellion is as the sin of divination, and stubbornness is as wickedness and idolatry.** Because you have **rejected the word of יהוה,** He also does reject you as sovereign." |
| **Divination:** | stg's **#H7081** "qesem", From H7080; a lot; also divination (including its fee), oracle: - (reward of) divination, divine sentence, **witchcraft**. |
| **Wickedness:** | stg's **#H205** "âven", From an unused root perhaps meaning properly to pant (hence to exert oneself, usually in vain; to come to naught); **strictly nothingness**; also trouble, vanity, wickedness; specifically an idol: - affliction, evil, false, idol, iniquity, mischief, mourners (-ing), naught, sorrow, unjust, unrighteous, vain, **vanity**, wicked (-ness.) Compare H369 (non-existent). |

Notice, that **OBEDIENCE** is better than sacrifice! Samuel is admonishing the king because of his disobedience to the Word of YHWH. He says that disobedience is the same thing as witchcraft in the eyes of YHWH and

585

stubbornness, i.e., refusing to obey the Word of YHWH, is the same thing as vanity and idolatry. Consider brother Ya'aqob (James):

| | |
|---|---|
| **Jam 2:17** | So also belief, if it does not have works, is in itself dead. |
| **Jam 2:18** | But someone might say, "You have belief, and I have works." Show me your belief without your works, and I shall show you my belief by my works. |
| **Jam 2:19** | You believe that Elohim is one. You do well. The demons also believe – and shudder! |

We see that there is a distinction made between belief and works, which are the two parts of scriptural salvation. Now we know that both are required to be "complete" in Yahushua Messiah and that if any part of this is lacking then we are no longer living in the truth.

This is exactly what brother James is saying here, belief without the accompanying works is dead. "Belief" refers to our trust in Yahushua Messiah for our deliverance from past sin and its penalty, death.

"Works" refers to how we LIVE as believers in Yahushua Messiah and refers to the Torah (consider again: 2 Timothy 3:15-16) for without which our declaration of belief is empty, being dead.

To be dead is to be void of life and in this context, is referring to the same thing that Samuel is referring to in his admonishment of King Saul. To disobey the commandments of YHWH is vanity and death.

James goes on to say that he shows his belief **by** his works, meaning that his obedience to the Torah is evidence of the belief in which he stands and of the trust in which he lives. His trust in YHWH and His promises is so complete that it not only affects the way he lives but dictates it.

Samuel said this kind of attitude, this attitude of obedience, is better than sacrifice for if we had lived in obedience from the start there would've been no need for sacrifice.

However, since we, like our father Adam, tend to listen to voices other than YHWH's, we have condemned ourselves through our disobedience (sin). It is only by trusting and depending upon the shed blood of Yahushua Messiah that we have any hope at all.

Lastly, James tells us that even the demons believe and yet they shudder (tremble). Why?

They tremble because they are disobedient, and the price of disobedience is death (the Second Death, i.e., the Lake of Fire – App. 3, pg. 554).

Just believing that Yahushua is the Messiah, the Savior, is not sufficient in and of itself to bring complete redemption, because even the demons believe the Yahushua is the Messiah and that He died to save His people, but that belief will not save them because they are rebellious.

This holds true for us as well, for if we claim that Yahushua is our Messiah, our Savior, and yet we refuse to walk in obedience to the Torah, our lack of Torah works prove that our belief is dead. If this is the case, then we too shall end up in the Lake of Fire, just like the branches that bore no fruit in John 15.

Now, going back to Hebrews 10:26 we see what the writer says to those who "sin purposely AFTER they come to the knowledge of the truth", he tells them, "...there no longer remains a sacrifice for sin but a **fearsome anticipation of judgment and a fierce fire that consumes the opponents.**

The phrase "no longer remains" would be better understood to mean, no other sacrifice remains. See, once we've been justified (made right) from sin, and its penalty of death, by belief in Yahushua Messiah and then turn away from Him to walk in disobedience to the Torah, we have rejected the sacrifice of Yahushua Messiah to go our own way.

The writer of Hebrews, later in this passage, states that this kind of attitude is the same thing as "trampling the blood of the Son of Elohim under your feet, counting the blood of the covenant by which he WAS set apart as common".

Earlier, in chapter 6, the writer of Hebrews said that a person with this kind of attitude has "impaled for themselves the Son of Elohim again and put Him to open shame". And, as we've mentioned above, brother Peter said it would've been better for them to never have known the truth than to know it and turn from it.

Also, an interesting passage to consider an association with Hebrews 10:26-31 is the one just before it in Chapter 10:1-18.

| | |
|---|---|
| **Heb 10:1** | For the Torah, having a shadow of the good *matters* to come, and not the image itself of the matters, was never able to make perfect those who draw near with the same slaughter *offerings* which they offer continually year by year. |
| **Heb 10:2** | Otherwise, would they not have ceased to be offered? Because those who served, once cleansed, would have had no more consciousness of sins. |
| **Heb 10:3** | But in those *offerings* is a reminder of sins year by year. |
| **Heb 10:4** | For it is impossible for blood of bulls and goats to take away sins. |

The book of Hebrews is grossly misunderstood by most teachers, even some Messianic teachers, because they do not closely follow the context of the discussion. The entirety of the book of Hebrews contrasts the "two" priesthoods, the priesthood of Aaron (physical) and the priesthood of Yahushua (spiritual).

The Aaronic priesthood could not grant eternal forgiveness for several reasons, first and foremost is that the priest themselves were sinners and so had to offer up sin offerings for themselves first before they could offer up any for the people.

Secondly, as humans, the priest died and were buried, being replaced by their descendants. Because these men died the effect of their offering was temporary.

And lastly, the blood of bulls and goats cannot take away sin nor the penalty of sin which is death.

**REMEMBER**, completeness requires both the physical element and the spiritual element, so the Aaronic priesthood and the sacrifices it offered were strictly physical in nature and only fulfilled one half of the requirement. Consider:

588

| | |
|---|---|
| **Heb 9:13** | For if the blood of bulls and goats and the ashes of a heifer, sprinkling the defiled, **sets apart for the cleansing of the flesh,** |
| **Heb 9:14** | how much more shall the blood of the Messiah, who through the everlasting Spirit offered Himself unblemished to Elohim, **cleanse your conscience from dead works to serve the living Elohim**? |

Notice that the blood of bulls and goats and the ashes of the heifer only cleanses the flesh (physical part) and remember that the Aaronic priesthood had two major flaws, one was that the priests were sinners themselves and the other was that they were mortal (died).

The priesthood of Yahushua was distinctly different in these two areas. Firstly, He was "unblemished", meaning that He had no sin of His own. Consider what the apostle Peter said about Him.

| | |
|---|---|
| **1Pe 2:21** | For to this you were called, because Messiah also suffered for us, **leaving us an example, that you should follow His steps,** |
| **1Pe 2:22** | **"who committed no sin,** nor was deceit found in His mouth," |

Furthermore, though Messiah did experience physical death for **our** sins, the Father resurrected Him into His eternal, spirit-body, that is promised to all who will inherit the Kingdom. In His resurrected form He can act as High Priest eternally.

So, the renewal of the covenant that YHWH made with Abraham (Gen 15:1-6) and with Yisra'el (Exo 19:1-8) through the death, burial and resurrection of Yahushua Messiah is a "better covenant" with "better promises" (Heb 8:6) because our High Priest is eternal and the blood of the covenant which He poured out for us was "unblemished", free from the taint of sin.

We see here two covenants of priesthood, the Aaronic, which sets apart according to the physical, and the Messianic, which sets apart according to the spiritual.

Notice also, it says the blood of Messiah has the power to "cleanse your conscience from dead works to serve the living Elohim" (Heb 9:14) which the Aaronic priesthood could not do with their offerings of bulls and goats (Heb 10:2).

**Conscience:**     stg's **#G4893 "suneidēsis"**, From a prolonged form of **G4894**; co-perception, that is, moral consciousness: - conscience.

    stg's **#G4894 "suneidō"**, From G4862 and G1492; to see completely; used (like its primary) only in two past tenses, respectively meaning to understand or become aware, and to be conscious or (clandestinely) informed of: - consider, know, be privy, beware of.

Sometimes the use of this word can be confusing to people and rightly so, however, the writer here is trying to express to us that the blood of Yahushua has the power to cleanse our inner-spirit-man, the part of us that has the capacity of rational thought. Also, this cleansing allows us to move forward in service to YHWH without the guilt and shame of our past sins.

Basically, it re-creates the distinction between our spirit mind and physical mind, which had been confused because of sin. Some people call this confusion "spiritual death" and use it in the context of the state of mind in which Adam and his descendants fell into because of his disobedience.

In a way, this point of view is not entirely incorrect, because when Adam sinned and was cast out of the garden, he was separated from the presence of YHWH and became more susceptible to his instinctual nature.

Humanity is in a constant state of double mindedness, between the angel on one shoulder, telling us what to do right and the demon on the other, telling us to do wrong. This double mindedness is a function of the two sides of our mentality, the rational part (spirit) versus the instinctual part (flesh).

The rational part of our mind makes choices based on **facts** or what it believes to be the facts, while the instinctual part of our mind makes choices based on **feelings** or what profits it the most.

Paul distinguishes these two parts of our mind by calling one the spiritual and the other the fleshly, admonishing us to follow the dictates of the spiritual or rational mind that knows the right thing to do, according to the Torah of YHWH, and does it.

Paul says that we who will walk according to the spirit (mind) will not receive condemnation when we struggle, due to our belief in Yahushua Messiah (Rom 8:1).

It is our **commitment** to living righteously, through obedience to the Torah, as believers in Yahushua Messiah that protects us from future condemnation if we fail. Our belief is proved by our works and ends in eternal life (Rom 6:17-23; Ya'aqob [James] 2:14-26).

However, Paul also says that those of us who walk according to the flesh shall die (Rom 8:13) which is the same thing the writer of Hebrews is saying here in 10:26.

**REMEMBER**, the Aaronic priesthood is physical, for the cleansing of the flesh, while the Messianic priesthood is spiritual, for the cleansing of the inner-spirit-man.

| | |
|---|---|
| **Heb 10:5** | Therefore, coming into the world, He says, "Slaughtering and meal offering You did not desire, but a body You have prepared for Me. |
| **Heb 10:6** | "In ascending offerings and *offerings* for sin You did not delight. |
| **Heb 10:7** | "Then I said, 'See, I come – in the roll of the book it has been written concerning Me – **to do Your desire, O Elohim.'"** |
| **Heb 10:8** | Saying above, "Slaughter and meal offering, and ascending offerings, and *offerings* for sin You did not desire, nor delighted in," which are offered according to the Torah, |
| **Heb 10:9** | then He said, "See, I come to do Your desire, O Elohim." **He takes** |

591

**away the first to establish the second**.

Heb 10:10    By that desire we have been set apart through the offering of the body of יהושע Messiah **once for all**.

If YHWH is the one who commanded the sacrificial system be established, why does He turn around and say that these offerings and sacrifices are something He doesn't desire?

He says this because His true desire for us is that we trust Him and walk in obedience to His Torah.

Remember, Samuel told King Saul that obedience was better than sacrifice. Why? Where there is obedience there is no need for sacrifice, sacrifice is a product of disobedience because it's only through a blood sacrifice that disobedience could be atoned for (Heb 9:22).

In verse 9, where it says that Elohim "takes away the first to establish the second" it is **NOT** saying that the "Old Covenant of Law" has been replaced by a "New Covenant of Grace", as many modern teachers would have you believe.

Favor (grace) and the Law/Torah have always worked together to accomplish His will, which is the fulfillment of the promises of YHWH to His people. The giving of the Torah at Mount Sinai was an act of favor (grace) towards the people of Yisra'el because it taught the people how to live righteously and acceptable unto YHWH.

In verse 9, the writer of Hebrews tells us that Elohim has taken away the first "priesthood", with all of its sacrifices and rituals and established the second "Priesthood" which has been established in the blood of Messiah.

This **DOES NOT** mean that He has "done away" with the Aaronic priesthood and Temple services forever, it just means that He has suspended the operation of it.

At the time of the Messiah, He prophesied the destruction of the Temple and the city, which took place in 70 CE. This book of Hebrews was written sometime prior to 70 CE; however, the author knew of this prophecy and is referencing it, not intending the phrase "takes away" to apply to a permanent condition.

People have not only misunderstood the writer's intent concerning the priesthood but have thoroughly confused the issue concerning the phrase "once for all" in verse 10. The author does **NOT** intend for us to understand him to mean that our belief in Messiah has set us apart "once and for all", as the "once saved, always saved" proponents suggest.

He is simply stating that our belief in Messiah sets us apart and that the sacrifice of Messiah is the "once and for all" sacrifice, meaning that there is no other sacrifice, He is the **ONLY** one.

This is an important concept to understand because of what he says in 10:26, "For if we sin purposely AFTER we have received the knowledge of the truth, **there no longer remains** a slaughter offering for sins". Once you've rejected the sacrifice of Yahushua Messiah through willful disobedience there is no other sacrifice, His is the **ONLY** one.

| | |
|---|---|
| **Heb 10:11** | And indeed every priest stands day by day doing service, and repeatedly offering the same slaughter *offerings* which are never able to take away sins. |
| **Heb 10:12** | But He, having offered one slaughter *offering* for sins for all time, sat down at the right hand of Elohim, |
| **Heb 10:13** | waiting from that time onward until His enemies are made a footstool for His feet. |
| **Heb 10:14** | For by one offering He has perfected for all time those who are **being** set apart. |

Once again, the author here contrasts the Aaronic priesthood with that of Yahushua. The Aaronic High Priests die and are replaced by another human High Priest, but Yahushua died and was raised again, and sits on the right hand of the Father, the place of authority, interceding for those of us who have called on Him for salvation.

Now verse 14 raises havoc in the minds of those aforementioned "once saved, always saved" adherents because it really sounds like he is saying here that Messiah has perfected believers "for all time".

The conviction of this belief seems justifiable; however, they misunderstand what is being said here because, among other things, they do not understand the *Two-Part Principle* and how it's at work in this passage. Let's compare this verse with what was said about Messiah's blood in the previous section.

| | |
|---|---|
| **Heb 10:10** | By that desire we **have been** set apart through the offering of the body of יהושע Messiah once for all. |

***

| | |
|---|---|
| **Heb 10:14** | For by one offering He has perfected for all time those who **are being** set apart. |

Notice, that verse 10 says "have been set apart" through His death, while verse 14 says "are being set apart".

These two phrases represent the two parts of complete redemption, the part He did for us through His death (spiritual set apartness through belief) and the part we do through obedience to the Torah (physical set apartness through obedience).

The confusion here stems from the authors point of view concerning "who" is responsible ultimately for our redemption and he says Messiah, which is true. However, the first set apartness mentioned has to do with something Messiah Himself did directly, through the offering up of His body.

The phrase "being set apart" has to do with a process through which we are declared set apart in the Last Day and receive the inheritance of the Kingdom. Ultimately, He alone deserves all the esteem because without His sacrifice we would have no hope at all.

What needs to be understood however, is that during this period between our confession of belief that **sets us apart in the spirit man** (making us born again in the inner man) and being **completely set apart (spirit and body)** at His return and the resurrection (making us born again in the outer man) we are wandering in the wilderness of this life, of which the wilderness wandering of Yisra'el is a shadow picture.

Just like Yisra'el was delivered "out of Egypt" but spent 40 years (a generation) wandering in the wilderness before they were delivered (into the Promised Land), so too are we, who have been delivered "from the condemnation of death", wandering through the wilderness of this life awaiting Messiah's return to deliver us (into the Messianic Kingdom).

And, just as many of those Yisra'elis died in the wilderness, never entering the Promised Land, because of their rebellion and hard heartedness, so too will many believers today miss the Messianic Kingdom and die the second death (Lake of Fire), because of their hard heartedness and rebellion.

YHWH delivered them all "out of Egypt" and He delivered some of them "into the Promise Land", but only those who had set themselves apart by living in obedience to His commands.

YHWH perfected them, Joshua and Caleb, for all time, preserving them and delivering them into the Promise Land. It was their whole-hearted commitment to believing/trusting in and obeying the Word/Torah of YHWH that justified them in the end.

In the same way, Messiah **has** delivered us "from the condemnation of death" and He **will** come again and deliver some of us "into the Messianic Kingdom", but only those who have submitted their heart fully to trusting in Him and obeying His Torah with a heart of compassion towards the brethren.

| | |
|---|---|
| **Heb 10:15** | And the Set-apart Spirit also witnesses to us, for after having said before, |
| **Heb 10:16** | "This is the covenant that I shall make with them after those days, says יהוה, giving My laws into their hearts, and in their minds I shall write them," |
| **Heb 10:17** | and, "Their sins and their lawlessnesses I shall remember no more." |
| **Heb 10:18** | Now where there is forgiveness of these, there is no longer a slaughter *offering* for sin. |

"The covenant" that is being referred to here comes from Jeremiah 31:31-33.

| | |
|---|---|
| **Jer 31:31** | "See, the days are coming," declares יהוה, "when I shall make **a renewed covenant with the house of Yisra'ĕl and with the house of Yehuḏah,** |
| **Jer 31:32** | not like the covenant I made with their fathers in the day when I strengthened their hand to bring them out of the land of Mitsrayim, My covenant which they broke, though I was a husband to them," declares יהוה. |
| **Jer 31:33** | "For this is the covenant I shall make with the house of Yisra'ĕl after those days, declares יהוה: **I shall put My Torah in their inward parts, and write it on their hearts.** And I shall be their Elohim, and they shall be My people. |
| **Jer 31:34** | "And no longer shall they teach, each one his neighbour, and each one his brother, saying, 'Know יהוה,' for they shall all know Me, from the least of them to the greatest of them," declares יהוה. **"For I shall forgive their crookedness, and remember their sin no more."** |

Notice, the "New Covenant", which the so-called "Gentile Church" is relying on, is a promise in the Tanak (Old Testament) given to the House of Yisra'el and the House of Yahudah, **NOT** to some man-made religious dogma called the "Gentile Church".

The promise is that YHWH would put His Law/Torah into their "inward parts and write it upon their hearts". I find it interesting that the very people that claim this promise upon themselves, calling themselves the "New Covenant Church" (Christianity), thinks that having the Torah put inside them and having it written upon their hearts, somehow excuses them from having to obey it.

596

To have the Torah placed in your inward parts is referring to the new birth of the inner spirit-man, who, according to Paul, delights in the Torah of YHWH and serves it (Rom 7:22 and 25) and our belief in the Good News of Messiah Yahushua, who is the "Law/Torah" made flesh, is what has made our inner man (spirit man) alive again, this is the spiritual part of the "New Covenant".

By bringing our inner-spirit-man back to life, YHWH has given him a fresh start and placed within him the mind of a servant.

The Messiah promised in John 14 that He would come to the believer and dwell within them, however, there was a condition that had to be met for Him to do so.

| | |
|---|---|
| **Joh 14:23** | יהושע answered him, "**If** anyone loves Me, **he shall guard My Word**. And My Father shall love him, and We shall come to him and **make Our stay with him**. |
| **Joh 14:24** | "He who does not love Me does not guard My Words. And **the Word which you hear is not Mine but of the Father Who sent Me.** |

The requirement for having Messiah "in us" is that we show our love toward Him by guarding His Word, the Words the Father had given Him, the Torah of YHWH.

While the spiritual part of the "New Covenant" has to do with how our belief in Yahushua has made our inner man alive again, with the mind to serve Him, the physical part of the "New Covenant" has to do with HOW we are to serve Him, and He has written the Torah on our hearts so that we desire to do so.

This does not mean that the Torah was literally written on the surface of our heart, no more than Paul saying the "circumcision of the heart", is a literal thing (Rom 2:29). Just as the phrase "circumcision of the heart" is a reference to a submissive heart condition, so too does the phrase "written on their heart" refer to a heart submitted to obeying it.

The "New Covenant" promise of the Torah being placed in our inner man and written upon our hearts is a reference to what YHWH does for us in our belief in

597

Yahushua Messiah, so that we can live in Him. He has given us a mind and a heart to serve Him in the renewed (inner) man of belief.

**REMEMBER**, the primary purpose behind our requirement to obey the Torah as believers, **IS NOT** about absolute perfect adherence to it, but an **absolute commitment** to adhere to it, with all our heart and mind and strength, day in and day out, for as long as we live.

Back in Hebrews 10:18, it says something that ties in to both verses 10 and 26, so let's quote it again here and have a look.

> **Heb 10:18**    Now where there is forgiveness of these, there is no longer a slaughter *offering* for sin.

Hebrews 10:10 told us that Messiah was the "once and for all" sacrifice through which we can be set apart and here in verse 18 we see that once there is forgiveness for sins there is no longer a sacrifice for sin. Why?

Verse 10 told us that Messiah was the only sacrifice that can take away sin, and once you've received the forgiveness of sin through that sacrifice, and reject it through disobedience, there is no other sacrifice that you can trust in, that will free you from the condemnation for your willful disobedience, which is death.

> **Heb 10:26**    For if **we** sin purposely after **we** have received the knowledge of the truth, **there no longer remains a slaughter *offering* for sins,**
>
> **Heb 10:27**    **but some fearsome anticipation of judgment, and a fierce fire which is about to consume the opponents.**
>
> **Heb 10:28**    Anyone who has disregarded the Torah of Mosheh dies without compassion on the witness of two or three witnesses.
>
> **Heb 10:29**    How much worse punishment do you think shall he deserve **who has trampled the Son of Elohim underfoot, counted the blood of**

|  | the covenant by which he WAS set apart as common, and insulted the Spirit of favour? |
| Heb 10:30 | For **we** know Him who has said, **"Vengeance is Mine, I shall repay, says יהוה."** And again, **"יהוה shall judge His people."** |
| Heb 10:31 | It is fearsome to fall into the hands of the living Elohim. |

Once again, the pronoun here is **WE**, which is a reference to believers. If **WE** (believers) disobey the Torah with intent, meaning that we have no intention of obeying it or that we just ignored it, then we have trampled the blood of the covenant by which **WE WERE** set apart (saved) under our foot and called His sacrifice common (unclean).

We are guilty of insulting His Spirit that came in and gave our spirit man new life, the One whose job it was to "cause you to walk in My laws and guard My right-rulings" and to do them (Eze 36:27).

Having said all this, we have a better understanding of what Paul means back in our original text, Galatians 2:18.

| Gal 2:18 | **"For if I rebuild what I _once_ overthrew, I establish myself a transgressor.** |

Yes, unfortunately, it is possible to confess Yahushua as our Savior, be justified from the penalty death because of our sin and be "born again" in the inner-spirit-man, and then reestablish ourselves as transgressors (sinners) by willfully disobeying the Torah. The penalty of which is a "fearsome anticipation of judgment, and a fierce fire which is about to consume the opponents", i.e., the "Second Death" (the Lake of Fire).

At this point, Paul says something interesting that he has already mentioned in Romans 6 and is going to elaborate on further in chapter 4, but let's look at it here as he has laid it out for us.

| Gal 2:19 | "For through Torah I died to Torah, in order to live to Elohim. |

599

| | |
|---|---|
| **Gal 2:20** | "I have been impaled with Messiah, and I no longer live, but Messiah lives in me. And that which I now live in the flesh I live by belief in the Son of Elohim, who loved me and gave Himself for me. |
| **Gal 2:21** | "I do not set aside the favour of Elohim, for if righteousness is through Torah, then Messiah died for naught." |

Let's briefly review what Paul said in Romans chapter 6.

| | |
|---|---|
| **Rom 6:1** | What, then, shall we say? Shall we continue in sin, to let favour increase? |
| **Rom 6:2** | Let it not be! How shall we who died to sin still live in it? |
| **Rom 6:3** | Or do you not know that as many of us as were immersed into Messiah יהושע were immersed into His death? |
| **Rom 6:4** | We were therefore buried with Him through immersion into death, that as Messiah was raised from the dead by the esteem of the Father, so also we should walk in newness of life. |

**REMEMBER**, "sin is the transgression of the law" or lawlessness (1 John 3:4). So, what is Paul asking us here? He is asking, "… Shall we continue to (disobey the Law/Torah), to let favor (grace) increase? His answer?

## ABSOLUTELY NOT!!!

How can those of us who have taken on the death of Messiah Yahushua, who delivered us from the death penalty we owed for disobeying the Law/Torah in the first place, continue to live in disobedience to the Law/Torah?

Paul often uses the word "sin" as if it was an entity, like evil, having its own personality and authority. To be "dead to sin" means that at some point sin had authority over us and now it no longer does, we are dead to it, it has no life in us.

So, being "dead to sin" essentially means that sin no longer has authority over us, to kill us, as it did before we believed that Messiah died for us.

It is important that we understand that baptism is a shadow picture, which we are commanded to act out, because it portrays us as having died with Messiah from the authority of sin and death, just like the children of Yisra'el were removed from the authority of Pharaoh and bondage in Egypt when they crossed the Red Sea.

Just like Pharaoh and his army died while chasing Yisra'el through the Red Sea, sin died in the life of the believer through the washing of the blood of Yahushua Messiah and baptism is a picture of that in our lives.

It also represents His resurrection, for just as He was raised back to life to the Father (verse 10) so too are we raised from the water as a sign of the resurrection (new birth) of the inner-spirit-man to "walk in the newness of life".

What does it mean to "walk in the newness of life"? Consider the following:

Before we believed in Messiah, we were guilty of sin (disobeying the Law/Torah) and condemned to death, we were "dead in trespasses and sins".

Now that we believe in Messiah and have had the guilt of our sin removed, we are now alive in Him to live in a "new" Way, having Him as our example.

| | |
|---|---|
| **Eph 2:1** | And **you were dead in trespasses and sins,** |
| **Eph 2:2** | in **which you once walked** according to the **course of this world**, according to the **ruler of the authority of the air**, of the spirit that is now **working in the sons of disobedience,** |
| **Eph 2:3** | among whom also **we all once lived** in the **lusts of our flesh, doing the desires of the flesh and of the mind,** and were by nature **children of wrath**, as also the rest. |

| Eph 2:4 | But Elohim, who is rich in compassion, because of His great love with which He loved us, |
| Eph 2:5 | even when we **were dead in trespasses**, **made us alive together with Messiah** – by favour you have been saved |
| Eph 2:6 | and **raised us up together**, and made us sit together in the heavenlies in Messiah יהושע, |

As you can see, Paul is saying the same thing in Ephesians 2 that he said in Romans 6 and a closer comparison of what's being said in both passages shows you a couple of important things. Before we believed in Messiah:

a.     We walked in trespasses and sins,
b.     We lived like the world lives,
c.     We walked according to the authority of another ruler (Satan),
d.     We walked according to the spirit of disobedience,
e.     We walked according to the lusts of our flesh,
f.     We did the desires of the flesh and the mind,
g.     We were children of wrath.

**BUT NOW**, we have been raised from the dead with Messiah, in the inner man, to "walk in the newness of life", where we don't walk in the old way.

As believers in Messiah:

a.     We **do not** walk in trespasses and sins,
b.     We **do not** live like the world lives,
c.     We **do not** walk according to the authority any other ruler,
d.     We **do not** walk according to the spirit of disobedience,
e.     We **do not** walk according to the lusts of our flesh,
f.     We **do not** do the desires of the flesh and

the mind,

g.    We **are not** children of wrath.

As believers in Yahushua Messiah, we serve YHWH only, according to His Torah, without additions or subtractions, in an attitude of love for one another. If you're doing anything else, you are not of Him.

Now, back in Galatians 2:19-21 we see Paul saying the same thing that was said in Romans 6 and Ephesians 2, just in a different way. The first verse is the most difficult for people to understand, but it's not clear why.

The phrase "through Torah I died to Torah" is simply a reference to what Paul has said, throughout his writings, concerning the effect the Torah had on the unbeliever and what believing in Messiah did for the believer, as it regards the Torah.

It was the Torah that condemned us to death when we disobeyed it, which caused us to seek out a way of justification other than the Torah itself, which we could no longer live justified in because of sin.

The Torah became a teacher, that taught us that we were condemned to death and needed someone to help us. The Torah also, through shadow pictures, told us what was necessary to overcome the death penalty for disobeying it, i.e., sacrifice.

It not only taught us that we needed a sacrifice to cover our sins but also revealed to us, in many diverse ways, Who that sacrifice would be. So, "through the Torah" we learned that we were sinners and needed to believe in Yahushua Messiah, so that in Him we could "die to Torah", which had condemned us for our disobedience.

Now, in Messiah, we can live to please YHWH, through obedience to His Torah, just as He did.

Yes, the Torah condemned us when we disobeyed it, but it also taught us the Way of Salvation in Yahushua Messiah, through whom we are set free from the condemnation of death commanded in the Torah for sin. Torah also teaches us how to live unto YHWH as believers.

Let's quote again verse 20:

**Gal 2:20**    "I have been impaled with Messiah, and I no longer live, but **Messiah lives in me**. And **that which I now**

603

**live in the flesh I live by belief in
the Son of Elohim**, who loved me
and gave Himself for me.

Two interesting things said here:

1)      "Messiah lives in me",
2)      The life "I now live in the flesh; I live by
belief"

How do we know that Messiah lives in us when we
believe? What are the criteria through which Messiah comes
into us and dwells within us? Is it belief only?

| | |
|---|---|
| **Joh 14:23** | יהושע answered him, "If anyone loves Me, **he shall guard My Word**. And My Father shall love him, and **We shall come to him and make Our stay with him**. |
| **Joh 14:24** | "He who does not love Me does not guard My Words. **And the Word which you hear is not Mine but of the Father Who sent Me.** |

Messiah Himself says that the criteria upon which
He and the Father would come to the believer and dwell in
them, is that they guard (protect and obey) His Word, which
is the Father's Word (Torah).

Paul's reference to living in the flesh, is about living
out our life in this physical body with all its trials and
temptations, but it also refers to our walking in obedience to
the Torah, which is why Messiah lives in us.

He mentions that Messiah dwells in us, which
requires we live in obedience to His Word, so His reference
to "in the flesh" is about striving to obey the Torah in this
fleshly body, which wants to disobey the Torah (Rom 7:7-
8:8; Gal 5:16-17).

So, even though we are in this fleshly body, we are
striving daily to obey the Torah, however, our trust is never
in our Torah obedience, it remains steadfast in our belief that
Yahushua is the Messiah and Savior, for **BY** that and **IN** that
we stand, for **THERE IS NO HOPE IN ANY OTHER**.

Paul's statement in Romans 7:6, "But now we have been released from the Torah, having died to what we were held by, so that we should **serve in newness of Spirit and not in oldness of letter**", is **NOT** about no longer having to obey the Torah, as some say.

"Newness of the Spirit" is a reference to **obedience through belief,** while "oldness of the letter" is a reference to <u>obedience for acceptance</u> (works acceptance/legalism). Paul vehemently states repeatedly that we are not accepted because of our works, but because of our belief.

If we could be accepted because of the works of the Torah, Messiah did not have to die. So then, if we begin trusting in the works of Torah for redemption, Messiah died for nothing and we're still under the curse.

Again, Galatians 2:21, "I do not set aside the favour of Elohim, for **if righteousness is through Torah, then Messiah died for naught.**"

See, it's all about where we put our trust, specifically our heart trust, for if we say we have put our trust in Yahushua Messiah, yet we begin trusting in the works themselves, then our heart is no longer set on Him.

This is exactly what is happening here in the book of Galatians, because some Jews came and told the brethren that they needed to be circumcised after the custom of Moses **"TO BE SAVED"**.

# Chapter 3: Galatians 3

Now we are going to get into the meat of Paul's letter to the Galatians.

| | |
|---|---|
| **Gal 3:1** | O senseless Galatians! Who has put you under a spell, not to obey the truth – before whose eyes יהושע Messiah was clearly portrayed among you as impaled? |

We see that Paul considers any teaching concerning salvation that is not solely and completely founded in the death, burial and resurrection of Yahushua Messiah, as a "spell" cast by false teachers.

| | |
|---|---|
| **Gal 3:2** | This only I wish to learn from you: Did you receive the Spirit by works of Torah, or by the hearing of belief? |

He is questioning the Galatians concerning whether or not they had experienced the working of the Spirit of YHWH in their lives because he had taught them to obey the Torah or because he had taught them to believe in Yahushua as Messiah.

| | |
|---|---|
| **Gal 3:3** | Are you so senseless? Having begun in the Spirit, do you now end in the flesh? |
| **Gal 3:4** | Have you suffered so much in vain – if indeed in vain? |
| **Gal 3:5** | Is He, then, who is supplying the Spirit to you and working miracles among you, doing it by works of Torah, or by hearing of belief? |

He repeats the same question again in a slightly different way, which is typical of Paul. It is important here to see two things;

Paul is adamant they remember that they received this redemption and the power that comes with it because of what they believed in and not because of any works they did to receive it.

Paul does not say anywhere that obeying the works of Torah is no longer required, only that they did not receive the Spirit because of the works of Torah.

| | |
|---|---|
| **Gal 3:6** | Even so Abraham **"did believe Elohim, and it was reckoned unto him as righteousness."** |
| **Gal 3:7** | Know, then, that those who are of belief are sons of Abraham. |

Paul references Genesis 15:6, where YHWH declares Abraham righteous based on what he believed.

Abraham (Abram) had just returned from rescuing Lot when the Word of YHWH appeared to him in a vision, saying that He was Abraham's shield and exceedingly great reward. In response, Abraham asked YHWH, what would He give him, seeing that he had no heirs of his own house and that his servant would be his heir.

YHWH told Abraham that he would have an heir from his own body and that his seed would be like the stars of heaven in number. The Scripture says that Abraham believed this promise of YHWH and because of it, YHWH declared him righteous.

Abraham did not do anything to earn righteousness, it was his belief alone that earned him this righteousness.

The word "reckoned" in Galatians 3:6, translates the Greek word "logizomai" (G3049), which refers to placing something on another's account, or declaring something to be true of another and comes from another Greek word, "logos", which refers to something said, i.e., a word.

Galatians 3:6 is a quote from Genesis 15:6 where the word "reckoned", translates the Hebrew word "châshab" (H2803), which means to plait or interpenetrate, to weave or fabricate, think or regard.

> **Note**: It is important we recognize that many times the Greek words don't actually express the actual meaning of the Hebrew words used in the same context. In such cases, we must allow the Hebrew words to take precedent when understanding doctrinal truths.

This fact is nowhere more important than in this case, for the difference between the Greek word "logizomai" and the Hebrew word "chasab" is like the difference between the sun and the moon.

As mentioned above, "logizomai" refers to placing something on another's account, like making an anonymous deposit into a friends bank account. However, "chashab" is a primitive root meaning to plait or interpenetrate, to weave or fabricate, two things together.

This means much, much more than just considering one righteous, it refers to weaving righteousness into us. In the messianic understanding, it refers to making righteousness part of us and is specifically a reference to the new birth of the inner-spirit-man.

In both cases, the context requires us to understand that it was because Abraham's belief alone, that YHWH granted him righteousness.

Paul then goes on to state that those who have the same belief that Abraham had, are sons of Abraham. The phrase "of belief" denote a position upon which a person stands.

Paul has already asked the Galatians whether they received the Spirit, and had miracles done among them, because of the Torah works they had done or because of the belief in Yahushua that they had. He is asking them; upon what position or circumstance did they receive these things.

As mentioned before, He is reminding them that it was through belief in Yahushua Messiah that they received the spirit and had miracles done among them. The foundation or position upon which they stand, is belief in Yahushua Messiah and NOT obedience to the Torah.

We know that belief in Yahushua Messiah justifies us (makes us right) from sin and death, so to be "of belief" is to be trusting in Yahushua Messiah and not in works of

Torah, because by the works of Torah no man is justified (Rom 3:20).

> **Gal 3:8**   And the Scripture, having foreseen that Elohim would declare right the nations by belief, announced the Good News to Abraham beforehand, saying, **"All the nations shall be blessed in you,"**

Paul now mentions the promise YHWH made to Abraham in Genesis 12:1-4, where YHWH commanded Abraham to leave his country and his father's house and to go into a place where YHWH would lead him.

YHWH promised that He would make Abraham's seed a great nation and that He would bless those who blessed him and curse those who cursed him. Furthermore, he told Abraham that through his seed, He would bless all the clans of the earth.

Paul states that this promise to "bless all the clans of the earth" was a shadow picture showing us that YHWH was going to justify (declare right) from death, "the clans of the earth" (Gentiles) who would believe in Yahushua Messiah.

DO NOT miss what this is saying, because Paul is clearly stating that even the Gentile who believes as Abraham believed, is a son of Abraham, even though he's not part of Abraham's natural seed.

The doctrine of the Christian church has so distorted what is being said here that they think their belief in "Jesus" gives them the same status before YHWH as that of Abraham, yet they prove by their behavior that they do not have the heart of Abraham, of whom YHWH says:

> **Gen 26:5**   because Abraham obeyed My voice and guarded My Charge: My commands, My laws, and My Torot."

> **Note:**   The Hebrew word "Torot" is the plural form of the word "Torah", which is translated as Law in English Bibles but, in fact, means instruction.

| Gal 3:9 | so that those who are **of belief** are blessed with Aḇraham, the believer. |
|---|---|
| Gal 3:10 | For as many as are **of works of Torah** are under the curse, for it has been written, **"Cursed is everyone who does not continue in all that has been written in the Book of the Torah, to do them."** |

Once again we see the phrase "of belief" as a reference to a position upon which we stand, it's a matter of what we are trusting in. If we, like Abraham, are trusting in the promises of YHWH, through belief in Yahushua Messiah, then we shall be blessed alongside father Abraham.

In the Messianic writings the Messiah said:

| Mat 8:11 | "And I say to you that **many shall come from east and west**, and sit down with Aḇraham, and Yitsḥaq, and Yaʿaqoḇ in the reign of the heavens, |
|---|---|
| Mat 8:12 | but **the sons of the reign** shall be cast out into outer darkness – there shall be weeping and gnashing of teeth." |

When Messiah mentions those who would come from the East and the West, He is referring to the Gentiles, all those not the physical seed of Abraham, Yitschaq (Isaac) and Ya'aqob (Jacob), i.e., native born Yisra'elis.

The "sons of the reign" is a reference to the native-born seed, Yisra'el, that will not believe in Yahushua for justification. These shall not inherit the Kingdom that YHWH promised Abraham because they did not have the belief that Abraham had in YHWH.

Unfortunately, modern Judaism has a deep **trust** in the works of Torah, as taught by their rabbis. It is to them that Paul is prophetically speaking when he says, "as many as are **of works of Torah** are under the curse, for it has been written, 'Cursed is everyone who does not continue in all that has been written in the Book of the Torah, to do them.'"

Here we see the contrast of position, between those who are "of belief" and those who are "of the works of

Torah". This contrast is about the foundation upon which we are **trusting** for our justification from death.

Those who are trusting in Torah works to be justified are still under the curse because "by the works of the law no man shall be justified" (Rom 3:20). However, those who are trusting in the shed blood of Yahushua Messiah, the Passover Lamb, are no longer under the curse of Torah, which is death.

| | |
|---|---|
| **Gal 3:11** | And that no one is declared right by Torah before Elohim is clear, for **"The righteous shall live by belief."** |
| **Gal 3:12** | And the Torah is not of belief, but **"The man who does them shall live by them."** |

Even in the Tanak (Old Testament), it was those who had placed their belief (trust) in the promises of YHWH, that He considered to be righteous men, and not those who walk in perfect obedience to His Torah, because no one had.

Scripture clearly states that, "all have sinned and fallen short of the esteem of Elohim" (Rom 3:23) and "there is none righteous, no not one" (Psa 14 and 53).

Even David, a man that YHWH said was a "man after His own heart", committed adultery with another man's wife and conspired to kill her husband Uriah, dragging Joab down with him.

Paul quotes from Habakkuk 2:4, showing that righteousness has always been associated to our steadfast belief in the promises of YHWH. Being "right" before YHWH was never about perfect adherence to the Torah, it was instead, about a heart perfectly surrendered to Him.

However, those who have a heart perfectly surrendered to Him strive diligently every day to obey His Torah, because the Torah says, in Leviticus 18:5, "the man who does them shall live by them".

| | |
|---|---|
| **Gal 3:13** | Messiah redeemed us from the curse of the Torah, having become a curse for us – for it has been written, |

|  | **"Cursed is everyone who hangs upon a tree."** – |
|---|---|
| Gal 3:14 | in order that the blessing of Abraham might come upon the nations in Messiah יהושע, to receive the promise of the Spirit through belief. |

**REMEMBER**, the "curse of the Torah" is death, because the Torah says, "the person that sins (violates the Torah) shall die". The price for disobeying the Torah (sinning) is death.

We have been redeemed from the Curse of the Law/Torah (death) because Messiah died for us on the tree. When Yahushua Messiah was nailed on that tree (cross/pole/whatever?) He took the curse of death from us and placed it upon Himself.

When He did this it made the promise of the Spirit available to everyone who would believe in Him, whether native born Yisra'eli or a Gentile. His death paid for all sin, even the sin of the people that will not believe in Him. Unfortunately, for them, it requires a belief that is worked out day by day to inherit the promise.

Something else that needs to be remembered, is that Paul's calling was to bring the Good News of Yahushua Messiah to the Gentiles (nations). Yes, he also preached the same Good News to Jews, but his primary calling was to bring it to the Gentiles and all his writings must be understood from that perspective.

The message of the Good News is the same to both the native-born Yisra'eli and the Gentile in order that the two can become one body of believers, with no distinction between them.

The only difference between the native-born Yisra'eli and the Gentile is that the native-born Yisra'elis have had the Torah since Mount Sinai, and unfortunately, they made a religion out of it that blinded them to the Messiah when He came to them.

When Messiah appeared, He needed to accomplish two things to fulfill the promises YHWH had made to Abraham.

1. He had to bring the native-born Yisra'elis out of the man-made religious trap that their leaders had caught them up in.
2. He had to bring the Gentiles out of the man-made paganism that they had been practicing.

Once these two groups were free from their false religious practices, they could serve YHWH in purity and in truth (Colossians 2:8-15).

His death made it possible for both groups to be redeemed from their sinful ways, so that they could be restored back to YHWH, their Creator. (See Ephesians 2)

**Gal 3:15** Brothers, as a man I say it: a covenant, even though it is man's, yet if it is confirmed, no one sets it aside, or adds to it.

This verse clarifies the principle of covenant, in that, once a covenant is confirmed it cannot be changed or done away with, until all parties in the covenant have fulfilled their part.

Many times YHWH has said, that the things He has spoken cannot be added to nor taken away from (Deut 4:2; 12:32; Ecc 3:14; Pro 30:6 and Rev 22:18-19) and this principle applies to all the covenants that YHWH has made with men.

**Gal 3:16** But the promises were spoken to Abraham, and to his Seed. He does not say, "And to seeds," as of many, but as of one, **"And to your Seed,"** who is Messiah.

Once again, Paul is referring to the promises made to Abraham in Genesis 12, where YHWH included the land (Promised Land) as part of what he would inherit. We will find in verse seven that the land was promised to Abraham's seed as well.

| Gen 12:7 | And יהוה appeared to Abram and said, "To your seed I give this land." And he built there a slaughter-place to יהוה, who had appeared to him. |
|---|---|

Now, when most people hear this, they assume that the "seed" referred to is all of Abraham's descendants, however, Galatians 3:16 Paul says that the seed spoken of, in that promise, is not the many descendants of Abraham but to a very specific Seed, that Seed being Yahushua Messiah.

So, the promise of inheriting the land belongs only to Abraham and to Yahushua, no one else is promised inheritance of that land.

All other people that would inherit the Kingdom, must become sons of Abraham through belief in Yahushua Messiah, just as Paul stated earlier in Galatians 3 and as he referenced in Romans 8 when he said that we are all "coheirs" with Messiah.

Yahushua Messiah is the Only Way, the Narrow Gate, through which men can inherit the Kingdom.

| Gal 3:17 | Now this I say, Torah, that came four hundred and thirty years later, does not annul a covenant previously confirmed by Elohim in Messiah, so as to do away with the promise. |
|---|---|
| Gal 3:18 | For if the inheritance is by Torah, it is no longer by promise, but Elohim gave it to Abraham through a promise. |

Paul is letting us know that the covenant at Mount Sinai, where the Torah was given, does not change the fact that the covenant that YHWH made to Abraham was based on His promises.

The covenant promise that YHWH made to Abraham was, He would bless those who blessed him and curse those who cursed him; it also included the promise that Abraham's seed would be more numerous than the stars of heaven and that he and a very specific seed of his (Messiah) would inherit the land.

615

The Torah has nothing whatsoever to do with this promise that YHWH gave to Abraham. YHWH made this covenant with Abraham and confirmed the covenant in Himself, ensuring the fulfillment of it.

However, according to Paul, that covenant promise does not apply to you and me, nor does it apply to any other human being except Abraham and Messiah.

The promise of the land of Canaan, is a reference to the Kingdom of Messiah. When He returns, He shall cleanse the land in the blood of His enemies, and He shall set up His throne to rule from Yerushalayim.

The Promised Land that Yisra'el conquered was a shadow picture of the Messianic Kingdom and would have lasted until His reign, if Yisra'el had been obedient to the Torah.

The Torah, which was given at Mount Sinai, was intended to teach the "many seeds" of Abraham how to live righteously before YHWH, so that they could inherit the Kingdom. The Torah applied to both the native-born Yisra'eli and the stranger (Gentile) who sojourned with them (Lev 19:33-34; Num 15:15-16).

**REMEMBER**, everything that took place from Yisra'el's exodus from Egypt to their entrance into the Promised Land are shadow pictures of how we receive redemption through Yahushua Messiah today.

Just as the Passover Lamb was a shadow picture of how the blood of Messiah delivers us from the death penalty for sin, so is the Promised Land a picture of the Messianic Kingdom. Yisra'el was to be the apostle of YHWH through whom He would teach the nations how to serve Him, but they failed in that task, never fulfilling their calling.

The twelve disciples were the fulfillment of the twelve spies, who were supposed to give Yisra'el a good report of the Land so that she would eagerly follow her Husband's command.

The 1st century believers were the start of how YHWH would fulfill His promises to Abraham, by sending them throughout the world to bring the whole world to the knowledge of Yahushua Messiah. As the book of Matthew says, "This message of the Kingdom will be proclaimed to the whole world as a witness to all nations, then the end will come." (Mat 24:14)

616

In verse 18, Paul says something he has said before in a slightly different way, let's see it again…

> **Gal 3:18**     For if the inheritance is by Torah, it is no longer by promise, but Elohim gave it to Abraham through a promise.

If we were to replace the word Torah with "works" and the word promise with "belief" it might be easier to understand what Paul is saying.

Basically, Paul wants us to know that we inherit the Land/Kingdom through the promises of YHWH by belief in Yahushua Messiah and NOT through the works of the Law/Torah.

> **Gal 3:19**     Why, then, the Torah? It was added because of transgressions, until the Seed should come to whom the promise was made. And it was ordained through messengers in the hand of a mediator.
>
> **Gal 3:20**     The Mediator, however, is not of one, but Elohim is one.

"Why the Torah?"
1.    In Leviticus, Mosheh says the man who keeps the Torah "shall live by it."
2.    Deuteronomy 4:5-6 says, obeying the Torah gives us wisdom and understanding and 6:24-25 says it is righteousness for us if we keep it.
3.    Proverbs 3:1-2 says long life and peace comes to those who watch over it.
4.    In Romans 2:18, Paul says the Jews "know the desire of Elohim, and approve what is superior, having been trained by the Torah."
5.    In Romans 3:20, Paul says "through the Torah is the knowledge of sin."
6.    Romans 5:20 says the Torah came so the transgression would increase.

Paul is going to call the Torah our "School Master" to lead us to Messiah.

There seems to be several reasons the Torah was given, all the above included, however Paul says in Galatians 3:19, it was given "because of transgressions" (like Rom 5:20). Then he says something that has been taken completely out of context to prove that the Torah no longer applies to the "New Covenant Believer".

He says the Torah was given "until the Seed would come to whom the promise was given." As you might imagine, modern teachers see this and say, "Jesus is the Seed, and since He has come the Torah no longer applies to us."

The problem with this rests in the context of the rest of the passage, i.e., "would come to whom the promise was given". This sentence clarifies the timeline of what Paul means by "until".

**REMEMBER**, the promise to Messiah was the inheritance of the Land. Has He come to inherit the Land? The answer is NO!

The word "until" does not apply to His first appearance but to His future return, when He takes His rulership and reigns (Rev 11:14-15).

Remember, the Torah was given "because of transgressions, until the Seed would come", this is not saying that when Messiah returns the Torah will no longer apply, because Isaiah 2:3 and Micah 4:2 says that in the Kingdom "the Torah shall go forth from Zion".

> **Mic 4:2**  And many nations shall come and say, "Come, and let us go up to the mountain of יהוה, to the House of the Elohim of Yaʿaqob̲, and let Him teach us His ways, and let us walk in His paths. **For out of Tsiyon comes forth the Torah, and the word of יהוה from Yerushalayim."**

When Paul says the Torah was given because of transgressions he is referring to knowledge, meaning that the Torah was given to reveal our sin and the penalty of death that is hanging over our heads because of it.

Knowing our sinful state motivates us to seek the Messiah in order to be justified and made right before YHWH, which Paul said in Romans 5:20 and is going to repeat at the end of Galatians 3 when he calls the Torah our schoolmaster.

The mediator mentioned in this passage is, of course, Mosheh, but it is important that we do not confuse the term mediator with how it is used today.

If you put the word "mediator" in your web browser you will get: "a person who attempts to make people involved in a conflict come to an agreement; a go-between."

This is hardly what took place at Mt. Sinai, there YHWH said that if you do this then I will do that! There was no mediation between parties and Mosheh wasn't trying to negotiate the terms of the Torah with Him.

Mosheh simply acted as the messenger that brought YHWH's instructions to the people and a time or two acted as an intercessor so that He would not destroy them for their stubbornness.

Messiah fulfills the office of Intercessor for us today so that the Father can forgive our unintentional transgressions.

There is some debate about the meaning of verse 20. Let's quote it again.

| | |
|---|---|
| **Gal 3:20** | The Mediator, however, is not of one, but Elohim is one. |
| **Mediator:** | stg's #**G3316** "mesites", From G3319 (middle); a go between, that is, (simply) an internunciator [a messenger between parties], or (by implication) a reconciler (intercessor): - mediator. This word does not carry the meaning of negotiator. |

The word "mediator" is capitalized here because the translator assumed that it applied to Messiah, which may or may not be accurate. This translation also suggests that the first word of the verse is the definitive article "the", which it is not.

619

The first Greek word in this verse is (G1161) "de", which is a primary particle (adversative or continuative); but, and etc.: - also, and, but, moreover, now [often unexpressed in English]. It is used in this passage as a continuative of the previous verse and is NOT the definitive article. This word is translated as "Now" in the (KJV).

Some have interpreted this verse to mean that a mediator does not decide the facts of a case but only mediates between the parties, in this case Mosheh didn't decide what the Torah would say, he only reported the facts of the Torah as it was given to him.

YHWH, however, is not a negotiator, He states the facts and requires the receiving party to act upon them. He alone has the authority to determine what is Right and True.

Others have interpreted this verse by applying the word "mediator" to the Messiah and then using the fact that Messiah declared that He and the Father were One. The Greek word for one in this passage is (G1520) "heis" referring to the primary numeral "1".

The Hebrew word for One, as it is used to refer to YHWH, is (H259) "echad", meaning One in absolute unity.

This being the case, verse 20 could mean "The Mediator", Yahushua, is not alone but He and the Father are One, they are in absolute agreement.

Whatever the case may be, YHWH did not give man a choice as to how we were to serve Him. He simply declared how He expected to be served and demands nothing less. The reward for doing so is life and blessing, while the alternative is cursing and death. There will be no negotiation involved.

| | |
|---|---|
| **Gal 3:21** | Is the Torah then against the promises of Elohim? Let it not be! For if a torah had been given that was able to make alive, truly righteousness would have been by Torah. |

At no time in the history of the Belief was the Torah ever in a position contrary to the promises of YHWH, which includes belief in Yahushua. Even today, the Torah is in complete agreement with the principle of salvation known as "grace through faith".

620

The only problem with the idea that we have been granted His favor solely because of our belief in Yahushua, is how the church has interpreted it.

To the church, this "grace through faith" doctrine has somehow been interpreted to mean that the Torah of YHWH is to be rejected as how believers LIVE righteously before Him.

The Torah was given to teach us how to live as righteous men, but we all have chosen to live our lives contrary to it. By doing so we have brought the curse of death upon our own heads, just as the Torah said we would (Deut 30).

Since we are all guilty before YHWH the Torah cannot make us righteous before Him, even if we obey it. Our state of condemnation prevents us from being righteous no matter how well we behave.

The Torah was given with the presumption of willingness among its adherents. It does not provide a way to be made right from our guilt other than the penalty, i.e., death.

However, YHWH also gave us the Sacrificial System in the Torah, to teach us how to be made right again before Him. Though the sacrifices are in the Torah they are not a part of the Torah in the same way the other commands are.

The commands of the Torah represent the physical part of the belief through which we can live righteous lives. The sacrifices in the Torah represent the spiritual part of the belief through which we can find atonement for our sins when we stumble.

The spiritual is about belief, while the physical part is about how believers live. Paul has alluded to this when he said, the "Torah is not of belief" back in verse 12.

He quoted from Habakkuk 3:4 when he said, "The righteous shall live by belief" in verse 11 and finished off verse 12 by saying of Torah, "The man who does them shall live by them."

These two principles represent the *Two-Part Principle* of salvation. The spiritual part upon which we stand, Yahushua Messiah, and the physical part in which we live, the Torah. It takes both to be complete in the Belief and to inherit eternal life.

Concerning false priests and prophets in Yisra'el the prophet Isaiah (YeshaYahu) had this to say.

| | |
|---|---|
| **Isa 8:13** | "יהוה of hosts, Him you shall set apart. Let Him be your fear, and let Him be your dread. |
| **Isa 8:14** | "And He shall be for a set-apart place, **but a stone of stumbling and a rock that makes for falling** to both the houses of Yisra'ĕl, as a trap and a snare to the inhabitants of Yerushalayim. |
| **Isa 8:15** | "And many among them shall stumble and fall, and be broken and snared and taken." |
| **Isa 8:16** | **Bind up the witness, seal the Torah among my taught ones**. |
| **Isa 8:17** | And I shall wait on יהוה, who hides His face from the house of Ya'aqoḇ. And I shall look for Him. |
| **Isa 8:18** | Look, **I and the children whom יהוה has given me** – for signs and wonders in Yisra'ĕl from יהוה of hosts, who dwells in Mount Tsiyon. |
| **Isa 8:19** | And when they say to you, "Seek those who are mediums and wizards, who whisper and mutter," should not a people seek their Elohim? Should they seek the dead on behalf of the living? |
| **Isa 8:20** | **To the Torah and to the witness! If they do not speak according to this Word, it is because they have no daybreak** (light). |

This is an end time prophesy concerning both houses of Yisra'el and those who dwell in Yerushalayim.

The title "YHWH of hosts" is a reference to Yahushua. Whenever we see it in the Tanak it is telling us something about what Yahushua is going to accomplish in the Name of the Father.

It tells us specifically to make Him our fear and our dread. This is the same thing that Paul means when he says

that our boast should be in Yahushua and not in the Torah.
However, obedience to His Torah is how we live before Him
in fear.

Paul instructs us to work out our salvation in fear
and trembling" (Php 2:12)

**Php 2:12**     So than, my beloved, as you always
                 obeyed – not only in my presence,
                 but now much rather in my absence
                 – work out your own deliverance
                 with **fear and trembling,**
**Php 2:13**     for it is Elohim who is working in
                 you both to desire and to work for
                 *His* good pleasure.

Paul indicates here that the Philippians have "always
obeyed". Obeyed what, we might ask? In verse 13 he tells us
that Elohim is working in them both to desire and to do his
good pleasure.

This is very similar to the "New Covenant" promise,
given in Jeremiah 31:31-33, where it says that YHWH
would put His Torah in our inner parts (spirit mind) and
write it upon our heart.

Desire is a heart issue, while the intent to do His will
is a rational choice. So, Paul is saying that YHWH is
working in us to both desire Him and to do the things that
please Him, i.e., obey His Torah.

What must we do to "please" YHWH? According to
Paul, in Romans 8:7-8, the mind of the flesh does not subject
itself to the Law/Torah, neither can it, and so it cannot
"please" Elohim.

In Romans 8, Paul is contrasting things of the spirit
with things of the flesh, so if the mind of the flesh cannot
"please" Elohim" because it is not subject to the Torah, then
by contrast the mind of the spirit can "please" Elohim by
being subject to the Torah, i.e., obeying it.

Consider what Peter (Kepha) has to say concerning
Isaiah 8:14.

**1Pe 2:6**     Because it is contained in the
                Scripture, "See, I lay in Tsiyon a
                chief corner-stone, chosen, precious,

|          | and he who believes on Him shall by no means be put to shame." |
| 1Pe 2:7  | This preciousness, then, is for you who believe; but to those who are disobedient, "The stone which the builders rejected has become the chief corner-stone," |
| 1Pe 2:8  | and "**A stone of stumbling and a rock that makes for falling,**" **who stumble because they are disobedient to the Word**, to which they also were appointed. |

In verse 8, Peter quotes from Isaiah, saying that the stone of stumbling and the rock that makes for falling (Yahushua) caused the people to stumble because they were "disobedient to the Word", which is a reference to the Torah of YHWH as it was given at Mt Sinai.

In Isaiah 8:16, the prophet says to "bind up the witness, seal up the Torah among my taught ones". **REMEMBER**, this passage is a reference to the work of Yahushua (YHWH of hosts) in the Last Day.

This quoted phrase has the *Two-Part Principle* in it, the witness, which is a reference to our belief in Yahushua Messiah, the spiritual part, and the Torah, which is a reference to the physical part that we live by.

In verse 18, the prophet says, "I and the children whom YHWH has given me", which is quoted in the book of Hebrews 2:13 concerning the work of Messiah and then in verse 20, he says something very important.

| Isa 8:20 | **To the Torah and to the witness**! If they do not speak according to this Word, it is because they have no daybreak (light). |

"To the Torah AND to the Witness" is a *Two-Part Principle*, that requires both parts to find fulfillment. In fact, this verse says that to be of the light, a teaching must contain both the Torah (physical) and the Witness (spiritual).

The Christian church claims to be of the light, and though it declares the witness, it rejects the Torah.

624

In John (Yochanan) 1:4, Yahushua is called the "light of men" and later in 8:12 and 9:5, Yahushua refers to Himself as "the light of the world".

According to the prophet Isaiah, for Messiah to refer to Himself as the Light, any teaching concerning Him must contain both the Torah and the Witness. Any doctrine that says you can have the Witness of Messiah without having to obey the Torah, is not a teaching of the light, but darkness.

| | |
|---|---|
| **Gal 3:22** | But the Scripture has shut up all *mankind* under sin, that the promise by belief in יהושע Messiah might be given to those who believe. |

What does it mean that "the Scripture has shut up all mankind under sin"? Well, the Scripture says that there is not a righteous man among us and the price of our unrighteousness is death.

| | |
|---|---|
| **Rom 3:10** | As it has been written, **"There is none righteous, no, not one!** |
| **Rom 3:11** | **"There is no one who is understanding, there is none who is seeking Elohim.** |
| **Rom 3:12** | **"They all have turned aside, they have together become worthless. There is none who does good, no, not one."** |
| **Rom 3:13** | **"Their throat is an open tomb, with their tongues they have deceived," "The poison of adders is under their lips,"** |
| **Rom 3:14** | **"Whose mouth is filled with cursing and bitterness."** |
| **Rom 3:15** | **"Their feet are swift to shed blood,** |
| **Rom 3:16** | **ruin and wretchedness are in their ways,** |
| **Rom 3:17** | **and the way of peace they have not known."** |
| **Rom 3:18** | **"There is no fear of Elohim before their eyes."** |

| | |
|---|---|
| **Rom 3:19** | And we know that whatever the Torah says, it says to those who are in the Torah, **so that every mouth might be stopped, and all the world come under judgment before Elohim.** |

(See: Psalms 5:9; 10:7; 14:1-3; 36:1; 53:1-4; 140:3; Pro 1:16. Isa 59:7)

| | |
|---|---|
| **Eze 18:4** | "See, all beings are Mine, the being of the father as well as the being of the son is Mine. **The being that is sinning shall die.**<br>\*\*\* |
| **Rom 3:23** | for **all have sinned** and fall short of the esteem of Elohim,<br>\*\*\* |
| **Rom 6:23** | For **the wages of sin is death**, but the favourable gift of Elohim is everlasting life in Messiah יהושע our Master. |

When Paul says that the Scripture has "shut up all mankind under sin" he is stating that the Scripture has condemned all mankind to death because of sin and he says it has done this so the promise (inheritance) can be given to all those who believe in Yahushua Messiah.

| | |
|---|---|
| **Gal 3:23** | But before belief came, we were being guarded under Torah, having been shut up for the belief being about to be revealed. |
| **Gal 3:24** | Therefore the Torah became our trainer unto Messiah, in order to be declared right by belief. |

"Before belief came" is a reference to personal belief, not belief as a synonym for Messiah. This needs to be stated because some teachers out there would have us believe that this statement is a reference to Messiah coming in the 1st century, and use it to say that since He has come there is no longer any need for Torah. This is not what Paul meant by this phrase.

He means us to understand, before we as individuals believed in Messiah, we had been "guarded under Torah", which means the exact same thing as "shut up...under sin" in verse 22.

**Guarded:** stg's #G5432 "phroureō", from two words meaning, (G4253) in front of and (G3708); similar to another word meaning, (G5083) to guard. This word can refer to being watched over the protection or being hemmed in like a prisoner.

This word needs to be understood in the same context as verse 22, which states that all mankind were "shut up" under sin.

**Shut up:** stg's #G4788 "sugkleiō", from two words meaning, (G4862) a union and (G2808) to close; i.e., to be closed up together. Refers to placing all men in the same category, i.e., sinners.

These two words are meant to be similar, that we were closed up together, hemmed in like prisoners, awaiting the penalty of death we deserve for our sin.

The Torah then, became our trainer (schoolmaster), which teaches us we were sinners (Rom 3:20, 23) and under the condemnation of death (Romans 6:23). It also teaches us our need of Messiah and reveals to us, in many diverse ways, Who the Messiah would be.

It is easy to think this passage is saying that the Torah was "watching over us" in some positive way until Messiah would come and "set us free" from having to obey it, which is how the modern church interprets it.

However, Paul does not refer to our being "under the Torah" as a positive thing, anywhere in his writings. He continually uses the idea of being "under the Torah" as a thing to be freed from and always in the context of condemnation.

627

To suggest that being "guarded by the Torah" was a positive thing, is to ignore everything else Paul has said concerning the Torah's authority over the sinner, which is clearly the context here.

Also, Messiah has not redeemed everyone who is "under the Torah", but only those who have believed in Him. So, the belief being revealed is about personal revelation within everyone.

| | |
|---|---|
| **Gal 3:25** | And after belief has come, we are no longer under a trainer. |

Once we believe in Yahushua Messiah, we are no longer under the condemnation of death because of sin, but have been set free from sin, so we are no longer condemned by the trainer.

This is the exact same thing Paul said in Romans 6:1-15, where he concluded that our baptism was a picture of dying with Messiah, He having died in our place, which set us free from the condemnation of death we were under because of our disobedience to the Torah (sin).

However, he asked whether we should continue to sin, since we are no longer under the condemnation of Torah, and his answer was **ABSOLUTELY NOT**!!!

He then told us we are servants to whom we obey. If we serve sin (disobedience) we will die, but if we serve obedience (to the Torah) we will be righteous, and that righteousness will end in eternal life (6:22).

There is no way to take all Paul's writings and legitimately conclude that our belief in Yahushua Messiah no longer requires us to obey the Law/Torah of YHWH, unless we choose to be willingly blind to the Truth, so that we can be comfortable in our own religion, the end of which is the Second Death.

| | |
|---|---|
| **Gal 3:26** | For you are all sons of Elohim through belief in Messiah יהושע. |
| **Gal 3:27** | For as many of you as were immersed into Messiah have put on Messiah. |
| **Gal 3:28** | There is not Yehuḏi nor Greek, there is not slave nor free, there is |

|            | not male and female, for you are all one in Messiah יהושע. |
|------------|-----------------------------------------------------------|
| **Gal 3:29** | And **if** you are of Messiah, then you are seed of Abraham, and heirs according to promise. |

Paul clearly believes that all the Galatians will hear his warning and do what he has instructed them. He declares all the believers in Galatia to be sons of YHWH, because they have "put on Messiah", which refers to accepting His substitutionary death on their behalf.

He also mentions how baptism is the shadow picture of dying with Him, which is what he taught the Romans in Chapter 6. To fully understand what Paul is saying here one must understand what he said there.

There is no distinction between believers as far as our standing before YHWH is concerned, we are all equal in salvation. However, this is not meant to imply that there are not positions of authority within the body of Messiah.

For instance, a man is the head of his household, even though his wife has a part in all the same promises that he does in the belief and will receive her part in the inheritance at Yahushua's return.

Their equality as believers does not change the principles of headship required by the Torah. Nothing in the belief has changed what is written in the Torah and nothing and no one in the belief will ever have the authority to do so.

All believers, native born and stranger, are the seed of Abraham, through Yahushua Messiah!

# Chapter 4: Galatians 4

Paul (Sha'ul) is now going to use a different metaphor for the same discussion in the previous chapter, however, from a slightly different perspective. He is going to use the heirship that comes to us through belief in Yahushua Messiah.

| | |
|---|---|
| **Gal 4:1** | And I say, for as long as the heir is a child, he is no different from a slave, though he is master of all, |
| **Gal 4:2** | but is under guardians and trustees till the time prearranged by the father. |

The phrase "under guardians and trustees" means the same thing as being "shut up…under sin" and "guarded by the Law/Torah" in the last chapter.

He equates being "under guardians and trustees" as slavery, even though we are called to be heirs, until the time "prearranged by the father". This is an allusion to what he said in Romans 8:29-30.

| | |
|---|---|
| **Rom 8:29** | Because **those whom He knew beforehand, He also ordained beforehand to be conformed to the likeness of His Son**, for Him to be the first-born among many brothers. |
| **Rom 8:30** | And whom He ordained beforehand, these He also called, and whom He called, these He also declared right. And whom He declared right, these He also esteemed. |

If you remember our discussion earlier in Romans 8, this section has to do with YHWH's sovereignty and foreknowledge, in that He knew us, and our future desire for Him, before we were even born, and chose us or preordained us at that time (See what Paul says about his own preordination in Galatians 1:15-16).

Simply speaking, he is telling us that even though we were going to be heirs of the Kingdom, because of our belief in Yahushua Messiah, we were being kept "under" the condemnation of the Law/Torah, which was our trainer/guardian and trustee to lead us into the knowledge of Messiah.

| | |
|---|---|
| **Gal 4:3** | So we also, when we were children, were **under the elementary matters of the world, being enslaved**. |

The phrase "elementary matters of the world" is generally used as a reference to idol worship, the worship of the sun, the moon and the stars, as well as other things made of wood and rocks, etc.

He uses this phrase in Colossians 2:8 in connection with man-made theology and ideology.

| | |
|---|---|
| **Col 2:8** | See to it that no one makes a prey of you through **philosophy and empty deceit, according to the tradition of men, according to the elementary matters of the world**, and not according to Messiah. |

Two things we need to notice, these things are **NOT** of Messiah and Paul is warning us not to let anyone else make a "prey" of us through them.

His use of this phrase in Galatians, where he says that we are "under the elementary matters of the world", is intended to be a direct correlation to what he said about being "under guardians and trustees".

Furthermore, it gives proof to the position that both of these references concern things that are not of YHWH and have no connection to Yahushua Messiah.

Basically, Paul is trying to tell us, before we came to the understanding of who Yahushua Messiah was and our need for Him, the Father had allowed us to be "under" the tutelage of all the false doctrines in all the false religions and man-made ideologies, which themselves are sin.

The sin of idolatry, whether religious or secular, brings us under the condemnation of death commanded by the Law/Torah and so we see that both this metaphor and the one in the previous chapter are referring to our position "under" (enslaved to) the condemnation of Law/Torah for sin.

| | |
|---|---|
| **Gal 4:4** | **But** when the completion of the time came, Elohim sent forth His Son, **born of a woman, born under Torah,** |
| **Gal 4:5** | **to redeem those who were under Torah, in order to receive the adoption as sons.** |
| **Gal 4:6** | And because you are sons, Elohim has sent forth the Spirit of His Son into your hearts, crying, "**Abba, Father!**" |

The word "but" denote a change has taken place and that change is directly connected to the fact that YHWH sent forth His Son to redeem us.

Let's take a closer look however, at the phrase **"born of a woman, born under the Law/Torah, to redeem those who are under the Law/Torah, in order to receive the adoption of sons"**.

The phrase "born of a woman" is a reference to the very first messianic prophecy, found in Genesis 3:15.

At the time this phrase was used in the book of Genesis, YHWH was condemning the Nachash (serpent) for beguiling Chawwah (Eve) into eating of the tree of the Knowledge of Good and Evil.

| | |
|---|---|
| **Serpent:** | stg's **#H5175** "**nachash**", meaning snake; from a word (**H5172**) meaning to hiss, that is, whisper a (magic) spell; generally meaning to prognosticate (to tell the future). |
| **Note:** | The Nachash in Genesis 3 is a shadow reference to the great serpent, the devil and adversary of YHWH's people, Ha-Satan, mentioned in the book of Revelation (Ch. 12). |
| **Gen 3:15** | "And I put enmity between you and the woman, and between your seed |

and **her Seed**. He shall crush your head, and you shall crush His heel."

In this verse, the Creator placed enmity (hostility) between the serpent and the woman, which is a reference to the hostility, the ongoing battle, between women and the adversary. There is no greater tool the enemy can wield against a son of Elohim than a woman, especially a wife.

> **Note**: More specifically, this is a reference to the hostility between man and sin and can be seen in our personal battle to be righteous before YHWH, which we strive to do in our inner-spirit-man, while our bodies desire to fulfill its own pleasures.

Paul refers to this very thing in Romans 7-8 and Galatians 5, where he makes a clear distinction between our spirit and our flesh, and the seed of the woman represents the spiritual part, the way we should be (like Yahushua) and the seed of the serpent represents the physical part, the way we are in our flesh, i.e., rebellious.

He goes on to say that this enmity will exist between the serpent's seed and her seed. The serpent tricked the woman into disobeying the commandment of YHWH concerning not eating the fruit of that tree, so then the serpent's seed is a reference to what the serpent produces, i.e., disobedience (sin).

So, there is open hostility between the seed of the serpent (sin) and the seed of the woman (Messiah).

**REMEMBER**, sin is the "transgression of the Law/Torah", so this "seed of a woman" – Messiah, would be staunchly against any teaching that advocated violating or disobeying the Law/Torah.

This verse concludes by saying that the "Seed of the woman" would crush the head of the seed of the serpent, but that the seed of the serpent would strike His heel.

Metaphorically speaking, the "head" is a reference to authority and so Messiah would crush the authority of sin.

Messiah, "came in the likeness of sinful flesh, concerning sin, condemning sin in the flesh" (Rom 8:3), meaning that He came in a fleshly body like ours to defeat sin and condemn it in this body, which must die.

633

Messiah's purpose was to defeat sin and overcome the consequences of sin, i.e., death, in the lives of all who would believe in Him, which is what Paul says repeatedly in all his writings.

When YHWH said that the serpent's seed would strike the "heel" of the woman's seed, it was a reference to the Messiah death. Since the "wages of sin is death", a death had to take place to overcome the authority of sin, thus Messiah had to die in our place.

This ties in to what Paul says in Galatians 4:4, where he says, Messiah was "born under the Law/Torah" so that He could "redeem those who are under the Law/Torah".

For Him to redeem those of us who were under the penalty of death for disobeying the Law/Torah, He had to die in our place. Messiah was born for this very purpose, to die for us as the Law/Torah required, so He was born "under" the condemnation of the Law/Torah, even though He had never committed any sin of His own.

Notice what Paul says in 2 Corinthians concerning this.

| | |
|---|---|
| **2Co 5:18** | And all *matters* are from Elohim, who **has restored us to favour with Himself through יהושע Messiah**, and has given us the service of restoration to favour, |
| **2Co 5:19** | that is, **that Elohim was in Messiah restoring the world to favour unto Himself**, not reckoning their trespasses to them, and has committed to us the word of restoration to favour. |
| **2Co 5:20** | Therefore we are envoys on behalf of Messiah, as though Elohim were pleading through us. We beg, on behalf of Messiah: Be restored to favour with Elohim. |
| **2Co 5:21** | **For He made Him who knew no sin to be sin for us, so that in Him we might become the righteousness of Elohim.** |

YHWH made Messiah "to be sin for us" even though He Himself had no sin. This is what Paul is referring to when he said that Messiah was "born under the Law/Torah", He was born to die so that through His death, we might have access to the adoption of sons.

> **Gal 4:7** So you are no longer a slave but a son, and if a son, also an heir of Elohim through Messiah.

Once again, Paul is confident that he is speaking to those who have placed their trust in Messiah and so he has no problem declaring that they are no longer slaves to sin, but sons of Elohim and heirs according to the promise because of their belief in Yahushua Messiah.

> **Gal 4:8** **But then**, indeed, not knowing Elohim, you served those which by nature are not mighty ones.

"But then" is a reference to the state all believers were in BEFORE they came to the knowledge of Messiah. More specifically, to the state the Galatian believers were in before they believed in Messiah.

Before the Galatians believed in Messiah, they were part of a pagan, idol worshiping society, much like the whole world is today. This is what Paul meant when he said that they "serve those which by nature are not mighty ones", that they were idol worshipers, not knowing YHWH.

Once again, the reference to false mighty ones ties back to what he said earlier concerning the "elementary matters of the world"(v3).

> **Gal 4:9** **But now** after you have known Elohim, or rather are known by Elohim, how do you turn again to the weak and poor elementary matters, to which you wish to be enslaved again?
>
> **Gal 4:10** You closely observe days and months and seasons and years.

"But now" denote a change, specifically their movement away from idolatry and into the true belief.

The phrase "have known Elohim, or rather are known by Him" is extremely significant because it makes a distinction between us saying we know Him and Him declaring He knows us.

You might wonder why this is significant, but the distinction between these two points of view can't be stressed enough, because the whole world claims to know Him by various ways and means, but He declares He only knows those who are His, those who have been "set apart" to Him according to the guidelines that He set forth.

If we go back to YHWH's relationship to Abraham we will see something very interesting.

1. YHWH first spoke to Abraham in chapter 12.
2. Abraham called on the name of YHWH in chapter 13 (vs.4).
3. Abraham swore an oath in the Name of YHWH in chapter 14, concerning the booty he had won in his battle, while saving Lot.
4. YHWH made a covenant with Abraham in verse 15.
5. YHWH blessed the birth of Abraham's son Yishma'el in chapter 16.
6. YHWH gave Abraham the covenant of circumcision in chapter 17.
7. YHWH sat down and had dinner with Abraham and negotiated with him over the destruction of YHWH spared Lot during the destruction of Sodom and Gomorrah because of Abraham's love and concern for him.
8. YHWH caused Abimelech to bless Abraham in chapter 20, even though he had deceived Abimelech.
9. YHWH then blessed Abraham and Sarah with the birth of Isaac (Yitschaq), even though Sarah had a barren womb, in Chapter 21.

By now you would think it quite evident that YHWH knows Abraham pretty well, however, it was not until **AFTER** Abraham lifted the knife to sacrifice his son Yitschaq in chapter 22, that YHWH declares that He knows Abraham will serve Him.

| | |
|---|---|
| **Gen 22:10** | And Abraham stretched out his hand and took the knife to slay his son, |
| **Gen 22:11** | but the Messenger of יהוה called to him from the heavens and said, "Abraham, Abraham!" And he said, "Here I am." |
| **Gen 22:12** | And He said, "Do not lay your hand on the boy, nor touch him. For **now I know that you fear Elohim, seeing you have not withheld your son, your only son, from Me.**" |

It wasn't until Abraham was ready to slaughter the thing he loved most in this world that he proved his commitment to YHWH.

This is a shadow picture of the kind of commitment required from every believer, especially those of us who will endure to the end. Because the enemy is at hand and the time is nearer than it once was.

Messiah warned us that our service to Him would cost us even the most intimate relationships of our lives.

| | |
|---|---|
| **Mat 10:34** | "Do not think that **I have come to bring peace on earth**. I did not come to bring peace **but a sword**, |
| **Mat 10:35** | **for I have come to bring division,** a man against his father, a daughter against her mother, and a daughter-in-law against her mother-in-law – |
| **Mat 10:36** | and **a man's enemies are those of his own household**. |
| **Mat 10:37** | "He who loves father or mother more than Me is not worthy of Me, and he who loves son or daughter more than Me is not worthy of Me. |

| | |
|---|---|
| **Mat 10:38** | "And he who does not take up his stake and follow after Me is not worthy of Me. |
| **Mat 10:39** | **"He who has found his life shall lose it, and he that has lost his life for My sake shall find it.** |

It is not until we have proven, **BY OUR ACTIONS**, that pleasing YHWH is our number one priority in this life, that He acknowledges that He knows us, just as He did with Abraham.

In Galatians 4:9 we see Paul indicating that these people were "known by Elohim", meaning they had proved by their behavior that He was their Elohim, yet they had begun to do something strange.

He asked them, "how do you **turn again** to the weak and poor **elementary matters**, to which you wish to be **enslaved again**?".

As we have already shown, the "elementary matters of the world" generally refers to idolatry, however, we have also shown that the context of this book has to do specifically with the Jewish religious dogma that demands Law/Torah observance as a pre-requisite "TO BE SAVED" (Acts 15:1).

What needs to be understood, is YHWH's perspective concerning disobedience.

| | |
|---|---|
| **Deu 28:14** | "And **do not turn aside from any** of the Words which I am commanding you today, right or left, **to go after other mighty ones to serve them.** |

YHWH considers disobedience to be an act of serving someone or something else, which is idolatry, spiritual adultery. Hear this, **DISOBEYING THE TORAH/LAW OF YHWH IS IDOLATRY** (1 Samuel 15:22-23).

So, saying that we "know Him", but refusing to obey His Law/Torah (Instructions), for whatever reason, proves that we are liars!

| | |
|---|---|
| **1Jn 2:3** | And by this we know that we know Him, **if** we guard His commands. |
| **1Jn 2:4** | The one who says, "I know Him," and does not guard His commands, **is a liar**, and **the truth is not in him**. |
| **1Jn 2:5** | But whoever guards His Word, truly the love of Elohim has been perfected in him. By this we know that we are in Him. |
| **1Jn 2:6** | The one who says he stays in Him ought himself also to walk, even as He walked. |

The Truth of the Good News is, without having both parts of the *Two-Part Principle* working in us (belief lived out in obedience to the Law/Torah of YHWH) there is "no truth in us", and neither is there any light (Isa 8:20).

Going back to Galatians 4, verses 10-11, Paul refers to "…closely observe(ing) days and months and seasons and years".

The church would have you believe that this is a reference to the Sabbaths and Feast Days commanded in the Law/Torah (Lev 23), however, the "days and months and seasons and years" referred to here are connected to the "elementary matters" mentioned in verse 9, which Paul says we used to be enslaved by.

Considering the context and purpose of the book of Galatians, he can only be referring to the man-made dogmas of religious men who DO NOT DO, OR TEACH OTHERS TO DO, the Law/Torah of YHWH, of which the Messiah had something to say.

| | |
|---|---|
| **Mat 5:17** | "**Do not think** that I came to destroy the Torah or the Prophets. I did not come to destroy but to complete. |
| **Mat 5:18** | "For truly, I say to you, till the heaven and the earth pass away, one yod or one tittle shall by no means pass from the Torah till all be done. |
| **Mat 5:19** | "Whoever, then, breaks one of the least of these commands, and |

teaches men so, shall be called least in the reign of the heavens; but whoever does and teaches them, he shall be called great in the reign of the heavens.

Mat 5:20    "For I say to you, that unless **your righteousness exceeds that of the scribes and Pharisees, you shall by no means enter into the reign of the heavens.**

**Destroy:**    stg's **#G2647** "**kataluō**", from two words meaning, (**G2596**) to loosen and (**G3089**) down; (disintegrate), that is, (by mplication) to demolish (literally or figuratively). Refers to the loosening of something that had been fixed, i.e., to remove the authority of, in this context.

**Complete:**    stg's **#G4137** "**plēroō**", from a word meaning (**G4134**) replete or full; **to make replete,** that is, (literally) to cram (a net), level up (a hollow). Refers to the act of filling something up that had been incomplete, i.e., increasing the understanding of something.

**Done:**    stg's **#G1096** "**ginomai**", A prolonged and middle form of a primary verb; to cause to be ("gen" -erate), used with great latitude (literally, figuratively, intensively, etc.). In this context it refers to absolute completion, i.e., when all things are finished.

The Hebrew mind immediately understands what the Messiah means here because the Law/Torah states several times that **it cannot be added to nor taken away from** (Deut 4:2; 12:32; Pro 30:6 and Ecc 3:14) and the Messianic Writings say so as well (Rev 22:18:19).

Let's look at two of these passages to see if we can get a glimpse into the mind of YHWH concerning the importance of His Word/Law/Torah in its pure form.

**Ecc 3:14**    I know that **whatever Elohim does is forever**. There is **no adding to it, and there is no taking from it**. Elohim does it, **that men should fear before Him**.

"Whatever Elohim does is forever" includes everything He has said and done. He established His Law/Torah as the only way to **LIVE** righteously before Him (Deut 6:24-24) and gave it to His people Yisra'el , both native born and stranger that sojourns with them (Lev 19:33-33; Num 15:15-16), as an **everlasting covenant, to ALL their generations** (Exod 31:16).

There can be no adding to it, by anyone, and there can be no taking away from it, by anyone because it is eternal just as He is eternal. What did Messiah say in Matthew 5:18?

The Greek word for "destroy" in 5:17, is "**kataluō**" and would best be understood to mean, diminish or take away from.

The Greek word for "complete" in 5:17, is "**plēroō**" and has the meaning of filling something up and in this context should be understood to mean that Messiah was going to increase our knowledge or understanding of the purpose of the Law/Torah and its place in our life.

Yes, He came to live it out Himself, so that He could be the perfect "Passover Lamb" that would die to take away our sin and free us from the death penalty required for disobedience, as a fulfillment of all the Law/Torah taught concerning the remission of sin.

He was also showing us how to live it out in our own lives as believers in Him. He lived as the example of how a believer in Him, one of His disciples, should live out their life in righteousness and set apartness.

**Remember**, Brother John (Yochanan) said the one who says they are in Him, "should walk as He walked" (1 John 2:4-6).

It is important that we don't lose sight of what Messiah said in Matthew 5:17-19 concerning what He DID NOT COME TO DO. He said that He did not come to "destroy" the Torah or the Prophets, but to complete them.

**Mat 5:17** **"Do not think that I came to destroy the Torah or the Prophets**. I did not come to destroy **but to complete.**

**Mat 5:18** "For truly, I say to you, **till the heaven and the earth pass away**, one yod or one tittle shall **by no means pass from the Torah till all be done.**

Now most Christian teachers will tell you that He didn't destroy the Law but by believing in Him, the Law no longer has authority over us, so we are no longer required to obey it.

Like all deception, it has a modicum of truth in it. The idea that believing in Him means the Torah no longer has authority over us IS TRUE, in the context of the condemnation of death we owed because of Adam's sin and then our own personal sin. This idea is the same thing Paul means when he says that we are no longer "under the Torah".

This DOES NOT, however, mean that we are no longer required to obey it AFTER we have been justified FROM sin and death, because we are still told to live Holy (Set-apart) and righteous, which is why the Torah was given, i.e., to teach us how.

This is the same thing Messiah is saying here when He says that He did not come to destroy the Torah or the Prophets. The word "destroy" comes from the Greek word "kataluo", which means to 'loosen down', i.e., destroy, demolish, diminish, and from the Hebraic Mindset, to 'take away from' (Deuteronomy 4:2, 12:32; Ecclesiastes 3:14, Revelation 22:19).

Messiah DID NOT come to diminish from or loosen any part of the Torah or the Prophets, not even a "jot or tittle" of them. This means that all of the commands and prophesies of the Tanak (OT) are both relevant and authoritative today, and applies to everyone, both native born and Gentile, equally (Galatians 3:28; Deuteronomy 19:33-34; Numbers 15:15-26).

The entire teaching in Matthew 5 is about the understanding of the Torah and the Prophets, not application of them. Once YHWH has set something down as true, it is true forever, in every generation!

***

| | |
|---|---|
| **Gal 4:11** | I fear for you, lest by any means I have laboured for you in vain. |
| **Gal 4:12** | Brothers, I beg you to become as I am, because I am as you are. You did not wrong me at all. |
| **Gal 4:13** | But you know that through weakness of the flesh I brought the Good News to you before. |
| **Gal 4:14** | And my trial which was in my flesh you did not despise or reject, but you received me as a messenger of Elohim, as Messiah יהושע. |
| **Gal 4:15** | What then was your blessedness? For I bear you witness, that if possible, you would have plucked out your own eyes and given them to me. |

Paul is concerned that the brethren, whom he had worked so diligently to teach the truth, are walking away from the truth as he has taught it to them.

643

He begs them to be "as I am" and then follows up with "because I am as you are".

This is not the first time that Paul has told us to be like him. In first Corinthians 11:1 he told the brethren to "Become imitators of me, as I also am of Messiah."

Now we know that Paul was firmly founded in the necessity of trusting in the Messiah by belief to receive the favor (grace) of YHWH and we know that he himself says "that according to the Way which they call a sect, so I worship the Elohim of my fathers, believing **all** that has been written in **the Torah and in the Prophets**" (Act 24:14).

We know that the Messiah Himself kept the Law/Torah in its entirety and that John told us that if we are in Him then we should also "walk as He walked" (1 John 2:6), which is the same thing Paul is saying when he tells us to imitate him as he does Messiah.

Clearly both John and Paul intended us to live our lives in the same type of righteousness that Yahushua lived His, according to the Law/Torah of YHWH, His Father.

So, Paul was telling the Galatians to be like he is, the Law/Torah obedient believer in Yahushua Messiah, and goes on to let them know it is not difficult because he is just like them, struggling daily to know and live the right way.

Paul told them that their struggles did not offend him because it's a natural process within the belief and then goes on to recount to them the fact that they themselves saw him struggling in his own flesh and did not reject him but received him like a brother.

Now the Christian church has interpreted Paul's "issue" of the flesh, something he called a thorn in the flesh in another place (2 Corinthians 12:7), to be a problem with his eyes because of what he says in verse 15, that "if possible, you would have plucked out your own eyes and given them to me."

We have heard many possible explanations for this, some say that because of his first confrontation with Messiah on the road to Damascus, where he was temporarily blinded, that he had a lifelong issue with his eyes, which the Scripture does not say.

In fact the Scripture clearly says that when Ḥananyah (Ananias) laid his hands on him the scales of his eyes were removed and he could see.

644

They believe that this physical issue of his body, bad eyes, is the fleshly issue that Paul is referring to here, however we could not disagree more.

Paul clearly tells us in Romans 7:7-21, that he personally struggled against his flesh to overcome sin. He very specifically refers to himself when he said "I find then a law, that, when I would do good, evil is present with me."

The context of Galatian 4 is struggling against the sin of man-made doctrine, which is just another form of sin, one in which Paul could easily relate. Because of his zeal to serve YHWH according to the "traditions of the fathers" and not the Word itself, he was guilty of persecuting the people of YHWH (1Co 15:9; Gal 1:13-14; Php 3:6).

It seems clear that Paul had an issue associated to his fleshly desires, just like we all do, and this is the thorn in his flesh that kept him humble (1 Cor 12:7), and it was this fleshy issue that he struggled with when bringing the Good News of Yahushua to the people in Antioch.

When he says, "you would have plucked out your own eyes and given them to me", he was likely referring, not to problems with his physical sight, but to some fleshly desire involving his eyes, likely covetousness (Romans 7:7), which is a 'lust of the eyes' (1 John 2:16) issue.

He praises them for their lack of judgment against him in his struggles to overcome his flesh and bring the Good News of Yahushua to them.

**Gal 4:16**      So then, have I become your enemy, speaking truth to you?

Has Paul now become the enemy of those who had once loved him because he's confronting their error with the truth?

**Gal 4:17**      They are ardent towards you, for no good, but they wish to shut you out, that you might be ardent towards them.

**THEY**, is a reference to those "certain men" that had come from Yahudah to spy out their freedom and draw them away from the truth of Messiah. These men had zeal for the believers in Galatia, but not for their good.

These men, false teachers, were teaching the brothers at Galatia doctrines that would shut them out of the belief so that they had nowhere else to turn but to these false teachers.

These teachers wanted the people to be zealous for them and their teachings and not for Yahushua Messiah. They wanted the people dependent on them, just like the heads of every religious group stand as "pillars" for the layman to trust in.

This idea that there are men in the assembly who are heads above the people, like bishops and cardinals and popes, is a doctrine of the Nikolaites (Nicolaitans).

> **Nicolaitans:** stg's #**G3531** "Nikolaitēs", from **G3532** which comes from two words meaning (**G3534**) a conquest and (**G2004**) to arrange upon. Refers to being victorious over the people.

The "teaching of the Nikolaites" is something the Messiah says He "hates" (Rev 2:15). There is only ONE Authority and that is YHWH, who has granted all power and authority to His Son, Yahushua.

> **Gal 4:18** And it is good always to be ardent in what is good, and not only when I am present with you.
>
> **Gal 4:19** My little children, for whom I am again in birth pains until Messiah is formed in you,
>
> **Gal 4:20** even now I wish to be present with you and to change my voice, for I have doubts about you.

"It is good to be ardent in what is good." What in the Scripture is called "good"?

1. Messiah said that there was none good but the Father (Matthew 19:17; Mark 10:18).
2. Paul says that the Law/Torah is good (Romans 7:12).
3. Mosheh (Moses), speaking of the Torah

646

said, it is "life and good".

| Deu 30:11 | "For this command which I am commanding you today, **it is not too hard for you, nor is it far off.** |
| Deu 30:12 | "It is not in the heavens, to say, 'Who shall ascend into the heavens for us, and bring it to us, and cause us to hear it, so that we do it?' |
| Deu 30:13 | "Nor is it beyond the sea, to say, 'Who shall go over the sea for us, and bring it to us, and cause us to hear it, so that we do it?' |
| Deu 30:14 | **"For the Word is very near you, in your mouth and in your heart – to do it.** |
| Deu 30:15 | "See, **I have set before you today life and good**, and death and evil, |
| Deu 30:16 | **in that I am commanding you today to love** יהוה **your Elohim, to walk in His ways, and to guard His commands, and His laws, and His right-rulings. And you shall live and increase**, and יהוה your Elohim shall bless you in the land which you go to possess. |

Paul is glad that the Galatians are zealous to do good (obey the Law/Torah) even when he is not there to supervise them, but he now desires to be with them so that he can "change his voice" because he's beginning to doubt their sincerity.

Paul is striving to train them up to the point that Messiah is "formed in them", which is a reference to them having a full understanding of what it means to be "in Messiah".

Once Messiah is formed in us, we are a shining example of Messiah in the world, full of love and mercy towards our fellow man and joyously adherent to the Law/Torah of YHWH, while trusting fully and only the Good News of Messiah through belief.

The phrase "change my voice" is a reference to his tone of voice towards them. So far in this letter, he has called them foolish, and his tone has been harsh and critical, so he wants to be with them so he can speak to them of the truth in a more compassionate tone, less aggressive.

> **Gal 4:21**  Say to me, you who wish to be **under Torah**, do you not hear the Torah?

As has been stated, the phrase "under Torah" has to do with being condemned by it, yet in this context Paul's reference to this phrase is more about trusting in the Torah, then the result of doing so.

He is basically asking all these people who want to put their trust in the Torah, if they actually understand what the Torah says, that being "of the works of Torah" means they are still under the curse of Torah, i.e., death.

We are now going to go into a passage that clearly refers to itself as allegorical.

> **Allegory:**  1: the expression by means of symbolic fictional figures and actions of truths or generalizations about human existence * a writer known for his use of *allegory*; also: an instance (as in a story or painting) of such expression * The poem is an *allegory* of love and jealousy.
> 2: a symbolic representation: EMBLEM

(https://www.merriam-webster.com/dictionary/allegory)

> **Gal 4:22**  For it has been written that Abraham had two sons, one by a female servant, the other by a free woman.
>
> **Gal 4:23**  But he who was of the female servant was born according to the flesh, and he of the free woman through promise.
>
> **Gal 4:24**  This is **allegorical**, for these are the **two covenants**: one indeed from

Mount Sinai which brings forth
slavery, which is Haḡar,

The word allegorical here comes from the Greek
word "allēgoreo" (G238) and is connected to another word
meaning "else" as in, something else. Refers to a form of
speech that sounds like one thing but means something else.

Modern scholars have thoroughly confused the
meaning of this passage, not understanding the allegory. To
understand it, we will need to clarify the elements within the
allegory that are actually factual and then compare them with
the parts of the allegory that are not factual.

Sometime after YHWH made the covenant with
Abraham in Genesis 15, his wife Sarai encouraged Abraham
to have a child with her maid servant Hagar.

| | |
|---|---|
| **Gen 16:1** | And Sarai, Aḇram's wife, had borne him no child. And she had a Mitsrian female servant whose name was Haḡar. |
| **Gen 16:2** | And Sarai said to Aḇram, "See, יהוה has kept me from bearing children. Please, go in to my female servant. It might be that I am built up by her." And Aḇram listened to the voice of Sarai. |

The child born to Abraham, through the servant
Hagar, was named Yishma'el, meaning "El hears" and then
later, in Genesis 21, Sarai gives birth to Isaac (Yitschaq),
meaning "laughter".

In Galatians 4:23, Paul says the son of the female
servants was born "according to the flesh" but that the son of
the free woman was born "through promise". Now, we must
understand what this means before we move on.

Abraham was promised that he would have a son
from his own body in Genesis 15. This was based on the
promise of YHWH, who would give him a son even though
his wife was barren, unable to bear children.

Yishma'el was born to Abraham through the
scheming of his barren wife Sarai, who saw that she was
unable to bear children of her own, convinced Abraham to
have a child through another woman, her servant Hagar.

649

This was an attempt by Abraham and Sarai to have a child through purely fleshly means, thinking to fulfill the promise of YHWH according to their own understanding.

Isaac, however, was born to Abraham through his barren wife Sarai, later called Sarah, as a fulfillment of the promise YHWH had made with him.

Yishma'el was born according to Abraham's fleshly (natural) attempt, while Isaac was born according to the promise (supernatural) of YHWH.

Paul goes on in Galatians 4:24 to say that these two sons represent two covenants.

Now, this is where modern teachers start getting off course. Paul is NOT saying that there are two covenants, one old covenant and one new covenant, as modern Christian dogma says.

He is referring to what we "trust" in, which is what the entire context of the book of Galatians is about.

Let's see verse 24 again, along with 25-26.

| | |
|---|---|
| **Gal 4:24** | This is allegorical, for these are the two covenants: one indeed from Mount Sinai which brings forth slavery, which is Haḡar, |
| **Gal 4:25** | for this Haḡar is Mount Sinai in Araḇia, and **corresponds to Yerushalayim which now is,** and is in slavery with her children. |
| **Gal 4:26** | But the Yerushalayim above is free, which is the mother of us all. |

The first thing we must ask ourselves is, does the servant Hagar actually have anything to do with Mount Sinai? The answer is no. Hagar died centuries before Yisra'el stood at the base of Mount Sinai receiving the Torah.

So, the connection of Hagar with Mount Sinai is allegorical, meaning that they are both actual events that have no real connection to one another but are used together to teach a spiritual principle.

We have already been told that the son of Hagar represents a "fleshly" attempt to fulfill the promise of YHWH. We have already seen that the entire book of

Galatians is about what we are "trusting" in to be justified from death.

This allegory harkens back to what Paul said in chapter 3, concerning the two options of being "of Abraham" or of being "of the works of Law/Torah".

Those who are of the belief of Abraham, refers to those who are trusting in Yahushua Messiah for justification, while those who are trusting in the works of Law/Torah are those who shall be cursed by the Law/Torah (Galatians 3:7-10).

Hagar represents those who are attempting to be justified through the works of the Law/Torah, which is why Paul associates her to Mount Sinai. She, symbolically, represents the fleshly attempt to justify ourselves by the works of the Law/Torah.

Hagar was a female servant (slave) and Paul teaches that those who are trusting in the Torah are under the curse, or in bondage to sin and death.

Paul goes on to connect Hagar and the Yerushalayim that existed in his time, i.e., religious Judaism that taught adherence to the Torah as a means of acceptance.

**REMEMBER**, the book of Galatians was written to answer the question "by what are we saved" because certain men from Judea had come to Antioch telling the Gentiles that they had to do the works of the Law/Torah, **TO BE SAVED**.

Paul is using this allegory to distinguish, in the minds of believers, the difference in trusting in our own fleshly attempts to obey the Law/Torah and trusting in the work of Yahushua Messiah.

What Paul is **NOT** saying is that the "old covenant" (Old Testament) no longer applies to believers today because we are under the "new covenant" (New Testament).

Paul is not saying that there are two covenants by which man can find redemption but that there are two ways men are attempting to find justification from death, one by works and one by belief.

As Paul has already said, "by the works of the Law/Torah no flesh shall be justified". This is about justification from death and **NOT** about how we live as justified people. The Torah was **NEVER** given to us to justify us from death, it was given to us to teach us how to live righteously before YHWH.

Because we believers have placed our trust firmly and completely in YHWH, through belief in His Son Yahushua Messiah, we are no longer in bondage to sin and death but have become children of the free woman, i.e., Sarah, and are citizens of the Yerushalayim that is above.

Once again, the context is how we escape the bondage of sin and death that we were in because of our past disobedience.

It is only through belief in Yahushua Messiah that we escaped condemnation and gain access to the Yerushalayim of YHWH, **IF** we offer our bodies as a living sacrifice, holy and acceptable to YHWH, through obedience to His Torah, which is the least we can do for what He has done for us (Rom 12:1-2).

| | |
|---|---|
| **Gal 4:27** | For it has been written, "Rejoice, O barren, you who do not bear! Break forth and shout, you who do not have birth pains! For the deserted one has many more children than she who has a husband." |
| **Gal 4:28** | And we, brothers, as Yitshaq was, are children of promise. |
| **Gal 4:29** | But, as he who was *born* according to the flesh then persecuted him born according to the Spirit, so also now. |

Paul is assuring us that, just as Yishma'el mocked Isaac, so too were the religious Jews of his time, who are trusting in the Law/Torah, mocking and persecuting the believers in Yahushua Messiah.

In these Last Days, those who are not of the truth, but think they are, shall persecute and destroy those who are of the truth.

| | |
|---|---|
| **Gal 4:30** | But what does the Scripture say? **"Cast out the female servant and her son, for the son of the female servant shall by no means be heir with the son of the free woman."** |

**Gal 4:31** Therefore, brothers, we are not children of the female servant but of the free woman.

This Belief is all about where you place your TRUST and the 'laws' you obey are PROOF of what you say. No matter how well you obey the Torah, if your trust is not in Yahushua Messiah OR if you claim to believe in Him but refuse to obey the Torah of the Father, then you shall be cast out as well.

# Chapter 5: Galatians 5-6

**Gal 5:1**  In the freedom with which Messiah
has made us free, stand firm, then,
and do not again be held with a yoke
of slavery.

In what way did Messiah make us free? He made us
free from the penalty for sin, which is death. He freed us
from the condemnation prescribed by Torah for those who
disobey it.

Paul tells us to stand firm in this freedom, no longer
being held with a yoke of slavery, which is the
condemnation of death.

How are we again held with a yoke of slavery? Two
ways:

1. Begin trusting and boasting in the
   Law/Torah instead of Yahushua.
2. Sin (disobey the Law/Torah) willfully
   (Hebrews 6:4-8; 10:26-31)

This is how Paul followed up his teaching in chapter
4. He told us that we were no longer sons of the
bondwoman, but sons of the free woman and in 5:1, he tells
us to remain there steadfastly.

**Gal 5:2**  See, I, Paul, say to you that if you
become circumcised, Messiah shall
be of no use to you.

**Gal 5:3**  And I witness again to every man
being circumcised that he is a debtor
to do the entire Torah.

**Gal 5:4**  You who are **declared right by
Torah** have severed yourselves
from Messiah, you have fallen from
favour.

Modern Christian teachers use this section to teach
that believers in the Messiah no longer need to be
circumcised, even though the Law/Torah says that
circumcision is for both the native born and the stranger who
are part of the household of Abraham.

To understand what Paul is saying, we have to understand the context of Galatians, again, which is being "circumcised, according to the practice of Mosheh" **TO BE SAVED**.

This reference to being "saved", concerns justification from death.

To be accepted into the household of the belief one must first believe in Yahushua Messiah for justification from death.

Once this has happened, that person is free to join the assembly and learn the ways of Torah and how to live by them, which is what Acts 15 is actually saying.

Here in Galatians 5, it sounds as if Paul is saying that when a believer gets circumcised they are now debtors to the entire Torah, because they have severed themselves from Messiah.

Yes, that is what it sounds like he is saying, which is why the church today thinks it's what he means, unfortunately that is NOT what he is saying.

He is saying, those who get circumcised according to the command of the Law/Torah, **to be declared right or justified by it**, have become debtors to obey the whole Torah, because they have severed themselves from Messiah.

This is another example of Paul's intellectualism being misunderstood. He is **NOT** telling people that they should no longer be circumcised or that they should no longer circumcise their children, he's telling them that if they put their TRUST in circumcision, then they have fallen from favor (grace).

Once again, the discussion is about what we are trusting in; and "if" our trust is in anything other than Yahushua Messiah, we have condemned ourselves again. This has nothing to do with how we live after we believe in Messiah.

Circumcision is an act of obedience done **AFTER** justification and not something we do **TO BE JUSTIFIED**. Just as most modern teachers believe that baptism is something that a believer does after his confession of Yahushua as Messiah, so too is circumcision.

Circumcision is something that people within the household of Abraham, which believers are according to Paul, do as a sign of their spiritual heritage.

Yes, the circumcision that YHWH is actually after is that of the heart (Rom 2:28-29), however, physical circumcision is a sign of the covenant. What, then, is Paul saying?

He is saying that any attempt to obey the Law/Torah as a means of justification is futile and a sign that we have transferred our trust from Messiah to works of the Law/Torah, which can only bring us back under the curse of death (Galatians 3:10).

| | |
|---|---|
| **Gal 5:5** | For we, in Spirit, by belief, eagerly wait for the expectation of righteousness. |
| **Gal 5:6** | For in Messiah יהושע neither circumcision nor uncircumcision has any strength, but belief working through love. |

Once again, the word spirit here should be small case, referring to our spirit and not the Spirit of YHWH, and refers to our position in Messiah, because of our belief.

It says, that we "eagerly wait" the expectation (hope) of righteousness. So, the righteousness that we receive from Yahushua Messiah is something that we are still hoping for, something in the future.

He goes on to say, neither circumcision nor uncircumcision has any strength but he prefaced that by saying "in Messiah".

Circumcision has no redeeming value in and of itself, redemption is only achieved through belief in Yahushua Messiah and no work of the Law/Torah changes that.

However, circumcision is a command of the Law/Torah for those who are in the household of Abraham (Genesis 17), whether stranger or native born, and Paul says our strength is "belief working through love".

Our belief must be "working" and that work must be done from a heart of love.

Here we see the *Two-Part Principle*, belief (spiritual part) and works (physical part) through the binding element (heart condition/attitude) of love.

In 1st Corinthians 13, the love chapter, Paul told believers that at this time we see through a glass darkly, meaning that we don't have full understanding, but then, when we are face-to-face with Him, we will know even as we are known (12).

Then he says:    And now belief, expectation, and love remain - these three. But the greatest of these is love (1Co 13:13**).**

Again, we see the *Two-Part Principle* at work.

1.    Belief is the spiritual part,
2.    Expectation (hope) is why we do the work, which is the physical part,
3.    Love is the binding element or attitude in which we do all things.

**1Jn 2:6**        The one who says he stays **in Him** ought himself also to **walk, even as He walked.**

Here we see the two parts; being in Him, in the belief (spiritual part) and walking as He walked, in obedience to the Law/Torah (physical part).

**1Jn 2:9**        The one who says he is in the light, and hates his brother, is in the darkness until now.
                                    ***
**1Jn 2:11**       But the one who hates his brother is in the darkness and walks in the darkness, and does not know where he is going, because the darkness has blinded his eyes.
                                    ***
**1Jn 4:20**       If someone says, "I love Elohim," and hates his brother, he is a liar. For the one not loving his brother whom he has seen, how is he able to love Elohim whom he has not seen?

An attitude of love completes the work of Messiah in us, it's the last piece that needs to be put in place to make us like Him. It's interesting that the word "light" is used in 1 John 2:9 to contrast hate and darkness, because love is light.

If we go back to Genesis 1:1 we see that YHWH created the "heavens and the earth", i.e., spiritual things and physical things, the *Two-Part Principle*. However, before He did any other creative work, YHWH brought forth light (v. 3).

Light has to do with revelation, because through it we see or perceive things. Love is light in the heart of the believer, because it is only through it that we can see Him or be like Him.

| | |
|---|---|
| **1Jn 4:7** | Beloved ones, let us love one another, because love is of Elohim, and everyone who loves has been born of Elohim, and knows Elohim. |
| **1Jn 4:8** | The one who does not love does not know Elohim, for Elohim is love. |
| | *** |
| **Gal 5:7** | You were running well, who held you back from obeying the truth? |
| **Gal 5:8** | That persuasion does not come from Him who calls you. |
| **Gal 5:9** | A little leaven leavens all the lump. |

What truth? The truth that Yahushua is the only way to the Father (John 14:6) and that no amount of works of Torah, including circumcision, can make us right before Him (Rom 3:20).

Any idea or teaching that requires Torah obedience, of any kind, as a means of justification from death, is not of Yahushua or the Father.

However, any idea or teaching that declares a belief that is NOT accompanied by the works of the Law/Torah, is not of Yahushua or the Father as well (James 2:14-26) .

The truth is, we are declared right or justified by the favor (grace) of YHWH, through our belief in Yahushua Messiah and that in Him, as His disciples, we have an obligation to walk in obedience to the "Good Works" of the Law/Torah, which the Father prepared before Messiah's coming that all his people should live by (Ephesians 2:8-11).

Any other doctrine is a lie and the Scripture refers to it as leaven.

| | | |
|---|---|---|
| **Leaven:** | 1 a: | a substance (such as yeast) |

658

used to produce fermentation in dough or a liquid; especially: SOURDOUGH.

b:    a material (such as baking powder) used to produce a gas that lightens dough or batter

2:    Something that modifies or lightens

(https://www.merriam-webster.com/dictionary/leaven)

Scripturally, leaven represents false doctrine, a doctrine that **modifies or lightens**, i.e., adds to or takes away from, the totality of what Scripture teaches about any given subject.

Paul says, even a little leaven (false doctrine) leavens/contaminates the entire thing, and the Scripture tells us to get the leaven out of our houses, our life, our doctrine et al…

**1Co 5:7**    Therefore cleanse out the old leaven, so that you are a new lump, as you are unleavened. For also Messiah our Pĕsaḥ was slaughtered for us.

\*\*\*

**Gal 5:10**    I trust in you, in the Master, that you shall have no other mind. And he who is troubling you shall bear his judgment, whoever he is.

This person troubling them is a reference to the "false brothers" of 2:4.

**Gal 5:11**    And I, brothers, if I still proclaim circumcision, why am I still persecuted? Then the stumbling-block of the stake has been set aside.

659

Paul is referring to himself as having once proclaimed circumcision as a means of acceptance, for which he was esteemed by those in his former religion, but that now he teaches the death, burial and resurrection of Yahushua Messiah as the only means of justification (acceptance).

He states, if he still proclaimed circumcision (as a means of acceptance) than the stake of Messiah, which is the stumbling block for the Jews, because of their trust in the Law/Torah, has been set aside.

There's only one way to be justified and that Way is Yahushua Messiah.

| | |
|---|---|
| **Gal 5:12** | O that those who disturb you would even cut themselves off! |
| **Gal 5:13** | For you, brothers, have been called to freedom, only do not use freedom as an occasion for the flesh, but through love serve one another. |
| **Gal 5:14** | For the entire Torah is completed in one word, in this, **"You shall love your neighbour as yourself."** |

The freedom that Paul is referring to, is a duality of freedom, meaning that we are free from the condemnation of death imposed on us by the Law/Torah for our disobedience because of the blood of Yahushua Messiah and from the dogma of man-made religion.

However, being free from these things does not allow us to just live anyway we want according to our own fleshly desires, because the flesh cannot please Elohim (Romans 8:7) and those of us who walk according flesh shall die (Romans 8:13).

As brethren, we are to serve one another in an attitude of love, the binding element, because we complete the Law/Torah when we love our neighbor as ourselves.

Loving someone is a fulfillment of the Law/Torah but it does not do away with the Law/Torah, for the Law/Torah teaches us how to love our neighbor as ourselves.

It is false doctrine to say, "if I love someone with all my heart, then I no longer have to obey the Law/Torah, because I fulfilled it".

This statement is predicated on the idea that we, as human beings, understand how to love one another properly, which is not the case, because our flesh is desperately wicked and selfish. The only way that we can love someone properly is to love them according to the instruction of the Law/Torah.

You cannot say that you love someone but treat them in a way that is contrary to the Torah because the Torah is how we love one another. If you love your neighbor you will not do any evil towards him, like murder him or steal his wife or slander him or any other such sin against a person.

| Gal 5:15 | And if you bite and devour one another, beware lest you be consumed by one another! |
|---|---|

This is a very good piece of advice, because it's only a matter of time before our hate for one another boils over and through it we destroy our lives, and ultimately suffer the destruction of the Lake of Fire.

| Gal 5:16 | And I say: **Walk in the Spirit**, and you shall not accomplish the lust of the flesh. |
|---|---|

As stated above, the word spirit here should be small case, referring to our spirit man.

This phrase, "walk in the spirit, and you shall not accomplish the lust of the flesh" is a repeat of something Paul said earlier in Romans 8:13, where he said " if by the spirit you put to death the deeds of the body, you shall live".

Remember, the words "flesh" and "body" in Romans 8 are synonymous with one another and refer to the outer fleshly man, that does not subject itself to the Law/Torah of YHWH (Romans 8:7).

The word "spirit" refers to our inner spiritual man, that delights in the Law/Torah of YHWH (Romans 7:22) and serves it (Romans 7:25).

| Gal 5:17 | For the flesh lusts against the Spirit, and the Spirit against the flesh. And these are opposed to each other, so |
|---|---|

that you do not do what you desire to do.

This verse is a reference to what Paul said in Romans 7:7-21, where he states that "though I would do good, evil is present in me".

This is a reference to the principle that mankind has two minds, the spiritual mind that wishes to obey and the physical mind that wishes to disobey, and these two are at odds with one another, continually battling one another for supremacy over the body (Rom 8:1-7).

This is why Paul admonishes the brethren in Romans 12:1-2 to offer their "body" as a living sacrifice, holy and acceptable.

It is the responsibility of the spirit man that dwells within us, to take control of the physical man that would destroy us, through a heartfelt commitment to obey the Torah every day with all of our heart and mind and strength.

**Gal 5:18**    But if you are led by the Spirit, you are not under Torah.

If we are "led by the spirit ", through obedience to the Torah, we are no longer under the condemnation of Torah, when we stumble.

**Gal 5:19**    And **the works** of the flesh are well-known, which are *these*: adultery, whoring, uncleanness, indecency,
**Gal 5:20**    idolatry, drug sorcery, hatred, quarrels, jealousies, fits of rage, selfish ambitions, dissensions, factions,
**Gal 5:21**    envy, murders, drunkenness, wild parties, and the like – of which **I forewarn you**, even as I also said before, that those who practise such as these shall not inherit the reign of Elohim.

Here Paul lists many of the works of the flesh, and we highlighted the word "works" because it is going to contrast with something said later on. Here though, it refers

662

to specific things that we do, all of which are a violation of the Law/Torah.

It is interesting, that Paul is telling BELIEVERS to beware because those who practice these things "**SHALL NOT INHERIT THE KINGDOM OF ELOHIM**".

He is warning BELIEVERS, if they practice these things they will not inherit the Kingdom.

There is **NO** "once saved, always saved" doctrine in the Scripture, for all Scripture teaches one thing, that man is justified by a belief in Yahushua Messiah, and does the works of the Torah, from a heart of love.

| | |
|---|---|
| **Gal 5:22** | But **the fruit** of the Spirit is love, joy, peace, patience, kindness, goodness, trustworthiness, |
| **Gal 5:23** | gentleness, self-control. Against such there is no Torah. |

Notice, the word is "fruit", not works. This is important because the "works" of the spirit is the Law/Torah of YHWH, as we have shown in Romans 8. Paul is saying the same thing here in Galatians 5 that he said in Romans 8, concerning the flesh and the spirit.

The mind of the flesh, he said in Romans 8:7, **does not subject itself to the Law/Torah of Elohim** and neither can it, which, according to the principle of contrast, means that the mind of the spirit is subject to the Law/Torah of Elohim and can be.

| | |
|---|---|
| **Rom 7:22** | For I delight in the Torah of Elohim according to the inward man, |
| **Rom 7:23** | but I see another torah in my members, battling against the torah of my mind, and bringing me into captivity to the torah of sin which is in my members. |
| **Rom 7:24** | Wretched man that I am! Who shall deliver me from this body of death? |
| **Rom 7:25** | Thanks to Elohim, through יהושע Messiah our Master! So then, **with the mind I myself truly serve the Torah of Elohim**, but with the flesh the torah of sin. |

Paul is referring to the intent of our heart. He is committed to walk in obedience to the Torah of YHWH with all his heart and mind and strength, as commanded in the Torah. However, his body desires to serve disobedience, the result of which is death, and he is in continual battle with this other side of himself.

He shall gain the victory, because though his body wishes to do evil, his heart is committed to walk in obedience to the Torah. It is because of his heartfelt intent to obey the Law/Torah that the blood of Messiah will cover him when he stumbles.

This is the doctrine Paul is teaching the brethren. He is not telling them they no longer have to obey the Law/Torah, he's just saying that you can't put your trust in it, because if you trust in it, it will destroy you.

To place your trust in the Law/Torah, is to place yourself in a position of having to obey every single letter of it perfectly, every day of your life, without fail, or be condemned to eternal death when you fail, and you will!

Paul's position is, if we place in our trust in Yahushua Messiah and strive with all of our heart to obey the Law/Torah completely, every day of our life, then we will not be condemned by the Law/Torah when we fail.

In both these scenarios, it is a requirement to obey the Law/Torah, all the Law/Torah, with all our heart, mind and strength, but only in one of these scenarios are we protected from condemnation if we stumble and violate one of the principles of Law/Torah. And…that scenario is the one of belief.

When we are walking in the belief of Yahushua Messiah, through obedience to the Law/Torah of YHWH, our spirit will produce in us these gifts; love, joy, peace, patience, kindness, goodness, trustworthiness, gentleness, self-control.

These gifts represent the character of Messiah and as we grow into the fullness of Messiah through obedience to the Torah, as He did, this character will be formed in us.

**Note**:    There is a misconception among Christians concerning the character of Messiah, for they wrongly believe that He was the way

He was because He is the Son of YHWH, but this is not true.

Yes, He is the Son of YHWH, but that had no bearing on the development of His character. His Sonship meant that He was born without the curse of death on Him, which the rest of us inherit from Adam. Since He had no human father that curse did not apply to Him.

The development of His character happened the same exact way our character is developed once we believe, through the renewing of our mind, the washing of the Word, i.e., obedience to the Torah.

Messiah was born into a household where both His mother and human stepfather were declared to be righteous by YHWH. The ONLY way YHWH could have declared them to be "righteous" people is if they had exhibited a trust in Him that was lived out in obedience to the Torah from a sincere heart.

It is that kind of household that produced a man with the character described in Galatians 5, and by following His example that same character can be formed in us.

There is no command in the Law/Torah that requires us to act in any way contrary to these fruits of the Spirit, in fact it teaches us how to live in them.

**Gal 5:24**   And those who are of Messiah have impaled the flesh with its passions and the desires.

Here we see Paul saying the same thing he said in Romans 6, concerning our having died with Messiah through baptism and further alludes to Romans 12:1-2.

As Messiah gave His body up to die to pay our sin debt, so are we to consider this body dead to its own desires, that we may use the members of this body for righteous purposes, in obedience to the Law/Torah.

| | |
|---|---|
| **Gal 5:25** | If we live in the Spirit, let us also walk in the Spirit. |

If we can claim to be believers in Messiah, then we are in the spirit, for through Him our spirit man has been made alive again and as such we should live out our lives according to the guidance of our spirit man, which delights in the Law/Torah (Romans 7:22) and serves it (Romans 7:25).

When we do this, the fruit of the spirit is born in us, and then His Spirit will cry out on our behalf when we do not know what to say (Romans 8:26-27).

| | |
|---|---|
| **Gal 5:26** | Let us not become conceited, provoking one another, envying one another. |

This again, is very good advice, and is something that all of us should be very careful of in our interaction with other people. However, this verse was not placed here simply as good advice, it was placed here as a contextual lead into chapter 6.

## Chapter 6

The context of chapter 6 is going to be about how we interact with one another, and Paul instructs us to not be conceited, not to provoke one another and not to envy one another.

Let's keep this in mind as we move forward in chapter 6.

| | |
|---|---|
| **Gal 6:1** | Brothers, if a man is overtaken in some trespass, you the spiritual ones, set such a one straight in a spirit of meekness, looking at yourself lest you be tried too. |
| **Gal 6:2** | Bear one another's burdens, and so complete the Torah of Messiah. |

666

**Gal 6:3**    For if anyone thinks himself to be somebody, when he is not, he deceives himself.

Paul is instructing the brothers on counseling one another, specifically a brother that is struggling with sin in his life.

He instructs the "spiritual ones" to give counsel to this brother. There are a lot of people out there that consider themselves spiritual people, however, being a "spiritual one", according to the Scripture, refers to a believer who is living in a very specific way.

In Romans 7:14, Paul calls the Law/Torah, "spiritual". From Paul's point of view, it is impossible to call oneself "spiritual" if one is not walking according to the Law/Torah of YHWH.

As we have mentioned numerous times in this book, the "new covenant" promise to believers consisted of a few specific things.

**Jer 31:31**    "See, the days are coming," declares יהוה, **"when I shall make a renewed covenant with the house of Yisra'ĕl and with the house of Yehudah,**

**Jer 31:32**    not like the covenant I made with their fathers in the day when I strengthened their hand to bring them out of the land of Mitsrayim, My covenant which they broke, though I was a husband to them," declares יהוה.

**Jer 31:33**    "For this is the covenant I shall make with the house of Yisra'ĕl after those days, declares יהוה: **I shall put My Torah in their inward parts, and write it on their hearts.** And I shall be their Elohim, and they shall be My people.

**Jer 31:34**    "And no longer shall they teach, each one his neighbour, and each one his brother, saying, 'Know יהוה,' for they shall all know Me, from the least of them to the greatest of them," declares יהוה. "For I shall forgive their crookedness, and remember their sin no more."

... And,

| | |
|---|---|
| **Eze 36:22** | "Therefore say to **the house of Yisra'ěl**, 'Thus said the Master יהוה, "I do not do this for your sake, O house of Yisra'ěl, but for My set-apart Name's sake, which you have profaned among the nations wherever you went. |
| **Eze 36:23** | "And I shall set apart My great Name, which has been profaned among the nations, which you have profaned in their midst. And the nations shall know that I am יהוה," declares the Master יהוה, "when I am set-apart in you before their eyes. |
| **Eze 36:24** | "And I shall take you from among the nations, and I shall gather you out of all lands, and I shall bring you into your own land. |
| **Eze 36:25** | **"And I shall sprinkle clean water on you, and you shall be clean** – from all your filthiness and from all your idols I cleanse you. |
| **Eze 36:26** | "And **I shall give you a new heart** and **put a new spirit within you**. And I shall take the heart of stone out of your flesh, and I shall give you a heart of flesh, |
| **Eze 36:27** | and **put My Spirit within you. And I shall cause you to walk in My laws and guard My right-rulings and shall do them.** |

Now, if we look closely, this new or renewed covenant that YHWH has promised is to the house of Yisra'el and the House of Yahudah, not some Gentile Church.

The church today might try to convince you that this new covenant spoken of by Jeremiah (Yirmeyahu) is

668

different than the one the church clings to, but that's not true. The new covenant promise was always for the people of Yisra'el and to any stranger (Gentile) that would join them (Numbers 15:15-16).

Next, notice that the Law/Torah would be placed in their inner parts and that the Law/Torah would be written upon their heart.

Now, did YHWH mean that He was really going to open their chests and place a copy of the Law/Torah inside them or was He going to literally write it on the surface of their heart?

No, of course not. If we look carefully at what it says here in Jeremiah and Ezekiel (Yeḥezqěl), we will see what YHWH intends us to understand.

The "inner parts" in Jeremiah is the same thing as the "new spirit" in Ezekiel, so the new covenant was going to make new our spirit man and place within him a desire for the Torah.

Remember what Paul said in Romans 7:22?

**Rom 7:22**     For I delight in the Torah of Elohim according to the inward man,

**Note:**   This is a partial quote by Paul from Psalms 119.

**Psa 119:9**     **How would a young man cleanse his path?** To guard it according to Your word.

**Psa 119:10**    I have sought You **with all my heart**; Let me not stray from Your commands!

**Psa 119:11**    **I have treasured up Your word in my heart, That I might not sin against You.**

**Psa 119:12**    Blessed are You, O יהוה! Teach me Your laws.

**Psa 119:13**    With my lips I have recounted All the right-rulings of Your mouth.

**Psa 119:14**    I have rejoiced in the way of Your witnesses, As over all riches.

**Psa 119:15**    I meditate on Your orders, And regard Your ways.

**Psa 119:16**    I delight myself in Your laws; I do not forget Your word.

**Note**:    This passage starts out by asking, "How would a young man cleanse his path" and the Word is the answer. The Torah of YHWH is the path we walk to be clean (righteous) before YHWH, and it has nothing to do with how we are made right or justified FROM sin and death.

Next, we see the heart is mentioned in both Jeremiah and Ezekiel, and that the Law/Torah would be written on the surface of our heart, a heart that had been turned from stone (hard and rebellious) to flesh (soft and pliable/obedient).

Lastly, we are told that YHWH would put His Spirit within us and He would "cause you to walk in My laws and guard My right-rulings and shall do them".

The "new covenant" has to do with cleansing us from past sin and making us alive again in the inner man with a new heart to obey the Law/Torah of YHWH, through belief in Yahushua Messiah.

So, a "spiritual" man is one who has been cleansed from past sin through belief in Yahushua Messiah and cleanses his path daily through obedience to the Law/Torah of YHWH.

Once again we see the *Two-Part Principle* at work, belief plus obedience equals spiritual completeness.

Paul goes on in Galatians 6:1 to advise this "spiritual one" to "set straight" the wayward brother with a " spirit of meekness, looking at yourself lest you be tried too".

Correcting a brother should be done in meekness, judging our own attitude first. Why would Paul instruct us to look at ourselves first, lest we be tried also?

Many teachers today might say that Paul is referring to falling into the same type of sin the brother was involved in or falling into sin of any kind due to the brothers influence. However, we must remember what is the context of the passage.

The last thing Paul instructed us in chapter 5. was not to be conceited. This is what he's warning the "spiritual one" to be careful of when setting the other brother straight.

670

This is proven out in verse 3 when he warns about someone thinking himself to be something when he's not. Paul is warning the "spiritual one" to look within himself and to be humble, so that he doesn't place himself above the brother as if he was better than them.

In verse 2 he told us to bear one another's burdens and by doing so we would complete the Torah of Messiah.

Don't get this twisted, because many people have. There is no difference between the Law/Torah of YHWH in the Tanak and the Torah of Messiah mentioned here by Paul
.

Paul uses this language to express the point that we, as brethren, should be willing to sacrifice of ourselves for a brother, just as Messiah sacrificed Himself for us.

Consider what Brother John (Yochanan) had to say about this matter.

| | |
|---|---|
| **1Jn 3:16** | By this we have known love, because He laid down His life for us. And we ought to lay down *our* lives for the brothers. |

***

| | |
|---|---|
| **Gal 6:4** | But let each one examine his own work, and then he shall have boasting in himself alone, and not in another. |
| **Gal 6:5** | For each one shall bear his own burden. |

First he tells us to examine our own work, which is the same thing he said earlier about looking at ourselves. This is sound judgment considering what else he has said about judging ourselves.

| | |
|---|---|
| **1Co 11:31** | For if we were to examine ourselves, we would not be judged. |

Next Paul says something that seems to contradict other things he has said. After telling us that a man should examine his own work, he goes on to say "he shall have boasting in himself alone, and not in another. For each one shall bear his own burden."

Has not Paul told us, on numerous occasions, that our boasting must always be in Yahushua and in Him alone? Why then does he now say that a man would have "boasting in himself alone, and not another"?

Paul is not saying that we should ever boast in our work, however, he is saying that we should examine our own work, because we will not be able to compare our works to anyone else's at the judgment.

You've all heard this; someone sees a brother sinning and points their finger saying, "At least I'm not like him".

In the first three verses Paul told us, we should bear each other's burdens and then in the next three verses he tells us, each of us must bear our own burden, and the contrast between these two is what this teaching's about.

We should all be willing to bear the burden of another brother's struggles and yet we never want to place ourselves over that brother in any way, shape or form, because if we do we must stand before the Father and answer for it; that other brother is not going to be there on judgment day to compare ourselves to.

**Gal 6:6**     And let him who is instructed in the Word share in all that is good, with him who is instructing.

Now, this does not necessarily mean that the person who is being instructed in the Word should pay the person instructing, as some would have us believe.

Yes, it is true that within the totality of Scripture there is a place for those who are learning the Scripture to make some type of provision for those who are teaching the Word, however, it is not necessarily what is being referred to here

It is our belief, that what is being said in verse 6 must be understood within the general context of this passage.

That being said, the phrase "all that is good" is associated to the good that comes from the counsel given by the "spiritual" brother to the brother that is struggling.

To be clear, it was expected among the brotherhood in the 1st century, for the local congregation to make provision for any brother or brothers that had traveled to their location for the purpose of teaching or ministry, and so should it be now, if possible.

| | |
|---|---|
| **Gal 6:7** | Do not be led astray: Elohim is not mocked, for whatever a man sows, that he shall also reap. |
| **Gal 6:8** | Because he who sows to his own flesh shall reap corruption from the flesh, but he who sows to the Spirit shall reap everlasting life from the Spirit. |

Verse 7 is a clear warning to all believers, even today, but was specifically to the spiritual brother about thinking himself better than his brother, for whatever reason.

Conceit, provocation and envy are all attitudes of the heart that prove a lack of love and compassion for a brother and, as Brother John said so clearly:

| | |
|---|---|
| **1Jn 3:14** | We know that we have passed out of death into life, because we love the brothers. **The one not loving his brother stays in death**. |
| **1Jn 3:15** | Everyone hating his brother is a murderer, and you know that no murderer has everlasting life staying in him. |

Though verse 7 must be understood in the context, it is a general principle throughout all of Scripture that the way a person lives their life determines their judgment. So, if a person sows' disobedience, his disobedience shall reap death.

Verse 8 carries on the theme, but unfortunately the translators capitalized the word "spirit" both times it was used, when they shouldn't have.

**REMEMBER**, the *Two-Part Principle* is at work everywhere all the time, and Paul refers to it here when he, talking to believers, says that if we sow to the flesh we shall reap corruption (death) from the flesh. Why?

| | |
|---|---|
| **Rom 8:6** | For the **mind of the flesh is death**,... |

| **Rom 8:7** | Because the mind of the flesh is enmity towards Elohim, for **it does not subject itself to the Torah** of Elohim, neither indeed is it able, |
|---|---|

*** 

| **Rom 8:13** | For if you live according to the flesh, **you are going to die**;... |
|---|---|

**Compare:**

| **1Jn 3:4** | Everyone doing sin also does lawlessness, and **sin is lawlessness** .(Not obeying the Law/Torah) |
|---|---|

*** 

| **Rom 6:23** | For the **wages of sin is death**,... |
|---|---|

Paul goes on to say, if we sow to the spirit, we shall reap from the spirit, why?

| **Rom 8:6** | ...but the **mind of the Spirit is life** and peace. |
|---|---|

| **Rom 8:13** | ...; but if by the Spirit you put to death the deeds of the body, you shall live. |
|---|---|

It's very simple, we were all guilty of sin and deserve death because we had not obeyed the Law/Torah of YHWH and because we inherited the curse of death from our father Adam, who also did not obey the command of YHWH.

Messiah came and died to redeem us from the curse of death that the Law/Torah required for anyone who disobeyed it.

Those who believe in Yahushua Messiah have been redeemed from the curse of death and been born again in the inner man (spirit man) which delights in the Law/Torah of YHWH (Romans 7:22) and serves it (Romans 7:25).

The new believer that walks in the spirit, through obedience to the Law/Torah, with all of his heart and mind and strength, will reap eternal life.

This is the essence of the *Two-Part Principle*, belief + Torah obedience = life.

| | |
|---|---|
| **Gal 6:9** | And let us not lose heart in **doing good**, for in due season we shall reap if we do not grow weary. |

Again, Paul admonishes us to obey the Law/Torah!

| | |
|---|---|
| **Deu 30:11** | "For this command which I am commanding you today, it is not too hard for you, nor is it far off. |
| **Deu 30:12** | "It is not in the heavens, to say, 'Who shall ascend into the heavens for us, and bring it to us, and cause us to hear it, so that we do it?' |
| **Deu 30:13** | "Nor is it beyond the sea, to say, 'Who shall go over the sea for us, and bring it to us, and cause us to hear it, so that we do it?' |
| **Deu 30:14** | "For the Word is very near you, in your mouth and in your heart – **to do it.** |
| **Deu 30:15** | **"See, I have set before you today life and good, and death and evil,** |
| **Deu 30:16** | in that I am commanding you today to love יהוה your Elohim, to walk in His ways, and to guard His commands, and His laws, and His right-rulings. **And you shall live and increase,** and יהוה your Elohim shall bless you in the land which you go to possess. |
| **Deu 30:17** | "**But** if your heart turns away, **and you do not obey,** and shall be drawn away, and shall bow down to other mighty ones and serve them, |
| **Deu 30:18** | "I have declared to you today that **you shall certainly perish,** you shall not prolong your days in the land which you are passing over the Yardĕn to enter and possess. |
| **Deu 30:19** | "I have called the heavens and the earth as witnesses today against you: I have set before you life and |

|  | death, the blessing and the curse. Therefore you shall **choose life**, so that you live, both you and your seed, |
|---|---|
| **Deu 30:20** | to love יהוה your Elohim, to obey His voice, and to cling to Him – for He is your life and the length of your days – to dwell in the land which יהוה swore to your fathers, to Abraham, to Yitsḥaq, and to Yaʿaqoḇ, to give them." |

To Paul, and all the Messianic writers, "doing good" is just another way of telling us to obey the Law/Torah.

***

| **Gal 6:10** | So then, as we have occasion, **let us do good to all**, especially to those who are of the household of the belief. |
|---|---|

It is our duty as believers in Yahushua Messiah to live our lives in the same way He lived His, in complete obedience to the Law/Torah of YHWH with all of our heart, mind and strength. To be kind and selfless in our interactions with other people, both those of the belief and those outside of it.

| **Gal 6:11** | See with what big letters I have written to you with my own hand! |
|---|---|
| **Gal 6:12** | **As many as wish to make a good show in the flesh, these compel you to be circumcised**, only so that they should not be persecuted for the stake of Messiah. |
| **Gal 6:13** | For those who are circumcised do not even watch over the Torah, but they wish to have you circumcised **so that they might boast in your flesh**. |

Again, Paul 's teaching concerning circumcision in this chapter, was not to say that new believers should not be circumcised, only that circumcision is not something to be trusted in.

He is referring to those people that had come from Yehudah saying that Gentiles had to be circumcised "**TO BE SAVED**" (Acts 15:1).

The phrase, "wish to make a good show in the flesh" is a roundabout way of saying they've placed their trust in circumcision, because they want to be able to say, "See I've been circumcised", as if it had eternal value.

Paul says that these people, those who trust in the circumcision of the flesh, compelled Gentiles to be circumcised so that they themselves would not be persecuted for teaching the true "Good News" of Yahushua Messiah, which is acceptance by belief only and not works of the Law/Torah.

He goes on to say, even those who would compel the Gentiles to be circumcised did not keep the rest of the Torah, which is a clue that these people were trusting in circumcision.

Lastly, they provoke the Gentiles to be circumcised so that they can boast in the work they had done among the Gentiles.

| | |
|---|---|
| **Gal 6:14** | And for me, let it not be that I should boast except in the stake of our Master יהושע Messiah, through whom the world has been impaled to me, and I to the world. |
| **Gal 6:15** | For in Messiah יהושע neither circumcision nor uncircumcision has any strength, but a renewed creature. |

Again, Paul is **NOT** saying that believers should not be circumcised, he's just saying that circumcision has no redemptive strength. Being circumcised does not save you, it is a work of belief.

Circumcision is an act done AFTER we come into the household to show that we are part of the household, it's a sign that we are children of Abraham.

Paul emphasizes our need to boast in the work of Messiah, which is evidence that what he said before concerning those who make a "good show" in the flesh had to do with boasting in or trusting in circumcision.

Paul's reference here to a renewed creature, is a reference to the inner man, NOT the whole man, because the outer man is still condemned to death (Romans 8:3).

The way Paul framed this verse may suggest, though circumcision has no strength, it is evidence of the renewed man, just as circumcision is a sign that we are of the household of Yisra'el, the children of Abraham.

> **Gal 6:16**    And as many as walk according to this rule, peace and compassion be upon them, and upon the Yisra'ĕl of Elohim.

Walk according to what rule?

1.    That our boast remains in Messiah.
2.    That we live as if we have died to the world, and it to us.
3.    That the only value we give circumcision, is that of a command of YHWH to His people, which it is a sign of.

> **Gal 6:17**    From now on let no one trouble me, for I bear in my body the scars of the Master יהושע.
>
> **Gal 6:18**    The favour of our Master יהושע Messiah be with your spirit, brothers. Amĕn.

We trust in Messiah Yahushua; we live in obedience to the Torah and love one another as He loved us

# SECTION 4

Section 4:

Hard Sayings

2 Corinthians 3

Colossians 2

Philippians 3

Food

# Hard Sayings

Among Paul's other writings, there are many passages that have been taken out of context and used to teach something contrary to the actual meaning Paul intended his readers to derive from them.

Notice what Brother Peter said concerning this matter.

| | |
|---|---|
| **2Pe 3:14** | So then, beloved ones, looking forward to this, do your utmost to be found by Him in peace, **spotless and blameless,** |
| **2Pe 3:15** | and **reckon the patience of our Master as deliverance,** as also our beloved brother Paul wrote to you, according to the wisdom given to him, |
| **2Pe 3:16** | as also in all *his* letters, speaking in them concerning these *matters*, **in which some are hard to understand,** which those who are **untaught and unstable** twist to their own destruction, as they do also the other Scriptures |
| **2Pe 3:17** | You, then, beloved ones, being forewarned, watch, **lest you also fall** from your own steadfastness, being **led away with the delusion of the lawless,** |
| **2Pe 3:18** | but grow in the favour and knowledge of our Master and Saviour יהושע Messiah. To Him be the esteem both now and to a day that abides. Amĕn. |

The first thing we notice in this passage is that Brother Peter encourages us to do our "utmost" to be found by the Messiah, "spotless and blameless".

Paul uses this phrase, or something like it, in most of his writings as a reference to how believers are to live. His desire for us is that we live in a way which is consistent with

681

the Law/Torah of YHWH, so that on the day Messiah returns the Torah has nothing in which to condemn us.

It is the Word/Torah that shall judge the thoughts and intents of our hearts on the day Yahushua administers His judgment (Heb 4:12).

Peter's reference to Messiah's patience has to do with the amount of time He waits to return. This time is evidence of His mercy, so that as many as will, can come to salvation, as well as time for us to grow into the maturity necessary to walk before Him.

Paul said something like this in Romans 2, where he admonished the knowledgeable (Jewish) believers about condemning the less knowledgeable (Gentile) brethren.

> **Rom 2:4**    Or do you despise the riches of His kindness, and tolerance, and patience, not knowing that the kindness of Elohim leads you to repentance?

Peter then talks about some of Paul's writings as hard to understand, which those who are "untaught and unstable" twist to their own destruction. Warning the rest of us not to listen to them lest we too **fall away**, being led away by the "delusion" of these "lawless" men.

> **Untaught:**    stg's #**G261** "amathēs", from a compound word meaning (G1) no, not and (G3129) to learn; *ignorant*. Refers to a person that does not have knowledge and/or understanding of any given topic.

> **Unstable:**    stg's #**G793** "astēriktos", from a compound word meaning (G1) no/not and (a presumed derivation of G4741) to set fast; *unfixed*. Refers to someone who's knowledge and/or understanding is not based firmly in some foundational truth.

Peter is telling us that these men **DO NOT** have Paul's knowledge and understanding, and the knowledge and understanding they do have is **NOT** based on the same foundational truth that Paul's was, i.e., the Torah.

Because of this, they do not read Paul's writings and understand them in the way he intended them to be understood. Instead, they read Paul's writings and make presumptions concerning what Paul meant based on their own understanding.

Lastly, Peter warns us not to be "led away" by the "delusion of the lawless". Unfortunately, most English bibles translate this phrase as "error of the wicked", which is true, but the true essence of what Peter is saying is lost in these words.

| | |
|---|---|
| **Error/Delusion:** | stg's **#G4106** "planē", feminine of **G4108** (as abstraction); objectively **fraudulence**; subjectively **a straying** from orthodoxy or piety: - deceit, to deceive, delusion, error. |

The word "planos" (G4108, the masculine form) has the meaning of "roving" (like a tramp), so from a strictly Scriptural way of thinking, this word refers to something deceitful, like an adulterous bride who strays from her husband.

| | |
|---|---|
| **Wicked/Lawless:** | stg's **#G113** "athesmos", from G1 (as a negative particle) meaning, no or not, and a derivative of G5087 (in the sense of enacting); **lawless**, that is, (by implication) criminal: - wicked. |

Together, these two words make it clear what Peter is saying, IF you let the totality of Scripture define your perspective. Peter was a Torah obedient Jew and his mindset or perspective was founded in what had been handed down to him in the Torah and the Prophets, just like Paul.

| Deu 28:14 | "And do not turn aside from **any of the Words** which I am commanding you today, right or left, **to go after other mighty ones to serve them**. |

To YHWH, turning to the right or left of ANY of His commands is the same thing as serving another Elohim, an idol. In the Tanak (OT) Yisra'el is referred to as an "Adulterous Bride" because she had fornicated with false elohim, idols.

Peter understood that any teaching of the GOOD NEWS of Yahushua Messiah that DID NOT include obedience to the Torah was a false teaching, a lie, deception or delusion.

It is his intention for us to understand that any teaching, claiming to be from Paul, that comes from men who live and teach that you no longer need obey the Torah is a delusion, a lie, and we are to flee from it.

There is one more passage of Scripture that we need to look at before we get into the hard sayings of Paul, and that comes from something he said to Timothy.

| 2Ti 2:15 | Study to shew thyself approved unto God, a workman that needeth not to be ashamed, rightly **dividing** the word of truth. (KJV) |

We have quoted this from the King James Version because it translates this verse in a way that has caused a tremendous amount of error in modern doctrine.

The use of the word "dividing" has led modern theologians to believe that they can "divide" Scripture, some for the Jews and some for the Gentiles, which is ridiculous.

As we have shown many times, the Scripture cannot be "added to nor taken away from" (Deut 4:2; 12:32; Eccl 3:14; Pro 30:6 and Rev 22:18-19), for it is settled in heaven for ever (Psa 119:89).

From this verse in 1st Timothy, modern theologians have divided the so-called "Old Testament" from the so-called "New Testament", saying that the "Old Testament" belongs to the Jews, while the "New Testament" belongs to Christians.

Nothing could be farther from the Truth!

| | |
|---|---|
| **Rightly Dividing**: | stg's #**G3718** "orthotomeō", from two words meaning (G3717) right, and the base of (G5114) to cut; to *make* **a** *straight cut*, that is, (figuratively) **to** *dissect* (*expound*) *correctly* (the divine message): - rightly divide. |

To "rightly divide" Scripture, is to correctly discern what it's saying. This **DOES NOT** mean to say some parts belonged to one group (Jews) and another part belongs to a different group (Gentile believers), for Paul himself said that in Messiah there is neither "Jew nor Greek".

What modern teachers have done is take Paul's message to Timothy and "twisted" it (2 Pet 3:14-17) teaching a false doctrine of dispensationalism, which teaches that YHWH has treated mankind differently during different eras of time.

Paul wanted Timothy to study the Scripture himself, so that no one else could deceive him, telling him to correctly dissect what the Scripture said, so that he could understand it properly. What is the purpose of dissecting something?

When we were in science class and had to dissect a frog, or some other creature, did we dissect the frog to figure out how each individual piece worked, or did we dissect the frog to figure out how all the pieces work together to give that creature life?

Of course, the purpose of dissection is to identify all the pieces of the creature and determine how all the individual pieces fit together properly so that we may correctly understand how the entire thing works, to give life.

Back when the King James Version was translated the word "divide" carried more than just the meaning of "division", as in separation. It also carried the meaning of "divining" or "discerning" but as in many other cases, the complete meaning has been lost over time.

685

So, instead of "rightly dividing" what the Scripture teaches we're supposed to **correctly discern** what the Scripture is saying, in its totality, so we can understand how to receive eternal life from it.

Now, the first "hard sayings" of Paul that we are going to dissect comes from Colossians.

# 2 Corinthians 3

Of the hard sayings of Paul, 2 Corinthians 3 can be the most confusing because of the nature of his writings. Keep in mind that Paul is a scholar who is most often writing to either other scholars or learned Jews, as well as learned Gentiles who had been attending the Synagogues. There are only a few cases in which he was writing to assemblies that he had not yet met, such as Romans, which was founded by learned Jews that had been at Shavuot (Pentecost) on the day the Spirit overshadowed the disciples, and Colossians.

So, let's go through 2 Corinthians 3 and see how it relates to other things we have said in this work.

First off, in the previous chapter (2), Paul is consoling them concerning his first letter wherein he had rebuked them for allowing a brother among them to be with his father's wife. He wrote to them (1 Corinthians 5) saying that they needed to remove the man so that the entire assembly would not become infected by such behavior, i.e., "a little leaven leavens the entire lump".

| | |
|---|---|
| **1Co 5:4** | In the Name of our Master יהושע Messiah, when you are gathered together, and my spirit, with the power of our Master יהושע Messiah, |
| **1Co 5:5** | **deliver such a one to Satan for destruction of the flesh, in order that his spirit be saved in the day of the Master יהושע.** |
| **1Co 5:6** | Your boasting is not good. **Do you not know that a little leaven leavens the entire lump?** |
| **1Co 5:7** | Therefore **cleanse out the old leaven**, so that you are a new lump, as you are unleavened. For also Messiah our Pěsaḥ was slaughtered for us. |

The "old leaven" Paul is referring to is lawlessness, i.e., sin, which we were delivered from (Romans 3:23-25) and were warned no longer to live in (John 5:14; 8:11; Romans 6:1-2, 14-16; Hebrews 10:26-31; 1 John 2:1).

By allowing scripture to define itself, we know that sin, by definition, is the "transgression of the Torah/Law" (1 John 3:4) and Messiah saved us FROM our old sin and it's penalty, i.e., death (Romans 3:23-25; Ephesians 2:1-7) When the "New Testament" writers, including Messiah Himself, instruct us NOT TO SIN, they must obviously expect us to obey the Torah/Law, and it is from this obvious truth that all Messianic doctrine must be understood.

In chapter 2, Paul tells the assembly that the reason he wrote such a harsh letter the last time, was so when he came to them there wouldn't be any sadness between them. He then encourages them not to be too harsh on the young man, saying his punishment (exile) was sufficient and that they should forgive him so that he would not be swallowed up by sadness.

It is imperative that we understand what discipline within the Body looks like. First, if a brother or sister sins against us, we are to go to them privately, or to her husband if she is married or her father if she is not married, and IF the sinner CONFESSES their sin and FORSAKES it (Proverbs 28:13b), we have gained a brother/sister.

However, if they refuse, we are to take two or three others and confront them. If they still refuse, we are to bring them before the congregation for judgment (Matthew 18:15-17).

The judgment for willful (intentional) sin is expulsion (Hebrews 6:4-8; 10:26-31 and others), but the purpose of discipline should ALWAYS be motivated by love, with the goal being restoration. It should always be in our hearts to make judgments and execute discipline in a way that is consistent with what the totality of Scripture teaches. Never deviate!

Furthermore, it should always be in our heart to receive that brother or sister back again, when they have confessed and forsaken their previous disobedience. If ever our own hearts hold a grudge and are not willing to extend forgiveness, then we ourselves are in sin and have no right to judge another.

Lastly, Paul talks about his ministering in Troas and that some had accused him of "adulterating the Word of Elohim for gain", which he rejects, and it is from this context we begin Chapter 3.

\*\*\*

| | |
|---|---|
| **2Co 3:1** | Are we to begin to recommend ourselves again? Or do we need, as some, letters of recommendation to you, or from you? |
| **2Co 3:2** | You are our letter, having been written in our hearts, known and read by all men, |
| **2Co 3:3** | making it obvious that you are a letter of Messiah, served by us, written not with ink but by the Spirit of the living Elohim, not on tablets of stone but on fleshly tablets of the heart. |
| **2Co 3:4** | And such trust we have toward Elohim, through the Messiah. |

Paul begins this portion by telling the Corinthians that they themselves are the evidence that his message is sincere and correct. This is proved out by their witness among those surrounding them. Others have seen the effect of the Belief in the lives of these brothers.

Their belief in Messiah has changed them, specifically their heart condition. They are the letter/witness of Messiah and because their lives have changed, from lawlessness to faithfulness, Paul's trust in YHWH is strengthened in Messiah.

| | |
|---|---|
| **2Co 3:5** | Not that we are competent in ourselves to reckon any matter as from ourselves, but our competence is from Elohim, |
| **2Co 3:6** | who also made us competent as servants of a renewed covenant, not of the letter but of the Spirit, for the letter kills but the Spirit gives life. |

Here's where the confusion begins! Ever since the Word was first given, people have interpreted these verses according to their own thoughts and feelings and having done so, "they changed the truth of Elohim into a falsehood" (lie – Romans 1:25a).

Paul says in verse 5 that we, meaning the teachers, are not "competent in ourselves to reckon any matter as from ourselves", which merits closer examination, if we are to gain correct understanding.

**Competent:** stgs #**G2425** "ἱκανός – hikanos", from ἵκω hikō (ἱκάνω or ἱκνέομαι; akin to G2240; **to arrive**); competent (as if coming in season), that is, ample (in amount) or fit (in character).

The word "reckon" here is "logizomai" (to take an inventory, i.e., estimate) and so Paul is saying that they don't consider themselves to have figured out the truth of the Good News by their own ability, but that the ability to understand it came directly from Elohim. This is similar to what he says in the first chapter of Galatians.

**Gal 1:11** And I make known to you, brothers, that the Good News announced by me **is not according to man**.
**Gal 1:12** For I did not receive it from man, **nor was I taught it**, **but through a revelation of יהושע Messiah.**

He goes on in verse 5 to say that Elohim, through Messiah, "made us competent as servants of a renewed covenant". First of all, he is referring to himself and other teachers when referring to "us" as "servants". They share the Good News of Yahushua, who is the Mediator of the "New" covenant (Hebrews 9:15).

**Renewed (New):** stgs #**G2537** "καινός – kainos", of uncertain affinity; new (especially in **freshness**; while G3501 (youthful or fresh) is properly so with respect to age): - new.

Some debate whether this word means 'new' as in brand new, not having existed before, or 'new' in the since of being made new or renewed. This phrase, "new covenant" comes from the Hebrew of Jeremiah 31:31-33.

690

| | |
|---|---|
| Jer 31:31 | "See, the days are coming," declares יהוה, "when I shall make a **renewed covenant** with the **house of Yisra'ĕl and with the house of Yehudah,** |
| Jer 31:32 | **not like the covenant** I made with their fathers in the day when I strengthened their hand to bring them out of the land of Mitsrayim, My covenant **which they broke,** though I was a husband to them," declares יהוה. |
| Jer 31:33 | "For this is the covenant I shall make with **the house of Yisra'ĕl** after those days, declares יהוה: I shall **put My Torah in their inward parts, and write it on their hearts.** And I shall be their Elohim, and they shall be My people. |

The most obvious thing here is that this "new covenant" promise is to the "House of Yisra'el" and the "House of Yehudah" (Jews). It does NOT say anything about this "new covenant" being for the Gentiles, though the Messianic Writings (NT) clearly say that Gentiles can take part in it. Gentiles join Yisra'el in covenant with YHWH through belief in Yahushua.

**\*\*\*THERE IS NO SUCH THING AS A GENTILE CHURCH!!!\*\*\***

Gentiles are the "little dogs" that eat the children's (Yisra'el) bread (Messiah) that falls from the Master's (YHWH) table (Matthew 15:21-28). Believing Gentiles are adopted into YHWH's family, having been grafted into His tree. That is to say, they are joined with Yisra'el to Himself. (Leviticus 19:33-34; Romans 11:11-24; Ephesians 2:11-19; Galatians 3:26-29).

| | |
|---|---|
| **Renewed (New):** | stgs #**H2319** "שָׁדָח - châdâsh", from **H2318**; new: - fresh, new thing. |

691

stgs #**H2318** "שָׁדַח -
châdash", a primitive root;
**to be new**; causatively **to
rebuild**: - renew, repair.

It is the opinion of this author that this
Hebrew word should be translated as "renewed" in this
context for, at least, two reasons.

1.     The Hebrew word "chadash" translated here
       (H2319) as 'new' and the word "chodesh"
       (H2320) which is translated 'new moon' or
       'month', both come from "chadash"
       (H2318). Now we call the beginning of the
       month the 'new moon', but is the moon
       actually new or is it simply renewing its
       cycle?

The author believes this idea of renewal is what is
meant in the context of the Good News of Messiah, where
believers are "born again" in the same body unto a 'new
man', and will be 'made new' or given a 'new' body at the
resurrection, etc.

2.     **Amo 3:7**     For the Master יהוה **does no
                       matter** unless **He reveals
                       His secret to His servants
                       the prophets.**

You can search the Scriptures until your life ebbs
away and your corpse rots, but you will not find any
evidence in the Tanak (OT) which teaches that this, or any
other "new" covenant allows the children of Elohim to claim
that His Law/Torah no longer applies to them.
Whether a person was born a Jew or a Gentile,
whether they practice Judaism or Christianity, the scripture
clearly teaches that BOTH the "**native born and the
stranger that sojourns with them**" are to be considered
native born Yisra'elis (Leviticus 19:33-34; also, Ephesians
2:8-19 and Romans 11:11-24). Furthermore, it teaches that
there is **ONE** Law/Torah for both, **FOREVER,
THROUGH-OUT YOUR GENERATIONS** (Numbers
15:15-16).

692

Nowhere in Scripture is it revealed to us that there ever was or ever will be a time when YHWH, or His "Messiah", will turn a blind eye to those who disobey His Torah/Law as it was given to Yisra'el, through Moses. In fact, the complete opposite is taught in both the Tanak (OT) and the Messianic Writings (NT). Any teaching that or doctrine that teaches otherwise is heresy. **IS JUST NOT TRUE!!!**

Even the Messianic Writings (NT) say so clearly.

| | |
|---|---|
| **Jas 2:24** | You see, then, that a man is declared right by works, and **not by belief alone**. |
| **Jas 2:25** | In the same way, was not Raḥab the whore also declared right by works when she received the messengers and sent them out another way? |
| **Jas 2:26** | For as the body without the spirit is dead, so also the **belief is dead without the works**. |

Anyone trusting in a belief system, whether Jewish or Christian, or Islam, etc., that teaches that the Torah/Law of YHWH no longer has any place in their life is trusting in a "Covenant of Death" (Isaiah 28).

In Jeremiah 31:32, YHWH says that this "new covenant" will not be like the one He made with their fathers when He brought them out of Egypt. Some would suggest that this is surely evidence that it is something 'brand new', since it is not like the 'old' covenant. Let's allow the context to tell us what is "new" about this covenant instead of just assuming something that cannot be proven through an honest and exhaustive examination of the whole of Scripture from Genesis 1 to Revelation 22:21.

In verse 33, He says that He will "put (His) Torah in their inward parts, and write it on their hearts", meaning it would **not** be written on stone and lambskin like it was the first time. Yes, that is different than the covenant He made with their fathers, yet it is still the SAME Torah/Law.

When He says that He is going to put it in their "inward parts", He is referring to our inner-spirit-man

693

who was born again when we believed in Messiah. This is consistent with something we have already talked about several times: He would "impute" righteousness to us.

Remember the difference in what the Greek word, "logizomai" (take inventory/place on account) means and what the Hebrew word, "chashab" (plait or weave) means. When we believe in the Lamb of Elohim (Messiah), the Spirit of YHWH makes righteousness a part of us, i.e., weaves it into this natural body.

This righteous part of us, i.e., the inner-spirit-man, will desire the Torah of Elohim and serve (guard and do)it.

| | |
|---|---|
| **Rom 7:18** | For I know that in me, that is in **my flesh**, dwells no good. For to wish is present with me, but to work the good I do not find. |
| **Rom 7:19** | For the good that I wish to do, I do not do; but the evil I do not wish to do, this I practice. |
| **Rom 7:20** | And if I do that which I do not wish, it is no longer I who work it, but the sin dwelling in me. |
| **Rom 7:21** | I find therefore this law, that when I wish to do the good, that the evil is present with me. |
| **Rom 7:22** | **For I delight in the Torah of Elohim according to the inward man**, |
| **Rom 7:23** | but I see another torah in my members, battling against the torah of my mind, and bringing me into captivity to the torah of sin which is in my members. |
| **Rom 7:24** | Wretched man that I am! Who shall deliver me from this body of death? |
| **Rom 7:25** | Thanks to Elohim, **through יהושע Messiah** our Master! So then, **with the mind I myself truly serve the Torah of Elohim**, but with the flesh the torah of sin. |

Now, some have erroneously taught that as long as a person is serving "God" in their mind, he/she no longer has

694

to obey the Torah/Law of YHWH. This doctrine is demonic and emphatically contradicted in the very next verse.

| | |
|---|---|
| **Rom 8:1** | There is, then, now no condemnation to those who are in Messiah יהושע, **who do not walk according to the flesh**, but according to the Spirit. |

There is no longer any condemnation for those who **DO NOT** live in obedience to their sinful flesh! It is "obeying sin" (Romans 6:15;) or "walking in the flesh" that leads to death (Romans 8:13; Galatians 2:15-18). What does it mean to live in the flesh?

| | |
|---|---|
| **Rom 8:5** | For those who **live according to the flesh set their minds on the matters of the flesh**, but those who live according to the Spirit, the matters of the Spirit. |
| **Rom 8:6** | **For the mind of the flesh is death**, but the mind of the Spirit is life and peace. |
| **Rom 8:7** | **Because the mind of the flesh is enmity** towards Elohim, for **it does not subject itself to the Torah of Elohim,** neither indeed is it able, |
| **Rom 8:8** | and those who are in the flesh are unable to please Elohim. |

Living in obedience to the flesh is to live in disobedience to the Torah/Law of YHWH. Sadly, this is exactly what many, if not most teachers within the 'Church' are teaching believers today. A vast majority of 'churches' today are guilty of teaching believers to sin (1 John 3:4 – transgress the Law [KJV]).

"The wages of sin is death" (Romans 6:23) and its punishment is a "fierce fire which is about to consume the opponents". In fact, there will be "much worse punishment" for those who know the truth and turn from it by sinning "willfully". (Hebrews 6:4-8; 10:26-31).

Furthermore, when YHWH says that He will "write it on (our) hearts", He is not saying that it will literally be inscribed on our hearts any more than He will literally "circumcise" our hearts (Romans 2:29). This phrase refers to placing the **desire to obey** in our hearts.

Every one of us who sincerely confessed the blood of Messiah rose from our knees desiring to please Him. Unfortunately, many so-called teachers within the 'Church' taught us to serve Him according to their own man-made dogma (Isaiah 29:13; quoted in Matthew 15:8-9 and Mark 7:6-7), before we really had a chance to be taught by YHWH from His own Word.

One of the reasons Messiah was so hard on the religious leaders of His day was because the Torah of YHWH had been with them for nearly fifteen centuries (1500 years), yet they had still developed their own man-made laws and teachings (traditions of the elders/fathers). This set them and all who heard them on a man-made path and not the ancient Path/Way of YHWH, the Elohim of their fathers.

These man-made traditions blinded both them and the people, keeping nearly all the Yahudim (Jews) in darkness even though the Light Himself walked among them. A darkness that still blinds them today.

> **Note**: It is a bad thing to have some traditions, however, if those traditions add to, take away from or in any way contradict the Torah of YHWH, or we make the traditions a 'requirement of participation', we have crossed the line and are guilty of the same sin as the Scribes and Pharisees.

Today, that darkness (man-made laws and traditions) not only blinds the adherents of Judaism but has convinced nearly a billion of our 'Christian' brothers and sisters that their faith ALONE is enough to make them heirs of the Kingdom.

This teaching is opposed to the teachings all of the Messianic Writers. It is even in opposition to the teachings of Messiah, Himself, yet many so-called leaders within the 'Church' continue to repeat the errors of the first century Jewish leaders, just in a different way.

What both of these man-made religions misunderstand is that the Torah of YHWH was **NOT** given to 'manage our behavior', it was given to **TEST OUR HEARTS**.

| | |
|---|---|
| **Deu 8:1** | "**Guard to do every command** which I command you today, that you might **live**, and shall **increase**, and **go in**, and shall **possess** the land of which יהוה swore to your fathers. |

a. **Guard** (Observe in KJV): "shamar" (H8104) meaning 'to hedge about' or protect, refers to putting the word in our heart and not allowing anyone to take it from us i.e., corrupt it or misuse it.

b. **Do**: "asah" (H6213) meaning 'to do or make', refers to the application of it in our daily life, i.e., obeying it.

When the Father instructs His people (believers) to "guard" every command here in chapter 8, He is referring to what He had already told them in chapter 6.

| | |
|---|---|
| **Deu 6:5** | "And you shall love יהוה your Elohim with all your heart, and with all your being, and with all your might. |
| **Deu 6:6** | "And these Words which I am commanding you today shall be in your heart, |

This refers to the spiritual part of belief and when He says, "to do" every command, He is referring to the physical part, obedience to His instructions (Torah), which leads to life (everlasting), to increase (prosperity/blessing), and to possession (inheritance) of the Promised Land (Kingdom).

| | |
|---|---|
| **Deu 8:2** | "And you **shall remember** that יהוה your Elohim led you all the way these forty years in the wilderness, **to humble you**, prove you, to know what is in your heart, whether you guard His commands or not. |

The wilderness wandering is a shadow picture of our lives today that begins when we paint the blood of the Lamb of Elohim on the door posts and lintel of our **heart** and ends when Messiah returns to fulfill the shadow picture of Joshua and takes us across the final baptism (River Jordon – resurrection) into the Promised Land (Kingdom).

The Torah of YHWH, which He gave us through Moses at Mt. Sinai, is the PATH a believer walks in AFTER he has been justified (freed from death) by Messiah, the Lamb of YHWH, "every command" of which leads us to life, blessing and inheritance because it is the TEST of a sincere heart.

The Torah of YHWH is given to humble us and prove us, for it reveals the true condition of our hearts. It will judge whether we truly listened/loved/trusted/honored YHWH in sincerity or whether we listened/loved/trusted/honored another.

**Deu 8:3**  "And He humbled you, and let you suffer hunger, and fed you with manna which you did not know nor did your fathers know, to make you know **that man does not live by bread alone, but by every Word that comes from the mouth of** יהוה.

When Messiah was challenged by Ha'Satan to turn stones into bread, He answered him by quoting the highlighted portion above. What makes this quote all the more interesting is that in John 6:33-51 Messiah refers to Himself as the "Bread of Life".

We see then that man DOES NOT live by bread (Messiah – spiritual/belief) alone but by "every word" (Torah – physical/works) that proceeds from the Mouth of YHWH, i.e., the two parts (See: James 2:14-26).

\*\*\*

**2Co 3:7**  But if the administering of death in letters, engraved on stones, was esteemed, so that the children of Yisra'ěl were unable to look steadily at the face of Mosheh

698

because of the esteem of his face, which was passing away,

2Co 3:8    how much more esteemed shall the administering of the Spirit not be?

Before we explain this passage, which, to be honest, is one of Paul's most difficult to interpret, we will look at how and when the "letter" of the Torah is administering death.

Deu 30:15    "See, I have set before you today **life and good**, and **death and evil**,
Deu 30:16    in that I am commanding you today to **love** יהוה your Elohim, to **walk** in His ways, and to **guard** His **commands**, and His **laws**, and His **right-rulings**. And you shall **live and increase**, and יהוה your Elohim shall **bless** you in the land which you go to **possess**.
Deu 30:17    "**But if your heart turns away**, and you **do not obey**, and shall be **drawn away**, and **shall bow down to other mighty ones and serve them**,
Deu 30:18    "I have declared to you today that **you shall certainly perish**, you shall not prolong your days in the land which you are passing over the Yardĕn to enter and possess.

As we have mentioned before, obedience to the Torah/Law of YHWH through belief in His Son, leads to life, prosperity, blessing and inheritance. In contrast, not obeying the Torah/Law of YHWH leads to death. Why? Because the "wages of sin is death" (Romans 6:23a) and "sin is the transgression (violation) of the Torah/Law", i.e., lawlessness (1 John 3:4).

So, the Torah of YHWH IS the administration of death **to those who disobey it**, however, it is also the administration of life **to those who obey it**. Unfortunately, "all have sinned and fallen short" (Romans 3:23), thus we are all under the administration of death. However, that does NOT mean there is a problem with the Torah, it means there is a problem within us, in our flesh (Romans 8:3a).

In the specific context of the Messianic Writings, Paul's argument is that the Torah cannot be trusted to justify us or make us righteous in and of itself, because it has already condemned all men "under sin", i.e., guilty.

Because of this fact, something greater than the Torah was needed to justify us from our sin and the death penalty which it carries, making us right before YHWH, and that something was blood, for there is no forgiveness of sin without the shedding of blood (Hebrews 9:22).

YHWH, however, so loved His creation that He gave His only begotten Son, so that whosoever will believe in the Son shall not perish but gain access to everlasting life (John 3:16).

| | |
|---|---|
| **Rom 8:3** | For the Torah being powerless, in that it was weak through the flesh, Elohim, **having sent His own Son** in the **likeness of flesh** of sin, and **concerning sin, condemned sin in the flesh,** |
| **Rom 8:4** | so **that the righteousness of the Torah should be completed in us WHO DO NOT WALK ACCORDING TO THE FLESH but according to the Spirit.** |

Remember, the argument Paul makes here in Romans MUST be consistent with what he is saying in 2 Corinthians 3, so let's analyze what is being said here and then compare the two.

As mentioned earlier, the Torah has no power to justify or make us right before YHWH because the desires of our fleshly man are both very strong and in direct opposition to the righteousness of YHWH.

| | |
|---|---|
| **Rom 8:6** | For **the mind of the flesh is death,** but the mind of the Spirit is life and peace. |
| **Rom 8:7** | Because **the mind of the flesh is enmity towards Elohim, FOR IT** |

700

|            | **DOES NOT SUBJECT ITSELF** |
|------------|------------------------------|
|            | **TO THE TORAH** of Elohim, |
|            | **neither indeed is it able**, |
| **Rom 8:8** | and those who are **in the flesh are** |
|            | **unable to please Elohim.** |

The righteousness of YHWH, which He teaches us in His Torah, is contrary to our fleshly man and so, when we "walk" or live in a way that is NOT SUBJECT to His Torah, i.e., in disobedience to it, we prove ourselves to be "transgressors" (Galatians 2:17-18), living according to the desires of the fleshly man and rather than as servants of YHWH, regardless of who or what we say we believe in.

There is a condition connected to our belief in Yahushua that keeps us "under grace" once we have gained access to it through belief in Him, and that condition is obedience. This is exactly what Paul is teaching here in Romans 8.

In verse 4 he clearly says that "the righteousness of the Torah should be completed in us WHO DO NOT WALK ACCORDING TO THE FLESH but according to the Spirit. If the fleshly man does not "subject itself to the Torah of Elohim", the law of contrast teaches that the spiritual man DOES "subject itself to the Torah of Elohim".

This is consistent with what Paul teaches about the Torah, for it is he who says the Torah is "holy, just, and good" (Romans 7:12 – KJV) and that it is also "spiritual" (Romans 7:14a). Unfortunately, however, we ourselves are fleshly men, because when Messiah came "in the **likeness of flesh** of sin", having become a man just like us, His primary purpose was "**concerning sin**", meaning that He came to set us free from it, in the inner-man, and in doing so He "**condemned sin in the flesh**," outer-man (Romans 8:3).

There is a constant battle going on within every believer that pits our inner-spiritual-man who has been "born again" against our outer-fleshly-man who is still "condemned in the flesh" (Galatians 5:17). But if we "walk in the spirit (man)" we shall "not accomplish the lust of the flesh" (Galatians 5:16, also see Romans 8:13).

To be "walking according to the spirit", means to walk in the Path/Way of the Torah through belief in Messiah, and "NOT according to the flesh", which is believing in the Torah alone or not at all, which includes a few different groups.

There are those who neither believe in Messiah nor obey the Torah, i.e., atheist, Muslims, Buddhist, etc., and there are those who obey the Torah but do not believe in Yahushua Messiah, i.e., Judaism.

Unfortunately, there are also those who believe they are "walking in the Spirit" because they believe in Jesus, but they do not obey the Torah, which Paul himself calls spiritual (Romans 7:14), and thus they are actually walking in the flesh and not the spirit (Romans 8:7-8).

It is only those who believe in Yahushua Messiah for justification FROM sin and death AND walk in obedience to the Torah/Law of YHWH, with a sincere heart of compassion for his fellowman that shall escape both spiritual and physical death (the Second Death) at the resurrection of the just, i.e., the First Resurrection (Revelations 20).

Going back now to 2 Corinthians 3:6, we see Paul making the statement that we are servants of a "renewed covenant" wherein we DO NOT live in the "letter of the Torah" alone because it alone kills. Rather, we who have the mind of the spirit, subjects ourselves to the Torah of Elohim, through belief in Messiah. Once again, verses 7-8).

| | |
|---|---|
| **2Co 3:7** | But if the **administering of death** in letters, engraved on stones, was esteemed, so that the children of Yisra'ĕl were unable to look steadily at the face of Mosheh because of the esteem of his face, which was passing away, |
| **2Co 3:8** | how much **more esteemed shall** the administering of the Spirit not be? |

As we have said, the Torah administers death only to those who disobey it and since we all have disobeyed it (sinned), it can no longer administer life to us. Paul says that the "letter" was esteemed, so much so that "Yisra'el were unable to look steadily at the face of Mosheh". This is a reference to the 'veil of Mosheh", which we will talk more about in a bit.

He goes on to say that the "administering of the Spirit" has more esteem than the Torah and, of course, we agree. Unfortunately, many within the 'Church' remain in the dark as to what this actually means. defines it. Many teach that once you get "in the spirit", by belief, meaning that your inner-spirit-man has been born again, that you are "sealed" for the day of a future redemption no matter what. This dogma is heresy.

The "administering of the Spirit" has more esteem because it is founded, NOT in the Torah itself, but in our belief in Messiah which is proven out by our submission to YHWH through obedience to His Torah.

It is belief in the blood of Messiah that gives us atonement from past sins and the penalty of death (Romans 3:25) and gives life to the inner-spirit-man. When this "new man" continues to struggle in his obedience, he will find no more condemnation, IF his intent is to "walk according to the spirit" (obedience), and NOT "according to the flesh" (disobedience).

Here we see the Two-Part Principle clearly taught. The inner man "delights" in the Torah of YHWH and "serves" it (Romans 7:22, 25), but it is belief in Yahushua Messiah that "saves me from this body of death" (Romans 7:24), when I "DO NOT walk according to the flesh, but according to the Spirit" (Romans 8:1).

Avoiding future condemnation is conditional and the condition has to do with HOW we administer the Torah in our lives. IF we walk "according to (our) spirit", which is led by His Spirit, into obedience (Ezekiel 36:27), we will live in righteousness (Romans 6:15-16) and inherit everlasting life (Romans 6:22).

However, if we walk "according to the (our) flesh", "serving sin" (Romans 6:16 and 8:7) we shall die.

| | |
|---|---|
| **Rom 8:12** | So then, **brothers**, we are not debtors to the flesh, **to live according to the flesh.** |
| **Rom 8:13** | For **IF** you live according to the flesh, **you are going to die**; **BUT** if by the Spirit **you put to death the deeds of the body, you shall live.** |

703

If the flesh "does not subject itself to the Torah of Elohim", then, by contrast, the spirit DOES subject itself to the Torah of Elohim, and we can "put to death the deeds of the body (flesh)" by subjecting ourselves to the Torah of Elohim THROUGH belief in Messiah.

In the Messianic Writings, the Jewish Leaders were teaching the people to do the works of Torah as a means of salvation. Their trust/hope was placed in the Torah itself and not in YHWH, the Law Giver. Paul's argument, as well as that of all the writers, in both "old" and "new", teaches that the righteous man lives by belief (Hab 2:4, quoted in Galatians 3:11).

Thus, trusting/hoping in the Torah alone is an act of sin. The covenant at Sinai is founded on the condition that "IF you **diligently obey My voice** (Torah), AND shall **guard My covenant** (Blood), THEN **you shall be My treasured possession** above all the peoples" (Exodus 19:5-6). This is a clear reference from the Torah itself, of the Two-Part Principle at work.

| | |
|---|---|
| 2Co 3:9 | For if the administering of condemnation had esteem, the administering of righteousness exceeds **much more** in esteem. |
| 2Co 3:10 | For indeed what was made esteemed **had no esteem in this respect, in view of the esteem that excels.** |
| 2Co 3:11 | For if that which is **passing away** was esteemed, much more that which remains in esteem. |
| 2Co 3:12 | Having then such expectation, we use much boldness of speech, |
| 2Co 3:13 | and not like Mosheh, **who put a veil over his face so that the children of Yisra'ĕl should not look steadily at the end of what was passing away.** |
| 2Co 3:14 | But their **minds were hardened**, for to this day, when the old covenant is being read, **that same veil remains**, not lifted, because **in Messiah it is taken away.** |

| | |
|---|---|
| **2Co 3:15** | But to this day, when Mosheh is being read, **a veil lies on their heart**. |

The Torah was and shall always be esteemed, unfortunately our disobedience to it caused it to condemn us, thus, we are unable to fulfill the righteous requirements of Torah. However, our belief in Messiah has more esteem because it accomplishes two things; 1) it delivers us from past sin and the condemnation of death, and 2) it can renew us daily in the mercy and grace of YHWH, thus allowing us to live in the righteousness of Torah.

There is, however, a condition imposed on #2 that IS NOT imposed on #1 and that condition is, IF we WALK according to the spirit and NOT according to the flesh. The word "walk" is about how we live and NOT about what we believe. Your walk proves what you believe.

Can we legitimately say we love our wife if we cheat on her and are always deceiving her? Absolutely Not!! And the same holds true in our relationship to the Father. We cannot say that we trust Him or fear Him or reverence Him or serve Him or love Him, if we don't "guard to do" ALL He has commanded of us.

So, we first gain access to the favour of YHWH through belief (Messiah) but we remain in that favour by how we live (Torah). However, our trust/hope is ALWAYS in the atoning blood of Yahushua Messiah and NEVER in the works of Torah themselves.

| | |
|---|---|
| **Jas 2:21** | Was not Aḇraham our father **declared right by works** when he offered Yitsḥaq his son on the slaughter-place? |
| **Jas 2:22** | Do you see that **the belief was working with his works**, and **by the works the belief was perfected**? |
| **Jas 2:23** | And the Scripture was filled which says, "Aḇraham believed Elohim, and it was reckoned to him for righteousness." And He called him, "he who loves Elohim." |

| Jas 2:24 | You see, then, that **a man is declared right by works, and not by belief alone**. |
|---|---|

When Paul says "passing away" in 2 Corinthians 3:11 as it refers to what is esteemed, we must ask ourselves, what is actually passing away and how is it related to Moses?

| Exo 34:29 | And it came to be, when Mosheh came down from Mount Sinai, while the two tablets of the Witness were in Mosheh's hand when he came down from the mountain, that Mosheh did not know that the skin of his face shone since he had spoken with Him. |
|---|---|
| Exo 34:30 | And Aharon and all the children of Yisra'ěl looked at Mosheh and saw the skin of his face shone, and they were afraid to come near him. |
| Exo 34:31 | But Mosheh called out to them, and Aharon and all the rulers of the congregation returned to him, and Mosheh spoke to them. |
| Exo 34:32 | And afterward all the children of Yisra'ěl came near, and he commanded them all that יהוה had spoken with him on Mount Sinai. |
| Exo 34:33 | And when Mosheh **ended speaking** with them, he put a veil on his face. |
| Exo 34:34 | But whenever Mosheh went in before יהוה to speak with Him, he would remove the veil until he came out. And when he came out he spoke to the children of Yisra'ěl what he had been commanded, |
| Exo 34:35 | and the children of Yisra'ěl would see the face of Mosheh, that the skin of Mosheh's face shone, and Mosheh would put the veil on his face again, until he went in to speak with Him. |

Notice that when Moses was in the Presence of YHWH his face shone brightly and when he spoke the Word of YHWH his face shone brightly, it was only after the Word went forth and he stopped speaking that he covered his face so the people could not look at it continually.

The Torah is the "Knowledge of good and evil", it is a light (Psalms 119:105; Proverbs 6:23). It's not until we look into the light of Torah that we get knowledge of the Most High (Proverbs 2:1-9) and walking out (doing) the works of Torah is how we gain wisdom and understanding (Deuteronomy 4:5-6, Psalms 119:100).

The "light" that shone on Mosheh's face was enlightenment or understanding and when he put on the veil the people no longer had the light of understanding shinning on them.

Later, after they got into the Land, Yisra'el substituted Torah light with the darkness of idolatry, and later still, after they returned from Babylonian captivity, they substituted Torah light with the blindness of man-made rabbinical dogma.

It was wisdom and understanding, which can only be gained through Torah obedience, that was "passing away" and NOT the Torah itself. The Torah is forever (Psalms 119:142), it cannot be added to or taken away from (Deuteronomy 4:2; 12:32; Ecclesiastes 3:14; Proverbs 30:6; Revelation 22:18-19). The Torah/Law is "holy, just and good" (Romans 7:12), and it is spiritual (Romans 7:14).

This passage in Exodus is similar to what James (Ya'aqob) says in his letter.

| | |
|---|---|
| **Jas 1:23** | Because if anyone is a **hearer** of the Word and **not a doer**, he is like a man who looks at his natural face in a mirror, |
| **Jas 1:24** | for he looks at himself, and goes away, and **immediately forgets what he was like.** |

We see that James is referring to those who DO NOT OBEY the Word, they are like someone looking in a mirror but when they look away they forget what they were like. The Torah is the mirror in this metaphor, for when we

707

are looking at the Word/Torah we see the light but when we look away, we forget the Way that we are to walk.

Why? Because of the flesh, which has "enmity towards Elohim, for it **DOES NOT SUBJECT** itself to the Torah of Elohim, neither indeed is it able" (Romans 8:7). When the disobedient read the Bible, the message of righteousness that it teaches does not remain in them once they close the book and walk away.

This is the same message YHWH is explaining to us in Exodus concerning the veil. When Moses was reading the Torah to the people, the righteousness of YHWH was being revealed to them, but once Moses finished speaking and put on the veil, the people could no longer see the light of righteousness and went their own way.

However,…

| | |
|---|---|
| **Jas 1:25** | But he that **looked into the perfect Torah**, that of freedom, **and continues in it**, not becoming a hearer that forgets, but a doer of work, **this one shall be blessed in his doing of the Torah**. |

The phrase "looked into the perfect Torah" is "παρακυψας εις νομον τελειον τον" in Greek and is "looked into instruction complete the". It refers to the 'completeness' or fulness of the Torah, which includes the Good News of Yahushua Messiah.

The Torah is the foundation of the Belief, Messiah being the Chief Cornerstone of that foundation, meaning that it is from Him that all the Torah is measured.

The word "looked" is past tense and contextually refers to someone who has heard the Good News of Messiah, which is revealed in the Torah, i.e., a Believer.

| | |
|---|---|
| **Note**: | It is important to remember that there was no 'New Testament" when these books were first penned. When these writers were putting these "NT" books together, the "word/law/scripture" they were referring to is the Tanak (OT). |

Next, the phrase "of freedom" (ἐλευθερία – G1657) has two parts, one spiritual, what YHWH has done for us through Messiah, and one physical, which is what we do in response to what He has done.

The "looked into" portion of this verse refers to the spiritual part that sets us freedom FROM past sin, and the sentence of death (Romans 8:2). It is our belief in Messiah that sets us free from sin and death..

The "continues in it" portion of this verse pertains to the physical part, referring to the Way we LIVE, i.e., the "doer of the work" (Torah obedience), which sets us free from the fear of condemnation when we stumble (Romans 8:15).

So, the Torah is NOT "done away with" or has not "passed away", in fact, our belief in Messiah removes the veil of blindness and misunderstanding, establishing the Torah (Romans 3:31) as the Way all believers are to 'walk in' (Numbers 8:1-3; Matthew 4:4), without additions or subtractions (Ecclesiastes 3:24; Revelation 22:18-19), as the Path of wisdom and understanding (Deuteronomy 4:5-6) that we are to live by to receive all the blessings in the Scripture, including inheritance.

| | |
|---|---|
| **2Co 3:16** | And when one turns to the Master, **the veil is taken away**. |
| **Note**: | The veil represents both walking in our own way as well as the "philosophy and empty deceit, according to the **tradition of men**, according to the **elementary matters** of the world (idolatry)" (Colossians 2:8), whether we call it 'theology' or 'ideology', whether we call it 'faith' or 'atheism', whether the 'truth' or a 'lie'. It is any dogma (teaching, opinion, rule) of men that adds to or takes away from the Word of YHWH and the simplicity of the Good News, i.e., obedience to the Word/Torah of YHWH through belief in Yahushua Messiah. |
| **2Co 3:17** | Now יהוה is the Spirit, and where the Spirit of יהוה is, there is freedom. |
| **2Co 3:18** | And we all, **as with unveiled face** we see as in a mirror the esteem of |

709

יהוה, are **being transformed into the same likeness** from esteem to esteem, as from יהוה, the Spirit.

As we are told in verse 16, belief in Messiah has removed the veil of our blindness (disobedience), giving us "freedom" from "the torah of sin and death".

| | |
|---|---|
| **Rom 8:2** | For the torah of the Spirit of the life in Messiah יהושע has set me free from the torah of sin and of death. |

Believers have been "born again" in the inner-spirit-man, having died with Messiah.

| | |
|---|---|
| **Rom 6:3** | Or do you not know that as many of us as were **immersed into Messiah יהושע were immersed into His death**? |
| **Rom 6:4** | We were therefore **buried with Him** through immersion into death, that as Messiah was raised from the dead by the esteem of the Father, so also **we should walk in newness of life**. |

The "freedom" we have in the Spirit of YHWH, is NOT freedom from the **requirement** to obey the Torah/Law, it is freedom FROM the condemnation of death the Torah/Law requires from all who disobey it (sin - 1 John 3:4 and Romans 6:23) and the freedom from fear (Romans 8:15) of condemnation when our flesh brings us "into captivity to the torah of sin which is in my members" (Romans 7:23).

We were "dead in trespasses and sins" but now we have been "made alive" again in Yahushua Ha-Mashiach (the Messiah).

| | |
|---|---|
| **Eph 2:1** | And you **were dead in trespasses and sins,** |
| **Eph 2:2** | in which you once **walked** according to the course of this world, according to the ruler of the authority of the air, of the spirit that |

| | |
|---|---|
| | is now working in the **sons of disobedience,** |
| Eph 2:3 | among whom **also we all once lived** in the **lusts of our flesh**, doing the desires of the flesh and of the mind, and were by nature **children of wrath**, as also the rest. |
| Eph 2:4 | **BUT** Elohim, who is rich in compassion, because of His great love with which He loved us, *(emphasis mine)* |
| Eph 2:5 | even when we **were** dead in trespasses, **made us alive together with Messiah** - by favour you have been saved - |
| Eph 2:6 | and raised us up together, and made us sit together in the heavenlies in Messiah יהושע, |
| Eph 2:7 | in order to show in the coming ages the exceeding riches of His favour in kindness toward us in Messiah יהושע. |

We were not physically dead before we believed, so this is talking about spiritual death and our belief in Messiah has made us alive again in the spirit man. It is in this state of 'new birth' that we are to "delight in the Torah of Elohim" (Romans 7:22) and serve it (obey – Romans 7:25).

As Paul says here in Ephesians, we **were** "dead" because of "trespasses and sins" (1 John 3:4), living out our lives according to the "lust of the flesh", that "does not subject itself to the Torah of Elohim" (Romans 8:7), following the "spirit that is now working in the SONS OF DISOBEDIENCE" and "were by nature the CHILDREN OF WRATH".

"BUT Elohim" has "made us alive together with Messiah" to "walk in the newness of life" (Romans 6:4) and "to serve sin (disobedience) no longer" (Romans 6:6, 11a), but to present our "members as instruments of righteousness to Elohim (Romans 6:13c), in which we serve "obedience" leading to "righteousness" (Romans 6:16d).

711

This newness of a life, lived in obedience to the Torah of YHWH through belief in His Son, Yahushua Messiah, bears in us "fruit resulting in set-apartness" (holiness, sanctification), the final outcome being "everlasting life" (Romans 6:22).

Our belief in Messiah begins a process of salvation that first, makes us alive again in the inner man, covering us in the 'spiritual' righteousness of Messiah. Then, while boasting or trusting in Messiah, we live out 'physical' righteousness through obedience to the Torah of YHWH, which sets us apart to Him in this life and leads to the new birth of the outer-physical-man at the resurrection of the Just unto the Kingdom of Messiah and everlasting life.

These Two-Parts, spiritual and physical, represent what He has done for us in Messiah and what we do in response to that, because we Love Him. And, as Jeremiah told us concerning the "new covenant";

| Jer 31:33 | "For this is the covenant I shall make with the house of Yisra'ĕl after those days, declares יהוה: I shall **put My Torah in their inward parts, and write it on their hearts**. And I shall be their Elohim, and they shall be My people. |

See, the "New Covenant" does not 'do away with' the Torah of YHWH, it puts it in our 'inner man' that will "delight" in it and serve it (Romans 7:22, 25). And YHWH will "write it on (our) hearts", so that we desire to obey it.

| Php 2:12 | So that, my beloved, as you always **obeyed** – not only in my presence, but now much rather in my absence – **work** out your own deliverance with **fear and trembling**, |
| Php 2:13 | for it is Elohim who is working in you **both to desire and to work for His good pleasure**. |

Then, after He has given us a "new spirit" and a "new heart", He puts His Spirit within us.

| | |
|---|---|
| **Eze 36:26** | "And I shall give you a **new heart and put a new spirit within you**. And I shall take the heart of stone out of your flesh, and I shall give you a heart of flesh, |
| **Eze 36:27** | and put **My Spirit within you**. And I shall **cause you to walk in My laws and guard My right-rulings and shall do them.** |

This is the "New Covenant" promise, a new inner-spirit-man and a new heart of obedience. Scripturally, a "heart of stone" is one that is stubborn and rebellious, disobedient and the opposite of a "heart of flesh", which is humble and contrite.

The phrase "fleshly heart" is NOT the same thing as a "heart of flesh", because the former is one that desires the lusts of the flesh and does not subject itself to the Torah of YHWH (Romans 8:7), while the latter is a heart to do the will of YHWH, i.e., to "walk in My laws and guard My right-rulings and shall do them".

The Messianic Writings (NT) tell us that the Spirit of YHWH that dwells within the heart of the Believer, is the Spirit of Truth that comes from the Father (John 14:17) and the Messiah asks the Father to give us this Helper because we love Him.

| | |
|---|---|
| **Joh 14:15** | "**IF** you love Me, **you shall guard My commands**. |
| **Joh 14:16** | "**And I shall ask the Father**, and He shall give you another Helper, to stay with you forever – |

You see, we prove our love by obeying and when we do, Messiah works on our behalf.

| | |
|---|---|
| **Joh 14:21** | "He who **possesses My commands and guards them**, it is he who loves Me. And he who loves Me shall be loved by My Father, and I shall love him and manifest Myself to him." |

***

713

| | |
|---|---|
| **Joh 14:23** | יהושע answered him, "If anyone loves Me, **he shall guard My Word**. And My Father shall love him, and We shall come to him and make Our stay with him. |
| **Joh 14:24** | "He who does not love Me **does not guard My Words. And the Word which you hear is NOT MINE but of the Father Who sent Me.**<br>\*\*\* |
| **Joh 15:7** | "**IF** you stay in Me, and **My Words stay in you**, you shall ask whatever you wish, and it shall be done for you. |

In conclusion, 2 Corinthians 3 DOES NOT support the heresy of a Law/Torah-less grace, as a majority of the 'Church' teaches today. It does, in fact, support a Law/Torah obedient 'grace', wherein we have access to the wisdom and understanding of the Torah, which the adherents of Judaism and Christianity lack, because we are obedient to what the Torah requires (Deuteronomy 4:5-6).

Just like every other scripture passage they use to attempt to prove that believers in "Jesus" no longer have to obey the 'Mosaic Law', this passage actually confirms our responsibility to "guard and do" it, for doing so is our righteousness" before a righteous Elohim (Deuteronomy 6:24-25).

| | |
|---|---|
| **Deu 6:24** | And יהוה commanded us to do **All** these laws, **to fear יהוה our Elohim, for our good always, to keep us alive,** as it is today. |
| **Deu 6:25** | And it is **righteousness for us when we guard to do all this command before יהוה** our Elohim, as He has commanded us.' (See also: Psalms 119:142, 172 and Isaiah 51:7) |

714

# Colossians 2

STOP!!! Before going on, read all of Colossians 1 and 2 carefully and remember that Chapter 1 will give us important contextual information to help us fully understand what Paul intended his readers to learn from Chapter 2. We will wait....

In Colossians 1, Paul introduces himself (vs. 1-2), which is important because the Assembly at Colossae (Kolossai) had never actually met him personally and neither had the Assembly in Laodikeia, to whom this letter was to be shared.

Paul goes on (vs. 3-14) to give thanks for the work the Father has done among them and to explain his prayers for them. In this section he says a couple things that are very interesting, things that need to be understood.

Having heard of the belief of the Assembly of Colossae and about their love (v.3-4), Paul was praying for them because of the expectation (hope) that had been laid up for them in heaven, which they had heard through the preaching of the "word of truth" that is the "Good News" of Yahushua Messiah.

The expectation or hope that he is referring to here is the same expectation that he referred to concerning himself in Philippians 3, the resurrection of the dead. Furthermore, it is a reference to the "New Yerushalayim" (Rev 21-22), the eternal abode of the resurrected believers, that shall descend from heaven.

Paul states that he is praying for them daily, that they "be filled with the knowledge of His desire in all wisdom and spiritual understanding" (v. 9), and that they "walk worthily of the Master" so they will be "bearing fruit in every good work and increasing in the knowledge of Elohim" (v. 10).

The three statements made in these two verses, have a very specific meaning. They represent a pattern or process that all believers are to follow, **AFTER** they have believed in Yahushua Messiah.

The first statement, "being filled with the knowledge of His desire in all wisdom and spiritual understanding" is a very specific reference to the Torah (Law) that YHWH gave to His people at Mount Sinai. Consider Romans 2:17-18.

| | |
|---|---|
| **Rom 2:17** | See, you are called a Yehuḏi, and rest on the Torah, and make your boast in Elohim, |
| **Rom 2:18** | and **know the desire** *of Elohim*, and approve what is superior, **being instructed out of the Torah,** |

Here we see that Paul, while admonishing the Yahudi (Jews), states that they know the desire of YHWH because they have been instructed or trained by the Torah. It is the Torah that teaches us the desire of YHWH in all wisdom and spiritual understanding.

To "walk worthily of the Messiah" means to live out our lives in the same manner He lived out His. Messiah lived His entire life in **complete obedience** to everything the Torah said, for if He had not, He would not have qualified as the Passover Lamb of YHWH. Consider 1 John 2:

| | |
|---|---|
| **1Jn 2:3** | And by this **we know that we know Him, if we guard His commands.** |
| **1Jn 2:4** | The one who says, "I know Him," and does **not guard His commands, is a liar**, and the truth is not in him. |
| **1Jn 2:5** | But whoever guards His Word, truly the love of Elohim has been perfected in him. By this we know that we are in Him. |
| **1Jn 2:6** | The one who says he stays in Him **ought himself also to walk, even as He walked.** |

Notice, John (Yochanan) says that if we know Him, we will guard His commands and that if we say we know Him but do not guard His commands we are a **liar, not having the Truth in us.**

He further admonishes us, if we say we stay in Him, we should be living our lives in the same way He lived His, in complete obedience to the Torah of YHWH.

What happens when we walk in complete obedience to the Torah, with all our heart and mind and strength?

| Deu 4:2 | "**Do not add to the Word which I command you, and do not take away from it, so as to guard the commands of** יהוה your Elohim which I am commanding you. |
| | \*\*\* |
| Deu 4:6 | "And you shall **guard and do them, for this is your wisdom and your understanding** before the eyes of the peoples who hear all these laws, and they shall say, 'Only a wise and understanding people is this great nation!' |
| | \*\*\* |
| Deu 6:24 | And יהוה commanded us to do **all** these laws, **to fear** יהוה our Elohim, for **our good always**, to **keep us alive**, as it is today. |
| Deu 6:25 | And **it is righteousness for us when we guard to do all this command** before יהוה our Elohim, as He has commanded us.' |

You see, it's through walking in obedience to what the Torah commands, without additions or subtractions, that we gain the wisdom and understanding that YHWH desires us to have. It is how we live our lives in fear or reverence of Him and it is how we live righteously before Him.

When we live in complete obedience to the Torah, with all our heart and mind and strength, as believers in Yahushua Messiah, we then bear the fruit of all our good works, which YHWH had prepared before Messiah came, that His people should live by (Ephesians 2:10).

For "All Scripture", including the Torah, "is breathed out by Elohim and profitable **for teaching, for reproof, for setting straight, for instruction in righteousness**, that the man of Elohim might be fitted, **equipped for every good work**" (2 Timothy 3:16-17).

Interestingly, in the Hebrew mindset, we understand that breath and spirit are connected, so when the Scripture says it has been "breathed out by Elohim", we understand that it is His Spirit that inspires the writing of the Word, and that Word has been settled in heaven forever, and it cannot be added to or taken away from, by **ANYONE**.

It is important to remember, Paul has told us clearly in Galatians 5:25, that those of us who are **in the spirit** (believers in Yahushua Messiah) should also **walk in the spirit** (live in obedience to the Torah) and that is how we produce the **fruit of the Spirit** in our lives.

Paul goes on in Colossians 1, to say that Messiah "is the likeness of the invisible Elohim, the first-born of all creation".

Notice the word "is", which refers to Messiah's present state, years after His resurrection. Also notice that Messiah is referred to here as the "firstborn of all creation".

The word here for "creation" is the Greek word "ktisis", which means formation, and can be translated as both creation and creature, which is how the (KJV) translates it.

This is a statement that Messiah is, in His post-resurrection form, the "likeness of the invisible Elohim", which is similar to the form in which man was originally created.

Genesis 1:27 says that "Elohim created the man in His image, in the image of Elohim He created him". So, man was originally created in the image and likeness of YHWH and remained that way until he sinned.

Once man sinned, all his children were born in the likeness of their father Adam (Gen 5:3), under the condemnation of death (Rom 5:12-21).

Messiah, after His resurrection, became the firstborn "from the dead" of all creation. Any time you see a reference to Messiah being the "firstborn", it is a reference to His resurrection, Him being the firstborn from the dead.

This is the hope that all believers should be working towards, the resurrection from the dead, so that we too might attain the image and likeness of our Father, YHWH.

Paul goes on, in Colossians 1:24-25, to describe the purpose of his ministry, which is to bring the Gentiles into the Assembly of YHWH, His people Yisra'el. He speaks about a "secret which has been hidden from ages and from generations", but that has now been revealed.

This secret has to do with Gentile inclusion into the belief, specifically, the fact that Yahushua would dwell within Gentiles, just as He would within Yisra'el, so that

718

they too had the hope of eternal life as resurrected believers. Is Gentile inclusion truly a secret that no one knew about?

Modern theologians say that this secret that was hidden, this mystery, had not been revealed to the ages past but was now only being revealed to the "1st Century Church". We disagree!

We must discern the difference between what Paul is saying and what he is not saying. Paul is **NOT** saying that the knowledge of Gentile inclusion had never been given, only that the understanding of it had never been revealed.

The Tanak (OT) is replete with prophecies and shadow pictures concerning the Messiah and Gentile inclusion, the "mixed multitude" of people that came out of Mitsrayim (Egypt) with Yisra'el (Exodus 12:37-38) and stood at the base of Mount Sinai to hear the covenant, being just one of many.

Certain prophecies very specifically spoke concerning the fact that Messiah would draw all men to Himself (John 12:32; Mat 12:18-24 [Isa 42:1-4]), in fulfillment of YHWH's promise to Abraham that in Him, all the clans of the earth would be blessed (Gen 12:1-4).

What people need to understand is that there is "nothing new" in the so-called "New Testament", it is only the partial fulfillment of what had been prophesied in the Tanak, for there are still many things written therein, which have yet to be fulfilled by Messiah Yahushua.

The most important contextual element in Colossians 1 we need to take ahold of moving forward, is that Paul was exhorting them to live righteously, worthily of Messiah, which is a reference to obedience to the Torah (Law).

Yes, there are other contextual elements within chapter 1 that are important to understanding the complete belief, however, the reason this specific contextual element is important, is because of the way modern teachers have misinterpreted chapter 2.

Having now established, in chapter 1, that all believers should "walk worthy of Messiah", in obedience to the Torah of YHWH, so that they can be "filled with the knowledge of His desire in all wisdom and spiritual understanding", bearing "fruit in every good work and increasing in the knowledge of Elohim" (Col 1:9-10), we can now move on to chapter 2.

| Col 2:1 | For I wish you to know what a great struggle I have for you and those in Laodikeia, and for **as many as have not seen my face** in the flesh, |

Paul includes the Assembly at Laodikeia in this letter and states that neither had seen his face, i.e., they had never met him personally.

| Col 2:2 | in order that their hearts might be encouraged, being knit together in love, and to all riches of **the entire confirmation of understanding**, to a **true knowledge of the secret of Elohim**, and of the Father, **and of the Messiah,** |
| Col 2:3 | **in whom are hidden all the treasures of wisdom and knowledge**. |

Paul lets them know that it is his desire for them to be encouraged, "being knit together in love", which is the foundation of the Torah (loving YHWH, and your neighbor as yourself – Mat 22:36-40).

He also mentions the riches of the "entire confirmation of understanding, to a true knowledge of the secret" mentioned in chapter 1, i.e., Messiah in the Gentile believer. It is important to see that Paul says, "in (Messiah) **ARE** hidden all the treasures of wisdom and knowledge".

Just as he said in chapter 1, that Messiah "is", in His resurrected form, "the likeness of the invisible Elohim, the first-born of all creation", so too, within Him, His resurrected form, "are hidden all the treasures of wisdom and knowledge".

What Paul means here, is that Messiah, in His resurrected form, is the fulfillment of all wisdom and knowledge taught in the Torah, He is the cornerstone upon which all of the Torah and the Prophets are built.

This **DOES NOT** mean that since Messiah has come, the Torah and the Prophets are no longer relevant or have in any way lost their authority.

Messiah, in His present resurrected form, is the goal of all those who believe in Him, we are all striving to be like Him at the resurrection. To receive this reward, we must be transformed from the image of Adam, our earthly father, into the image of our Heavenly Father, of whom Yahushua is the embodiment.

There is only one way for this transformation to happen, but this one way has two parts. The first part is spiritual and has to do with being saved (delivered) from the guilt of sin and the penalty of death we all inherited from our earthly father, Adam, and that we all walked in of our own free will.

This first part, spiritual justification, is accomplished through the sacrifice of Yahushua as our Passover Lamb, who is the Lamb of YHWH, sent to pay the price for sin through His own death. His sacrifice is the **ONLY** way this first part of the transformation can be fulfilled.

The second part of the transformation, physical justification, is fulfilled when we as individual believers, choose of our own free will, to walk in obedience to the Way our Master lived out His life, i.e., in complete obedience to the Torah of YHWH as it was given at Mt. Sinai, without additions or subtractions.

As we have stated many times in this writing, the *Two-Part Principle* represents what He did for us, i.e., "grace through faith" and what we do in response to it, i.e., obey His Word with all of our heart, mind and strength.

This principle, lived out in compassion for one another, ends in the "entire conformation" of understanding and knowledge of the secret of Elohim and Messiah.

Christian teachers today have no CONCEPT of this principle because they have thrown the "Old Testament" into the trash bin of history, claiming the Torah no longer applies in the life of the believer today, thereby isolating themselves, and all who hear them, from any hope of true understanding.

Interestingly though, these teachers who say, believers no longer have to consider part of the "Old Testament" (the Torah) to be important in our lives today, will tell you the prophecies of the last days, written in the Tanak, are still important for believers today, so that we can know what will happen in the future.

They can't have it both ways, either everything in the so-called "Old Testament" has been done away with or everything in it still applies today.

***

| | |
|---|---|
| **Col 2:4** | And this I say, **so that no one deceives you with enticing words**. |
| **Col 2:5** | For though I am absent in the flesh, yet I am with you in spirit, rejoicing to see your good order and the steadfastness of your belief in Messiah. |

**NOTICE**, he begins this section with a warning not to be deceived by "enticing words".

| | |
|---|---|
| **Enticing words:** | stg's #**G4086** "pithanologia", a compound word meaning, (derivative of G3982) to convince or persuade, and (G3056) something said; persuasive language. Refers to a convincing or persuasive argument (teaching). |

Paul warned Brother Timothy that this very thing would happen within the Assembly.

| | |
|---|---|
| **2Ti 4:3** | For the time will come when they will **not endure sound doctrine**; but **after their own lusts** shall they heap to themselves teachers, **having itching ears;** |
| **2Ti 4:4** | And **they shall turn away** *their* **ears from the truth**, and **shall be turned unto fables.** |

This passage in Colossians 2 is a prime example of how modern teachers have interpreted Paul's writings to pacify themselves and those who hear them, teaching them untruths disguised as righteousness.

It is important to see that Paul says he is "rejoicing to see your good order and steadfastness of your belief in Messiah".

There are two things being said, which are technically one thing, but the church misses it because it has rejected the first part and sold itself out completely to the second part, which without the first part is dead. Let us explain.

His reference to "good order" is associated to how they are living their lives, while their "steadfastness of your belief" refers to their firm foundation in the death, burial and resurrection of Yahushua Messiah, the Good News.

**REMEMBER**, the True Belief is founded solely and completely on the death, burial and resurrection of Yahushua Messiah, yet as believers in Messiah we are to live out our lives in diligent obedience to the Torah of YHWH, just as Messiah did.

The *Two-Part Principle* requires a belief (spiritual) lived out in obedience to the Torah (physical) with an attitude of love towards others. What did Brother James say about this?

| | |
|---|---|
| **Jam 2:14** | My brothers, what use is it for anyone to say he has belief but does not have works? This belief is unable to save him. |
| **Jam 2:15** | And if a brother or sister is naked and in need of daily food, |
| **Jam 2:16** | but one of you says to them, "Go in peace, be warmed and be filled," but you do not give them the bodily needs, what use is it? |
| **Jam 2:17** | So also belief, if it does not have works, is in itself dead. |
| **Jam 2:18** | But someone might say, "You have belief, and I have works." Show me your belief without your works, and **I shall show you my belief by my works.** |
| **Jam 2:19** | You believe that **Elohim is one** You do well. **The demons also believe – and shudder!** |

| | |
|---|---|
| **Jam 2:20** | But do you wish to know, **O foolish man, that the belief without the works is dead?** |
| **Jam 2:21** | Was not Aḇraham our father **declared right by works when he offered Yitsḥaq his son on the slaughter-place?** |
| **Jam 2:22** | Do you see that the **belief was working with his works, and by the works the belief was perfected?** |
| **Jam 2:23** | **And the Scripture was filled which says, "Aḇraham believed Elohim, and it was reckoned to him for righteousness."** And He called him, "he who loves Elohim." |
| **Jam 2:24** | You see, then, **that a man is declared right by works, and not by belief alone.** |
| **Jam 2:25** | In the same way, was not Raḥaḇ the whore also declared right by works when she received the messengers and sent them out another way? |
| **Jam 2:26** | For as the body without the spirit is dead, so also the belief is dead without the works. |

Christians read this all the time and yet they still don't get it because their understanding is not based on the same foundational principles as that of the early Messianic writers.

In this passage, we see clearly that we should **NOT** think that belief alone fulfills the redemption plan of YHWH, however, a belief **worked out** does fulfill it. Why?

Belief is not perfect (complete) unless it is lived out in obedience to the righteous standards upon which the redemption is founded, i.e., the Torah.

We see here that even the demons believe that "Elohim is One", but they still tremble because they know He will not accept them due to their disobedience (rebellion).

The reference to Elohim being One comes from the Shema (Deuteronomy 6:4-9), which Messiah Himself declared to be the Greatest Commandment.

| | |
|---|---|
| **Deu 6:4** | "Hear, O Yisra'ĕl: יהוה our Elohim, יהוה **is one**! |
| **Deu 6:5** | "And you shall love יהוה your Elohim with all your heart, and with all your being, and with all your might. |
| **Deu 6:6** | "And these Words which I am commanding you today shall be in your heart, |
| **Deu 6:7** | and you shall impress them upon your children, and shall speak of them when you sit in your house, and when you walk by the way, and when you lie down, and when you rise up, |
| **Deu 6:8** | and shall bind them as a sign on your hand, and they shall be as frontlets between your eyes. |
| **Deu 6:9** | "And you shall write them on the doorposts of your house and on your gates. |

**Hear**: stg's # **H8085** "shâma", a primitive root; to hear intelligently (often with implication of attention, obedience, etc. Refers to hearing with intent and would be better understood if translated as the English word "listen", which itself carries the implication of obedience.

**One**: stg's # **H259** "echâd", from a word meaning (H258) to unify; properly *united*, that is, *one*; or (as an ordinal) *first*. Refers to complete and absolute unity **in** one, as well as complete and absolute unity **as** one.

Paul's use of the phrase "itching ears" in 1 Timothy 4:3, refers to someone who is double minded, who hears the way they should go, but doesn't like it. Because of this

725

fleshly (rebellious), stubborn (idolatrous) attitude, they are easily susceptible to false teaching, which will lead them astray.

**Note**: Paul says the fleshly mind cannot please YHWH, why?

**Rom 8:6**     For **the mind of the flesh is death**, but the mind of the Spirit is life and peace.

**Rom 8:7**     Because the mind of the flesh is **enmity towards Elohim, for it does not subject itself to the Torah of Elohim**, neither indeed is it able,

**Rom 8:8**     and those who are in the flesh **are unable to please Elohim**.

Refusing to **subject oneself** to the laws or teachings of one's superior is an act of rebellion. Here in Romans 8, we see that the fleshly mind rebels specifically against the Torah (Law) of YHWH.

Also, let's consider what the prophet Shemu'el (Samuel) had to say to King Saul concerning this.

**1Sa 15:22**     Then Shemu'ĕl said, "Does יהוה delight in ascending offerings and slaughterings, as in obeying the voice of יהוה? Look, **to obey is better than a slaughtering, to heed is** *better* **than the fat of rams**.

**1Sa 15:23**     "**For rebellion is as the sin of divination, and stubbornness is as wickedness and idolatry**. Because you have rejected the word of יהוה, He also does reject you as sovereign."

To YHWH, refusing to obey His Torah is the same thing as witchcraft and to be stubborn against the true teaching of the Good News of Yahushua Messiah, which includes the requirement to obey the Torah of YHWH in our belief, is idolatry.

When Paul said that they would "turn away their ears from the truth" in 2 Timothy 4:4, he meant, their heart attitude made them unwilling to obey the truth when they heard it.

The people Paul is referring to in 2 Timothy 4 are just like the demons James is talking about (Jam 2:19), they know that YHWH is "echad" (one), but they do not obey Him.

As shown above, the Hebrew word "echad" refers to complete and absolute unity, so when the Scripture says the Messiah and the Father are one, it means They are in complete and absolute unity with one another, both in thought and action.

Thus, the Messiah, Yahushua, can do and say **NOTHING** that would in

any way change or diminish what the Father has already said. When YHWH instituted His Torah as the Way of righteous living for His people at Mount Sinai, Messiah **could not and did not** in any way change how the people of YHWH were to live their lives before Him.

**ANY OTHER TEACHING**, is of the enemy, designed for those who are unwilling to walk in obedience to the Torah, without additions or subtractions.

The Christian church today is in a similar position as the demons mentioned in James 2:14 because they claim to know that YHWH is "echad" (One) and they believe that Yahushua and the Father are One (echad), just as He said, but they do not live as if this were true, for if they were, they would be obeying the Torah of YHWH, not rejecting it.

Unfortunately, the church is in a much more dangerous place then those demons because the demons at least **KNOW** they are destined for the Lake of Fire, but the church **BELIEVES** it is the Righteous Bride of Messiah and destined for the Kingdom, despite its refusal to obey the Torah.

**Note**:   Among the Messianic Assembly today, there is a movement against the Trinitarian idea of oneness (3 in 1) held by the Christian church, and rightly so.

However, Messianic teachers today, in their zeal to quash the false doctrine of

727

Trinitarianism, have went so far that they have ignored certain truths concerning the nature of YHWH, His power and His Son (For more information on this see Appendix 1: "Echad", pg. 543).

James, in 2:20, implies that the man who thinks his belief does not need to be followed by works, is a foolish man.

He goes on in vs. 21-23 to explain how the righteousness that YHWH imputed to Abraham in Genesis 15 was not perfected (completed) until Abraham was about to offer his son Isaac (Yitschaq) to YHWH as a burnt offering in Genesis 22.

If you remember, we talked about the difference in men claiming to know YHWH and YHWH claiming to know them, and we used the same passage of Scripture to explain it.

Even though YHWH had declared Abraham righteous because of his belief in Genesis 15, YHWH did not claim to know Abraham would serve Him, until **AFTER** Abraham was about to plunge the knife into his son.

In both cases, it was not until Abraham was acting out (doing) what he had been commanded to do that YHWH considered his belief complete.

> **Note**: There are many other examples of this principle in the Tanak, even in the life of Abraham:
>
> 1.  When YHWH called Abram out of Haran to go into a land he did not know, Abram went (Gen 12:1-4)
> 2.  When YHWH told Abram that He was giving the land to his seed, Abram built an altar in His Name, as a remembrance (Gen 12:7).
> 3.  When YHWH promised Abram that He would give Him an heir from his own body, it says he believed, and YHWH declared him righteous (Gen 15:1-6).

Other examples:

1. YHWH requires blood sacrifices and Abel (Hebel) gave one and was accepted.
2. YHWH commanded Noah to build an ark, he built it and saved himself and his family.
3. YHWH sent Moses back to Egypt, he went and accomplished miracles and the deliverance of his people.
4. YHWH commanded Joshua (Yahushua) concerning Jericho, he obeyed and saw its walls crumble before him.
5. David trusted the promises of YHWH more than he feared. men and defeated Goliath with a small stone.
6. Yahushua trusted the promises of YHWH so completely that He obeyed the Torah His entire life and suffered the pain of a horrible death. In doing so He became the Savior of the world and was resurrected act as High Priest for the set-apart ones until He returns as their King.

Our works prove or perfect (complete) our belief and scripturally these two terms, belief and works, refer to very specific things.

In the singular, the One, we know that there is the written Torah (Law/Word) that was given at Mount Sinai and there is the living Torah (Law/Word) that was born to the maiden, Miryam.

Understand this, the living Torah and the written Torah cannot be separated and thus, to say you believe in the Messiah, and yet refuse to obey the Torah, makes your belief in Messiah, dead (empty, of no value).

Belief is always about Yahushua, while works is always about the Torah, and the two cannot be separated.

So, when James says that belief without works is dead, he's referring to those people who claim the death, burial and resurrection of Yahushua in their lives, yet refuse to obey the Torah of YHWH as it was given at Mount Sinai, without additions or subtractions.

He is telling these people that their belief has no value, it's empty, meaning nothing, because their willful disobedience proves they are not sons, but transgressors.

This is the same thing Paul said in Galatians 2:17-18.

**Gal 2:17** "And if, while seeking to be declared right by Messiah, **we ourselves also are found sinners**, is Messiah then a servant of sin? Let it not be!

**Gal 2:18** "For if I rebuild what I *once* overthrew, **I establish myself a transgressor**.

To these types of people the writer of Hebrews had something else to say.

**Heb 10:26** For if **we sin purposely after we have received the knowledge of the truth**, there no longer remains a slaughter *offering* for sins,

**Heb 10:27** but some fearsome anticipation of judgment, and a fierce fire which is about to consume the opponents.

**Heb 10:28** Anyone who has disregarded the Torah of Mosheh dies without compassion on the witness of two or three witnesses.

**Heb 10:29** How much **worse punishment** do you think shall he deserve who **has trampled the Son of Elohim underfoot, counted the blood of the covenant by which he <u>was</u> set apart as common, and insulted the Spirit of favour?**

**Heb 10:30** For we know Him who has said, **"Vengeance is Mine, I shall repay, says יהוה."** And again, **"יהוה shall judge His people."**

**Heb 10:31** It is fearsome to fall into the hands of the living Elohim.

Notice, the writer starts off with the pronoun "we", because if you go further up in the text to verse 19 you'll see he is talking to the brethren.

"If we **sin purposely**", is a reference to knowing what the Torah says and refusing to obey it, i.e., rebellion. It can be referring to nothing but Torah obedience because in the writings of Brother John (1 John 3:4) we are told that the definition of "sin" is "anomia", lawlessness.

The Greek word "a-nom-ia", literally means "no law doing" and is a specific reference to the Torah of YHWH. The word "Nomos" is the Greek word that translators use for the Hebrew word "Torah".

The "nom" is the conjugated form of the word "Nomos", so the word "anomia" actually means "no Torah doing", referring to the Torah that YHWH gave at Mount Sinai.

So, those who have believed in Yahushua (we), but **INTENTIONALLY REFUSE** to obey the Torah of YHWH, have **REJECTED** the only sacrifice that could save them, having "trampled the Son of Elohim underfoot" and are counting the blood of the covenant by which they **WERE** set apart as common (unclean), thus insulting the Spirit of favor (grace) that made them born again in the inner man.

This type of person has only one thing to look forward to, a **"fearsome anticipation of judgment, and a fierce fire which is about to consume the opponents"**, when **"יהוה shall judge His people"** and they **"fall into the hands of the living Elohim"**.

Consider what Paul told the Thessalonians about Messiah's return.

| | |
|---|---|
| **2Th 1:7** | and to give you who are afflicted rest with us when the Master יהושע **is revealed from heaven with His mighty messengers**, |
| **2Th 1:8** | **in flaming fire taking vengeance** on those **who do not know Elohim, and on those who do not obey the Good News of our Master** יהושע **Messiah,** |
| **2Th 1:9** | **who shall be punished with everlasting destruction** from the presence of the Master and from the esteem of His strength, |

731

**REMEMBER**, "The one who says, 'I know Him', and **does not guard His commands**, is a **liar**, and **the truth is not in him**" (1Jn 2:4), because "The one who says he stays in Him ought himself also to walk, even as He walked (1Jn 2:6).

Messiah, "knew no sin", meaning that He never violated the Torah of YHWH in any way.

He was made "*to be* sin for us", meaning that He took all of our sin upon Himself so that we could be set free from the penalty of sin and death, when we believed in His death, burial and resurrection.

He did this so "we might be made the righteousness of Elohim in Him", meaning that through our belief in Messiah Yahushua we can achieve the righteous standard (Torah) that YHWH expects of His people (2 Co 5:21).

Can we accomplish the righteousness of Elohim by our own works? **NO**!!! Does that mean that we are no longer required to do the righteous works of Torah? **NO**!!!

How then, can we accomplish the righteousness of Elohim as believers in

Yahushua Messiah? The answer to this question is **NOT** founded in doing the works of Torah, it is founded in where we place our **TRUST**.

If we obey the righteous works of Torah, trusting in them for our ultimate redemption, then our trust has been misplaced and we shall be judged by the Torah as sinners and condemned.

However, if our trust is firmly, completely and unwaveringly founded in the GOOD NEWS of Yahushua Messiah, then, and only then, will our obedience to the righteous works of Torah accomplish in us the righteousness of Elohim.

The righteousness of YHWH can only be accomplished in the fully committed heart of an obedient believer, for it is in this state of commitment that His mercy and grace is extended to us when we stumble.

Having said all this, let's move on to verse 6 of Colossians 2, remembering Paul's exhortation to "walk worthily of Messiah" as the "righteousness of Elohim".

**Col 2:6**     Therefore, as you accepted Messiah יהושע the Master, walk in Him,

732

| Col 2:7 | having been rooted and built up in Him, and established in the belief, as you were taught, overflowing in it with thanksgiving. |
|---|---|

Here again we see Paul exhorting the believers to "walk in Him", which means the same thing as "walk as He walked" (1John 2:6).

Being "rooted and built up in Him and established in the belief" is a clear reference to their walk of obedience, for it is through obedience to the Torah (Law) of YHWH that we confirm or establish (perfect) our belief.

| Rom 3:28 | For we reckon that a man is declared right by belief without works of Torah. |
|---|---|
| Rom 3:29 | Or *is He* the Elohim of the Yehudim only, and not also of the nations? Yes, of the nations also, |
| Rom 3:30 | since it is one Elohim who shall declare right the circumcised by belief and the uncircumcised through belief. |
| Rom 3:31 | **Do we then nullify the Torah through the belief? Let it not be! On the contrary, we establish the Torah.** |

Paul's argument in Romans 3 concerned how we are justified (made right) from the condemnation of death for sin and so he is rejecting the Torah as a means of justification **ONLY**.

Just because the Torah cannot justify a man from condemnation **DOES NOT** mean that the Torah no longer applies to the man as a means of righteous living, as modern teachers claim.

In Romans 3, Paul is referring to a very specific thing, i.e., justification **FROM** death, and there is only one way to be justified from death, through the blood of Yahushua.

The Torah cannot justify a man from death because it was the Torah that condemned the man when he sinned (disobeyed the Torah-1 John 3:4), it is the Torah that gives sin the power (authority) to kill the disobedient (1 Cor 15:55).

The sacrificial system was established to show us the principle of substitutionary death, where only the blood of a worthy sacrifice could atone for disobedience to the Torah.

Paul goes on to ask, if belief alone justifies us, does our belief nullify our responsibility to obey the Torah and his answer is, **ABSOLUTELY NOT!!!**

In fact, he says, the opposite is true. Belief establishes the Torah in the life of the believer by making a way for him to live in obedience to the Torah without having to fear condemnation when he stumbles.

This is the same thing Paul means in Colossians 2:6-7 when he tells them to "walk in Him" (Obey the Torah as He did), being "rooted and grounded" in Him through belief. This is what it means to be "established in the belief" (belief followed by obedience without fear).

| | |
|---|---|
| **Rom 8:14** | For as many as are led by the Spirit of Elohim, these are sons of Elohim. |
| **Rom 8:15** | For **you did not receive the spirit of bondage again to fear, but you received the Spirit of adoption** by whom we cry out, "Abba, Father." |
| **Rom 8:16** | The Spirit Himself bears witness with our spirit that we are children of Elohim, |
| **Rom 8:17** | and if children, also heirs – truly heirs of Elohim, and co-heirs with Messiah, if indeed we suffer with Him, in order that we also be exalted together. |

When our inner-spirit-man is committed to walking in obedience to the leading of the Spirit of YHWH, whose job it is to "cause" believers to "walk in [His] laws and guard [His] right-rulings and … do them (Ezek 36:27), we have no reason to fear being condemned when we stumble because we have rejected the leading of the outer-fleshly-man, who "does not subject itself to the Torah of Elohim" (Rom 8:7).

**REMEMBER**, the True Belief is a belief that is walked out in obedience to the Torah of YHWH, without additions or subtractions, trusting **ONLY** in the Good News of Yahushua Messiah and **NEVER** in the works of Torah, from a heart attitude of mercy and compassion for each other.

Now, verse 8 of Colossians 2 is going to set the context upon which the rest of the chapter is to be understood.

**Col 2:8**    See to it that no one makes a prey of you through **philosophy and empty deceit, according to the tradition of men, according to the elementary matters of the world, and not according to Messiah**

Paul tells the Colossians to make sure that no one "makes a prey" of them, meaning that there are wolves that will come in among the sheep and devour them through false teaching. The false teaching that he is referring to is the "teachings of men" that are contrary to the true teachings of the Scripture.

Paul specifically references "philosophy" and the "elementary matters of the world", which are a reference to man-made theologies and ideologies.

**"Philosophy**:    (from Greek φιλοσοφία, philosophia, literally "love of wisdom") is the study of general and fundamental problems concerning matters such as existence, knowledge, values, reason, mind, and language. The term was probably coined by Pythagoras (c. 570–495 BCE).

"Philosophical methods include questioning, critical discussion, rational argument, and systematic presentation." (Wikipedia)

735

As the above definition says, philosophy is the study of general fundamental issues concerning matters such as existence, knowledge, values, reason, mind, and language.

However, the methods by which philosophers come to their conclusions is based in the intellectual capacity of the finite human mind, and not in the infinite and superior mind of YHWH, the Creator of all things.

The phrase "elementary matters of the world" is a reference to man-made religion's, i.e., idolatry and such.

| | |
|---|---|
| **Gal 4:8** | But then, indeed, not knowing Elohim, you served those **which by nature are not mighty ones.** |
| **Gal 4:9** | But now after you have known Elohim, or rather are known by Elohim, how do you **turn again to the weak and poor elementary matters**, to which you wish to be enslaved again? |

"But then" is a reference to the time before the Galatians believed in Yahushua for justification from death, when they served false deities (idols).

"But now" is a reference to their present state of belief in Yahushua and Paul is asking them why they "turn again" to the "elementary matters" of idolatry.

Paul equates philosophy with "empty deceit" because the conclusions the philosophers come to have no eternal value; they are based in man-made reasoning.

He warns the Colossians to be careful not to be taken in by any teaching, no matter how much sense it seems to make, that is not based solely in the "Good News" of Yahushua Messiah.

| | |
|---|---|
| **Col 2:9** | Because in Him dwells all the completeness of Elohim-ness bodily, |
| **Col 2:10** | and you have been made complete in Him, who is the Head of all principality and authority. |

"In Him dwells" is a present tense phrase, referring to His present resurrected form, in which He is the completeness of Elohim bodily.

Yahushua is the Word of YHWH in resurrected human form and as such the fulness of what it is to be YHWH resides within Him and as His people we are made complete through our belief in Him, a belief that is "worked out".

This is true because He has been granted power and authority over all creation by the Father, YHWH.

| | |
|---|---|
| **Mat 28:18** | And יהושע came up and spoke to them, saying, "All authority has been given to Me in heaven and on earth. |

Paul makes this statement, concerning the Colossians being "complete in Him", based on his personal knowledge of their spiritual condition.

It is possible for someone to believe that Yahushua is the Messiah and yet not be "complete in Him", because they did not bear the fruit of righteousness, as Messiah Himself says in John 15.

| | |
|---|---|
| **Joh 15:1** | "I am the true vine, and My Father is the gardener. |
| **Joh 15:2** | **"Every branch in Me that bears no fruit He takes away**. And every branch that bears fruit He prunes, so that it bears more fruit. |
| **Joh 15:3** | "You are already clean because of the Word which I have spoken to you. |
| **Joh 15:4** | "Stay in Me, and I *stay* in you. As the branch is unable to bear fruit of itself, unless it stays in the vine, so neither you, unless you stay in Me. |
| **Joh 15:5** | "I am the vine, you are the branches. He who stays in Me, and I in him, he bears much fruit. Because without Me you are able to do naught! |

| Joh 15:6 | "If anyone does not stay in Me, he is thrown away as a branch and dries up. And they gather them and throw them into the fire, and they are burned. |
| Joh 15:7 | "If you stay in Me, and My Words stay in you, you shall ask whatever you wish, and it shall be done for you. |
| Joh 15:8 | "In this My Father is esteemed, **that you bear much fruit, and you shall be My taught ones.** |

In this passage, the Messiah refers to Himself as the true vine, which is a reference to Him being the "Righteous Branch" prophesied in Jeremiah (YirmeYahu) 23:5; 33:15.

As the Righteous Branch, all His taught ones (the branches) must bear the fruit of righteousness, and those who don't bear this fruit are taken away, thrown away as a branch and thrown into the fire.

Since Paul already knows the spiritual state of the Colossians, he can say their belief in Yahushua makes them complete in Him, and since He has all power and authority, He can keep them till the end, if they remain in Him.

| Col 2:11 | In Him you were also circumcised with a circumcision not made with hands, in the putting off of the body of the sins of the flesh, by the circumcision of Messiah, |
| Col 2:12 | having been buried with Him in immersion, in which you also were raised with Him through the belief in the working of Elohim, who raised Him from the dead. |

The circumcision Paul is referring to here is that of the heart, which is a heart committed to obedience, having submitted to the Torah of YHWH.

Verse 12 is a restatement of what he taught in Romans 6:1-2, where he used baptism as a shadow picture of our dying with Messiah and being raised up again to the "newness of life".

| | |
|---|---|
| **Col 2:13** | And you, being dead in your trespasses and the uncircumcision of your flesh, He has made alive together with Him, having forgiven you all trespasses, |
| **Col 2:14** | having blotted out that which was written by hand against us – **by the dogmas** – which stood against us. And He has taken it out of the way, having nailed it to the stake. |
| **Col 2:15** | Having stripped the principalities and the authorities, He made a public display of them, having prevailed over them in it. |

Here's the point where Christian teachers begin to lose their way in their interpretation of what Paul means in this passage. The context of Colossians 2 is the false teachings of man-made theologies and ideologies, which are empty deceit and idolatry.

This passage then, must be understood in that context. Yes, our belief in Messiah cleanses us from all sin of every kind, however, in this case Paul is referring to the trespasses associated to what we used to trust in and were obedient to, i.e., false man-made, religion and ideology.

This would refer to any man-made religious practice, whether it be that of the idolatrous religions of the Gentile world or the pseudo-righteous practices of the Jewish religion of the time, which required adherence to the "traditions of the elders".

It is these man-made religious and ideological traditions (dogmas) that has trapped man in the cycle of misunderstanding of, and disobedience to, the Torah of YHWH. It is these man-made dogmas that have been nailed to the tree (stake, cross) and **NOT** the Torah of YHWH.

Because of His sacrifice, Messiah stripped all authority, physical and spiritual, from these theological and ideological dogmas, and from the beings that created them, and in His resurrection, He prevailed over them.

| | |
|---|---|
| **Col 2:16** | Let no one therefore judge you in eating or in drinking, or in respect of |

| | a festival or a new moon or Sabbaths – |
|---|---|
| **Col 2:17** | which **are** a shadow of what **is to come** – but the Body of the Messiah. |

Keeping in mind the context of this chapter, which was spelled out in verse 8, concerning man-made religious doctrine and secular ideology, we must consider versus 16-17 as a contrast to the warning against these man-made teachings.

So, when Paul says "let no one therefore judge you" he's referring to allowing those people that he warned us about, to judge us in how we live in Yahushua.

Basically, he's telling the Gentile believers, now that they are in Messiah Yahushua, they need to stop listening to the doctrines of their former beliefs and not let anyone from their past dictate to them how they should live.

Believers in Messiah live in obedience to the Torah of YHWH and no one from our past belief system has any authority to tell us how to live or to judge us in our belief in Yahushua.

Paul goes on to say in verse 17 that the eating, drinking, festivals, new moons and Sabbaths "are a shadow picture of what is to come". Notice, the language, "are" a present tense word and "what is to come", is a future tense word.

Paul, many years after Messiah's ascension, says that the commands of the Torah still have future significance, meaning that everything the Torah commands are still pictures of things yet to come.

Christian teachers like to use prophecy from the Tanak to warn people about what's coming in the future, which is appropriate, and they also claim the promises written in the Tanak for themselves, yet they reject all the requirements of the Torah even though those promises hinge on our submission to the Torah.

Now, as important as understanding the future tense of what he said in verse 17 is, the most important part of that verse are the last six words.

We are going to quote verse 17 again from both the King James version and the Scriptures version so that you can see the difference in how they are translated.

740

| Col 2:17 | Which are a shadow of things to come; but the body *is* of Christ. (KJV) |
|---|---|

***

| Col 2:17 | which are a shadow of what is to come – but the Body of the Messiah. |
|---|---|

Notice, in the King James version there is an "is", which does not exist in the Scriptures version.

If the publisher and translators of your Bible have any integrity at all, in the beginning of your Bible there will be a section on translation and in it they will tell you that words in italics have been added for clarification.

Unfortunately, most of the time these italicized words don't actually give the proper meaning of the passage, but they do give you the meaning of the passage according to what the translators want you to get from it.

Yes, we are saying that the translators took liberties and added words to manipulate the meaning of the passages in which they're used, so that the reader would get the understanding the translators wanted them to get.

Was this done intentionally, we don't know, but what we do know is they have caused no end of confusion and false doctrine.

For example, in John 1:17 we find this statement in the King James version:

| Joh 1:17 | For the law was given by Moses, *but* grace and truth came by Jesus Christ. |
|---|---|

Notice that the word "but" is italicized. If you find a good Greek interlinear Bible, like the J. P. Green interlinear Bible, you'll find that this word is not in the Greek but was added by translators. The word "but" is a conjunction just like the word "and" except that the word "but" is used to show a contrast between two points.

The translators added the word "but" because they wanted to show that there is a contrast between the Law/Torah that was given through Moses and the "grace and truth" that comes from Yahushua Messiah, basically putting the two in opposition to one another.

741

This is clearly and undeniably a theological addition to the passage and not a legitimate one, because the verse does not need the word "but" to be understood correctly. Here is the verse in the Scriptures version.

**Joh 1:17**     for the Torah was given through Mosheh – the favour and the truth came through יהושע Messiah.

In this version the translators used a hyphen, which was not necessary, a comma would've worked just fine. The point is, these two statements are not in opposition to one another, they are in fact in agreement with one another because the Torah of YHWH is the truth.

**Psa 119:142**     Your righteousness is righteousness **forever**, And Your **Torah is truth**.

You see, John is not telling us the Messiah gave us something greater than the Torah, he is saying that Messiah gave us favor (grace) and the Torah, meaning that those who are in Yahushua Messiah are able to accomplish the righteousness of the Torah because the favor (grace) of YHWH is extended to us when we stumble.

Now, don't let anyone tell you that those in the Tanak (OT) who strove to obey the Torah, did not receive the favor (grace) of YHWH.

Abraham was accepted by YHWH even though he lied to Pharaoh and King David was a man after YHWH's own heart, even though he stole Uriah's wife and ordered Joab to put him in the worst fighting so that he would be killed.

Both these men dedicated their hearts to serving YHWH, in obedience to His Word/Torah, every day of their lives and because of that, their mistakes were not counted against them. The same principle works for us, in our belief in Yahushua Messiah, who gave Himself for our sin.

The word "is" in verse 17 of Colossians 2, in the King James Version, is italicized or should be, which means it is not in the Greek text, it was added by the translators.

The end of verse 17 should say, "but the body of Messiah". Why is this important? The passage starts out, "let no one judge you" and finishes with, "but the body of Messiah".

742

Everything between these two phrases are what you are not to let outsiders judge you about, because only those in the Body of Messiah have the authority to judge these matters.

Christianity has twisted the meaning of this passage to say that the Law/Torah of YHWH no longer has significance in the life of the believer because Messiah "nailed it to His tree", "taking it away".

They could not be more wrong, because this passage is telling us that Messiah took all power and authority over all man-made teachings, both religious and secular, having nailed them to His tree, removing them from the lives of His people.

In His resurrection, He showed his superiority over all teachers, both spiritual and physical, who taught these false doctrines.

This being true, none of those teachers, nor any people associated to their false teaching, has the authority to judge the believer when he obeys the Torah of YHWH, in the things he eats or drinks, or in the festivals he keeps or the new moons or the Sabbath, because they are shadow pictures to show the believer what is to come in the future.

The only people that have the authority to make judgments on how a believer is living out the Torah is other believers in the body, and they better know what they're talking about.

| | |
|---|---|
| Col 2:18 | **Let no one deprive you of the prize**, one who takes delight in **false humility and worship of messengers**, taking his stand on what he has not seen, **puffed up by his fleshly mind,** |
| Col 2:19 | and **not holding fast to the Head**, from whom all the Body – nourished and knit together by joints and ligaments – grows with the growth of Elohim. |

Here again, Paul warns us not to let anyone "make a prey" of us and "deprive" us of the "prize", which is the resurrection. The ones that would "make a prey" are those who take delight in "false humility and worship of messengers".

"False humility" is a specific reference to those people who seem, by their actions and their attitudes, to be humble but are not humble according to the scriptural definition, because they do not subject themselves to the Law/Torah of YHWH, a mind of the flesh, according to Paul in Romans 8:7.

"Worship of messengers (angels/demons)" is a specific reference to idolatry, which encompasses much more than the reverence of statues or created things. Idolatry is any form of trust or reference (honor) given to something or someone other than YHWH, which does not always mean a carved image.

> **Deu 28:14**  And **do not turn aside from any of the Words which I am commanding you** today, right or left, **to go after other mighty ones to serve them**.

Notice, in YHWH's way of thinking, turning to the left or to the right of **ANY** of the commands in His Word is the same thing as serving some other elohim (authority).

There are only two kinds of authority in the world, YHWH, as the Creator, is the only true authority, however, there is another being in authority on this planet, because mankind granted him authority by obeying him, and that being is known as the Adversary, Ha-Satan. Paul says in 1 Corinthians 10 that idols are demons.

> **1Co 10:19**  What then do I say? That an idol is of any *value*? Or that which is slaughtered to idols is of any *value*?
>
> **1Co 10:20**  No, but what the nations slaughter **they slaughter to demons** and not to Elohim, and I do not wish you to become sharers with demons. (See also: Lev 17:7; Deut 32:17)

This passage is used in connection to eating things that have been offered to idols, however there is an important principle here, which teaches that by offering things to anyone other than YHWH is to be a servant of that being to whom you give the offering, even if that offering is just your obedience or reverence/respect (Romans 6:16).

For example, the religion of Judaism is not a scriptural religion for it does not adhere strictly to what the Scripture says. Judaism is a religious practice created by rabbis who, though they give a nod to the Torah of YHWH as the foundation of their belief, violate the Torah through the additions or subtractions of man-made religious opinion (dogma).

So, those who practice Judaism are not serving YHWH, but are serving the rabbis instead, their rabbis have become their idols.

The same thing is true for the Christian church, Christianity does not worship YHWH in obedience to His Torah, even though they claim to believe in His Son, Yahushua, who did keep the Torah of YHWH all His life, as an example of how we are to live. WWJD? He would obey the Torah!

Because they have rejected the Torah of YHWH, they have turned the true Messiah, Yahushua, into a false messiah named Jesus, and Jesus is their idol.

Both these, so-called, great religions shall answer to the Messiah at His return and many of their adherents shall be rejected on that day and find themselves in the Lake of Fire, if they don't hear and repent.

In Colossians 2:18, we see that the one who would "make a prey" of the believer is "puffed up in his fleshly mind". What is a "fleshly mind"?

| | |
|---|---|
| **Rom 8:6** | For the **mind of the flesh is death**, but the mind of the Spirit is life and peace. |
| **Rom 8:7** | Because the **mind of the flesh is enmity towards Elohim**, for it **does not subject itself to the Torah of Elohim,** neither indeed is it able, |
| **Rom 8:8** | and those who are in the flesh **are unable to please Elohim**. |

According to Paul, a "fleshly mind" is one that does not subject itself to the Law/Torah of YHWH.

Here again is evidence that what was nailed to the tree is NOT the Torah of YHWH, because the ones that would "make a prey" of the believer and "deprive" them of the prize, do not subject themselves to the Torah of YHWH and so they are unable to please Him.

In this paragraph we have two things contrasted, the truth of the Torah of YHWH and the lie of man-made theologies (idolatry) and ideologies (philosophy), and we will see that contrast again in the next passage.

Before we go there though, Paul says these false teachers were "not holding fast to the Head, from whom all the Body – nourished and knit together by joints and ligaments – grows with the growth of Elohim". "The Head" that he is referring to is Yahushua Messiah, and not holding fast to the Head has a two-part meaning.

First, it's a reference for our need to place our boast or our trust solely and completely in Him.

Secondly, it is a reference to the believers need to live in obedience to the Torah of YHWH just as Yahushua Himself did. It is through obedience to the Torah that the love of YHWH is perfected in us.

| | |
|---|---|
| **1Jn 2:3** | And by this we know that we know Him, **if we guard His commands**. |
| **1Jn 2:4** | The one who says, "I know Him," and does not guard His commands, **is a liar, and the truth is not in him.** |
| **1Jn 2:5** | But whoever guards His Word, **truly the love of Elohim has been perfected in him**. By this we know that we are in Him. |
| **1Jn 2:6** | The one who says he stays in Him **ought himself also to walk, even as He walked**. |

So, we see that Paul is warning us, not to allow people that do not obey the Torah to judge us on whether we should obey the Torah, or how we obey it.

| | |
|---|---|
| **Col 2:20** | **If,** then, **you died with Messiah from the elementary matters of the world**, why, as though living in |

746

| | the world, do you subject yourselves to dogmas |
|---|---|
| Col 2:21 | "Do not touch, do not taste, do not handle" – |
| Col 2:22 | which are all to perish with use – according to the **commands and teachings of men?** |

Once again, the church today will tell you that "do not touch, do not taste, do not handle" is a reference to things written in the Torah, and interpret this to mean that believers no longer have to obey the Torah.

However, does this say that these three commands come from the Torah? **No!!!**

In Messiah, we have died **FROM** the elementary matters of the world (man-made theologies and ideologies) so why do we go back to these worldly "commands and teachings of men" and subject ourselves to them?

| | |
|---|---|
| Col 2:23 | These indeed have an **appearance of wisdom in self-imposed worship**, **humiliation and harsh treatment of the body** – of no **value at all**, *only* **for satisfaction of the flesh.** |

Look closely at this verse now, these "commands and teachings of men", which include the traditions of the rabbis and the doctrines of the Christian church, **APPEAR** to be wisdom in **SELF-IMPOSED WORSHIP.**

To appear to be wisdom, means that it's **NOT** wisdom, it only appears to be. Self-imposed worship is a form of worship **we impose upon ourselves** that is **NOT** required by YHWH.

One of the things we impose upon ourselves, that is **NOT** required by YHWH, is the humiliation and harsh treatment of the body, which may be excessive fasting or any form of flagellation or some other such thing.

| | |
|---|---|
| **Note**: | Flagellation, flogging, whipping or lashing is the act of beating the human body with special implements such as whips, lashes, |

rods, switches, the cat o' nine tails, the sjambok, etc.

Typically, flogging is imposed on an unwilling subject as a punishment; however, it can also be submitted to willingly, or performed on oneself, in religious or sadomasochistic contexts.

According to Paul, this kind of behavior is "of no value at all, only for satisfaction of the flesh". The things we impose upon ourselves, that are **NOT** required by YHWH in His Torah, have no value whatsoever in our attempts to please YHWH, because the only way to please Him is to walk in obedience to His Torah, without additions or subtractions, through belief in His Son, Yahushua, in a heart attitude of mercy and compassion for a fellow man, especially those in the belief.

What these self-imposed regulations do, is make us feel better about ourselves, they please our flesh. An example of this self-imposed worship prevalent today, is the high-octane, emotionally fueled forms of "worship" in church services, meetings, retreats, etc. that raise goose bumps on our flesh, which many adherents think are a sign of the "Spirit moving". Hogwash!!!

Anyone who has ever went to an Ozzy Osbourne concert, or any other high physically or emotionally powered experience, has had this same experience. Goose bumps ARE NOT a sign that the Spirit of YHWH is moving.

Going to "Church" today has become, more and more, about (fleshly) entertainment value and virtually nothing of ANY spiritual value. It's all about feeling good in the flesh!

**REMEMBER**, your flesh is trying to kill you, for "the mind of the flesh is death" (Romans 8:6).

> **Pro 28:26**  He who **trusts in his own heart is a fool**, but he who **walks wisely is delivered**.

It is important to remember what the Scripture says about a man's heart.

748

| | |
|---|---|
| **Gen 6:5** | And יהוה saw that the wickedness of man was great in the earth, and that **every inclination of the thoughts of his heart was only evil continually**. |
| | *** |
| **Jer 17:9** | "The heart is **crooked above all, and desperately sick** – who shall know it? |

(See also: Jer 7:24; 16:12; 18:12; 23:17)

This is still true today, just look around you. Our own thoughts and our own feelings cannot be trusted, it is only when our heart and our mind has been conformed to the righteous principles of the Torah, that they can help us walk in the truth and find deliverance.

| | |
|---|---|
| **Rom 12:1** | I call upon you, therefore, brothers, through the compassion of Elohim, to present your bodies a **LIVING OFFERING** – set-apart, well-pleasing to Elohim – your reasonable worship. |
| **Rom 12:2** | And do not be conformed to this world, but be transformed by the renewing of your mind, so that you prove what is that good and well-pleasing and perfect desire of Elohim. |

# Philippians 3

Another hard saying of Paul which has been thoroughly misunderstood comes from Philippians 3, but before we go there, let's set some context of the book of Philippians.

After introducing himself and giving thanks to YHWH for the remembrance of the Philippians and their fellowship in the "Good News", Paul says something interesting.

| | |
|---|---|
| **Php 1:6** | being persuaded of this, **that He who has begun a good work in you shall perfect it until the day of** יהושע **Messiah**. |
| **Php 1:7** | It is right for me to think this of you all, **because I have you in my heart**, all of you being sharers of the favour with me, both in my chains and in the defense and confirmation of the Good News. |

Many teachers have misunderstood the context of this passage and have taught that verse 6 means that because of our belief in Messiah, YHWH will perfect our good work of belief for us, because they begin with a false presumption that the Law/Torah no longer applies to the believer. However, in verse 7 he says, it is right for him to think this of them "because I have you in my heart".

Paul is **NOT** saying, because of their belief in Yahushua, the Father will perfect them until the day of His return, but because he has them in his heart, he loves them so much, that he believes this will happen.

He believes they are righteous believers, because of all he has heard concerning them, has convinced him of their "good work" of belief. It is the believers "good work" that perfects his belief, unto eternal life as heirs of the Kingdom.

As we have said many times and as Brother James has said (2:14-26), our belief in Yahushua Messiah **MUST** be followed by works of the Torah or our belief is dead (has no life).

Paul is going to say this very thing, just not in so many words, which is his habit.

750

| Php 1:8 | For Elohim is my witness, how I long for you all with the affection of יהושע Messiah. |
| Php 1:9 | And this I pray, that **your love might extend more and more in knowledge and all discernment**, |
| Php 1:10 | for you to **examine the *matters* that differ**, **in order to be sincere, and not stumbling, until the day of Messiah,** |
| Php 1:11 | being filled with **the fruit of righteousness, through** יהושע **Messiah**, to the esteem and praise of Elohim. |

(See also: Mat 3:8-10; Rom 6:22; Rom 14:17; 2Co 9:10; Eph 5:9; Gal 5:22; Col 1:10; Heb 12:11; Jam 3:18 and compare to John 15:1-7)

Paul wants our love to extend (grow) in "knowledge and discernment" so that we are be able to "examine matters that differ" and be "sincere, and not stumbling".

How could he mean in verse 6, that YHWH would perfect our good works FOR us and then turn around and warn us not to be "stumbling"? If the FATHER is doing the work, how can WE stumble?

Paul is saying, his belief in them gives him confidence to say that YHWH will finish a good work in them until Messiah returns and his belief in them is based on the good things he has heard about them from others, concerning how they are living out their belief.

He encourages them to continue so that they can grow in knowledge and discernment (understanding), and there is only ONE scriptural way to do that.

| Deu 4:5 | "See, I have taught you laws and right-rulings, as יהוה my Elohim commanded me, **to do** thus in the land which you go to possess. |
| Deu 4:6 | "And **you shall guard and do them, for this is your wisdom and your understanding before the** |

**eyes of the peoples who hear all these laws**, and they shall say, 'Only a wise and understanding people is this great nation!'

It is the guarding and doing of the Law/Torah that is our wisdom and understanding, and it is only through guarding and doing the Law/Torah that we get wisdom and understanding, for the Torah is the wisdom of Elohim given to us, to show us how to live before Him, which was fully manifested in Yahushua Messiah.

Paul says something very similar to Timothy.

> 2Ti 2:15 **Do your utmost to present yourself approved to Elohim**, a worker who does not need to be ashamed, **rightly handling the Word of Truth.**

Then he defined what he meant by the "Word of Truth".

> 2Ti 3:14 But you, stay in what you have learned and trusted, having known from whom you have learned,
> 2Ti 3:15 and that from a babe **you have known the Set-apart Scriptures, which are able to make you wise for deliverance through belief in Messiah יהושע.**
> 2Ti 3:16 **All Scripture** is breathed out by Elohim and **profitable for teaching, for reproof, for setting straight, for instruction in righteousness,**
> 2Ti 3:17 that the man of Elohim might be fitted, **equipped for every good work.**

> Note: Carefully read Ephesians 2:8-10 and ask yourself, "What 'good works' did YHWH prepare BEFORE Messiah came that His people were to live by?"

The "All Scripture" Paul is referring to here, not only includes the Torah, but is a very specific reference to the Torah. Notice also, "All Scripture" (Torah) is good for teaching how to find deliverance in Yahushua and teaches us how to discern (examine) error (matters that differ) and correct them.

The Law/Torah also teaches us what it means to walk straight and be righteous, so that we can accomplish "every good work" that YHWH desires of us.

Paul knows, it is only the knowledge of the Torah of YHWH, in the heart of sincere and obedient believer, that keeps us from stumbling.

| Psa 119:165 | Great peace have those **loving Your Torah**, And **for them there is no stumbling-block**. |
|---|---|

When speaking of himself and the struggles he had in his belief, Paul said the following:

| Rom 7:22 | For I **delight in the Torah of Elohim** according to the inward man, |
|---|---|
| Rom 7:23 | but I see another torah in my members, battling against the torah of my mind, and bringing me into captivity to the torah of sin which is in my members. |
| Rom 7:24 | Wretched man that I am! Who shall deliver me from this body of death? |
| Rom 7:25 | Thanks to Elohim, through יהושע Messiah our Master! **So then, with the mind I myself truly serve the Torah of Elohim**, but with the flesh the torah of sin. |

Paul loves the Torah and diligently seeks to obey it, however, his body only wishes to serve itself and its own desires, so there is a constant battle within himself, he is struggling to obey while his body strives to disobey.

If we are honest, we all have this issue, but it is only through a diligent (sincere) commitment to obey the Torah that the favor (grace) of YHWH is extended to the believer.

If we think that we can be justified from death by belief in Yahushua Messiah and still walk in disobedience to the Torah (sin), we are mistaken, for our disobedience proves that we are not sons but transgressors (Galatians 2:17-18).

The result of willful disobedience to the Torah of YHWH, even for a believer, is the expectation of a fiery judgment (Hebrews 10:26-31; See also: Hebrews 6:4-8).

As believers in Yahushua Messiah, it is our duty to bear the "fruit of righteousness", which only comes through obedience to the Torah.

| | |
|---|---|
| **Deu 6:24** | **And יהוה commanded us to do all these laws**, to fear יהוה our Elohim, **for our good always**, to keep us alive, as it is today. |
| **Deu 6:25** | And **it is righteousness for us when we guard to do all this command** before יהוה our Elohim, as He has commanded us. |

Messiah Himself said as much and told the consequences of not doing so.

| | |
|---|---|
| **Joh 15:1** | "I am the true vine, and My Father is the gardener. |
| **Joh 15:2** | **Every branch in Me that bears no fruit He takes away**. And every branch that bears fruit He prunes, so that it bears more fruit. |
| **Joh 15:3** | "You are already clean because of the Word which I have spoken to you. |
| **Joh 15:4** | "Stay in Me, and I *stay* in you. **As the branch is unable to bear fruit of itself**, unless it stays in the vine, so neither you, unless you stay in Me. |
| **Joh 15:5** | "I am the vine, you are the branches. He who stays in Me, and I in him, |

he bears much fruit. Because without Me you are able to do naught!

**Joh 15:6** "**If anyone does not stay in Me, he is thrown away as a branch and dries up. And they gather them and throw them into the fire, and they are burned.**

Any believer, who does not bear the fruit of righteousness, shall be taken away (cut out) and dried up, to be gathered and thrown into the fire to be burned.

We want no part of that, and I'm sure you, the reader, don't either, but it is true that a believer can turn from the truth and be destroyed. We have already mentioned Hebrews 6:4-8 and 10:26-31, but, for clarity, let's quote them both here.

**Heb 6:4** For **it is impossible for those who were once enlightened**, and have tasted the heavenly gift, and have become partakers of the Set-apart Spirit,

**Heb 6:5** and have tasted the good Word of Elohim and the powers of the age to come,

**Heb 6:6** **and fall away, to renew them again to repentance – having impaled for themselves the Son of Elohim again, and put Him to open shame**.

**Heb 6:7** For ground that is drinking the rain often falling on it, and is bearing plants fit for those by whom it is tilled, receives blessing from Elohim,

**Heb 6:8** but if it brings forth thorns and thistles, **it is rejected and near to being cursed, and ends up by being burned**.

\*\*\*

**Heb 10:26** For **if <u>we</u> sin purposely after we have received the knowledge of**

755

| | the truth, there no longer remains a slaughter *offering* for sins, |
|---|---|
| Heb 10:27 | **but some fearsome anticipation of judgment, and a fierce fire which is about to consume the opponents.** |
| Heb 10:28 | Anyone who has disregarded the Torah of Mosheh dies without compassion on the witness of two or three witnesses. |
| Heb 10:29 | How much **worse punishment** do you think shall **he deserve who has trampled the Son of Elohim underfoot, counted the blood of the covenant <u>by which he was</u> set apart as common, and insulted the Spirit of favour**? |
| Heb 10:30 | For we know Him who has said, "Vengeance is Mine, I shall repay, says יהוה." And again, "יהוה **shall judge His people.**" |
| Heb 10:31 | It is fearsome to fall into the hands of the living Elohim. |

*** 

| Php 1:27 | Only, **behave yourselves worthily of the Good News of Messiah**, in order that whether I come and see you or am absent, I hear about you, that you stand fast in one spirit, with one being, **striving together** for the belief of the Good News, |
|---|---|

Throughout his writings, Paul describes a principle of the Scripture that most modern teachers misunderstand, which we call the *Two-Part Principle* (see Pg. 26).

As we've described many times in this writing, the *Two-Part Principle* refers to the spiritual part and the physical part of the belief, working together to accomplish eternal life.

The first part, the spiritual part, can only be achieved through belief in Yahushua Messiah, because it is only through belief in Him that we are "born again" in the inner man.

Once this has happened, we are a "new man" in Messiah, yet we still live in this physical (fleshly) body, which requires of us a diligent commitment to bring this body into subjection to the Torah of YHWH, so that we live righteously and set apart (holy) onto Him, the physical part.

If we say we have been "born again" in Messiah through belief, but we do not produce the "fruit of righteousness" that ONLY comes through obedience to the works of the Torah, then our belief is dead (James 2:14-26).

This is the meaning of the *Two-Part Principle*; it is to the second (physical) part of the principle that Paul is referring when he tells us to "behave yourselves worthily of the Good News of Messiah".

Behaving ourselves is a reference to the way we live, our works and these works we do must be the kind of works that are worthy of the Messiah, which can only refer to the Torah of YHWH, which Messiah Himself lived perfectly.

We as a community of believers need to "strive together" to come to a full understanding and set apart (holy) walk before YHWH. It is only through the fulfillment of both parts of this principle that we fulfill the belief.

| | |
|---|---|
| **Php 2:12** | So that, my beloved, as **you always obeyed** – not only in my presence, but now much rather in my absence – **work out your own deliverance with fear and trembling,** |
| **Php 2:13** | for it is Elohim who is working in you **both to desire and to work** for *His* good pleasure. |
| **Php 2:14** | Do all *matters* without grumblings and disputings, |
| **Php 2:15** | in order that you be **blameless and faultless**, children of Elohim **without blemish** in the midst of a **crooked and perverse generation,** among whom you shine as lights in the world, |
| **Php 2:16** | holding on to **the Word of life**, for a boast to me in the day of Messiah, that I have not run in vain or laboured in vain. |

757

The "New Covenant" promise is found in Jeremiah 31:31-33 and the promise of the Spirit is found in Ezekiel 36:24-27.

| | |
|---|---|
| **Jer 31:31** | "See, the days are coming," declares יהוה, "when **I shall make a renewed covenant with the house of Yisra'ĕl and with the house of Yehuḏah,** |
| **Jer 31:32** | not like the covenant I made with their fathers in the day when I strengthened their hand to bring them out of the land of Mitsrayim, **My covenant which they broke, though I was a husband to them,**" declares יהוה. |
| **Jer 31:33** | "For this is the covenant **I shall make with the house of Yisra'ĕl after those days**, declares יהוה: **I shall put My Torah in their inward parts, and write it on their hearts.** And I shall be their Elohim, and they shall be My people. |
| **Jer 31:34** | "And no longer shall they teach, each one his neighbour, and each one his brother, saying, 'Know יהוה,' for they shall all know Me, from the least of them to the greatest of them," declares יהוה. **"For I shall forgive their crookedness, and remember their sin no more."** |

| | |
|---|---|
| **Renewed (New):** | stg's #**H2319** "חָדָשׁ" (châdâsh), from H2318 (to be new; renew); *new:* - fresh, new thing. Refers, not to a brand-new thing, but to the renewal or restoration of a thing. |

It is not YHWH's intention here for us to think of this "new" covenant as something that has not existed before, but that we view this "new" covenant as better in the sense that He is doing something slightly different than He did with the tablets of stone.

We are not saying that He's changed the covenant in any way, because the covenant was always based first in the redemption that would come through belief in Yahushua Messiah. The Torah has always been for those who are already in the household of YHWH.

This phrase, "new covenant" refers to the fact that YHWH is going to put the Torah into our inner man, our spirit man, and that He was going to write it on our hearts.

This does not mean that He is going to literally, physically write it on our hearts or put it inside of us like the tablets of stone went into the ark of the covenant but is a reference to having a new spirit and a new heart that desires to obey Him.

This is proven out by what He says in Ezekiel.

| | |
|---|---|
| **Eze 36:24** | "And I shall take you from among the nations, and I shall gather you out of all lands, and I shall bring you into your own land. |
| **Eze 36:25** | "And I shall sprinkle clean water on you, and you shall be clean – **from all your filthiness and from all your idols I cleanse you.** |
| **Eze 36:26** | "And I shall **give you a new heart** and **put a new spirit within you.** And **I shall take the heart of stone out of your flesh, and I shall give you a heart of flesh,** |
| **Eze 36:27** | and **put My Spirit within you.** And **I shall cause you to walk in My laws and guard My right-rulings and shall do them.** |

First, He says that He will cleanse us from our filthiness, which is the same thing He said concerning forgiving our crookedness in Jeremiah 31:34. Then, He would give us a new heart and a new spirit, which is a reference to our inner-spirit-man, that is renewed or made new in our belief.

Notice, He says, "I shall take the heart of stone out of your flesh, and I shall give you a heart of flesh".

759

A "heart of stone" is a reference to a stubborn and rebellious heart and the "heart of flesh" refers to a heart that is pliable, willing and obedient. Then, He would put His Spirit within us, and He would "cause" us to walk in obedience to His Law and His right rulings.

> **Cause**: stg's # **H6213** "עָשָׂה" ('âśâh), a primitive root; to *do* or *make*. Refers to the making, accomplishing and appointing of something, and could be understood to mean, establishing something.

Remember what Paul said in Romans 3:31.

> **Rom 3:31**     Do we then nullify the Torah through the belief? Let it not be! On the contrary, **we establish the Torah**.

This is the purpose of His Spirit within us, to establish the Torah as the way believers live in Yahushua Messiah, and He gave us a new spirit and a new heart that would desire to obey His Torah.

> **Rom 7:22**     For I delight in the Torah of Elohim according to the **inward man**,

Lastly, notice that in both Jeremiah and Ezekiel these promises were to Yisra'el and there is no mention of Gentiles at all.

It was always YHWH's intention to restore all mankind back to Himself through the man Abraham and his seed (Genesis 12:1-4). And the Seed He was referring to, according to Paul, was Yahushua Messiah (Galatians 3:16).

Therefore, when YHWH gave the Torah to Yisra'el at Mount Sinai, He said it applied to both the native-born and the stranger that sojourned with them (Leviticus 19:33-34; Numbers 15:15-16).

This is what Paul meant when he said, in Messiah, there is neither Jew nor Gentile because we are all one, one body, one Yisra'el.

**Remember** what Messiah Himself said to the Gentile woman who requested that He cast demons out of her daughter.

| | |
|---|---|
| **Mat 15:21** | And יהושע went out from there and withdrew to the parts of Tsor and Tsidon. |
| **Mat 15:22** | And see, a **woman of Kenaʻan** came from those borders and cried out to Him, saying, "Have compassion on me, O Master, Son of Dawiḏ! My daughter is badly demon-possessed." |
| **Mat 15:23** | But He did not answer her a word. And His taught ones came and asked Him, saying, "Send her away, because she cries after us." |
| **Mat 15:24** | And He answering, said, "**I was not sent except to the lost sheep of the house of Yisra'ĕl.**" |
| **Mat 15:25** | But she came and was bowing to Him, saying, "Master, help me!" |
| **Mat 15:26** | And He answering, said, "It is not good to take the **children's** bread and throw it to the **little dogs**." |
| **Mat 15:27** | But she said, "Yes Master, for **even the little dogs eat the crumbs which fall from their masters' table.**" |
| **Mat 15:28** | And יהושע answering, said to her, "O woman, **your belief is great!** Let it be to you as you desire." And her daughter was healed from that hour. |

The "woman/little dogs" here represent the Gentiles, while the "children" represent the native born Yisra'elis.

The "bread" represents the Word of restoration or the Good News of Yahushua Messiah, while the "table" represents the Kingdom.

This is about salvation, coming into covenant with YHWH. The covenant was originally set up with Yisra'el at Mount Sinai and included both the native-born and the stranger that had sojourned with them, meaning they had come into covenant with YHWH alongside them.

The covenant was not for them, but it did apply to them when they joined Yisra'el in service to YHWH.

Gentiles get into the covenant just like the little dogs eat the bread of the children, the bread was not meant for them, meaning that Messiah didn't come for the Gentiles, He had come to restore the "lost house of Yisra'el" that was scattered among the nations in 722 BCE.

However, a Gentile who believes that Yahushua is the Messiah and will confess Him for the remission of their sins, joins Yisra'el as a servant of YHWH, which was His intent all along.

The purpose of the Torah is twofold. First, it was given to teach the children (Yisra'el) how to live before the Father (YHWH) and second, it was given to show that we had all violated the requirements of the Father when we did not obey it, having fallen short of what He expected of us, so that we would reach out to Him, through belief in His Son, Yahushua Messiah.

This is what Paul meant in Philippians 2, when he told us to "work out your own deliverance with fear and trembling" so we will be "blameless and faultless, children of Elohim without blemish in the midst of a crooked and perverse generation, among whom you shine as lights in the world, holding on to the Word of life".

This is **NOT** legalism, as some would ignorantly accuse us, for legalism is not obedience to the Torah, it is placing your trust in the Torah, which leads to death.

Paul is adamant throughout his writings that our boast (trust) should always be in Yahushua Messiah and never in the Torah.

Now, to our primary text.

**Php 3:1**      For the rest, my brothers, rejoice in יהוה. To write the same *matters* to you is truly no trouble to me, and for you it is safe.

Obviously, this is not the first time he has had this discussion.

**Php 3:2**      Look out for dogs, look out for the evil workers, look out for the mutilation!

Paul's warning is interesting here because he refers to three types of people, which are actually just one type of person, the unbelieving, however, these three people are unbelieving in three different ways.

First, the "dogs", is generally a reference to unbelieving Gentiles, while "evil workers" refers to those that, by claiming to be in the covenant, refuse to obey the Torah.

The "mutilation" is a very specific reference to unbelieving Jews who have placed their trust (boast) in physical things, i.e., circumcision, bloodlines and Torah obedience.

**Php 3:3**      For we are the circumcision, who are serving Elohim in the Spirit, and boasting in Messiah יהושע, and do not trust in the flesh,

The circumcision Paul is referring to here is that of the heart (Romans 2:25-29), however, this does not mean that Paul teaches that physical circumcision no longer matters.

Paul is referring to a position of belief (trust) and he uses the word "circumcision" as a contrast to the word "mutilation" in the verse before it.

Remember, the word "mutilation" is a reference to those who are trusting in physical circumcision, and we as believers in Yahushua place our trust only in Yahushua Messiah, not in physical or fleshly things.

Paul means this very thing when he says we serve "Elohim in the spirit" and not trusting in the flesh, emphasizing that we do so while "boasting in Messiah Yahushua", not in the Torah.

The word "spirit" in this verse is generally capitalized, a reference to His Spirit; however, Paul is referring to our inner-spirit-man who was "born again" through belief in Yahushua Messiah.

It's the same thing Paul says in Romans 8 where he contrasts being in the spirit and being in the flesh, where he

763

says our inner spirit man "delights in the Torah of Elohim" (Rom 7:22) and "serves" it (Rom 7:25).

"Serving Elohim", means that we obey Him by living according to the path He set forth in His Torah, that all His people should follow, while "boasting in Messiah Yahushua" refers to where we place our trust.

Now, Paul is going to compare himself to those of the mutilation who have placed their trust in their physical attributes such as circumcision, bloodlines and Torah obedience.

| | |
|---|---|
| **Php 3:4** | though I too might have **trust in the flesh**. If anyone else **thinks to trust in the flesh**, I more – |
| **Php 3:5** | **circumcised the eighth day, of the race of Yisra'ěl, of the tribe of Binyamin, a Hebrew of Hebrews, according to Torah a Pharisee,** |
| **Php 3:6** | according to ardour, persecuting the assembly; **according to righteousness that is in the law, having become blameless**. |

The term "Hebrew of Hebrews" is important because it refers to Paul's mindset, meaning that he thinks more like a Hebrew than most Hebrews. This is telling us that Paul was more zealous for the Tanak, which includes the Torah, then most anyone else.

| | |
|---|---|
| **Pharisee**: | stg's #**H6567** "שָׁרַף" (pârâsh), a primitive root; to separate. Literally (to disperse) or figuratively (to specify); also (by implication) to wound: - scatter, declare, distinctly, shew, sting. Refers to a person that has been separated or set apart for a purpose. |

A Pharisee was someone whose life had been dedicated to studying and teaching the Torah, generally these people began their studies at a very young age and by the time they reached maturity have an extensive knowledge of not just the Torah, but also the Tanak as a whole.

764

Paul says, according to the righteous standard of the Torah, he was without blame, meaning that he obeyed the whole of the Torah all of his life. If anyone had a right to boast/trust in the flesh (physical issues), it was Paul.

**Php 3:7**     But what might have been a gain to me, **I have counted as loss**, because of Messiah.

**Php 3:8**     What is more, **I even count all to be loss because of the excellence of the knowledge of Messiah** יהושע my Master, for whom I have suffered the loss of all, **AND COUNT THEM AS REFUSE**, in order to gain Messiah,

Does the fact that Paul counted all those physical attributes of his as loss, mean that they have no value at all?

No, these things have value, especially his blamelessness in the Torah, however when it comes to what we are trusting in for redemption, these things have no value at all, so they are no better than garbage.

There is **no redemptive value in anything other than the work of Yahushua Messiah!!!**

However, once we are **IN** Messiah, the physical things do have value, especially the righteous works of the Torah from an obedient heart, for without it our belief is dead.

**Php 3:9**     and be found in Him, not having my own righteousness, which is of the law, but that which is through belief in Messiah, the righteousness which is from Elohim on the basis of belief,

Again, does Paul mean that there's no value in living in the righteousness of the Torah? Absolutely not! Paul is referring to the type of righteousness in which we TRUST.

We cannot trust in our own righteousness as it is defined in the Torah, we must always, always keep our trust in the righteous work of Yahushua, for in Him only is redemption.

765

The righteousness of the Torah is how we are to live AFTER we've believed, keeping our eye on the prize through belief.

| | |
|---|---|
| **Php 3:10** | to know Him, and the power of His resurrection, and the fellowship of His sufferings, being conformed to His death, |
| **Php 3:11** | if somehow I might attain to the resurrection from the dead. |

To say that we "know Him", means that we also "walk as He walked", obedient to the Torah of YHWH. (1 John 2:3-6)

To understand what it means to be "conformed to his death", we must understand what Paul taught in Romans 6 (See: Sec 2, Ch. 4, on Pg. 135).

To summarize, Paul teaches, when we go through the rite of baptism, it is a symbol of having died with Messiah from the sins of the past and being raised again to new life, to walk in obedience to life, which refers to the Torah.

To know the "power of His resurrection", refers to His power to make us "new men" or "born again", both in the inner man now and the outer man at the resurrection, while the phrase "fellowship of His sufferings", means more than just the persecution He received under the Jewish religious leadership, but includes the sufferings of denying this body the things it craves.

Remember what Paul says in Romans 12,

| | |
|---|---|
| **Rom 12:1** | I call upon you, therefore, brothers, through the compassion of Elohim, to **present your bodies a living offering – set-apart, well-pleasing to Elohim** – your reasonable worship. |
| **Rom 12:2** | And do not be conformed to this world, but **be transformed by the renewing of your mind**, so that you prove what is that good and well-pleasing and perfect desire of Elohim. |

766

This is not easy because it requires a complete denial of our fleshly desires and determined intent to walk in obedience to the Torah of YHWH regardless of the consequences, which eventually will include the severing of our head.

Paul is willing to set aside all the things he had **trusted in before**, i.e., physical stuff, so he might come to the knowledge of Yahushua Messiah and is willing to suffer the things Messiah suffered so he might attain the resurrection from the dead, which is our hope/expectation.

| | |
|---|---|
| **Php 3:12** | Not that I have already received, or already been perfected, but I press on, to lay hold of that for which Messiah יהושע has also laid hold of me. |

Paul does not consider that his belief, by itself, guarantees him this promise of resurrection, but he presses forward so that he can take hold of the promise of the resurrection, for which Messiah gave Himself, so that we might attain it also.

| | |
|---|---|
| **Php 3:13** | Brothers, I do not count myself to have laid hold of it yet, but only this: forgetting what is behind and reaching out for what lies ahead, |
| **Php 3:14** | I press on toward the goal for the prize of the high calling of Elohim in Messiah יהושע. |

Again, Paul does not consider himself to have attained this promise as yet, but he forgets all the little things he had trusted in before and is reaching forward to the things that lie ahead (the Kingdom), so that he might attain the goal of the resurrection, which is the high calling to which YHWH has called us, through our belief in Messiah Yahushua.

This is a very specific reference to obeying the Torah through belief, because the promises of life and blessing are and always have been, conditional, based on our commitment to obeying the Torah of YHWH (Deuteronomy 30).

| Php 3:15 | As many, then, as are perfect, should have this mind. And if you think differently in any respect, Elohim shall also reveal this to you. |

Paul is telling them, all who are perfect (complete) in Yahushua should have the same mind as Paul, forgetting the things they trusted in before and striving forward in obedience to attain the promise ahead.

Furthermore, he tells them, if they think differently in any way, YHWH will reveal it to them. This is interesting and has two sides to it, the first being Paul's inference that they don't fully understand and the second being their need to continue obeying the Torah, from which all wisdom and understanding comes (Deut 4:5-6).

| Php 3:16 | But to what we have *already* attained – walk by the same rule, be of the same mind. |
| Php 3:17 | Become joint imitators of me, brothers, and look at those who so walk, as you have us for a pattern. |

What we as believers have "already attained" is the new birth of the inner man who "delights in the Torah of YHWH" (Rom 7:22) and "serves" it (Rom 7:25).

We are to walk by this "same rule" and be of the "same mind" as Paul, who set aside all the things he used to believe and trust in, laying hold of Yahushua Messiah and walking in obedience to the righteousness of Torah, that he might receive the prize of the resurrection.

"Become joint imitators of me" refers to imitating Messiah, who walked in obedience to the Torah, and we know this because Paul has already told us in 1 Corinthians 11:1 to "be imitators of me as I am of Messiah". (See also: 1Co 4:16; 1Co 11:1; Eph 5:1; 1Th 1:6; 1Th 2:14; 2Th 3:7; 2Th 3:9; Heb 6:12; Heb 13:7)

He encourages them to walk the same way that he and others like him walk, using them as a pattern of behavior.

768

| | |
|---|---|
| **Php 3:18** | For many – of whom I have often told you, and now say to you even weeping – **walk as enemies of the stake of Messiah**. |
| **Php 3:19** | Their end is destruction, their mighty one is their stomach, and their esteem is in their shame – **they mind the earthly**. |

This is also a reference to the Torah, but it refers to disobeying the Torah of YHWH, because to turn to the left or the right of anything it says is to serve another Elohim (mighty one – Deut 28:14).

To "mind the earthly" has a twofold meaning, the first being someone who has the "mind of the flesh" that does not "subject itself to the Torah of Elohim" (Rom 8:7) and secondly being those who follow the "lust of the eyes, the lust of the flesh and the pride of life" (1 John 2:17).

| | |
|---|---|
| **Php 3:20** | For our citizenship is in the heavens, from which we also eagerly wait for the Saviour, the Master יהושע Messiah, |
| **Php 3:21** | who shall change our lowly body, to be conformed to His esteemed body, according to the working by which He is able even to bring all under His control. |

Here's a promise of the resurrection in the last day and also refers to those who are still alive when this resurrection takes place (1 Thes 4:13-18).

Lastly, in Chapter 4, Paul admonishes all believers to do what is right (Deut 6:24-25).

| | |
|---|---|
| **Php 4:8** | For the rest, brothers, **whatever is true, whatever is noble, whatever is righteous, whatever is clean, whatever is lovely, whatever is of good report, if there is any uprightness and if there is any praise – think on these**. |

769

| | |
|---|---|
| Php 4:9 | And **what you have learned and received and heard and saw in me, practise** these, and **the Elohim of peace shall be with you**. |

***

| | |
|---|---|
| Deu 30:15 | "See, I have set before you today **life and good**, and death and evil, |
| Deu 30:16 | in that I am commanding you today **to love יהוה your Elohim, to walk in His ways, and to guard His commands, and His laws, and His right-rulings**. And you shall live and increase, and יהוה your Elohim shall bless you in the land which you go to possess. |
| Deu 30:17 | "But if your heart turns away, and you do not obey, and shall be drawn away, and shall bow down to other mighty ones and serve them, |
| Deu 30:18 | "I have declared to you today that **you shall certainly perish**, you shall not prolong your days in the land which you are passing over the Yardĕn to enter and possess. |
| Deu 30:19 | "I have called the heavens and the earth as witnesses today against you: I have set before you **life** and death, the **blessing** and the curse. Therefore you shall choose life, so that you live, both you and your seed, |
| Deu 30:20 | **to love יהוה your Elohim, to obey His voice, and to cling to Him – for He is your life and the length of your days** – to dwell in the land which יהוה swore to your fathers, to Aḇraham, to Yitsḥaq, and to Yaʿaqoḇ, to give them." |

***

| | |
|---|---|
| Pro 3:1 | My son, **do not forget my Torah**, And let your heart watch over my commands; |

770

| Pro 3:2 | **For length of days and long life And peace they add to you**. |
| Pro 3:3 | Let not loving-commitment and truth forsake you – Bind them around your neck, Write them on the tablet of your heart, |
| Pro 3:4 | **Thus finding favour and good insight In the eyes of Elohim and man**. |
| Pro 3:5 | Trust in יהוה with all your heart, And **lean not on your own understanding**; |
| Pro 3:6 | **Know Him in all your ways**, And He makes all your paths straight. |

# Food?

As we have already said, the greatest error in Christian understanding is rooted in the belief that the Torah/Law, given at Mount Sinai, no longer applies to believers. Christians have relegated the Torah of YHWH to the dust bin of history, refusing to apply it to their belief.

Because of this they almost completely misunderstand what the Messianic writers are teaching them in the Messianic Writings (New Testament). One of their primary misunderstandings concerns what the Messianic Writings say about food.

Because they have relegated the Torah to history and do not apply the principles of Torah to their belief, they don't even understand the definition of what food is, scripturally, and so they cannot understand what the Messianic Writings are saying concerning what can be eaten.

**REMEMBER**, the Tanak (Old Testament) was given to man by YHWH so that we would know Him and understand what He expects of His people. It is an instruction (Torah) book for His people.

Let's see what the instruction book considers "food".

| | |
|---|---|
| **Lev 11:1** | And יהוה spoke to Mosheh and to Aharon, saying to them, |
| **Lev 11:2** | "Speak to the children of Yisra'ĕl, saying, '**These are the living creatures which you do eat among all the beasts that are on the earth**: |
| **Lev 11:3** | 'Whatever has a split hoof **completely divided**, chewing the cud, among the beasts, **that you do eat**. |
| **Lev 11:4** | 'Only, these **you do not eat** among those that chew the cud or those that have a split hoof: the camel, because it chews the cud but does not have a split hoof, **it is unclean to you**; |
| **Lev 11:5** | and the rabbit, because it chews the cud but does not have a split hoof, it **is unclean to you;** |

| | |
|---|---|
| **Lev 11:6** | and the hare, because it chews the cud but does not have a split hoof, **it is unclean to you;** |
| **Lev 11:7** | and the pig, though it has a split hoof, completely divided, yet does not chew the cud, **it is unclean to you**. |
| **Lev 11:8** | 'Their flesh you do not eat, and their carcasses you do not touch. They are unclean to you. |
| **Lev 11:9** | 'These you **do eat** of all that are in the waters: any one that has fins and scales in the waters, in the seas or in the rivers, **that you do eat**. |
| **Lev 11:10** | 'But **all that have not fins and scales in the seas and in the rivers, all that move in the waters or any living being which is in the waters, they are an abomination to you.** |
| **Lev 11:11** | 'They are an abomination to you – of their flesh you **do not eat**, and their carcasses you abominate. |
| **Lev 11:12** | 'All that have not fins or scales in the waters are **an abomination to you**. |
| **Lev 11:13** | 'And these you do abominate among the birds, **they are not eaten, they are an abomination**: the eagle, and the vulture, and the black vulture, |
| **Lev 11:14** | and the hawk, and the falcon after its kind, |
| **Lev 11:15** | every raven after its kind, |
| **Lev 11:16** | and the ostrich, and the nighthawk, and the seagull, and the hawk after its kind, |
| **Lev 11:17** | and the little owl, and the fisher owl, and the great owl, |
| **Lev 11:18** | and the white owl, and the pelican, and the carrion vulture, |
| **Lev 11:19** | and the stork, the heron after its kind, and the hoopoe, and the bat. |

| Lev 11:20 | 'All flying insects that creep on all fours is an abomination to you. |
| Lev 11:21 | 'Only, these **you do eat** of every flying insect that creeps on all fours: those which have jointed legs above their feet with which to leap on the earth. |
| Lev 11:22 | 'These of them **you do eat**: the arbeh-locust after its kind, and the solam-locust after its kind, and the hargol-locust after its kind, and the hagab-locust after its kind. |
| Lev 11:23 | **'But all other flying insects which have four feet are an abomination to you.** |
| Lev 11:24 | 'And **by these you are made unclean**, anyone touching the carcass of any of them is unclean until evening, |
| Lev 11:25 | and anyone picking up part of the carcass of any of them has to wash his garments, and **shall be unclean** until evening. |
| Lev 11:26 | 'Every beast that has a split hoof not completely divided, or does not chew the cud, is **unclean to you**. Anyone who touches their carcass is unclean. |
| Lev 11:27 | 'And whatever goes on its paws, among all the creatures that go on all fours, **those are unclean to you**. Anyone who touches their carcass is unclean until evening, |
| Lev 11:28 | and he who picks up their carcass has to wash his garments, and shall be unclean until evening. **They are unclean to you.** |
| Lev 11:29 | 'And **these are unclean to you** among the creeping creatures that creep on the earth: the mole, and the mouse, and the tortoise after its kind, |

| | |
|---|---|
| Lev 11:30 | and the gecko, and the land crocodile, and the sand reptile, and the sand lizard, and the chameleon. |
| Lev 11:31 | '**These are unclean to you** among all that creep. Anyone who touches them when they are dead becomes unclean until evening. |
| Lev 11:32 | 'And whatever any of them in its dead state falls upon, becomes unclean, whether it is any wooden object or garment or skin or sack, any object in which work is done, it is put in water. And **it shall be unclean** until evening, then it shall be clean. |
| Lev 11:33 | 'Any earthen vessel into which any of them falls, whatever is in it becomes **unclean**, and you break it. |
| Lev 11:34 | '**Any of the food which might be eaten**, on which water comes, becomes **unclean**, and any drink which might be drunk from it becomes unclean. |
| Lev 11:35 | 'And on whatever any of their carcass falls becomes **unclean** – an oven or cooking range – it is broken down. They are unclean and are **unclean to you**. |
| Lev 11:36 | 'But a fountain or a well, a collection of water, is clean, but whatever touches their carcass is **unclean**. |
| Lev 11:37 | 'And when any of their carcass falls on any planting seed which is to be sown, it is **clean**. |
| Lev 11:38 | 'But when any water is put on the seed and any part of any such carcass falls on it, it is **unclean to you**. |
| Lev 11:39 | 'And when any of the beasts which **are yours for food** dies, he who touches its carcass becomes unclean until evening. |

| | |
|---|---|
| Lev 11:40 | 'And he who eats of its carcass has to wash his garments, and shall be unclean until evening. And he who picks up its carcass has to wash his garments, and shall be unclean until evening. |
| Lev 11:41 | 'And every swarming creature – the one that swarms on the earth is an abomination, **it is not eaten.** |
| Lev 11:42 | 'Whatever crawls on its stomach, and whatever goes on all fours, and whatever has many feet among all swarming creatures – the ones swarming on the earth, **these you do not eat**, for they are an abomination. |
| Lev 11:43 | 'Do not make yourselves abominable with any swarming creature – the one swarming, and **do not make yourselves unclean with them, lest you be defiled by them.** |
| Lev 11:44 | **'For I am יהוה your Elohim, and you shall set yourselves apart. And you shall be set-apart, for I am set-apart. And do not defile yourselves with any swarming creature – the one creeping on the earth.** |
| Lev 11:45 | **'For I am יהוה who is bringing you up out of the land of Mitsrayim, to be your Elohim. And you shall be set-apart, for I am set-apart.** |
| Lev 11:46 | 'This is the Torah of the beasts and the birds and every living being – the creeping creature in the waters, and of every being that swarms on the earth, |
| Lev 11:47 | **to make a distinction between the unclean and the clean**, and **between the living creature that is eaten and the living creature that is not eaten.' "** |

776

(See: also, Deuteronomy 14)

Those things that **CAN BE EATEN** are the things considered food, however, the things that **CAN NOT BE EATEN** are the things that are **NOT** food, scripturally.

Firstly, after saying what can and cannot be eaten, YHWH clearly demands that we be set apart (holy) onto Him and a part of being set apart (holy) unto Him concerns the things we eat.

| | |
|---|---|
| **Lev 20:22** | 'And you shall **guard all My laws and all My right-rulings, and do them,** so that the land where I am bringing you to dwell does not vomit you out. |
| **Lev 20:23** | 'And **do not walk in the laws of the nation which I am driving out before you,** for they do all these, and therefore I loathed them. |
| **Lev 20:24** | 'But I say to you, "You are going to possess their land, and I Myself give it to you to possess it, a land flowing with milk and honey." I am יהוה your Elohim, who has separated you from the peoples. |
| **Lev 20:25** | 'And **you shall make a distinction** between clean beasts and unclean, and between unclean birds and clean. And do not make yourselves abominable by beast or by bird, or whatever creeps on the ground, **which I have separated from you as unclean.** |
| **Lev 20:26** | 'And **you shall be set-apart to Me, for I יהוה am set-apart, and have separated you from the peoples to be Mine.** |

**REMEMBER**, what is written in the Tanak are shadow pictures, examples for us to follow according to Paul (Romans 15:4) and the "land which you are going in to possess" is a shadow picture of the Kingdom of Messiah, which all believers are striving to inherit.

As a shadow picture, these truths still apply today. You cannot say that you are now clean through belief in Yahushua Messiah and continue to do things or eat things that are unclean. Messiah Himself never put any unclean thing in His mouth, for if He had, He would have been unclean and unqualified to be the Passover Lamb.

Now Christians, instead of just accepting the truth of our need to remain clean through obedience to what is food, have searched the Messianic Writings and found passages that **SEEM** to say, believers are no longer required to obey these "dietary laws".

They misunderstand the fact that the things referred to in the Messianic Writings, that can be eaten, are only things the Scripture declares as food. The Messianic Writings are never referring to things that are not considered food in the Torah.

We know, that Acts 10 refers to things that are unclean and that Peter is told to eat of them, but we shall show in this writing that it was **NOT** YHWH's intention for him to understand this vision to mean he could eat what is unclean.

But that comes later, for now let's look at a few other Scriptures that are significant to this discussion. Before we go on though let's review some of the things the Scripture says are **NOT** food for the believer.

Of the creatures that primarily live on land, Pigs are **NOT FOOD**, and neither are rabbits. This is because ONLY the animals that have BOTH a split hoof, fully divided, AND chew the cud are food.

Pigs have a split hoof, fully divided, but do not to the cud and rabbits chew the cud, but do not have a split hoof.

Other creatures that fit into this category would be squirrels, dogs, cats of any size, tortoises, alligators and crocodiles, reptiles of any kind, anything with the paw or a pad or a claw or a foot.

Of the creatures we consider birds that are NOT FOOD, the Scripture gives a specific list, which includes: eagles, ravens, vultures, hawks, seagulls, owls, ostriches, falcons, storks, herons, pelicans, including bats.

Of the creatures that swim in the water that are NOT FOOD, those that do not have **BOTH** fins **AND** scales, which include sharks, dolphins, porpoises, whales, shellfish of every kind, including lobster and crab, etc. These creatures are **NOT** food, according to Scripture.

According to the passage above, they are all considered UNCLEAN and to eat of them makes us unclean, furthermore, to touch their carcass makes us unclean.

In verse 39 it says, "And when any of the beasts which **are yours for food dies**, he who touches its carcass becomes unclean until evening", which tells us clearly that some of these things are food and some of them are not.

When it says, "beasts which are yours for food **dies**", it is referring to one that dies on its own or is killed by some other way, not the one that we kill for food.

So, not only can we NOT eat the snake, but we can't wear boots or belts made from its skin.

This passage clearly teaches that YHWH told us these things so that we would know the difference between what is clean before Him and what is not clean before Him.

In His condemnation of Yisra'el, YHWH said this of the priesthood:

> **Eze 22:26** "Her priests **have done violence to My teaching and they profane My set-apart matters**. They have **not distinguished** between the set-apart and profane, **nor have they made known the difference between the unclean and the clean**. And they have **hidden their eyes from My Sabbaths, and I am profaned in their midst**.

Sounds eerily like what Christianity teaches today, doesn't it?

> **Job 14:4** Who brings the clean out of the unclean? **No one!**

Notice, according to Job, **NO ONE** can make a clean thing out of an unclean thing!

Once YHWH has declared a thing to be true, it is true forever and cannot be added to nor taken away from (changed).

779

Christians believe that Messiah's death allows them to do what the Scripture clearly says they cannot do, i.e., make unclean things clean. They say that the food laws, among others, have been cleansed by Messiah, which is nonsense.

It was the sin of NOT obeying these and other laws that He died to free us from, not the laws themselves.

> **Ecc 3:14** I know that whatever Elohim does is **forever**. There is **no adding to it, and there is no taking from it**. Elohim does it, **that men should fear before Him**.

YHWH established the food laws, among other things, as a way for us to prove that we fear (respect/reverence) Him, and these laws are FOREVER, can NOT be added to or taken away from. What then, is Acts 10 really all about?

> **Act 10:1** Now there was a certain man in Caesarea called Cornelius, a captain of what was called the Italian Regiment,
>
> **Act 10:2** **dedicated, and fearing Elohim with all his household, doing many kind deeds to the people, and praying to Elohim always.**
>
> **Act 10:3** He clearly saw in a vision, about the ninth hour of the day, a messenger of Elohim coming to him, and saying to him, "Cornelius!"
>
> **Act 10:4** And looking intently at him, and becoming afraid, he said, "What is it, master?" And he said to him, "Your prayers and your kind deeds have come up for a remembrance before Elohim.
>
> **Act 10:5** "And now send men to Yapho, and send for Shim'on who is also called Kĕpha.

| | |
|---|---|
| **Act 10:6** | "He is staying with Shim'on, a leather-tanner, whose house is by the sea." |
| **Act 10:7** | And when the messenger who spoke to him went away, Cornelius called two of his household servants, and a dedicated soldier from among those who waited on him continually. |
| **Act 10:8** | And having explained to them all, he sent them to Yapho. |

Notice, this passage says Cornelius, a Gentile, was "dedicated, and fearing Elohim with all his household, doing many kind deeds to the people, and praying to Elohim always".

This man **already believed in YHWH and had been serving Him** to the best of his understanding, for which YHWH heard his prayer and told him to send for Peter, from whom he would later learn the true Good News of Yahushua Messiah.

| | |
|---|---|
| **Act 10:9** | And on the next day, as they were on their way and approaching the city, Kĕpha went up on the house-top to pray, about the sixth hour. |
| **Act 10:10** | **And he became hungry and wished to eat**. But while they were preparing, he fell into a trance, |

It is interesting that the Scripture tells us specifically that Peter was "hungry and wished to eat", seemingly such a trivial thing.

On the contrary, this phrase explains why YHWH used unclean animals to teach Peter a principle of belief, while not actually referring to unclean animals at all, He only used them metaphorically to explain Himself.

Peter was already thinking about food when he went into his trance, so YHWH used that to teach him something deeper.

| | |
|---|---|
| **Act 10:11** | and he saw the heaven opened and a certain vessel like a great sheet bound at the four corners, |

781

| | |
|---|---|
| | descending to him and let down to the earth, |
| Act 10:12 | in which were all kinds of four-footed beasts of the earth, and wild beasts, and creeping creatures, and the birds of the heaven. |
| Act 10:13 | And a voice came to him, "Rise up, Kĕpha, slay and eat." |
| Act 10:14 | But Kĕpha said, "**Not at all, Master! Because I have never eaten whatever is common or unclean**." |
| Act 10:15 | And a voice came to him again the second time, "**What Elohim has cleansed you do not consider common**." |
| Act 10:16 | And this took place three times, and the vessel was taken back to the heaven. |
| Act 10:17 | And while **Kĕpha was doubting within himself about what the vision might mean**, look, the men who had been sent from Cornelius, having asked for the house of Shim'on, stood at the gate, |
| Act 10:18 | and calling out, they enquired whether Shim'on, also known as Kĕpha, was staying there. |

This Voice from the vision told Peter to do something that he absolutely knew the Scripture commanded him not to do.

Notice, many years after Messiah's death and ascension, one of His chief apostles was still convinced that he was required to keep the food laws of the Torah. It seems interesting that if the Messiah had intended us to believe we no longer had to keep these food laws in our belief, He would've mentioned it to His apostles.

Now, Christian teachers today are going to say, this is for the Nation of Yisra'el and not for the Gentile church, however, we have shown earlier in this writing that there is no such thing as a "Gentile Church", it is a fiction of modern man-made religious dogma.

The Torah, as it was given by YHWH to the children of Yisra'el, through Moses (Mosheh), is an instruction book for **ALL** His people, both native born and stranger (Num 15:15-16).

Also, notice Peter's confusion at being told to "kill and eat" these unclean creatures and YHWH's admonishment that what He had cleansed, Peter was to not refer to as unclean.

Verse 17 says, "Kĕpha was doubting within himself about what the vision might mean", which seems strange considering he had spent so much time with Messiah, if indeed Messiah had made "unclean animals" clean through His death.

| | |
|---|---|
| **Act 10:19** | And as Kĕpha was thinking about the vision, the Spirit said to him, "See, three men seek you. |
| **Act 10:20** | **"But rise up, go down and go with them, not doubting at all, for I have sent them.**" |
| **Act 10:21** | So Kĕpha went down to the men who had been sent to him from Cornelius, and said, "Look, I am the one you seek. Why have you come?" |
| **Act 10:22** | And they said, "Cornelius the captain, **a righteous man and one who fears Elohim and well spoken of by the entire nation of the Yehuḏim**, was instructed by a set-apart messenger to send for you to his house, and to hear words from you." |
| **Act 10:23** | **So inviting them in, he housed them**. And on the next day Kĕpha went away with them, and some brothers from Yapho went with him. |

Now the Spirit of YHWH does not explain Himself, but just tells Peter to go with the men that He had sent, not doubting.

783

This must've been very perplexing to Peter, because he knows that the Spirit of YHWH cannot contradict what has already been spoken by Him, it is the Spirit of YHWH that inspired the Word to be written in the first place (2 Timothy 3:16-17).

YHWH cannot lie (Hebrews 6:18) and neither does He change (Malachi 3:6), so it must've been very difficult to just go with these men, doubting nothing.

Again, we see that Cornelius is called a "righteous man who fears Elohim", but to this is added a very interesting statement, he is "well-spoken of by the entire nation of Yehudim (Jews)".

The first statement clearly emphasizes that he was obedient to the Torah, for it is through obedience to the Torah we are declared righteous in how we live (Deut 6:24-25), but the second statement is the most interesting because for a Gentile, especially a Roman centurion, to be well spoken of among the Jews speaks volumes.

There is no way on heaven or on earth a religious Jew would consider speaking well about a Roman centurion, especially to consider him a righteous man, unless his devotion to the Torah of YHWH was impeccable, without single flaw.

So, we see, again, that Cornelius was already a servant of the Most High, long before he heard the Good News of Yahushua Messiah.

There is a clue in verse 23 that suggests Peter figured out what the Spirit was trying to tell him as he spoke to these men.

The very fact that he invited these men, these Gentile men, into the house of a Jew to spend the night is evidence that he understood the deeper meaning of his vision, and his understanding is revealed in the next part of this passage.

| | |
|---|---|
| **Act 10:24** | And the following day they entered into Caesarea. And Cornelius was waiting for them, having called together his relatives and close friends. |
| **Act 10:25** | And it came to be, that when Kěpha entered, Cornelius met him and fell |

784

| | down at his feet and bowed before him. |
|---|---|
| Act 10:26 | But Kĕpha raised him up, saying, "Stand up, I myself am also a man." |
| Act 10:27 | And talking with him, he went in and found many who had come together. |
| Act 10:28 | And he said to them, "**You know that a Yehuḏi man is not allowed to associate with, or go to one of another race. But Elohim has shown me that I should not call any man common or unclean**. |
| Act 10:29 | "**That is why I came without hesitation when I was sent for**. So I ask, why have you sent for me?" |

Though **NOWHERE** in the Scripture does it say that a Jew cannot give hospitality to a Gentile or receive it in kind, the religious Jews of the time were adhering to man-made regulations that forbade Jews to interact with Gentiles in an informal way, like friendship.

It is this nonsense, this ethnic division, that YHWH was addressing when He gave Peter this vision. Peter clearly, and unambiguously, understood his vision to mean that he could no longer consider Gentile believers as common or unclean.

Even though YHWH used unclean creatures as a metaphor for unclean men, He **WAS NOT** telling Peter, or us, for that matter, that believers could now eat unclean animals.

We have had Christians tell us that He was referring to both men and animals when He gave him this vision, however, there is absolutely nothing anywhere in the entire book of Scripture to suggest such a thing.

Yes, there are plenty of references to "food" in the Messianic Writings, but these references are always about what is food, and not about unclean animals.

**UNCLEAN ANIMALS** are **NOT FOOD**, and **NOTHING** in the Messianic Writings changes that, or even suggests it. But one might ask, didn't "Jesus make all foods clean?" **NO!!!**

785

"**ALL foods**" were already clean, because only clean meat from clean animals, is food.

Below, is the verse that is referred to when people say that "Jesus declared all foods clean", let's review it.

**Mar 7:19**     for it doesn't go into their heart but into their stomach, and then out of the body." (In saying this, Jesus declared all foods clean.) **NIV**

                        \*\*\*

**Mar 7:19**     Because it entereth not into his heart, but into the belly, and goeth out into the draught, purging all meats? **(KJV)**

                        \*\*\*

**Mar 7:19**     because it does not enter his heart but his stomach, and is eliminated, thus purging all the foods?" **TS**

Notice, in the NIV the last part of this verse is in parentheses, which is an indication that what it says is not actually part of the original Greek. However, looking at the (KJV) and the TS we see something similar that is not in parentheses. This is what the Greek says:

**Mar 7:19**     ὅτι οὐκ εἰσπορεύεται αὐτοῦ εἰς τὴν καρδίαν, ἀλλ᾽ εἰς τὴν κοιλίαν, καὶ εἰς τὸν ἀφεδρῶνα ἐκπορεύεται, καθαρίζων πάντα τὰ βρώματα.

The specific portion that is relevant here is: **καθαρίζων πάντα τὰ βρώματα**, which means, "to cleanse all food".

Now, we must figure out if the phrase, "cleanse all food", is referring to making all "unclean" meat clean.

As we have said that which YHWH has declared to be true **CAN NOT CHANGE**, so Messiah has no authority to cleanse "unclean meat" and make it clean, so that believers can eat it. Let's consider carefully what is being said in Mark 7:19

The "it" being referred to is dirt from unwashed hands, but we will get to that in a moment. "It" does not

786

enter the heart but enters the stomach and is eliminated. What does this mean?

When we eat something, we put it in her mouth and chew it, we swallow it so that it goes down our esophagus into our stomach, where it digests and moves out of our stomach into our colon, through our intestines to eventually exit our body when we go to the toilet.

Thus, everything we have eaten (all foods) gets purged from our body, as does any dirt that might have been on our hands when we ate it.

This passage is talking about "cleansing food" from our body and is **NOT** referring to making unclean meat, clean.

What then, is Mark 7 (also Matthew 15) really saying?

| | |
|---|---|
| **Mar 7:1** | And the Pharisees and some of the scribes assembled to Him, having come from Yerushalayim. |
| **Mar 7:2** | And seeing some of **His taught ones eat bread with defiled, that is, with unwashed hands**, they found fault. |
| **Mar 7:3** | For the Pharisees, and all the Yehuḏim, **do not eat unless they wash their hands thoroughly, holding fast the tradition of the elders**, |
| **Mar 7:4** | and coming from the market-place, they do not eat unless they wash. And there are many other traditions which they have received and hold fast – the washing of cups and utensils and copper vessels and couches. |

Right away we are told that the context of this passage is, "eating with unwashed hands", and that this requirement to wash the hands is a "tradition of the elders", meaning a man-made
rule.

The Pharisees noticed that the disciples of Yahushua would eat bread without washing their hands first, now this

787

idea of requiring handwashing before eating stems from a belief that a demon could enter a person if they ate with unwashed hands, and so **the rabbis** forbade eating with unwashed hands.

Sounds reasonable right, I mean if they really believe that, unfortunately we are told multiple times in the Scripture to never add to or take away from what it says, and to do so and require others to do so is a violation of the Torah, i.e., sin.

| | |
|---|---|
| **Mar 7:5** | Then the Pharisees and scribes asked Him, "**Why do Your taught ones not walk according to the tradition of the elders,** but eat bread with unwashed hands?" |
| **Mar 7:6** | And He answering, said to them, "**Well did Yeshayahu prophesy concerning you hypocrites, as it has been written, 'This people respect Me with their lips, but their heart is far from Me.** |
| **Mar 7:7** | **And in vain do they worship Me, teaching as teachings the commands of men.**' |

Messiah then quotes Isaiah (YeshaYahu) 29, where YHWH said that the people say they respect (fear, love, worship) Him, but their hearts are far from Him. What does this mean?

Verse 7 clarifies it a bit, saying, "in vain they worship Me, teaching as teachings the commands of men", which is a clear reference to the fact that Yisra'el had stopped worshiping YHWH according to the Way He had instructed them (Torah).

Instead, they claimed to be worshipping Him but were not, choosing to obey the teachings of men.

The rabbis had stopped teaching the purity of the Torah as a means of worshiping YHWH and had begun to teach the people to worship YHWH in the way they thought proper, and this practice is still going on today in both Judaism and Christianity.

| Mar 7:8 | "**Forsaking the command of Elohim**, you hold fast the tradition of men." |
| Mar 7:9 | And He said to them, "**Well do you set aside the command of Elohim**, in order to guard your tradition. |

Once again, we see that the church today is guilty of the same exact thing Yahushua accused the Jewish leadership of doing, forsaking the command (Torah) of YHWH and obeying the teachings of men instead.

The church teaches a false doctrine called "dispensationalism", which basically says, YHWH has dealt with mankind differently during different stages or ages (dispensations) of time.

> **Note**: "Dispensationalism is a method of interpreting history **that divides God's work and purposes toward mankind into different periods of time**. Usually, there are seven dispensations identified, although some theologians believe there are nine. Others count as few as three or as many as thirty-seven dispensations."

(https://www.gotquestions.org/seven-dispensations.html)

It seems that the church cannot even agree among themselves as to how many "dispensations" there might be, but below are the seven most commonly agreed upon.

The 7 dispensations are:

1. Innocence: The Garden of Eden
2. Conscience: The fall to the flood
3. Government: The flood to Abraham
4. Promise: Abraham to Moses
5. Law: Moses to Messiah
6. Grace: $1^{st}$ coming to $2^{nd}$ coming
7. Kingdom: Future 1000 years

Consider what YHWH says about this idea that His work and purposes toward mankind are different throughout time.

> **Ecc 3:14**  I know that **whatever Elohim does is forever**. There is **no adding to it, and there is no taking from it**. Elohim does it, that men should fear before Him.

So, who do we believe?

Christianity, like Judaism before it, has chosen to pick and choose the parts of the Tanak (OT) that they want to apply to them, like prophecies and blessings, and to reject the parts of the Tanak, especially the Torah, that requires something of them, that they don't want to do.

The problem is, all these prophecies and promises and blessings are conditional, and are based on how those who say they believe in YHWH, prove they believe, which is by obeying His Torah without additions or subtractions.

Now, Messiah is going to give us an example of what He means by them setting aside the Torah of YHWH to follow their tradition.

> **Mar 7:10**  "For Mosheh said, 'Respect your father and your mother,' and, 'He who curses father or mother, let him be put to death.'
> **Mar 7:11**  "**But** you say, 'If a man says to his father or mother, "Whatever profit you might have received from me, is Qorban (that is, a gift),"
> **Mar 7:12**  you no longer let him do any matter at all for his father or his mother,
> **Mar 7:13**  **nullifying the Word of Elohim through your tradition which you have handed down.** And many such traditions you do."

Though the Scripture clearly teaches that children are to honor (respect) their father and their mother, the rabbis have said, the person who does not care for his parents, especially in their old age, but gives what is due them as an offering, is no longer required to take care of the matters concerning their mother and father.

Thus, the man-made tradition was put in place to supersede or nullify the Word of Elohim, His Torah.

| | |
|---|---|
| **Mar 7:14** | And calling the crowd to Him, He said to them, "Hear Me, everyone, and understand: |
| **Mar 7:15** | **"There is no matter that enters a man from outside which is able to defile him, but it is what comes out of him that defiles the man**. |
| **Mar 7:16** | "If anyone has ears to hear, let him hear!" |
| **Mar 7:17** | And when He went from the crowd into a house, His taught ones asked Him concerning the parable. |
| **Mar 7:18** | And He said to them, "Are you also without understanding? **Do you not perceive that whatever enters a man from outside is unable to defile him,** |
| **Mar 7:19** | **because it does not enter his heart but his stomach, and is eliminated, thus purging all the foods?"** |

This is where the church makes its error, they say that "whatever" enters the man from the outside, includes unclean meat, such as pork. The discussion, however, concerns eating bread with unwashed hands, the specific contextual element here is dirt not meat.

A man that eats food with unwashed hands risks allowing dirt into his body, however, getting dirt inside the body does not defile a man because it goes into the belly, through the intestines and out into the waste, when he uses the toilet.

Everything that goes into a man's mouth will eventually be purged from his body through the work of the digestive system.

What does defile a man however is the "dirt" that resides in his heart.

| | |
|---|---|
| **Mar 7:20** | And He said, "**What comes out of a man, that defiles a man**. |
| **Mar 7:21** | "For from within, **out of the heart of men**, proceed evil reasonings, adulteries, whorings, murders, |
| **Mar 7:22** | thefts, greedy desires, wickednesses, deceit, indecency, an evil eye, blasphemy, pride, foolishness. |
| **Mar 7:23** | "**All these wicked matters come from within and defile a man**." |

This same discussion is seen in Matthew 15, where the Messiah concludes the discussion in verse 20.

| | |
|---|---|
| **Mat 15:20** | "These defile the man, **but to eat with unwashed hands does not defile the man**." |

The discussion here is not what you can eat or what you can't eat, concerning food, it's about whether dirt on our hands defiles us when we eat it.

The answer is no, it's the dirt within our heart, the wickedness and selfishness of our own desires, that defiles us.

Now, there are plenty of other passages in the Messianic Writings concerning things eaten and if we read through them with a Hebrew mindset, one founded in the Torah, just like those men who authored these writings, we will see that none of them have to do with unclean creatures.

\*\*\*

| | |
|---|---|
| **Note**: | This passage is referring to dirt on the hands and not meat (Matthew 15:1-2 and Mark 7:1-2), but ever if it was talking about meat, unclean meats enter the body from outside and then go back outside the body as waste, however, it is not the meat that defiles us but the rebelliousness of our heart (Compare Matthew 5:27-28). |

| | |
|---|---|
| **Rom 14:1** | And receive him who is **weak in the belief,** not criticising his thoughts. |

The phrase, "weak in the belief" refers to someone who believes but lacks understanding. Those who have understanding are not supposed to criticize the ignorance of our brothers but edify them.

| Rom 14:2 | One indeed believes to eat all food, but **he who is weak eats only vegetables**. |
| Rom 14:3 | He that eats, let him not despise him who does not eat, and he that does not eat, let him not judge him who eats, for Elohim received him. |

The church has used this passage, again falsely, to say that believers can eat the things declared unclean in the Torah, however, this passage has nothing to do with what is considered unclean in the Scripture, it is an argument about whether we should eat meat or not.

We will explain the importance of this distinction a bit later, for now though it is important to understand that weak brothers think they should only eat vegetables while stronger brothers know they can eat meat, but only clean meat.

| Rom 14:4 | Who are you that judges another's servant? To his own master he stands or falls. But he shall be made to stand, for Elohim is able to make him stand. |
| Rom 14:5 | One indeed **judges one day above another, another judges every day alike.** Let each one be completely persuaded in his own mind. |
| Rom 14:6 | He who minds the day, minds it to יהוה. And he who does not mind the day, to יהוה he does not mind it. He who eats, eats to יהוה, for he gives Elohim thanks. And he who does not eat, to יהוה he does not eat, and gives Elohim thanks. |
| Rom 14:7 | **For not one of us lives to himself, and not one dies to himself.** |

| | |
|---|---|
| **Rom 14:8** | For both, if we live, **we live unto the Master**, and if we die, we die unto the Master. Therefore, whether we live or die, we are the Master's. |
| **Rom 14:9** | For unto this Messiah died and rose and lived again, to rule over both the dead and the living. |

Once again, the church has used this passage to teach that believers are no longer required to keep the 7th day (Saturday) Sabbath, because "whatever day we decide to worship, we do so to honor God".

Well, that's true, you can worship YHWH any day you want, and each man has the right to worship Him on any day he likes, however **ALL MEN EVERYWHERE** who claim Yahushua as their Messiah **MUST** obey the Sabbath, for it is a **SIGN** that He is our Elohim, and we are His people (Exodus 31:13).

| | |
|---|---|
| **Rom 14:10** | But why do you judge your brother? Or why do you despise your brother? For we shall all stand before the judgment seat of Messiah. |
| **Rom 14:11** | For it has been written, "As I live, says יהוה, every knee shall bow to Me, and every tongue shall confess to Elohim." |
| **Rom 14:12** | Each one of us, therefore, shall give account of himself to Elohim. |
| **Rom 14:13** | Therefore let us not judge one another any longer, but rather judge this, **not to put an obstacle or a stumbling-block in our brother's way**. |

All right, the discussion at hand concerns whether we are to eat meat or only vegetables and it is Paul's conclusion that the stronger, more knowledgeable, brother should not do anything that would cause the weaker brother to stumble.

| Rom 14:14 | I know and am persuaded in the Master יהושע that **none at all is common of itself. But to him who regards whatever to be common, to him it is common**. |
| Rom 14:15 | And if your brother is grieved because of your food, you are no longer walking in love. **Do not by your food ruin the one for whom Messiah died**. |
| Rom 14:16 | Do not then allow your good to be spoken of as evil. |
| Rom 14:17 | For the reign of Elohim is not eating and drinking, **but righteousness and peace and joy in the Set-apart Spirit**. |
| Rom 14:18 | For he who is **serving Messiah** in these matters is well-pleasing to Elohim and approved by men. |

Here's where the confusion begins, because Paul says, in Messiah, he is persuaded that there is nothing common (unclean) unto itself, but if we consider something to be common (unclean) then it is common (unclean) to us.

Does Paul's statement here change anything that YHWH has already said be true? Does he have that authority?

The answer to both these questions is an emphatic **NO!!! NO ONE** has the authority to add to, take away from or in **ANY WAY** change what YHWH has spoken. What then can Paul mean here?

The discussion concerns whether believers can eat meat or should only eat vegetables, so what he is saying here must be associated to that question.

Before we get to that though, we see that we are not to allow our **food** to ruin one who Messiah has died for. Only the Scripture decides what food is and unclean animals are **NOT FOOD.**

Also, this begs the question as to, "How can the things we eat, ruin a brother?" Part of the answer resides in what he says next concerning "righteousness and peace and joy in the set apart Spirit".

**REMEMBER**, the Spirit of YHWH was given to **cause** us to walk in His Law and His right rulings (Ezekiel 36:27) and guarding and obeying ALL He has commanded is how we live righteously (Deut 6:24-25).

Also, consider this.

| | |
|---|---|
| **Pro 3:1** | My son, **do not forget my Torah**, And **let your heart watch over my commands**; |
| **Pro 3:2** | For **length of days and long life And <u>peace</u> they add to you.** |
| **Pro 3:3** | Let not loving-commitment and truth forsake you – Bind them around your neck, write them on the tablet of your heart, |
| **Pro 3:4** | **Thus finding favour and good insight In the eyes of Elohim and man.** |
| **Pro 3:5** | Trust in יהוה with all your heart, And lean not on your own understanding; |
| **Pro 3:6** | **Know Him in all your ways**, And He makes all your paths straight. |
| **Pro 3:7** | Do not be wise in your own eyes; **Fear** יהוה and turn away from evil. |

Doesn't Paul tell us that serving Messiah in these matters pleases Elohim and is approved by men?

We see that if we obey the Torah of YHWH it gives us long life and peace, and that if we do not forsake this truth and the mercy that it teaches us, we will find favor with Elohim and men.

Don't be foolish enough to think that these things are not connected, everything is connected, and must be understood within that connection.

The other thing that we could do, that can cause a weaker brother to be ruined, is to behave in a way, though it is within our right, that would cause a weaker brother to stumble because of what he believes but doesn't know.

In our ignorance, we sometimes give honor where no honor is due and by doing so, we dishonor the One to whom all honor belongs.

| Rom 14:19 | So, then, let us pursue the matters of peace and the matters for building up one another. |
| Rom 14:20 | Do not destroy the work of Elohim for the sake of food. **All indeed are clean**, but evil to that man who eats so as to cause stumbling. |
| Rom 14:21 | It is good not to eat meat or drink wine, nor to do whatever by which your brother stumbles. |
| Rom 14:22 | Do you have belief? Have it to yourself before Elohim. Blessed is he who does not condemn himself in what he approves. |
| Rom 14:23 | But he who doubts, if he eats, is condemned, because it is not of belief, and all that is not of belief is sin. |

Okay, again we're talking about food, and all "food" is clean because no unclean thing is food. However, there is some "food" that we could eat that would make a brother stumble because, as we've said, if a brother eats of this "food" having doubt about whether he should eat it, he is condemned for his lack of belief, and that condemns us because we have become approvers of what is evil through our selfishness.

One of the reasons this passage is so extremely difficult for people to understand is because chapter 14 is making a discussion about something that was going on in the assemblies of belief throughout the world and yet is not specifically referenced in Romans 14.

To find out exactly what this passage is referring to, you must go somewhere else, specifically 1 Corinthians.

| 1Co 8:1 | **And concerning food offered to idols**: We know that we all have knowledge. **Knowledge puffs up, but love builds up**. |
| 1Co 8:2 | If anyone thinks that he knows somewhat, **he does not yet know as he should know**. |

797

| 1Co 8:3 | But if anyone loves Elohim, **this one is known by Him**. |

The context of nearly all discussion on "food" in the Messianic Writings concerns animals that have been offered to idols.

What Paul said in Romans, what he says here in Corinthians as well as what he says later to Timothy, is all centered around **clean animals** that had been offered to idols.

He talks about knowledge here and warns that knowledge alone puffs up, but love is meant to build up and it's upon this idea that he speaks to the more knowledgeable members of the congregation as to how they should behave around the weaker, less knowledgeable members of the congregation, concerning this matter of **clean animals** offered to idols.

Understanding this context, we can look back at Romans 14 and see why there was a discussion concerning whether we should eat meat or only eat vegetables, because we don't always know where the meat we eat comes from, which is going to be addressed more specifically later.

Notice, Paul warns us that whatever we think we know, there's always more to know, and we should not get puffed up in our own mind or our own heart concerning what we do know, so we can deal with lesser knowledgeable brethren in an attitude of compassion and love.

Verse 3 goes back to something we have said earlier in this book concerning the difference between knowing YHWH and Him knowing us, a distinction that is associated to our obedience.

Love is associated to obedience throughout the Scripture, we cannot say we love YHWH if we are not keeping His commandments (John 14:15-24) and if we say we know Him but don't keep His commandments we prove we are liars, having no truth in us (1 John 2:3-6).

| 1Co 8:4 | So then, **concerning the eating of food offered to idols**, we know that an idol is **no matter at all** in the world, and that there **is no other Elohim but one**. |

| | |
|---|---|
| **1Co 8:5** | For even if there are so-called mighty ones, whether in heaven or on earth – as there are many mighty ones and many masters – |
| **1Co 8:6** | **for us there is one Elohim**, the Father, **from** whom all came **and for** whom we live, and one Master יהושע Messiah, **through** whom all came **and through** whom we live. |
| **1Co 8:7** | However, **not all have this knowledge**. But some, **being aware of the idol**, until now eat it **as having been offered to an idol, so their conscience, being weak, is defiled.** |

Once again, we see the context of the food issue, meat offered to idols. Of course, what the Scripture has declared unclean **IS NOT** food, and does not apply to this discussion.

Idols have no real authority in the world unless we grant it to them. There is only One true authority (Elohim), YHWH.

"For us" is a reference to believers, and there is only one Authority for believers, as we have said. However, we need to pay attention to what Paul is saying here concerning the Father and Son.

Paul says that we all came "from" the Father, and it is "for" the Father we all live. This is important when it comes to the question of, who we worship, because Christian doctrine has confused the issue with half-truths.

All creation came into being by an act of YHWH, the Father and the purpose of our creation was to give honor to the Father.

Because Christianity does not understand the nature of YHWH and the nature of His relationship to the Son, Yahushua, they don't really understand what the Messianic Writings say about the nature of Yahushua.

We have spoken on this matter other places in this book and shall not dig into it here again, however, Paul explains in 1 Corinthians about the structure of authority as it exists in His (YHWH's) Creation (1 Cor 11:3).

Messiah's purpose was to bring all men back to YHWH, the Father, and so it is "through" Him we all come to the Father, and it is "through" Him we all live.

All mankind is guilty of sin and has been condemned to death. It is only through belief in Yahushua Messiah that we have been delivered from this condemnation and restored to the Father.

It is through Yahushua that we come to the Father, however, it is also through Him that we live unto the Father.

This means, not only were we restored to the Father through belief in Yahushua, but we can also live unto the Father, by obeying His Torah, through our belief in Yahushua, without fear of condemnation if we stumble.

All praise and worship belong to YHWH, this has always been and always will be the truth, however, in our failure to worship Him according to the Way He requires us to (Torah), we needed a way to be restored to Him that would also allow us to serve Him, even though we struggle obeying His Torah at times. Yahushua is the answer!

This is the same thing Paul meant in Romans 7:22-25.

| | |
|---|---|
| Rom 7:22 | For **I delight in the Torah of Elohim according to the inward man,** |
| Rom 7:23 | **but I see another torah in my members,** battling against the torah of my mind, and **bringing me into captivity to the torah of sin** which is in my members. |
| Rom 7:24 | **Wretched man that I am! Who shall deliver me from this body of death?** |
| Rom 7:25 | Thanks to Elohim, **through יהושע Messiah our Master!** So then, with the mind **I myself truly serve the Torah of Elohim,** but with the flesh the torah of sin. |

As we have noted in our study of Romans, our inner-spirit-man was born again through belief in Yahushua Messiah and he delights in the Torah of YHWH, to obey it.

800

However, there is another part of us, the outer-fleshly-man, that does not desire to be subjected to the Torah of YHWH (Rom 8:7) and battles with our inner man continually trying to bring us into disobedience and the condemnation of death that comes with it.

The ONLY way to overcome this body that is trying to kill us, is to place our trust in the work of Yahushua Messiah. So now, being restored to the Father by belief, we can serve YHWH by striving to obey His Torah with all our heart, mind and strength, without fear of being condemned if we fail. Paul confirms this in Romans 8:1.

**Rom 8:1**   There is, then, now no condemnation to those who are in Messiah יהושע, **who do not walk according to the flesh**, but according to the Spirit.

There is no longer a need to fear condemnation for those believers who "do not walk according to the flesh", meaning those that do not obey the fleshly desires.

We are free from the fear of condemnation if we walk "according to the spirit", which delights in the Torah of YHWH and serves it.

It is to this principle, Paul is referring in 1 Corinthians 8, where he is talking to the brethren concerning things eaten, that may have been offered to idols.

We live to honor the Father through belief in the Son and this knowledge keeps us from fearing the consequences of what might happen if we **UNKNOWINGLY** eat something offered to idols.

This is the important part, we never KNOWINGLY eat something offered to idols, but we do not shrink from eating something, something clean, if we have no previous knowledge whether it had been offered to idols, because the idol is nothing, but YHWH is ALL.

This is about what we know, our knowledge.

**1Cor 8:7**   However, **not all have this knowledge**. But some, **being aware of the idol**, **until now eat it as having been offered to an idol**, so their conscience, being weak, is defiled.

The phrase "being aware of the idol", refers to having reverence towards it, because these lesser knowledgeable believers, don't know that the idol is nothing, so that when they eat things that have been offered to idols, their conscience becomes defiled because of their ignorance.

> **1Co 8:8** But food does not commend us to Elohim, for we are none the better if we eat, nor any worse for not eating.
>
> **1Co 8:9** But look to it, lest somehow this right of yours becomes a stumbling-block to those who are weak.

Here again we see the warning concerning a knowledgeable believer doing something that causes a less knowledgeable believer to stumble.

**Remember,** just because we think we know something, doesn't mean we really understand it as fully as we should, and our knowledge is not meant to puff us up, it is meant to build up others.

> **Note:** FOOD ONLY refers to animals that YHWH has granted us permission to eat. **UNCLEAN ANIMALS ARE NOT FOOD!!!**

Food, whether it's offered to idols or not, does not commend us to YHWH, meaning, it gives us no standing before Him, for our position before Him is based in Yahushua, and is not determined by whether we eat it or not.

When most people read this they still think, "It doesn't matter if I knowingly eat an animal that had been sacrificed to an idol", which is not true.

We are very specifically commanded in the Torah not to eat things offered to idols, and this will be borne out as we go further into what Paul has to say on this matter.

We are not to allow our "right", which is something we're allowed to do, to cause another brother to stumble, because they don't understand the "rights" we have, causing them, in their ignorance, to condemn themselves.

| | |
|---|---|
| **1Co 8:10** | For if anyone **sees you who have knowledge eating in an idol's place**, shall not his conscience, if he is weak, **be built up to eat food offered to idols**? |
| **1Co 8:11** | So this weak brother, for whom Messiah died, **shall perish through your knowledge!** |

If this passage is telling us that we can knowingly eat things offered idols, why would a weak brother who ate something offered to idols perish because of it?

As we shall see, this discussion is not referring to intentionally eating things offered to idols, it is only referring to eating things that may or may not have been offered to idols.

Now, the King James Version translates "an idol's place" as "an idol's Temple" but the Torah absolutely condemns the practice of participating in any form of idol worship, which would include being in their temples and eating things they offered to their idol.

The Greek word here translated as place is "eidōleion" (G1493) and refers to where an idol resides. This may or may not be a temple, because people in ancient times kept replicas of the idols they worshipped right inside their houses.

If you remember, Jacob's wife, Rachel, stole her father's idols when they fled Laban (Gen 31:19), also, many people today keep statues of angels and other religious icons in their houses.

So, it is most likely that Paul's reference to "an idol's place" concerns a home or business that had an idol present, but not a temple that is designed specifically for the worship of that idol.

The phrase, "be built up to eat food offered to idols" means the same thing as 8:7, about being "aware of the idol", and eating the offering to it "as to an idol". It is a reference to eating the sacrifice, giving honor to the idol.

803

There is a consequence to those of us who have knowledge, for leading weaker brothers into error through our knowledge.

> **1Co 8:12**      **Now sinning in this way against the brothers**, and wounding their weak conscience, **you sin against Messiah**.

To "sin against Messiah", refers to living or behaving in a manner that is contrary to both the Commands (Torah) and the principle of selflessness lived out and taught by Messiah.

> **1Co 8:13**      Therefore, if food makes my brother stumble, I am never again going to eat meat, lest I make my brother stumble.

In Paul's mind it would be better to never eat meat again then to eat meat that would cause someone else to stumble, for their blood would be on our hands.

**REMEMBER**, the "meat" he is referring to is **NOT** meat from an unclean animal! **UNCLEAN ANIMALS ARE NOT FOOD!!!**

Moving on, Paul has more to say on this matter in Chapter 10 that will clarify a lot of what has been said here.

> **1Co 10:1**      For I do not wish you to be ignorant, brothers, that all our fathers were under the cloud, and all passed through the sea,
>
> **1Co 10:2**      and all were immersed into Mosheh in the cloud and in the sea,
>
> **1Co 10:3**      and all ate the same spiritual food,
>
> **1Co 10:4**      and all drank the same spiritual drink. For they drank of that spiritual Rock that followed, and **the Rock was Messiah**.
>
> **1Co 10:5**      However, with most of them Elohim was not well pleased, for they were laid low in the wilderness.

| 1Co 10:6 | And these became examples for us, so that we should not lust after evil, as those indeed lusted. |

This is another example of where Paul tells us, everything that happened during the Exodus from Mitsrayim (Egypt) are shadow pictures that we are to learn from, so we don't stumble in the same when they did when they worshiped the golden calf (Exodus 32).

| 1Co 10:7 | And do not become idolaters as some of them, as it has been written, "The people sat down to eat and to drink, and stood up to play." |

Or, when they committed fornication with the daughters of Moab (Num 25:9).

| 1Co 10:8 | Neither should we commit whoring, as some of them did, and in one day twenty-three thousand fell, |

| Note: | There is a scribal error in verse 8, the actual number was twenty-four thousand (Num 25:9). |

| 1Co 10:9 | neither let us try Messiah, as some of them also tried, and were destroyed by serpents, (Num 21:4-9) |
| 1Co 10:10 | neither grumble, as some of them also grumbled, and were destroyed by the destroyer. |
| 1Co 10:11 | And all these came upon them as examples, and they were written as a warning to us, on whom the ends of the ages have come, |
| 1Co 10:12 | so that he who thinks he stands, let him take heed lest he fall. |

All these examples of the misbehavior and willful disobedience of Yisra'el during the Exodus are warnings to those of us who live in the last day, not to think too highly of ourselves lest we fall.

Obviously, Paul wants us to remember, it is still possible to fall as a believer, which is taught again in Hebrews 6:4-5 and 10:26-31, among other places.

It is imperative that we carefully review every element and every story written in the Torah (Genesis-Deuteronomy) because everything written therein are shadow pictures and parables and allegories through which we can learn the truth of the Good News of Yahushua Messiah and our responsibility to YHWH, the Father in our belief.

> **1Co 10:13**  **No trial has overtaken you except such as is common to man**, and Elohim is trustworthy, who shall not allow you to be tried beyond what you are able, but with the trial shall also make the way of escape, enabling you to bear it.

This passage has a twofold meaning, the first and most obvious being that there is no trial or temptation that we may undergo that someone hasn't already been through, or is going through, but that YHWH is trustworthy to deliver us out of our trials or to comfort us during them so that we can overcome them.

The second meaning here is less obvious, but every bit as important for believers to understand and it has to do with remembering that there is no kind of sin that is not common among men.

That we should never, ever, say to ourselves, "I can't believe he did that, I would never do such a thing", because we can never put ourselves in the shoes of someone else and understand the whys and wherefores of their motivations.

It is our firm belief, and experience, that there is absolutely no sin, to include the worst atrocities you can imagine, that every single one of us wouldn't commit under the right circumstances, circumstances that may differ from person to person.

> **1Co 10:14**  Therefore, my beloved ones, flee from idolatry.

Ugh, I thought he just said that if we eat meat offered idols or whether we don't eat them doesn't really affect our standing before YHWH?

This is an example of where its vitally imperative to know what the Torah says, otherwise, the things Paul says will confuse us, because we do not naturally have his mindset nor are taught by the church to be founded in the same things that he was founded in.

We, as believers, are **NEVER** to participate in any kind of pagan idol worship, or any false worship of any kind, in fact, we are to flee from it with all haste.

| | |
|---|---|
| **1Co 10:15** | I speak as to wise men, judge for yourselves what I say. |
| **1Co 10:16** | The cup of blessing which we bless, is it not a sharing in the blood of Messiah? The bread that we break, is it not a sharing in the body of Messiah? |
| **1Co 10:17** | Because there is one bread, we, who are many, are one body, for we all partake of the one bread. |

This, of course, is a reference to what Messiah said when He claimed to be the "bread of life" and that whoever should eat of Him would attain eternal life.

Our love feasts, which is generally referred to as "the Lord's supper", is a shadow picture of us taking part in His death so that we may also take part in His resurrection, which baptism is also a shadow picture of.

We are all "one body" of believers, both the native-born (a Jew) and the stranger (Gentile).

| | |
|---|---|
| **1Co 10:18** | Look at Yisra'ĕl after the flesh: Are not those who eat of the slaughterings sharers in the slaughter-place? |
| **1Co 10:19** | What then do I say? That an idol is of any value? Or that which is slaughtered to idols is of any value? |
| **1Co 10:20** | No, but what the nations slaughter they slaughter to demons and not to |

| | Elohim, and I do not wish you to become sharers with demons. |
| 1Co 10:21 | You are not able to drink the cup of the Master and the cup of demons, you are not able to partake of the table of the Master and of the table of demons. |
| 1Co 10:22 | Do we provoke the Master to jealousy? Are we stronger than He? |

In the Torah, Yisra'el was able to eat a portion of the sacrifices that they had offered and by doing so they had taken part in the offering, in that it reflected to whom they had placed their trust and to whom they had committed their obedience, namely YHWH.

Paul uses this shadow picture to express the principle, that eating things that have been offered to some authority figure (elohim, god) is evidence that you are placing your trust and obedience in that authority, whether that authority is YHWH or some other authority (elohim).

He goes on to explain that those who offer sacrifices to an authority figure other than YHWH are making offerings to demons and that he in no way intends us to think that it is okay to intentionally eat things that have been offered to idols, which some have interpreted his writings to mean.

Paul goes on to say that we as believers are not able to drink the cup of Messiah (reference to the cup of the "Last Supper") and any kind of offering made to demons.

**REMEMBER**, the reference to the "cup of Messiah" concerns His blood, which he gave for the redemption of all men. It is not possible for a believer to legitimately share in both the blood of Messiah and the blood of pagan idols nor is it legitimate to eat of the "bread of life" that is Messiah and eat of the sacrifices made to pagan idols.

To eat the "bread" and drink the "cup" of Messiah is a matter of trust and obedience so that if we are drinking the "cup" of demons and eating the "bread" of demons we are saying that we are serving both Messiah and demons, which is not possible.

He asks, "Do we provoke the master to jealousy? Are we stronger than He?" **Remember** what the Torah says concerning jealousy.

| | |
|---|---|
| **Exo 20:2** | "I am יהוה your Elohim, who brought you out of the land of Mitsrayim, out of the house of slavery. |
| **Exo 20:3** | "You have no other mighty ones against My face. |
| **Exo 20:4** | "You do not make for yourself a carved image, or any likeness of that which is in the heavens above, or which is in the earth beneath, or which is in the waters under the earth, |
| **Exo 20:5** | you do not bow down to them nor serve them. For I, יהוה your Elohim am a jealous Ěl, visiting the crookedness of the fathers on the children to the third and fourth generations of those who hate Me, |
| **Exo 20:6** | but showing loving-commitment to thousands, to those who love Me and guard My commands. |

It is important to remember that Paul himself says, the things in Scripture concerning Yisra'el are for our instruction, and they are examples for us so that we do not fall by the same errors that Yisra'el did (1 Cor 10:11).

So, when YHWH says in Exodus 20:2, that He "brought you out of the land of Mitsrayim and from the house of slavery", it is the shadow picture of Him bring us out from under the authority of Ha-Satan and this world and the bondage of sin and death, through Yahushua Messiah.

The rest of the quoted section above defines what it means to "provoke Him to jealousy" and gives the consequences of doing so.

Paul's question about whether we are "stronger than Him" is about authority, are we capable of overruling His commandments to live anyway we want and still be accepted.

This is the same type of question he asked the Galatians in Chapter 2:17.

**Gal 2:17**   "And if, while seeking to be declared right by Messiah, we ourselves also are found sinners, is Messiah then a servant of sin? Let it not be!"

Here again we see Paul asking whether we who are seeking to be declared right (justified) through belief in Yahushua Messiah and yet still sin (disobey the Law/Torah- 1 John 3:4) have we made Messiah our servant so that we can disobey and still be accepted, and his answer is NO!

The idea that there is only one Elohim (authority) but that there are many ways to get to Him is a lie straight from the pit of hell, likewise, is the teaching that those of us who believe in Messiah are no longer required to obey the Law/Torah.

These are both derived from the same spirit of deception and are part of the same error of lawlessness.

If we take everything Paul has written in Romans 14 and 1 Corinthians 8-10 in the context of what was happening within the assemblies in that time concerning "foods" offered to idols, it becomes clear that he is not saying it is okay for a believer to eat something offered idols.

What he is saying, however, is that if we go to purchase clean meat from the butcher shop or from the market, or if we go to someone's house that does not worship YHWH but does in fact worship some other authority, and that person offers us clean meat to eat, and we do not know or are not told whether that meat had been offered to an idol, then we are free to eat it because the idol itself has no power over us.

Not all believers understand this principle however, so when they see a more mature believer eating this food that **MIGHT** have been offered idols, they will be emboldened to eat this clean meat while still thinking or believing that the idol is of some significance in the world.

A mature believer that does this has put a stumbling block in the path of the immature believer and has sinned against Yahushua by leading this immature believer into disobedience. Thus, the immature believer will be judged because of his disobedience and we the mature believer will be judged for leading them astray.

> **1Co 10:23** All is permitted me, but **not all do profit**. All is permitted me, but **not all build up**.

This is another verse that people use out of context to say that believers are now permitted to do whatever, but they don't understand what it means that "not all do profit, ... not all build up".

Once a person has believed in Yahushua Messiah and been delivered from the penalty of death, that person is free to do whatever he wants to do, however, not everything he could do will profit him, because the wages of sin is still death.

Go back and read Galatians 2:17 again, carefully.

\*\*\*

> **1Co 10:24** Let no one seek his own, but each one that of the other.
>
> **1Co 10:25** You **eat whatever is sold in the meat market, asking no questions because of conscience**,
>
> **1Co 10:26** for "**The earth belongs to יהוה, and all that fills it**."
>
> **1Co 10:27** And if any of the **unbelievers invite you, and you wish to go, you eat whatever is set before you, asking no question on account of the conscience**.
>
> **1Co 10:28** And if anyone says to you, "**This was slaughtered to idols," do not eat** it because of the one pointing it out to you, and on account of the conscience, for "The earth belongs to יהוה, and all that fills it."
>
> **1Co 10:29** Now I say conscience, not your own, but that of the other. For why is my freedom judged by another's conscience?
>
> **1Co 10:30** But if I partake with thanks, why am I evil spoken of for what I give thanks?

| 1Co 10:31 | Therefore, whether you eat or drink, or whatever you do, do all to the esteem of Elohim. |
|-----------|---------------------------------------------------------------|
| 1Co 10:32 | Cause no stumbling, either to the Yehuḏim or to the Greeks or to the assembly of Elohim, |
| 1Co 10:33 | as I also please all men in all matters, not seeking my own advantage, but that of the many, that they might be saved. |

We see here that the context is clearly meat that has been offered to idols, that we might find in the meat market or at the house of some unbeliever.

This is **NOT** a reference to eating meat that is considered unclean, it is about clean meat that has been offered idols. We are **NEVER** allowed to eat unclean meat regardless of where it comes from or who invites us to eat it.

Another instance where the word "food" is used in the Scripture comes from Hebrews 9:10 and 13:9, which we will look at briefly just to show how this word is applied there.

| Heb 9:7 | But into the second part the high priest went alone once a year, not without blood, which he offered for himself and for sins of ignorance of the people, |
|---------|---------------------------------------------------------------|
| Heb 9:8 | the Set-apart Spirit signifying this, that the way into the Most Set-apart Place was not yet made manifest while the first Tent has a standing, |
| Heb 9:9 | which was a parable for the present time in which both gifts and slaughters are offered which are unable to perfect the one serving, **as to his conscience**, |
| Heb 9:10 | only as to foods and drinks, and different washings, and fleshly regulations **imposed until a time of setting matters straight**. |

Use of the word "foods" in verse 10 is clearly a reference to foods offered on the altar of YHWH which are undeniably a reference to clean meat.

In this passage the writer is expressing the difference between the physical Aaronic priesthood and the spiritual Messianic priesthood and the difference in them concerning cleansing.

There are two key phrases here that must be understood, the first being "as to his conscience", which refers to the fact that Aaronic priesthood was not able to offer a sacrifice that could cleanse the inner man.

A man's "conscience" refers to the inter-spirit-man that was dead because of sin but that has been made alive again through belief in Yahushua Messiah (See: Ephesians 2:1-7).

The purpose of the Aaronic priesthood and the sacrifices of bulls and goats performed by them was never intended to cleanse the inner man but were however, intended to cleanse the fleshly-outer-man.

**Heb 9:11** But Messiah, having become a High Priest of the coming good matters, through the greater and more perfect Tent not made with hands, that is, not of this creation,

**Heb 9:12** entered into the Most Set-apart Place **once for all, not with the blood of goats and calves, but with His own blood, having obtained everlasting redemption**.

**Heb 9:13** For if the blood of bulls and goats and the ashes of a heifer, sprinkling the defiled, **sets apart for the cleansing of the flesh,**

**Heb 9:14** **how much more shall the blood of the Messiah, who through the everlasting Spirit offered Himself unblemished to Elohim, cleanse your conscience from dead works to serve the living Elohim?**

We see here what the writer of Hebrews intends us to understand about what was written before it, which is the difference between the physical Aaronic priesthood and its duty to cleanse the outer-physical-man and the spiritual Messianic priesthood, which duty it is to cleanse the inner-spiritual-man (our conscience)

Notice, that the blood of Messiah cleansed our conscience from "dead works" to "serve" YHWH.

The phrase "dead works" refers to a standard of works that leads to death, which the Scripture clearly teaches are works of disobedience to the Law/Torah of YHWH.

| | |
|---|---|
| **Deu 30:15** | "See, I have set before you today **life and good**, and **death and evil**, |
| **Deu 30:16** | in that I am commanding you today **to love יהוה your Elohim, to walk in His ways, and to guard His commands, and His laws, and His right-rulings**. And you shall live and increase, and יהוה your Elohim shall bless you in the land which you go to possess. |
| **Deu 30:17** | "But **if your heart turns away, and you do not obey, and shall be drawn away, and shall bow down to other mighty ones and serve them**, |
| **Deu 30:18** | "I have declared to you today that **you shall certainly perish**, you shall not prolong your days in the land which you are passing over the Yardĕn to enter and possess. |

To not obey the Law/Torah of YHWH is to commit sin (1 John 3:4) and the wages of sin is death (Romans 6:23).

To walk in disobedience to the Law/Torah of YHWH is to have a life full of "dead works", which condemns to death the inner-spirit-man and leads to the condemnation and judgment of this body in the Lake of Fire.

Belief in Yahushua Messiah has released us from this condemnation and has made us alive again in the inner-spirit-man who delights in the Law/Torah of YHWH (Romans 7:22), however, once we are made alive again from those "dead works" through belief in Him, we are to then

814

"serve" YHWH in our "mind" (conscience/inner-spirit-man, Romans 7:25).

Now to Hebrews 13.

| | |
|---|---|
| **Heb 13:7** | Remember those leading you, who spoke the Word of Elohim to you. Consider the outcome of their behaviour and imitate their belief. |
| **Heb 13:8** | **יהושע Messiah is the same yesterday, and today, and forever.** |
| **Heb 13:9** | Do not be borne about by various and strange teachings. For it is good **for the heart to be established** by favour, not with foods which have not profited those who have been **occupied with them**. |

This reference to "foods" is used in association to both what a believer has placed their trust in and how they are to walk as believers.

The fact that the writer of Hebrews says that Messiah is the same "yesterday, and today and forever" is significant because it establishes the supremacy of the Law/Torah in the lives of believers as it relates to walking out their belief.

The Messiah Himself, kept the entire Law/Torah completely and we are told many times to do the same. We are told to imitate Him and to walk as He walked and the standard in which He lived doesn't change and neither does our requirement to be conformed into His image.

There are two key phrases in this passage that must be understood, which are "the heart is established" and "occupied by them".

These two phrases are references to what we have believed in, what we place our trust in, and has nothing to do directly with whether the meat restrictions apply today or that they ever had significance in of themselves.

What the writer is saying here is that our heart must be established on the favor that we received from YHWH because of our belief, hence our trust is always in the work of Yahushua Messiah and not in the works of the law, such as food restrictions or the Sabbath or any such thing.

815

We are **NEVER, EVER** to place our hope or trust in the works of the Law/Torah, regardless of what they are. Our hope and trust must be wholly and completely centered on the work of Yahushua Messiah.

The phrase "occupied by them" is a reference to those people who have placed their heart, their hope and their trust in the observations of Law/Torah commands and **NOT** in the work of Yahushua Messiah.

Neither of these two passages in Hebrews has anything to do with unclean meat or whether we should eat or not eat things that **MIGHT** have been offered to idols.

The next passage we need to address concerns what is called the "Noahide laws".

It is a fallacy within Judaism that Gentiles who would come into the Jewish religion are only required to keep the Noahide laws. The Noahide laws, refers to the set of instructions YHWH gave Noah (Noach) concerning food in Genesis 9.

After the flood, YHWH established a covenant with Noah, promising that He would no longer destroy the earth with the flood and in this section of the Scripture He gave mankind the right to take animals as food.

| | |
|---|---|
| **Gen 9:1** | And Elohim blessed Noaḥ and his sons, and said to them, "Be fruitful and increase,   and fill the earth. |
| **Gen 9:2** | "And the fear of you and the dread of you is on every beast of the earth, on every bird of the heavens, on all that creeps on the ground, and on all the fish of the sea – into your hand they have been given. |
| **Gen 9:3** | "Every creeping creature that lives is food for you. I have given you all, as I gave the green plants. |
| **Gen 9:4** | "But do not eat flesh with its life, its blood. |
| **Gen 9:5** | "But only your blood for your lives I require, from the hand of every beast I require it, and from the hand of man. From the hand of every man's brother I require the life of man. |

| | |
|---|---|
| **Gen 9:6** | "Whoever sheds man's blood, by man his blood is shed, for in the image of Elohim has He made man. |
| **Gen 9:7** | "As for you, be fruitful and increase, bring forth teemingly in the earth and increase in it." |
| **Gen 9:8** | And Elohim spoke to Noaḥ and to his sons with him, saying, |
| **Gen 9:9** | "And I, see, I establish My covenant with you and with your seed after you, |
| **Gen 9:10** | and with every living being that is with you: of the birds, of the cattle, and of every beast of the earth with you, of all that go out of the ark, every beast of the earth. |
| **Gen 9:11** | "And I shall establish My covenant with you, and never again is all flesh cut off by the waters of the flood, and never again is there a flood to destroy the earth." |

Notice verses 3-5, where it says that "every creeping creature" was given to man as food. Now, many people believe that this statement gives man the authority to eat absolutely any kind of animal, unfortunately that is not the case.

Because people do not understand the very nature of YHWH nor the intrinsic reality of His Word, and neither do they accept what He says about Himself and His word, they do not understand this passage.

By His very nature, YHWH can never declare something to be true and then change it, because once something has been declared to be true, it is true forever, it cannot be added to or taken away from.

There is evidence here in Genesis 8-10 showing that Noah would've understood what YHWH meant by "every creeping creature" and know that YHWH was NOT referring to animals that are later declared unclean in the Torah.

Part of this evidence is the fact that Noah knew the distinction between clean and unclean animals even though the Scripture had not yet declared such.

| Gen 8:20 | And Noaḥ built a slaughter-place to יהוה, and **took of every clean beast and of every clean bird**, and offered ascending offerings on the slaughter-place. |
| Gen 8:21 | And יהוה smelled a soothing fragrance, and יהוה said in His heart, "Never again shall I curse the ground because of man, although the inclination of man's heart is evil from his youth, and never again strike all living creatures, as I have done, |
| Gen 8:22 | as long as the earth remains, seedtime and harvest, and cold and heat, and summer and winter, and day and night shall not cease." |

Notice here that he knew what a clean animal was, and this knowledge would influence his understanding of what YHWH said concerning food in the next chapter.

Before we go on, let's make a statement concerning the Noahide laws.

"The **Seven Laws of Noah** (Hebrew: שבע מצוות בני נח□ *Sheva Mitzvot B'nei Noah*), also referred to as the **Noahide Laws** or the **Noachide Laws** (from the Hebrew pronunciation of "Noah"), are a set of imperatives which, according to the **Talmud**, were given by God[1] as a binding set of laws for the "children of Noah" – that is, all of humanity.[2][3]

"Accordingly, any non-Jew who adheres to these laws because they were given by Moses[4] is regarded as a *righteous gentile*, and is assured of a place in the world to come (עולם הבא□ *Olam Haba*), the final reward of the righteous.[5][6]

"The seven Noahide laws as traditionally enumerated are the following:[7][8]

1.    Not to worship idols.
2.    Not to curse God.
3.    To establish courts of justice.
4.    Not to commit murder.

5.      Not to commit adultery or sexual immorality.
6.      Not to steal.
7.      Not to eat flesh torn from a living animal.

According to the **Talmud**,[7] the rabbis agree that the seven laws were given to the sons of Noah. However, they disagree on precisely which laws were given to Adam and Eve. Six of the seven laws are exegetically derived from passages in Genesis,[9] with the seventh being the establishing of courts"

(An excerpt from:
https://en.wikipedia.org/wiki/Seven_Laws_of_Noah)

The Talmud is the primary text upon which Judaism defines itself. It consists of man-made religious traditions, commentaries and other types of rules and ways of living required by the rabbis.

Though it is associated to the Torah, it only actually gives lip service to the Torah because it is a culmination of teachings that are in violation of the Torah.

We are told clearly in Scripture not to add to nor take away from anything the Scripture says, but the Talmud is full of "takanot" (enactments and decrees, specifically man-made decrees, much of which contradict the Torah) and "ma'asim" (handed down tradition or legal precedent).

Though the Talmud was not actually written down until centuries after the ascension of Messiah, much of it was known in the time of Messiah as the "oral traditions" or "oral law".

It is this standard of rabbinic thought that is called the "tradition of the elders" in Matthew 15 and Mark 7, as well as the "traditions of the fathers" in Galatians 2.

Earlier we spoke concerning Acts 10, where Peter mentioned to the house of Cornelius that according to the Jews it was unlawful for him to go into one of another nation. He says this because it had been taught them by the rabbis and it was from of these "oral traditions" that this error was taught.

If you look carefully at these seven commands of the Noahide law, you will see that only two or three of them can be inferred from the passage in Genesis 9, make no mistake, the concept of Noahide law is foreign to the Scripture, for it is a man-made religious tradition.

Somehow, some sects within the Christian church have adopted this practice and yet have somehow redefined it to fit their own agenda, and they have tied this error to what Brother James said in Acts 15.

Acts 15 is where we find the Jerusalem Council, which was set up because the Jews had gone to Antioch in Galatia and taught the Gentile believers there that it was a pre-requisite for them to be circumcised "TO BE SAVED".

Paul had argued against this idea of work acceptance, teaching that we are accepted by the favor (grace) of YHWH through belief in Yahushua Messiah, our initial acceptance/justification is a matter of belief and not of works.

At the end of this debate Brother James explains to the Council that they have no business imposing restrictions upon new believers, but he encourages new believers to refrain certain things.

| | |
|---|---|
| **Act 15:13** | And after they were silent, Ya'aqoḇ answered, saying, "Men, brothers, listen to me: |
| **Act 15:14** | "Shim'on has declared how Elohim first visited the nations to take out of them a people for His Name. |
| **Act 15:15** | "And the words of the prophets agree with this, as it has been written: |
| **Act 15:16** | 'After this I shall return and rebuild the Booth of Dawiḏ which has fallen down. And I shall rebuild its ruins, and I shall set it up, |
| **Act 15:17** | so that the remnant of mankind shall seek יהוה, even all the nations on whom My Name has been called, says יהוה who is doing all this,' |
| **Act 15:18** | who has made this known from of old. |
| **Act 15:19** | "Therefore I judge that **we should not trouble those from among the nations** who are turning to Elohim, |

| Act 15:20 | but that **we write to them to abstain from the defilements of idols, and from whoring, and from what is strangled, and from blood.** |

**Note:**

| 1. | Idols: | Exo 22:20; Lev 17:7; Deu 32:17; 32:21;   1Co 10:14, 20-21. |
| 2. | Whoring: | Num 25:1-3; Lev 17:7. |
| 3. | Strangling: | Gen 9:4; Eze 33:25 (strangulation: blood saturation) Pro 21:25. |
| 4. | Blood: | Lev 17:10-14. |

Now, these things are all a reference to pagan idol worship, where an animal would be strangled to death which would cause the meat to be saturated with blood and adrenaline, then the blood would be drained into a cup of some kind, from which the adherents would later drink.

The meat then would be roasted but not completely, so the blood was still thick in the meat, and then after the meal they would participate in some form of whoring, some would perform orgies while others laid with the temple prostitutes both male and female.

James was simply telling the new believers, many of whom had come from this form of pagan worship, to no longer participate in idol temple worship. Why?

| Act 15:21 | "For from ancient generations Mosheh has, in every city, those proclaiming him – being read in the congregations every Sabbath." |

If a Gentile continued to participate in pagan temple services they would not be allowed into the congregation's, which is the only place they could hear the Torah spoken.

The apostles are **NOT** telling new Gentile believers they are not required to obey the Torah, they were instructing the Jewish brethren not to force the Gentiles into submission to the Torah as a prerequisite of acceptance.

It is not submission to the Torah that allows a Gentile admittance into the congregation, it is belief in Messiah.

However, once in the congregation, a Gentile believer can hear the Torah of YHWH, as was given through Moses to the people, and learn to obey it.

It was important to the apostles, as it should be to us, that new believers hear directly from the mouth of YHWH what is required of them.

Now, going back to the line, "Every creeping creature that lives is food for you", from Genesis 9:3, we need to ask ourselves whether YHWH has two different standards of what is food.

Some might say; originally, in the garden of Eden, man was given plants to eat as food, as well as the fruit of the trees (Genesis 1:29), then, after the flood, YHWH gave men "every creeping creature" as food, which was true until He gathered Yisra'el out of Mitsrayim (Egypt), at which time He gave them the dietary laws.

That, in and of itself, seems like a reasonable explanation, except the fact that YHWH doesn't change (Malachi 3:6) and in Him there is no shadow of turning (James 1:17).

Furthermore, as we have already shown, Noah understood the difference between clean animals and unclean animals (Genesis 8:20), which, all things being equal, must lead us to the conclusion that he understood YHWH to mean every "clean" creature.

Many will have a problem with this because it clearly does not say that in this passage, however, it is the responsibility of all who would diligently seek YHWH to interpret any single passage of Scripture in light of the totality of what Scripture says on any given subject.

We must remember that YHWH is not restrained by time or space and so the Scripture alone must interpret itself notwithstanding the timeline in which we received it.

Whatever the intent of YHWH in Genesis 9, it is clear through the totality of Scripture that those who would come into covenant with YHWH through belief in Yahushua Messiah, whether native born or stranger, are required to keep the dietary laws as they were given at Mount Sinai.

Now, it is understandable how a person might not understand how the phrase "every creeping creature" does not apply to every single creature, because though we were taught that YHWH doesn't change and that His Word is established in the heavens forever and that it cannot contradict itself, statements that seem as clear as this one tests our ability to see beyond the statement itself.

Also, as mentioned, there has been some question concerning YHWH changing His definition of "food" from only fruits and vegetables in Genesis 1:29 to animals in Genesis 9.

In Genesis 1, Adam was told by YHWH that He had given him ( and all creatures) vegetation to eat as food. He did not say that meat could not be eaten because He didn't need to, there was no death in the garden.

After Adam sinned, death was now in the world and man had to offer a sacrifice to YHWH in remembrance of the mercy YHWH had shown to Adam, when He threw him out of the Garden.

The first death was committed by YHWH Himself when He killed animals to cover the nakedness of Adam and his wife. This sacrifice is the first shadow picture of the need for a sacrifice to cover sin, and it came right on the heels of the first Messianic prophesy ever given in Genesis 3:15.

Once death came into the world, meat was now available as food for man. Vegetation was the only food available to man before death entered the world.

It is clear that Noah knew the difference between what animals were clean and which were not clean, because he knew which animals to sacrifice.

We are not given specific information concerning when Adam's children began eating meat, but it is clear that YHWH allowed it beginning in Genesis 9. It is important to remember that is was never YHWH's intent for man to disobey and be kicked out of the Garden.

YHWH placed the Tree of Life in the Garden, right next to the Tree of the Knowledge of Good and Evil, it was man that chose to eat of the tree of disobedience and the consequence of his actions was death to himself, his children and all living creatures.

YHWH's response to man's sin, though He knew it and prepared for it ahead of time, was to offer a sacrifice to cover him, a life for a life.

Giving the meat of that life to man as food is another shadow picture of Messiah, the Passover Lamb, that we eat once a year.

What's interesting about this phrase "every creeping creature", is that it is very similar to what Paul said to Timothy.

| | |
|---|---|
| **1Ti 4:1** | But the Spirit distinctly says that in latter times **some shall fall away** from the belief, paying attention to **misleading spirits, and teachings of demons**, |
| **1Ti 4:2** | speaking lies in hypocrisy, having been branded on their own conscience, |
| **1Ti 4:3** | forbidding to marry, **saying to abstain from foods which Elohim created to be received with thanksgiving by those who believe and know the truth**. |
| **1Ti 4:4** | Because **every creature** of Elohim is good, and none is to be rejected if it is received with thanksgiving, |
| **1Ti 4:5** | **for it is set apart by the Word of Elohim and prayer**. |

Christianity has totally mangled the meaning of this passage, trying to interpret it outside the context of the totality of what Scripture says in the matter of what is "food".

As we have shown, **UNCLEAN CREATURES ARE NOT FOOD**!!!

Christians like to say, that because of their belief in "Jesus Christ" they no longer have to obey the "Old Testament law", but as we've shown multiple times in this writing, this is not true. Their perspective allows them to reinterpret or better yet, to misinterpret what Paul means here in 1 Timothy.

From their point of view, their Greco-Roman mindset, those who "fall away" because of "misleading spirits, and the teachings of demons" are those of us who claim that we are supposed to keep the dietary laws commanded in the Torah.

Unfortunately, there mindset causes them to interpret what is said throughout the Messianic Writings to mean the opposite of what the Hebrew minded writers meant.

In fact, any Hebrew minded person can easily refute their anti-law position and prove a believer's responsibility to obey the Torah, from the exact same passages Christians use to teach that they don't have to.

This passage in 1 Timothy is a perfect example. Though Christians believe this passage of Scripture is evidence that believers are no longer required to keep the dietary laws, this passage, in fact, teaches believers to keep the dietary laws, however, as in the other passages in the Messianic Writings concerning food, Paul is referring to "clean" meat that **MIGHT** have been offered to idols.

**Remember**, the arguments in Romans 14 and 1st Corinthians 8 and 10, concern the eating of clean meat that **MIGHT** have been offered to idols, and that some of the immature brethren were saying that they should not eat of it while the mature brethren knew they could eat of it.

Paul is warning Timothy that in the last days men would come along forbidding the eating of food that **MIGHT** have been offered idols. It is simply a matter of men commanding us to do things that YHWH has told us not to do or to not do things that YHWH has told us to do.

This has to do with men making up commands that contradict what YHWH has already spoken, so it's unlawful for anyone to tell us that we cannot eat what YHWH has already ordained for us to eat, which is **NEVER** unclean meat.

In the same sentence as food, he also mentions that these same men would forbid marriage, which has been done in certain religious circles within Christianity, however, in most "Christian cultures" we have not been forbidden to marry, only to redefine the meaning of it.

**NO ONE** has the authority to forbid marriage or to redefine its meaning, for only the Giver of life, the Creator of all things, the Creator of man, has the right to declare what is or is not acceptable.

It is easy to discern from this passage in 1st Timothy that Paul intends us to understand that he is referring only to clean meats.

Paul says that "every creature of Elohim is good" because it is "set apart by the Word of Elohim and prayer".

What creatures did YHWH "set apart" in His Word to be "good for food" for His people?

The torot (teachings/laws) concerning creatures to be eaten in Leviticus 11 and Deuteronomy 14 are the **ONLY** creatures that YHWH has set apart for His people Yisra'el, whether native born or stranger.

Technically, these two passages tell us more specifically what is forbidden to eat and gives us a basic instruction on how to determine what cannot be eaten and what can be.

For instance, the only land creatures that can be eaten must have both a split hoof **AND** chew the cud, which eliminates pork, rabbits, squirrels, raccoons, etc.

Furthermore, the only water creatures eaten must have both fins **AND** scales, which eliminates all shellfish, shark, porpoise, whale and the like.

All flying creatures can be eaten **EXCEPT** those that have been specifically forbidden in these passages, most of which are predatory or scavenger birds, but also includes ostriches, storks and bats.

No insects can be eaten **EXCEPT** locusts, specifically those creatures that have two sets of legs for walking and one set of legs for jumping.

All these creatures have been set apart by the Word of Elohim as food for the people of YHWH, both native born and stranger. **NO** creature that has been declared as unclean in these passages is food.

Obviously, Paul is not referring to unclean animals when he says "every creature" is good for food, when YHWH has declared the opposite to be true.

The question then, is "if the Word has set the food apart, why is prayer relevant to the food being acceptable?"

How does prayer "set apart" food that has already been "set apart" by the Word?

Notice again what Paul specifically says in verses 4-5.

| | |
|---|---|
| **1Ti 4:4** | Because every creature of Elohim is good, and none is to be rejected **if it is received with thanksgiving,** |
| **1Ti 4:5** | **for it is set apart by the Word of Elohim and prayer**. |

Now, compare this to what Paul said about "clean meat" offered to idols in Romans 14 and 1ˢᵗ Corinthians 10.

| | |
|---|---|
| **Rom 14:6** | He who minds the day, minds it to יהוה. And he who does not mind the day, to יהוה he does not mind it. He who eats, eats to יהוה, **for he gives Elohim thanks**. And he who does not eat, to יהוה he does not eat, and gives Elohim thanks. |
| | *** |
| **1Co 10:30** | But if I partake **with thanks**, why am I evil spoken of for what **I give thanks**? |
| **1Co 10:31** | Therefore, whether you eat or drink, or whatever you do, **do all to the esteem of Elohim.** |

Paul is simply telling us that the creatures that YHWH has set aside for His people to eat in Leviticus 11 and Deuteronomy 14 cannot be forbidden to us by the teachings or doctrines of men.

Furthermore, the fact that some people or religious group **MIGHT** have offered one of these clean creatures to some demon, does not change the fact that YHWH gave these creatures to His people to eat as food.

Now we are **NEVER** allowed to **KNOWINGLY** eat meat that has been offered to idols, however, if there is a question as to whether it was offered to an idol, we are free to eat of it if we give thanks for it, because YHWH has set it apart in His Word as food for us and our prayer of thanksgiving cleanses it of any taint of idol worship.

This is what the Messianic Writings say about food, it **NEVER** refers to unclean meat as it is defined in Leviticus 11 and Deuteronomy 14.

Lastly, I want to talk about the love feast, specifically what 1st Corinthians 11 says about the taking of the bread and the cup of Messiah.

We are only going to talk about this because Paul's discussion in 1st Corinthians 10 included the phrase cup of Messiah and our inability to participate in it and in the cup of demons (idol worship) and his teaching on it directly following chapter 10.

The general teaching of Chapter 11, like most everything else Christians teach, is inaccurate.

| | |
|---|---|
| **1Co 11:17** | And in declaring this I do not praise you, **since you come together not for the better but for the worse**. |
| **1Co 11:18** | For in the first place, I hear that **when you come together as an assembly, there are divisions among you,** and to some extent I believe it. |
| **1Co 11:19** | For **there have to be factions even among you**, so that the approved ones might be revealed among you. |

So, this is the context upon which he's going to begin teaching about the cup of Messiah and it revolves around divisions in the body and factions vying for supremacy and favor instead of coming together in the spirit in which Messiah gave Himself.

| | |
|---|---|
| **1Co 11:20** | So when you come together in one place, it is not to eat the Master's supper. |
| **1Co 11:21** | For, when you eat, **each one takes his own supper first**, and one is hungry and another is drunk. |
| **1Co 11:22** | Have you not houses to eat and drink in? Or **do you despise the assembly of Elohim and shame those who have not**? What shall I say to you? Shall I praise you in this? I do not praise! |

Now we see the context bared out here, in that some people are focused on feeding their own bellies and getting their fill of drink, while caring nothing at all for others among them who may not have enough at home. The cup and bread of Messiah is about His self-sacrificial act, done for the good of those of us who had nothing and no hope.

He is the Word of YHWH made flesh, the Son of the living Elohim, yet He gave His own life for those of us who had shown His Father no love and no respect.

| Rom 5:6 | For **when we were still weak**, Messiah in due time died for the wicked. |
| Rom 5:7 | For one shall hardly die for a righteous one, though possibly for a good one someone would even have the courage to die. |
| Rom 5:8 | **But Elohim proves His own love for us, in that while we were still sinners, Messiah died for us**. |

Do not lose sight of this, because it is with this frame of mind, we are supposed to take part in the supper of Messiah. We are to have this same frame of mind towards our brethren, especially the weaker among us, that Messiah had towards us when He gave His life for us.

| 1Co 11:23 | For I received from the Master that which I also delivered to you: that the Master יהושע in the night in which He was delivered up took bread, |
| 1Co 11:24 | and having given thanks, He broke it and said, "**Take, eat, this is My body which is broken for you; do this in remembrance of Me**." |
| 1Co 11:25 | In the same way also the cup, after supper, saying, "**This cup is the renewed covenant in My blood. As often as you drink it, do this in remembrance of Me**." |
| 1Co 11:26 | For **as often as you eat this bread and drink this cup, you proclaim** |

| | the death of the Master until He comes. |
|---|---|
| 1Co 11:27 | So that **whoever should eat this bread or drink this cup of the Master unworthily shall be guilty of the body and blood of the Master**. |
| 1Co 11:28 | But **let a man examine himself**, and so let him eat of that bread and drink of that cup. |
| 1Co 11:29 | For the one who is eating and drinking unworthily, **eats and drinks judgment to himself, not discerning the body of the Master**. |
| 1Co 11:30 | Because of this many are weak and sick among you, and many sleep. |

Most of us were taught as young Christians, that this referred to those of us who might still be struggling with sin in our lives, that if we were, we were unworthy of the cup of Messiah and should refrain from taking part in it because of the possible consequences.

This could not be farther from the truth; this cup is for the sinner to remind them of sins cost. To partake of this cup "unworthily" has nothing to do with struggling against some fleshly issue and has everything to do with drinking of it with a divisive, arrogant and selfish attitude.

It is taking part in this sacrificial meal, drinking of this sacrificial cup in a selfish manner, filling our own belly and getting our own drink, while other brothers, who have little or nothing, hunger and thirst.

| 1Co 11:31 | **For if we were to examine ourselves, we would not be judged.** |
|---|---|
| 1Co 11:32 | But when we are judged, we are disciplined by the Master, that we should not be condemned with the world. |
| 1Co 11:33 | So then, my brothers, when you come together to eat, **wait for one another**. |

**1Co 11:34**    And if anyone is hungry, let him eat at home, lest you come together for judgment. And the rest I shall set in order when I come.

Our belief is about sacrifice, what Yahushua Messiah did for us and how we are to treat others, especially those in the household of Elohim, in the light of His sacrifice.

# The Conclusion of the Matter

As we have shown, both the Jewish rabbis and the Christian theologians have errored in their interpretation of Scripture due to their disobedience.

Judaism adheres primarily to the teachings and traditions of rabbinical thought, and not to the Scripture strictly. Because of this, Judaism has become a veil over the eyes of the people, so they cannot see the truth of their need of Yahushua and turn towards Him.

Christians adhere to doctrines that are not founded in the Tanak, having founded their beliefs on what the Messianic Writings or New Testament says, outside of the foundational context in which was given.

Jews reject Yahushua and Christians reject the Torah, both make these two religions, false religions. They each have a modicum of truth to them and yet they fail to understand the totality of truth, because of their refusal to be absolutely set apart unto YHWH and Him alone, according to the Way He set forth from the beginning.

Yes, they claim to be His servants, His people, but they do not live their lives in the way He commanded them to. Instead, they follow a path of pseudo righteousness, that comes from the teachings and doctrines of man-made thoughts and feelings. In the end, this will destroy them.

Neither Judaism, nor Christianity, adhere to the totality of Scripture strictly, without additions or subtractions, and so they are incapable of gaining the wisdom and understanding promised in the Scripture.

Wisdom and understanding of the Scripture, comes from obedience to it, without additions or subtractions (Deuteronomy 4:1-6).

Neither of these religions actually read the Scripture from a strictly Hebrew mindset, even though Judaism is an ethnically Hebrew religion. There is a distinct difference between a physically descendent Hebrew and someone who thinks like a scriptural Hebrew.

Judaism does not view the Tanak from a distinctly Hebrew mindset because they have been led astray by the rabbis and sages of the past, which has caused them to have a distinctly "Jewish" mindset, i.e., founded in the teachings of religious Judaism.

832

The only way to view and interpret the Scripture properly, is to conform our way of thinking to what the Scripture in its totality actually says and then live it out strictly with all of our heart and mind and strength. It is only then that we gain access to the wisdom and understanding taught therein.

According to the Messianic Writings, there is a veil over the eyes of Judaism and that veil is Moses (Mosheh).

2Co 3:1    Are we to begin to recommend ourselves again? Or do we need, as some, letters of recommendation to you, or from you?

2Co 3:2    You are our letter, having been written in our hearts, known and read by all men,

2Co 3:3    making it obvious that you are **a letter of Messiah**, served by us, written not with ink but by the Spirit of the living Elohim, **not on tablets of stone but on fleshly tablets of the heart.**

2Co 3:4    And such **trust** we have toward Elohim, through the Messiah.

2Co 3:5    Not that we are competent in ourselves to reckon any matter as from ourselves, but our competence is from Elohim,

2Co 3:6    who also made us competent as servants of a renewed covenant, **not of the letter but of the Spirit, for the letter kills but the Spirit gives life.**

2Co 3:7    But if the **administering of death in letters, engraved on stones,** was esteemed, so that the children of Yisra'ěl were unable to look steadily at the face of Mosheh because of the esteem of his face, **which was passing away,**

2Co 3:8    how much more esteemed shall the administering of the Spirit not be?

2Co 3:9    For if the **administering of condemnation** had esteem, the

833

| | administering of righteousness exceeds much more in esteem. |
|---|---|
| 2Co 3:10 | For indeed what was made esteemed had no esteem in this respect, in view of the esteem that excels. |
| 2Co 3:11 | For if that which is **passing away** was esteemed, much more that which remains in esteem. |
| 2Co 3:12 | Having then such expectation, we u se much boldness of speech, |
| 2Co 3:13 | and not like Mosheh, **who put a veil over his face so that the children of Yisra'ĕl should not look steadily at the end of what was passing away.** |
| 2Co 3:14 | But **their minds were hardened,** for to this day, when the old covenant is being read, **that same veil remains**, not lifted, because **in Messiah it is taken away.** |
| 2Co 3:15 | But to this day, when Mosheh is being read, **a veil lies on their heart.** |
| 2Co 3:16 | And **when one turns to the Master, the veil is taken away.** |
| 2Co 3:17 | Now יהוה is the Spirit, and where the Spirit of יהוה is, **there is freedom.** |
| 2Co 3:18 | And we all, as with unveiled face we see as in a mirror the esteem of יהוה, are being **transformed into the same likeness** from esteem to esteem, as from יהוה, the Spirit. |

Now, Christians believe that this veil that has blinded the Jews, is the Torah, however, it is not the Torah itself that is being referred to here, it is the consequence of trusting in the Torah that Paul is referring to.

Let's take a look at what the Torah says about Mosheh and the veil.

| **Exo 34:29** | And it came to be, when Mosheh came down from Mount Sinai, while the two tablets of the Witness were |
|---|---|

| | in Mosheh's hand when he came down from the mountain, **that Mosheh did not know that the skin of his face shone since he had spoken with Him**. |
|---|---|
| Exo 34:30 | And Aharon and all the children of Yisra'ĕl looked at **Mosheh and saw the skin of his face shone, and they were afraid to come near him**. |
| Exo 34:31 | But Mosheh called out to them, and Aharon and all the rulers of the congregation returned to him, and Mosheh spoke to them. |
| Exo 34:32 | And afterward all the children of Yisra'ĕl came near, and **he commanded them all that יהוה had spoken with him on Mount Sinai.** |
| Exo 34:33 | And **when Mosheh ended speaking with them, he put a veil on his face.** |
| Exo 34:34 | But whenever Mosheh went in before יהוה to speak with Him, he would remove the veil until he came out. **And when he came out he spoke to the children of Yisra'ĕl what he had been commanded,** |
| Exo 34:35 | **and the children of Yisra'ĕl would see the face of Mosheh, that the skin of Mosheh's face shone, and Mosheh would put the veil on his face again**, until he went in to speak with Him. |

Notice the progression here, Mosheh went before YHWH and received the commands, he then came down to the people with his face shining and told them what the Father had commanded of them, it was only after speaking the Words of YHWH that he put the veil on his face.

So, during the speaking of the Torah Mosheh's face shone brightly and the people all saw his face shining and were afraid. Only after Mosheh had given them the commands did he cover his face.

Think of this scenario, Mosheh speaking the Torah in light, for the Torah is light (Proverbs 6:23) and once he had spoken it, he covered his face, so the light was no longer visible.

When the Torah is spoken it not only teaches us the way to live but also the consequences for not living in obedience to it, and while it's being spoken the reality of it is like a light shining in our eyes, but once we stop hearing it, the light of it begins to fade.

The principle expressed here is very similar to what Brother James said in James 1.

| | |
|---|---|
| **Jam 1:21** | Therefore **put away all filthiness and overflow of evil**, and receive with meekness **the implanted Word**, which is able to save your lives. |
| **Jam 1:22** | And become **doers of the Word, and not hearers only, deceiving yourselves**. |
| **Jam 1:23** | **Because if anyone is a hearer of the Word and not a doer, he is like a man who looks at his natural face in a mirror,** |
| **Jam 1:24** | **for he looks at himself, and goes away, and immediately forgets what he was like.** |
| **Jam 1:25** | But he that looked **into the perfect Torah, that of freedom, and continues in it,** not becoming a hearer that forgets, **but a doer of work, this one shall be blessed in his doing** *of the Torah.* |

The command to "put away all filthiness and overflow of evil" is a reference to repentance (turning away from evil and re-turning to YHWH) and the phrase "implanted Word" has a very specific meaning, a meaning that has two parts.

The first part, the spiritual part, has to do with Yahushua Messiah being in us, as He promised in John 14:15-24. There He says that if we love Him, we will keep His commands (15) and that those who "possess" His

836

commands and "guards them", they are those who love Him (21).

Furthermore, Messiah says of those who love Him (guard His Word) the Father will love them, and He and the Father will make their stay with them (23). The promise of having Messiah in us is directly connected to our obedience to the commands.

Messiah is the Word made flesh, which is the first part of the "implanted Word", but the second part is the Torah itself, the physical part.

In Jeremiah 31:31-33, we see the promise of the new/renewed covenant and in it we are told that YHWH would put His Torah in our inner parts and write it upon our hearts. The Torah of YHWH is the second part of the "implanted Word" that Brother James is referring to in the above passage.

Going on, we see James commanding us to be "doers of the Word" because if we only hear the word and don't do it, **we are deceiving ourselves** (See: Rom 2:13).

**REMEMBER**, the "Word", as is used in the Scripture, refers to the totality of what YHWH has spoken, and not just to what is said in the Messianic Writings. The "Word" includes the Torah, the Prophets and the Writings (the Tanak). James is commanding us to obey the Torah, because if we only hear what the Torah says, but do not actually obey what it says, **we are deceiving ourselves** (Romans 2:13).

He goes on to say, someone who hears what the Torah says but does not obey it is like a man who sees what he looks like in a mirror, but the minute he walks away from the mirror, he forgets what he looks like.

This matches exactly the scenario in Exodus concerning the veil over Mosheh's face when he finished reading the Torah. As the people were hearing the Torah being spoken by Mosheh, the light of its righteousness shone from Mosheh's face for all to see.

During the reading of the Torah the people heard the command and the penalty for disobedience, so what was meant to give life to them, actually brought upon them the condemnation of death, just as brother Paul says of himself in Romans 7:7-11.

837

| Rom 7:7 | What, then, shall we say? Is the Torah sin? Let it not be! However, **I did not know sin except through the Torah. For also the covetousness I knew not if the Torah had not said, "You shall not covet."** |
|---|---|
| Rom 7:8 | But sin, having taken the occasion through the command, did work in me all sorts of covetousness. For apart from Torah sin is dead. |
| Rom 7:9 | **And I was alive apart from the Torah once, but when the command came, the sin revived, and I died.** |
| Rom 7:10 | **And the command which was to result in life, this I found to result in death.** |
| Rom 7:11 | For sin, **having taken the occasion through the command, deceived me, and through it killed me.** |

Do you see what Paul is saying here? Though we may have been guilty of disobeying the Torah before we knew what the Torah said, we still believed we were in life. However, once we heard all the command said, we realized we were guilty of disobeying it and that guilt condemned us to death.

It is in this context Paul uses the idea of the veil in 2<sup>nd</sup> Corinthians, but we will get back to that in a moment.

Brother James uses the mirror as a picture of the Torah. When we look into the Torah, we see the contrast between the kind of person we are and the kind of person it requires us to be, but when we are no longer looking in the Torah, when it is no longer in our face, a veil comes over our eyes that prevents us from seeing or understanding our unrighteousness in relationship to righteousness of Torah.

In verse 25, he's going to make a profound distinction between those who are trusting in the Torah and those who are trusting in Yahushua, as it relates to obedience to the Torah.

Let's see that verse again.

| Jam 1:25 | But he that looked **into the perfect Torah, that of freedom, and continues in it**, not becoming a hearer that forgets, **but a doer of work, this one shall be blessed in his doing** *of the Torah.* |
|---|---|

| Note: | The last three words in this verse, in this translation, have been italicized to show that they are not actually in the writings. The translators have added them to **correctly** express the intent of the author. |
|---|---|

The context of this verse is clearly the Torah, specifically the "perfect Torah", and our "continuing in it", being a "doer of the work", which brings blessing, as promised in Deuteronomy 30:11-20.

The person that looks into the perfect Torah, that of freedom, and continues in it, **doing the work** shall be blessed in his doing.

What does it mean to be looking into the "perfect Torah" and how does the Torah bring freedom when it actually condemns us for our disobedience?

The "perfect Torah" is the Torah that consists of both the spiritual part and the physical part, this is the complete Torah. What does this mean?

Yahushua Messiah is the Word/Torah made flesh, the spiritual part of the Torah, while the written Torah, as it was given by YHWH, through Mosheh, at Mount Sinai is the physical part of the Torah.

When we have these two things working in our lives (belief in Yahushua with a heart of obedience) then we can walk in freedom because the mistakes we make are not counted against us.

What must be emphatically stated here is that a "heart of obedience" refers to someone that never, ever intentionally violates the Torah!

"Willful sin (disobedience)" brings condemnation, even upon the believer. However, because of the intense battle going on between our spiritual man that wants to obey and the physical man that doesn't want to obey, unintentional sin (sin that takes place by accident or is stumbled into) can still be cleansed through confession (1st John 2:9).

Our belief in Messiah frees us from the condemnation of the Torah and clears our conscience (spirit man) of all wrongdoing, which is true freedom. However, this blessing only comes upon those who are living in the perfect or complete Torah from a sincere heart.

It is the believer who does the works of Torah who receives a blessing. However, the believer who only hears the Torah but does not obey it, heaps up condemnation upon themselves again (Galatians 2:17-18).

Judaism's eyes are still veiled because they have placed their trust in the Torah, even while they walk in disobedience to it, which adds condemnation onto condemnation. They are blind to what the Torah is trying to teach them about sin, death and redemption because they placed their trust in the Torah and not the Author of the Torah, and neither do they obey it.

Christians have the veil of condemnation lifted from them when they believe in the death, burial and resurrection of Messiah and confess Him, even if the multitude of their understanding is incorrect.

Then, however, they walk right back down the road towards condemnation because they are being taught, they no longer need to obey the Torah.

"...Sin is the transgression of the Law." (1 John 3:4 (KJV) and anyone NOT obeying the Law/Torah is guilty of sin and headed for judgment.

Where the Jews have placed their trust in the Torah, even though they don't walk in obedience to, the Christians have placed their trust in the Messiah, even though they don't walk in obedience to the Torah as He did.

Just like the Jews before them, Christians have turned the truth of YHWH, and His Son Yahushua, into a false, man-made religion, because they refuse to walk in the truth of the "Perfect Torah" as commanded by Messiah, Paul, Peter, James, etc.

Believers, who walk in obedience to the Torah, have had the veil (condemnation) removed and shall inherit the Everlasting Kingdom because they understand the difference between being justified from death through belief and living a justified life.

Belief in Yahushua Messiah justifies us from past sin and the penalty of death, while living a justified life in obedience to the Torah from a pure heart, protects us from condemnation for future mistakes.

**Isa 29:13**     And יהוה says, "Because this people has drawn near with its mouth, and with its lips they have esteemed Me, and **it has kept its heart far from Me**, and their fear of Me has **become a command of men that is taught!**

Both Judaism and Christianity are guilty of this passage for though they say they believe Him, and they say that they love Him, their hearts are far from Him. Why?

Because, instead of loving Him and serving Him according to the very specific way in which He taught them to, they have gone their own way, allowing themselves to be taught things by men that are not consistent with what He commanded of them.

They no longer fear YHWH, to obey Him, but they fear other men, obeying their teachings and traditions, which are additions or subtractions from what YHWH Himself has spoken and are direct violations of what He has commanded.

The truth is very simple, Judaism has missed their Messiah because they allowed their teachers to teach them things that are not consistent with what YHWH commanded of them.

Christianity, though it acknowledges the Messiah, shall not inherit the Kingdom unless they repent, because they have allowed their teachers to teach them things that are not consistent with what YHWH commanded of them. Does anyone see a pattern here?

The **ONLY WAY** to inherit the Kingdom, is to believe in Yahushua Messiah for the justification from death and walk in the justification of life, through obedience to the Torah of YHWH, as was given by Him through Moses at Mount Sinai, without additions or subtractions, with a sincere and compassionate heart.

841

| | |
|---|---|
| **2Co 11:13** | For such are false emissaries, deceptive workers, masquerading as emissaries of Messiah. |
| **2Co 11:14** | And no wonder! For Satan himself masquerades as a messenger of light! |
| **2Co 11:15** | It is not surprising, then, if his servants also masquerade as servants of righteousness, **whose end shall be according to their works**! |

There are many teachers out there that seem to be spiritual men and seem to teach us to live righteously, but beware, their master does not love you.

# Appendices

# Appendix

# Appendix 1: Echad

One or 3 in 1?

**Deu 6:4**  "Hear, O Yisra'ĕl: יהוה our Elohim,
יהוה is **one**!
\*\*\*

**Joh 10:30**  "I and My Father are **one**."

**One:**  Hebrew - stg's **#H259** "'echâd", a numeral
from H258 (to unify); properly united, that
is, one; or (as an ordinal) first: - a, alike,
alone, altogether, and, any (-thing), apiece, a
certain [dai-] ly, each (one), + eleven, every,
few, first, + highway, a man, once, one,
only, other, some, together.

Greek - stg's **#G1520** "heis", (Including the
neuter [etc.] ἕν hen); a primary numeral;
one: - a (-n, -ny, certain), + abundantly,
man, one (another), only, other, some.

**Note:**  Though these two words seem similar, they
do not express the exact same meaning. The
Greek word suggests a singularity, one
single thing, like the number one, while the
Hebrew expresses a unity of one and should
be understood to mean, absolute and
complete unity, as in no distinction or
difference.

It cannot be argued that Yahushua is the "Word" of
YHWH made flesh through the conception of a Yisra'eli
maiden, who had not yet known a man (a virgin), through
the power of His Spirit.

The problem comes from the fact that as men we do
not think the same way YHWH thinks and it is not until we
surrender our thoughts, our minds, our desires and our
actions completely to what He has said in His Word, and
concerning His Son, that we will begin to think more like
Him.

845

YHWH, His Son and His Spirit, is One, but not according to the Trinitarian definition taught by the Christian church.

To understand how the Son and the Father and the Spirit can be One and yet **NOT** be 3 in 1, we have to understand the nature of YHWH as He has revealed it to us through His Word and His creation.

In the beginning, YHWH spoke, "let there be" and there was, something out of nothing, which defines the scriptural idea of 'divinity'. He accomplished this through His Word that went forth from His lips carried on the wind of His breath.

Here we see the so-called "three" working to accomplish creation, by the act of one. There is not three here, there is only one. For out of the one came the other two and that is how we are to understand the "echad" (unity) of YHWH.

This teaching is not about this topic specifically, so we are not going to cover it very thoroughly, but we want to express the importance of not just accepting what other people tell you is true, so that you will investigate how things actually are for yourself.

The Word that went forth from the mouth of YHWH, being carried on His breath (Spirit), and it was that the same Word with which YHWH fertilized the ova of the maiden Miryam (Mary), through the power of His Spirit (breath).

In His humanity, the Word (Yahushua), became the full expression of the character of YHWH in a human being, which is revealed to us in the Torah of YHWH, and even though YHWH appeared in human form in the Torah, and we understand this to be a physical manifestation of the Word of YHWH, the Word born flesh in Yahushua was a new and very unique occurrence.

The Living Word, Yahushua, became subject to the authority of the Father in His humanity so He could fulfill the calling to which He was called, to be the Passover Lamb of YHWH that would deliver mankind from the condemnation of death and the authority of sin.

The Spirit of YHWH, His breath, is the power through which YHWH accomplishes His purposes and since YHWH Himself is Spirit, the Spirit of YHWH is the breath (life) of YHWH working in us unto everlasting life.

846

YHWH created all things and impregnated the Jewish virgin, Miriam, in the same way you and I might create a poem or a song. He thought it and then He spoke it and it came to be.

All the physical, mental and emotional attributes we use in the creating of a poem are expressions of who we are (one, not many of us in one) and we refer to all these attributes as "I" not "we". They represent everything that makes us, us.

> **Note**: We submit that in the book of Genesis, YHWH seems to refer to Himself as "Us" and this mystery is why there can be NO emphatic explanation of the relationship between YHWH, His Word and His Spirit prior to the Word tooking on humanity.

We must understand that our thoughts become our words and our breath then carries them from our mouth, giving them life in the ears of those who hear us.

The Father, in this simile, represents the thoughts, while the Messiah represents the Words and the Spirit is the Breath, which goes out to perform the action of generating life, not three in one, just One.

Don't forget, though, the person we know as Yahushua Messiah did not exist as Yahushua Messiah before the Father impregnated the ova of the Jewish maiden. It was not until He was conceived in her womb that He took on humanity and became Yahushua the Messiah, in what seems to us to be a separate form than the Father.

What confuses us when we try to explain this, is the distinction we make in our understanding, in our finite minds, between what is two distinct personalities that are absolutely One in heart and mind.

The limitations of our physical mental process and the lack of obedience to the physical righteousness we are commanded to live by, prevent us from understanding things greater than what is physically understandable.

Only those who walk in the spiritual, according to the process through which spiritual understanding is given, can see beyond the limitations of our physical mind to take hold of the reality of what it means to be echad.

Paul tells us that the Law/Torah is spiritual (Romans 7:14) and Moses tells us that obeying the Law/Torah is our wisdom and understanding (Deuteronomy 4:5-6).

The Torah, though it is written down in physical form, is, in fact, a spiritual document and it is through obedience to what is written, that we gain the wisdom and understanding of spiritual things.

However, all mankind has been born under the condemnation of death that we inherited from our father Adam, because of his disobedience in eating of the Tree of the Knowledge of Good and Evil

His disobedience condemned himself and all his descendant's to death, both physical death and spiritual death, so that we cannot gain spiritual understanding without the help of YHWH.

The Law/Torah of YHWH was given to us to teach us how to walk spiritually before YHWH, however, because we were already in a state of condemnation, we were unable to achieve spiritual righteousness.

To remedy this spiritual death, YHWH had to provide a way for the condemnation of death that overshadowed us because of disobedience (sin), to be removed so we could then walk in physical righteousness and gain spiritual understanding.

The remedy to our condemnation, was the death of that which had condemned us, i.e., His Law/Torah.

Now, it was His Law/Torah (His Word) that became flesh in Yahushua Messiah, and it was through the death of Yahushua that the condemnation for sin (death) required by His Law/Torah was removed from our account.

Think of it like a bank account, where life was deposited in our account when we were created, and disobedience (sin) became a debt against our account, which withdrew/took the life from us, because the Law/Torah commanded that death was the price for disobedience.

YHWH, the Banker, offered a life, in the form of His Law/Torah made flesh (Yahushua), as a substitute for the debt/death we owed, so that if we place our trust in that sacrifice, life is deposited back into our account.

Now that life has been deposited back into our account, we have access to wisdom, understanding and eventual inheritance, **If** we walk in obedience to the command of life (obedience to the Law/Torah) and not in obedience to the command of death (disobedience to the Law/Torah).

Read and carefully consider the following:

| | |
|---|---|
| **Deu 30:15** | "See, I have set before you today life and good, and death and evil, |
| **Deu 30:16** | in that I am commanding you today to love יהוה your Elohim, to walk in His ways, and to guard His commands, and His laws, and His right-rulings. And you shall live and increase, and יהוה your Elohim shall bless you in the land which you go to possess. |
| **Deu 30:17** | "But if your heart turns away, and you do not obey, and shall be drawn away, and shall bow down to other mighty ones and serve them, |
| **Deu 30:18** | "I have declared to you today that you shall certainly perish, you shall not prolong your days in the land which you are passing over the Yardĕn to enter and possess. |
| **Deu 30:19** | "I have called the heavens and the earth as witnesses today against you: I have set before you life and death, the blessing and the curse. Therefore you shall choose life, so that you live, both you and your seed, |
| **Deu 30:20** | to love יהוה your Elohim, to obey His voice, and to cling to Him – for He is your life and the length of your days – to dwell in the land which יהוה swore to your fathers, to Aḇraham, to Yitsḥaq, and to Yaʿaqoḇ, to give them." |

The process by which YHWH created all things and will eventually restore all things rests in the unity, the oneness, of His nature, regardless whether we understand it or not, but it is vital that we do not try to express the nature

849

of YHWH and His relationship to Yahushua in a way that makes sense to us but is not fully explainable Scripturally.

Especially, if the explanation we try to produce is much more consistent to ancient practices of idolatry and pagan religions. The Trinitarian concept of 3 in 1 existed long before the Messiah was born and is founded in the Babylonian deception.

Yes, the Babylonian Trinitarian "Godhead", which has been, in one way or another, copied in many different pagan religious societies, is a distorted mimicry of the true nature of YHWH, advanced by the adversary of our lives, Ha-Satan.

However, the similarities between Babylonian Trinitarianism and echad (Scriptural Unity) are minuscule compared to the vast differences between the Babylonian deception and Scriptural Truth.

When asked about the relationship between the Father, His Spirit and His Son, Yahushua, the best answer is that they are One in absolute and complete unity. Leave the rest to those who look for reasons to disbelieve and to those who like to waste their time debating things that cannot be proven emphatically.

# Appendix 2:      Jot and Tittle

**Mat 5:17**      Think not that I am come to destroy the law, or the prophets: I am not come to destroy, but to fulfil.

**Mat 5:18**      For verily I say unto you, Till heaven and earth pass, **one jot or one tittle** shall in no wise pass from the law, till all be fulfilled.

In this passage, Yahushua is making a statement concerning the Torah and the Prophets, a Hebrew expression referring to the Tanak (Old Testament).

Much of Christian dogma today teaches that the "Old Testament Law" is no longer relevant in the life of the believer today, despite what the Messiah says here.

Within this passage is the phrase "one jot and one tittle", which prompts many to ask what it means that not one jot nor one tittle shall pass from the Law.

Before we discuss the meaning of jot and tittle, we're going to dissect this verse so you, the reader, can understand how the meaning of jot and tittle should be understood in the context of Matthew 5.

First, let's define certain words.

**Destroy:**      stg's #**G2647** "kaluō", from two words meaning, (G2596) down and (G3089) to loosen; to loosen down, to demolish, to halt, destroy, dissolve, come to nought, overthrow, throw down. Refers to the act of making something less, as in diminishing its relevance or authority.

**Fulfill:** stg's #**G4137** "plēroō", from (G4134) replete; to make replete, to cram *full*, level up. Refers to the act of making something fuller, bringing it to completion.

**Jot:**      stg's #**G2503** "iōta", of Hebrew origin (the tenth letter of the Hebrew alphabet- yod "י"); "iota", the name of the eighth letter of

852

the Greek alphabet, put (figuratively) for a very small part of anything. Refers to the smallest letter of any alphabet, like the letter "i" in English.

**Tittle**:     stg's #G2762 "keraia", feminine of a presumed derivative of the base of G2768; something horn like, that is, (specifically) the apex of a Hebrew letter (figuratively the least particle). Refers to the tiniest brushstroke of a letter, like the dot (•) above the letter "i".

**Fulfilled**:     stg's #**G1096** "ginomai", A prolonged and middle form of a primary verb; to cause to be, to become, used with great latitude. Refers contextually to complete fulfillment, i.e., the glass being completely full.

The difference between the Greek words "plēroō" and "ginomai" is one of action. Pleroo is the act of filling up a glass, while ginomai is the glass completely filled.

What Yahushua is saying here, concerns our understanding of the will and purpose of YHWH in the lives of His people.

His people had a partial (half-full) understanding of His Word and purpose, so they're understanding was not complete. Like a glass half-full, there was still plenty of room left in the glass, plenty of things they did not yet understand.

Messiah did not come to change or in any way diminish the Law/Torah's relevance in the life of a believer, nor in any way diminish our responsibility to live in obedience to it as believers.

He did, however, come to increase our understanding of what YHWH had said in His Word through both His teaching and His behavior.

He not only came to give us more understanding of what the Law/Torah means, but He also came to live it out completely as our example, so we could walk it out through our belief in Him.

Following this passage, Messiah shows us a deeper meaning of what it means to murder, saying it was more than the act of killing, because having hate in your heart is what makes us murderers.

He also teaches that adultery is more than just the act of having sexual interaction with someone's spouse, but it's looking at someone to lust for (desire) them, etc.

The phrase, "jot and tittle" is equivalent to the English phrase, "dot the 'i' and cross the 't'".

Messiah is emphasizing the fact that the Law/Torah/Word of YHWH is eternal (Psalms 119:89; Ecclesiastes 3:14), it cannot be added to nor taken away from (Deuteronomy 4:2; 12:32; Ecclesiastes 3:14; Proverbs 30:6 and Revelation 22:18-19).

Not the smallest letter (jot) neither the slightest brushstroke (tittle) will pass away from the written Torah, as long as the heavens and the earth remain.

This is saying more than the Law/Torah will continue to exist, because it also refers to the Law/Torah's significance in the life of believers as the only means of "living righteously" before a set apart (holy) Elohim.

Technically, the word "jot" is referring specifically to the Hebrew letter "yod", the 10th letter of the Hebrew alphabet.

The "yod" is the smallest letter in the Hebrew alphabet and represents the English "Y". Consider the Name.

Hebrew language is written from right to left, so the first letter in the Name is "yod", as you can see it is the smallest letter and it is printed above the center line.

The other letters, "hey" - "waw" - "hey" represent the size of most of the rest of the Hebrew letters of the alphabet.

Note:   Most modern Hebrew speakers consider the "waw" to be "vav" and so they write the four letters of The Name as "YHVH" instead of "YHWH". They say that there are no vowels in the Hebrew language, yet the ancient historian Josephus, when talking about the high priest head covering, states that the Name consists of four vowels.

"A mitre also of fine linen encompassed his head, which was tied by a blue ribbon, about which there was another golden crown, in which was engraven the sacred name - it consists of four vowels."

Josephus (Flavius Yusef) in "War of the Jews" book 5, chapter 5 v.7.

The "jot and tittle" are the absolute smallest parts of any writing and Messiah is simply trying to say that absolutely nothing of the Law/Torah and Prophets will change, be done away with, or be diminished by Him, or anyone else for that matter, as long as the heavens and the earth remain.

Note:   Wikipedia defines "jot and tittle" as: smallest details.

(https://en.wiktionary.org/wiki/jot_and_tittle)

Below is a column from the "got questions.org" website, it is a Christian website that does not use the Name, however, despite this they give a good explanation of what "jot and tittle" means.

**What is a jot? What is a tittle?**

The following is quoted from:

**Question:** **"What is a jot? What is a tittle?
What does it mean that neither a
jot nor a tittle will disappear from
God's Law?"**

**Answer:**

"In Matthew 5:17, Jesus assures His audience on the
mount that He had not come to abolish the Law and the
Prophets; rather, He had come to fulfill them. Then, in verse
18, Jesus emphasizes the eternal nature of God's Word:
"For verily I say unto you, Till heaven and earth pass, one
jot or one tittle shall in no wise pass from the law, till all be
fulfilled" (KJV). His statement naturally prompts the
question of what's a jot? And what's a tittle?

"Most of us are unfamiliar with jots and tittles because most
of us do not read the Hebrew language. Jots and tittles have
to do with letters and pen strokes in Hebrew writing.

"A jot is the tenth letter in the Hebrew alphabet and the
smallest. It was written above the line and looks to us rather
like an apostrophe:

*"Jot* is related to our modern English word *iota*, meaning "a
very small amount." The Hebrew spelling is *yod* or *yodh*.
Many Bibles have a picture of a yod in Psalm 119. Check
out the section title coming just before verse 73.

"A tittle is even smaller than a jot. A tittle is a letter
extension, a pen stroke that can differentiate one Hebrew
letter from another. An example can be seen in the
comparison between the Hebrew letters resh and daleth (or
dalet):

856

"The resh (on the left) is made with one smooth stroke. The daleth (on the right) is made with two strokes of the pen. The letters are very similar to each other, but the distinguishing mark of the daleth is the small extension of the roof of the letter:

"That extension is a tittle. See Psalm 119:25 and 153 for pictures of the daleth and resh, respectively.

"When Jesus said, "Till heaven and earth pass, one jot or one tittle shall in no wise pass from the law, till all be fulfilled" in Matthew 5:18, He was stating emphatically that God's Word is true and trustworthy. God has spoken, His words have been written down accurately, and what God has said will surely come to pass. Fulfillment is inevitable. Even the smallest letter of the Law will be fulfilled. Even the smallest pen stroke of the Prophets will be accomplished. The NLT translates the verse this way: "Until heaven and earth disappear, not even the smallest detail of God's law will disappear until its purpose is achieved.

"Doubters will doubt, and mockers will mock, but God's Word will not change: "Your word, LORD, is eternal; it stands firm in the heavens" (Psalm 119:89). The gospel changes lives: "'The word of the Lord endures forever.' And this is the word that was preached to you" (1 Peter 1:25). God is reliable, and so is His Word—every jot and tittle of it."

Though we agree with how the author of the above article understands and explains the meaning of "one jot and one title", we believe he has omitted, perhaps ignorantly, that this phrase also implies to the authority and the relevance of the Torah in the lives of the Believer today.

Most Christian teachers today will agree with everything this article says about the Law/Word, yet they do not practice what it says because they no longer consider the Law relevant in the lives of believers today, believing that Messiah fulfilled the Law, so we no longer have to obey it.

This, and many like it, is a case where they know what it says and what it means, but they don't believe it applies to them and so they are saying one thing but doing another. The Scripture calls this hypocrisy, something YHWH hates.

# Appendix 3: The Second Death

**Rev 20:4** And I saw thrones – and they sat on them, and judgment was given to them – and the lives of those who had been beheaded **because of the witness they bore to יהושע and because of the Word of Elohim**, and **who did not worship the beast, nor his image, and did not receive his mark** upon their foreheads or upon their hands. And they lived and reigned with Messiah for a thousand years

**Rev 20:5** **(and the rest of the dead did not come to life until the thousand years were ended)** – this is **the first resurrection**.

**Rev 20:6** Blessed and set-apart is the one having part in the first resurrection. **The second death possesses no authority over these**, but they shall be priests of Elohim and of Messiah, and shall reign with Him a thousand years.

**Rev 20:7** And **when the thousand years have ended**, Satan shall be released from his prison,

**Rev 20:8** and he shall go out to lead the nations astray which are in the four corners of the earth, Goḡ and Maḡoḡ, to gather them together for battle, whose number is as the sand of the sea.

**Rev 20:9** And they came up over the breadth of the earth and surrounded the camp of the set-apart ones and the beloved city. And fire came down from Elohim out of the heaven and consumed them.

**Rev 20:10** **And the devil, who led them astray, was thrown into the lake of fire and sulphur where the**

| | beast and the false prophet are. **And they shall be tortured day and night forever and ever.** |
|---|---|
| Rev 20:11 | And I saw a great white throne and Him who was sitting on it, from whose face the earth and the heaven fled away, and no place was found for them. |
| Rev 20:12 | And I saw the dead, small and great, standing before the throne, and books were opened. And another book was opened, which is the Book of Life. **And the dead were judged from what was written in the books, according to their works**. |
| Rev 20:13 | And the sea gave up the dead who were in it, and Death and She'ol gave up the dead who were in them. And they were judged, **each one according to his works.** |
| Rev 20:14 | **And Death and She'ol were thrown into the lake of fire. This is the second death**. |
| Rev 20:15 | And if anyone was **not found written in the Book of Life**, he was thrown into the lake of fire. |

In verses 4-6 we see a group of people mentioned who had been beheaded for "**the witness** they bore to יהושע and because of **the Word** of Elohim, and **who did not worship the beast**, nor his image, and did not receive his mark.

We see the *Two-Part Principle* here (the Witness of Messiah and the Word [Torah] of YHWH) and we see that they were faithful to this principle even unto death (beheading), never granting authority and service to the Beast (Anti-Messiah).

Believing in Yahushua requires obedience to the Torah, which forbids giving authority and service to anything or anyone that opposes YHWH.

These Believers are those called up in the FIRST RESURRECTION, who will sit as judges and will live and reign with Messiah for a thousand years. These Believers are NOT subject to the judgment of the Second Death.

The Second Death is the Lake of Fire and the "rest of the dead" are subject to this judgment. This phrase, "rest of the dead", refers to those who will take part in the second resurrection.

There are two resurrections mentioned in the Scripture and they are characterized as follows.

| | |
|---|---|
| **Dan 12:2** | and many of those who sleep in the dust of the earth wake up, **some to everlasting life**, and some **to reproaches, everlasting abhorrence**. |

1. Everlasting Life
2. Reproaches and everlasting abhorrence

| | |
|---|---|
| **Reproaches:** | stg's **#H2781** "cherpah", from a word (H2778) meaning, to pull off; contumely (insolent or insulting language or treatment), disgrace. Refers to having all the hidden sins exposed and the shame associated to them. |
| **Abhorrence:** | stg's **#H1860** "dera'on", from an unused root (meaning to repulse [drive away or intense distaste]); an object of aversion (a strong dislike or disinclination). Refers to a strong sense of contempt. |
| **Joh 5:26** | "For as the Father possesses life in Himself, so He gave also to the Son to possess life in Himself, |
| **Joh 5:27** | and He has given Him authority also to do judgment, because He is the Son of Adam. |
| **Joh 5:28** | "Do not marvel at this, because the hour is coming in which **all those in the tombs shall hear His voice**, |

861

| Joh 5:29 | and shall come forth – those **who have done good, to the resurrection of life**, and **those who have practised evil matters, to a resurrection of judgment**. |
|---|---|

The first resurrection is for those who have the witness of Messiah and the Word/Torah of YHWH, those who have "done good" who are "righteous" (Luke 14:14) and "sons of Elohim" (Luke 20:26), these people who have the *Two-Part Principle* working in them will receive "everlasting life".

The second resurrection is for those who, by contrast, DO NOT have the witness of Messiah and the Word/Torah of YHWH, those who DO NOT do good, but instead practice evil, these people will face the judgment of the Second Death, which is "reproaches and everlasting abhorrence" in the Lake of Fire.

| Note: | The terms, "good" and "evil", have taken on relative meanings based on the viewpoint of the individual speaking them. However, YHWH defines these terms very specifically in His Torah. |
|---|---|

| Deu 30:15 | "See, I have set before you today **l ife and good**, and **death and evil**, |
|---|---|
| Deu 30:16 | in that I am commanding you today to **love יהוה** your Elohim, to **walk in His ways**, and to **guard His commands**, and **His laws**, and **His right-rulings. And you shall live** and increase, and יהוה your Elohim shall bless you in the land which you go to possess. |
| Deu 30:17 | "**But if your heart turns away, and you do not obey**, and shall be drawn away, and shall bow down to other mighty ones and serve them, |
| Deu 30:18 | "**I have declared to you today that you shall certainly perish**, you shall not prolong your days in the |

| | land which you are passing over the Yardĕn to enter and possess. |
|---|---|
| **Deu 30:19** | "I have called the heavens and the earth as witnesses today against you: **I have set before you life and death**, the blessing and the curse. Therefore you shall **choose life**, so that you live, both you and your seed, |
| **Deu 30:20** | to love יהוה your Elohim, to obey His voice, and to cling to Him – for He is your life and the length of your days – to dwell in the land which יהוה swore to your fathers, to Abraham, to Yitsḥaq, and to Yaʿaqoḇ, to give them." |

From YHWH's point of view, good represents EVERYTHING He has spoken, and evil represents EVERYTHING that is contrary to what He has spoken.

Thus, to obey EVERYTHING He has commanded is doing what is GOOD, and NOT obeying EVERYTHING He has commanded is doing what is EVIL.

So, the first resurrection is for those who have believed in Messiah Yahushua AND have obeyed EVERYTHING that YHWH has spoken, and the second resurrection is for those who DO NOT believe in Messiah Yahushua and have NOT obeyed EVERYTHING YHWH has spoken.

| | |
|---|---|
| **Act 24:15** | having an expectation in Elohim, which they themselves also wait for, that there **is to be a resurrection of the dead, both of the righteous and the unrighteous**. |
| **Righteous**: | stg's **#G1342** "dikaios", from a word (**G1349**) meaning, right or just; equitable (in character or act); by implication innocent, holy (absolutely or relatively): - just, meet, right (-eous). Refers to being |

863

in right standing (obedient) before YHWH.

**Unrighteous**:    stg's #**G94** "adikos", from G1 (as a negative particle) and **G1349**; unjust; by extension wicked; by implication treacherous; specifically heathen: - unjust, unrighteous. Refers to NOT being in right standing before YHWH, having been disobedient.

**Note**:    The Torah declares that righteousness comes from obeying ALL the Torah says.

**Deu 6:24**    And יהוה commanded us **to do all these laws, to fear יהוה** our Elohim, **for our good always, to keep us alive**, as it is today.

**Deu 6:25**    And **it is righteousness for us** when **we guard to do all this command before יהוה** our Elohim, as He has commanded us.'

Obeying EVERYTHING the Torah of YHWH commands is how we fear Him, it is for our good ALWAYS, including today, and it is meant to keep us alive. It is how we live righteously before Him.

It is vital that we understand that this Truth does not change after we believe in Yahushua Messiah as Savior. He came and died to free us from the penalty of death we owed for our past disobedience to the Torah (Rom 3:23-25).

Now, that we have been made free from that debt, the Torah of YHWH has been established in us as the Way we live righteously before Him by belief (Rom 3:31).

NOTHING has changed concerning how His people are to live righteously, the only thing that has changed is our position before Him, in that our past sin debt has been paid and our condemnation removed because of our belief in Messiah.

**Jud 1:4**    For **certain men have slipped in,** whose judgment was written about long ago, **wicked ones perverting the favour of our Elohim for indecency, and denying the only Master יהוה and our Master יהושע Messiah.**

**Jud 1:5** But I intend to remind you, though you once knew this, that יהוה, having saved a people out of the land of Mitsrayim, **afterward destroyed those who did not believe.**

\*\*\*

**Jud 1:8** In the same way, indeed, these dreamers **defile the flesh**, and **reject authority**, and **speak evil of esteemed ones**.

**Jud 1:9** But Miḵa'ĕl the chief messenger, in contending with the devil, when he disputed about the body of Mosheh, presumed not to bring against him a blasphemous accusation, but said, "יהוה rebuke you"!

**Jud 1:10** But these blaspheme that which they do not know. And that which they know naturally, **like unreasoning beasts, in these they corrupt themselves**.

**Jud 1:11** Woe to them! Because they have gone in **the way of Qayin**, and gave themselves to the **delusion of Bil'am for a reward**, and perished in **the rebellion of Qoraḥ**.

**Jud 1:12** These are **rocky reefs** in your love feasts, feasting with you, **feeding themselves without fear, waterless clouds borne about by the winds,** late autumn trees **without fruit, twice dead, pulled up by the roots,**

**Jud 1:13** **wild waves of the sea foaming up their own shame, straying stars** for whom **blackness of darkness is kept forever.**

(See also: 2Pet 2:9-15)

So far, we have mentioned two types of people, those who believe in Messiah and obey the Torah of YHWH and those who do not. We also talked about which resurrection either type belongs. There is a third type of person that we need to talk about.

Jude talks about a third type of person, one who is within the Body of Messiah but does not live as a member of the Body, i.e., they do not obey the Torah of YHWH.

He calls them "wicked ones" who are "perverting the favour of our Elohim for indecency and denying the only Master יהוה and our Master יהושע Messiah".

> **Wicked ones:** stg's #G765 "asebēs", from G1 (as a negative particle) and a presumed derivative of G4576 (to revere); irreverent, that is, (by extension) impious or wicked: - ungodly (man). Refers to a person that has no fear or respect for the things of YHWH, i.e., disobedient to His Torah.

To "pervert the favor (grace) of Elohim" is to use His favor as a license to disobey His Torah (something Paul speaks against - Gal 2:15-18).

**Heb 10:26**  For if **we sin purposely** after we have received the knowledge of the truth, there no longer remains a slaughter offering for sins,

**Heb 10:27**  **but some fearsome anticipation of judgment, and a fierce fire which is about to consume the opponents.**

**Heb 10:28**  Anyone who has disregarded the Torah of Mosheh dies without compassion on the witness of two or three witnesses.

**Heb 10:29**  **How much worse punishment do you think shall he deserve who has trampled the Son of Elohim underfoot, counted the blood of**

866

| | the covenant by which he was set apart as common, and insulted the Spirit of favour? |
|---|---|
| **Heb 10:30** | For we know Him who has said, "Vengeance is Mine, I shall repay, says יהוה." And again, "יהוה shall judge His people." |
| **Heb 10:31** | It is fearsome to fall into the hands of the living Elohim. |

The writer of Hebrews says, "if we sin purposely after we come to the knowledge of the truth, there no longer remains a slaughter offering for sins, but some fearsome anticipation of judgment". What "truth" is he referring to?

| | |
|---|---|
| **Joh 14:6** | יהושע said to him, "**I am the Way, and the Truth, and the Life**. No one comes to the Father except through Me. |
| | *** |
| **Joh 17:17** | "Set them apart in Your truth – **Your Word is truth**. |
| | *** |
| **Psa 119:142** | Your righteousness is righteousness forever, And **Your Torah is truth**. |

The Truth contains both Yahushua Messiah AND the Word/Torah, The *Two-Part Principle*. It is clearly expressed in Isaiah 8:20 and Revelation 14:12.

| | |
|---|---|
| **Isa 8:20** | **To the Torah and to the witness!** If they do not speak according to this Word, it is because they have no daybreak (light). |
| | *** |
| **Rev 14:12** | Here is the endurance of the set-apart ones, here are **those guarding the commands of Elohim and the belief of יהושע**. |

And, as we have seen, this characterizes the people of the first resurrection (Rev 20:4) who have "the witness they bore to יהושע and because of the Word of Elohim".

Those who have the knowledge of this Truth and yet "sin purposely" have rejected the only sacrifice that could deliver them, having "trampled the Son of Elohim underfoot, counted the blood of the covenant by which **he was set apart** as common, and **insulted the Spirit of favour**".

The definition of sin is "lawlessness" or "transgression of the Law" (KJV), and refers to disobeying the Torah of YHWH, which He gave to the people of Yisra'el at Mt. Sinai, through Moses. The Law/Torah that applied to both the 'native born and the stranger" (Gentile) that sojourns with them (Num 15:15-16).

So, to disobey the Law/Torah of YHWH, as a believer, is a denial of Yahushua Messiah and ends in fiery judgment, i.e., the Lake of Fire.

Jude says these people bear "no fruit" and are "pulled up by the roots", which correlates perfectly with what Messiah said about the "branches" that bear no fruit in John 15.

He says, "Every branch in Me that **bears no fruit** (the Father) **takes away** (Joh 15:2) and "If anyone does not stay in Me, **he is thrown away as a branch and dries up**. And **they gather them and throw them into the fire, and they are burned** (Joh 15:6).

Jude goes on to say that these people are "twice dead", which is a reference to the Second Death of the Lake of Fire.

Some people believe that their belief in Messiah (who they call Jesus) protects them from the Second Death, but that is only true if they "abide" in the Messiah by bearing the fruit of righteousness that comes ONLY through obedience to the Torah of YHWH.

Others say that the Second Death/Lake of Fire refers to complete annihilation (spirit, soul and body), because they do not believe that their "God" would make someone suffer forever.

Unfortunately, their "God" is not running the show, YHWH is, and He seems to suggest that He will.

> **Rev 19:19** And I saw the beast, and the sovereigns of the earth, and their armies, gathered together to fight Him who sat on the horse and His army.

| **Rev 19:20** | And the beast was seized, and with him the false prophet who worked signs in his presence, by which he led astray those who received the mark of the beast and those who worshipped his image. **The two were thrown alive into the lake of fire burning with sulphur.** |
|---|---|

We have already shown that the Second Death has to do with, "reproaches and everlasting abhorrence" (Dan 12:2) and those who go there "…shall be tortured day and night forever and ever" (Rev 20:10).

The Beast and the False Prophet are thrown into the Lake of Fire alive, which means they never actually die physical death like the rest of us, and yet their torment is still forever, in this physical body.

It seems obvious that the Lake of Fire isn't about total annihilation, if it doesn't even destroy our physical bodies, much less a resurrected body that cannot die.

When Paul talks about the resurrected body in 1 Corinthians 15, he does not differentiate between the resurrection of the good or the resurrection of the evil, he only states the difference between that physical body and the spiritual body.

If those who have rejected Messiah and those who have excepted Messiah but refused to live in obedience to the Torah of YHWH, get resurrected bodies, then they will suffer the judgment of the Lake of Fire, forever, unable to die and escape it.

This judgment is measured by the works they did while in this life, so not everyone will suffer to the same degree as someone like, say, Hitler, but they will still have to endure the penalty of their own disobedience.

# Appendix 4:    Religion

**Definition of Religion** <u>**noun**</u>    re·li·gion | \ri-ˈli-jǝn \

1a:    the state of a <u>religious</u> , a nun in her 20th year of *religion*

 b:    (1) the service and worship of God or the supernatural (2) commitment or devotion to religious faith or observance

2:    a personal set or institutionalized system of religious attitudes, beliefs, and practices

3:    *archaic* : scrupulous conformity : <u>CONSCIENTIOUSNESS</u>

4:    a cause, principle, or system of beliefs held to with ardor and faith

(https://www.merriam-webster.com/dictionary/religion)

**Note:**    The word religion comes from the Latin and while there are a few different translations, the most prevalent roots take you back to the Latin word "Re-Ligare". "Ligare" means "to bind" or to "connect". Adding the "re" before "ligare" causes the word to mean "Re-Bind" or "Re-Connect."

(https://www.gregtrimble.com/meaning-of-the-word-religion/)

By the definition above, the word religion carries a similar meaning to the Hebrew concept of Teshuva (repentance) in that it represents a "Re-turn" to the True Belief, and not just a turning away of something.

However, to re-turn to the True Belief, as it is taught in the Scripture, requires an absolute rejection of or turning away from the worldly or "religious" practices that are contrary to the True Belief as it is taught in the Scripture.

Here is the conundrum, the word "religion", in its basic meaning, assumes that there is only one true belief, because anything contrary to that is what you are turning from to be "Re-connected" to.

871

Since every religion believes it is the one True Belief it becomes very difficult to discern the actual "religion" from all the imitators. Thus, you have The Religion and a whole lot of man-made religions.

The Hebrew Scriptures (Tanak) claim to be inspired by YHWH, the Creator of all things and that HE alone is the True Authority. Thus, the Tanak can be the only source of truth by which man can know and serve their Creator.

The Messianic Writings (New Testament) is a continuation of what was revealed in the Tanak and must be interpreted from the foundation of the Tanak, in both the language and culture.

Unfortunately, most of the "religions" that have sprouted up around the Scriptures have made fatal flaws in the way they have used the Scripture in their religious practices.

The only way to know for sure that the things you are believing in and practicing are the True Belief, is to compare it to what the Tanak strictly says about what the True Belief is.

The Scripture is very clear, there is only ONE Truth and it was revealed by YHWH Himself to man. YHWH intended to speak to each man directly, but when He spoke to Yisra'el from Mt. Sinai they were afraid and asked Him for a mediator. He granted their request in the man Moses (Mosheh).

The True Belief must be founded in what the Tanak says from the very first words given to us concerning the creation and built upon everything that it says from there. Anything else is a deviation from the Truth.

The Tanak represents the actions taken by the Creator to reveal Himself to man and what man must do to have a relationship with his Creator. It also explains the consequences for deviating from the path that the Creator laid down for us.

According to the Tanak, YHWH is the Creator of all things and all life comes from Him. If this is true then, by definition, everything that is contrary to Him and the things He says and does is death.

Since YHWH states clearly that He is eternal and never changes, then anything that anyone may say or do that is contrary to what He has said and done, regardless of when

872

in time they do it, results in death to those people and to all those who would follow them.

This is, by definition, "False Religion" and includes any and all teachings that are contrary to the Tanak, regardless of the source.

In the Tanak, YHWH says repeatedly that the things He has said, are not to be added to or taken away from, for all that He has set forth is forever.

> **Ecc 3:14** I know that whatever Elohim does is **forever**. There is **no adding to it, and there is no taking from it**. Elohim does it, **that men should fear before Him**.

(See also: Deut 4:2; 12:32; Pro 30:6 and Rev 22:18-19)

He says that turning to the left or right of ANYTHING He has said, is to serve someone or something else (false religion).

> **Deu 28:14** "And do not turn aside from **any of the Words** which I am commanding you today, right or left, **to go after other mighty ones to serve them**.

He clearly tells us **not** to learn the ways of those who serve other elohim (mighty ones/gods) and do it unto Him.

> **Deu 12:30** guard yourself that you are not ensnared to follow them, after they are destroyed from before you, and that you do not inquire about their mighty ones, saying, 'How did these nations serve their mighty ones? And let me do so too.
>
> **Deu 12:31** "Do not do so to יהוה your Elohim, for every abomination which יהוה hates they have done to their mighty ones, for they even burn their sons and daughters in the fire to their mighty ones.

(See also: Deu 18:9; Lev 18:3; Jer 10:2; Eze 11:12; 20:32; Eph 4:17; and 1Pe 4:3)

He also clearly states that His Torah (Law) is life if we obey it and death if we do not.

| | |
|---|---|
| **Deu 30:11** | "For this command which I am commanding you today, **it is not too hard for you,** nor is it far off. |
| **Deu 30:12** | "It is not in the heavens, to say, 'Who shall ascend into the heavens for us, and bring it to us, and cause us to hear it, so that we do it?' |
| **Deu 30:13** | "Nor is it beyond the sea, to say, 'Who shall go over the sea for us, and bring it to us, and cause us to hear it, so that we do it?' |
| **Deu 30:14** | **"For the Word is very near you, in your mouth and in your heart – to do it.** |
| **Deu 30:15** | "See, I have set before you today **life and good, and death and evil,** |
| **Deu 30:16** | in that **I am commanding you today to love יהוה your Elohim, to walk in His ways, and to guard His commands, and His laws, and His right-rulings**. And you shall live and increase, and יהוה your Elohim shall bless you in the land which you go to possess. |
| **Deu 30:17** | **"But if your heart turns away, and you do not obey, and shall be drawn away, and shall bow down to other mighty ones and serve them,** |
| **Deu 30:18** | "I have declared to you today that **you shall certainly perish,** you shall not prolong your days in the land which you are passing over the Yardĕn to enter and possess. |
| **Deu 30:19** | **"I have called the heavens and the earth as witnesses today against you: I have set before you life and** |

874

**death, the blessing and the curse.**
Therefore, you shall **choose life**, so
that you live, both you and your
seed,

Deu 30:20     **to love** יהוה **your Elohim, to obey
His voice, and to cling to Him –
for He is your life and the length
of your days** – to dwell in the land
which יהוה swore to your fathers, to
Aḇraham, to Yitsḥaq, and to
Yaʿaqoḇ, to give them."

The Messiah Himself stated that He did not come to
diminish a single thing from the Tanak.

Mat 5:17     **"Do not think that I came to
destroy** the Torah or the Prophets. **I
did not come to destroy but to
complete**.

Mat 5:18     "For truly, I say to you, **till the
heaven and the earth pass away,
one yod or one tittle shall by no
means pass from the Torah till <u>all</u>
be done**.

Mat 5:19     "Whoever, then, breaks one of the
least of these commands, and
teaches men so, shall be called least
in the reign of the heavens; but
**whoever does and teaches them,
he shall be called great in the
reign of the heavens**.

Mat 5:20     "For I say to you, that **unless your
righteousness exceeds that of the
scribes and Pharisees, you shall by
no means enter into the reign of
the heavens**.

Now, of course, many men have misinterpreted this
passage to mean something it doesn't say but the language is
quite clear, even in the English.

NOTHING from the Torah (Law) and the Prophets
have been destroyed (diminished) by the work of Messiah,
and neither will they be diminished for as long as the heaven

and earth remain, until EVERYTHING they say has been fulfilled.

A lot of the things in the Tanak have been fulfilled but not everything it says, and the heaven and the earth are still around.

Also, He clearly says that those who DO the things written in the Torah and TEACHES others to DO them, shall be great in the Kingdom. So, Messiah DID NOT come to fulfill the Law so that you don't have to, as some men teach today.

Interestingly, the Scribes and Pharisees were the "religious leaders" of the time and yet Messiah says that if we want to enter the Kingdom, we must be MORE righteous than them. Why, what did they do that made them NOT righteous enough?

They had violated the command not to add or take away from the Word.

| | |
|---|---|
| **Mat 15:1** | Then there came to יהושע scribes and Pharisees from Yerushalayim, saying, |
| **Mat 15:2** | "Why do Your taught ones transgress the **tradition of the elders**? For they do not wash their hands when they eat bread." |
| **Mat 15:3** | But He answering, said to them, **"Why do you also transgress the command of Elohim because of your tradition**? |
| **Mat 15:4** | "For Elohim has commanded, saying, 'Respect your father and your mother,' 'He who curses father or mother, let him be put to death.' |
| **Mat 15:5** | "But you say, 'Whoever says to his father or mother, "Whatever profit you might have received from me has been dedicated," |
| **Mat 15:6** | is certainly released from respecting his father or mother.' **So you have nullified the command of Elohim by your tradition**. |
| **Mat 15:7** | "Hypocrites! Yeshayahu rightly prophesied about you, saying, |

876

| | |
|---|---|
| **Mat 15:8** | 'This people draw near to Me with their mouth, and respect Me with their lips, but **their heart is far from Me.** |
| **Mat 15:9** | '**But in vain do they worship Me, teaching as teachings the commands of men.**'" |

(See also: Isa 29:13; Mar 7:1-13)

This practice of following the teachings of men instead of the commands of YHWH as He laid them down has been the bane of Yisra'el's existence for millennia.

| | |
|---|---|
| **2Ki 17:13** | And יהוה warned Yisra'ĕl and Yehuḏah, through all of His prophets, and every seer, saying, "**Turn back from your evil ways, and guard My commands and My laws, according to all the Torah which I commanded your fathers, and which I sent to you by My servants the prophets.**" |
| **2Ki 17:14** | But **they did not listen** and hardened their necks, like the necks of their fathers, **who did not put their trust in יהוה their Elohim**, |
| **2Ki 17:15** | and **rejected His laws and His covenant** that He had made with their fathers, **and His witnesses which He had witnessed against them**, and **went after worthlessness, and became worthless, and after the nations who were all around them, of whom יהוה had commanded them not to do like them.** |
| **2Ki 17:16** | And **they left all the commands of יהוה their Elohim**, and **made for themselves** a moulded image, two calves, and made an Ashĕrah and bowed themselves to all the host of the heavens, and served Ba'al, |

877

| 2Ki 17:17 | and caused their sons and daughters to pass through the fire, and **practised divination and sorcery, and sold themselves to do evil** in the eyes of יהוה, **to provoke Him.** |
| 2Ki 17:18 | So יהוה was very enraged with Yisra'ĕl, **and removed them from His presence** – none was left but the tribe of Yehuḏah alone. |
| 2Ki 17:19 | Yehuḏah, also, **did not guard the commands of** יהוה their Elohim, **but walked in the laws of Yisra'ĕl which they made.** |

YHWH set down a clear and simple path by which His people were to please Him and yet they found it easier to follow the teachings of men instead and they are still doing it today.

And what is even more disturbing is the fact that the Christian church has fallen into this same trap of listening to men tell them what to believe, things like they no longer need to obey the Torah (Law), even though that teaching is contrary to everything the Tanak and the Messianic Writings declare.

The Torah has always applied to both the native born Yisra'eli (Jew) and the stranger who sojourned with them (Gentile), and it was a Law FOREVER, throughout the generations.

| Num 15:15 | **One law** is for **you of the assembly and for the stranger who sojourns with you – a law forever throughout your generations.** As you are, so is the stranger before יהוה. |
| Num 15:16 | **One Torah** and **one right-ruling** is for you and for the stranger who sojourns with you.' " |

The phrase "As you are, so is the stranger before YHWH" is a reference to what the Messianic Writings calls the adoption.

| Lev 19:33 | 'And when **a stranger sojourns with you** in your land, do not oppress him. |
| Lev 19:34 | '**Let the stranger who dwells among you be to you as the native among you**, and you shall love him as yourself. For you were strangers in the land of Mitsrayim. I am יהוה your Elohim. |

There is no distinction between the Native Born and the Stranger, the Jew and the Gentile, in the eyes of YHWH and there never has been. Everyone who claims YHWH as there Elohim is required to obey the Torah, A law **FOREVER, THROUGHOUT YOUR GENERATIONS!!!**

The Messianic Writings confirm this in Galatians.

| Gal 3:26 | For you are all sons of Elohim through belief in Messiah יהושע. |
| Gal 3:27 | For as many of you as were immersed into Messiah have put on Messiah. |
| Gal 3:28 | **There is not Yehuḏi nor Greek**, there is not slave nor free, there is not male and female, **for you are all one in Messiah** יהושע. |
| Gal 3:29 | And if you are of Messiah, **then you are seed of Aḇraham, and heirs according to promise.** |

Yes, believers are required to obey the Torah of YHWH just as it was given at Mt. Sinai, without additions or subtractions, HOWEVER, our TRUST is NEVER in our works!!!

Our TRUST and our HOPE are ALWAYS AND FOREVER in belief, that Yahushua is the Messiah, the Seed of the woman promised to Adam and Chawwah (Eve), and to Abraham, Yitschaq (Isaac) and Ya'aqob (Jacob).

# Appendix 5:

# The Great Deception Gentile Church?

### 2 Thessalonians 2:7-12 (KJV)

| | |
|---|---|
| **2 The 2:7** | For the **mystery of iniquity** doth already work: only he who now letteth *will let,* until he be taken out of the way. |
| **2 The 2:8** | And then shall that **Wicked** be revealed, whom the Lord shall consume with the spirit of his mouth, and shall destroy with the brightness of his coming: |
| **2 The 2:9** | *Even him,* whose coming is after the **working of Satan** with all **power** and **signs** and **lying wonders**, |
| **2 The 2:10** | And with all **deceivableness of unrighteousness** in them that perish; because they **received not the love of the truth**, that they might be saved. |
| **2 The 2:11** | And for this cause <u>God</u> shall send them strong delusion, **that they should believe a lie:** |
| **2 The 2:12** | That they all might be damned who **believed not the truth, but had pleasure in unrighteousness.** |

Well, here it is. Paul's warning to the modern "Church" which he calls a "mystery of iniquity". In this study we are going to dissect this passage to learn exactly what Paul meant. Then, we'll go to other places where he and other writers commented on this very thing.

First of all, let's find out the meaning of the words mystery and iniquity.

| | |
|---|---|
| **Mystery:** | stg's #**G3466** - "**musterion**", derived from the Greek word, "**muo**" (to shut the mouth); a *secret* or "mystery" (through the idea of |

881

*silence* imposed by *initiation* into religious rites).

**Iniquity**: stg's **#G458 -"anomia"**, meaning, no law doing; translated in 1 John 3:4 as "transgression of the law".

So, we see here, that Paul is referring to a "religious" (i.e., manmade ideas and traditions) rite or practice of **not obeying the law**, specifically a reference to what is generally called the Mosaic Law or Torah.

Now I know what you are thinking, all your lives you have been taught that Paul said that believers in the Messiah no longer had to obey the law, but this passage suggests that this idea of a lawless faith comes from someone other than the Messiah.

Verse 8 refers to "that Wicked" that was to be revealed. Before we go into dissecting this word wicked, we must recognize that it refers to a person, as the context suggests in verses 3 and 4.

**2 The 2:3** Let no man deceive you by any means: for that day shall not come, except there come a falling away first, and that **man of sin be revealed, the son of perdition**;

**2 The 2:4** Who opposeth and exalteth himself above all that is called God, or that is worshipped; so that he as God sitteth in the temple of God, **shewing himself that he is God**. (KJV)

This Person is all about sin and perdition (destruction or damnation) and as far as I know every so-called Christian scholar considers this person to be the coming Anti-Messiah or Anti-Christ. It is interesting to me that he is called the "Man" of Sin" because according to 1 John 3:4, "sin is the transgression of the law".

Here we see again this idea of No Law Doing in association with this Person who is coming claiming himself to be the Most High (v 4), the person in whom the Messiah Himself shall destroy at His return.

Going back to that word "wicked" in verse eight, we see this meaning.

| Wicked: | stg's **#G459** -"**anomos**", meaning, lawless; i.e., Not subject to law or without law. (Note: in Romans 8:7 we are told that the mind of the flesh, does not subject itself to the law.) |
|---|---|

Interestingly and obviously, the words "anomos" and "anomia" are related. In this context the word "wicked" should be translated as "lawless one" and the phrase "mystery of iniquity" should be translated as "secret of lawlessness".

| 2 The 2:7 | For the secret of lawlessness is already at work – only until he who now restrains comes out of the midst. |
|---|---|
| 2 The 2:8 | And then the lawless one shall be revealed, whom the Master **shall consume with the Spirit of His mouth** and bring to naught with the manifestation of His coming. (The Scriptures) |

Going back to verse 9 we see that this "Lawless One" is coming doing the works of "Satan, with all power and signs and lying wonders". Think about what that means for a second.

This Anti-Messiah will not only live contrary to the law or Torah that YHWH gave through Moses to Yisra'el at Mount Sinai, but he'll also be teaching it, encouraging others to live according to the same mystery. And he will be using all kinds of powers and signs and wonders that are based in and intended to trap us in The Lie.

So, in these last days, powers and signs and wonders that are going forth from teachers or churches that teach a doctrine of lawlessness or not keeping the law and are all based in a lie from the father of lies, Satan.

Remember, this passage of Scripture in 2 Thessalonians was written by Paul, who is the same man that wrote the book of Romans and the book of Galatians where we are told by him that we are not under the law.

So, one of two things must be true, either Paul is contradicting himself or our so-called Christian forefathers and teachers do not understand what Paul is saying when he says we are not under the law, for Paul himself kept the law (Acts 21:24).

In verse 10, we see the phrase "deceivableness of unrighteousness" in those who perish.

| | |
|---|---|
| **Deceivableness**: | stg's **#G539** -"**apate**", from the word "**apatao**" (to cheat), meaning, delusion or deceit. This word "apate" refers to a lie or deception. |
| **Unrighteousness**: | stg's **#G93** -"**adikia**", from the word "**adikos**" (unjust), meaning, injustice or wrong. |

Consider:

| | |
|---|---|
| **Deut 6:24** | And the LORD commanded **us to do all these statutes, to fear the LORD our God**, for our good always, that he might preserve us alive, as it is at this day. |
| **Deut 6:25** | And **it shall be our righteousness, if we observe to do all these commandment**s before the LORD our God, as he hath commanded us. (KJV) |

For us to live righteously is to obey all these commandments that YHWH gave to us through Moses. To not obey all these commandments is to live unrighteously or to be unrighteous. Back in verse 10 we see that the idea of unrighteousness or living unrighteously is a lie or delusion.

Verse 10 goes on to say that those who have been caught up in this lie of unrighteousness would perish because "they did not receive the love of the truth, that they might be saved."

Now the first thing the Christian with any Bible knowledge is going to do is quote John 14:6,

| John 14:6 | `Jesus saith unto him, I am the way, the truth, and the life: no man cometh unto the Father, but by me.(KJV) |

Then, they would say that their belief in Messiah, whose Hebrew name is Yahushua, shows that they have received the love of the truth, since He is the Truth. In this they would be half correct. He is the Truth; however, the Word is also the truth (John 17:17).

Also, the Law is the truth according to Psalms 119:142. Interesting enough, John chapter 1 says that Messiah is the Word made flesh, thus, also making Him the Law/Torah made flesh. Consider:

| Jam 2:14 | What doth it profit, my brethren, though a man say he hath faith, and have not works? can faith save him? |
| Jam 2:15 | If a brother or sister be naked, and destitute of daily food, |
| Jam 2:16 | And one of you say unto them, Depart in peace, be ye warmed and filled; notwithstanding ye give them not those things which are needful to the body; what doth it profit? |
| Jam 2:17 | yea though but **Even so faith, if it hath not works, is dead, being alone**. |
| Jam 2:18 | Yea, a man may say, Thou hast faith, and I have works: shew me thy faith without thy works, **and I will shew thee my faith by my works.** |
| Jam 2:19 | Thou believest that there is one God; thou doest well: the devils also believe, and tremble. |
| Jam 2:20 | But wilt thou know, O vain man, that faith without works is dead? |
| Jam 2:21 | Was not Abraham our father justified by works, when he had offered Isaac his son upon the altar? |

| Jam 2:22 | **Seest thou how faith wrought with his works, and by works was faith made perfect?** |
| Jam 2:23 | And the scripture was fulfilled which saith, Abraham believed God, and it was imputed unto him for righteousness: and he was called the Friend of God. |
| Jam 2:24 | **Ye see then how that by works a man is justified, and <u>not by faith only</u>.** (KJV) |

Many teachers today quote this passage and yet have no idea what it is actually saying. See in this example, belief in Yahushua is called faith, while obedience to the Law/Torah that YHWH gave to us through Mosheh on Mount Sinai is called works. You'll find this duality, this *Two-Part Principle*, in virtually every major passage in Scripture.

What brother James (Ya'aqob) is saying here is that belief in Yahushua Messiah alone, if not followed up by obedience to the Torah, is dead. Faith in Messiah alone, without a commitment of obedience afterward, is not true faith.

In our main passage of the study, 2 Thessalonians, we see that the Anti-Messiah is all about not obeying the law. The very concept of a faith in Messiah without a subsequent obedience to the law is an anti-Messiah doctrine, it is a delusion, a lie!

Consider now again, the last two verses of our passage.

| 2Th 2:11 | And for this cause God shall send them strong delusion, that they should believe A lie: |
| 2Th 2:12 | That they all might be damned who believed not the truth, but had pleasure in unrighteousness. (KJV) |

Notice, who does Paul says sends this great delusion upon them? It is the Almighty Himself that sends this delusion because the people believed the delusion of unrighteousness, the Satanic, demonic, Anti-Messiah lie that

886

once you believe in Messiah you no longer have to obey the Law/Torah.

And look at verse 12, that they all might be damned, referring to the Lake of Fire, who believe not the truth, but had pleasure in unrighteousness. Remember, the truth is both the Messiah and the Word/Torah, because Messiah is the Word/Torah made flesh. You can't have Messiah without the Torah nor the Torah without the Messiah, both are an error.

The Christian church boast on its salvation based on grace through faith without the works of the law, which is how we are justified from death, there is no other way (Romans 3:20), yet they deny the very Messiah that justified them from death when they refuse to walk in the justification of life, through obeying the Torah (Romans 2:13).

Christianity today, that teaches a faith without a corresponding obedience to the law, is The Great Delusion!

| | |
|---|---|
| **1Jn 3:1** | See what love the Father has given us, that we should be called children of Elohim! For this reason the world does not know us, because it did not know Him. |
| **1Jn 3:2** | Beloved ones, now we are children of Elohim. And it has not yet been revealed what we shall be, but we know that when He is revealed, **we shall be like Him**, for we shall see Him as He is. |
| **1Jn 3:3** | And everyone having this expectation in Him cleanses himself, as He is clean. |
| **1Jn 3:4** | Everyone doing sin also does lawlessness, and **sin is lawlessness**. |
| **1Jn 3:5** | And you know that He was manifested to take away our sins, **and in Him there is no sin.** |
| **1Jn 3:6** | Everyone staying in Him **does not sin**. Everyone sinning has **neither seen Him nor known Him.** |
| **1Jn 3:7** | Little children, let no one lead you astray. **The one doing righteousness is righteous**, even as He is righteous. |

| | |
|---|---|
| **1Jn 3:8** | **The one doing sin is of the devil**, because the devil has sinned from the beginning. For this purpose the Son of Elohim was manifested: to destroy the works of the devil. |
| **1Jn 3:9** | **Everyone having been born of Elohim does not sin,** because His seed stays in him, and he is powerless to sin, because he has been born of Elohim. |
| **1Jn 3:10** | In this the children of Elohim and the children of the devil are manifest: **Everyone not doing righteousness is not of Elohim, neither the one not loving his brother**. |

(Everything within parentheses added by author for clarification)

**Note**: In verse 3 it states that He (Messiah) is pure, while in verse 5 it says that He is without sin. Since sin is by definition the transgression of the law (Torah) and He did not ever transgress the law (Torah), than for us to purify ourselves as He is pure, means that we should obey the law (Torah) as He did.

It is the duty of all those who have Belief in Yahushua Messiah to struggle diligently every day to obey all that YHWH has spoken in His Torah, trusting not in the Torah, but in Yahushua Messiah, Who alone can keep us when we stumble. And lastly, we are to do these things in a heart of unbridled compassion and forgetful forgiveness, i.e., Love, which is the binding element.

Before we close this section, we want the reader to see the correlation between the "strong delusion" mentioned here in 2 Thessalonians 2 and the "covenant of death" mentioned in Isaiah 28:15.

In 2 Thessalonians we see that it is YHWH who brings this "delusion" upon the people "because they did not receive the love of the truth", but "delighted in the unrighteousness" instead.

The word "delusion" here is 'falsehood' in the KJV because it refers to a lie that YHWH is going to allow to rise within the 'church' that is associated "with all power and signs and wonders".

This power is a working of Ha-Satan and the lie he brings into the body will gel nicely with the coming Anti-Messiah, the lawless one. And the lie is that you can serve YHWH through His Son, "Jesus", and live lawless.

The Torah/Law of YHWH was given to show us how to live righteously before Him (Deuteronomy 6:24-25) and to show us that we are all sinners and condemned to death for violating it so we would turn to Messiah for deliverance (Galatians 3:22-29).

It fulfilled its primary duty of bringing us to Messiah and now its secondary duty is to teach us to walk righteously before Him, for our belief in Messiah as "established the Torah" as the way of life, blessing and inheritance for all who believe (Romans 3:31).

Now, in Isaiah 28 we are told that YHWH gave Yisra'el (a shadow of the Body today) His Word "Command upon command, command upon command, line upon line, line upon line, here a little, there a little," saying that it is the Rest and the Restoration, but "they would not hear".

**Hear**: stgs #**H8085** "עָמַשׁ - shâma'", a primitive root; to hear intelligently.

The Hebrew word "shama" is a verbal root that refers to the type of hearing that has intent behind it. "Hear" isn't the best English word for 'shama', the word 'Listen' is a better fit because it carries the underlaying requirement of obedience.

The Word of YHWH was NOT bringing rest for them because then didn't "hear" it with the intent of obeying it (hard or rebellious hearted), and so that which was meant to give them rest actually caused them to "stumble backward and be broken and snared and taken captive".

YHWH goes on to tell them that they are depending on a "covenant of death" that they believe will deliver them from the "overflowing scourge" (wrath), which He says is a "lying refuge" and "falsehood". Sound familiar?

He goes on to tell them that the covenant that they are trusting in is NOT going to save them, but when the "scourge" (wrath) comes they will be overcome by it, and it is so because they "believed the falsehood... and delighted in the unrighteousness" (2 Thessalonians 2:11-12).

What then, is a covenant of death? To answer that question, we must first ask another. What causes death?

| | |
|---|---|
| **1Co 15:56** | And the sting of death is the sin, and the power of the sin is the Torah. |

*\*\*\**

| | |
|---|---|
| **Rom 3:23** | for all have sinned and fall short of the esteem of Elohim, |

*\*\*\**

| | |
|---|---|
| **1Jn 3:4** | Everyone doing sin also does lawlessness, and sin is lawlessness (the transgression of the law – KJV). |

*\*\*\**

| | |
|---|---|
| **Rom 6:23a** | For the wages of sin is death, |

The rules are simple, YHWH is righteous and set-apart, He is also the ONLY giver of life, so to be righteous and set-apart, to have life, we have to be like Him. The first step to doing that is to believe in His Son who He gave to make us right (justify) FROM sin and death.

Then, in that belief, we MUST live in the righteousness of His Instructions (Torah/Law), just as His Son did so we can also inherit the Kingdom of His Son and everlasting life.

Because neither Judaism nor Christianity, in its many tentacles, have both belief in Yahushua Messiah AND obedience to the Torah of YHWH, without additions or subtractions, neither of them live in the love of Elohim nor will they inherit the Kingdom of Elohim, unless they repent and obey.

# Hebrew Mindset Ministries

YouTube Channel: www.Hebrewmindset.info

Email: Hebrewmindsetministries@gmail.com

Website: Hebrewmindsetministries.org

Facebook: Hebrew Mindset

Voicemail: (407) 720-8862

Author: M.W. Morris
Orlando, Florida

Made in the USA
Columbia, SC
08 September 2022

66809711R00413